DATE DUE

DEMCO 38-296

Guide To
FRENCH POETRY EXPLICATION

A
Reference
Publication
in
Literature

Nancy Martinez
Editor

Guide To
FRENCH POETRY EXPLICATION

KATHLEEN COLEMAN

G. K. HALL & CO.
An Imprint of Macmillan Publishing Company
New York

MAXWELL MACMILLAN CANADA
Toronto

MAXWELL MACMILLAN INTERNATIONAL
New York   Oxford   Singapore   Sydney

G. K. Hall & Co.
An Imprint of Macmillan Publishing Company
866 Third Avenue
New York, NY 10022

Maxwell Macmillan Canada, Inc.
1200 Eglinton Avenue East, Suite 200
Don Mills, Ontario M3C 3N1

Macmillan Publishing Company is part of the Maxwell Communication Group of Companies

Library of Congress Catalog Card Number: 92-22129

Printed in the United States of America

printing number
1 2 3 4 5 6 7 8 9 10

Library of Congress Cataloging-in-Publication Data

Coleman, Kathleen.
    Guide to French poetry explication / Kathleen Coleman.
        p.   cm.—(A Reference publication in literature)
    Includes bibliographical references and index.
    ISBN 0-8161-9075-5
    1. French poetry—Explication.   I. Title.   II. Series.
    PQ401.C65   1993
    841.009—dc20   92-22129
                                                    CIP

The paper used in this publication meets the minimum requirements of American National Standard for Information Sciences—Permanence of Paper for Printed Library Materials. ANSI Z39.48–1984. ∞™

Contents

The Author

Kathleen Coleman holds degrees from Stanford University and the University of Wisconsin at Madison. She is a former French teacher at secondary and university levels and is a reference librarian at San Diego State University. One of her current responsibilities is developing the library's collection in French language and literature. She has contributed to *Business Journals of the United States* (Westport, CT: Greenwood Press, 1991) and has written numerous articles for professional publications in library science.

Preface

This is the first publication in the Guides to Poetry Explication series to list explications of poetry in a language other than English. As with its predecessors in English and American poetry, the principal purpose of this *Guide* is to lead the user to published explications of poetry by major poets.

All periods in French literary history are represented in the *Guide,* from the Middle Ages to such contemporary poets as Yves Bonnefoy and Léopold Senghor. Among the medieval poets are representative southern troubadours who wrote in Provençal, such as Marcabru, Peire d'Alvernhe, and Arnaut Daniel. While these poets must today be read in French or English translation by most students, their influence on French lyric poetry has been significant, and the knowledgeable student of French literature should at least be aware of this body of work.

Primary emphasis is on poets generally included in the canon of French literary studies. The *Guide* includes only explications for poems of approximately 2,000 lines or less. The explications come from a variety of sources, including:

1. Volumes analyzing the works of several poets, by one or more critics
2. Books covering the work of a single poet
3. Conference proceedings

4. Edited volumes of critical essays

5. Scholarly journals widely held in American academic libraries

All sources consulted—both monographs and journals—were published between 1960 and 1990, and were limited to those in either English or French. Very brief explications have been excluded; all listed explications are at least twenty-five lines long. As even a cursory glance at any recent literary bibliography will reveal, the published literature on French poetry seems to grow exponentially each year. Therefore, it was impossible to include all relevant publications. Selection of materials to be included was based on listings in bibliographies such as David C. Cabeen's *Critical Bibliography of French Literature* (Syracuse, N.Y.: Syracuse University Press, 1947–), ease of use by American students, and availability in American academic libraries. As for the poets themselves, only those readily available in nineteenth- or twentieth-century editions were included. For this reason, a number of well-received poets, such as Louis Racine of the eighteenth century, have been excluded from the *Guide*.

In general, the *Guide* does not list explications of prose poems. The one exception is the *Illuminations* and a few other texts of Arthur Rimbaud. Rimbaud's prose poems are considered by many critics to be his finest work. Because of their importance and the significant influence they had on subsequent nineteenth- and twentieth-century poets, the prose poems of Rimbaud are included in nearly all scholarly analyses of his work, and are therefore listed in this *Guide*.

The explicatons listed here reflect many schools of critical thought. The traditional scholastic *explication de texte* is well represented in the checklist, as are conventional scholarly studies and newer means of literary analysis, such as close readings following structuralist or deconstructionist theories. The study of literary criticism has become an important subdiscipline among teachers and students of literature, and the *Guide* facilitates this work. Through the Index to Critics at the end of the *Guide* it is possible to identify the explications of individual scholars. Virtually all distinguished contemporary critics of French poetry are represented here, provided that their scholarship is published in either English or French. As every student of French poetry discovers, "What does this poem mean?" is a question with many answers, some of which have not yet been proposed.

To explicate a French poem it is essential to be familiar with the principles that guide both poets and scholars. Many books have been written to explain meter, rhyme, fixed forms, and other basic elements of French poetry. The bibliography at the end of this preface lists recent manuals about French verse study in both French and English.

For too many students of French, poetry is an arcane genre to be dealt with as quickly as possible. To appreciate poetry it is essential to understand its technical construction as well as the figurative and literal meanings of the words used. But although the discipline is sometimes demanding, the rewards of poetry study are great. Experiencing French poetry and understanding its meaning and structure can bring a lifetime of pleasure.

To find an explication in the *Guide* is easy. The volume is arranged as follows.

1. In the Checklist of Interpretation, the entries for each poet are arranged alphabetically by the poet's name, generally last name first. Poets known most often by a noble title or nickname are listed in the most familiar form. (For example, Charles d'Orléans is listed under "C," not "O.")

2. Running headings give the first poet mentioned on the page on the left hand page and the last poet mentioned on the page on the right hand page.

3. Within each poet's section, the poems analyzed are arranged alphabetically by title. Under each poem, the explications are alphabetized by the critic's name. Series of poems, such as sonnet cycles, are filed in numerical order after individual poems.

4. Because French spelling was not standardized until the latter part of the seventeenth century, poets used variant and even inconsistent spellings. Scholarly editions generally print poetry as written by the poet, therefore older poems are listed under traditionally spelled titles.

5. Journal titles are abbreviated according to the standard abbreviation used by the Modern Language Association (MLA). All abbreviated journal titles are spelled out in full in the Abbreviations list immediately preceding the Checklist.

6. The bibliography (Main Sources Consulted) follows the Checklist and lists major sources that include five or more explications. These titles are cited in shortened form in the Checklist. Journals that have been important sources for explications are also listed in the bibliography.

7. The last section of the Guide, the Index to Critics, permits access to all explications prepared by individual scholars.

Many people gave me valuable assistance, making the formidable task of preparing the *Guide* much easier. First, I wish to thank the staff of the Interlibrary Loan Office of San Diego State University for locating many sources that were not available locally. Second, I thank Dr. Nancy Martinez and the editorial staff at G. K. Hall for their excellent orientation to the project and prompt, thorough answers to all my questions. Finally, I am grateful to my husband, Phil, and sons, Nick and Curt, for their computer expertise, moral support, and practical assistance with the project.

PREFACE

NOTE: The poems of Ronsard's sonnet sequences are not numbered consistently throughout all editions of his poetry. This *Guide* follows the numbering used in the Gustave Cohen "Bibliotheque de la Pleiade" edition (Paris: Gallimard, 3d ed., 1958); some sonnets will have different numbers from those in the critical edtions referred to in explications. When in doubt, select explications from the first line of the sonnet rather than from its number in a sequence.

Select Bibliography of French Poetry Manuals

GRAMMONT, MAURICE. *Petit traité de versification française,* 13th ed. Paris: Armand Colin, 1987.

A recent edition of the classic French guide to the basic structural elements of French poetry. Discusses and illustrates rhyme, syllabification, characteristics of the line in French verse, and rhythm. In French.

LEWIS, ROY. *On Reading French Verse: A Study of Poetic Form.* Oxford: Clarendon Press, 1982.

Manual for British university students. Presents line length, phonetic patterning, stanza structure, principles of rhyme, and use of sonority to enhance meaning. Forty pages of sample commentaries for well-known poems. In Engish.

MAZALEYRAT, JEAN. *Eléments de métrique française.* Paris: Armand Colin, 1974.

A brief, readable guide to the basic characteristics of French poetry. Well illustrated with sample analyses. In French.

SCOTT, CLIVE. *French Verse-art: a Study.* Cambridge: Cambridge University Press, 1980.

An exhaustively illustrated guide to the French verse line, rhyme, stanzas, and fixed forms. Includes an extensive section on free verse. In English.

Abbreviations

AJFS   Australian Journal of French Studies

BHR   Bibliothèque d'Humanisme et Renaissance

CAIEF   Cahiers de L'Association Internationale des Etudes Françaises

CL   Comparative Literature

CLDS   Cahiers de Littérature du XVIIe Siècle

CLS   Comparative Literature Studies

ECr   Esprit Créateur

ABBREVIATIONS

ECS	Eighteenth Century Studies
EF	Etudes Françaises
ELit	Etudes Littéraires
Europe	Europe
Expl	Explicator
FMLS	Forum for Modern Language Studies
FR	French Review
FrF	French Forum
FS	French Studies
FSB	French Studies Bulletin
JES	Journal of European Studies
JML	Journal of Modern Literature
KRQ	Romance Quarterly (Former title: Kentucky Romance Quarterly)
LCL	Littérature Classique (Former title: Cahiers de Littérature du XVIIe Siècle)

NCFS   Nineteenth-Century French Studies

O&C   Œuvres et Critiques

PFSCL   Papers on French Seventeenth Century Literature

PMLA   Publications of the Modern Language Association of
           America

Poétique   Poétique

RHL   Revue d'Histoire Littéraire de la France

RLM   Revue des Lettres Modernes

RR   Romanic Review

RSH   Revue des Sciences Humaines

SFr   Studi Francesi

SFR   Stanford French Review

SubStance

YFS   Yale French Studies

Checklist of Interpretation

ADAM DE LA HALLE

"Congé"

Paul Zumthor, "Entre deux esthétiques: Adam de la Halle," in *Mélanges . . . offerts à Jean Frappier,* vol. 2, 1159–71 (Fr).

Zumthor, *Essai de poétique médiévale,* 412–15 (Fr).

"Merveille est quel talent j'ai"

Paul Zumthor, "Entre deux esthétiques: Adam de la Halle," in *Mélanges . . . offerts à Jean Frappier,* vol. 2, 1155–71 (Fr).

"Vers d'amour"

Zumthor, *Essai de poétique médiévale,* 416–18 (Fr).

ANONYMOUS

"Banquet du bois"

Winter, *Visual Variety and Spatial Grandeur,* 41, 43–44, 52 (Eng).

ANONYMOUS, "Cantilène de Sainte Eulalie"

"Cantilène de Sainte Eulalie"

F. J. Barnett, "Some Notes to the Sequence of Saint Eulalia," in *Oxford University Studies in Medieval French Presented to Alfred Ewert* (Oxford: Clarendon Press, 1961), 1–25 (Eng).

"Chanson de Saint Alexis"

Zumthor, *Essai de poétique médiévale*, 319–22 (Fr).

"La Châtelaine de Vergi"

Paula Clifford, *La Châtelaine de Vergi and Jean Renart, "Le Lai de l'Ombre"* (London: Grant and Cutler, 1986), 12–55 (Eng).

Linda Cooper, "Irony as Courtly Poetic Truth in 'La Châtelaine de Vergi,'" *RR* 75 (May 1984): 273–82 (Eng).

Renée Curtis, "The Châtelaine de Vergi's Husband," *FSB* 24 (Autumn 1987): 1–5 (Eng).

Frappier, *Du Moyen Age à la Renaissance*, 393–413 (Fr).

Laurence de Looze, "The Untellable Story: Language and Writing in 'La Châtelaine de Vergi,'" *FR* 59 (October 1985): 42–50 (Eng).

J. Reed, "La Châtelaine de Vergi: Another View," *FSB* 28 (Autumn 1988): 17–21 (Eng).

Zumthor, *Essai de poétique médiévale*, 194–205, 240–41, 380–383 (Fr).

"La Complainte d'amours"

Jacques Monfrin, "'La Complainte d'amours,' poème du XIIIe siècle," in *Mélanges offerts à Rita Lejeune, Professeur à l'Université de Liège*, vol. 2 (Gembloux: Editions Duculot, 1969) 1365–89 (Fr).

"La Complainte de Fualdès"

Marc Angenot, "La 'Complainte de Fantômas' et al 'Complainte de Fualdès,'" *EF* 4 (November 1968): 424–30 (Fr).

ANONYMOUS, "Lai de l'épervier"

"De Guillaume au faucon"

Gregg Lacy, "Form, Context, and Disjunction in the Fabliau World," in Lacy and Nash, eds., *Essays in Early French Literature,* 46–49 (Eng).

"Le Dit de l'éschassier"

Philippe Ménard, "Le Dit de l'eschassier," in *Mélanges de langue et de littérature françaises du moyen âge et de la Renaissance, offerts à M. Charles Foulon,* vol. 1, 251–8 (Fr).

"Doon"

Donovan, *The Breton Lay,* 72–74 (Eng).

"Epine"

Donovan, *The Breton Lay,* 75–77 (Eng).

"Graelent"

Donovan, *The Breton Lay,* 69–71 (Eng).

"Guingamor"

Sara Sturm, *The Lay of Guingamor: A Study* (Chapel Hill: University of North Carolina Press, 1968) (Eng).

"Lai de Désiré"

Donovan, *The Breton Lay,* 67–68 (Eng).

Jean Subrenat, "Le Lai de Désiré," in *Mélanges de langue et de littérature françaises du moyen âge et de la Renaissance, offerts à M. Charles Foulon,* vol. 1, 371–9 (Fr).

"Lai de l'épervier"

Donovan, *The Breton Lay,* 94–96 (Eng).

ANONYMOUS, "Lai de l'oiselet"

"Lai de l'oiselet"

Donovan, *The Breton Lay,* 86–87 (Eng).

"Lai d'Haveloc"

Donovan, *The Breton Lay,* 101–5 (Eng).

"Lai d'Ignaure"

Milad Doueihi, "The Lure of the Heart," *SFR* 14 (Spring–Fall 1990): 54–68 (Eng).

"Lai du conseil"

Donovan, *The Breton Lay,* 86–87 (Eng).

"Lai du cor"

Roger Middleton, "Ten Kings in the 'Lai du cor,' " *FS* 29 (Winter 1988–89): 15–18 (Eng).

"Lai du Lecheoir"

Donovan, *The Breton Lay,* 105–19 (Eng).

"Lai du Trot"

Donovan, *The Breton Lay,* 84–86 (Eng).

"Mélion"

Donovan, *The Breton Lay,* 74–75 (Eng).

"Quant vient en mai que l'on dit as lons jors"

Michel Zink, *Les Chansons de toile* (Paris: Honoré Champion, 1977), 38–41 (Fr).

"Remonstrance à la Royne, mère du Roy, sur les Discours de P. de
Ronsard des misères du Temps"

Charbonnier, *La Poésie française et les guerres de religion,* 60–63 (Fr).

"Response aux Calomnies contenues au Discours et Suyte du Discours
sur les Misères de ce temps, faits par Messire Pierre Ronsard"

Charbonnier, *La Poésie française et les guerres de religion,* 63–76 (Fr).

" Response de la Baronie" (Seconde)

Charbonnier, *La Poésie française et les guerres de religion,* 94–96, 101–4
(Fr).

"Le Temple de Ronsard"

Charbonnier, *La Poésie française et les guerres de religion,* 96–100 (Fr).

"Tydorel"

Donovan, *The Breton Lay,* 77–80 (Eng).

Jean Frappier, "A propos du lai de 'Tydorel' et de ses éléments mythiques,"
in *Mélanges de linguistique française et de philologie et littérature médié-
vales offerts à M. Paul Imbs* (Paris: Klinchsieck, 1973), 561–87 (Fr).

"Tyolet"

Donovan, *The Breton Lay,* 80–82 (Eng).

"Vie de Saint Alexis"

Brigitte Cazelles, "Outrepasser les normes: L'Invention de soi en France
médiévale," *SFR* 14 (Spring–Fall 1990): 81–85 (Fr).

James Chiampi, "The 'Vie de Saint Alexis' and the Weight of Paternity,"
KRQ 34, no. 2 (1987): 131–40 (Eng).

Evelyn B. Vitz, " 'La vie de Saint Alexis': Narrative Analysis and the Quest
for the Sacred Subject," *PMLA* 93 (1978): 396–408 (Eng).

ANONYMOUS, "Vie de Sainte Marie L'Egyptienne"

"Vie de Sainte Marie L'Egyptienne"

Brigitte Cazelles, "Modèle ou mirage: Marie L'Egyptienne," *FR* 53 (October 1979): 13–22 (Fr).

"Vie de Saint Léger"

Zumthor, *Essai de poétique médiévale,* 317–18 (Fr).

"Voyage de Charlemagne"

John Grigsby, "A Note on the Genre of the 'Voyage de Charlemagne,'" in Lacy and Nash, eds., *Essays in Early French Literature Presented to Barbara Craig,* 1–8 (Eng).

APOLLINAIRE, GUILLAUME

"L'Adieu"

Durry, *Guillaume Apollinaire: Alcools,* vol. 2, 154–56 (Fr).

"L'Adieu du cavalier"

Margaret Davies, "Le Médaillon toujours fermé," *RLM* 450–55 (1976): 96–97 (Fr).

"Arbre"

Leroy Breunig, "From Dada to Cubism: Apollinaire's 'Arbre,'" in Caws, ed., *About French Poetry from Dada to "Tel Quel,"* 25–41 (Eng).

Renaud, *Lecture d'Apollinaire,* 331–45 (Fr).

"Aussi bien que les cigales"

Arminel Marrow, "Form and Meaning in Apollinaire's Picture-Poems," *AJFS* 5 (September–December 1968): 296 (Eng).

APOLLINAIRE, GUILLAUME, "Le Brasier"

"La Blanche neige"

Mechthild Cranston, "A la découverte de 'Blanche neige' de Guillaume Apollinaire," *FR* 39 (April 1966): 684–93 (Fr).

Henri Jones, "Entre expressionnisme et cubisme: Apollinaire peintre de la plume," in De Fabry and Hilgar, eds., *Etudes autour d' "Alcools,"* 124–25 (Fr).

Mario Richter, "'La Blanche neige' d'Apollinaire," in De Fabry and Hilgar, eds., *Etudes autour d' "Alcools,"* 41–50 (Fr).

"Le Bœuf"

Couffignal, *Apollinaire,* 63–64 (Fr); 57–58 (Eng).

"La Boucle retrouvée"

Margaret Davies, "Le Médaillon toujours fermé," *RLM* 450–55 (1976): 82–85 (Fr).

"Le Brasier"

Bates, *Guillaume Apollinaire,* 85–87; rev. ed., 76–78 (Eng).

Mechthild Cranston, "Sortir d'Orkenise: Réflexions sur 'Onirocritique,' 'Le Brasier,' et 'Les Fiançailles,'" *RLM* 166–69 (1967): 53–72 (Fr).

Margaret Davies, "Le Brasier," in De Fabry and Hilgar, eds., *Etudes autour d' "Alcools,"* 1–13 (Fr).

Durry, *Guillaume Apollinaire: Alcools,* vol. 3, 162–65 (Fr).

Lawrence Lipson, "Apollinaire Student of Dante?" *SFr* 15 (April 1971): 99–100 (Eng).

S. I. Lockerbie, "Alcools et le symbolisme," *RLM* 85–89 (1963): 19–20 (Fr).

Morhangue-Bégué and Lartique, *Alcools Apollinaire,* 28–30, 59–60 (Fr).

Pauline Newman-Gordon, "Apothéoses solaires et astrales chez Apollinaire," in De Fabry and Hilgar, eds., *Etudes autour d' "Alcools,"* 85–89 (Fr).

Renaud, *Lecture d'Apollinaire,* 73–74, 116–17, 132–33 (Fr).

APOLLINAIRE, GUILLAUME, "C'est Lou qu'on la nommait"

Jean Richer, "Le Destin comme matière poétique chez Guillaume Apollinaire," *RLM* 166–69 (1967): 17–19 (Fr).

"C'est Lou qu'on la nommait"

Renaud, *Lecture d'Apollinaire*, 392–94 (Fr).

"La Chanson du Mal-Aimé"

Bates, *Guillaume Apollinaire*, 51–57; rev. ed., 38–46 (Eng).

Claude Bégué, "Le Champ lexico-sémantique de 'blanc' dans la 'Chanson du Mal-Aimé,'" *ELit* 5 (August 1972): 213–38 (Fr).

David Berry, "Apollinaire's Solar Imagery," in Cardinal, ed., *Sensibility and Creation*, 42–43, 53–54 (Eng).

Madeleine Boisson, "Orphée et anti-Orphée dans l'œuvre d'Apollinaire," *RLM* 249–53 (1970): 15–19, 25–29 (Fr).

"La Structure septenaire des 'Sept épées' à 'La Rose de Hildesheim,'" *RLM* 677–81 (1983): 61–66 (Fr).

Leroy Breunig, "Apollinaire et les sirènes," *RLM* 677–81 (1983): 43–59 (Fr).

Peter Collier, "Nerval in Apollinaire's 'La Chanson du Mal-Aimé,'" *FSB* 6 (1983): 9–13 (Eng).

Couffignal, *Apollinaire*, 53–54 (Eng); 59–60 (Fr).

Couffignal, *L'Inspiration biblique*, 81–85 (Fr).

Margaret Davies, "La 'Chanson du Mal-Aimé': Semblance et ressemblance," *RLM* 677–81 (1983): 9–30 (Fr).

Daniel Delbreil, "Remarques sur l'inspiration religieuse des 'Sept épées,'" *RLM* 677–81 (1983): 67–93 (Fr).

Françoise Dininman, "'Les Sept Epées'—une 'Alchimie du verbe'?" *RLM* 677–81 (1983): 95–114 (Fr).

Durry, *Guillaume Apollinaire: Alcools*, vol. 3, 136–40; 3d ed., vol. 1, 233–34 (Fr).

Lionel Follet, "Images et thèmes de l'amour malheureux dans 'Les Sept Epées,'" *Europe* 44 (November–December 1966): 206–39 (Fr).

APOLLINAIRE, GUILLAUME, "Chant de l'honneur"

Antoine Fongaro, "Encore 'Les Sept Epées,'" *RLM* 249–53 (1970): 123–33 (Fr).

James R. Lawler, "Apollinaire et 'La Chanson du Mal-Aimé,'" *AJFS* 1 (September–December 1964): 272–93 (Fr).

Lawler, *The Language of French Symbolism,* 233–62 (Eng).

S. I. Lockerbie, "Alcools et le symbolisme," *RLM* 85–89 (1963): 10–14 (Fr).

Morhangue-Bégué and Lartique, *Alcools Apollinaire,* 37–38, 52, 59 (Fr).

Jean Pernet, "La Place et la signification des 'Sept Epées' dans 'La Chanson du Mal-Aimé,'" in De Fabry and Hilgar, eds., *Etudes autour d' "Alcools,"* 15–24 (Fr).

Maurice Piron, "Sur quelques passages de 'La Chanson du Mal-Aimé,'" *RLM* 85–89 (1963): 90–100 (Fr).

Renaud, *Lecture d'Apollinaire,* 59–63, 111–12 (Fr).

Jean Richer, "Le Destin comme matière poétique chez Guillaume Apollinaire," *RLM* 166–69 (1967): 21–22, 26–31 (Fr).

Léon Somville, "La 'Chanson du Mal-Aimé: Du contenu à l'expression, enjeu d'une lecture," *RLM* 677–81 (1983): 31–41 (Fr).

Stamelman, *The Drama of Self,* 166–209 (Eng).

"Les Sept Epées"

Antoine Fongaro, "Les Sept Epées et le plaisir des dieux," *RLM* 327–30 (1972): 111–19 (Fr).

Pol Gossiaux, "Recherches sur 'Les Sept Epées,'" *RLM* 146–49 (1966): 41–83 (Fr).

"Le Chant d'amour"

Durry, *Guillaume Apollinaire: Alcools,* vol. 2, 99–101; 3d ed., vol. 2, 99–101 (Fr).

"Chant de l'honneur"

J. G. Clark, "La Poésie, la politique et la guerre," *RLM* 450–55 (1976): 33–46 (Fr).

APOLLINAIRE, GUILLAUME, "Chant de l'horizon en Champagne"

"Chant de l'horizon en Champagne"

Anne H. Greet, "Wordplay in Apollinaire's 'Calligrammes,'" *ECr* 10 (Winter 1970): 299–300, 305–6 (Eng).

Renaud, *Lecture d'Apollinaire,* 425–29 (Fr).

"Chantre"

Antoine Fongaro, "Un Vers univers," *RLM* 450–55 (1976): 109–18 (Fr).

Marc Poupon, "Un Parangon de poésie apollinarienne 'Chantre,'" *RLM* 450–55 (1976): 119–24 (Fr).

"Chevaux de frise"

Renaud, *Lecture d'Apollinaire,* 418–24 (Fr).

"Clair de lune"

Madeleine Boisson, "Orphée et anti-Orphée dans l'œuvre d'Apollinaire," *RLM* 249–53 (1970): 11–13 (Fr).

Durry, *Guillaume Apollinaire: Alcools,* vol. 2, 48–50; 3d ed., vol. 2, 48–50 (Fr).

"Cœur, couronne et miroir"

Arminel Marrow, "Form and Meaning in Apollinaire's Picture-Poems," *AJFS* 5 (September–December 1968): 296–99 (Eng).

Renaud, *Lecture d'Apollinaire,* 375–78 (Fr).

"Les Colchiques"

Jean Bellemin-Noël, "Petit supplément aux lectures des 'Colchiques,'" *Poétique* 9 (February 1978): 66–73 (Fr).

Michel Deguy, *Choses de la poésie et affaire culturelle* (Paris: Hachette, 1986), 66–73 (Fr).

Michel Deguy, "Encore une lecture des 'Colchiques,'" *Poétique* 5 (November 1974): 452–57 (Fr).

Françoise Dininman, "Toujours à propos des 'Colchiques,'" in De Fabry and Hilgar, eds., *Etudes autour d' "Alcools,"* 25–40 (Fr).

Durry, *Guillaume Apollinaire: Alcools,* vol. 2, 149–54; 3d ed., vol. 2, 149–52 (Fr).

Lawrence Lipson, "Apollinaire Student of Dante?" *SFr* 15 (April 1971): 98–99 (Eng).

Peter Por, "Notes en marge des textes d'Apollinaire," *RLM* 971–76 (1991): 135–37 (Fr).

D. C. Potts, "The Interpretation of Apollinaire's 'Les Colchiques,'" *FS* 26 (October 1972): 430–33 (Eng).

"Les Collines"

Bates, *Guillaume Apollinaire,* 146–49; rev. ed., 140–45 (Eng).

Scott Bates, "'Les Collines,' dernier testament d'Apollinaire," *RLM* 69–70 (Spring 1962): 25–39 (Fr).

Couffignal, *Apollinaire,* 97–98 (Eng), 102–3 (Fr).

Couffignal, *L'Inspiration biblique,* 102–3 (Fr).

S. I. Lockerbie, "'Alcools' et le symbolisme," *RLM* 85–89 (1963): 39–40 (Fr).

S. I. Lockerbie, "Le Rôle de l'imagination dans 'Calligrammes,'" *RLM* 166–69 (1967): 88–97, 103–4 (Fr).

Renaud, *Lecture d'Apollinaire,* 287–88, 449–54 (Fr).

"La Colombe poignardée"

Jean Lapacherie, "Ecriture et lecture du calligramme," *Poétique* 13 (April 1982): 198–200 (Fr).

"Cors de chasse"

Durry, *Guillaume Apollinaire: Alcools,* vol. 2, 156–67 (Fr).

Renaud, *Lecture d'Apollinaire,* 109–10, 201 (Fr).

APOLLINAIRE, GUILLAUME, "Cortège"

"Cortège"

Marguerite Bonnet, "A propos de 'Cortège': Apollinaire et Picabia," *RLM* 85–89 (1963): 62–75 (Fr).

Morhangue-Bégué and Lartique, *Alcools Apollinaire,* 30–32 (Fr).

Renaud, *Lecture d'Apollinaire,* 84–87, 153–57, 160–61 (Fr).

Stamelman, *The Drama of Self,* 39–55 (Eng).

Richard Stamelman, "The 'Fatal Shadow' of Otherness: Desire and Identity in the Poetry of Guillaume Apollinaire," *FrF* 8 (May 1983): 156–57. Reprinted in Stamelman, *Lost Beyond Telling,* 84–86 (Eng).

"La Cravate et la montre"

Jean Lapacherie, "Ecriture et lecture du calligramme," *Poétique* 13 (April 1982): 200–201 (Fr).

Longree, *L'Expérience idéo-calligrammatique,* 106–11 (Fr).

"Crépuscule"

Durry, *Guillaume Apollinaire: Alcools,* vol. 2, 59–61 (Fr).

Stamelman, *The Drama of Self,* 106–18 (Eng).

"Dans l'abri-caverne"

Renaud, *Lecture d'Apollinaire,* 415–18, 422–24 (Fr).

Richard Stamelman, "The 'Fatal Shadow' of Otherness: Desire and Identity in the Poetry of Guillaume Apollinaire," *FrF* 8 (May 1983): 153–55. Reprinted in Stamelman, *Lost Beyond Telling,* 80–83 (Eng).

"Deuxième canonnier conducteur"

Renaud, *Lecture d'Apollinaire,* 432–35 (Fr).

APOLLINAIRE, GUILLAUME, "L'Ermite"

"1909"

Michel Décaudin, " '1909': Obscurité et composition chez Apollinaire," *EF* 15 (March 1963): 119–25 (Fr).

Renée R. Hubert, "L'Elan vers l'actuel dans la poésie d'Apollinaire et de Breton," *RLM,* no. 183–88 (1968): 196 (Fr).

Jean Richer, "Une Prémonition d'Apollinaire: '1909,' " *FR* 39 (February 1966): 491–95 (Fr).

"Le Dôme de Cologne"

Couffignal, *L'Inspiration biblique,* 119–20 (Fr).

Durry, *Guillaume Apollinaire: Alcools,* 3d ed., vol. 1, 157–58 (Fr).

"Du coton dans les oreilles"

Renaud, *Lecture d'Apollinaire,* 424–25 (Fr).

"L'Eléphant"

Pol Gossiaux, "Sur léléphant du 'Bestiaire,' " *RLM* 217–22, no. 6 (1969): 211–12 (Fr).

"L'Emigrant de Landor Road"

Bates, *Guillaume Apollinaire,* 58–59; rev. ed., 46–47 (Eng).

Morhangue-Bégué and Lartigue, *Alcools Apollinaire,* 38–39, 57–58 (Fr).

Renaud, *Lecture d'Apollinaire,* 63–65 (Fr).

"L'Ermite"

Durry, *Guillaume Apollinaire: Alcools,* vol. 1, 192–207; 3d ed., vol. 1, 192–207 (Fr).

13

APOLLINAIRE, GUILLAUME, "Un Fantôme de nuées"

"Un Fantôme de nuées"

Margaret Davies, "Poetry as the Reconciliation of Contradictions in Apollinaire," in Beaumont, Cocking, and Cruickshank, eds., *Order and Adventure in Post–Romantic French Poetry*, 181–92 (Eng).

Renaud, *Lecture d'Apollinaire*, 277–80, 286 (Fr).

Philippe Renaud, " 'Ondes,' ou les métamorphoses de la musique," in Décaudin, ed., *Apollinaire et la musique*, 27–31 (Fr).

Stamelman, *The Drama of Self*, 117 (Eng).

"Les Femmes"

Durry, *Guillaume Apollinaire: Alcools*, vol. 3, 102–8 (Fr).

Philippe Renaud, "L'Effraie et le rossignol, ou Les Enigmes du tremblement," *RLM* 249–53 (1970): 60–62 (Fr).

"Les Fenêtres"

Bates, *Guillaume Apollinaire*, 113; rev. ed., 108–9 (Eng).

Kay W. Blandford, "Apollinaire's 'Les Fenêtres,' " *Expl* 22 (January 1964): 12–14 (Eng).

J. G. Clark, "Delaunay, Apollinaire, et 'Les Fenêtres,' " *RLM* 183–88 (1968): 100–11 (Fr).

K. R. Dutton, "Apollinaire and Communication," *AJFS* 5 (September–December 1968): 309–10 (Eng).

Renée Linkhorn, " 'Les Fenêtres': Propos sur trois poèmes," *FR* 44 (February 1971): 513–15, 518–21 (Fr).

S. I. Lockerbie, "Le Rôle de l'imagination dans 'Calligrammes,' première partie: 'Les Fenêtres' et le poème créé," *RLM* 146–49 (1966): 6–13, 16–22 (Fr).

S. I. Lockerbie, "Qu'est-ce que l'Orphisme d'Apollinaire?" in Décaudin, ed., *Apollinaire et la musique*, 81–87 (Fr).

Marc Poupon, "Remarques à propos d'une iconographie," *RLM* 166–69 (1967): 117–20 (Fr).

Renaud, *Lecture d'Apollinaire*, 296–303, 350–68 (Fr).

APOLLINAIRE, GUILLAUME, "La Grâce exilée"

Michael Rowland, "Apollinaire's 'Les Fenêtres,'" *Expl* 35 (Fall 1976): 24–25 (Eng).

"Les Feux du bivouac"

Margaret Davies, "Le Médaillon toujours fermé," *RLM* 450–55 (1976): 88–90 (Fr).

"Les Fiançailles"

Bates, *Guillaume Apollinaire,* 87–94; rev. ed., 78–85 (Eng).

David Berry, "Apollinaire's Solar Imagery," in Cardinal, ed., *Sensibility and Creation,* 50–51 (Eng).

Mechthild Cranston, "Sortir d'Orkenise: Réflexions sur 'Onirocritique,' 'Le Brasier,' et 'Les Fiançailles,'" *RLM* 166–69 (1967): 54–58, 72 (Fr).

Susan Harrow, "'Les Fiançailles,' cristallisation d'un amour," *RLM* 805–11 (1987): 119–34 (Fr).

S. I. Lockerbie, "Alcools et le symbolisme," *RLM* 85–89 (1963): 20–22 (Fr).

Renaud, *Lecture d'Apollinaire,* 73–74, 117–22, 125–26, 149–51 (Fr).

Jean Richer, "Le Destin comme matière poétique chez Guillaume Apollinaire," *RLM* 166–69 (1967): 19–20 (Fr).

"Fusée"

Anne H. Greet, "Wordplay in Apollinaire's 'Calligrammes,'" *ECr* 10 (Winter 1970): 302–3 (Eng).

"Fusée-signal"

Renaud, *Lecture d'Apollinaire,* 472–74 (Fr).

"La Grâce exilée"

Margaret Davies, "Le Médaillon toujours fermé," *RLM* 450–55 (1976): 79–82 (Fr).

Marc Poupon, "La Grâce exilée," *RLM* 327 (1972): 105–8 (Fr).

APOLLINAIRE, GUILLAUME, "Les Grenadines repentantes"

"Les Grenadines repentantes"

Margaret Davies, "Le Médaillon toujours fermé," *RLM* 450–55 (1976): 90–93 (Fr).

Anne H. Greet, "Wordplay in Apollinaire's 'Calligrammes,'" *ECr* 10 (Winter 1970): 298–99 (Eng).

"Il pleut"

Renaud, *Lecture d'Apollinaire,* 273–77 (Fr).

"Il y a"

Durry, *Guillaume Apollinaire: Alcools,* vol. 2, 101–4; 3d ed., vol. 2, 101–4 (Fr).

Renée R. Hubert, "L'Elan vers l'actuel dans la poésie d'Apollinaire et de Breton," *RLM* 183–88 (1968): 197–98 (Fr).

"Les Jeunes: Picasso peintre"

Longree, *L'Expérience idéo-calligrammatique,* 167–72 (Fr).

"La Jolie Rousse"

Anna Balakian, "Breton in the Light of Apollinaire," in Caws, ed., *About French Poetry,* 48–49 (Eng).

Couffignal, *Apollinaire,* 98–99 (Eng); 103–4 (Fr).

Couffignal, *L'Inspiration biblique,* 103–4 (Fr).

S. I. Lockerbie, "Le Rôle de l'imagination dans 'Calligrammes,'" *RLM* 166–69 (1967): 90–92, 104 (Fr).

Renaud, *Lecture d'Apollinaire,* 454–58 (Fr).

Jean Richer, "Le Destin comme matière poétique chez Guillaume Apollinaire," *RLM* 166–69 (1967): 24–25 (Fr).

"Le Larron"

Bates, *Guillaume Apollinaire,* 28–33; rev. ed., 14–19 (Eng).

Scott Bates, "The Identity of Apollinaire's 'Larron,'" *FR* 40 (October 1966): 56–64 (Eng).

Couffignal, *Apollinaire,* 28–29 (Eng); 34–36 (Fr).

Couffignal   *L'Inspiration biblique,* 78–79, 131–34 (Fr).

Mechthild Cranston, "Apprendre 'Le Larron' de Guillaume Apollinaire," *PMLA* 82 (October 1967): 325–32 (Fr).

Durry, *Guillaume Apollinaire: Alcools,* vol. 1, 223–33; 3d ed., vol. 1, 223–33 (Fr).

Antoine Fongaro, "Apollinaire et les rêveries de crapaud," *RLM* 276–79 (1971): 85–98 (Fr).

Claudine Gothot-Mersch, "Apollinaire et le symbolisme: 'Le Larron,'" *RHL* 67 (July–September 1967): 590–600 (Fr).

Morhangue-Bégué and Lartigue, *Alcools Apollinaire,* 21–25 (Fr).

Marc Poupon, "'Le Larron': Essai d'exégèse," *RLM* 166–69 (1976): 35–51 (Fr).

"Lettre-Océan"

Bates, *Guillaume Apollinaire,* rev. ed., 107 (Eng).

Willard Bohn, "Circular Poem—Paintings by Apollinaire and Carrà," *CL* 31 (1979): 247–60 (Eng).

K. R. Dutton, "Apollinaire and Communication," *AJFS* 5 (September–December 1968): 311–12 (Eng).

Longree, *L'Expérience idéo-calligrammatique,* 57–60 (Fr).

Renaud, *Lecture d'Apollinaire,* 371–72 (Fr).

"Liens"

Renaud, *Lecture d'Apollinaire,* 273–77, 457–58 (Fr).

APOLLINAIRE, GUILLAUME, "Loin du pigeonnier"

"Loin du pigeonnier"

Anna Whiteside, "Poèmes de guerre et d'amour, ou la double chevauchée d'Apollinaire," *FR* 54 (May 1981): 807–8 (Fr).

"La Loreley"

Durry, *Guillaume Apollinaire: Alcools,* vol. 3, 81–87 (Fr).

"Lul de Faltenin"

Bates, *Guillaume Apollinaire,* 59–60; rev. ed., 47–49 (Eng).

Jacqueline Bellas, "Lul de Faltenin," *RLM* 327 (1972): 95–100 (Fr).

David Berry, "Apollinaire's Solar Imagery," in Cardinal, ed., *Sensibility and Creation,* 51–52 (Eng).

Léon Cellier, "Lecture de 'Lul de Faltenin,' " *RLM* 327 (1972): 65–78 (Fr).

Margaret Davies, "Lul de Faltenin," *RLM* 327 (1972): 89–93 (Fr).

Renaud, *Lecture d'Apollinaire,* 70–72, 115, 199–200, 495–502 (Fr).

"Lundi rue Christine"

Hans-Robert Jauss, "1912: Threshold to an Epoch: Apollinaire's 'Zone' and 'Lundi rue Christine,' " *YFS,* no. 74 (1988): 44–53 (Eng).

Renaud, *Lecture d'Apollinaire,* 294–96, 314–24 (Fr).

"Mai"

Curnier, *Pages commentées d'auteurs contemporains,* vol. 2, 51–64 (Fr).

Katz and Hall, *Explicating French Texts,* 58–63 (Fr).

Stamelman, *The Drama of Self,* 62–78 (Eng).

"La Maison des morts"

Auffret and Auffret, *Le Commentaire composé,* 164–72 (Fr).

"La Mandoline, l'œillet et le bambou"

Longree, *L'Expérience idéo-calligrammatique,* 194–232 (Fr).

"Marie"

Henri Jones, "Entre expressionnisme et cubisme: Apollinaire peintre de la plume," in De Fabry and Hilgar, eds., *Etudes autour d'"Alcools,"* 123–124 (Fr).

"Marizibill"

Durry, *Guillaume Apollinaire: Alcools,* vol. 3, 112–17; 3d ed., vol. 3, 100, 108–9, 112–16 (Fr).

"Merlin et la vieille femme"

Durry, *Guillaume Apollinaire: Alcools,* vol. 1, 207–23; 3d ed., vol. 1, 207–23; vol. 3, 123–25 (Fr).

Morhangue-Bégué and Lartigue, *Alcools Apollinaire,* 21–22, 56–57 (Fr).

Renaud, *Lecture d'Apollinaire,* 46–50, 113, 158–60 (Fr).

Stamelman, *The Drama of Self,* 78–100 (Eng).

Richard Stamelman, "The Dramatic Structure of Apollinaire's 'Merlin et la vieille femme,' " *FR* 46 (Special Issue 5) (Spring 1973): 120–30 (Eng).

"Merveille de la guerre"

Renaud, *Lecture d'Apollinaire,* 144–46, 438–43 (Fr).

Richard Stamelman, "The 'Fatal Shadow' of Otherness: Desire and Identity in the Poetry of Guillaume Apollinaire," *FrF* 8 (May 1983): 158–59. Reprinted in Stamelman, *Lost Beyond Telling,* 87–88 (Eng).

"Minuit"

Longree, *L'Expérience idéo-calligrammatique,* 116–20 (Fr).

APOLLINAIRE, GUILLAUME, "La Mort du grand Pan"

"La Mort du grand Pan"

Raymond Pouilliart, "Sur 'La Mort du grand Pan,' " *RLM* 146–49 (1966): 23–26 (Fr).

"Le Musicien de Saint-Merry"

Antoine Fongaro, "Le vingt et un du mois de mai," *RLM* 380–84 (1973): 133–36 (Fr).

Jean Levaillant, "L'Espace dans 'Calligrammes,' " *RLM* 217–22 (1969): 54–56 (Fr).

S. I. Lockerbie, "Le Musicien de Saint-Merry," *CAIEF* 23 (May 1971): 197–209 (Fr).

Octavio Paz, " 'The Musician of Saint-Merry' by Apollinaire: A Translation and a Study," *ECr* 10 (Winter 1970): 269–84 (Eng).

Marc Poupon, "Le Musicien de Saint-Merry," *CAIEF* 23 (May 1971): 211–20 (Fr).

Renaud, *Lecture d'Apollinaire,* 280–86, 309 (Fr).

Philippe Renaud, "Le Musicien de Saint-Merry," *CAIEF* 23 (May 1971): 181–95 (Fr).

Philippe Renaud, " 'Ondes,' ou les métamorphoses de la musique," in Décaudin, ed., *Apollinaire et la musique,* 25–27, 30–31 (Fr).

Richter, *La Crise du logos,* 99–105 (Fr).

"Nuit rhénane"

Philippe Renaud, "L'Effraie et le rossignol, ou les énigmes du tremblement," *RLM* 249–53 (1970): 46–51 (Fr).

Stamelman, *The Drama of Self,* 56–61 (Eng).

"O ma jeunesse abandonnée"

William Wallace, "Apollinaire's 'O ma jeunesse abandonnée,' " *Expl* 28 (January 1970): 8–10 (Eng).

Renaud, *Lecture d'Apollinaire,* 406–8 (Fr).

"Océan de terre"

Durry, *Guillaume Apollinaire: Alcools,* 3d ed, vol. 2, 92–94 (Fr).

Renaud, *Lecture d'Apollinaire,* 406–8 (Fr.)

"Ombre"

David Berry, "Apollinaire's Solar Imagery," in Cardinal, ed., *Sensibility and Creation,* 55 (Eng).

Maryann De Julio, "The Drama of Self in Apollinaire and Reverdy: Play of Light and Shadow," *FrF* 6 (May 1981): 154–57 (Eng).

Renaud, *Lecture d'Apollinaire,* 126–27 (Fr).

Richard Stamelman, "The 'Fatal Shadow' of Otherness: Desire and Identity in the Poetry of Guillaume Apollinaire," *FrF* 8 (May 1983): 148–52. Reprinted in Stamelman, *Lost Beyond Telling,* 74–77 (Eng).

"Onirocritique"

Durry, *Guillaume Apollinaire: Alcools,* vol. 2, 92–94; 3d ed., vol. 2, 78–86 (Fr).

"Orphée"

Couffignal, *Apollinaire,* 58–59 (Eng); 64–5 (Fr).

Couffignal, *L'Inspiration biblique,* 64–65 (Fr).

"Pablo Picasso"

Longree, *L'Expérience idéo-calligrammatique,* 172–92 (Fr).

"Palais"

Bates, *Guillaume Apollinaire,* 60–62; rev. ed., 49–51 (Eng).

David Berry, "Apollinaire and the Tantalus Complex," *AJFS* 9 (January–April 1972): 55–79 (Eng).

Durry, *Guillaume Apollinaire: Alcools,* vol. 2, 27–48; 3d ed., vol. 2, 33–34 (Fr).

Antoine Fongaro, " 'Chantre,' 'Palais,' 'Annie' et 'Mallarmé,' " *SFr* 16 (January–April 1972): 82–87 (Fr).

APOLLINAIRE, GUILLAUME, "Paysage"

Morhangue-Bégué and Lartigue, *Alcools Apollinaire,* 26–27, 66–67 (Fr).

Renaud, *Lecture d'Apollinaire,* 67–69 (Fr).

Stamelman, *The Drama of Self,* 25–39 (Eng).

"Paysage"

Renaud, *Lecture d'Apollinaire,* 375–78 (Fr).

"La Petite auto"

J. G. Clark, "La Poésie, la politique et la guerre," *RLM* 450–55 (1976): 19–23, 30–31 (Fr).

Renaud, *Lecture d'Apollinaire,* 387–90 (Fr).

"Pipe"

Durry, *Guillaume Apollinaire: Alcools,* 3d ed., vol. 1, 162–63 (Fr).

"Poème lu au mariage d'André Salmon"

Henri Jones, "Entre expressionnisme et cubisme: Apollinaire peintre de la plume," in De Fabry and Hilgar, eds., *Etudes autour d' "Alcools,"* 125–28 (Fr).

"Poème"

Antoine Fongaro, "J'étais guidé par la chouette . . . ," *RLM* 166–69 (1967): 75–83 (Fr).

"Le Pont"

Renaud, *Lecture d'Apollinaire,* 474–77 (Fr).

Le Pont Mirabeau"

Robert Champigny, "Analyse du 'Pont Mirabeau,' " *PMLA* 78 (September 1963): 78 (Fr).

David Hill, "Apollinaire's 'Le Pont Mirabeau,' " *Expl* 36 (Spring 1978): 30–31 (Eng).

Jean Peytard, "Forme et de-forme du sens," *AJFS* 15 (January–April 1978): 28–41 (Fr).

Renaud, *Lecture d'Apollinaire,* 196–97 (Fr).

Richard Zakarian, "Apollinaire's 'Mirabeau Bridge,'" *Expl* 45 (Winter 1987): 45–48 (Eng).

"La Porte"

Durry, *Guillaume Apollinaire: Alcools,* 3d ed., vol. 1, 81–83, 93–96 (Fr).

"Prière"

Francis Burch, "Apollinaire's 'Prière'?" *Expl* 41 (Fall 1982): 43 (Eng).

Couffignal, *L'Inspiration biblique,* 122–23 (Fr).

"Que je m'ennuie entre ces murs tout nus"

Durry, *Guillaume Apollinaire: Alcools,* 3d ed., vol. 1, 174–75 (Fr).

"Refus de la colombe"

Margaret Davies, "Le Médaillon toujours fermé," *RLM* 450–55 (1976): 77–98 (Fr).

" Rosemonde"

Broome and Chesters, *The Appreciation of Modern French Poetry (1850–1950),* 134–36 (Eng).

Robert Guiette, "Rosemonde," in Décaudin, ed., *Apollinaire et la musique,* 33–38 (Fr).

"Salomé"

Auffret and Auffret, *Le Commentaire composé,* 158–63 (Fr).

APOLLINAIRE, GUILLAUME, "Saltimbanques"

"Saltimbanques"

Durry, *Guillaume Apollinaire: Alcools,* vol. 2, 55–57; 3d ed., vol. 2, 55–59 (Fr).

"Les Sapins"

Renaud, *Lecture d'Apollinaire,* 166–67 (Fr).

"Un Soir"

Bates, *Guillaume Apollinaire,* 19–22; rev. ed., 3–7 (Eng).

"Le Son du cor"

Jean Alter, "Apollinaire and Two Shakespearean Sonnets," *CL* 14 (Fall 1962): 377–85 (Eng).

"Sur les prophéties"

Renaud, *Lecture d'Apollinaire,* 325–30 (Fr).

"La Synagogue"

Couffignal, *L'Inspiration biblique,* 86–90 (Fr).

"Tierce rime pour votre âme"

Peter-P. Por, "Notes en marge des textes d'Apollinaire," *RLM* 143–48 (1991): 133–48 (Fr).

"La Tour"

Marc Poupon, "Remarques à propos d'une iconographie," *RLM* 166–69 (1967): 110–12 (Fr).

"Tourbillon de mouches"

Margaret Davies, "Le Médaillon toujours fermé," *RLM* 450–55 (1976): 93–96 (Fr).

APOLLINAIRE, GUILLAUME, "La Victoire"

"Tours"

S. I. Lockerbie, "Le Rôle de l'imagination dans 'Calligrammes,' première partie: 'Les Fenêtres' et le poème créé," *RLM* 146–49 (1966): 13–16 (Fr).

"La Tzigane"

Broome and Chesters, *The Appreciation of Modern French Poetry (1850–1950)*, 132–34 (Eng).

Durry, *Guillaume Apollinaire: Alcools*, vol. 3, 15–25 (Fr).

Marie Jeanne Durry, "Sur 'La Tsigane,' " *RLM* 85–89 (Autumn 1963): 76–89 (Fr).

"Vendémiaire"

Bates, *Guillaume Apollinaire*, 105–8; rev. ed., 99–102 (Eng).

Madeleine Boisson, "Orphée et anti-Orphée dans l'œuvre d'Apollinaire," *RLM* 249–53 (1970): 32–34 (Fr).

Couffignal, *L'Inspiration biblique*, 140–41 (Fr).

Durry, *Guillaume Apollinaire: Alcools*, vol. 3, 42–47 (Fr).

Henri Meschonnic, "Significance de 'Vendémiaire,' " *RLM* 327–30 (1972): 41–56 (Fr).

Renaud, *Lecture d'Apollinaire*, 84–87, 137–42, 151–53, 169–70 (Fr).

"Le Vent nocturne"

Bates, *Guillaume Apollinaire*, 48–49, rev. ed., 35–36 (Eng).

Durry, *Guillaume Apollinaire: Alcools*, vol. 3, 90–91 (Fr).

"La Victoire"

Margaret Davies, "Poetry as the Reconciliation of Contradictions in Apollinaire," in Beaumont, Cocking, and Cruickshank, eds., *Order and Adventure in Post-Romantic French Poetry*, 186–87 (Eng).

Renaud, *Lecture d'Apollinaire*, 458–65 (Fr).

Richter, *La Crise du logos*, 106–47 (Fr).

APOLLINAIRE, GUILLAUME, "Visée"

"Visée"

Anne H. Greet, "Wordplay in Apollinaire's 'Calligrammes,'" *ECr* 10 (Winter 1970): 300–301 (Eng).

"Vitam impendere amori"

S. I. Lockerbie, "Le Rôle de l'imagination dans 'Calligrammes,'" *RLM* 166–69 (1967): 90–94, 99–102 (Fr).

Renaud, *Lecture d'Apollinaire,* 467–71 (Fr).

"Voyage"

Renaud, *Lecture d'Apollinaire,* 372–75 (Fr).

"Le Voyageur"

Bates, *Guillaume Apollinaire,* 100–101; rev. ed., 92–93 (Eng).

Claude Bégué, "A propos du 'Voyageur': Quelques directions stylistiques de lecture," *RLM* 276–79 (1971): 69–82 (Fr).

Couffignal, *Apollinaire,* 59–61 (Eng).

Couffignal, *L'Inspiration biblique,* 65–67 (Fr).

Durry, *Guillaume Apollinaire: Alcools,* vol. 2, 74–78; 3d ed., vol. 2, 74–78 (Fr).

Henri Jones, "Entre expressionnisme et cubisme: Apollinaire peintre de la plume," in De Fabry and Hilgar, eds., *Etudes autour d'"Alcools,"* 120–23 (Fr).

S. I. Lockerbie, "'Alcools': 'Le Voyageur,'" in Nurse, ed., *The Art of Criticism,* 226–39 (Eng).

S. I. Lockerbie, "Alcools et le symbolisme," *RLM* 85–89 (1963): 30–33 (Fr).

"Zone"

David Berry, "Apollinaire's Solar Imagery," in Cardinal, ed., *Sensibility and Creation,* 45, 50–51 (Eng).

Couffignal, *Apollinaire,* 66–86 (Eng).

Couffignal, *L'Inspiration biblique,* 69–92, 137, 139–40, 147–76 (Fr).

Couffignal, *Zone d'Apollinaire,* 3–68 (Fr).

Robert Couffignal, "Genèse de 'Zone,' " in Décaudin, ed., *Apollinaire et la musique,* 73–80 (Fr).

Anne De Fabry, "Péripatétisme et amphionie: De l'esthétique d'"Alcools,' " in De Fabry and Hilgar, eds., *Etudes autour d' "Alcools, "* 163–65 (Fr).

Durry, *Guillaume Apollinaire: Alcools,* vol. 1, 234–301; v. 3, 41–42; 3d ed., vol. 1, 79–81, 234–36, 252–74 (Fr).

C. A. Hackett, *Autour de Rimbaud* (Paris: Klincksieck, 1967), 56–58 (Fr).

C. A. Hackett, "Rimbaud and Apollinaire," *FS* 19 (July 1965): 273–74 (Eng).

Hans-Robert Jauss, "1912: Threshold to an Epoch: Apollinaire's 'Zone' and 'Lundi rue Christine,' " *YFS,* no. 74 (1988): 39–44 (Eng).

Jeannine Kohn-Etiemble, "Sur 'Zone,' " *RLM* 576–81 (1980): 79–93 (Fr).

S. I. Lockerbie, " 'Alcools' et le symbolisme," *RLM* 85–89 (1963): 33–37 (Fr).

Moreau, *Six études de métrique,* 54–66 (Fr).

Morhangue-Bégué and Lartigue, *Alcools Apollinaire,* 41–44 (Fr).

Laurence Porter, "The Fragmented Self of Apollinaire's 'Zone,' " *ECr* 10 (Winter 1970): 285–95 (Eng).

Peter Read, "Christ the Pilot in Apollinaire's 'Zone,' " *FSB* 4 (Autumn 1982): 8–10 (Eng).

Garnet Ries, "Guillaume Apollinaire and the Search for Identity," in Beaumont, Cocking, and Cruickshank, eds., *Order and Adventure in Post-Romantic French Poetry,* 169–70 (Eng).

Stamelman, *The Drama of Self,* 121–64 (Eng).

Anna Whiteside, "De la dichotomie à la dialectique," in De Fabry and Hilgar, eds., *Etudes autour d' "Alcools, "* 67–73 (Fr).

ARAGON

"Ballade de celui qui chanta dans les supplices"

Dubosclard and Dubosclard, *Du surréalisme à la Résistance,* 64–72 (Fr).

"C"

Dubosclard and Dubosclard, *Du surréalisme à la Résistance,* 57–63 (Fr).

"Cantique à Elsa"

M. Adereth, *Aragon: The Resistance Poems* (London: Grant & Cutler, 1985), 30–31 (Eng).

"Le Conscrit des cent villages"

Ian Higgins, "Tradition and Myth in French Resistance Poetry: Reaction or Subversion?" *FMLS* 21 (January 1985): 52–54 (Eng).

"Hourra l'Oural"

Lucille F. Becker, *Louis Aragon* (New York: Twayne, 1971), 39–40 (Eng).

"Il n'y a pas d'amour heureux"

M. Adereth, *Aragon: The Resistance Poems* (London: Grant & Cutler, 1985), 24–27 (Eng).

"Madame Colette"

Norma Rinsler, "Louis Aragon and the Cage of Words," *AJFS* 5 (January–April 1968): 43–44, 47–49 (Eng).

"Mon cœur battait comme une voile dans ta voix"

Mary Ann Caws, "Aragon's 'Mon cœur battait comme une voile dans ta voix,'" *Expl* 25 (February 1967): 8–9 (Eng).

"Tes yeux sont si profonds qu'en me penchant pour boire"

M. Adereth, *Aragon: The Resistance Poems* (London: Grant & Cutler, 1985), 29–30 (Eng).

ARNAUT DANIEL

"En cest sonet coind'e leri"

Topsfield, *Troubadours and Love,* 208–210 (Eng).

"Lo ferm voler"

Erik S. Ryding, "Arnaut Daniel's 'Lo ferm voler,'" *Expl* 48 (Summer 1990): 236–37 (Eng).

Topsfield, *Troubadours and Love,* 213–18 (Eng).

AUBIGNE, AGRIPPA D'

"La Création"

Cameron, *Agrippa d'Aubigné,* 142–43 (Eng).

"Discours par stances avec l'esprit du feu Roy Henry Quatriesme"

Cameron, *Agrippa d'Aubigné, 90–91 (Fr).*

"Le Printemps"

H. Weber, *La Création poétique au XVIe siècle en France,* 302–3, 327–33 (Fr).

Le Printemps I: Hécatombe à Diane

Lapp, *The Brazen Tower,* 80–81 (Eng).

Robert Mélançon, "Le rite de 'l'Hécatombe': Le 'Printemps' d'Agrippa d'Aubigné," *EF* 11 (February 1975): 5–20 (Fr).

Le Printemps I: Hécatombe à Diane, Sonnet 4
"Combattu des vents et des flots"

Mitchell Greenberg, "D'Aubigné's Sacrifice: 'L'Hécatombe à Diane' and the Textuality of Desire," *SFR* 5 (Spring 1981): 53–54 (Eng).

Le Printemps I: Hécatombe à Diane, Sonnet 12
"Souhaitte qui voudra la mort inopinée"

Cameron, *Agrippa d'Aubigné,* 28–29 (Eng).

Le Printemps II, Stances 1
"Tous ceulx qui ont gousté combien de mortz on treuve"

Robert Griffin, "The Rebirth Motif in Agrippa d'Aubigné's 'Le Printemps,'" *FS* 19 (July 1965): 234–37 (Eng).

H. Weber, *A travers le seizième siècle,* 212–18 (Fr).

Le Printemps II, Stances 20
"Quand je voy ces monts sourcilleux"

Lafay, *La Poésie française du premier XVIIe siècle,* 229–45 (Fr).

H. Weber, *A travers le seizième siècle,* 218–23 (Fr).

Le Printemps II, Stances 3
"A longs filetz de sang, ce lamentable cors"

Robert Griffin, "The Rebirth Motif in Agrippa d'Aubigné's 'Le Printemps,'" *FS* 19 (July 1965): 233–34 (Eng).

Le Printemps II, Stances 7
"Puisque le cors blessé, mollement estendu"

Robert Griffin, "The Rebirth Motif in Agrippa d'Aubigné's 'Le Printemps,'" *FS* 19 (July 1965): 231 (Eng).

Le Printemps III, Ode 14
"Au temps qu la feuille blesme"

H. Weber, *A travers le seizième siècle,* 226–28 (Fr).

Le Printemps III, Ode 23
"Que je te plains, beauté divine!"

H. Weber, *A travers le seizième siècle,* 224–26 (Fr).

AUBIGNE, AGRIPPA D', *Les Tragiques, Préface* "Autheur à son livre"

Le Printemps III, Ode 36
"La douce agréable Cybelle"

Robert Griffin, "The Rebirth Motif in Agrippa d'Aubigné's 'Le Printemps,'" *FS* 19 (July 1965): 232–33 (Eng).

"Psaume 54" (Translation)

Jean Rousselot, "D'Aubigné, prosateur, novateur," *Europe* 54 (March 1976): 25–26 (Fr).

"La Sorcière"

Jacques Bailbé, "Agrippa d'Aubigné et les sorcières," *Europe* 54 (March 1976): 42–48 (Fr).

"Les Tragiques"

Edwin Duval, "The Place of the Present: Ronsard, Aubigné, and the 'Misères de ce temps,'" *YFS,* no. 80 (1991): 19–20, 25–29 (Eng).

Michel Jeanneret, " 'Les Tragiques': Mimésis et intertexte," in Kritzman, ed., *Le Signe et le texte,* 101–13 (Fr).

Lapp, *The Brazen Tower,* 77–80, 92 (Eng).

Malcolm Quainton, *D'Aubigné: Les Tragiques* (London: Grant & Cutler, 1990), 115 pp. (Eng).

Judith Sproxton, "D'Aubigné and Bunyan: The Experience of Sin," *JES* 18 (September 1988): 156–58, 160–62, 164 (Eng).

Judith Sproxton, "Perspectives of War in the Writings of Agrippa d'Aubigné," *JES* 15 (June 1985): 139–41 (Eng).

Les Tragiques, Préface
"Autheur à son livre"

Marc Bensimon, "Essaie sur Agrippa d'Aubigné," *SFr* 7 (1963): 419–28 (Fr).

Cameron, *Agrippa d'Aubigné,* 45–46 (Eng).

Regosin, *The Poetry of Inspiration,* 72–75 (Eng).

AUBIGNE, AGRIPPA D', *Les Tragiques* "La Chambre dorée"

Les Tragiques
"La Chambre dorée"

Marc Bensimon, "Essai sur Agrippa d'Aubigné," *SFr* 7 (September–Decemgber 1963): 428–31 (Fr).

Cameron, *Agrippa d'Aubigné,* 53–55 (Eng).

Elliott Forsyth, "Le Message prophétique d'Agrippa d'Aubigné," *BHR* 41 (January 1979): 38 (Fr).

Lapp, *The Brazen Tower,* 82–83 (Eng).

Lestringant, *Agrippa D'Aubigné: Les Tragiques,* 92–96 (Fr).

Regosin, *The Poetry of Inspiration,* 20–21, 43–45, 58–59, 70–71 (Eng).

Michel Simonin, "Agrippa d'Aubigné et les 'matras enflez du poil des orphelins': Sur un passage de 'La Chambre dorée' (vv. 218–226)," *BHR* 49 (September 1987): 537–46 (Fr).

Judith Sproxton, "D'Aubigné, Milton, and the Scourge of Sin," *JES* 11 (December 1981): 267–68 (Eng).

H. Weber, *La Création poétique au XVIe siècle en France,* 630–31, 637–38, 645–51, 669–71 (Fr).

Les Tragiques
"Fers"

Cameron, *Agrippa d'Aubigné,* 58–62 (Eng).

Elliott Forsyth, "Le Message prophétique d'Agrippa d'Aubigné," *BHR* 41 (January 1979): 35–36 (Fr).

Lestringant, *Agrippa D'Aubigné: Les Tragiques,* 40–47, 77–83, 91–92 (Fr).

Regosin, *the Poetry of Inspiration,* 23–24, 48–49, 82–84, 91–93 (Eng).

Marguerite Soulié, "L'Inspiration biblique dans 'Les Tragiques,'" *Europe* 54 (March 1976): 74–75 (Fr).

H. Weber, *La Création poétique au XVIe siècle en France,* 629–33, 677, 695–98 (Fr).

Les Tragiques
"Feux"

Marc Bensimon, "Essai sur Agrippa d'Aubigné," *SFr* 7 (September–December 1963): 429–30 (Fr).

Cameron, *Agrippa d'Aubigné,* 65–68 (Eng).

Claude Dubois, "Les Images de parenté dans 'Les Tragiques,'" *Europe* 54 (March 1976): 27–42 (Fr).

Lestringant, *Agrippa D'aubigné: Les Tragiques,* 44–47, 86–91 (Fr).

Regosin, *The Poetry of Inspiration,* 21–22, 64–65, 81 (Eng).

Judith Sproxton, "D'Aubigné, Milton, and the Scourge of Sin," *JES* 11 (December 1981): 268 (Eng).

H. Weber, La Création poétique au XVIe siècle en France, 619–21, 636–37, 699 (Fr).

Les Tragiques
"Jugement"

Marc Bensimon, "Essai sur Agrippa d'Aubigné," *SFr* 7 (September–December 1963): 432–37 (Fr).

Cameron, *Agrippa d'Aubigné,* 65–68 (Eng).

James Dauphiné, "Le Sang dans 'Les Tragiques,'" *Europe* 54 (March 1976): 55–67 (Fr).

Elliott Forsyth, "Le Message prophétique d'Agrippa d'Aubigné,' *BHR* 41 (January 1979): 38–39 (Fr).

Lestringant, *Agrippa D'Aubigné: Les Tragiques,* 64–69 (Fr).

Regosin, *The Poetry of Inspiration,* 25–26, 51–52, 59–60, 86–90 (Eng).

H. Weber, La Création poétique au XVIe siècle en France, 633–34, 638–42, 692, 695–97, 712–13, 718–19 (Fr).

Les Tragiques
"Misères"

Marc Bensimon, "Essai sur Agrippa d'Aubigné," *SFr* 7 (September–December 1963): 423–25 (Fr).

Cameron, *Agrippa d'Aubigné,* 48–50, 74 (Eng).

James Dauphiné, "Le Sang dans 'Les Tragiques,'" *Europe* 54 (March 1976): 59–60 (Fr).

Elliott Forsyth, "Le Message prophétique d'Agrippa d'Aubigné," *BHR* 41 (January 1979): 26–30, 38 (Fr).

AUBIGNE, AGRIPPA D', *Les Tragiques* "Princes"

Lapp, *The Brazen Tower,* 81, 83 (Eng).

Lestringant, *Agrippa D'Aubigné: Les Tragiques,* 55–56, 58–64, 112–19 (Fr).

Regosin, *The Poetry of Inspiration,* 17–20, 27–29, 33–42 (Eng).

Marguerite Soulié, "L'Inspiration biblique dans 'Les Tragiques,' " *Europe* 54 (March 1976): 70–74 (Fr).

Judith Sproxton, "D'Aubigné, Milton, and the Scourge of Sin," *JES* 11 (December 1981): 265–66 (Eng).

H. Weber, La Création poétique au XVIe siècle en France, 635–36, 643–45, 658–68, 685–86, 697, 716–17, 721 (Fr).

Jesse Zeldin, " 'Les Tragiques' and the Baroque," *ECr* 1 (Summer 1961): 68–71, 73–74 (Eng).

Les Tragiques
"Princes"

Cameron, *Agrippa d'Aubigné,* 51–53 (Eng).

Elliott Forsyth, "Le Message prophétique d'Agrippa d'Aubigné," *BHR* 41 (January 1979): 34–35 (Fr).

Lapp, *The Brazen Tower,* 85–89 (Eng).

Regosin, *The Poetry of Inspiration,* 20, 40–43, 77 (Eng).

Judith Sproxton, "D'Aubigné, Milton, and the Scourge of Sin," *JES* 11 (December 1981): 266–67, 269 (Eng).

H. Weber, La Création poétique au XVIe siècle en France, 601–2, 608, 611–14, 651–56, 665–66, 684–85, 715, 718 (Fr).

Les Tragiques
"Vengeances"

Marc Bensimon, "Essai sur Agrippa d'Aubigné," *SFr* 7 (September–December 1963): 432 (Fr).

Cameron, *Agrippa d'Aubigné,* 62–64 (Eng).

Elliott Forsyth, "Le Message prophétique d'Agrippa d'Aubigné," *BHR* 41 (January 1979): 30–33 (Fr).

Lapp, *The Brazen Tower,* 84–85 (Eng).

Lestringant, *Agrippa D'Aubigné: Les Tragiques,* 49–52, 54–55 (Fr).

Ian D. McFarlane, "D'Aubigné: 'Les Tragiques': 'Vengeances,' " in Nurse, ed., *The Art of Criticism,* 58–68 (Eng).

Regosin, *The Poetry of Inspiration,* 24–25, 51, 81–82 (Eng).

H. Weber, La Création poétique au XVIe siècle en France, 668–69, 713–14, 717–20 (Fr).

BAIF, JEAN-ANTOINE DE

"Amymone"

Jean Braybrook, "Obliquity in Baïf's Mythological Poems," *KRQ* 33, no. 2 (1986): 143–44 (Eng).

"Baltasar mon Baïf, et que fait ta maistresse"

Rigolot, Poétique et onomastique, 183–84 (Fr).

"Hier, cueillant ceste Rose En Autonne fleurie"

H. Weber, *La Création poétique au XVIe siècle en France,* 354–56 (Fr).

"L'Hippocrène"

Jean Braybrook, "Obliquity in Baïf's Mythological Poems," *KRQ* 33, no. 2 (1986): 139–41, 144–153 (Eng).

"Hymne de la paix"

Malcolm Quainton, "Some Sources and Techniques of Source Adaptation in the Poetry of Jean-Antoine de Baïf," *FMLS* 7 (October 1971): 380–94 (Eng).

BAIF, JEAN-ANTOINE DE, "Je n'entan point la Ligue sainte"

"Je n'entan point la Ligue sainte"

Mathieu Augé-Chiquet, *La Vie, les idées, et l'œuvre de Jean Antoine de Baïf* (Paris: Hachette, 1909; reprint, Geneva: Slatkine, 1969), 561–63 (Fr).

"Long temps ha que suis aux écoutes"

Edelgard Dubruck, "Jean-Antoine de Baïf, Poet of the Absurd," *ECr* 12 (Fall 1972): 196–97 (Eng).

"Le Meurier"

Moss, *Poetry and Fable,* 111–17 (Eng).

"Les Muses"

Jean Braybrook, "Obliquity in Baïf's Mythological Poems," *KRQ* 33, no. 2 (1986): 139–40, 142 (Eng).

Chamard, *Histoire de la Pléiade,* vol. 3, 177–81 (Fr).

"O doux plaisir plein de doux pensement"

H. Weber, *La Création poétique au XVIe siècle en France,* 390–91 (Fr).

"O qu'estre bien ouy je peusse!"

Mathieu Augé-Chiquet, *La Vie, les idées, et l'œuvre de Jean Antoine de Baïf* (Paris: Hachette, 1909; reprint, Geneva: Slatkine, 1969), 556–58 (Fr).

"Premier des météores"

Mathieu Augé-Chiquet, *La Vie, les idées, et l'œuvre de Jean Antoine de Baïf* (Paris: Hachette, 1909; reprint, Geneva: Slatkine, 1969), 236–48 (Fr).

Michael Riffaterre, "Un Faux problème: L'Erosion intertextuelle," in Kritzman, ed., *Le Signe et le texte,* 53–58 (Fr).

BANVILLE, THEODORE DE, "A ma mère"

"Psaume 6" (Translation)

Jeanneret, *Poésie et tradition biblique,* 214, 231, 238–39 (Fr).

"Psaume 42" (Translation)

Jeanneret, *Poésie et tradition biblique,* 216–17 (Fr).

"Psaume 66" (Translation)

Jeanneret, *Poésie et tradition biblique,* 219–21, 224, 229–30 (Fr).

"Psaume 115" (Translation)

Jeanneret, *Poésie et tradition biblique,* 215–16, 236 (Fr).

"Salmaci"

Moss, *Poetry and Fable,* 98–110 (Eng).

"Vie des chams"

Malcolm Quainton, "Some Sources and Techniques of Source Adaptation in the Poetry of Jean-Antoine de Baïf," *FMLS* 7 (October 1971): 375–80 (Eng).

BANVILLE, THEODORE DE

"L'Ame de la lyre"

Harms, *Théodore de Banville,* 30–31 (Eng).

"A ma mère"

H. Riffaterre, *L'Orphisme dans la poésie,* 86–87 (Fr).

BANVILLE, THEODORE DE, "A Méry"

"A Méry"

Harms, *Théodore de Banville,* 37–38 (Eng).

"A Roger de Beauvoir"

Harms, *Théodore de Banville,* 38–39 (Eng).

"Les Baisers"

Harms, *Théodore de Banville,* 69 (Eng).

"Les Baisers de pierre"

Harms, *Théodore de Banville,* 18, 24 (Eng).

"Baudelaire"

Francis Heck, "Théodore de Banville's Poem: 'Baudelaire,'" *NCFS* 16 (Fall–Winter 1987–88): 84–94 (Eng).

"Le Berger"

Harms, *Théodore de Banville,* 73–74 (Eng).

"Cariatides"

H. Riffaterre, *L'Orphisme dans la poésie,* 85–86 (Fr).

"La Cithare"

Harms, *Théodore de Banville,* 77–78 (Eng).

"Décor"

Harms, *Théodore de Banville,* 28 (Eng).

BANVILLE, THEODORE DE, "Querelle"

"L'Exil des Dieux"

Harms, *Théodore de Banville,* 72–73 (Eng).

"Le Festin des dieux"

Harms, *Théodore de Banville,* 78–79 (Eng).

"L'Invincible"

Harms, *Théodore de Banville,* 60–61 (Eng).

"Le Jugement de Paris"

Harms, *Théodore de Banville,* 66–67 (Eng).

"Malédiction de Cypris"

Harms, *Théodore de Banville,* 65–66 (Eng).

"Mascarades"

Harms, *Théodore de Banville,* 45–46 (Eng).

"La Nuit"

Harms, *Théodore de Banville,* 64 (Eng).

"La Nuit de printemps"

Harms, *Théodore de Banville,* 14–15 (Eng).

"Querelle"

Denommé, *The French Parnassian Poets,* 71–73 (Eng).

39

BANVILLE, THEODORE DE, "Le Saut du tremplin"

"Le Saut du tremplin"

Denommé, *The French Parnassian Poets,* 74–75 (Eng).

"Songe d'hiver"

Harms, *Théodore de Banville,* 19 (Eng).
H. Riffaterre, *L'Orphisme dans la poésie,* 126–27 (Fr).

"Les Souffrances de l'artiste"

Harms, *Théodore de Banville,* 61–62 (Eng).

"V——le baigneur"

Harms, *Théodore de Banville,* 47–49 (Eng).

"La Voie lactée"

Harms, *Théodore de Banville,* 19–21, 24 (Eng).

BAUDELAIRE, CHARLES

"Abel et Cäin"

Galand, *Baudelaire,* 417–18 (Fr).

"A celle qui est trop gaie"

Galand, *Baudelaire,* 435–37 (Fr).
Prévost, *Baudelaire,* 224–25 (Fr).
Turnell, *Baudelaire,* 129–31 (Eng).
Zilberberg, *Une Lecture des "Fleurs du mal,"* 97–99 (Fr).

"L'Albatros"

Galand, *Baudelaire*, 259 (Fr).

Frederick Locke, "L'Albatros," *Expl* 20 (January 1962): 44. Reprinted in Walcutt and Whitesell, eds., *The Explicator Cyclopedia*, vol. 2, 27–28 (Eng).

Richter, *La Crise du logos*, 11–24 (Fr).

André Spire, "Baudelaire esthéticien et précurseur du symbolisme," *Europe* 45 (April–May 1967): 84–85 (Fr).

"Alchimie de la douleur"

Galand, *Baudelaire*, 340–42 (Fr).

Quesnel, *Baudelaire solaire et clandestin*, 200–201 (Fr).

"Allégorie"

Galand, *Baudelaire*, 407–9 (Fr).

Prévost, *Baudelaire*, 151–52, 263 (Fr).

"L'Ame du vin"

Galand, *Baudelaire*, 389–90 (Fr).

"L'Amour du mensonge"

Aguettant, *Baudelaire*, 175–77 (Fr).

Galand, *Baudelaire*, 379–81 (Fr).

Prévost, *Baudelaire*, 218–19 (Fr).

"L'Amour et le crâne"

F. W. Leakey, "Baudelaire: The Poet as Moralist," in *Studies in Modern French Literature Presented to P. Mansell Jones*, 208–9 (Eng).

Prévost, *Baudelaire*, 138–39, 217–18, 252–53 (Fr).

BAUDELAIRE, CHARLES, "L'Aube spirituelle"

"L'Aube spirituelle"

Galand, *Baudelaire,* 301–2 (Fr).

Quesnel, *Baudelaire solaire et clandestin,* 190–91 (Fr).

"Au lecteur"

Carter, *Charles Baudelaire,* 56–58 (Eng).

Ross Chambers, "Poetry in the Asiatic Mode: Baudelaire's 'Au Lecteur,' " *YFS,* no. 74 (1988): 97–116 (Eng).

F. W. Leakey, "Baudelaire: The Poet as Moralist," in *Studies in Modern French Literature Presented to P. Mansell Jones* (Manchester: Manchester University Press, 1961), 204–7 (Eng).

Charles Mauron, "Premières recherches sur la structure inconsciente des 'Fleurs du mal,' " in *Baudelaire: Actes du Colloque de Nice, 25–27 ed. mai 1967* (Paris: Minard, 1968), 131–33 (Fr).

Prévost, *Baudelaire,* 176–77 (Fr).

Turnell, *Baudelaire,* 97–100 (Eng).

Nathaniel Wing, "The Stylistic Functions of Rhetoric in Baudelaire's 'Au lecteur,' " *KRQ* 19, no. 4 (1972): 447–60 (Eng).

"A une madone"

Jeanne Bem, "Psychanalyse et poétique baudelairiennes," *Poétique* 7 (February 1976): 30–35 (Fr).

Chesters, *Baudelaire and the Poetics of Craft,* 84–86 (Eng).

Galand, *Baudelaire,* 314–16 (Fr).

Prévost, *Baudelaire,* 147–48, 223 (Fr).

Turnell, *Baudelaire,* 147–52 (Eng).

"A une malabaraise"

F. W. Leakey, "Baudelaire: The Poet as Moralist," in *Studies in Modern French Literature Presented to P. Mansell Jones* 198–200 (Eng).

BAUDELAIRE, CHARLES, "Avec ses vêtements ondoyants et nacrés"

"A une mendiante rousse"

Cassou-Yager, *La Polyvalence du thème de la mort,* 48–49 (Fr).

Ross Chambers, "Baudelaire's Street Poetry," *NCFS* 13 (Summer 1985): 247–49 (Eng).

"A une passante"

Aguettant, *Baudelaire,* 157–59 (Fr).

Donald Aynesworth, "A Face in the Crowd: A Baudelairean Vision of the Eternal Feminine," *SFR* 5 (Winter 1981): 329–39 (Eng).

Ross Chambers, "Baudelaire's Street Poetry," *NCFS* 13 (Summer 1985): 247–49 (Eng).

Ross Chambers, "Pour une poétique de vêtement," in Gray, ed., *Poétiques,* 39–41 (Fr).

Galand, *Baudelaire,* 372–73 (Fr).

John Humphries, "Poetical History or Historical Poetry: Baudelaire's 'Epouvantable jeu' of Love and Art," *KRQ* 30, no. 3 (1983): 233–36 (Eng).

Porter, *The Crisis of French Symbolism,* 143–46 (Eng).

Timothy Raser, "Language and the Erotic in Two Poems by Baudelaire," *RR* 79 (May 1988): 449–51 (Eng).

Richard Stamelman, "The Shroud of Allegory: Death, Mourning, and Melancholy in Baudelaire's Work," *Texas Studies in Literature and Language* 25 (1983): 390–409. Reprinted in Stamelman, *Lost Beyond Telling,* 58–67 (Eng).

"Avec ses vêtements ondoyants et nacrés"

Ross Chambers, "Pour une poétique du vêtement," in Gray, ed., *Poétiques,* 36–38 (Fr).

Galand, *Baudelaire,* 282–83 (Fr).

F. W. Leakey, "The Amorous Tribute: Baudelaire and the Renaissance Tradition," in D. R. Haggis et al., eds., *The French Renaissance and Its Heritage. Essays Presented to Alan Boase* (London: Methuen, 1968), 107–8. Reprinted in Leakey, *Baudelaire,* 84–85 (Eng).

BAUDELAIRE, CHARLES, "Les Aveugles"

Mossop, *Pure Poetry,* 69–70 (Eng).

Turnell, *Baudelaire,* 122–24 (Eng).

"Les Aveugles"

Aguettant, *Baudelaire,* 154–56 (Fr).

Galand, *Baudelaire,* 369–72 (Fr).

Peter Nurse, "Baudelaire: 'Les Fleurs du mal': 'Les Aveugles,'" in Nurse, ed., *The Art of Criticism,* 194–203 (Eng).

Turnell, *Baudelaire,* 192–93, 254 (Eng).

"Le Balcon"

Bertocci, *From Symbolism to Baudelaire,* 115–17 (Eng).

Carter, *Charles Baudelaire,* 68–69 (Eng).

Georges Combet, "Les Parallélismes de 'Booz endormi,'" *RLM* 693–97 (1984): 85–86 (Fr).

Jean Duval, "Pages sur Baudelaire," *Europe* 45 (April–May 1967): 40–41 (Fr).

Helen R. Elam, "Temporality in Baudelaire," in Bloom, ed., *Charles Baudelaire,* 146–47 (Eng).

Galand, *Baudelaire,* 290 (Fr).

Doris Kadish and L. Brian Price, "A View From the Balconies of Baudelaire and Genêt," *FR* 48 (December 1974): 332–35, 339–42 (Eng).

Mossop, *Pure Poetry,* 86–89 (Eng).

Prévost, *Baudelaire,* 210–11, 274–75 (Fr).

Quesnel, *Baudelaire solaire et clandestin,* 76–83, 254–63 (Fr).

Jean-Pierre Richard, "Mettons-nous au 'Balcon'!" in Bowie, Fairlie, and Finch, eds., *Baudelaire, Mallarmé, Valéry,* 117–27 (Fr).

"La Béatrice"

Richard D. E. Burton, "Baudelaire and Shakespeare: Literary References and Meaning . . . ," *CLS* 26 (1989): 10–28 (Eng).

Galand, *Baudelaire,* 409–10 (Fr).

Prévost, *Baudelaire,* 125–26, 219–20, 259, 264 (Fr).

"Le Beau Navire"

Chesters, *Baudelaire and the Poetics of Craft,* 54–55 (Eng).

Galand, *Baudelaire,* 307–8 (Fr).

F. W. Leakey, "The Amorous Tribute: Baudelaire and the Renaissance Tradition," in D. R. Haggis et al., eds., *The French Renaissance and Its Heritage. Essays presented to Alan Boase* (London: Methuen, 1968), 93–97. Reprinted in Leakey, *Baudelaire,* 73–76 (Eng).

Prévost, *Baudelaire,* 246–47, 286 87 (Fr).

Turnell, *Baudelaire,* 143–47, 253, 274–75 (Eng).

"La Beauté"

Bertocci, *From Symbolism to Baudelaire,* 130–32 (Eng).

Antoine Fongaro, "La Beauté, fleur du mal," *SFr* 4 (September–December 1960): 489–93 (Fr).

Galand, *Baudelaire,* 272–73 (Fr).

René-Albert Gutmann, *Introduction à la lecture des poètes français* (Paris: Nizet, 1967), 84–86 (Fr).

Francis Heck, " 'La Beauté': Enigma of Irony," *NCFS* 10 (Fall–Winter 1981–82); 85–95 (Eng).

Andrea Moorhead, "Thanatos and Carnal Knowledge in Baudelaire's 'La Beauté,' " *ECr* 13 (Summer 1973): 124–28 (Eng).

Prévost, *Baudelaire,* 150 (Fr).

Quesnel, *Baudelaire solaire et clandestin,* 300–304 (Fr).

Zilberberg, *Une Lecture des "Fleurs du mal,"* 125–33 (Fr).

BAUDELAIRE, CHARLES, "Bénédiction"

"Bénédiction"

Galand, *Baudelaire,* 256–59, 359–60 (Fr).

Charles Mauron, "Premières recherches sur la structure inconsciente des 'Fleurs du mal,'" in *Baudelaire: Actes du Colloque de Nice, 25–27 mai 1967* (Paris: Minard, 1968), 134–36 (Fr).

Porter, *The Crisis of French Symbolism,* 162–63 (Eng).

Prévost, *Baudelaire,* 163–64 (Fr).

Quesnel, *Baudelaire solaire et clandestin,* 24–33 (Fr).

Turnell, *Baudelaire,* 103–5, 255 (Eng).

"Bien loin d'ici"

Anis Ghannam, "Sur le sonnet baudelairien: Du dessein extérieur au dessein intérieur," *Poétique* 20 (September 1989): 357–61 (Fr).

Scott, *Pictorialist Poetics,* 98–102 (Eng).

"Les Bijoux"

Carter, *Charles Baudelaire,* 64–65 (Eng).

Galand, *Baudelaire,* 432–34 (Fr).

F. W. Leakey, "The Amorous Tribute: Baudelaire and the Renaissance Tradition," in D. R. Haggis et al., eds., *The French Renaissance and Its Heritage. Essays presented to Alan Boase* (London: Methuen, 1968), 100–103. Reprinted in Leakey, *Baudelaire,* 79–81 (Eng).

Georges Poulet, *La Poésie éclatée* (Paris: Presses universitaires de France 1980), 57–59 (Fr).

Prévost, *Baudelaire,* 114–15, 209, 285–86 (Fr).

Timothy Raser, "Language and the Erotic in Two Poems by Baudelaire," *RR* 79 (May 1988): 444–49 (Eng).

M. Riffaterre, *Semiotics of Poetry,* 51–53 (Eng).

Richard Sieburth, "Poetry and Obscenity: Baudelaire and Swinburne," *CL* 36 (Fall 1984): 348–49 (Eng).

Turnell, *Baudelaire,* 110–12 (Eng).

"Bohémiens en voyage"

Galand, *Baudelaire,* 270 (Fr).

Melâhat Menemencioglu, "Le Thème des bohémiens en voyage dans la peinture et la poésie de Cervantes à Baudelaire," *EF* 18 (March 1966): 228–31 (Fr).

Prévost, *Baudelaire,* 133–34 (Fr).

"Brumes et pluies"

Aguettant, *Baudelaire,* 183–84 (Fr).

Chesters, *Baudelaire and the Poetics of Craft,* 138–40 (Eng).

"Le Cadre"

F. W. Leakey, "The Amorous Tribute: Baudelaire and the Renaissance Tradition," in D. R. Haggis et al., eds., *The French Renaissance and Its Heritage. Essays presented to Alan Boase* (London: Methuen, 1968), 103–4. Reprinted in Leakey, *Baudelaire,* 81 (Eng).

Marie Maclean, "Specularité et inversion transformationnelle chez Baudelaire: 'Un Fantôme,'" *AJFS* 21 (January–April 1984): 64–65 (Fr).

Scott, *Pictorialist Poetics,* 81–83 (Eng).

"Causerie"

Bertocci, *From Symbolism to Baudelaire,* 145–46 (Eng).

Anis Ghannam, "Sur le sonnet baudelairien: Du dessein extérieur au dessein intérieur," *Poétique* 20 (September 1989): 355–57 (Fr).

Prévost *Baudelaire,* 190, 205–6 (Fr).

Turnell, *Baudelaire,* 249–50 (Eng).

BAUDELAIRE, CHARLES, "Chanson d'après-midi"

"Chanson d'après-midi"

Galand, *Baudelaire*, 316–17 (Fr).

Freeman G. Henry, "Baudelaire's 'Chanson d'après-midi' and the Return of Jeanne Duval," *KRQ* 24, no. 1 (1977): 95–107 (Eng).

F. W. Leakey, "The Amorous Tribute: Baudelaire and the Renaissance Tradition," in D. R. Haggis et al., eds., *The French Renaissance and Its Heritage. Essays presented to Alan Boase* (London: Methuen, 1968), 99–100. Reprinted in Leakey, *Baudelaire*, 78–79 (Eng).

"Chant d'automne"

Chesters, *Baudelaire and the Poetics of Craft*, 21–23 (Eng).

Galand, *Baudelaire*, 313–14 (Fr).

Henri Meschonnic, *Pour la poétique, vol. 3: Une Parole écriture* (Paris: Gallimard, 1973), 298–336 (Fr).

Prévost, *Baudelaire*, 194–95, 206–7 (Fr).

Turnell, *Baudelaire*, 141–43, 250–51 (Eng).

Chant d'automne
"Bientôt nous plongerons dans les froides ténèbres"

Robert Cargo, "Baudelaire's 'Chant d'automne,' " in Robert Cargo, ed., *Studies in Honor of Alfred G. Engstrom* (Chapel Hill: University of North Carolina Press, 1972), 27–35, 41–3 (Eng).

Chant d'automne
"J'aime de vos longs yeux la lumière verdâtre"

Robert Cargo, "Baudelaire's 'Chant d'automne,' " in Robert Cargo, ed., *Studies in Honor of Alfred G. Engstrom* (Chapel Hill: University of North Carolina Press, 1972), 27–9, 35–43 (Eng).

"Une Charogne"

Carter, *Charles Baudelaire*, 67–68 (Eng).

Cassou-Yager, *La Polyvalence du thème de la mort*, 113–20 (Fr).

Fairlie, *Baudelaire: "Les Fleurs du Mal,"* 41–42 (Eng).

Galand, *Baudelaire,* 285–87 (Fr).

Knight, *Flower Poetics in Nineteenth-Century France,* 72–73 (Eng).

Catherine Osborne, "Mystic Fusion: Baudelaire and 'le sentiment du beau,'" *PMLA* 88 (October 1973): 1133–34 (Eng).

Porter, *The Crisis of French Symbolism,* 151–52 (Eng).

Prévost, *Baudelaire,* 290–91 (Fr).

Alain Ranwez, "Baudelaire's 'Une Charogne,'" *Expl* 35 (Summer 1977): 15–19 (Eng).

Turnell, *Baudelaire,* 281, 297–99 (Eng).

Le Chat
"Dans ma cervelle se promène"

Quesnel, *Baudelaire solaire et clandestin,* 291–300 (Fr).

Zilberberg, *Une Lecture des "Fleurs du mal,"* 141–45, 151–52 (Fr).

Le Chat
"Viens, mon beau chat, sur mon coeur amoureux"

Quesnel, *Baudelaire solaire et clandestin,* 282–90 (Fr).

Zilberberg, *Une Lecture des "Fleurs du mal,"* 140–45 (Fr).

"Châtiment de l'orgueil"

Pierre Emmanuel, *Baudelaire, la femme et Dieu* (Paris: Editions du Seuil, 1982), 125–26 (Fr).

Galand, *Baudelaire,* 272 (Fr).

Peter Hambly, "Notes sur deux poèmes de Baudelaire: 'Réversibilité' et 'Châtiment de l'orgueil,'" *RHL* 71 (May–June 1971): 487–88 (Fr).

Prévost, *Baudelaire,* 257–59 (Fr).

Quesnel, *Baudelaire solaire et clandestin,* 175–76 (Fr).

BAUDELAIRE, CHARLES, "Les Chats"

"Les Chats"

Jean-Michel Adam, "Encore 'Les Chats,'" *Poétique* 37 (February 1979): 43–55 (Fr). Reprinted in Delcroix and Geerts, eds., *Les "Chats" de Baudelaire,* 277–91 (Fr).

Léon Cellier, "'Les Chats' de Charles Baudelaire: Essai d'exégèse," *Revue des Sciences Humanines* 142 (April–June 1971): 207–16. Reprinted in Delcroix and Geerts, eds., *"Les Chats" de Baudelaire,* 177–85 (Fr).

Ross Chambers, "Situation de la recherche du temps des 'Chats' au temps du 'Cygne,'" *O&C* 9, no. 2 (1984): 12–16 (Fr).

W. Delsipech, "'Les Chats': Essai d'analyse formelle," in Delcroix and Geerts, eds., *Les "Chats" de Baudelaire,* 157–66 (Fr).

Gilbert Durand, "'Les Chats,' les rats et les structuralistes: Symbole et structuralisme figuratif," in Delcroix and Geerts, eds., *"Les Chats" de Baudelaire,* 91–115 (Fr).

Ida-Marie Frandon, "Le Structuralisme et les caractères de l'œuvre littéraire à propos des 'Chats'," *RHL* 72 (January–February 1972): 101–16. Reprinted in Delcroix and Geerts, eds., *"Les Chats" de Baudelaire,* 193–207 (Fr).

Galand, *Baudelaire,* 323 (Fr).

Walter Geerts, "Pour une herméneutique structurale," in Delcroix and Geerts, eds., *"Les Chats" de Baudelaire,* 315–20 (Fr).

Lucien Goldmann, and Norbert Peters "'Les Chats,' Charles Baudelaire," in Delcroix and Geerts, eds., *"Les Chats" de Baudelaire,* 153–56 (Fr).

Marie-Thérèse Goosse, "S + F/V = M: Note sur 'Les Chats' de Baudelaire," *Poétique* 3 (November 1972): 596–97; reprinted in Delcroix and Geerts, eds., *"Les Chats" de Baudelaire,* 241–42 (Fr).

Roman Jakobson, "Postscriptum," in Delcroix and Geerts, eds., *"Les Chats" de Baudelaire,* 265–68, 270–75 (Fr).

Roman Jakobson and Claude Lévi-Strauss, "'Les Chats' de Charles Baudelaire," in Delcroix and Geerts, eds., *"Les Chats" de Baudelaire,* 19–35 (Fr).

Georges Legros, "Du sexe des chats, ou De l'art de lire," in Delcroix and Geerts, eds., *"Les Chats" de Baudelaire,* 187–92 (Fr).

Georges Legros and Maurice Delcroix, "Une analyse textuelle des 'Chats,'" in Delcroix and Geerts, eds., *"Les Chats" de Baudelaire,* 293–304 (Fr).

Georges Mounin, "Baudelaire devant une critique structurale," in *Baudelaire: Actes du Colloque de Nice, 25–27 mai 1967* (Paris: Minard, 1968), 155–60 (Fr).

Morten Nøjgaard, "Une Machine à transposer le réel: Le Sonnet des 'Chats,'" in Delcroix and Geerts, eds., *"Les Chats" de Baudelaire,* 243–58 (Fr).

Jean Pellegrin, "Félices feles," *Poétique* 3 (February 1972): 89–101. Reprinted in Delcroix and Geerts, eds., *"Les Chats" de Baudelaire,* 89–101 (Fr).

François Pire, "Baudelaire entre chien et chat," in Delcroix and Geerts, eds., *"Les Chats" de Baudelaire,* 167–75 (Fr).

Quesnel, *Baudelaire solaire et clandestin,* 236–50 (Fr).

Michael Riffaterre, "Describing Poetic Structures; Two Approaches to Baudelaire's 'Les Chats,'" *YFS,* nos. 36–37 (1966): 200–242 (Eng).

Michael Riffaterre, "La Description des structures poétiques: Deux approches du poème de Baudelaire," in Delcroix and Geerts, eds., *"Les Chats" de Baudelaire,* 37–76 (Fr).

Graham Robb, " 'Les Chats' de Baudelaire: Une Nouvelle Lecture," *RHL* 85 (November–December 1985): 1002–10 (Fr).

Léon Somville, "Le Poème 'Les Chats' de Baudelaire: Essai d'exégèse," *ELit* 5 (August 1972): 189–211. Reprinted in Delcroix and Geerts, eds., *"Les Chats" de Baudelaire,* 225–40 (Fr).

Jean-Paul Weber, *Genèse de l'œuvre poétique,* 220–21 (Fr).

Zilberberg, *Une Lecture des "Fleurs du mal,"* 135–40 (Fr).

"La Chevelure"

Edward J. Ahearn, "Black Woman, White Poet: Exile and Exploitation in Baudelaire's Jeanne Duval Poems," *FR* 51 (December 1977): 216–20 (Eng).

Bertocci, *From Symbolism to Baudelaire,* 150–56, 160–61 (Eng).

Victor Brombert, "The Will to Ecstasy: The Example of Baudelaire's 'La Chevelure,'" *YFS,* no. 50 (1974): 55–63. Reprinted in Bloom, ed., *Charles Baudelaire,* 27–33 (Eng).

Robert G. Cohn, "Intimate Globality: Baudelaire's 'La Chevelure,'" *FS* 42 (July 1988): 292–301 (Eng).

BAUDELAIRE, CHARLES, "Ciel brouillé"

Fairlie, *Baudelaire: "Les Fleurs du Mal,"* 22–23 (Eng).

Galand, *Baudelaire,* 278–80 (Fr).

Mossop, *Pure Poetry,* 70–72, 100–101 (Eng).

Catherine Osborne, "Mystic Fusion: Baudelaire and 'le sentiment du beau,'" *PMLA* 88 (October 1973): 1131, 1134–35 (Eng).

Prévost, *Baudelaire,* 181–82, 242–45 (Fr).

Turnell, *Baudelaire,* 112–16, 286 (Eng).

Eléonore M. Zimmermann, "Un Héritage romantique dévoyé: L'Apostrophe dans 'Le Lac,' 'Tristesse d'Olympio,' et 'La Chevelure,'" *FrF* 13 (May 1988): 210–13 (Fr).

"Ciel brouillé"

Galand, *Baudelaire,* 306 (Fr).

F. W. Leakey, "The Amorous Tribute: Baudelaire and the Renaissance Tradition," in D. R. Haggis et al., eds., *The French Renaissance and Its Heritage. Essays Presented to Alan Boase* (London: Methuen, 1968), 110–12. Reprinted in Leakey, *Baudelaire,* 86–88 (Eng).

"La Cloche fêlée"

Peter Collier, "Baudelaire and Metaphor: Work in Regress," *FMLS* 26 (January 1990): 31 (Eng).

Pierre Emmanuel, *Baudelaire, la femme et Dieu* (Paris: Editions du Seuil, 1982), 74–75 (Fr).

Galand, *Baudelaire,* 330–31 (Fr).

Howarth and Walton, *Explications,* 162–74 (Eng).

William Sylvester, "La Cloche fêlée," *Expl* 10 (May 1952): 47. Reprinted in Walcutt and Whitesell, eds., *The Explicator Cyclopedia,* vol. 2, 28–29 (Eng).

Turnell, *Baudelaire,* 164–65 (Eng).

"Confession"

Galand, *Baudelaire,* 299–300 (Fr).

BAUDELAIRE, CHARLES, "Crépuscule du soir"

"Correspondances"

Aguettant, *Baudelaire,* 83–85, (Fr).

Kristine Anderson, "Two Translators of Baudelaire's 'Correspondances,' " *CLS* 17 (December 1980): 439–46 (Eng).

Jean-Pierre Boon, "Baudelaire, 'Correspondances' et le magnétisme animal," *PMLA* 86 (May 1971): 406–10 (Fr).

Jonathan Culler, "Intertextuality and Interpretation: Baudelaire's 'Correspondances,' " in Prendergast, ed., *Nineteenth-Century French Poetry,* 118–37 (Eng).

Paul De Man, "Anthropomorphism and Trope in the Lyric," in Bloom, ed., *Charles Baudelaire,* 125–42 (Eng).

Fairlie, *Baudelaire: "Les Fleurs du Mal,"* 20–22 (Eng).

Galand, *Baudelaire,* 261 (Fr).

Knight, *Flower Poetics in Nineteenth-Century France,* 84–85, 113–14 (Eng).

Porter, *The Crisis of French Symbolism,* 173–74 (Eng).

Laurence Porter, "The Invisible Worm: Decay in the Privileged Moments of Baudelaire's Poetry," *ECr* 13 (Summer 1973): 110–11 (Eng).

Quesnel, *Baudelaire solaire et clandestin,* 250–52 (Fr).

Raitt, *Life and Letters in France,* 84–91 (Eng).

"Le Crépuscule du matin"

Aguettant, *Baudelaire,* 191–95 (Fr).

Galand, *Baudelaire,* 387–88 (Fr).

Prévost, *Baudelaire,* 97–99 (Fr).

Turnell, *Baudelaire,* 197–99 (Eng).

"Crépuscule du soir"

Aguettant, *Baudelaire,* 159–64 (Fr).

Graham Chesters, "Baudelaire and the Limits of Poetry," *FS* 32 (October 1978): 423–27 (Eng).

BAUDELAIRE, CHARLES, "Le Cygne"

Graham Chesters, "The Transformation of a Prose-Poem: Baudelaire's 'Crépuscule du soir,' " in Bowie, Fairlie, and Finch, eds., *Baudelaire, Mallarmé, Valéry,* 24–37 (Eng).

Chesters, *Baudelaire and the Poetics of Craft,* 153–58 (Eng).

Galand, *Baudelaire,* 374–75 (Fr).

Marisa Gatti-Taylor, "Twi-light and the Anima," *NCFS* 11 (Fall–Winter 1982–83): 126–30 (Eng).

Catherine Osborne, "Mystic Fusion: Baudelaire and 'le sentiment du beau,' " *PMLA* 88 (October 1973): 1133 (Eng).

Prévost, *Baudelaire,* 97–99, 260–62 (Fr).

Turnell, *Baudelaire,* 193–94, 267–68 (Eng).

"Le Cygne"

Aguettant, *Baudelaire,* 122–31 (Fr).

Edward J. Ahearn, "Black Woman, White Poet: Exile and Exploitation in Baudelaire's Jeanne Duval Poems," *FR* 51 (December 1977): 219–20 (Eng).

Edward J. Ahearn, "Marx's Relevance for Second Empire Literature: Baudelaire's 'Le Cygne,' " *NCFS* 14 (Summer 1986): 269–77 (Eng).

Bertocci, *From Symbolism to Baudelaire,* 147–50 (Eng).

Carter, *Charles Baudelaire,* 95–97 (Eng).

Cassou-Yager, *La Polyvalence du thème de la mort,* 141–47 (Fr).

Ross Chambers, " 'Je' dans les 'Tableaux parisiens' de Baudelaire," *NCFS* 13 (Summer 1985): 63–66 (Fr).

Ross Chambers, "Situation de la recherche du temps des 'Chats' au temps du 'Cygne,' " *O&C* 9, no. 2 (1984): 16–23 (Fr).

Chesters, *Baudelaire and the Poetics of Craft,* 21–23 (Eng).

Christine Crow, " 'Le Silence au vol de cygne': Baudelaire, Mallarmé, Valéry, and the Flight of the Swan," in Bowie, Fairlie, and Finch, eds., *Baudelaire, Mallarmé, Valéry,* 2–4 (Eng).

Fairlie, *Baudelaire: "Les Fleurs du Mal,"* 24–25 (Eng).

Bernhard Frank, "Baudelaire's 'The Swan,' " *Expl* 48 (Summer 1990): 257–58 (Eng).

Galand, *Baudelaire,* 360–62 (Fr).

John Gale, "De Quincey, Baudelaire, and 'Le Cygne,'" *NCFS* 5 (Spring–Summer 1977): 296–307 (Eng).

Timothy Hampton, "Virgil, Baudelaire, and Mallarmé at the Sign of the Swan," *RR* 73 (November 1982): 442–46 (Eng).

Heather Ingman, "Joachim Du Bellay and Baudelaire's 'Tableaux parisiens,'" *NCFS* 15 (Summer 1987): 409–14 (Eng).

F. W. Leakey, "The Originality of Baudelaire's 'Le Cygne': Genesis as Structure and Theme," in Beaumont, Cocking, and Cruickshank, eds., *Order and Adventure in Post-Romantic French Poetry,* 38–55. Reprinted in Leakey, Baudelaire, 92–107 (Eng).

Laurent Le Sage and Eleanor Stewart, "Le Cygne," *Expl* 16 (June 1958): 52. Reprinted in Walcutt and Whitesell, eds., *The Explicator Cyclopedia,* vol. 2, 29–30 (Eng).

Lewis, *On Reading French Verse,* 210–33 (Eng).

Lowry Nelson, "Baudelaire and Virgil: A Reading of 'Le Cygne,'" *CL* 13 (Fall 1961): 332–45 (Eng).

Quesnel, *Baudelaire solaire et clandestin,* 83–86 (Fr).

Turnell, *Baudelaire,* 179–86, 279, 288–89, 293 (Eng).

"Danse macabre"

Aguettant, *Baudelaire,* 166–75 (Fr).

Cassou-Yager, *La Polyvalence du thème de la mort,* 32–39 (Fr).

Chesters, *Baudelaire and the Poetics of Craft,* 88–91 (Eng).

Galand, *Baudelaire,* 377–79 (Fr).

Knight, *Flower Poetics in Nineteenth-Century France,* 103–4 (Eng).

F. W. Leakey, "Baudelaire and Mortimer," *FS* 7 (April 1953): 116–18. Reprinted in Leakey, *Baudelaire,* 115–18 (Eng).

F. W. Leakey, "Baudelaire: The Poet as Moralist," in *Studies in Modern French Literature Presented to P. Mansell Jones* (Manchester: Manchester University Press, 1961), 210–11, 214–15 (Eng).

Prévost, *Baudelaire,* 145–47 (Fr).

BAUDELAIRE, CHARLES, "De profundis clamavi"

"De profundis clamavi"

Galand, *Baudelaire,* 287–88 (Fr).

Anis Ghannam, "Sur le sonnet baudelairien; Du dessein extérieur au dessein intérieur," *Poétique* 20 (September 1989): 352–54 (Fr).

"Delphine et Hippolyte"

Carter, *Charles Baudelaire,* 77–79 (Eng).

Galand, *Baudelaire,* 438–42 (Fr).

F. W. Leakey, " 'Les Lesbiennes': A Verse Novel?" *FMLS* 24 (January 1988): 1–2, 8–12. Reprinted in Leakey, *Baudelaire,* 30–31, 37–41 (Eng).

Prévost, *Baudelaire,* 200–201 (Fr).

"La Destruction"

Galand, *Baudelaire,* 397–98 (Fr).

Charles Mauron, "Premières recherches sur la structure inconsciente des 'Fleurs du mal,' " in *Baudelaire: Actes du Colloque de Nice, 25–27 mai 1967* (Paris: Minard, 1968), 133–34 (Fr).

Quesnel, *Baudelaire solaire et clandestin,* 56–59 (Fr).

Turnell, *Baudelaire,* 202–3, 252 (Eng).

"Don Juan aux enfers"

Galand, *Baudelaire,* 271–72 (Fr).

Prévost, *Baudelaire,* 112–13 (Fr).

Quesnel, *Baudelaire solaire et clandestin,* 134–36 (Fr).

"Duellum"

Prévost, *Baudelaire,* 121–23, 219 (Fr).

"Elévation"

Ivan Barko, "La Médiation chez Baudelaire ou l'accord de contraires," *AJFS* 16 (January–April 1979): 184–85 (Fr).

Galand, *Baudelaire,* 260–61 (Fr).

René-Albert Gutmann, *Introduction à la lecture des poètes français* (Paris: Nizet, 1967), 87–89 (Fr).

Lois B. Hyslop, *Baudelaire's 'Elévation' and E. T. A. Hoffman,"* FR 46 (April 1973): 951–59 (Eng).

M. Larroutis, "Le Sujet d'une 'Fleur du mal' chez Baudelaire," *RHL* 63 (January–March 1963): 110–13 (Fr).

Laurence Porter, "The Invisible Worm: Decay in the Privileged Moments of Baudelaire's Poetry," *ECr* 13 (Summer 1973): 111–12 (Eng).

Prévost, *Baudelaire,* 241–42 (Fr).

Quesnel, *Baudelaire solaire et clandestin,* 252–54 (Fr).

"L'Ennemi"

Gordon Browning, "Baudelaire's 'L'Ennemi': Convergence and Divergence . . . ," *NCFS* 15 (Fall–Winter 1986–87): 108–18 (Eng).

Knight, *Flower Poetics in Nineteenth-Century France,* 92–93 (Eng).

Emmanuel J. Mickel, "A Rebours' Trinity of Baudelairean Poems," *NCFS* 16 (Fall–Winter 1987–88): 155, 157 (Eng).

Alan Rosenthal, "Baudelaire's Mysterious 'Enemy,'" *NCFS* 4 (Spring 1976): 286–94 (Eng).

Zilberberg, *Une Lecture des "Fleurs du mal,"* 58–61, 72–73 (Fr).

"L'Examen de minuit"

Prévost, *Baudelaire,* 171–72 (Fr).

"Un Fantôme"

Mary Ann Caws, "Insertion in an Oval Frame: Poe Circumscribed by Baudelaire," *FR* 56 (May 1983): 885–95. Reprinted in Bloom, ed., *Charles Baudelaire,* 110–19 (Eng).

BAUDELAIRE, CHARLES, "Femmes damnées"

Helen Elam, "Temporality in Baudelaire," in Bloom, ed., *Charles Baudelaire,* 147–48 (Eng).

Marie Maclean, "Specularité et inversion transformationnelle chez Baudelaire: 'Un Fantôme,' " *AJFS* 21 (January–April 1984): 58–69 (Fr).

"Femmes damnées"

Galand, *Baudelaire,* 404–5 (Fr).

F. W. Leakey, " 'Les Lesbiennes': A Verse Novel?" *FMLS* 24 (January 1988): 12. Reprinted in Leakey, *Baudelaire,* 41–42 (Eng).

Turnell, *Baudelaire,* 206–11, 243, 295 (Eng).

"Les Fenêtres"

Renée Linkhorn, " 'Les Fenêtres': Propos sur trois poèmes,' " *FR* 44 (February 1971): 514–17 (Fr).

"La Fin de la journée"

Aguettant, *Baudelaire,* 207–8 (Fr).

Edward K. Kaplan, "Baudelaire and the Battle with Finitude: 'La Mort,' Conclusion of 'Les Fleurs du mal,' " *FrF* 4 (May 1979): 224 (Eng).

"Le Flacon"

Peter Collier, "Baudelaire and Metaphor: Work in Regress," *FMLS* 26 (January 1990): 30–31 (Eng).

Helen R. Elam, "Temporality in Baudelaire," in Bloom, ed., *Charles Baudelaire,* 148–51 (Eng).

Galand, *Baudelaire,* 303–5 (Fr).

Quesnel, *Baudelaire solaire et clandestin,* 151–57 (Fr).

Turnell, *Baudelaire,* 132–36, 252–53, 285 (Eng).

Zilberberg, *Une Lecture des "Fleurs du mal,"* 92–96, 103–5, 108 (Fr).

BAUDELAIRE, CHARLES, "Le Goût du néant"

"Le Flambeau vivant"

Elliott Forsyth, "Baudelaire and the Petrarchan Tradition," *AJFS* 16 (January–April 1979): 188–97 (Eng).

Galand, *Baudelaire,* 297 (Fr).

Quesnel, *Baudelaire solaire et clandestin,* 198–200 (Fr).

"La Fontaine de sang"

Galand, *Baudelaire,* 406–7 (Fr).

Prévost, *Baudelaire,* 216–17 (Fr).

"Franciscae meae laudes"

Galand, *Baudelaire,* 317 (Fr).

"La Géante"

Galand, *Baudelaire,* 275 (Fr).

Quesnel, *Baudelaire solaire et clandestin,* 102–5 (Fr).

Nicolas Ruwet, *Musique, langage, poésie* (Paris: Seuil, 1972), 217–27 (Fr).

"Le Gouffre"

Cassou-Yager, *La Polyvalence du thème de la mort,* 90–97 (Fr).

Galand, *Baudelaire,* 455–57 (Fr).

"Le Goût du néant"

Galand, *Baudelaire,* 339–40 (Fr).

Turnell, *Baudelaire,* 170–71 (Eng).

BAUDELAIRE, CHARLES, "Une Gravure fantastique"

"Une Gravure fantastique"

F. W. Leakey, "Baudelaire and Mortimer," *FS* 7 (April 1953): 101–15. Reprinted in Leakey, *Baudelaire,* 111–14 (Eng).

Prévost, *Baudelaire,* 139–40, 264–65 (Fr).

Quesnel, *Baudelaire solaire et clandestin,* 180–82 (Fr).

"Le Guignon"

Bertocci, *From Symbolism to Baudelaire,* 139–40 (Eng).

Galand, *Baudelaire,* 267–68 (Fr).

Prévost, *Baudelaire,* 280–81 (Fr).

Quesnel, *Baudelaire solaire et clandestin,* 141–44 (Fr).

"Harmonie du soir"

Aguettant, *Baudelaire,* 90–91 (Fr).

Bertocci, *From Symbolism to Baudelaire,* 156–60 (Eng).

Broome and Chesters, *The Appreciation of Modern French Poetry (1850–1950),* 77–79 (Eng).

Galand, *Baudelaire,* 302–3 (Fr).

Knight, *Flower Poetics in Nineteenth-Century France,* 85–86 (Eng).

F. W. Leakey, "Harmonie du soir," *RHL* 67 (April–June 1967): 343–56. Reprinted in Leakey, *Baudelaire,* 130–38 (Fr).

Mossop, *Pure Poetry,* 101–2 (Eng).

Eithne O'Sharkey, "A Note on Baudelaire's 'harmonie du soir,' " *FS* 33 (April 1979): 155–56 (Eng).

Porter, *The Crisis of French Symbolism,* 146–47 (Eng).

Prévost, *Baudelaire,* 273, 283–85 (Fr).

Quesnel, *Baudelaire solaire et clandestin,* 178–80 (Fr).

Turnell, *Baudelaire,* 131–32, 275, 293 (Eng).

Janine Wickers, "Baudelaire's 'Harmonie du soir,' " *Expl* 33 (September 1974): 14–16 (Eng).

BAUDELAIRE, CHARLES, "Horreur sympathique"

"L'Héautontimoraúménos"

Galand, *Baudelaire,* 344–49 (Fr).

Eric Gans, "Mon semblable, mon frère," *SFR* 8 (Spring 1984): 79, 81–82 (Eng).

Deborah Harter, "Divided Selves, Ironic Counterparts," *CLS* 26, no. 1 (1989): 28–38 (Eng).

Robert Wilcocks, "Towards a Re-examination of 'L'Héautontimorou-ménos,'" *FR* 48 (February 1975): 566–79 (Eng).

"Les Hiboux"

F. W. Leakey, "Baudelaire: The Poet as Moralist," in *Studies in Modern French Literature Presented to P. Mansell Jones* (Manchester: Manchester University Press, 1961), 200–203 (Eng).

"L'Homme et la mer"

Galand, *Baudelaire,* 270–71 (Fr).

"L'Horloge"

Galand, *Baudelaire,* 355–56 (Fr).

John Jackson, "Baudelaire lecteur de Théophile Gautier: Les Deux 'Hor-loges,'" *RHL* 84 (May–June 1984): 444–49 (Fr).

Robert L. Mitchell, "Baudelaire's 'Feline': The Lady or the Tiger?' *NCFS* 6 (Fall–Winter 1977–78): 94–103 (Eng).

Porter, *The Crisis of French Symbolism,* 174–76 (Eng).

Turnell, *Baudelaire,* 174–75, 289 (Eng).

"Horreur sympathique"

Galand, *Baudelaire,* 342–44 (Fr).

Quesnel, *Baudelaire solaire et clandestin,* 201–5 (Fr).

BAUDELAIRE, CHARLES, "Hymne à la beauté"

"Hymne à la beauté"

Bertocci, *From Symbolism to Baudelaire,* 131–32 (Eng).

Chesters, *Baudelaire and the Poetics of Craft,* 133–35 (Eng).

Galand, *Baudelaire,* 277 (Fr).

Lois B. Hyslop, "Baudelaire's 'Hymne à la beauté,'" *NCFS* 7 (Spring–Summer 1979): 202–12 (Eng).

Quesnel, *Baudelaire solaire et clandestin,* 304–8 (Fr).

Eléonore M. Zimmermann, "'Hymne à la beauté': Un Art poétique," *CAIEF* 41 (May 1989): 237–350 (Fr).

"L'Idéal"

Galand, *Baudelaire,* 273–75 (Fr).

Frances Heck, "Baudelaire's 'L'Idéal,'" *Expl* 38 (Spring 1980): 31–34 (Eng).

"L'Invitation au voyage"

Aguettant, *Baudelaire,* 97–101 (Fr).

Ivan Barko, "La Médiation chez Baudelaire, ou L'Accord de contraires," *AJFS* 16 (January–April 1979): 185–86 (Fr).

Barrère, *Le Regard d'Orphée,* 83–99 (Fr).

Martine Bercot, "Poèmes et contre-poèmes," *CAIEF* 41 (May 1989): 285–99 (Fr).

Galand, *Baudelaire,* 308–10 (Fr).

Knight, *Flower Poetics in Nineteenth-Century France,* 88–89, 114–16 (Eng).

James McLaren, "The Imagery of Light and Darkness in 'Les Fleurs du mal,'" *NCFS* 7 (Fall–Winter 1978–79): 35–37 (Eng).

Emilie Noulet, "D'un seul poème . . . ," in *Baudelaire: Actes du Colloque de Nice, 25–27 mai 1967* (Paris: Minard, 1968), 61–65 (Fr).

Prévost, *Baudelaire,* 188, 252, 272–73 (Fr).

BAUDELAIRE, CHARLES, "Je n'ai pas oublié, voisine de la ville"

Quesnel, *Baudelaire solaire et clandestin*, 268–74 (Fr).

Turnell, *Baudelaire*, 138–40 (Eng).

"L'Irrémédiable"

Cassou-Yager, *La Polyvalence du thème de la mort*, 84–90 (Fr).

Galand, *Baudelaire*, 349 55 (Fr).

Eleanor Manheim, and Leonard Manheim, "L'Irrémédiable," *Expl* 12 (June 1954): 52. Reprinted in Walcutt and Whitesell, eds., *The Explicator Cyclopedia*, vol. 2, 30–31 (Eng).

Quesnel, *Baudelaire solaire et clandestin*, 216–21 (Fr).

"L'Irréparable"

Galand, *Baudelaire*, 310–12 (Fr).

Quesnel, *Baudelaire solare et clandestin*, 214–16 (Fr).

Turnell, *Baudelaire*, 140–41 (Eng).

"J'aime le souvenir de ces époques nues"

Galand, *Baudelaire*, 262–63 (Fr).

Turnell, *Baudelaire*, 105, 236–38 (Eng).

"Je n'ai pas oublié, voisine de la ville"

Aguettant, *Baudelaire*, 177–79 (Fr).

Bernard Delmay and Maria C. Lori, "Baudelaire et le vrai visage de sa mère," *SFr* 21 (January–August 1977): 200–203 (Fr).

Galand, *Baudelaire*, 381–82 (Fr).

Prévost, *Baudelaire*, 159–60 (Fr).

Quesnel, *Baudelaire solaire et clandestin*, 14–19 (Fr).

BAUDELAIRE, CHARLES, "Je n'ai pas pour maîtresse . . ."

"Je n'ai pas pour maîtresse une lionne illustre"

Prévost, *Baudelaire,* 230–32 (Fr).

"Je t'adore à l'égale de la voûte nocturne"

Galand, *Baudelaire,* 280–81 (Fr).
Turnell, *Baudelaire,* 119–20, 239–40 (Eng).

"Je te donne ces vers afin que si mon nom"

Cassou-Yager, *La Polyvalence du thème de la mort,* 63–66 (Fr).
Chesters, *Baudelaire and the Poetics of Craft,* 83–84 (Eng).
Galand, *Baudelaire,* 294 (Fr).
Lewis, *On Reading French Verse,* 6–7 (Eng).
Nicolas Ruwet, "'Je te donne ces vers'; esquisse d'analyse linguistique," *Poétique* 2 (September 1971): 355–401. Reprinted in Austin, ed., *Poetic Principles and Practice,* 228–47 (Fr).

"Le Jet d'eau"

Galand, *Baudelaire,* 451–52 (Fr).
Turnell, *Baudelaire,* 256–58 (Eng).

"Le Jeu"

Aguettant, *Baudelaire,* 164–66 (Fr).
Ross Chambers, "'Je' dans les 'Tableaux parisiens' de Baudelaire," *NCFS* 13 (Summer 1985): 66–68 (Fr).
Galand, *Baudelaire,* 375–76 (Fr).
Prévost, *Baudelaire,* 141–43 (Fr).

"Lesbos"

Antoine Fongaro, "Baudelaire: 'Le Noir mystère,'" *SFr* 17 (September–December 1973): 483–84 (Fr).
Galand, *Baudelaire,* 437–38 (Fr).
F. W. Leakey, "'Les Lesbiennes': A Verse Novel?" *FMLS* 24 (January 1988): 2–7. Reprinted in Leakey, *Baudelaire,* 31–36 (Eng).
Prévost, *Baudelaire,* 200, 275 (Fr).

BAUDELAIRE, CHARLES, "Les Métamorphoses du vampire"

Quesnel, *Baudelaire solaire et clandestin,* 43–51 (Fr).

Turnell, *Baudelaire,* 205–6, 276–77 (Eng).

"Les Litanies de Satan"

Galand, *Baudelaire,* 418–20 (Fr).

"La Lune offensée"

Prévost, *Baudelaire,* 123–24 (Fr).

"Madrigal triste"

Galand, *Baudelaire,* 446–47 (Fr).

"Une Martyre"

Galand, *Baudelaire,* 399–404 (Fr).

Knight, *Flower Poetics in Nineteenth-Century France,* 71–72 (Eng).

F. W. Leakey, " 'Les Lesbiennes': A Verse Novel?" *FMLS* 24 (January 1988): 13–14. Reprinted in Leakey, *Baudelaire,* 44–45 (Eng).

"Le Masque"

Galand, *Baudelaire,* 276–77 (Fr).

Richard Stamelman, "L'Anamorphose baudelairienne: L'Allégorie du 'Masque,' " *CAIEF* 41 (May 1989): 251–67 (Fr).

Turnell, *Baudelaire,* 244–47 (Eng).

"Le Mauvais Moine"

Prévost, *Baudelaire,* 131–32, 172–73 (Fr).

"Les Métamorphoses du vampire"

Galand, *Baudelaire,* 442–43 (Fr).

BAUDELAIRE, CHARLES, "Moesta et errabunda"

"Moesta et errabunda"

Galand, *Baudelaire,* 319 (Fr).

Prévost, *Baudelaire,* 211–12, 276 (Fr).

Turnell, *Baudelaire,* 152–55 (Eng).

"La Mort des amants"

Aguettant, *Baudelaire,* 200–202 (Fr).

Cassou-Yager, *La Polyvalence du thème de la mort,* 69–73 (Fr).

Galand, *Baudelaire,* 420–21 (Fr).

Jean-Louis Joubert, *La Poésie* (Paris: Armand Colin/Gallimard, 1977), 102–8 (Fr).

Edward K. Kaplan, "Baudelaire and the Battle with Finitude: 'La Mort,' Conclusion of 'Les Fleurs du mal,' " *FrF* 4 (May 1979): 220–21 (Eng).

F. W. Leakey, " 'Les Lesbiennes': A Verse Novel?" *FMLS* 24 (January 1988): 15–16. Reprinted in Leakey, *Baudelaire,* 45–46 (Eng).

Emmanuel J. Mickel, " 'A Rebours' Trinity of Baudelairean Poems," *NCFS* 16 (Fall–Winter 1987–88): 155–56 (Eng).

Quesnel, *Baudelaire solaire et clandestin,* 274–79 (Fr).

Turnell, *Baudelaire,* 219–21, 291 (Eng).

"La Mort des artistes"

Aguettant, *Baudelaire,* 205–7 (Fr).

Cassou-Yager, *La Polyvalence du thème de la mort,* 130–35 (Fr).

Galand, *Baudelaire,* 422–23 (Fr).

Edward K. Kaplan, "Baudelaire and the Battle with Finitude: 'La Mort,' Conclusion of 'Les Fleurs du mal,' " *FrF* 4 (May 1979): 222–23 (Eng).

"La Mort des pauvres"

Aguettant, *Baudelaire,* 203–5 (Fr).

Bertocci, *From Symbolism to Baudelaire,* 98–99 (Eng).

Turnell, *Baudelaire,* 221–22 (Eng).

BAUDELAIRE, CHARLES, "Parfum exotique"

"Le Mort joyeux"

Cassou-Yager, *La Polyvalence du thème de la mort,* 55–59 (Fr).

Galand, *Baudelaire,* 328–29 (Fr).

"La Muse malade"

Chesters, *Baudelaire and the Poetics of Craft,* 140–41 (Eng).

Galand, *Baudelaire,* 265–66 (Fr).

Zilberberg, *Une Lecture des "Fleurs du mal,"* 77–78, 147–50 (Fr).

"La Musique"

Galand, *Baudelaire,* 324–26 (Fr).

Prévost, *Baudelaire,* 235–37 (Fr).

"Une Nuit que j'étais près d'une affreuse Juive"

Turnell, *Baudelaire,* 263–65 (Eng).

"Obsession"

Galand, *Baudelaire,* 338–39 (Fr).

Quesnel, *Baudelaire solaire et clandestin,* 169–70 (Fr).

"Le Parfum"

Marie Maclean, "Specularité et inversion transformationnelle chez Baudelaire: 'Un Fantôme,'" *AJFS* 21 (January–April 1984): 62–63 (Fr).

"Parfum exotique"

Edward J. Ahearn, "Black Woman, White Poet: Exile and Exploitation in Baudelaire's Jeanne Duval Poems," *FR* 51 (December 1977): 216–20 (Eng).

Quesnel, *Baudelaire solaire et clandestin,* 266–68 (Fr).

BAUDELAIRE, CHARLES, "Paysage"

"Paysage"

Aguettant, *Baudelaire,* 112–18 (Fr).

Galand, *Baudelaire,* 357–58 (Fr).

Prévost, *Baudelaire,* 140–41, 166–67 (Fr).

Quesnel, *Baudelaire solaire et clandestin,* 184–87 (Fr).

"Les petites vieilles"

Aguettant, *Baudelaire,* 138–54 (Fr).

Bertocci, *From Symbolism to Baudelaire,* 118–21, 126 (Eng).

Chesters, *Baudelaire and the Poetics of Craft,* 105–17 (Eng).

Fairlie, *Baudelaire: "Les Fleurs du Mal,"* 51–52 (Eng).

Galand, *Baudelaire,* 365–69 (Fr).

John Jackson, "Rilke et Baudelaire," *SFR* 3 (Winter 1979): 325–41 (Fr).

Prévost, *Baudelaire,* 96–97 (Fr).

Quesnel, *Baudelaire solaire et clandestin,* 87–99 (Fr).

Turnell, *Baudelaire,* 191–92, 273–74, 285–86 (Eng).

"Les Phares"

Jean-Loup Bourget, "Une Lecture des 'Phares,' " *ECr* 13 (Summer 1973): 129–36 (Fr).

Léon Cellier, " 'Les Phares' de Baudelaire: Etude de structure," *Revue des Sciences Humaines* 121 (January–March 1966): 97–103 (Fr).

Galand, *Baudelaire,* 263–65 (Fr).

A. E. Pilkington, "Baudelaire's 'Les Phares': Structure and Statement," *FMLS* 25 (April 1989): 95–106 (Eng).

Laurence Porter, "The Anagogic Structure of Baudelaire's 'Les Phares,' " *FR* 46 (Special Issue 5) (Spring 1973): 49–54 (Eng).

Prévost, *Baudelaire,* 110–12, 118–20, 153–54, 289–90 (Fr).

Turnell, *Baudelaire,* 105–6, 109, 273 (Eng).

"La Pipe"

Ross Chambers, "Le Poète fumeur," *AJFS* 16 (January–April 1979): 145–46 (Fr).

Jean Hytier, " 'Les Fleurs du mal': Evénement poétique," *RR* 59 (December 1968): 251–52 (Fr).

Arden Reed, "Baudelaire's 'La Pipe': 'De la vaporisation du 'moi,' " *RR* 72 (May 1981): 274–84 (Eng).

"Les Plaintes d'un Icare"

Galand, *Baudelaire,* 457–59 (Fr).

Prévost, *Baudelaire,* 130–31 (Fr).

"Le Poison"

Galand, *Baudelaire,* 305–6 (Fr).

F. W. Leakey, "The Amorous Tribute: Baudelaire and the Renaissance Tradition," in D. R. Haggis et al., eds., *The French Renaissance and Its Heritage. Essays Presented to Alan Boase* (London: Methuen, 1968), 108–10. Reprinted in Leakey, *Baudelaire,* 85–86 (Eng).

"Le Portrait"

Galand, *Baudelaire,* 293–94 (Fr).

Marie Maclean, "Specularité et inversion transformationnelle chez Baudelaire: 'Un Fantôme,' " *AJFS* 21 (January–April 1984): 65–67 (Fr).

"Le Possédé"

Herbert Gershman, "Baudelaire's 'Le Possédé': A Nineteenth-Century Example of 'L'Amour fou,' " *FR* 39 (December 1965): 354–60 (Eng).

F. W. Leakey, "The Amorous Tribute: Baudelaire and the Renaissance Tradition," in D. R. Haggis et al., eds., *The French Renaissance and Its Heritage. Essays Presented to Alan Boase* (London: Methuen, 1968), 112–14. Reprinted in Leakey, *Baudelaire,* 88–89 (Eng).

BAUDELAIRE, CHARLES, "Que diras-tu ce soir, pauvre âme solitaire"

"Que diras-tu ce soir, pauvre âme solitaire"

Galand, *Baudelaire,* 296–97 (Fr).

"La Rançon"

Galand, *Baudelaire,* 453–55 (Fr).
Prévost, *Baudelaire,* 134–37, 288 (Fr).

"Le Rebelle"

Galand, *Baudelaire,* 450–51 (Fr).

"Recueillement"

W. T. Bandy, "Recueillement," *Expl* 20 (February 1962): 51. Reprinted in Walcutt and Whitesell, eds., *The Explicator Cyclopedia,* vol. 2, 31–32 (Eng).

Bertocci, *From Symbolism to Baudelaire,* 127–29 (Eng).

Chesters, *Baudelaire and the Poetics of Craft,* 135–38 (Eng).

Fairlie, *Baudelaire: "Les Fleurs du Mal,"* 25–26 (Eng).

Galand, *Baudelaire,* 454–55 (Fr).

Jacques Geninasca, "Forme fixe et forme discursive dans quelques sonnets de Baudelaire," *CAIEF* 32 (May 1980): 132–36 (Fr).

Lawler, *The Language of French Symbolism,* 52–55 (Eng).

Porter, *The Crisis of French Symbolism,* 171–72 (Eng).

Prévost, *Baudelaire,* 276–79 (Fr).

Quesnel, *Baudelaire solaire et clandestin,* 317–23 (Fr).

"Remords posthume"

Cassou-Yager, *La Polyvalence du thème de la mort,* 61–63 (Fr).

Prévost, *Baudelaire,* 269–70 (Fr).

Quesnel, *Baudelaire solaire et clandestin,* 146–48 (Fr).

BAUDELAIRE, CHARLES, "Réversibilité"

"Le Reniement de Saint Pierre"

Carter, *Charles Baudelaire,* 81–82 (Eng).

Pierre Emmanuel, *Baudelaire, la femme et Dieu* (Paris: Editions du Seuil, 1982), 131–32, 134, 136 (Fr).

Galand, *Baudelaire,* 415–17 (Fr).

Prévost, *Baudelaire,* 101, 282–83 (Fr).

"Le Rêve d'un curieux"

Aguettant, *Baudelaire,* 209–10 (Fr).

Galand, *Baudelaire,* 424–25 (Fr).

Edward K. Kaplan, "Baudelaire and the Battle with Finitude: 'La Mort,' Conclusion of 'Les Fleurs du mal,' " *FrF* 4 (May 1979): 224–25 (Eng).

"Rêve parisien"

Aguettant, *Baudelaire,* 184–91 (Fr).

Cassou-Yager, *La Polyvalence du thème de la mort,* 153–61 (Fr).

Galand, *Baudelaire,* 383–87 (Fr).

Turnell, *Baudelaire,* 195–97 (Eng).

Zilberberg, *Une Lecture des "Fleurs du mal,"* 41–43, 45–50 (Fr).

"Le Revenant"

Prévost, *Baudelaire,* 221–22 (Fr).

Quesnel, *Baudelaire solaire et clandestin,* 211–12 (Fr).

"Réversibilité"

Galand, *Baudelaire,* 297–99 (Fr).

Peter Hambly, "Notes sur deux poèmes de Baudelaire: 'Réversibilité' et 'Châtiment de l'orgueil,' " *RHL* 71 (May–June 1971): 485–87 (Fr).

Prévost, *Baudelaire,* 186–87, 224 (Fr).

BAUDELAIRE, CHARLES, "Révolte"

"Révolte"

Galand, *Baudelaire,* 414–15 (Fr).

"Sed non satiata"

Chesters, *Baudelaire and the Poetics of Craft,* 91–94 (Eng).

Galand, *Baudelaire,* 282 (Fr).

Prévost, *Baudelaire,* 214–15, 268–69 (Fr).

Turnell, *Baudelaire,* 120–21 (Eng).

"Semper eadem"

Cassou-Yager, *La Polyvalence du thème de la mort,* 59–61 (Fr).

Galand, *Baudelaire,* 295 (Fr).

"Les Sept Vieillards"

Aguettant, *Baudelaire,* 131–38 (Fr).

Bertocci, *From Symbolism to Baudelaire,* 121–23, 126 (Eng).

Richard D. E. Burton, "Baudelaire et Shakespeare: Literary References and Meaning . . . ," *CLS* 26 (1989): 1–27 (Eng).

Cassou-Yager, *La Polyvalence du thème de la mort,* 147–53 (Fr).

Ross Chambers, "Baudelaire's Street Poetry," *NCFS* 13 (Summer 1985): 252–53 (Eng).

Fairlie, *Baudelaire: "Les Fleurs de Mal,"* 51–52 (Eng).

Galand, *Baudelaire,* 362–64 (Fr).

F. W. Leakey and Claude Pichois, "Les Sept Versions des sept vieillards," in James Patty and Claude Pichois, eds., *Etudes Baudelairiennes III: Hommage à W. T. Bandy* (Neuchâtel: A la Baconnière, 1973), 262–89. Reprinted in Austin, ed., *Poetic Principles and Practice,* 139–58 (Fr).

Quesnel, *Baudelaire solaire et clandestin,* 223–30 (Fr).

Turnell, *Baudelaire,* 186–91 (Eng).

BAUDELAIRE, CHARLES, "Le Soleil"

"Sépulture"

Quesnel, *Baudelaire solaire et clandestin,* 212–14 (Fr).

"Le Serpent qui danse"

Fairlie, *Baudelaire: "Les Fleurs du Mal,"* 28–29 (Eng).

Galand, *Baudelaire,* 284–85 (Fr).

F. W. Leakey, "The Amorous Tribute: Baudelaire and the Renaissance Tradition," in D. R. Haggis et al., eds., *The French Renaissance and Its Heritage. Essays Presented to Alan Boase* (London: Methuen, 1968), 97–99. Reprinted in Leakey, *Baudelaire,* 76–77 (Eng).

"La Servante au grand cœur dont vous étiez jalouse"

Augettant, *Baudelaire,* 177, 179–82 (Fr).

Bernard Delmay and Maria C. Lori, "Baudelaire et le vrai visage de sa mère," *SFr* 21 (January–August 1977): 200–203 (Fr).

Galand, *Baudelaire,* 382–83 (Fr).

Prévost, *Baudelaire,* 160–62 (Fr).

Quesnel, *Baudelaire solaire et clandestin,* 19–24 (Fr).

"Le Soleil"

Aguettant, *Baudelaire,* 118–21 (Fr).

Ross Chambers, "Baudelaire's Street Poetry," *NCFS* 13 (Summer 1985): 245–47 (Eng).

Chesters, *Baudelaire and the Poetics of Craft,* 141–43 (Eng).

Galand, *Baudelaire,* 358–60 (Fr).

Quesnel, *Baudelaire solaire et clandestin,* 182–84 (Fr).

Timothy Raser, "Barthes and Riffaterre: The Dilemmas of Realism in the Light of Baudelaire's 'Le Soleil,' " *FR* 59 (October 1985): 61–64 (Eng).

BAUDELAIRE, CHARLES, "Sonnet d'automne"

"Sonnet d'automne"

Galand, *Baudelaire,* 320–22 (Fr).

Prévost, *Baudelaire,* 207–08 (Fr).

Spleen 1
"Pluviôse, irrité contre la ville entière"

Broome and Chesters, *The Appreciation of Modern French Poetry (1850–1950),* 80–82 (Eng).

Fairlie, *Baudelaire: "Les Fleurs de Mal,"* 49–50 (Eng).

Galand, *Baudelaire,* 332–33 (Fr).

Jacques Geninasca, "Forme fixe et forme discursive dans quelques sonnets de Baudelaire," *CAIEF* 32 (May 1980): 130–32 (Fr).

Quesnel, *Baudelaire solaire et clandestin,* 144–46 (Fr).

M. Riffaterre, *Semiotics of Poetry,* 67–70 (Eng).

Turnell, *Baudelaire,* 165–68, 261 (Eng).

Spleen 2
"J'ai plus de souvenirs que si j'avais mille ans"

Ian Alexander, "The Consciousness of Time in Baudelaire," in *Studies in Modern French Literature Presented to P. Mansell Jones* (Manchester: Manchester University Press, 1961), 4–5 (Eng).

P. W. M. Cogman, "The Paradoxical Image in Baudelaire," *FSB* 26 (Spring 1988): 10–14 (Eng).

Galand, *Baudelaire,* 333–35 (Fr).

Prévost, *Baudelaire,* 148–49, 194, 262–263 (Fr).

Quesnel, *Baudelaire solaire et clandestin,* 164–68 (Fr).

Turnell, *Baudelaire,* 158–63, 260–61 (Eng).

Spleen 3
"Je suis comme le roi d'un pays pluvieux"

Bertocci, *From Symbolism to Baudelaire,* 129–30 (Eng).

Galand, *Baudelaire,* 335–36 (Fr).

Quesnel, *Baudelaire solaire et clandestin,* 157–63 (Fr).

Spleen 4
"Quand le ciel bas et lourd pèse comme un couvercle"

Aguettant, *Baudelaire,* 102–8 (Fr).

Jean-Dominique Biard, "Baudelaire, son spleen et son couvercle," *FSB* 22 (Spring 1987): 9–12 (Fr).

A. J. L. Busst, "Spleen 4: Baudelaire's 'Couvercle,'" *FSB* 23 (Summer 1987): 21 (Eng).

Jean Cohen, "Poésie et redondance," *Poétique* 7 (November 1976): 419–22 (Fr).

Galand, *Baudelaire,* 336–38 (Fr).

Katz and Hall, *Explicating French Texts,* 40–45 (Fr).

Prévost, *Baudelaire,* 127–28, 193, 245–246 (Fr).

Quesnel, *Baudelaire solaire et clandestin,* 310–17 (Fr).

Michael Riffaterre, "Sémantique du poème," *CAIEF* 23 (May 1971): 127–30 (Fr).

Turnell, *Baudelaire,* 163–64, 262–63 (Eng).

William Weaver, "Spleen," *Expl* 12 (December 1953): 19. Reprinted in Walcutt and Whitesell, eds., *The Explicator Cyclopedia,* vol. 2, 32–33 (Eng).

Bernard Weinberg, "Les Limites de l'hermétisme, ou Hermétisme et intelligibilité," *CAIEF* 15 (March 1963): 152–55 (Fr).

"Le Squelette laboureur"

Galand, *Baudelaire,* 373 (Fr).

"Sur le Tasse en prison d'Eugène Delacroix"

Prévost, *Baudelaire,* 108–10 (Fr).

"Les Ténèbres"

Marie Maclean, "Specularité et inversion transformationnelle chez Baudelaire: 'Un Fantôme,'" *AJFS* 21 (January–April 1984): 60–62 (Fr).

BAUDELAIRE, CHARLES, "Le Tonneau de la haine"

"Le Tonneau de la haine"

Galand, *Baudelaire,* 329–30 (Fr).

"Toute entière"

Galand, *Baudelaire,* 295–96 (Fr).

F. W. Leakey, "The Amorous Tribute: Baudelaire and the Renaissance Tradition," in D. R. Haggis et al., eds., *The French Renaissance and Its Heritage. Essays Presented to Alan Boase* (London: Methuen, 1968), 104–7. Reprinted in Leakey, *Baudelaire,* 82–83 (Eng).

"Tu mettrais l'univers entier dans ta ruelle"

Galand, *Baudelaire,* 281–82 (Fr).

"La Vie antérieure"

Auffret and Auffret, *Le Commentaire composé,* 142–52 (Fr).

Galand, *Baudelaire,* 268–70 (Fr).

Louis Morice, "La Vie antérieure," *ELit* 1 (April 1968): 29–49 (Fr).

Prévost, *Baudelaire,* 182–83 (Fr).

Quesnel, *Baudelaire solaire et clandestin,* 101–2, 263–66 (Fr).

"Le Vin"

Galand, *Baudelaire,* 388–89 (Fr).

"Le Vin de l'assassin"

Abraham Avni, "A Revaluation of Baudelaire's 'Le Vin': Its Originality and Significance for 'Les Fleurs du mal," *FR* 44 (December 1970): 316–17 (Eng).

Galand, *Baudelaire,* 392–93 (Fr).

Prévost, *Baudelaire,* 226 (Fr).

"Le Vin des amants"

Galand, *Baudelaire,* 395–96 (Fr).

"Le Vin des chiffonniers"

Galand, *Baudelaire,* 390–92 (Fr).

"Le Vin du solitaire"

Galand, *Baudelaire,* 394–95 (Fr).

"La Voix"

Galand, *Baudelaire,* 449–50 (Fr).

Prévost, *Baudelaire,* 155–56, 162–163 (Fr).

"Le Voyage"

Aguettant, *Baudelaire,* 211–34 (Fr).

Lloyd J. Austin, "Baudelaire: "Poet or Prophet?" in Lloyd J. Austin, Garnet Rees, and Eugène Vinaver, eds., *Studies in Modern Literature Presented to P. Mansell Jones* (Manchester: Manchester University Press, 1961), 1–18. Reprinted in Austin, ed., *Poetic Principles and Practice,* 8–17 (Eng).

Carter, *Charles Baudelaire,* 97–101 (Eng).

Cassou-Yager, *La Polyvalence du thème de la mort,* 97–106 (Fr).

Chesters, *Baudelaire and the Poetics of Craft,* 94–95 (Eng).

Fairlie, *Baudelaire: "Les Fleurs du Mal,"* 58 (Eng).

Galand, *Baudelaire,* 425–32 (Fr).

Eric Gans, "Mon semblable, mon frère," *SFR* 8 (Spring 1984): 84–85 (Eng).

Freeman G. Henry, " 'Les Fleurs du mal' and the Exotic: The Escapist Psychology of a Visionary Poet," *NCFS* 8 (Fall–Winter 1979–80): 73–74 (Eng).

BAUDELAIRE, CHARLES, "Un Voyage à Cythère"

Edward K. Kaplan, "Baudelaire and the Battle with Finitude: 'La Mort,' Conclusion of 'Les Fleurs du mal,'" *FrF* 4 (May 1979): 225–28 (Eng).

Edward K. Kaplan, "The Courage of Baudelaire and Rimbaud: The Anxiety of Faith," *FR* 52 (December 1978): 297–99, 305 (Eng).

F. W. Leakey, "Baudelaire: the Poet as Moralist," in Lloyd Austin, Eugène Vinaver, and Garnet Rees, eds., *Studies in Modern French Literature Presented to P. Mansell Jones* (Manchester: Manchester University Press, 1961), 211–12, 214 (Eng).

James McLaren, "The Imagery of Light and Darkness in 'Les Fleurs du mal,'" *NCFS* 7 (Fall–Winter 1978–79): 47–48 (Eng).

Porter, *The Crisis of French Symbolism,* 178–79 (Eng).

Quesnel, *Baudelaire solaire et clandestin,* 192–95 (Fr).

Turnell, *Baudelaire,* 82–88, 160, 223–24, 242–43, 248, 294–95 (Eng).

"Un Voyage à Cythère"

Cassou-Yager, *La Polyvalence du thème de la mort,* 39–45 (Fr).

Peter Collier, "Baudelaire and Metaphor: Work in Regress," *FMLS* 26 (January 1990): 31–34 (Eng).

Galand, *Baudelaire,* 410–13 (Fr).

Edward K. Kaplan, "The Courage of Baudelaire and Rimbaud: The Anxiety of Faith," *FR* 52 (December 1978): 295–97 (Eng).

Knight, *Flower Poetics in Nineteenth-Century France,* 77–78 (Eng).

Catherine Osborne, "Mystic Fusion: Baudelaire and 'le sentiment du beau,'" *PMLA* 88 (October 1973): 1134 (Eng).

Prévost, *Baudelaire,* 195–96 (Fr).

Turnell, *Baudelaire,* 212–16, 242–43, 280–81 (Eng).

"Les Yeux des pauvres"

Georges Poulet, *La Poésie éclatée* (Paris: Presses universitaires de France, 1980), 66–67 (Fr).

BELLEAU, RÉMY

"L'Améthyste"

Eckhardt, *Rémy Belleau, sa vie, sa Bergerie,* 185–87 (Fr).

"L'Amour ambitieux d'Ixion"

Jean Braybrook, "Rémy Belleau and the Figure of the Artist," *FS* 37 (January 1983): 4–8, 10–13 (Eng).

"Avril"

Eckhardt, *Rémy Belleau, sa vie, sa Bergerie,* 144–47 (Fr).

Bergerie, première journée
"Il estoit nuit, et la trace cornue"

Jean Braybrook, " Les Sonnets pétrarchistes de Rémy Belleau," in Bellenger, ed., *Le Sonnet à la Renaissance,* 169–71, 177 (Fr).

Bergerie, deuxième journée
"Yeux non pas yeux, mais celestes flambeaux"

Jean Braybrook, " Les Sonnets pétrarchistes de Rémy Belleau," in Bellenger, ed., *Le Sonnet à la Renaissance,* 172–73 (Fr).

"Chant pastoral de la paix"

Eckhardt, *Rémy Belleau, sa vie, sa Bergerie,* 127–29 (Fr).

"Eclogues sacrées 7, 'Noble et gente Princesse, et de beauté divine' "

H. Weber, *La Création poétique au XVIe siècle en France,* 284–86 (Fr).

"L'Eté"

Eckhardt, *Rémy Belleau, sa vie, sa Bergerie,* 187–88 (Fr).

BELLEAU, RÉMY, "La Gagate"

"La Gagate"

Marcel Tetel, "La Poétique de la réflexivité chez Belleau," *SFr* 29 (January–April 1985): 4 (Fr).

"Je voy dessus la porte une lumière belle"

Jean Braybrook, "Les Sonnets pétrarchistes de Remy Belleau," in Bellenger, ed., *Le Sonnet à la Renaissance,* 173–74 (Fr).

"Lune porte-flambeau, seule fille heritière"

Jean Braybrook, " Les Sonnets pétrarchistes de Remy Belleau," in Bellenger, ed., *Le Sonnet à la Renaissance,* 176–77 (Fr).

"Le Mulet"

Marcel Tetel, "La Poétique de la réflexivité chez Belleau," *SFr* 29 (January–April 1985): 9 (Fr).

"Oeil, non pas oeil, mais esclair qui foudroye"

Jean Braybrook, " Les Sonnets pétrarchistes de Remy Belleau," in Bellenger, ed., *Le Sonnet à la Renaissance,* 174–75 (Fr).

"Le Papillon"

Marcel Tetel, "La Poétique de la réflexivité chez Belleau," *SFr* 29 (January–April 1985): 2 (Fr).

"Prométhée premier inventeur des anneaux
et de l'enchasseure des pierres"

Jean Braybrook, "Rémy Belleau and the Figure of the Artist," *FS* 37 (January 1983): 8–10 (Eng).

BERTAUT, JEAN, "Psaume 1" (Translation)

"Le Rubis"

Marcel Tetel, "La Poétique de la réflexivité chez Belleau," *SFr* 29 (January–April 1985): 16–17 (Fr).

"Les Vendangeurs"

Eckhardt, *Rémy Belleau, sa vie, sa Bergerie,* 188–89 (Fr).

BERNART DE VENTADORN

"Lo tems vai e ven e vire"

Topsfield, *Troubadours and Love,* 133–35 (Eng).

"Non es meravelha s'eu chan"

Eliza Miruna Ghil, "Topic and Tropeic:" Two Types of Syntagmatic Development in the Old Provençal Canzo," *ECr* 19 (Winter 1979): 54–69 (Eng).

William D. Paden, "Utrum Copularentum of Cors," *ECr* 19 (Winter 1979): 74–77 (Eng).

BEROALDE DE VERVILLE, FRANÇOIS

"Psaume 20" (Translation)

Jeanneret, *Poésie et tradition biblique,* 469–70, 472 (Fr).

BERTAUT, JEAN

"Félicité passée"

Lafay, *La Poésie française du premier XVIIe siècle,* 261–64 (Fr).

"Psaume 1" (Translation)

Jeanneret, *Poésie et tradition biblique,* 474, 478, 483 (Fr).

BERTAUT, JEAN, "Psaume 6" (Translation)

"Psaume 6" (Translation)

Jeanneret, *Poésie et tradition biblique,* 478, 480 (Fr).

"Psaume 45" (Translation)

Jeanneret, *Poésie et tradition biblique,* 465–67, 471, 479 (Fr).

BERTRAN DE BORN

"Un sirventes on motz non faill"

Patricia Harris-Stablein, "The Rotten and the Burned: Normative and Nutritive Structures in the Poetry of Bertran de Born," *ECr* 19 (Winter 1979): 107–19 (Eng).

BEZE, THEODORE DE

"Psaume 16" (Translation)

Jeanneret, *Poésie et tradition biblique,* 99–100, 102–03 (Fr).

"Psaume 47" (Translation)

Jeanneret, *Poésie et tradition biblique,* 98, 100 (Fr).

"Psaume 81" (Translation)

Jeanneret, *Poésie et tradition biblique,* 95–97 (Fr).

"Psaume 148" (Translation)

Jeanneret, *Poésie et tradition biblique,* 96, 99 (Fr).

BODEL, JEAN

"Les Congés d'Arras"

Jean-Charles Payen, "L'Aveu pudique de l'écriture dans les 'Congés' de Jean Bodel, ou Le Charme discret de la bourgeoisie en face du malheur et de la pauvreté," in *Mélanges de langue et de littérature françaises . . . offerts à M. Charles Foulon,* vol. 1 (Rennes: Institut de Français, 1980), 267–275 (Fr).

BOILEAU, NICOLAS

"L'Arrêt burlesque"

White, *Nicolas Boileau,* 45–48 (Eng).

"L'Art poétique"

Bray, *Boileau,* 49, 64–87 (Fr).

Pocock, *Boileau and the Nature of Neo-Classicism,* 83–145 (Eng).

White, *Nicolas Boileau,* 135–51 (Eng).

"Dialogue des héros de romans"

White, *Nicolas Boileau,* 77–83 (Eng).

"Discours au Roi"

Pocock, *Boileau and the Nature of Neo-Classicism,* 39–42 (Eng).

Epître 1
"Au Roy"

Pocock, *Boileau and the Nature of Neo-Classicism,* 60–69 (Eng).

White, *Nicolas Boileau,* 92–95 (Eng).

BOILEAU, NICOLAS, *Epître 2* "A Monsieur l'Abbé des Roches"

Epître 2
"A Monsieur l'Abbé des Roches"

Pocock, *Boileau and the Nature of Neo-Classicism,* 73–74 (Eng).

White, *Nicolas Boileau,* 44–45 (Eng).

Epître 3
"A Monsieur Arnauld, Docteur de Sorbonne"

Pocock, *Boileau and the Nature of Neo-Classicism,* 70–71 (Eng).

White, *Nicolas Boileau,* 95–98 (Eng.)

Epître 4
"Au Roy"

Bray, *Boileau,* 56, 58 (Fr).

Pocock, *Boileau and the Nature of Neo-Classicism,* 74–81 (Eng).

White, *Nicolas Boileau,* 65–67 (Eng).

Epître 5
"A. M. de Guilleragues"

Pocock, *Boileau and the Nature of Neo-Classicism,* 81–82 (Eng).

White, *Nicolas Boileau,* 98–100 (Eng).

Epître 6
"A. M. de Lamoignon"

White, *Nicolas Boileau,* 100–103 (Eng).

Epître 7
"A. M. Racine"

Pocock, *Boileau and the Nature of Neo-Classicism,* 159–62 (Eng).

White, *Nicolas Boileau,* 68–69 (Eng).

Epître 8
"Au Roy"

White, *Nicolas Boileau,* 69–71 (Eng).

Epître 9
"A. M. le Marquis de Seignelay"

Pocock, *Boileau and the Nature of Neo-Classicism,* 152–59 (Eng).

White, *Nicolas Boileau,* 151–53 (Eng).

Epître 10
"A mes vers"

Bray, *Boileau,* 134–35 (Fr).

White, *Nicolas Boileau,* 71–74 (Eng).

Epître 11
"A mon jardinier"

White, *Nicolas Boileau,* 74–76 (Eng).

Epître 12
"Sur l'amour de Dieu"

Bray, *Boileau,* 142–44 (Fr).

White, *Nicolas Boileau,* 103–8 (Eng).

"Le Lutrin"

Bray, *Boileau,* 90–96 (Fr).

Calin, *In Defense of French Poetry,* 80–82 (Eng).

Pocock, *Boileau and the Nature of Neo-Classicism,* 148–52 (Eng).

White, *Nicolas Boileau,* 48–57, 76–77 (Eng).

BOILEAU, NICOLAS, "Ode sur la Prise de Namur"

"Ode sur la Prise de Namur"

Pocock, *Boileau and the Nature of Neo-Classicism,* 162–64 (Eng).

Satire 1
"Damon ce grand auteur, dont la muse fertile"

Bray, *Boileau,* 17–18 (Fr).

White, *Nicolas Boileau,* 35–37 (Eng).

Satire 2
"A. M. de Molière"

Pocock, *Boileau and the Nature of Neo-Classicism,* 31–35 (Eng).

White, *Nicolas Boileau,* 59–61 (Eng).

Satire 3
"A. 'Quel sujet inconnu vous trouble et vous altère?' "

Bray, *Boileau,* 41–42 (Fr).

Pocock, *Boileau and the Nature of Neo-Classicism,* 47–48 (Eng).

White, *Nicolas Boileau,* 38–40 (Eng).

Satire 4
"A Monsieur l'Abbé Le Vayer"

White, *Nicolas Boileau,* 85–87 (Eng).

Pocock, *Boileau and the Nature of Neo-Classicism,* 42–46 (Eng).

Satire 5
"A Monsieur le Marquis de Dangeau"

Pocock, *Boileau and the Nature of Neo-Classicism,* 46–47 (Eng).

White, *Nicolas Boileau,* 87–89 (Eng).

Satire 6
"Qui frappe l'air, bon Dieu! de ces lugubres cris?"

Bray, *Boileau,* 17–22 (Fr).

Pocock, *Boileau and the Nature of Neo-Classicism,* 25–27 (Eng).

White, *Nicolas Boileau,* 37–38 (Eng).

Satire 7
"Muse, changeons de style, et quittons la satire"

Pocock, *Boileau and the Nature of Neo-Classicism,* 27–31 (Eng).

White, *Nicolas Boileau,* 57–59 (Eng).

Satire 8
"A Monsieur M ***, Docteur de Sorbonne"

Bray, *Boileau,* 44–46 (Fr).

Pocock, *Boileau and the Nature of Neo-Classicism,* 56–58 (Eng).

White, *Nicolas Boileau,* 89–92 (Eng).

Satire 9
"A son Esprit"

Bray, *Boileau,* 44–47, 49, 98–99 (Fr).

Pocock, *Boileau and the Nature of Neo-Classicism,* 48–56 (Eng).

White, *Nicolas Boileau,* 61–65 (Eng).

Satire 10
"Enfin bornant le cours de tes galanteries"

Pocock, *Boileau and the Nature of Neo-Classicism,* 164–66 (Eng).

White, *Nicolas Boileau,* 40–44 (Eng).

BOILEAU, NICOLAS, *Satire 11* "A Monsieur de Valincour"

Satire 11
"A Monsieur de Valincour"

White, *Nicolas Boileau,* 108–12 (Eng).

Satire 12
"Discours de l'auteur pour servir d'apologie"

Bray, *Boileau,* 146–47 (Fr).

White, *Nicolas Boileau,* 113–19 (Eng).

BONNEFOY, YVES

"A une terre d'aube"

Caws, *Yves Bonnefoy,* 19–20 (Eng).

"Dans le leurre du seuil"

M. Bishop, *The Contemporary Poetry of France,* 132 (Eng).

Caws, *Yves Bonnefoy,* 32–43, 55–57 (Eng).

Richard Stamelman, "The Crack in the Mirror: The Subversion of Image and Representation in the Poetry of Yves Bonnefoy," *FrF* 13 (January 1988):77–78 (Eng).

Richard Stamelman, "The Syntax of the Ephemeral," *Dalhousie French Studies* 2 (October 1980): 101–17. Reprinted in Stamelman, *Lost Beyond Telling,* 164–70 (Eng).

Richard Vernier, "Dans la certitude du seuil: Yves Bonnefoy aujourd'hui," *SFR* 2 (Spring 1978): 140–42 (Fr).

Dans le leurre du seuil 1
"Deux couleurs"

M. Bishop, *The Contemporary Poetry of France,* 132–33 (Eng).

Caws, *Yves Bonnefoy,* 36 (Eng).

BONNEFOY, YVES, "Le Feuillage éclairé"

Dans le leurre du seuil 2
"Deux barques"

M. Bishop, *The Contemporary Poetry of France,* 132–33 (Eng).

Caws, *Yves Bonnefoy,* 36–37 (Eng).

Dans le leurre du seuil 3
"La Terre"

M. Bishop, *The Contemporary Poetry of France,* 133–34 (Eng).

Caws, *Yves Bonnefoy,* 37–38 (Eng).

"Douve parle"

Stephen Winspur, "Bonnefoy Cartesien?" *FrF* 9 (May 1984): 241–42 (Fr).

"Du mouvement et de l'immobilité de Douve"

Caws, *Yves Bonnefoy,* 5–13, 43–47 (Eng).

John E. Jackson, *Yves Bonnefoy* (Paris: Seghers, 1976), 9–22, 24–25, 27–30 (Fr).

Annie Prothin, "The Substantive Language of Yves Bonnefoy," *SubStance,* no. 20 (Fall 1978): 45–57 (Eng).

Richard Stamelman, "Landscape and Loss in Yves Bonnefoy and Philippe Jaccottet," *FrF* 5 (January 1980): 36–37 (Eng).

"L'Epars, l'indivisible"

M. Bishop, *The Contemporary Poetry of France,* 135–36 (Eng).

Caws, *Yves Bonnefoy,* 39–43 (Eng).

"Le Feuillage éclairé"

Caws, *Yves Bonnefoy,* 17–19 (Eng).

BONNEFOY, YVES, "Le Fleuve"

"Le Fleuve"

M. Bishop, *The Contemporary Poetry of France,* 130–32 (Eng).

"Hic es locus patriae"

Caws, *Yves Bonnefoy,* 44 (Eng).

"Hier règnant désert"

Marc Hofstadter, "From Alienation to Incarnation: Yves Bonnefoy's 'Hier règnant désert,'" *RR* 72 (May 1981): 333–48 (Eng).

John E. Jackson, *Yves Bonnefoy* (Paris: Seghers, 1976), 30 (Fr).

John Price," Yves Bonnefoy: The Sense of Things," in Cardinal, ed., *Sensibility and Creation,* 211–16 (Eng).

Hier règnant désert 1
"Ménaces du témoin"

Caws, *Yves Bonnefoy,* 14–15 (Eng).

Hier règnant désert 2
"Le Visage mortel"

Caws, *Yves Bonnefoy,* 15–17 (Eng).

Hier règnant désert 3
"Le Chant des sauvegards"

Caws, *Yves Bonnefoy,* 17 (Eng).

Hier règnant désert 4
"Le Feuillage éclairé"

Caws, *Yves Bonnefoy,* 17–19 (Eng).

BONNEFOY, YVES, "Pierre écrite"

Hier règant désert 5
"A une terre d'aube"

Caws, *Yves Bonnefoy,* 19 (Eng).

"Menaces du témoin"

Caws, *Yves Bonnefoy,* 14–15 (Eng).

"Nous n'aurons pas parlé"

Caws, *Yves Bonnefoy,* 44–47 (Eng).

"Les Nuées"

M. Bishop, *The Contemporary Poetry of France,* 134–35 (Eng).

Caws, *Yves Bonnefoy,* 38–39 (Eng).

"O de ton aile de terre et d'ombre éveille-nous"

Sarah Lawall, "Yves Bonnefoy and Denis Roche: Art and the Art of Poetry," in Caws, ed., *About French Poetry,* 74–80 (Eng).

"L'Orangerie"

John E. Jackson, *Yves Bonnefoy* (Paris: Seghers, 1976), 22–24 (Fr).

Annie Prothin, "The Substantive Language of Yves Bonnefoy," *Sub-Stance,* no. 20 (Fall 1978): 48–50 (Eng).

"Pierre écrite"

Caws, *Yves Bonnefoy,* 20–32 (Eng).

John Price, "Yves Bonnefoy: the Sense of Things," in Cardinal, ed. *Sensibility and Creation,* 213–16 (Eng).

BONNEFOY, YVES, *Pierre écrite 1* "L'Eté de nuit"

Pierre écrite 1
"L'Eté de nuit"

Caws, *Yves Bonnefoy,* 20–3 (Eng).

Pierre écrite 2
"Un Feu devant nous"

Caws, *Yves Bonnefoy,* 25–29 (Eng).

Pierre écrite 3
"La Lumière changée"

Caws, *Yves Bonnefoy,* 29–30 (Eng).

Pierre écrite 4
"Le Dialogue d'Angoisse et de Désir"

Caws, *Yves Bonnefoy,* 30–32 (Eng).

"Rive d'une autre mort"

Caws, *Yves Bonnefoy,* 44–45 (Eng).

Le Seul Témoin II
"Elle fuit vers les saules: Le Sourire"

R. A. York, "Bonnefoy and Mallarmé: Aspects of Intertextuality," *RR* 71 (May 1980): 308–11 (Eng).

"Théâtre"

Caws, *Inner Theatre,* 154–56 (Eng).

"Le Visage mortel"

Caws, *Yves Bonnefoy,* 16–17 (Eng).

BRETON, ANDRE, "Au beau demi-jour de 1934"

BOSQUET, ALAIN

"Hésitation"

Antonio Rodriguez, "A Propos d'"Hesitation' de A. Bosquet," *FR* 44 (March 1971): 665–76 (Fr).

BRETON, ANDRE

"Age"

Michael Sheringham, " 'Mont de Piété' and André Breton's Early Poetic Development," *FMLS* 15 (Jan 1979): 50–51 (Eng).

"André Derain"

Michael Sheringham, " 'Mont de Piété' and André Breton's Early Poetic Development," *FMLS* 15 (Jan 1979): 53–55 (Eng).

"Arcane 17"

Audouin, *Breton,* 152–55, 158–60, 210–13 (Fr).

Balakian, *André Breton,* 201–13 (Eng).

Michel Beaujour, "André Breton ou la transparence: Sur 'Arcane 17,' " in *Les Critiques de notre temps et Breton* (Paris: Garnier, 1974), 141–45 (Fr).

Mary Ann Caws, *André Breton* (New York: Twayne, 1971), 84–86 (Eng).

Jean Schoenfeld, "André Breton, Alchemist," *FR* 57 (March 1984): 496–502 (Eng).

"L'Art magique"

Audouin, *Breton,* 221–23 (Fr).

"Au beau demi-jour de 1934"

Roger Cardinal, "Breton: 'Au beau demi-jour de 1934,' " in Nurse, ed., *The Art of Criticism,* 256–71 (Eng).

BRETON, ANDRE, "Cette anné-là, un chasseur . . ."

"Cette anné-là, un chasseur . . ."

Michael Riffaterre, "Semantic Incompatibilities in Automatic Writing," in Caws, ed., *About French Poetry,* 224–33 (Eng).

"Cette femme, je l'ai connue"

Michael Riffaterre, "Semantic Incompatibilities in Automatic Writing," in Caws, ed., *About French Poetry,* 233–38 (Eng).

"Les Champs magnétiques"

Balakian, *André Breton,* 60–64 (Eng).

"Château étoilé"

Jean Ethier-Blais, "Borduas et Breton," *EF* 4 (November 1968): 369–82 (Fr).

"Coqs de bruyère"

Michael Sheringham, " 'Mont de Piété' and André Breton's Early Poetic Development," *FMLS* 15 (Jan 1979): 50–53 (Eng).

"Le Corset mystère"

Michael Sheringham, " 'Mont de Piété' and André Breton's Early Poetic Development," *FMLS* 15 (Jan 1979): 62–64 (Eng).

"Décembre"

Michael Sheringham, " 'Mont de Piété' and André Breton's Early Poetic Development," *FMLS* 15 (Jan 1979): 49–50 (Eng).

"Dernière levée"

Mary Ann Caws, *André Breton* (New York: Twayne, 1971), 100–101 (Eng).

BRETON, ANDRE, "Il faut aller voir"

"Les Etats généraux"

Audouin, *Breton,* 214–15 (Fr).

Balakian, *André Breton,* 189–93 (Eng).

Anna Balakian, "André Breton's 'Les Etats généraux': Revolution and Poetry," *FR* 62 (May 1989): 1008–16 (Eng).

"Fata Morgana"

Audouin, *Breton,* 209–10 (Fr).

Balakian, *André Breton,* 184–89 (Eng).

Mary Ann Caws, *André Breton* (New York: Twayne, 1971), 102–5 (Eng).

Neal Oxenhandler, "Cocteau, Breton, and Ponge: The Situation of the Self," in Caws, ed., *About French Poetry,* 60–62 (Eng).

"Forêt noire"

Michael Sheringham, " 'Mont de Piété' and André Breton's Early Poetic Development," *FMLS* 15 (January 1979): 56–57 (Eng).

Michael Sheringham, "Rimbaud in 1875 and André Breton's 'Forêt noire,' " *FS* 35 (January 1981): 32–44 (Eng).

"L'Herbage rouge"

Keith Aspley, "André Breton's Poems for Denise," *FS* 41 (January 1987): 52–53 (Eng).

"Un Homme et une femme absolument blancs"

Neal Oxenhandler, "Cocteau, Breton, and Ponge: The Situation of the Self, in Caws, ed., *About French Poetry,* 59–60 (Eng).

"Il faut aller voir"

Dubosclard and Dubosclard, *Du surréalisme à la Résistance,* 16–21 (Fr).

BRETON, ANDRE, "Il n'y a pas à sorti de là"

"Il n'y a pas à sorti de là"

Michael Sheringham, "Breton and the Language of Automation: Alterity, Allegory, Desire," *FMLS* 18 (April 1982): 145–47 (Eng).

"Il y aura une fois"

Jacqueline Chénieux, "Pour une imagination poétique et pratique," in *Les Critiques de notre temps et Breton* (Paris: Garnier, 1974), 83–97 (Fr).

"Je reviens"

M. Riffaterre, *Semiotics of Poetry,* 93–94 (Eng).

"La Lampe dans l'horloge"

Audouin, *Breton,* 217–19 (Fr).

"Langue des pierres"

Jean Schoenfeld, "André Breton, Alchemist," *FR* 57 (March 1984): 494–96 (Eng).

"Ligne brisée"

Michael Sheringham, "Breton and the Language of Automation: Alterity, Allegory, Desire," *FMLS* 18 (April 1982): 149–50 (Eng).

"Mieux vaut recommencer toujours. La Cavalcade"

Keith Aspley, "André Breton's Poems for Denise," *FS* 41 (January 1987): 57 (Eng).

"Monsieur V"

Michael Sheringham, " 'Mont de Piété' and André Breton's Early Poetic Development," *FMLS* 15 (Jan 1979): 60–62 (Eng).

"Nœud des miroirs"

J. Gratton, "Runaway: Textual Dynamics in the Surrealist Poetry of André Breton," *FMLS* 18 (April 1982): 130–38 (Eng).

"Ode à Charles Fourier"

Audouin, *Breton,* 215–17 (Fr).

Balakian, *André Breton,* 193–99 (Eng).

Anna Balakian, "André Breton et l'hermétisme: Des 'Champs magnétiques' à 'La Clé des champs," *CAIEF* 15 (March 1963): 137–38 (Fr).

Clifford Browder, *André Breton, Arbiter of Surrealism* (Geneva: Droz, 1967), 130–32 (Eng).

Gérald Schaeffer, "Un Petit Matin de 1937," in *André Breton,* ed. Marc Eigeldinger (Neuchâtel: La Baconnière, 1970), 241–78 (Fr).

Gérald Schaeffer, "Un Petit Matin de 1937 (sur l'"Ode à Charles Fourier')," in *Les Critiques de notre temps et Breton* (Paris: Garnier, 1974), 145–51 (Fr).

"On me dit que là-bas les plages sont noires"

J. D. Hubert, "André Breton et le paradis perdu," *FR* 37 (December 1963): 200–202 (Fr).

"Page blanche"

M. Riffaterre, *Semiotics of Poetry,* 141–43 (Eng).

See also René Char, Paul Elvard (q.v.).

"La Parure des voix silencieuses dort"

Keith Aspley, "André Breton's Poems for Denise," *FS* 41 (January 1987): 55–56 (Eng).

"Poisson soluble"

Balakian, *André Breton,* 64–68 (Eng).

Julien Gracq, "Spectre du 'Poisson soluble,'" in *Les Critiques de notre temps et Breton* (Paris: Garnier, 1974), 117–21 (Fr).

BRETON, ANDRE, "Poisson soluble #28"

"Poisson soluble #28"

M. Riffaterre, *Semiotics of Poetry,* 70–72 (Eng).

"Pour Lafcadio"

Michael Sheringham, " 'Mont de Piété' and André Breton's Early Poetic Development," *FMLS* 15 (January 1979): 57–59 (Eng).

"Rano Raraku"

Edgar Knowlton, "Breton's 'Rano Raraku,' " *Expl* 40 (Summer 1982): 50–52 (Eng).

"Signe ascendant"

Jean-Louis Houdebine, "L'Idéologie du 'Signe ascendant,' " in *Les Critiques de notre temps et Breton* (Paris: Garnier, 1974), 100–7 (Fr).

Roger Navarri, "Une Autre lecture du 'Signe ascendant,' " in *Les Critiques de notre temps et Breton* (Paris: Garnier, 1974), 108–10 (Fr).

"Sur le tranchant éveil bel oiseau de malice"

Keith Aspley, "André Breton's Poems for Denise," *FS* 41 (January 1987): 57–58 (Eng).

"Tournesol"

Curnier, *Pages commentées d'auteurs contemporains,* vol. 2, 65–78 (Fr).

"Tout paradis n'est pas perdu"

J. D. Hubert, "André Breton et le paradis perdu," *FR* 37 (December 1963): 202–4 (Fr).

CENDRARS, BLAISE, "Natures mortes"

"L'Union libre"

Elza Adamowicz, "Narcisse se noie: Lecture de 'L'Union libre' d'André Breton," *RR* 80 (November 1989): 571–81 (Fr).

Balakian, *André Breton,* 139–42 (Eng).

CAILLER, RAOUL

"Auprès des beaux yeux de Phyllis"

Lafay, La Poésie française du premier XVIIe siècle, 266–70 (Fr).

CENDRARS, BLAISE

"Aux cinq coins"

Mary Ann Caws, "Blaise Cendrars: A Cinema of Poetry," *KRQ* 17, no. 4 (1970): 349–50 (Eng).

"Contrastes"

Tatiana Greene, "La 'Pure Poésie' de Blaise Cendrars," *FR* 57 (May 1984): 817–18 (Fr).

"La Guerre au Luxembourg"

Mary Ann Caws, "Blaise Cendrars: A Cinema of Poetry," *KRQ* 17, no. 4, (1970): 350–52 (Eng).

Caws, *The Inner Theatre,* 40–44 (Eng).

"Natures mortes"

Caws, *The Inner Theatre,* 40–44 (Eng).

CENDRARS, BLAISE, "Panama, ou Les Aventures de mes sept oncles"

"Panama, ou Les Aventures de mes sept oncles"

Jay Bochner, *Blaise Cendrars: Discovery and Re-Creation* (Toronto:University of Toronto Press, 1978), 109–20 (Eng).

Monique Chefdor, *Blaise Cendrars* (Boston: Twayne, 1980), 46–48 (Eng).

"Les Pâques à New York"

Jay Bochner, *Blaise Cendrars: Discovery and Re-Creation* (Toronto: University of Toronto Press, 1978) 91–97 (Eng).

Monique Chefdor, *Blaise Cendrars* (Boston: Twayne, 1980), 37–41 (Eng).

Couffignal, *Zone d'Apollinaire,* 25–30 (Fr).

Durry, *Guillaume Apollinaire: Alcools,* vol. 1, 234–247, 254–301 (Fr).

Tatiana Greene, "La 'Pure Poésie' de Blaise Cendrars," *FR* 57 (May 1984): 813–15 (Fr).

Richter, *La Crise du logos,* 63–95 (Fr).

"Prose du Transsibérien et de la petite Jeanne de France"

Jay Bochner, *Blaise Cendrars: Discovery and Re-Creation* (Toronto: University of Toronto Press, 1978) 97–109 (Eng).

Mary Ann Caws, "Blaise Cendrars: A Cinema of Poetry," *KRQ* 17, no. 4, (1970): 346–47 (Eng).

Caws, *The Inner Theatre,* 28–31 (Eng).

Monique Chefdor, *Blaise Cendrars* (Boston: Twayne, 1980), 41–46 (Eng).

Tatiana Greene, "La 'Pure Poésie' de Blaise Cendrars," *FR* 57 (May 1984): 815–17 (Fr).

"Vie dangereuse"

Tatiana Greene, "La 'Pure Poésie' de Blaise Cendrars," *FR* 57 (May 1984): 813 (Fr).

CESAIRE, AIME

"Afrique"

Arnold, *Modernism and Negritude,* 267–69 (Eng).

"A l'Afrique"

Arnold, *Modernism and Negritude,* 213–17 (Eng).

"A la mémoire d'un syndicaliste noir"

Arnold, *Modernism and Negritude,* 275–77 (Eng).

"Antipode"

Cailler, *Proposition poétique,* 170–71 (Fr).

"Les Armes miraculeuses"

Arnold, *Modernism and Negritude,* 111–12 (Eng).
Cailler, *Proposition poétique,* 90–93 (Fr).

"Au-delà"

Arnold, *Modernism and Negritude,* 109–11 (Eng).

"Avis de tirs"

Arnold, *Modernism and Negritude,* 125–26 (Eng).

"Batouque"

Arnold, *Modernism and Negritude,* 128–29, 230–234 (Eng).

Cailler, *Proposition poétique,* 73–74, 78–81, 130 (Fr).

Lilyan Kesteloot, "Première Lecture d'un poème de Césaire, 'Batouque,'" *ELit* 6 (April 1973): 50–71 (Fr).

CESAIRE, AIME, "Beau Sang giclé"

"Beau Sang giclé"

Arnold, *Modernism and Negritude,* 253–55 (Eng).

Cailler, *Proposition poétique,* 87–89 (Fr).

Aliko Songolo, " 'Cadastre' et 'Ferrements' de Césaire: Une Nouvelle Poétique," *ECr* 17 (Summer 1977): 154–55 (Fr).

"Blanc à remplir sur la carte voyageuse du pollen"

Davis, *Non-Vicious Circle,* 54–55(Eng).

"Blues de la pluie"

Davis, *Non-Vicious Circle,* 40–41 (Eng).

"Cahier d'un retour au pays natal"

Arnold, *Modernism and Negritude,* 133–68 (Eng).

Cailler, *Proposition poétique,* 133, 159–62, 195–99 (Fr).

Frederick Case, "Aimé Césaire et l'occident chrétien," *ECr* 10 (Fall 1970): 247–50, 252–54 (Fr).

Thomas Hale, "Bibliographie commentée," *EF* 14 (October 1978): 224–29 (Fr).

Lilyan Kesteloot, *Aimé Césaire* (Paris: Seghers, 1962), 24–27 (Fr).

Jacqueline Leiner, "Césaire et les problèmes du langage chez un écrivain francophone," *ECr* 17 (Summer 1977): 138–42 (Fr).

Scharfman, *"Engagement" and the Language of the Subject in the Poetry of Aimé Césaire,* 29–64 (Eng).

Emile Snyder, "A Reading of Aimé Césaire's 'Return to My Native Land,'" *ECr* 10 (Fall 1970): 197–212 (Eng).

"Cercle non vicieux"

Davis, *Non-Vicious Circle,* 144–45 (Eng).

"Chevelure"

Cailler, *Proposition poétique,* 172–74, 179 (Fr).

"Comptine"

Davis, *Non-Vicious Circle,* 62–64 (Eng).

"Corps perdu"

Arnold, *Modernism and Negritude,* 235–42 (Eng).

Cailler, *Proposition poétique,* 97–105 (Fr).

Scharfman, *"Engagement" and the Language of the Subject in the Poetry of Aimé Césaire,* 74–85 (Eng).

"Le Coup de couteau du soleil dans le dos des villes surprises"

Arnold, *Modernism and Negritude,* 193–204 (Eng).

Aliko Songolo, " 'Cadastre' et 'Ferrements' de Césaire: Une Nouvelle Poétique," *ECr* 17 (Summer 1977): 149–53 (Fr).

"Le Cristal automatique"

Scharfman, *"Engagement" and the Language of the Subject in the Poetry of Aimé Césaire,* 66–69 (Eng).

"Depuis Akkad, depuis Elam, depuis Sumer"

Arnold, *Modernism and Negritude,* 220–21 (Eng).

Davis, *Non-Vicious Circle,* 132 (Eng).

"Dit d'errance"

Arnold, *Modernism and Negritude,* 242–51 (Eng).

Davis, *Non-Vicious Circle,* 108–12 (Eng).

CESAIRE, AIME, "Elégie"

"Elégie"

Cailler, *Proposition poétique,* 95–96 (Fr).

"Et les chiens se taisaient"

Thomas Hale, "Bibliographie commentée," *EF* 14 (October 1978): 260–62 (Fr).

"Ex-voto pour un naufrage"

Davis, *Non-Vicious Circle,* 124–25 (Eng).

"Ferment"

Arnold, *Modernism and Negritude,* 255–59 (Eng).

"Ferrements"

Davis, *Non-Vicious Circle,* 58–59 (Eng).

"Grand Sang sans merci"

Scharfman, *"Engagement" and the Language of the Subject in the Poetry of Aimé Césaire,* 101–11 (Eng).

"Le Griffon"

Davis, *Non-Vicious Circle,* 136–37 (Eng).

"Hors des jours étrangers"

Arnold, *Modernism and Negritude,* 277–79 (Eng).
Scharfman, *"Engagement" and the Language of the Subject in the Poetry of Aimé Césaire,* 93–101 (Eng).

"Intimité marine"

Scharfman, *"Engagement" and the Language of the Subject in the Poetry of Aimé Césaire,* 71–73 (Eng).

CESAIRE, AIME, "Ode à la Guinée"

"Lynch I"

Arnold, *Modernism and Negritude,* 208–11 (Eng).

"Magique"

Davis, *Non-Vicious Circle,* 32–36 (Eng).

"Mémorial de Louis Delgrès"

Arnold, *Modernism and Negritude,* 274–75 (Eng).
Davis, *Non-Vicious Circle,* 86–91 (Eng).

"Mort à l'aube"

Davis, *Non-Vicious Circle,* 50–51 (Eng).

"Mot"

Arnold, *Modernism and Negritude,* 224–29, 235 (Eng).
Davis, *Non-Vicious Circle,* 118–19 (Eng).
Scharfman, *"Engagement" and the Language of the Subject in the Poetry of Aimé Césaire,* 85–92 (Eng).

"Nocturne d'une nostalgie"

Davis, *Non-Vicious Circle,* 128–29 (Eng).
Ronnie Scharfman, "Repetition and Absence: The Discourse of Deracination in Aimé Césaire's 'Nocturne d'une nostalgie,'" *FR* 56 (March 1983): 572–78 (Eng).

"Ode à la Guinée"

Arnold, *Modernism and Negritude,* 217–19 (Eng).
Davis, *Non-Vicious Circle,* 98–100 (Eng).

CESAIRE, AIME, "Pour saluer le tiers monde"

"Pour saluer le tiers monde"

Jacqueline Leiner, "Etude comparative des structures de l'imaginaire d'Aimé Césaire et de Léopold Senghor," *CAIEF* 30 (May 1978): 209–24 (Fr).

"Les Pur-sang"

Arnold, *Modernism and Negritude,* 77–88, 108 (Eng).

Cailler, *Proposition poétique,* 116–18 (Fr).

Joan Dayan, The Figure of Negation: Some Thoughts on a Landscape by Césaire," *FR* 56 (February 1983): 413, 416–23 (Eng).

"Quelconque"

Davis, *Non-Vicious Circle,* 74–76 (Eng).

"Réponse à Depestre poète haïtien"

Arnold, *Modernism and Negritude,* 181–84 (Eng).

"Salut à la Guinée"

Arnold, *Modernism and Negritude,* 265–67 (Eng).

"Séisme"

Davis, *Non-Vicious Circle,* 94–95 (Eng).

"Spirales"

Davis, *Non-Vicious Circle,* 44–46 (Eng).

"Statue de Lafcadio Hearn"

Davis, *Non-Vicious Circle,* 68–71 (Eng).

CHAR, RENE, "A une sérénité crispée"

"Ton portrait"

Cailler, *Proposition poétique,* 93–95 (Fr).

"La Tornade"

Arnold, *Modernism and Negritude,* 207–7 (Eng).
Davis, *Non-Vicious Circle,* 140 (Eng).

"Totem"

Scharfman, *"Engagement" and the Language of the Subject in the Poetry of Aimé Césaire,* 69–71 (Eng).

CHAR, RENE

"****"

La Charité, *The Poetry and the Poetics of René Char,* 70–73 (Eng).

"A ***"

La Charité, *The Poetry and the Poetics of René Char,* 137–39 (Eng).
Diana Festa McCormick, "Réflexions sur la création cosmique de René Char: Le Poème 'A***,' " *FR* 46 (Special Issue 5) (Spring 1973): 131–40 (Fr).

"A la santé du serpent"

Mechthild Cranston, " 'Arrière-histoire du poème pulverisé': René Char's 'Winterreise,' " *FR* 46 (Special Issue 5) (Spring 1973): 153–55 (Eng).

"A une sérénité crispée"

Caws, *The Presence of René Char,* 26–27 (Eng).

CHAR, RENE, "Affres, détonation, silence"

"Affres, détonation, silence"

Dubosclard and Dubosclard, *Du surréalisme à la Resistance,* 73–79 (Fr).

"L'Allusion imitée"

La Charité, *The Poetry and the Poetics of René Char,* 47 (Eng).

"L'Alouette"

Lawler, *René Char,* 91–96 (Eng).

James Lawler, "René Char's 'Quatre fascinants,' " in Caws, ed., *About French Poetry,* 214–17 (Eng).

"Argument"

Caws, *The Presence of René Char,* 212–14 (Eng).

Robert Nugent, "The 'Argument' of René Char's 'L'Avant-Monde,' " *FR* 45 (March 1972): 789–99 (Eng).

"Aromates chasseurs"

Caws, *The Presence of René Char,* 304–14 (Eng).

Eric Marty, "René Char: Sade et Saint-Just," *FR* 62 (May 1989): 1029–31 (Fr).

"Artine"

Virginia de La Charité, "Char's Surrealist Experience: An Appraisal of 'Artine,' " in George B. Daniel, ed., *Renaissance and Other Studies in Honor of William L. Wiley* (Chapel Hill: University of North Carolina Press, 1968), 191–201 (Eng).

La Charité, *The Poetry and the Poetics of René Char,* 48–57 (Eng).

Lawler, *René Char,* 12–13 (Eng).

'm

"Aux portes d'Aerea"

Caws, *The Presence of René Char,* 34–35, 267–68 (Eng).

"La Bête innommable"

Lawler, *René Char,* 63–69 (Eng).

"La Bibliothèque est en feu"

Caws, *The Presence of René Char,* 226–29 (Eng).
La Charité, *The Poetry and the Poetics of René Char,* 176–79 (Eng).

"Biens égaux"

Daniel Bergez, "Lecture de René Char," *Europe* 66 (January–February 1988): 93–101 (Fr).
La Charité, *The Poetry and the Poetics of René Char,* 100–102 (Eng).

"Le Bois de l'Epte"

Philip Cranston, "René Char, poète outil: À l'instant du poème," *FR* 43 (Special Issue 1) (Winter 1970): 17–24 (Fr).

"Le Bouge de l'historien"

Lawler, *René Char,* 35–37 (Eng).

"Le Carreau"

Nancy K. Piore, "The Sexualized Poetic Universe of René Char," *SFR* 2 (Spring 1978): 52–53 (Eng).

"Ce soir"

Mechthild Cranston, "René Char 1923–1928: The Young Poet's Struggle for Communication," *PMLA* 87 (October 1972): 1016–17 (Eng).

CHAR, RENE, "Les Cerfs noirs"

"Les Cerfs noirs"

Lawler, *René Char,* 58–62 (Eng).

"Cet amour à tous retiré"

Mechthild Cranston, "Violence and Magic: Aspects of René Char's Surrealist Apprenticeship," *FMLS* 10 (Jan 1974): 1–18 (Eng).

"Chaîne"

Caws, *René Char,* 62–64 (Eng).

"Chant du refus"

Caws, *René Char,* 25 (Eng).

"Chérir Thouson"

Caws, *The Presence of René Char,* 265–66 (Eng).

"Le Climat de la chasse ou l'accomplissement de la poésie"

La Charité, *The Poetry and the Poetics of René Char,* 60–61 (Eng).

"Commune présence"

Caws, *René Char,* 18–19 (Eng).
La Charité, *The Poetry and the Poetics of René Char,* 73–74 (Eng).
Lawler, *René Char,* 23–28 (Eng).

"Les Compagnons dans le jardin"

La Charité, *The Poetry and the Poetics of René Char,* 180–81 (Eng).

"Contre une maison sèche"

Caws, *The Presence of René Char,* 295–305 (Eng).

Courbet
"Les Casseurs de cailloux"

Philippe Berthier, "De Courbet à Char: Casser des cailloux, peindre, ecrire," *SFR* 6 (Fall–Winter 1982): 262–69 (Eng).

"Débris mortels et Mozart"

La Charité, *The Poetry and the Poetics of René Char,* 182–83 (Eng).

Lawler, *René Char,* 28–31 (Eng).

"Le Deuil des Névons"

La Charité, *The Poetry and the Poetics of René Char,* 183–84 (Eng).

"Dire aux miens"

Eric Marty, "René Char: Sade et Saint-Just," *FR* 62 (May 1989): 1018–19 (Fr).

"Domaine"

Eric Marty, "René Char: Sade et Saint-Just," *FR* 62 (May 1989): 1021–22 (Fr).

"La Double Tresse"

La Charité, *The Poetry and the Poetics of René Char,* 171–72 (Eng).

"Dyne"

Caws, *The Presence of René Char,* 291–92 (Eng).

Lawler, *René Char,* 31–33 (Eng).

CHAR, RENE, "L'Esprit poétique"

"L'Esprit poétique"

La Charité, *The Poetry and the Poetics of René Char,* 59–60 (Eng).

"L'Extravagant"

Mechthild Cranston, " 'Arrière-histoire du poème pulverisé': René Char's 'Winterreise,' " *FR* 46 (Special Issue 5) (Spring 1973): 147–48 (Eng).

John P. Houston, "Modes of Symbolism in René Char's Poetry," *FrF* 10 (September 1985): 346–47 (Eng).

"Fastes"

Caws, *René Char,* 83–84 (Eng).

"Fenaison"

John P. Houston, "Modes of Symbolism in René Char's Poetry," *FR* 10 (September 1985): 345 (Eng).

"Flexibilité de l'oubli"

La Charité, *The Poetry and the Poetics of René Char,* 30–33 (Eng).

"Fréquence"

Caws, *René Char,* 85–86 (Eng).

"Front de la rose"

Caws, *The Presence of René Char,* 63–64 (Eng).

Caws, *René Char,* 98–100 (Eng).

"Grège"

Caws, *The Presence of René Char,* 76–77 (Eng).

"Hommage et famine"

Lawler, *René Char,* 37–39 (Eng).

"Homme-oiseau mort et bison mourant"

Lawler, *René Char,* 53–58 (Eng).

"L'Inoffensif"

Nathan Bracher, "Char et l'écriture de l'autre: Une Poétique de l'absence," *FrF* 15 (May 1990): 231–33 (Fr).

"Jeune Cheval à la crinière vaporeuse"

Lawler, *René Char,* 70–74 (Eng).

"J'habite une douleur"

Mechthild Cranston, " 'Arrière-histoire du poème pulverisé': René Char's 'Winterreise,' " *FR* 46 (Special Issue 5) (Spring 1973): 146–47 (Eng).

Lawler, *René Char,* 42–48 (Eng).

"Jouvence"

Mechthild Cranston, "René Char 1923–1928: The Young Poet's Struggle for Communication," *PMLA* 87 (October 1972): 1019–21 (Eng).

"Léonides"

Caws, *The Presence of René Char,* 74–76 (Eng).

"Lettera amorosa"

Mechthild Cranston, "René Char and Georges Braque: Poets of Metamorphosis," *KRQ* 23, no. 1 (1976): 114–20 (Eng).

La Charité, *The Poetry and the Poetics of René Char,* 153–63 (Eng).

CHAR, RENE, "Louis Curel de la Sorgue"

Lawler, *René Char*, 16–23 (Eng).

Nelly Stéphane, "L'Amour," *Europe* 66 (January–February 1988): 26–29 (Fr).

"Louis Curel de la Sorgue"

Caws, *The Presence of René Char*, 200–202 (Eng).

"Lutteurs"

Caws, *The Presence of René Char*, 279–81 (Eng).

"Lyre"

Mechthild Cranston, "Arrière-histoire de poème pulverisé: René Char's 'Winterreise,'" *FR* 46 (Special Issue 5) (Spring 1973): 157–58 (Eng).

"Madeleine à la veilleuse"

Lawler, *René Char*, 39–42 (Eng).

Nelly Stéphane, "L'Amour," *Europe* 66 (January–February 1988): 25–26 (Fr).

"Marmonnement"

Nathan Bracher, "Char et l'écriture de l'autre: Une Poétique de l'absence," *FrF* 15 (May 1990): 228–30 (Fr).

Caws, *The Presence of René Char*, 69–72 (Eng).

"Le Martinet"

Serge Gaulupeau, "Le Savoir de coeur dans la poésie de René Char," *EF* 5 (November 1969): 410–18 (Fr).

"Les Matinaux"

Caws, *The Presence of René Char*, 66–67 (Eng).

"La Minutieuse"

Lawler, *René Char,* 96–103 (Eng).

"Mirage des aiguilles"

Caws, *The Presence of René Char,* 33–34 (Eng).

"Mission et révocation"

Caws, *The Presence of René Char,* 77–78 (Eng).

"La Nuit talismanique"

Caws, *The Presence of René Char,* 236–61 (Eng).

"L'Ouest derrière soi perdu"

Caws, *The Presence of René Char,* 282–85 (Eng).

"Page blanches"

See André Breton.

"Poème fin du monde"

Eric Marty, "René Char: Sade et Saint-Just," *FR* 62 (May 1989): 1020–21 (Fr).

"Prêt au dépouillement"

Mechthild Cranston, "René Char 1923–1928: The Yount Poet's Struggle for Communication," *PMLA* 87 (October 1972): 1018–19 (Eng).

"Quatre fascinants"

Nancy K. Piore, "The Sexualized Poetic Universe of René Char," *SFR* 2 (Spring 1978): 55–60 (Eng).

CHAR, RENE, "Le Rempart de brindilles"

"Le Rempart de brindilles"

La Charité, *The Poetry and the Poetics of René Char*, 167–69 (Eng).

"Le Requin et la mouette"

Lawler, *René Char*, 9–11 (Eng).

"Robustes météores"

Mechthild Cranston, "Violence and Magic: Aspects of René Char's Surrealist Apprenticeship," *FMLS* 10 (January 1974): 16–17 (Eng).

"Rougeur des matinaux"

Gilles Guégan, "Pour une lecture de 'Rougeur des matinaux,' " *EF* 8 (May 1972): 131–52 (Fr).

La Charité, *The Poetry and the Poetics of René Char*, 128–30 (Eng).

"Sept parcelles de Luberon"

Caws, *The Presence of René Char*, 262–64 (Eng).

"Le Serpent"

Lawler, *René Char*, 87–91 (Eng).

James Lawler, "René Char's 'Quatre fascinants,' " in Caws, ed., *About French Poetry*, 211–14 (Eng).

"Sillage"

Mechthild Cranston, "René Char 1923–1928: The Young Poet's Struggle for Communication," *PMLA* 87 (October 1972): 1017–18, 1021 (Eng).

"Le Sujet"

La Charité, *The Poetry and the Poetics of René Char*, 36–37 (Eng).

CHAR, RENE, "Les Utopies sanglantes du XXe siècle"

"Sur une nuit sans ornement"

La Charité, *The Poetry and the Poetics of René Char,* 184–85 (Eng).

"Le Taureau"

Lawler, *René Char,* 80–84 (Eng).

James Lawler, "René Char's 'Quatre fascinants,'" in Caws, ed., *About French Poetry,* 206–9 (Eng).

"Tous compagnons de lit"

Eric Marty, "René Char: Sade et Saint-Just," *FR* 62 (May 1989): 1023–24 (Fr).

"Tracé sur le gouffre"

Caws, *The Presence of René Char,* 264–65 (Eng).

"Transir"

Caws, *The Presence of René Char,* 94–97 (Eng).

Lawler, *René Char,* 74–80 (Eng).

"La Truite"

Lawler, *René Char,* 84–87 (Eng).

James Lawler, "René Char's 'Quatre fascinants,'" in Caws, ed., *About French Poetry,* 209–11 (Eng).

"Les Utopies sanglantes du XXe siècle"

Eric Marty, "René Char: Sade et Saint-Just," *FR* 62 (May 1989): 1029 (Fr).

CHAR, RENE, "Le Visage nuptial"

"Le Visage nuptial"

Caws, *René Char,* 86–89 (Eng).

La Charité, *The Poetry and the Poetics of René Char,* 84–86 (Eng).

Lawler, *René Char,* 13–16 (Eng).

CHARLES D'ORLEANS

"A ma Dame je ne sçay que je dye"

John Fox, *The Lyric Poetry of Charles d'Orléans* (Oxford: Clarendon Press, 1969), 59–60 (Eng).

"Ainsi que chassoye aux sangliers"

Planche, *Charles d'Orléans,* 276–78 (Fr).

"Aussi bien laides que belles"

Planche, *Charles d'Orléans,* 143–44 (Fr).

"L'Autre jour tenoit son conseil"

Cholakian, *Deflection/Reflection,* 36–37 (Eng).

"C'est la prison Dedalus"

Cholakian, *Deflection/Reflection,* 66–67 (Eng).

"Ce n'est que chose acoustumee"

Harrison, *Charles d'Orléans,* 27–28 (Eng).

"Ce n'est riens qui ne puist estre"

Planche, *Charles d'Orléans,* 141–43 (Fr).

CHARLES D'ORLEANS, "D'Espoir? Il n'en est nouvelles"

"Ce qui m'entre par une oreille"

Planche, *Charles d'Orléans*, 162–63 (Fr).

"Chiere contrefaicte de cueur"

Planche, *Charles d'Orléans*, 268–70 (Fr).

"Comme j'oy que chascun devisc"

Planche, *Charles d'Orléans*, 80–81 (Fr).

"Comment se peut un povre cueur deffendre"

Harrison, *Charles d'Orléans*, 45–46 (Eng).

"Comment voy je ses Anglois esbays!"

Goodrich, *Charles of Orléans*, 156–57 (Eng).

"Cueur endormy en pensée"

Planche, *Charles d'Orléans*, 104–5 (Fr).

"De riens ne sert à cueur en desplaisance"

Planche, *Charles d'Orléans*, 152–53 (Fr).

"Dedans mon livre de pensée"

Sara Sturm-Maddox, "Charles d'Orléans devant la critique—vers une poétique de l'allégorie," *O&C* 5 (Autumn 1980): 21–22 (Fr).

"D'Espoir? Il n'en est nouvelles"

Harrison, *Charles d'Orléans*, 55–56 (Eng).

CHARLES D'ORLEANS, "Desploiez vostre baniere"

"Desploiez vostre baniere"

John Fox, *The Lyric Poetry of Charles d'Orléans* (Oxford: Clarendon Press, 1969), 107–8 (Eng).

Goodrich, *Charles of Orléans,* 150 (Eng).

"Dieu vueille celle nef garder"

Daniel Poirion, "La Nef d'esperance: Symbole et allégorie chez Charles d'Orléans," in *Mélanges de langue et de littérature . . . offerts à Jean Frappier,* vol. 2 (Geneva: Droz, 1970), 919–22 (Fr).

"L'Eaue de Pleur, de Joye ou de Douleur"

Planche, *Charles d'Orléans,* 175–77 (Fr).

"En la forest de Longue Actente"

Planche, *Charles d'Orléans,* 204–5, 511–12, 524 (Fr).

"En la forêt d'ennuyeuse Tristesse"

Calin, *In Defense of French Poetry,* 88–90 (Eng).

"En la nef de Bonne Nouvelle"

Daniel Poirion, "La Nef d'esperance: Symbole et allégorie chez Charles d'Orléans," in *Mélanges de langue et de littérature . . . offerts à Jean Frappier,* vol. 2 (Geneva: Droz, 1970), 918–22 (Fr).

Zumthor, *Essai de poétique médiévale,* 283–84 (Fr).

"En mes païs, quant me treuve à repos"

Planche, *Charles d'Orléans,* 160–61 (Fr).

CHARLES D'ORLEANS, "Jaulier des prisons de Pensée"

"En regardant vers le païs de France"

Fein, *Charles d'Orléans,* 43–46 (Eng).

Daniel Poirion, "La Nef d'esperance: Symbole et allégorie chez Charles d'Orléans," in *Mélanges de langue et de littérature . . . offerts à Jean Frappier,* vol. 2 (Geneva: Droz, 1970), 914–17 (Fr).

"En tirant d'Orléans à Blois"

Cholakian, *Deflection/Reflection,* 34–36 (Eng).

Fein, *Charles d'Orléans,* 107–9 (Eng).

Planche, *Charles d'Orléans,* 167–69 (Fr).

Daniel Poirion, "La Nef d'esperance: Symbole et allégorie chez Charles d'Orléans," in *Mélanges de langue et de littérature . . . offerts à Jean Frappier,* vol. 2 (Geneva: Droz, 1970), 915–18 (Fr).

Friedrich Wolfzettel, "La Poésie lyrique en France comme mode d'appréhension de la réalité," in *Mélanges de langue et de littérature françaises . . . offerts à M. Charles Foulon,* vol. 1 (Rennes: Institut de Français, 1980), 418–19 (Fr).

"Escollier de Merencolie"

Planche, *Charles d'Orléans,* 316–17 (Fr).

"France, jadis on te souloit nommer"

Fein, *Charles d'Orléans,* 54–62 (Eng).

Goodrich, *Charles of Orléans,* 155–56 (Eng).

Enid McLeod, *Charles of Orléans, Prince and Poet* (London: Chatto and Windus, 1962), 171–72 (Eng).

"Jaulier des prisons de Pensée"

Cholakian, *Deflection/Reflection,* 64–66 (Eng).

CHARLES D'ORLEANS, "J'ay aux eschés joué devant Amours"

"J'ay aux eschés joué devant Amours"

Harrison, *Charles d'Orléans,* 72–73 (Eng).

"J'ay fait l'obsèque de ma Dame"

Fein, *Charles d'Orléans,* 52–53 (Eng).

"J'ay ou tresor ma pensée"

Fein, *Charles d'Orléans,* 29–33 (Eng).

"Je fu en fleur ou temps passé d'enfrance"

Calin, *In Defense of French Poetry,* 90–92 (Eng).
Planche, *Charles d'Orléans,* 239–41 (Fr).

"Je meurs de soif en couste la fontaine"

Planche, *Charles d'Orléans,* 688–96 (Fr).

"Jennes amoureux nouveaulx"

Planche, *Charles d'Orléans,* 132–33 (Fr).

"Laissez moy penser à mon ayse"

Planche, *Charles d'Orléans,* 28–29 (Fr).

"Le Lendemain de premier jour de May"

Goodrich, *Charles of Orléans,* 138–39 (Eng).
Harrison, *Charles d'Orléans,* 50–52 (Eng).

CHARLES D'ORLEANS, "Patron vous fays de ma galee"

"Le Livre contre tout peché"

Harrison, *Charles d'Orléans,* 78 (Eng).

Enid McLeod, *Charles of Orléans, Prince and Poet* (London: Chatto and Windus, 1962), 24–25 (Eng).

"Mon cueur est devenu hermite"

Harrison, *Charles d'Orléans,* 43–45, 48–49 (Eng).

"Mon cueur plus ne volera"

Cholakian, *Deflection/Reflection,* 69–70 (Eng).

"Monseigneur, pource que sçay bien"

Planche, *Charles d'Orléans,* 591–92 (Fr).

"On parle de religion"

Planche, *Charles d'Orléans,* 288–90 (Fr).

"Ou puis parfont de ma merencolie"

Calin, *In Defense of French Poetry,* 92–94 (Eng).

Kelly, *Medieval Imagination,* 220–22 (Eng).

"Par le commandement d'Amours"

Planche, *Charles d'Orléans,* 228–29 (Fr).

"Patron vous fays de ma galee"

Zumthor, *Essai de poétique médiévale,* 283–84 (Fr).

123

CHARLES D'ORLEANS, "Petit mercier, petit pannier!"

"Petit mercier, petit pannier!"

Cholakian, *Deflection/Reflection,* 74–75 (Eng).

"Plus de desplaisir que de joye"

Planche, *Charles d'Orléans,* 76–77 (Fr).

"Une Poore ame tourmentee"

Planche, *Charles d'Orléans,* 70, 292–293 (Fr).

"Portant harnoys rouillé de Nonchaloir"

Fein, *Charles d'Orléans,* 96–97 (Eng).
Planche, *Charles d'Orléans,* 304–5 (Fr).

"Pres la, briquet aus pendantes oreilles"

Planche, *Charles d'Orléans,* 145–46 (Fr).

"Priez pour paix doulce Vierge Marie"

Goodrich, *Charles of Orléans,* 158 (Eng).

"Puis ça, puis la"

Planche, *Charles d'Orléans,* 156–60 (Fr).

"Quant commanceray a voler"

Planche, *Charles d'Orléans,* 214–16 (Fr).

"Quant je suis couschié en mon lit"

Kelly, *Medieval Imagination,* 207–9 (Eng).

CHARLES D'ORLEANS, "Rien ne valent ses mirliques"

"Quant n'ont assez fait dodo"

Planche, *Charles d'Orléans,* 133–35 (Fr).

"Quant Souvenir me ramentoit"

Harrison, *Charles d'Orléans,* 69–72 (Eng).

"Que je vous aime maintenant"

Planche, *Charles d'Orléans,* 275–76 (Fr).

"Qui? quoy? comment? a qui? pourquoy?"

Planche, *Charles d'Orléans,* 155–56 (Fr).

"Rafrœchissez le chastel de mon cueur"

Goodrich, *Charles of Orléans,* 153–55 (Eng).

"La Retenue d'Amours"

Fein, *Charles d'Orléans,* 63–65 (Eng).

John Fox, *The Lyric Poetry of Charles d'Orléans* (Oxford: Clarendon, 1969), 58, 84–85, 87 (Eng).

Harrison, *Charles d'Orléans,* 78–80 (Eng).

Kelly, *Medieval Imagination,* 204–6 (Eng).

Enid McLeod, *Charles of Orléans, Prince and Poet* (London: Chatto and Windus, 1962), 105–8 (Eng).

Planche, *Charles d'Orléans,* 321–27 (Fr).

"Rien ne valent ses mirliques"

Cholakian, *Deflection/Reflection,* 74–75 (Eng).

125

CHARLES D'ORLEANS, "Salués moy toute la compaignie"

"Salués moy toute la compaignie"

Cholakian, *Deflection/Reflection,* 70–72 (Eng).

"Se Dieu plaist, brief ment la nuée"

Harrison, *Charles d'Orléans,* 47–48 (Eng).

"Se je vous dy bonne nouvelle"

Harrison, *Charles d'Orléans,* 52–54 (Eng).

"Songe en complainte"

Fein, *Charles d'Orléans,* 65–74 (Eng).

Goodrich, *Charles of Orléans,* 140–43 (Eng).

Harrison, *Charles d'Orléans,* 82–88 (Eng).

Enid McLeod, *Charles of Orléans, Prince and Poet* (London: Chatto and Windus, 1962), 221–24 (Eng).

Planche, Charles d'Orléans, 321–27 (Fr).

Shigemi Sasaki, "L'Emergence des temps dans la poésie de Charles d'Orléans," in *Mélanges de langue et de littérature françaises . . . offerts à M. Charles Foulon,* vol. 2 (Rennes: Institut de Français, 1980), 255–58 (Fr).

Shigemi Sasaki, *Sur le thème du nonchaloir dans la poésie de Charles d'Orléans* (Paris: Nizet, 1974), 71–73, 84–88, 90–91 (Fr).

"Sont des oreilles estouppees?"

Planche, *Charles d'Orléans,* 663–64 (Fr).

"Le Temps a laissé son manteau"

Fein, *Charles d'Orléans,* 120–21 (Eng).

"Temps et temps m'ont emblé Jennesse"

Cholakian, *Deflection/Reflection,* 67–69 (Eng).

CHARTIER, ALAIN, "Débat des deux fortunes d'amour"

"Visage de baffe venu"

Planche, *Charles d'Orléans,* 135–36 (Fr).

"Yver, vous n'estes qu'un villain"

Planche, *Charles d'Orléans,* 64–65 (Fr).

CHARTIER, ALAIN

"La Belle Dame sans mercy"

Champion, *Histoire poétique du XVe siècle,* vol. 1, 65–72 (Fr).

John Fox, *The Lyric Poetry of Charles d'Orléans,* (Oxford: Clarendon, 1969), 39–41 (Eng).

Johnson, *Poets as Players,* 122–27 (Eng).

Kelly, *Medieval Imagination,* 190–91 (Eng).

William Kibler, "The Narrator as Key to Alain Chartier's 'La Belle Dame sans mercy,'" *FR* 52 (April 1979): 714–23 (Eng).

Shapley, *Studies in French Poetry,* 97–120 (Eng).

Zumthor, *Essai de poétique médiévale,* 308–10 (Fr).

"Breviaire des nobles"

Shapley, *Studies in French Poetry,* 45–48 (Eng).

"Complainte contre la mort"

Johnson, *Poets as Players,* 146–62 (Eng).

"Débat des deux fortunes d'amour"

Champion, *Histoire poétique du XVe siècle,* vol. 1, 78–84 (Fr).

Johnson, *Poets as Players,* 131–34 (Eng).

CHARTIER, ALAIN, "Débat du herault, du vassault et du villain"

"Débat du herault, du vassault et du villain"

Johnson, *Poets as Players,* 129–31 (Eng).

"Débat du Réveille-matin"

Champion, *Histoire poétique du XVe siècle,* vol. 1, 63–65 (Fr).

Johnson, *Poets as Players,* 126–29 (Eng).

Shapley, *Studies in French Poetry,* 50–54 (Eng).

"Débat patriotique"

Shapley, *Studies in French Poetry,* 60–62 (Eng).

Julian White, "The Conflict of Generations in the 'Débat patriotique,'" *FR* 39 (November 1965): 230–33 (Eng).

"Deux fortunés"

Shapley, *Studies in French Poetry,* 54–60 (Eng).

"L'Excusacion aux dames"

Johnson, *Poets as Players,* 143–45 (Eng).

"Le Lay de Paix"

Champion, *Histoire poétique du XVe siècle,* vol. 1, 118–120 (Fr).

Shapley, *Studies in French Poetry,* 42–45 (Eng).

"Le Lay de Plaisance"

Johnson, *Poets as Players,* 145–46 (Eng).

Shapley, *Studies in French Poetry,* 39–42 (Eng).

CHENIER, ANDRE, "Hymne aux Suisses de Châteauvieux"

"Le Livre des quatre dames"

Champion, *Histoire poétique du XVe siècle,* vol. 1, 11–17 (Fr).

Shapley, *Studies in French Poetry,* 62–92 (Eng).

CHENIER, ANDRE

"L'Aveugle"

René Guise, "Souvenirs florentins dans 'L'Aveugle' d'André Chénier," *SFr* 8 (May–August 1964): 284–88 (Fr).

Smernoff, *André Chénier,* 67–73 (Eng).

"Comme un dernier rayon"

Smernoff, *André Chénier,* 147–50 (Eng).

"Epître sur ses ouvrages"

Smernoff, *André Chénier,* 54–57 (Eng).

"Fanny, l'heureux mortel qui près de toi respire"

Henri Coulet, "Le Pouvoir expressif des strophes et des iambes chez André Chénier," in *Approches des lumières; mélanges offerts à Jean Fabre* (Paris: Klincksieck, 1974), 83–86 (Fr).

Smernoff, *André Chénier,* 130–31 (Eng).

"La Fête de l'Etre Suprême"

Smernoff, *André Chénier,* 144–45 (Eng).

"Hymne aux Suisses de Châteauvieux"

Henri Coulet, "Le Pouvoir expressif des strophes et des iambes chez André Chénier," in *Approches des lumières; mélanges offerts à Jean Fabre* (Paris: Klincksieck, 1974), 89–91 (Fr).

CHENIER, ANDRE, "L'Invention"

"L'Invention"

Smernoff, *André Chénier,* 44–54 (Eng).

"J'étais un faible enfant"

Smernoff, *André Chénier,* 75–76 (Eng).

"Jeu de paume"

Henri Coulet, "Le Pouvoir expressif des strophes et des iambes chez André Chénier," in *Approches des lumières; mélanges offerts à Jean Fabre* (Paris: Klincksieck, 1974), 81–82 (Fr).

"La Jeune Captive"

Smernoff, *André Chénier,* 143–44 (Eng).

"La Jeune Locrienne"

Smernoff, *André Chénier,* 76–77 (Eng).

"La Jeune Tarentine"

Smernoff, *André Chénier,* 77–80 (Eng).

"Liberté"

Annabel Patterson, *Pastoral and Ideology: Virgil to Valéry* (Berkeley and Los Angeles: University of California Press,1987), 222–24 (Eng).

"Le Malade"

Smernoff, *André Chénier,* 80–82 (Eng).

"Mârat au Panthéon"

Smernoff, *André Chénier,* 141–42 (Eng).

"Le Mendiant"

Smernoff, *André Chénier*, 82–86 (Eng).

"La Mort d'Hercule"

Smernoff, *André Chénier*, 73–74 (Eng).

"Les Noyades de Nantes"

Smernoff, *André Chénier*, 142–43 (Eng).

"Nymphe tendre et vermeille, ô jeune Poésie"

Smernoff, *André Chénier*, 66–67 (Eng).

"Ode à Marie-Anne Charlotte Corday"

Smernoff, *André Chénier*, 132–34 (Eng).

"Ode à son frère"

Smernoff, *André Chénier*, 145–46 (Eng).

"Ode au Jeu de Paume"

Smernoff, *André Chénier*, 120–23 (Eng).

"Ode à Versailles"

Smernoff, *André Chénier*, 134–35 (Eng).

"Pannychis"

Smernoff, *André Chénier*, 74–75 (Eng).

CHENIER, ANDRE, "Pasiphaé"

"Pasiphaé"

Howarth and Walton, *Explications,* 114–24 (Eng).

"Quand au mouton bêlant la sombre boucherie"

Francis Scarfe, "Chénier: 'Iambes X': 'Quand au mouton bêlant,' " in Nurse, ed., *The Art of Criticism,* 170–79 (Eng).

"La République des lettres"

Henri Coulet, "Le Pouvoir expressif des strophes et des iambes chez André Chénier," in *Approches des lumières; mélanges offerts à Jean Fabre* (Paris: Klincksieck, 1974), 91–92 (Fr).

Smernoff, *André Chénier,* 57–60 (Eng).

"Saint-Lazare"

Smernoff, *André Chénier,* 146–47 (Eng).

"Versailles"

Richard Fargher, *Life and Letters in France: The Eighteenth Century* (New York: Scribner's, 1979), 199–208 (Eng).

"Xanthus"

Smernoff, *André Chénier,* 64–66 (Eng).

CHRISTINE DE PISAN

"Amys, venez ancore nuit"

Johnson, *Poets as Players,* 76–78 (Eng).

CHRISTINE DE PISAN, "Dit de Poissy"

"Le Débat de deux amants"

McLeod, *The Order of the Rose,* 58–61 (Eng).

Willard, *Christine de Pisan,* 65–66 (Eng).

"Débat sur le 'Roman de la Rose' "

Kevin Brownlee, "Discourses of the Self: Christine de Pisan and the 'Rose,' " *RR* 79 (January 1988): 213–21 (Eng).

"Dieu est"

Johnson, *Poets as Players,* 84–85 (Eng).

"Dit de la Pastoure"

Joël Blanchard, "La Pastourale et le ressourcement des valeurs courtoises au XVe siècle," *CAIEF* 39 (May 1987): 9–14 (Fr).

McLeod, *The Order of the Rose,* 88–90 (Eng).

Willard, *Christine de Pisan,* 68–70 (Eng).

Winter, *Visual Variety and Spatial Grandeur,* 42–43, 53 (Eng).

Michel Zink, *La Pastourelle: Poésie et folklore au Moyen Age* (Paris: Bordas, 1972), 106–8 (Fr).

"Dit de la rose"

Kevin Brownlee, "Discourses of the Self: Christine de Pisan and the 'Rose,' " *RR* 79 (January 1988): 207–13 (Eng).

McLeod, *The Order of the Rose,* 75–76 (Eng).

Willard, *Christine de Pisan,* 167–69 (Eng).

"Dit de Poissy"

Barbara Altmann, "Diversity and Coherence in Christine de Pisan's 'Dit de Poissy,' " *FrF* 12 (September 1987): 261–71 (Eng).

McLeod, *The Order of the Rose,* 54–57 (Eng).

Willard, *Christine de Pisan,* 67–68 (Eng).

CHRISTINE DE PISAN, "Le Duc des vrais amants"

"Le Duc des vrais amants"

McLeod, *The Order of the Rose,* 62–65 (Eng).

"Enseignemens moraux"

McLeod, *The Order of the Rose,* 42 (Eng).

"L'Epistre au Dieu d'Amours"

Kevin Brownlee, "Discourses of the Self" Christine de Pisan and the 'Rose'," *RR* 79 (January 1988): 200–7 (Eng).

McLeod, *The Order of the Rose,* 46–48 (Eng).

"L'Epistre de Thea la deesse que elle envoya à Hector de Troie quand il estoit an l'aage de quinze ans"

McLeod, *The Order of the Rose,* 51–52 (Eng).

"Livre de la cité des dames"

Maureen Quilligan, "Allegory and the textual body: female authority in Christine de Pisan's 'Livre de la cité des dames,' " *RR* 79 (1988): 222–42 (Eng).

"Le Livre des trois jugemens"

Willard, *Christine de Pisan,* 66 (Eng).

"Mutacion de Fortune"

McLeod, *The Order of the Rose,* 91 (Eng).

"Oroyson Nostre Dame"

McLeod, *The Order of the Rose,* 91 (Eng).

CLAUDEL, PAUL, "Cinq grandes odes"

"Plourez, Francoys"

McLeod, *The Order of the Rose,* 100 (Eng).

"Sur la Mort du Duc de Bourgogne (27 avril 1404)"

McLeod, *The Order of the Rose,* 100–104 (Eng).

"Venez vers moy, tres doulz amy"

Johnson, *Poets as Players,* 78–80 (Eng).

CLAUDEL, PAUL

"Abeille"

Lawler, *The Language of French Symbolism,* 137–40 (Eng).

"L'Architecte"

Barrère, *Claudel,* 187–88 (Fr).

"Cantate à trois voix"

Emery, *Trois poètes cosmiques,* 124–25 (Fr).

Yves-Alain Favre, "Musique du temps et temps de la musique dans 'La Cantate à trois voix,' " *Europe* 60 (March 1982): 137–46 (Fr).

Lawler, *The Language of French Symbolism,* 146–84 (Eng).

"Cent phrases pour éventails"

Barry Laine, "Tradition and Innovation in Paul Claudel's 'Cent phrases pour éventails,' " *FR* 49 (December 1975): 234–46 (Eng).

"Cinq grandes odes"

Michel Autrand, "Claudel poète de la négation dans les 'Cinq grandes odes,' " *Europe* 60 (March 1982): 124–37 (Fr).

Nina Hellerstein, "Myth and the Sacrifice of the Son in the Structure of Paul Claudel's 'Cinq grandes odes,' " *FMLS* 23 (April 1987): 151–60 (Eng).

CLAUDEL, PAUL, Cinq grandes odes 1 "Les Muses"

Nina Hellerstein, "Le Mythe de la muse dans les 'Cinq grandes odes,'" *RLM* 747–52 (1985): 121–42 (Fr).

Cinq grandes odes 1
"Les Muses"

Gérald Antoine, "L'Image de la femme chez Claudel," in Georges Cattaui and Jacques Madaule, eds., *Entretiens sur Paul Claudel* (Paris, The Hague: Mouton, 1968), 274–78, 280–81 (Fr).

E. M. Beaumont, "A Note on 'Cinq grandes odes': Some Ambiguities of Order and Adventure," in Beaumont, Cocking, and Cruickshank, eds., *Order and Adventure in Post-Romantic French Poetry*, 108–11 (Eng).

Emery, *Trois poètes cosmiques*, 93–94 (Fr).

Hume, *Two Against Time*, 66–68, 72–73, 77 (Eng).

Moreau, *Six études de métrique*, 80–92 (Fr).

Cinq grandes odes 2
"L'Esprit et l'eau"

E. M. Beaumont, "A Note on 'Cinq grandes odes': Some Ambiguities of Order and Adventure," in Beaumont, Cocking, and Cruickshank, eds., *Order and Adventure in Post-Romantic French Poetry*, 111–13 (Eng).

Emery, *Trois poètes cosmiques*, 94–95 (Fr).

Hume, *Two Against Time*, 68, 70–71, 73–77 (Eng).

Cinq grandes odes 3
"Magnificat"

E. M. Beaumont, "A Note on 'Cinq grandes odes': Some Ambiguities of Order and Adventure," in Beaumont, Cocking, and Cruickshank, eds., *Order and Adventure in Post-Romantic French Poetry*, 113–14 (Eng).

Emery, *Trois poètes cosmiques*, 95–96 (Fr).

Marius-François Guyard, "La Bible et la liturgie: Sources du 'Magnificat' de Claudel," *RHL* 61 (January–March 1961): 72–80 (Fr).

Hume, *Two Against Time*, 71–72, 77 (Eng).

Cinq grandes odes 4
"La Muse qui est la Grâce"

Gérald Antoine, "L'Image de la femme chez Claudel," in Georges Cattaui and Jacques Madaule, eds., *Entretiens sur Paul Claudel* (Paris, The Hague: Mouton, 1968), 279–80 (Fr).

Barrère, *Claudel,* 113–15 (Fr).

E. M. Beaumont, "A Note on 'Cinq grandes odes': Some Ambiguities of Order and Adventure," in Beaumont, Cocking, and Cruickshank, eds., *Order and Adventure in Post-Romantic French Poetry,* 114–16 (Eng).

Emery, *Trois poètes cosmiques,* 96 (Fr).

Hume, *Two Against Time,* 69–70, 77 (Eng).

Moreau, *Six études de métrique,* 80–92 (Fr).

Cinq grandes odes 5
"La Maison fermée"

E. M. Beaumont, "A Note on 'Cinq grandes odes': Some Ambiguities of Order and Adventure," in Beaumont, Cocking, and Cruickshank, eds., *Order and Adventure in Post-Romantic French Poetry,* 116–19 (Eng).

Emery, *Trois poètes cosmiques,* 96–97 (Fr).

Hume, *Two Against Time,* 78–79 (Eng).

"Connaissance du temps"

Maurice de Gandillac, " 'Scission' et 'co-naissance' d'après l''Art poétique' de Claudel," in Georges Cattaui and Jacques Madaule, eds., *Entretiens sur Paul Claudel* (Paris, The Hague: Mouton, 1968), 115–18 (Fr).

"La Messe là-bas"

Barrère, *Claudel,* 181–86 (Fr).

Emery, *Trois poètes cosmiques,* 123 (Fr).

137

CLAUDEL, PAUL, "Ode jubiliaire"

"Ode jubiliaire"

Barrère, *Claudel,* 191–93 (Fr).

"Ouverture ancienne"

Yves-Alain Favre, "Musique du temps et temps de la musique dans 'La Cantate à trois voix,' " *Europe* 60 (March 1982): 137–46 (Fr).

"Saint Louis"

Barrère, *Claudel,* 189–90 (Fr).

"Sainte Geneviève"

Barrère, *Claudel,* 188 (Fr).

"Splendeur de lune"

M. Riffaterre, *Semiotics of Poetry,* 119–20 (Eng).

"Traité de la co-naissance au monde et de soi-même"

Maurice de Gandillac, " 'Scission' et 'co-naissance' d'après l'Art poétique' de Claudel," in Georges Cattaui and Jacques Madaule, eds., *Entretiens sur Paul Claudel* (Paris, The Hague: Mouton, 1968), 118–27 (Fr).

COCTEAU, JEAN

"A force de plaisirs"

Neal Oxenhandler, "Cocteau, Breton, and Ponge: The Situation of the Self," in Caws, ed., *About French Poetry,* 56–58 (Eng).

"L'Hôtel"

Neal Oxenhandler, "Cocteau, Breton, and Ponge: The Situation of the Self," in Caws, ed., *About French Poetry,* 55–56 (Eng).

CONDE, JEAN DE

"Dit du lévrier"

J. Ribard, "Des Lais au XIVème siècle?" in *Mélanges de langue et de littérature du Moyen âge et de la Renaissance offerts à Jean Frappier,* vol. 2 (Geneva: Droz, 1970), 948–50, 952–54 (Fr).

Jacques Ribard, *Un Ménestrel du XIVe siècle: Jean de Condé* (Geneva: Droz, 1969), 262, 264–265, 272 (Fr).

"Lai de l'ourse"

J. Ribard, "Des Lais au XIVème siècle?" in *Mélanges de langue et de littérature . . . offerts à Jean Frappier,* vol. 2 (Geneva: Droz, 1970), 949, 951–52 (Fr).

"Lai du blanc chevalier"

J. Ribard, "Des Lais au XIVème siècle?" in *Mélanges de langue et de littérature . . . offerts à Jean Frappier,* vol. 2 (Geneva: Droz, 1970), 948–51 (Fr).

Jacques Ribard, *Un Ménestrel du XIVe siècle: Jean de Condé* (Geneva: Droz, 1969), 260–61, 267–268, 272 (Fr).

CORBIERE, TRISTAN

"A une camarade"

Mitchell, *Tristan Corbière,* 124–26 (Eng).

"A une demoiselle"

Angelet, *La Poétique de Tristan Corbière,* 128–29 (Fr).

Robert L. Mitchell, "Corbière, Hélas!: A Case of Antirayonnement," *FR* 51 (February 1978): 362–66 (Eng).

Mitchell, *Tristan Corbière,* 82–88 (Eng).

CORBIERE, TRISTAN, "Au vieux Roscoff"

"Au vieux Roscoff"

Angelet, *La Poétique de Tristan Corbière,* 122–23 (Fr).
Mitchell, *Tristan Corbière,* 133–35 (Eng).

"Bonne fortune et fortune"

Mitchell, *Tristan Corbière,* 50–51 (Eng).

"Ça?"

Mitchell, *Tristan Corbière,* 42–47 (Eng).

"Cris d'aveugle"

Angelet, *La Poétique de Tristan Corbière,* 129–34 (Fr).
Albert Sonnenfeld, "Tristan Corbière: The Beatific Malediction," *ECr* 9
(Spring 1969): 42–43 (Eng).

"Epitaphe"

Mitchell, *Tristan Corbière,* 26–34 (Eng).

"La Fin"

Angelet, *La Poétique de Tristan Corbière,* 123–25 (Fr).
Mitchell, *Tristan Corbière,* 142–43 (Eng).

"Litanie du sommeil"

Angelet, *La Poétique de Tristan Corbière,* 88–89, 92, 97–99 (Fr).
Mitchell, *Tristan Corbière,* 53–60 (Eng).

"Mirliton"

Mitchell, *Tristan Corbière,* 145–46 (Eng).

CORBIERE, TRISTAN, "Sonnet, avec la manière de s'en servir (I)"

"Le Pardon de Sainte Anne"

Albert Sonnenfeld, "Tristan Corbière: The Beatific Malediction," *ECr* 9 (Spring 1969): 43–45 (Eng).

"Paria"

Robert L. Mitchell, "Hemorrhoids/Splenectomy/Gestation: Towards Authorial Manipulation, Reader Expectation, and the Perversion of Complicity," *FR* 53 (October 1979): 41–43 (Eng).

Mitchell, *Tristan Corbière,* 94–102 (Eng).

"Paysage mauvais"

Mitchell, *Tristan Corbière,* 130–31 (Eng).

"Petit mort pour rire"

Mitchell, *Tristan Corbière,* 147–48 (Eng).

"Le Poète contumace"

Mitchell, *Tristan Corbière,* 102–13 (Eng).

"La Rapsode foraine et le pardon de Sainte-Anne"

Mitchell, *Tristan Corbière,* 137–40 (Eng).

"Rapsodie du sourd"

Mitchell, *Tristan Corbière,* 113–19 (Eng).

"Sonnet, avec la manière de s'en servir (I)"

Robert L. Mitchell, "The Muted Fiddle: Tristan Corbière's 'I Sonnet' as 'Ars (Im)poetica,'" *FR* 50 (October 1976): 35–45 (Eng).

Mitchell, *Tristan Corbière,* 72–81 (Eng).

CROS, CHARLES

"Conquérant"

Broome and Chesters, *The Appreciation of Modern French Poetry (1850–1950)*, 89–91 (Eng).

"Distrayeuse"

Mitchell, *The Poetic Voice of Charles Cros,* 144–45 (Eng).

"Hiéroglyphe"

Broome and Chesters, *The Appreciation of Modern French Poetry (1850–1950)*, 91–95 (Eng).

"Madrigal"

Mitchell, *The Poetic Voice of Charles Cros,* 144 (Eng).

"Pluriel feminin"

Mitchell, *The Poetic Voice of Charles Cros,* 134–35 (Eng).

"Les Quatre Saisons"

Mitchell, *The Poetic Voice of Charles Cros,* 122–25 (Eng).

"Sonnet madrigal"

Mitchell, *The Poetic Voice of Charles Cros,* 139–41, 179–81 (Eng).

"Tableau de sainteté"

Mitchell, *The Poetic Voice of Charles Cros,* 128–29 (Eng).

DEGUY, MICHEL, "Ecrire 'Au reveil' "

"Valse"

Mitchell, *The Poetic Voice of Charles Cros,* 124–26 (Eng).

"La Vision du grand canal royal des deux mers"

Mitchell, *The Poetic Voice of Charles Cros,* 148–49, 160–61, 174–75 (Eng).

DEGUY, MICHEL

"Achronique"

Michael Bishop, "The Coherence of Revolution: The Poetics of Michel Deguy," *FMLS* 19 (January 1983): 12–13 (Eng).

"Les Ages"

Joan Brandt, "Le Problème de l'allégorie: Michel Deguy et ses critiques," *O&C* 15, no. 1 (1990): 35–37 (Fr).

"A Hobbema"

Michael Bishop, "The Coherence of Revolution: The Poetics of Michel Deguy," *FMLS* 19 (January 1983): 2–3 (Eng).

M. Bishop, *The Contemporary Poetry of France,* 86 (Eng).

"Antiphonaire"

Michael Bishop, "The Coherence of Revolution: The Poetics of Michel Deguy," *FMLS* 19 (January 1983): 9 (Eng).

M. Bishop, *The Contemporary Poetry of France,* 94–95 (Eng).

"Ecrire 'Au reveil' "

M. Bishop, *The Contemporary Poetry of France,* 98 (Eng).

DEGUY, MICHEL, "Et ainsi sommes-nous éclairés"

"Et ainsi sommes-nous éclairés"

M. Bishop, *The Contemporary Poetry of France,* 98–99 (Eng).

"Paroi la mort adamantine"

Groupe Mu (Jacques Dubois, Francis Edeline, Jean-Marie Klinkenberg, Philippe Minquet), *Rhétorique de la poésie: Lecture linéaire, lecture tabulaire* (Bruxelles: Editions Complexe, 1977), 247–61 (Fr).

"La Reconnaissance"

Michael Bishop, "The Coherence of Revolution: The Poetics of Michel Deguy," *FMLS* 19 (January 1983): 8–9 (Eng).

"Symptômes"

M. Bishop, *The Contemporary Poetry of France,* 95–96 (Eng).

"Utopiques"

Michael Bishop, "The Coherence of Revolution: The Poetics of Michel Deguy," *FMLS* 19 (January 1983): 11 (Eng).

M. Bishop, *The Contemporary Poetry of France,* 96–97 (Eng).

"La Vigie"

M. Bishop, *The Contemporary Poetry of France,* 85–86 (Eng).

DELILLE, JACQUES

"Les Jardins"

Richard Fargher, *Life and Letters in France: The Eighteenth Century* (New York: Scribner's, 1970), 177–88 (Eng).

DESBORDES-VALMORE, MARCELINE, "Eau douce"

DEPESTRE, RENE

"Minerai noir"

Frederick Case, "Aimé Césaire et l'occident chrétien," *ECr* 10 (Fall 1970): 249–50, 253–54 (Fr).

"Ouvrons les portes du temple pour [Atibon Legba]"

Bernadette Cailler, "L'Efficacité poétique du Vaudou dans 'Un Arc-en-ciel pour l'occident chrétien' de René Depestre," *FR* 53 (October 1979): 52–56 (Fr).

DESBORDES-VALMORE, MARCELINE

"A Madame Tastu"

Jasenas, *La Poétique,* 78–80 (Fr).

"Ame errante"

Jasenas, *La Poétique,* 64–69 (Fr).

"Cigale"

Jasenas, *La Poétique,* 108–9 (Fr).

"Couronne effeuillée"

Jasenas, *La Poétique,* 113–16 (Fr).

"Dans l'été"

Jasenas, *La Poétique,* 51–54 (Fr).

"Eau douce"

Jasenas, *La Poétique,* 80–81 (Fr).

DESBORDES-VALMORE, MARCELINE, "Fileuse et l'enfant"

"Fileuse et l'enfant"

Jasenas, *La Poétique,* 109–13, 130 (Fr).

"Halte sur le Simplon"

Jasenas, *La Poétique,* 47–51 (Fr).

"Imitation libre de Thomas Moore 'When the first summer bee' "

Michael Danahy, "Marceline Desbordes-Valmore and the Engendered Canon," *YFS,* no. 75 (1989): 145–46 (Eng).

"Ines"

Jasenas, *La Poétique,* 106–7 (Fr).

"Jeune comédienne à Fontenay–Les Roses"

Jasenas, *La Poétique,* 100–104 (Fr).

"Jeune fille et le ramier"

Jasenas, *La Poétique,* 54–56 (Fr).

"Jour d'orient"

Jasenas, *La Poétique,* 32–33 (Fr).

"Jours d'été"

Jasenas, *La Poétique,* 28–32 (Fr).

"Laisse-nous pleurer"

Jasenas, *La Poétique,* 34–35 (Fr).

DESBORDES-VALMORE, MARCELINE, "Rêve intermittent"

"Loin du monde"

Jasenas, *La Poétique,* 77–78 (Fr).

"Maison de ma mère"

Jasenas, *La Poétique,* 85–88 (Fr).

"Nid solitaire"

Jasenas, *La Poétique,* 37–38 (Fr).

"Nouveau-né"

Jasenas, *La Poétique,* 83–85 (Fr).

"Nuit de mon âme"

Jasenas, *La Poétique,* 89–93 (Fr).

"Puits de Notre-Dame à Douai"

Jasenas, *La Poétique,* 81–83 (Fr).

"Renoncement"

Jasenas, *La Poétique,* 116–19 (Fr).

"Retour dans une église"

Jasenas, *La Poétique,* 63–64 (Fr).

"Rêve intermittent d'une nuit triste"

Jasenas, *La Poétique,* 119–24 (Fr).

DESBORDES-VALMORE, MARCELINE, "Roses de Saadi"

"Roses de Saadi"

Jasenas, *La Poétique,* 56–61 (Fr).

"Ruelle de Flandre"

Jasenas, *La Poétique,* 38–43 (Fr).

"Un Ruisseau de la Scarpe"

Wendy Greenberg, "An Aspect of Desbordes-Valmore's Life in Her Poetry," *NCFS* 17 (Spring–Summer 1989): 299–306 (Eng).

"Sanglots"

Jasenas, *La Poétique,* 36, 93–97 (Fr).

"Secret perdu"

Jasenas, *La Poétique,* 72–77 (Fr).

"Sol natal"

Jasenas, *La Poétique,* 43–47 (Fr).

"Son image"

Barbara Johnson, "Gender and Poetry: Charles Baudelaire and Marceline Desbordes-Valmore," in Joan De Jean and Nancy K. Miller, eds., *Displacements: Women, Tradition, Literatures in French* (Baltimore: Johns Hopkins University Press, 1991), 172–73 (Eng).

"La Tombe lointaine"

Michael Danahy, "Marceline Desbordes-Valmore and the Engendered Canon," *YFS,* no. 75 (1989): 141–42 (Eng).

DESNOS, ROBERT, "Le Bain avec Andromède"

"Tristesse"

Jasenas, *La Poétique,* 97–100 (Fr).

"La Voix perdue"

Michael Danahy, "Marceline Desbordes-Valmore and the Engendered Canon," *YFS,* no. 75 (1989): 138–39 (Eng).

Jasenas, *La Poétique,* 104–6 (Fr).

DESCHAMPS, EUSTACHE

"Armes, amours, dames, chevalerie"

Jean-Claude Mühlethaler, "Un Poète et son art face à la postérité: Lecture de deux ballades de Deschamps," *SFr* 33 (September–December 1989): 389–410 (Fr).

"Lai de franchise"

Joël Blanchard, *La Pastorale en France aux XIVe et XVe siècles: Recherches sur les structures de l'imaginaire médiévale* (Paris: Champion, 1983), 56–58 (Fr).

"O fleur des fleurs de toute mélodie"

Jean-Claude Mühlethaler, "Un Poète et son art face à la postérité: Lecture de deux ballades de Deschamps," *SFr* 33 (September–December 1989): 390–410 (Fr).

DESNOS, ROBERT

"Le Bain avec Andromède"

Carmen Vasquez, "A travers la forêt obscure et touffue," in Dumas, ed., *Moi qui suis Robert Desnos,* 180–83 (Fr).

DESNOS, ROBERT, "Calixto"

"Calixto"

Carmen Vasquez, "A travers la forêt obscure et touffue," in Dumas, ed., *Moi qui suis Robert Desnos,* 185–89 (Fr).

"Chant du ciel"

Michel Murat, "Robert Desnos poète lyrique," in Dumas, ed., *Moi qui suis Robert Desnos,* 92–93 (Fr).

"Comme une main à l'instant de la mort"

Broome and Chesters, *The Appreciation of Modern French Poetry (1850–1950),* 160–63 (Eng).

"Elégant cantique de Salomé Solomon"

Robert Favre, "Desnos danse Des Esseintes," *Europe* 50 (May–June 1972): 105–12 (Fr).

"Espaces du sommeil"

Michel Murat, "Robert Desnos poète lyrique," in Dumas, ed., *Moi qui suis Robert Desnos,* 95–96 (Fr).

"Idéal maîtresse"

K. R. Dutton, "The Text and the Sense of Desnos' 'Idéal maîtresse,'" *AJFS* 16 (January–April 1979): 258–69 (Eng).

Arthur Evans, "Catachresis in Early Surrealist Poetry: Robert Desnos's 'Idéal maîtresse,'" *RR* 79 (November 1988): 622–32 (Eng).

"L'Idée fixe"

Adelaide Russo, "Le Tombeau de Robert ou la tradition encrystée," in Dumas, ed., *Moi qui suis Robert Desnos,* 47–51 (Fr).

DESPORTES, PHILIPPE, "Icare est cheut icy le jeune audacieux"

"Il fait nuit"

Adelaide Russo, "Le Tombeau de Robert ou la tradition encrystée," in Dumas, ed., *Moi qui suis Robert Desnos,* 42–46 (Fr).

"Le Legs"

Ian Higgins, "Tradition and Myth in French Resistance Poetry: Reaction or Subversion?" *FMLS* 21 (January 1985): 54–5 (Eng).

"Non, l'amour n'est pas mort"

Broome and Chesters, *The Appreciation of Modern French Poetry (1850–1950),* 156–60 (Eng).

"Le Paysage"

Mary Ann Caws, "Desnos's 'Le Paysage,'" *Expl* 26 (May 1968): 6–7 (Eng).

"Prose Sélavy"

Manuela Girod, "Mécanique métaphysique: Prose Sélavy (1922–1923)," *Europe* 50 (May–June 1972): 97–104 (Fr).

"La Ville de Don Juan"

Reinhard Pohl, "Robert Desnos et la Mythologie," in Dumas, ed., *Moi qui suis Robert Desnos,* 168–71 (Fr).

DESPORTES, PHILIPPE

"Icare est cheut icy le jeune audacieux"

Marc Eigeldinger, "Le Mythe d'Icare dans la poésie française du XVIe siècle," *CAIEF* 25 (May 1973): 275–78 (Fr).

DESPORTES, PHILIPPE, "Las! qui languit jamais en si cruel martyre"

"Las! qui languit jamais en si cruel martyre"

Jeanneret, *Poésie et tradition biblique,* 282–83 (Fr).

"Plainte de l'autheur durant une sienne longue maladie"

Cave, *Devotional Poetry,* 114–19 (Eng).

"Prière"

Cave, *Devotional Poetry,* 111–14, 125 (Eng).

"Prière en forme de confession"

Cave, *Devotional Poetry,* 120–23, 125 (Eng).

"Sommeil, paisible fils de la nuict solitaire"

Terence Cave, "Desportes and Maynard: Two Studies in the Poetry of Wit," in Bayley and Coleman, eds., *The Equilibrium of Wit,* 87–91 (Eng).

DIOP, DAVID

"Nègre clochard"

Enid Peschel Rhodes, "David Diop: Poet of Passion," *ECr* 10 (Fall 1970): 235–36 (Eng).

"Rama Kam"

Enid Peschel Rhodes, "David Diop: Poet of Passion," *ECr* 10 (Fall 1970): 240–41 (Eng).

DU BARTAS, GUILLAUME

"La Judit"

Jean-Dominique Biard, "La Fontaine et Du Bartas," *SFr* 7 (May–August 1963): 280–82 (Fr).

DU BELLAY, JOACHIM, *Les Antiquitez 1*

"La Première Sepmaine"

Jean-Dominique Biard, "La Fontaine et Du Bartas," *SFr* 7 (May–August 1963): 282–85 (Fr).

H. Weber, *La Création poétique au XVIe siècle en France,* 537–55 (Fr).

"La Seconde Sepmaine"

Jean-Dominique Biard, " La Fontaine et Du Bartas," *SFr* 7 (May–August 1963): 285–86 (Fr).

DU BELLAY, JOACHIM

"A Bertran Bergier, poète dithyrambique"

Hall and Wells, *Du Bellay: Poems,* 93–94 (Eng)

Helen O. Platt, "Structure in Du Bellay's 'Divers jeux rustiques,' " *BHR* 35 (January 1973): 31–32 (Eng).

"A Olivier de Magni sur les perfections de sa dame"

Hall and Wells, *Du Bellay: Poems,* 90–91 (Eng).

Les Amours 20
"Je ne souhaitte poinct me pouvoir transformer"

François Rigolot, "Du Bellay et la poésie du refus," *BHR* 36 (September 1974): 494–97 (Fr).

Les Antiquitez 1
"Divins esprits, dont la poudreuse cendre"

Richard Katz, "The Collapse of the City: The 'Vision' of the 'Antiquités de Rome,' " *ECr* 19 (Fall 1979): 14 (Eng).

DU BELLAY, JOACHIM, *Les Antiquitez 3*

Les Antiquitez 3
"Nouveau venu qui cherches Rome en Rome"

Coleman, *The Chaste Muse,* 102–5 (Eng).

Les Antiquitez 4
"Celle qui de son chef les estoilles passoit"

Gray, *La Poétique de Du Bellay,* 49–51 (Fr).

Les Antiquitez 6
"Telle que dans son char la Berecynthienne"

Coleman, *The Chaste Muse,* 105–9 (Eng).

Les Antiquitez 7
"Sacrés coteaux, et vous saintes ruines"

Bots, *Joachim Du Bellay entre l'histoire littéraire,* 71–75, 86–87 (Fr).

Les Antiquitez 8
"Par armes et vaisseaux Rome dompta le monde"

Hall and Wells, *Du Bellay: Poems,* 49 (Eng).

Les Antiquitez 12
"Telz que lon vid les enfans de la Terre"

Daniel Russell, "Du Bellay's Emblematic Vision of Rome," *YFS,* no. 47 (1973): 102–5 (Eng).

Les Antiquitez 15
"Palles esprits, et vous umbres pouldreuses"

Dorothy G. Coleman, "Allusiveness in the 'Antiquitez de Rome,'" *ECr* 19 (Fall 1979): 6–11 (Eng).

Coleman, *The Chaste Muse,* 109–11 (Eng).

DU BELLAY, JOACHIM, "La Complainte du Déscspéré"

Les Antiquitez 16
"Comme l'on voit de loin sur la mer courroucée"

Bots, *Joachim Du Bellay entre l'histoire littéraire,* 69–92 (Fr).

Hall and Wells, *Du Bellay: Poems,* 51 (Eng).

Daniel Russell, "Du Bellay's Emblematic Vision of Rome," *YFS,* no. 47 (1972): 105–7 (Eng).

Les Antiquitez 18
"Ces grands monceaux pierreux, ces vieux murs que tu vois"

Philip Ford, "Du Bellay et le sonnet satirique," in Bellenger, ed., *Le Sonnet à la Renaissance,* 208–9 (Fr).

Les Antiquitez 19
"Tout le parfait dont le ciel nous honore"

Gilbert Gadoffre, "Structures des mythes de Du Bellay," *BHR* 36 (May 1974): 276–77 (Fr).

"Chant de l'amour et du printemps"

Hall and Wells, *Du Bellay: Poems,* 86–88 (Eng).

"Chant du Désespéré"

H. Weber, *La Création poétique au XVIe siècle en France,* 400–403 (Fr).

"Le Combat d'Hercule et d'Acheloys"

Hall and Wells, *Du Bellay: Poems,* 85 (Eng).

Helen O. Platt, "Structure in Du Bellay's 'Divers jeux rustiques,' " *BHR* 35 (January 1973): 26–27 (Eng).

"La Complainte du Désespéré"

Bots, *Joachim Du Bellay entre l'histoire littéraire,* 4–68, 106–7 (Fr).

Chamard, *Histoire de la Pléiade,* vol. 1, 298–301 (Fr).

H. Weber, *La Création poétique au XVIe siècle en France,* 403–13 (Fr).

DU BELLAY, JOACHIM, "Contre les envieux poètes"

"Contre les envieux poètes"

Hall and Wells, *Du Bellay: Poems,* 41–42 (Eng).

"Contre les Pétrarchistes"

Bernard Weinberg, "Du Bellay's 'Contre les Pétrarchistes,' " *ECr* 12 (Fall 1972): 159–77 (Eng).

"De l'immortalité des poètes"

Hall and Wells, *Du Bellay: Poems,* 37–38 (Eng).

Mark Whitney, "Du Bellay in April 1549: Continuum and Change," *FR* 44 (April 1971): 859–61 (Eng).

"Discours au Roy sur la trefve de 1555"

Keating, *Joachim Du Bellay,* 110–12 (Eng).

"Discours au Roy sur le faict de ses quatre estats"

Keating, *Joachim Du Bellay,* 113–14 (Eng).

"Discours sur le sacre du Tres-chrestien Roy François II"

Chamard, *Histoire de la Pléiade,* vol. 2, 340–43 (Fr).

"D'un berger, à Pan"

Coleman, *The Chaste Muse,* 73–74 (Eng).

"D'un vanneur de blé, aux vents"

Coleman, *The Chaste Muse,* 66–67 (Eng).

Keating, *Joachim Du Bellay,* 99–100 (Eng).

DU BELLAY, JOACHIM, "Musagnœomachie"

"Epitaphe de l'Abbé Bonnet"

Hall and Wells, *Du Bellay: Poems,* 95 (Eng).

Helen O. Platt, "Structure in Du Bellay's 'Divers jeux rustiques,'" *BHR* 35 (January 1973): 31–32 (Eng).

"Epitaphe d'un flambeau"

Hall and Wells, *Du Bellay: Poems,* 97–98 (Eng).

Keating, *Joachim Du Bellay,* 106–7 (Eng).

"Les Furies contre les infracteurs de Foy"

Keating, *Joachim Du Bellay,* 112–13 (Eng).

"Hymne de la surdité"

Chamard, *Histoire de la Pléiade,* vol. 2, 323–25 (Fr).

Hall and Wells, *Du Bellay: Poems,* 94–95 (Eng).

Keating, *Joachim Du Bellay,* 107–8 (Eng).

Helen O. Platt, "Structure in Du Bellay's 'Divers jeux rustiques,'" *BHR* 35 (January 1973): 24–25 (Eng).

"Métamorphose d'une Rose"

Helen O. Platt, "Structure in Du Bellay's 'Divers jeux rustiques,'" *BHR* 35 (January 1973): 25–26 (Eng).

"Le Moretum de Virgile"

Hall and Wells, *Du Bellay: Poems,* 82–83 (Eng).

"Musagnœomachie"

Hall and Wells, *Du Bellay: Poems,* 40–41 (Eng).

Lapp, *The Brazen Tower,* 32–37 (Eng).

DU BELLAY, JOACHIM, *Olive 1* "Je ne quiers pas la fameuse couronne"

Olive 1
"Je ne quiers pas la fameuse couronne"

Coleman, *The Chaste Muse,* 34–36 (Eng).

Jo Ann Della Neva, "Du Bellay, Reader of Scève, Reader of Petrarch," *RR* 79 (May 1988): 402–6 (Eng).

Olive 11
"Des ventz emeuz la raige impetueuse"

H. Weber, *La Création poétique au XVIe siècle en France,* 296–97 (Fr).

Olive 13
"La Belle main, dont la forte foiblesse"

Jo Ann Della Neva, "Variations in a Minor Key: Du Bellay's Imitations of the Giolito Anthology," *FrF* 14 (May 1989): 136–38 (Eng).

Olive 14
"Fort sommeil, que celeste on doibt croyre"

Coleman, *The Chaste Muse,* 46–47 (Eng).

H. Weber, *La Création poétique au XVIe siècle en France,* 359–60 (Fr).

Olive 16
"Qui a peu voir celle que Déle adore"

Jo Ann Della Neva, "Du Bellay, Reader of Scève, Reader of Petrarch," *RR* 79 (May 1988): 407–9 (Eng).

Olive 19
"Face le ciel (quand il vouldra) revivre"

Jo Ann Della Neva, "Variations in a Minor Key: Du Bellay's Imitations of the Giolito Anthology," *FrF* 14 (May 1989): 134–36 (Eng).

DU BELLAY, JOACHIM, *Olive 64* "Comme jadis l'âme de l'univers"

Olive 20
"Puis que les cieux m'avoient prédestiné"

Jo Ann Della Neva, "Variations in a Minor Key: Du Bellay's Imitations of the Giolito Anthology," *FrF* 14 (May 1989): 138–40 (Eng).

Olive 24
"Piteuse voix, qui écoutes mes pleurs"

Deguy, *Tombeau de Du Bellay*, 62–63 (Fr).

Rigolot, *Poétique et onomastique*, 142–44 (Fr).

Olive 26
"La Nuit m'est courte, et le jour trop me dure"

Cameron, *Louise Labé*, 32–34 (Eng).

Mark Whitney, "Du Bellay in April 1549: Continuum and Change," *FR* 44 (April 1971): 856–58 (Eng).

Olive 40
"Si des sainctes yeulx que je vois adorant"

Rigolot, *Poétique et onomastique,* 147–48 (Fr).

Olive 45
"Ores qu'en l'air le grand Dieu du Tonnerre"

Coleman, *The Chaste Muse*, 40–42 (Eng).

Olive 62
"Qui voudra voir le plus précieux arbre"

Jo Ann Della Neva, "Illustrating the 'Deffence': Imitation and Poetic Perfection in Du Bellay's 'Olive,'" *FR* 61 (October 1987): 39–49 (Eng).

Olive 64
"Comme jadis l'âme de l'univers"

Deguy, *Tombeau de Du Bellay,* 61–62 (Fr).

DU BELLAY, JOACHIM, *Olive 67*

Olive 67
"Sus, chaulx soupirs, allez à ce froid cœur"

D. J. Shaw, "Two Sixteenth-Century Versions of a Petrarchan Sonnet," *FSB* 6 (Spring 1983): 4–5 (Eng).

Olive 80
"Toy, qui courant à voile haulte et pleine"

Rigolot, *Poétique et onomastique,* 151–52 (Fr).

Olive 83
"Déjà la nuit en son parc amassoit"

Gray, *La Poétique de Du Bellay,* 36–37 (Fr).

H. Weber, *La Création poétique au XVIe siècle en France,* 304–6 (Fr).

Olive 91
"Rendez à l'or cette couleur qui dore"

Deguy, *Tombeau de Du Bellay,* 59–60 (Fr).

Olive 97
"Qui a peu voir la matinale rose"

H. Weber, *La Création poétique au XVIe siècle en France,* 337–38 (Fr).

Olive 104
"O Citherée! ô gloire Paphienne!"

Coleman, *The Chaste Muse,* 36–38 (Eng).

Olive 105
"Esprit divin, que la troupe honnorée"

Jo Ann Della Neva, "Du Bellay, Reader of Scève, Reader of Petrarch," *RR* 79 (May 1988): 406–7 (Eng).

Olive 113
"Si nostre vie est moins qu'une journée"

Coleman, *The Chaste Muse,* 43–45 (Eng).

Fernand Hallyn, "Du Bellay: 'Si nostre vie . . . ,' " *BHR* 39 (January 1977): 51–65 (Fr).

"Par un sentier inconnu à mes yeux"

Coleman, *The Chaste Muse,* 32–34 (Eng).

"Le Poète courtisan"

Chamard, *Histoire de la Pléiade,* vol. 2, 335–40 (Fr).

Keating, *Joachim Du Bellay,* 122–25 (Eng).

"Quand je suis près de la flamme divine"

H. Weber, *La Création poétique au XVIe siècle en France,* 251–52 (Fr).

"Quand ton col de couleur de rose"

H. Weber, *La Création poétique au XVIe siècle en France,* 379–81 (Fr).

Les Regrets 5
"Ceux qui sont amoureux, leurs amours chanteront"

Hall and Wells, *Du Bellay: Poems,* 64–65 (Eng).

C. E. Nelson, "Enumeration and Irony in 'Les Regrets' of Du Bellay," *FR* 36 (January 1963): 268–70 (Eng).

Les Regrets 6
"Las où est maintenant ce mespris de Fortune?"

Coleman, *The Chaste Muse,* 77–78 (Eng).

Les Regrets 8
"Ne t'ébahis, Ronsard, la moitié de mon âme"

Gray, *La Poétique de Du Bellay,* 80–82 (Fr).

Les Regrets 9
"France, mère des arts, des armes et des loix"

Coleman, *The Chaste Muse,* 78–79 (Eng).

H. Weber, *La Création poétique au XVIe siècle en France,* 438–40 (Fr).

Les Regrets 14
"Si l'importunité d'un créditeur me fâche"

Gray, *La Poétique de Du Bellay,* 73–75 (Fr).

Les Regrets 15
"Panjas, veulx-tu sçavoir quels sont mes passetemps?"

H. Weber, *La Création poétique au XVIe siècle en France,* 444–45 (Fr).

Les Regrets 19
"Ce pendant que tu dis ta Cassandre divine"

Gray, *La Poétique de Du Bellay,* 86–88 (Fr).

Les Regrets 20
"Heureux de qui la mort de la gloire est suivie"

Gray, *La Poétique de Du Bellay,* 84–86 (Fr).

Les Regrets 22
"Ores, plus que jamais, me plaît d'aimer la Muse"

Gray, *La Poétique de Du Bellay,* 88–89 (Fr).

Les Regrets 31
"Heureux qui, comme Ulysse, a fait un beau voyage"

Auffret and Auffret, *Le Commentaire composé,* 112–20 (Fr).

Yvonne Bellenger, *Du Bellay: Ses "Regrets" qu'il fit dans Rome . . . Etude et documentation* (Paris: Nizet, 1975), 69–74, 90 (Fr).

Bots, *Joachim Du Bellay entre l'histoire littéraire,* 93–127 (Fr).

Coleman, *The Chaste Muse,* 80–84 (Eng).

Howarth and Walton, *Explications,* 25–40 (Eng).

Guy Mermier and Yvette Boilly-Widmer, *Explication de texte, théorie et pratique* (Glenview, Ill.: Scott, Foresman, 1972), 65–68 (Fr).

G. H. Tucker, "Ulysses and Jason: A Problem of Allusion in Sonnet 31 of 'Les Regrets,'" *FS* 36 (1982): 385–96 (Eng).

H. Weber, *La Création poétique au XVIe siècle en France,* 428–30, 442–443 (Fr).

Les Regrets 53
"Vivons (Gordes) vivons, vivons, et pour le bruit"

H. Weber, *La Création poétique au XVIe siècle en France,* 449–51 (Fr).

Les Regrets 54
"Maraud, qui n'est maraud que de nom seulement"

Gray, *La Poétique de Du Bellay,* 128–29 (Fr).

Les Regrets 63
"Quel est celuy qui veult faire croire de soy"

Jacques Pineaux, "Sur un sonnet des 'Regrets,'" *RHL* 74 (April 1974): 254–56 (Fr).

Les Regrets 68
"Je hais de Florentin l'usurière avarice"

Gray, *La Poétique de Du Bellay,* 139–40 (Fr).

Les Regrets 79
"Je n'écris point d'amour, n'étant point amoureux"

Deguy, *Tombeau de Du Bellay,* 80–81 (Fr).

C. E. Nelson, "Enumeration and Irony in 'Les Regrets' of Du Bellay," *FR* 36 (January 1963): 270–71 (Eng).

Les Regrets 80
"Si je monte au Palais, je n'y trouve qu'orgueil"

H. Weber, *La Création poétique au XVIe siècle en France,* 456–57 (Fr).

Les Regrets 81
"Il fait bon voir (Paschal) un conclave serré"

Coleman, *The Chaste Muse,* 85–86 (Eng).

H. Weber, *La Création poétique au XVIe siècle en France,* 455–56 (Fr).

Les Regrets 85
"Flatter un crediteur, pour son terme allonger"

H. Weber, *La Création poétique au XVIe siècle en France,* 452–54 (Fr).

Les Regrets 86
"Marcher d'un grave pas et d'un grave sourci"

H. Weber, *La Création poétique au XVIe siècle en France,* 454–55 (Fr).

Les Regrets 87
"D'ou vient cela (Mauny) que tant plus on s'efforce"

Julia Lupton, "Undressing Alcina: The 'Orlando Furioso' in Du Bellay's 'Les Regrets,'" *FrF* 14 (September 1989): 292–95 (Eng).

Les Regrets 91
"O beaux cheveux d'argent mignonnement retors"

C. E. Nelson, "Enumeration and Irony in 'Les Regrets' of Du Bellay," *FR* 36 (January 1963): 271–73 (Eng).

Les Regrets 100
"Ursin, quand j'oy nommer de ces vieux noms romains"

Gray, *La Poétique de Du Bellay,* 124–28 (Fr).

Les Regrets 103
"Si la perte des tiens, si les pleurs de la mère"

Philip Ford, "Du Bellay et le sonnet satirique," in Bellenger, *Le Sonnet à la Renaissance,* 209–11 (Fr).

Gray, *La Poétique de Du Bellay,* 130 (Fr).

Les Regrets 104
"Si fruicts, raisins, et bledz, et autres telles choses"

Philip Ford, "Du Bellay et le sonnet satirique," in Bellenger, *Le Sonnet à la Renaissance,* 211–13 (Fr).

Les Regrets 109
"Comme un qui veult curer Cloaque immunde"

William Panici, *Three French Short-Verse Satirists: Marot, Magny, and Du Bellay* (New York and London: Garland, 1990), 110–12 (Eng).

Les Regrets 133
"Il fait bon voir (Magny) ces Coïons magnifiques"

Coleman, *The Chaste Muse,* 86–88 (Eng).

C. E. Nelson, "Enumeration and Irony in 'Les Regrets' of Du Bellay," *FR* 36 (January 1963): 273–75 (Eng).

Les Regrets 156
"Par ses vers Teïens Belleau me fait aymer"

Gray, *La Poétique de Du Bellay,* 91–92 (Fr).

DU BELLAY, JOACHIM, *Les Regrets 157*

Les Regrets 157
"En cependant, Clagny, que de mille arguments"

Hall and Wells, *Du Bellay: Poems,* 76–77 (Eng).

"Si par peine, et sueur, et par fidélité"

Deguy, *Tombeau de Du Bellay,* 90–91 (Fr).

"Songe"

Alexandre Amprimoz, "Du Blason et du songe," *ELit* 20 (Autumn 1987): 106–15 (Fr).

Gilbert Gadoffre, *Du Bellay et le sacré* (Paris: Gallimard, 1978), 151–82 (Fr).

Michael Giordano, "Du Bellay's 'Songe' and the Ambiguity of Narrative Authority," *O&C* 11, no. 1, (1986): 61–77 (Fr).

Margaret Wells, "Du Bellay's Sonnet Sequence 'Songe,' " *FS* 26 (January 1972): 1–8 (Eng).

Songe 1
"C'était alors que le présent"

Gilbert Gadoffre, "Structures des mythes de Du Bellay," *BHR* 36 (May 1974): 284–85 (Fr).

Songe 4
"Je vy hault eslevé sur columnes d'ivoire"

Richard Katz, "The Collapse of the City: The 'Vision' of the 'Antiquités de Rome,' " *ECr* 19 (Fall 1979): 18–19 (Eng).

Songe 7
"Je vis l'oiseau qui le soleil contemple"

Marc Eigeldinger, "Le Mythe d'Icare dans la poésie française du XVIe siècle," *CAIEF* 25 (May 1973): 267–68 (Fr).

Hall and Wells, *Du Bellay: Poems,* 57–58 (Eng).

Michael Riffaterre, "Le Tissu du texte: Du Bellay, 'Songe VII,' " *Poétique* 9 (April 1978): 193–203 (Fr).

Songe 12
"Je vy sourdre d'un roc une vive Fontaine"

Sharlene Poliner, "Du Bellay's 'Songe': Strategies of Deceit, Poetics of Vision," *BHR* 43 (September 1981): 516–19 (Eng).

Songe 13
"Plus riche assez que ne se monstroit celle"

Sharlene Poliner, "Du Bellay's 'Songe': Strategies of Deceit, Poetics of Vision," *BHR* 43 (September 1981): 523–25 (Eng).

Songe 15
"Finablement sur le point que Morphée"

Gilbert Gadoffre, "Structures des mythes de Du Bellay," *BHR* 36 (May 1974): 279–80 (Fr).

"Sus, ma petite Columbelle"

H. Weber, *La Création poétique au XVIe siècle en France,* 373–74 (Fr).

"La Terre y est fertile, amples les édifices"

Gray, *La Poétique de Du Bellay,* 137–38 (Fr).

"La Vieille courtisane"

Hall and Wells, *Du Bellay: Poems,* 95–97 (Eng).

Helen O. Platt, "Structure in Du Bellay's 'Divers jeux rustiques,' " *BHR* 35 (January 1973): 26–27 (Eng).

DU BELLAY, JOACHIM, "Villanelle"

"Villanelle"

Helen O. Platt, "Structure in Du Bellay's 'Divers jeux rustiques,'" *BHR* 35 (January 1973): 25–26 (Eng).

"Vœux rustiques du latin de Naugerius"

Helen O. Platt, "Structure in Du Bellay's 'Divers jeux rustiques,'" *BHR* 35 (January 1973): 24–25 (Eng).

DU BOUCHET, ANDRE

"Fraction"

Robert Greene, "André du Bouchet and Jacques Dupin, Poets of *L'Ephémère,*" *FrF* 1 (January 1976): 53–56 (Eng).

DU GUILLET, PERNETTE

"Celle clarté mouvante sans umbrage"

Donaldson-Evans, *Love's Fatal Glance,* 60–61 (Eng).

"Combien de fois ay-je en moy souhaicté"

Lance Donaldson-Evans, "The Taming of the Muse: The Female Poetic Voice in Pernette Du Guillet's 'Rymes,'" in J. C. Nash, ed., *Pre-Pléiade Poetry,* 93–95 (Eng).

T. Anthony Perry, "Pernette Du Guillet's Poetry of Love and Desire," *BHR* 35 (May 1973): 265–68 (Eng).

"Conde claros de Adonis"

V. L. Saulnier, "Mellin de Saint-Gelais, Pernette Du Guillet et l'air 'Conde Claros,'" *BHR* 32 (September 1970): 525, 528–31 (Fr).

DU GUILLET, PERNETTE, "Sans congnoissance"

"Le Corps ravy, l'ame s'en esmerveille"

T. Anthony Perry, "Pernette Du Guillet's Poetry of Love and Desire," *BHR* 35 (May 1973): 261–62, 264 (Eng).

"Esprit celeste et des dieux transformé"

Donaldson-Evans, *Love's Fatal Glance,* 54–55 (Eng).

"Le Hault pouvoir des Astres"

Robert D. Cottrell, "Pernette Du Guillet's 'Rymes': An Adventure in Ideal Love," *BHR* 31 (September 1969): 558–61 (Eng).

"Je suis la journée"

Donaldson-Evans, *Love's Fatal Glance,* 56–58 (Eng).

"La Nuict"

Christine M. Scollen, *The Birth of the Elegy in France* (Geneva: Droz, 1967), 127–8 (Eng).

"La Nuict estoit pour moy si tresobscure"

Robert D. Cottrell, "Pernette Du Guillet's 'Rymes': An Adventure in Ideal Love," *BHR* 31 (September 1969): 562–63 (Eng).

Donaldson-Evans, *Love's Fatal Glance,* 52–54 (Eng).

"Sans congnoissance aucune en mon Printemps j'estois"

Donaldson-Evans, *Love's Fatal Glance,* 58–60 (Eng).

Lance Donaldson-Evans, "The Taming of the Muse: The Female Poetic Voice in Pernette Du Guillet's 'Rymes,'" in Nash, ed., *Pre-Pléiade Poetry,* 92–93 (Eng).

DU PERRON, JACQUES

"Cantique de la Vierge"

Cave, *Devotional Poetry,* 287–89 (Eng).

"Psaume 104" (Translation)

Jeanneret, *Poésie et tradition biblique,* 462, 470–78, 481–84 (Fr).

DUPIN, JACQUES

"Ballast"

Maryann De Julio, "Jacques Dupin and a New Kind of Lyricism," *FrF* 14 (May 1989): 209–17 (Eng).

"Ecrire, est-ce un sommeil plus mobile"

M. Bishop, *The Contemporary Poetry of France,* 44 (Eng).

"Forêt seconde"

Roger Cardinal, "Jacques Dupin," in Cardinal, ed., *Sensibility and Creation,* 237–38 (Eng).

"Grand vent"

M. Bishop, *The Contemporary Poetry of France,* 48–49 (Eng).

"L'Irréversible"

M. Bishop, *The Contemporary Poetry of France,* 43–44 (Eng).

"Moraines"

Georges Raillard, *Jacques Dupin* (Paris: Seghers, 1974), 64–65 (Fr).

ELUARD, PAUL, "Ailleurs, ici et partout"

"Saccades"

Roger Cardinal, "Jacques Dupin," in Cardinal, ed., *Sensibility and Creation*, 224–27 (Eng).

Georges Raillard, *Jacques Dupin* (Paris: Seghers, 1974), 48–50 (Fr).

"Sang"

M. Bishop, *The Contemporary Poetry of France,* 51 (Eng).

"Le Soleil substitué"

M. Bishop, *The Contemporary Poetry of France,* 44–46, 49–51 (Eng).

ELUARD, PAUL

"A Chastel"

Jean-Charles Gateau, "Morale de la lumière à propos du poème d'Eluard: 'A Chastel,' " *SFr* 16 (January–April 1972): 87–90 (Fr).

"A Fernand Léger"

Renée R. Hubert, "Eluard's 'A Fernand Léger,' " *Expl* 24 (February 1966): 11–13 (Eng).

"L'Absolue Nécessité, l'absolu désir"

Gisèle Manoury, "Deuxième étude," *Europe* 51 (January 1973): 261–79 (Fr).

"Ailleurs, ici et partout"

Jacques Gaucheron, "Poésie et imagination: Étude sur 'Ailleurs, ice et partout,' " *Europe* 51 (January 1973): 20–35 (Fr).

ELUARD, PAUL, "L'Amoureuse"

"L'Amoureuse"

Broome and Chesters, *The Appreciation of Modern French Poetry (1850–1950),* 143–45 (Eng).

Daniel E. Rivas, "Eluard's 'L'Amoureuse': Mimesis and Semiosis," *FR* 55 (March 1982): 489–96 (Eng).

"Au cœur de mon amour"

Perche, *Paul Eluard,* 41 (Fr).

"Au premier mot limpide"

A. Kibedi Varga, "Syntaxe et rythme chez quelques poètes contemporains," in Monique Parent, ed., *Le Vers français au XXème siècle* (Paris: Klincksieck, 1967), 182–83 (Fr).

"Berceuse"

Frank Coppay, "Natural History versus Natural Science in Paul Eluard's 'Berceuse,'" *SubStance,* no. 16 (Spring 1987): 11–18 (Eng).

"Celle de toujours, toute"

Nugent, *Paul Eluard,* 62–64 (Eng).

"Chant du dernier délai"

Nugent, *Paul Eluard,* 119–22 (Eng).

"Le Château des pauvres"

Perche, *Paul Eluard,* 68–70 (Fr).

"Le Cinquième Poème visible"

Nugent, *Paul Eluard,* 40–41, 90–95 (Eng).

"Le Cœur sur l'arbre"

Nugent, *Paul Eluard,* 30–31 (Eng).

"Comme deux gouttes d'eau"

Nugent, *Paul Eluard,* 51, 81–82 (Eng).

"La Courbe de tes yeux"

Dubosclard and Dublsclard, *Du surréalisme à la Résistance,* 29–36 (Fr).

Antoine Fongaro, "Eluard et Hugo, encore," *SFr* 27 (May–August 1983): 302–4 (Fr).

"Cours naturel"

Jacques Gaucheron, "Eluard et la morale: Contre les faiseurs de morale." *Europe* 40 (November–December 1962): 103–4 (Fr).

"Crépuscule"

Nugent, *Paul Eluard,* 71–72 (Eng).

"Croyez-moi, je suis la loi"

Francis Carmody, "Eluard's Rupture with Surrealism," *PMLA* 76 (September 1961): 445 (Eng).

"L'Egalité des sexes"

Perche, *Paul Eluard,* 38–41 (Fr).

"L'Extase"

C. H. Wake, "Eluard: 'L'Extase,'" in Nurse, ed., *The Art of Criticism,* 288–99 (Eng).

ELUARD, PAUL, "Georges Braque"

"Georges Braque"

Anne H. Greet, "Paul Eluard's Early Poems for Painters," *FMLS* 9 (January 1973): 89–90 (Eng).

"Giorgio de Chirico"

Anne H. Greet, "Paul Eluard's Early Poems for Painters," *FMLS* 9 (January 1973): 90–94 (Eng).

"La Halte des heures"

Groupe Mu, "Rhétorique poétique: Le Jeu des figures dans un poème de Paul Eluard," *RR* 63 (April 1972): 125–51 (Fr).

"Immobile"

Perche, Paul Eluard, 79–80 (Fr).

"Jardin perdu"

Nugent, *Paul Eluard,* 73–76 (Eng).

"Je te l'ai dit pour les nuages"

Malcolm Bowie, "Paul Eluard," in Cardinal, ed., *Sensibility and Creation,* 150–52 (Eng).

"Joan Mirò"

Anne H. Greet, "Paul Eluard's Early Poems for Painters," *FMLS* 9 (January 1973): 98–101 (Eng).

"Liberté"

"Nugent, *Paul Eluard,* 26–28 (Eng).

"Le Miroir d'un moment"

Nugent, *Paul Eluard,* 33–34 (Eng).

"Notre mouvement"

Malcolm Bowie, "Paul Eluard," in Cardinal, ed., *Sensibility and Creation,* 157–59 (Eng).

"Les Oiseaux parfument les bois"

Malcolm Bowie, "Paul Eluard," in Cardinal, ed., *Sensibility and Creation,* 152–53 (Eng).

"On ne peut me connaître"

Perche, *Paul Eluard,* 62–63 (Fr).

"Taille"

Michael Riffaterre, "Sémantique du poème," *CAIEF* 23 (May 1971): 136–38 (Fr).

"La Parole"

Marie-Noëlle Balavoine, Arlette Besnard and Pascale Busson, "Deux Études sur 'Capitale de la douleur': Première Étude," *Europe* 51 (January 1973): 244–60 (Fr).

Perche, *Paul Eluard,* 73–75 (Fr).

"Une Personnalité toujours nouvelle . . ."

Nugent, *Paul Eluard,* 131–33 (Eng).

"Picasso"

Nugent, *Paul Eluard,* 82–85 (Eng).

ELUARD, PAUL, "Poésie ininterrompue"

"Poésie ininterrompue"

Michel Beaujour, "Analyse de 'Poésie ininterrompue,'" *Europe* 21 (November–December 1962): 74–87 (Fr).

Malcolm Bowie, "Paul Eluard," in Cardinal, ed., *Sensibility and Creation*, 160–66 (Eng).

Curnier, *Pages commentées d'auteurs contemporains*, vol. 2, 87–102 (Fr).

Nugent, *Paul Eluard*, 107–16, 129–130 (Eng).

Richard Vernier, "La Prosodie d'Eluard," *FR* 43 (Winter 1970): 29–32 (Fr).

"Pour vivre ici"

Pierre Emmanuel, "Commentaire," *Europe* 40 (November–December 1962): 44–50 (Fr).

Perche, *Paul Eluard*, 47–49, 59–60, 94 (Fr).

"Première du monde"

Malcolm Bowie, "Paul Eluard," in Cardinal, ed., *Sensibility and Creation*, 153–57 (Eng).

Nugent, *Paul Eluard*, 60–62 (Eng).

"Quelques-uns des mots qui, jusqu'ici, m'étaient mystérieusement interdits"

Francis Carmody, "Eluard's Rupture with Surrealism," *PMLA* 76 (September 1961): 440–43 (Eng).

Georges Mounin, "Paul Eluard's Forbidden Words," *FMLS* 18 (April 1982): 98–105 (Eng).

"Règnes"

Nugent, *Paul Eluard*, 48, 97 (Eng).

ELUARD, PAUL, "L'Univers-Solitude"

"Salvador Dali"

Nugent, *Paul Eluard,* 76–79 (Eng).

"Sans âge"

Broome and Chesters, *The Appreciation of Modern French Poetry (1850–1950),* 146–49 (Eng).

"Les Semblables"

Nugent, *Paul Eluard,* 126–27 (Eng).

"Le Sixième Poème visible"

Nugent, *Paul Eluard,* 128–29 (Eng).

"Sous la menace rouge d'une épée"

Jean Breton, "Notes sur le poème en prose dans 'Capitale de la douleur,' " *Europe* 51 (January 1973): 120–25 (Fr).

"Tout aiguisé de soif, tout affamé de froid"

Dorothy Aspinwall, "Eluard's 'Tout aiguisé de soif, tout affamé de froid,' " *Expl* 26 (November 1967): 4–5 (Eng).

"Tu te lèves l'eau se déplie"

Perche, *Paul Eluard,* 57–60 (Fr).

"L'Univers-Solitude"

Claudine Rousseau, "Francis Ponge et Paul Eluard à la flamme d'une bougie . . . Lecture à deux voix," *SFr* 25 (September–December 1981): 496–97 (Fr).

ELUARD, PAUL, "La Victoire de Guernica"

"La Victoire de Guernica"

Nugent, *Paul Eluard,* 24–25 (Eng).

"Vivre"

Nugent, *Paul Eluard,* 18–21, 46–47 (Eng).

"Volé!"

Michel Launay, "Analyse du premier écrit d'Eluard: 'Volé! Nouvelle iné-dite,'" in *Approches: Essais sur la poésie moderne de langue française* (Paris: Les Belles Lettres, 1971), 165–74 (Fr).

EMMANUEL, PIERRE

"Mes pas si longtemps ont neigé"

Pierre-Ivan Laroche, "Rythme et expressivité dans un poème de Pierre Em-manuel," in Monique Parent, ed., *Le Vers français au XXème siècle* (Paris: Klincksieck, 1967), 245–60 (Fr).

FAVRE, ANTOINE

"Sur le premier mystère douleureux"

Lance K. Donaldson-Evans, "The Theme of Blood and the Agony of Christ in the Work of French Baroque Poets," *FR* 45 (Special Issue 3) (Fall 1971): 130–32 (Eng).

FRENAUD, ANDRE

"L'Agonie du Général Krivitski"

Clancier, *André Frénaud,* 82–84 (Fr).

GARNEAU, SAINT-DENYS, "Accompagnement"

"Enorme figure de la déesse Raison"

Clancier, *André Frénaud,* 76–79 (Fr).

"Epitaphe"

Clancier, *André Frénaud,* 53–54 (Fr).

"La Noce noire"

Clancier, *André Frénaud,* 67–72 (Fr).

"Nul ne s'égare"

Michael Bishop, "Cela qui nous em/porte: À propos de 'Nul ne s'égare,' "
Europe 68 (1990): 57–63 (Fr).

"Les Paysans"

Clancier, *André Frénaud,* 79–82 (Fr).

FROISSART, JEAN DE

"L'Horloge amoureuse"

Peter Dembowski, " 'L'Horloge amoureuse' de Froissart," *ECr* 18 (Spring
1978): 19–31 (Fr).

Claire Nouvet, "La Mecanique du diffèrement lyrique: 'L'Orloge amoureuse' de Jean Froissart," *SFr* 30 (May–August 1986): 259–67 (Fr).

GARNEAU, SAINT-DENYS

"Accompagnement"

Philippe Haeck, "Naissance de la poésie moderne au Québec," *EF* 9 (May
1973): 97–101 (Fr).

GARNEAU, SAINT-DENYS, "L'Arbre fleuri"

"L'Arbre fleuri"

Dujka Smoje, "Lorsque le verbe se fait musique: Saint-Denys Garneau," *ELit* 15 (April 1982): 74–75 (Fr).

"Musique"

Dujka Smoje, "Lorsque le verbe se fait musique: Saint-Denys Garneau," *ELit* 15 (April 1982): 77–93 (Fr).

GAUTIER DE COINCI

"Quant ces floretes florir voi"

Calin, *In Defense of French Poetry*, 109–15 (Eng).

GAUTIER, THEOPHILE

"Affinités secrètes"

Denommé, *The French Parnassian Poets*, 54–57 (Eng).

David Kelley, "Gautier et Baudelaire: 'Emaux et camées' et les 'Petits poèmes en prose,'" in Bowie, Fairlie, and Finch, eds., *Baudelaire, Mallarmé, Valéry*, 60–62 (Fr).

"Albertus"

Grant, *Théophile Gautier*, 22–24 (Eng).

"L'Art"

Denommé, *The French Parnassian Poets*, 10–12, 52–53 (Eng).

"A une robe rose"

Ross Chambers, "Pour une poétique du vêtement," in Gray, ed., *Poétiques*, 29–32 (Fr).

GAUTIER, THEOPHILE, "La Fumée"

"Aux vitraux diaprés des sombres basiliques"

Denommé, *The French Parnassian Poets,* 42–44 (Eng).

"Banc de pierre"

Jean Dubu, "Du 'Banc de pierre' de Gautier au 'Colloque sentimental' de Verlaine," *SFr* 11 (September–December 1967): 486–87 (Fr).

"Ce que disent les hirondelles"

Denommé, *The French Parnassian Poets,* 60–62 (Eng).

"Coerulei oculi"

Grant, *Théophile Gautier,* 141–43 (Eng).

"La Comédie de la Mort"

H. Riffaterre, *L'Orphisme dans la poésie,* 127–30 (Fr).

"Contralto"

Denommé, *The French Parnassian Poets,* 58–60 (Eng).

"La Diva"

Monica Nurnberg, "Inspiration and Aspiration: Gautier's 'La Diva' and Musset's 'Une Soirée perdue,'" *AJFS* 15 (September–December 1978): 234–42 (Eng).

"La Fumée"

Ross Chambers, "Le Poète fumeur," *AJFS* 16 (January–April 1979): 141–44, 146–48 (Fr).

GAUTIER, THEOPHILE, "L'Hippopotame"

"L'Hippopotame"

Fernande Bassan, "Une Source bouddhiste possible d'un poème de Théophile Gautier," *NCFS* 2 (Fall 1973): 24–28 (Fr).

"L'Horloge"

John Jackson, "Baudelaire lecteur de Théophile Gautier: Les Deux 'Horloges,' " *RHL* 84 (May–June 1984): 440–44 (Fr).

"L'Impassible"

Grant, *Théophile Gautier,* 143–44 (Eng).

"In deserto"

M. Riffaterre, *Semiotics of Poetry,* 6–12, 59 (Eng).

"Melancholia"

H. Riffaterre, *L'Orphisme dans la poésie,* 121–22 (Fr).

"Nostalgies d'obélisques"

Nichola Haxell, "Hugo, Gautier, and the Obelisk of Luxor," *NCFS* 18 (Fall–Winter 1989–90): 69–71 (Eng).

"Notre Dame"

David Burnett, "The Architecture of Meaning: Gautier and Romantic Architectural Visions," *FrF* 7 (May 1982): 110–14 (Eng).

"La Nue"

Christopher Prendergast, "Questions of Metaphor: Gautier's 'La Nue,' " in Prendergast, ed., *Nineteenth-Century French Poetry,* 138–56 (Eng).

GAUTIER, THÉOPHILE, "La Vie dans la mort"

"Pastel"

Denommé, *The French Parnassian Poets,* 44–46 (Eng).

"Le Poème de la femme"

Joan Driscoll, "Visual Allusion in the Work of Théophile Gautier," *FS* 27 (October 1973): 426–28 (Eng).
Knight, *Flower Poetics in Nineteenth-Century France,* 169–70 (Eng).

"Portail"

Grant, *Théophile Gautier,* 66–67 (Eng).

"La Robe pailletée"

Ross Chambers, "Pour une poétique du vêtement," in Gray, ed., *Poétiques,* 42–45 (Fr).

"Symphonie en blanc majeur"

John Van Eerde, " 'La Symphonie en blanc majeur': An Interpretation," *ECr* 3 (Spring 1963): 26–33 (Eng).
David Kelley, "Gautier et Baudelaire: 'Emaux et camées' et les 'Petits poèmes en prose,' " in Bowie, Fairlie, and Finch, eds., *Baudelaire, Mallarmé, Valéry,* 67–68 (Fr).

"Ténèbres"

H. Riffaterre, *L'Orphisme dans la poésie,* 84–85 (Fr).

"Variations sur le carnaval de Venise"

David Kelley, "Gautier et Baudelaire: 'Emaux et camées' et les 'Petits poèmes en prose,' " in Bowie, Fairlie, and Finch, eds., *Baudelaire, Mallarmé, Valéry,* 62–63 (Fr).

"La Vie dans la mort"

Grant, *Théophile Gautier,* 67–69 (Eng).

GOLL, YVAN, "La Roche percée"

GOLL, YVAN

"La Roche percée"

Jean-Jacques Thomas, "Michel Leiris, Yvan Goll: 'Touristes nous nous sommes promenés,'" *FrF* 3 (May 1978): 217–18 (Fr).

GRANDBOIS, ALAIN

"Avec ta robe"

Philippe Haeck, "Naissance de la poésie moderne au Québec," *EF* 9 (May 1973): 105–10 (Fr).

"Poème"

N. Beauchemin, "Etude du rythme d'un poème de Grandbois, d'après la lecture de l'auteur," in Monique Parent, ed., *Le Vers français au XXème siècle* (Paris: Klincksieck, 1967), 233–44 (Fr).

GREVIN, JACQUES

Gélodacrye
"C'est aujourd'hui vertu que sçavoir courtiser"

Bots, *Joachim Du Bellay entre l'histoire littéraire,* 128–35 (Fr).

Zoé Samaras, "La Gélodacrye de Grévin: etude stylistique," *BHR* 40 (May 1978): 272–73 (Fr).

Gélodacrye
"Je me ris de ce monde et n'y trouve que rire"

Zoé Samaras, "La Gélodacrye de Grévin: etude stylistique," *BHR* 40 (May 1978): 274–75 (Fr).

Gélodacrye
"Lubin comme l'on dit, n'est que trop courageux"

Zoé Samaras, "La Gélodacrye de Grévin: etude stylistique," *BHR* 40 (May 1978): 275–76 (Fr).

GUILLAUME IX D'AQUITAINE, "Compaign, non pus mudar"

Gélodacrye
"Qu'est-ce que ceste vie? un public eschafault"

Zoé Samaras, "La Gélodacrye de Grévin: etude stylistique," *BHR* 40 (May 1978): 263–79 (Fr).

GRINGOIRE, PIERRE

"Lettres nouvelles de Milan avec les regretz du seigneur Ludovic"

Brown, *The Shaping of History and Poetry in Late Medieval France,* 38–41, 70 (Eng).

"L'Union des Princes"

Brown, *The Shaping of History and Poetry in Late Medieval France,* 55–58, 71 (Eng).

GUILLAUME IX D'AQUITAINE

"Ben vuelh que sapchon li pluzor"

Topsfield, *Troubadours and Love,* 14–16 (Eng).

"Companho, farai un vers tot covinen"

Stephen G. Nichols, "Canso → Conso: Structure of Parodic Humor in Three Songs of Guilhem IX," *ECr* 16 (Spring 1976): 17–20, 22–25 (Eng).

Charles Camproux, "Feray un vers tot covinon" in *Mélanges de langue et de littérature du Moyen Age et de la Renaissance offerts à Jean Frappier, Professeur à la Sorbonne, par ses collègues, ses élèves et ses amies,* vol. 1 (Geneva: Droz, 1970), 159–72 (Fr).

Topsfield, *Troubadours and Love,* 18–20 (Eng).

"Compaign, non pus mudar qu'eu no m'effrei"

Stephen G. Nichols, "Canso → Conso: Structure of Parodic Humor in Three Songs of Guilhem IX," *ECr* 16 (Spring 1976): 25–27 (Eng).

GUILLAUME IX D'AQUITAINE, "Companho, tant ai agutz"

"Companho, tant ai agutz d'avols conres"

Stephen G. Nichols, "Canso → Conso: Structure of Parodic Humor in Three Songs of Guilhem IX," *ECr* 16 (Spring 1976): 27–28 (Eng).

Topsfield, *Troubadours and Love,* 20–23 (Eng).

"Farai un vers de dreyt nien"

Topsfield, *Troubadours and Love,* 30–35 (Eng).

"Farai un vers pos mi sonelh"

Topsfield, *Troubadours and Love,* 16–18 (Eng).

"Mout jauzens me prenc en amar"

Topsfield, *Troubadours and Love,* 36–39 (Eng).

HADJ ALI, BACHIR

"Nuits algériennes"

Eric Sellin, "The Poetry of Bachir Hadj Ali; or, The Aesthetics of the Footnote," *ECr* 12 (Winter 1972): 293–95 (Eng).

HEBERT, ANNE

"Je suis une fille maigre"

Robert Giroux and Hélène Dame, "Les Critères de poéticité dans l'histoire de la poésie québécoise (sémiotique littéraire)," *ELit* 14 (April 1981): 136–41 (Fr).

"Marine"

Philippe Haeck, "Naissance de la poésie moderne au Québec," *EF* 9 (May 1973): 101–5 (Fr).

HEREDIA, JOSE-MARIA DE, "Le Cydnus"

"Neige"

Jean-Michel Adam, "Sur cinq vers de 'Mystère de la parole,' " *ELit* (December 1972): 466–80 (Fr).

HEDELIN, CLAUDE

"Royaume de la fève"

J. D. Hubert, "Un Poème burlesque au temps de Malherbe," *ECr* 6 (Winter 1966): 283–91 (Fr).

HEREDIA, JOSE-MARIA DE

"Antoine et Cléopâtre"

Alexander Fischler, "The Decadent Side of Aestheticism: Heredia's Anthony and Cleopatra Triptych," *NCFS* 4 (Spring 1976): 280–83 (Eng).

Rachel Killick, "José-Maria de Heredia and the Descriptive Sonnet: An Appreciation of 'Le Tepidarium,' 'Antoine et Cléopâtre,' and 'Fuite de Centaures,' " *AJFS* 22 (September–December 1985): 258–62 (Eng).

"Après Cannes"

Denommé, *The French Parnassian Poets,* 118–20 (Eng).

"Les Conquérants"

Denommé, *The French Parnassian Poets,* 122–23 (Eng).

"Le Cydnus"

Alexander Fischler, "The Decadent Side of Aestheticism: Heredia's Anthony and Cleopatra Triptych," *NCFS* 4 (Spring 1976): 278–79 (Eng).

HEREDIA, JOSE-MARIA DE, "Fuite de Centaures"

"Fuite de Centaures"

Rachel Killick, "José-Maria de Heredia and the Descriptive Sonnet: An Appreciation of 'Le Tepidarium,' 'Antoine et Cléopâtre,' and 'Fuite de Centaures,'" *AJFS* 22 (September–December 1985): 262–66 (Eng).

"Maris stella"

Denommé, *The French Parnassian Poets,* 126–28 (Eng).

"La Mort de l'aigle"

Denommé, *The French Parnassian Poets,* 129–31 (Eng).

"L'Oubli"

Richard Berrong, "The Image of the Hero . . . in Heredia's 'Les Trophées,'" *NCFS* 11 (Spring–Summer 1983): 278–84 (Eng).

Denommé, *The French Parnassian Poets,* 116–18 (Eng).

"Le Récif de corail"

Denommé, *The French Parnassian Poets,* 123–25 (Eng).

"Soir de bataille"

Alexander Fischler, "The Decadent Side of Aestheticism: Heredia's Anthony and Cleopatra Triptych," *NCFS* 4 (Spring 1976): 279–80 (Eng).

"Le Tépidarium"

Rachel Killick, "José-Maria de Heredia and the Descriptive Sonnet: An Appreciation of 'Le Tepidarium,' 'Antoine et Cléopâtre,' and 'Fuite de Centaures,'" *AJFS* 22 (September–December 1985): 251–57 (Eng).

Scott, *Pictorialist Poetics,* 93–96 (Eng).

HOPIL, CLAUDE

"Vol d'Esprit"

Lafay, *La Poésie française du premier XVIIe siècle,* 288–91 (Fr).

HUGO, VICTOR

"A Albert Durer"

Gaudon, *Le Temps de la contemplation,* 76–81 (Fr).

Edward K. Kaplan, "Victor Hugo and the Poetics of Doubt: The Transition of 1835–1837," *FrF* 6 (May 1981): 147–49 (Eng).

Py, *Les Mythes grecs,* 132–34 (Fr).

"A André Chénier"

S. Nash, *"Les Contemplations" of Victor Hugo,* 86–87 (Eng).

"Abîme"

Gaudon, *Le Temps de la contemplation,* 198 (Fr).

"A celle qui est restée en France"

Frey, *"Les Contemplations,"* 110, 124, 127–30, 141 (Eng).

Gaillard, *"Les Contemplations": Victor Hugo,* 65–66 (Fr).

Gaudon, *Le Temps de la contemplation,* 267–69, 295–96 (Fr).

Glauser, *La Poétique de Hugo,* 492–93 (Fr).

Houston, *Victor Hugo,* rev. ed.,103–8, 138–40 (Eng).

John P. Houston, "Design in 'Les Contemplations,'" *FrF* 5 (May 1980): 137–38 (Eng).

S. Nash, *"Les Contemplations" of Victor Hugo,* 194–204 (Eng).

Py, *Les Mythes grecs,* 206–8 (Fr).

HUGO, VICTOR, "L'Aigle du casque"

"L'Aigle du casque"

Glauser, *La Poétique de Hugo,* 292–95 (Fr).

"A la fenêtre, pendant la nuit"

Cogman, *Hugo: Les Contemplations,* 71–72 (Eng).

"A l'Arc de Triomphe"

Pierre Citron, *La Poésie de Paris dans la littérature française de Rousseau à Baudelaire,* vol. 2 (Paris: Editions de Minuit, 1961), 32–34 (Fr).

Gaudon, *Le Temps de la contemplation,* 94–96 (Fr).

"A ma fille"

S. Nash, *"Les Contemplations" of Victor Hugo,* 58–59 102–4 (Eng).

"A Monsieur de D. De***"

Wendy Greenberg, "En Passant dans la place Louis XV un jour de fête," *NCFS* 13 (Summer 1985): 229–33 (Fr).

"A M. de Lamartine"

Jean Gaudon, "Les Grandes Manœuvres de 1829," *CAIEF* 38 (May 1986): 220–23 (Fr).

Glauser, *La Poétique de Hugo,* 322–24 (Fr).

"A. M. Louis B."

Jean Gaudon, "Les Grandes manœuvres de 1829, *CAIEF* 38 (May 1986): 223–24 (Fr).

"L'Ange"

Glauser, *La Poétique de Hugo,* 73–74 (Fr).

"A Olympio"

Jean-Marie Gleize, "L'Ouverture lyrique: 'Voix intérieures,'" *Europe* 63 (March 1985): 20–26 (Fr).

"Après une lecture de Dante"

Edward K. Kaplan, "Victor Hugo and the Poetics of Doubt: The Transition of 1835–1837," *FrF* 6 (May 1981): 149–50 (Eng).

"A propos d'Horace"

Frey, *"Les Contemplations,"* 78–80, 90–91 (Eng).

Glauser, *La Poétique de Hugo,* 341–43 (Fr).

"A Théophile Gautier"

Glauser, *La Poétique de Hugo,* 336–37 (Fr).

Houston, *Victor Hugo,* 140–42; rev. ed., 136–37 (Eng).

"Au Cheval"

Albouy, *La Création mythologique,* 109–11 (Fr).

Patricia A. Ward, "Hugo's Private and Public Personae in 'Les Chansons des rues et des bois,'" *ECr* 16 (Fall 1976): 207–9 (Eng).

"A Villequier"

Cogman, *Hugo: Les Contemplations,* 52–55 (Eng).

Denommé, *Nineteenth-Century French Romantic Poets,* 116–17 (Eng).

Gaillard, *"Les Contemplations": Victor Hugo,* 37–40 (Fr).

"A Virgile"

Gaudon, *Le Temps de la contemplation,* 67–68 (Fr).

Edward K. Kaplan, "Victor Hugo and the Poetics of Doubt: The Transition of 1835–1837," *FrF* 6 (May 1981): 145–47 (Eng).

HUGO, VICTOR, "Bièvre"

"Bièvre"

Gaudon, *Le Temps de la contemplation,* 58–61 (Fr).

"Booz endormi"

Jean-Bertrand Barrère, "Hugo: Extract from 'Booz endormi,'" in Nurse, ed., *The Art of Criticism,* 182–91 (Eng).

Barrère, Le Regard D'Orphée, 69–81 (Fr).

Elizabeth Beaujour, "'Booz Endormi' and the Epic of Man," *FR* 44 (Special Issue 2) (Winter 1971): 1–11 (Eng).

Georges Combet, "Les Parallélismes de 'Booz endormi,'" *RLM* 693–97 (1984): 91–99 (Fr).

Michel Grimaud, "Structures des mythes de Du Bellay," *FR* 51 (October 1977): 15–21 (Fr).

Jean Onimus, "'Booz endormi' dans l'esthétique et la théologie de Péguy," *RLM* 731–34 (1985): 59–76 (Fr).

"Le Calcul, c'est l'abîme"

Glauser, *La Poétique de Hugo,* 52–54 (Fr).

"Les Cariatides"

Albouy, *La Création mythologique,* 141–43, 231–32 (Fr).

"Ce que dit la bouche d'ombre"

Albouy, *La Création mythologique,* 276–77 (Fr).

Bays, *The Orphic Vision,* 120, 122–24 (Eng).

Cogman, *Hugo: Les Contemplations,* 68–71 (Eng).

Denommé, *Nineteenth-Century French Romantic Poets,* 120–21, 123–24 (Eng).

Frey, *"Les Contemplations,"* 18–20, 32–33, 58, 81, 141–42 (Eng).

Gaillard, *"Les Contemplations": Victor Hugo,* 62–65 (Fr).

Gaudon, *Le Temps de la contemplation,* 231–35, 260–61, 304–5 (Fr).

Glauser, *La Poétique de Hugo,* 62–64, 161–62 (Fr).

John P. Houston, "Design in 'Les Contemplations,' " *FrF* 5 (May 1980): 135–36 (Eng).

Houston, *Victor Hugo,* 99–103; rev. ed., 71–75, 105–6 (Eng).

Bettina L. Knapp, "What the Mouth of Darkness Says," *ECr* 16 (Fall 1976): 178–97 (Eng).

S. Nash, *"Les Contemplations" of Victor Hugo,* 23–24, 171–76 (Eng).

"Ce qu'on entend sur la montagne"

Glauser, *La Poétique de Hugo,* 159–61 (Fr).

"Cérigo"

Glauser, *La Poétique de Hugo,* 194–99 (Fr).

S. Nash, *"Les Contemplations" of Victor Hugo,* 163–65 (Eng).

"Charles Vacquerie"

S. Nash, *"Les Contemplations" of Victor Hugo,* 139–40, 145–47 (Eng).

"La Chouette"

Frey, *"Les Contemplations,"* 37–38 (Eng).

"Le Cirque de Gavarnie"

Glauser, *La Poétique de Hugo,* 349–57 (Fr).

"La Conscience"

Gaudon, *Le Temps de la contemplation,* 180–81 (Fr).

HUGO, VICTOR, "Crépuscule"

"Crépuscule"

Denommé, *Nineteenth-Century French Romantic Poets,* 112–14 (Eng).

"Demain, dès l'aube"

William Beauchamp, "An Introduction to French Poetry: Hugo's 'Demain dès l'aube,' " *FR* 49 (February 1976): 381–87 (Eng).

Cogman, *Hugo: Les Contemplations,* 56–57 (Eng).

Howarth and Walton, *Explications,* 143–50 (Eng).

Neal Oxenhandler, "The Discourse of Emotion in Hugo's 'Demain dès l'aube,' " *FrF* 11 (January 1986): 29–39 (Eng).

"Le Dénombrement"

Glauser, *La Poétique de Hugo,* 206–8 (Fr).

"Le Dévouement"

Léon-François Hoffmann, "Autour d'une ode de Victor Hugo, 'Le Dévouement,' " *RR* 55 (April 1964): 91–97 (Fr).

"Dicté en présence du glacier du Rhône"

Glauser, *La Poétique de Hugo,* 314–15 (Fr).

"Les Djinns"

Denommé, *Nineteenth-Century French Romantic Poets,* 95 (Eng).

Richard B. Grant, "Sequence and Theme in Victor Hugo's 'Les Orientales,' " *PMLA* 94 (October 1979): 902–3 (Eng).

Houston, *Victor Hugo,* 27–29 (Eng).

Py, *Les Mythes grecs,* 59–60 (Fr).

"Dolor"

Gaudon, *Le Temps de la contemplation,* 209–10 (Fr).

"Eblouissements"

Gaudon, *Le Temps de la contemplation,* 169, 174–177 (Fr).

"Eclaircie"

Frank Bowman, "Lectures de Victor Hugo, 'Eclaircie': New Criticism, Nouvelle Critique, ou . . . ," *CAIEF* 23 (May 1971): 145–62 (Fr).

"Ecrit au bas d'un crucifix"

Gaillard, *"Les Contemplations": Victor Hugo,* 69–70 (Fr).

"Ecrit sur la vitre d'une fenêtre flamande"

Michael Riffaterre, "Le Poème comme représentation," *Poétique* 1 (November 1970): 402–18 (Fr).

"L'Egout de Rome"

Glauser, *La Poétique de Hugo,* 67–68 (Fr).

"Elle était déchausée, elle était décoiffée"

Ross Chambers, "Pour une poétique de vêtement," in Gray, ed., *Poétiques,* 22–24 (Fr).

Jean Joseph, " 'Galatea bifrons': Étude structurale d'un poème de Victor Hugo," *AJFS* 17 (September–December 1980): 241–61 (Fr).

"Entre géants et dieux"

Albouy, *La Création mythologique,* 253–60 (Fr).

HUGO, VICTOR, "Envoi des feuilles d'automne"

"Envoi des feuilles d'automne"

M. Riffaterre, *Semiotics of Poetry,* 157–59 (Eng).

"L'Epopée du ver"

Glauser, *La Poétique de Hugo,* 489–91 (Fr).

"L'Esprit humain"

Gaudon, *Le Temps de la contemplation,* 270–73 (Fr).
Glauser, *La Poétique de Hugo,* 83–89 (Fr).

"Est-ce que tu serais par hasard un poète?"

Glauser, *La Poétique de Hugo,* 138–39 (Fr).

"Et d'abord, de quel Dieu veux-tu parler? Précis"

Glauser, *La Poétique de Hugo,* 82–83 (Fr).

"Et Nox facta est"

Houston, *Victor Hugo,* rev. ed., 65–67 (Eng).
Michael Riffaterre, "La Poétisation du mot chez Victor Hugo," *CAIEF* 19 (March 1967): 182–85 (Fr).

"Eviradnus"

Glauser, *La Poétique de Hugo,* 284–88 (Fr).

"L'Expiation"

Denommé, *Nineteenth-Century French Romantic Poets,* 106–8 (Eng).
Gaudon, *Le Temps de la contemplation,* 178–79, 181 (Fr).
Moreau, *Six Études de métrique,* 18–25 (Fr).

"Extase"

Robert L. Mitchell, "Poetry of Religion to Religion of Poetry: Hugo, Mallarmé, and the Problematics of Preservation," *FR* 55 (March 1982): 483–84 (Eng).

"La Fête chez Thérèse"

Frey, *"Les Contemplations,"* 28–29, 73, 79 (Eng).

John P. Houston, "Design in 'Les Contemplations,'" *FrF* 5 (May 1980): 125–26 (Eng).

Houston, *Victor Hugo,* rev. ed., 89–91 (Eng).

S. Nash, *"Les Contemplations"* of Victor Hugo, 97–100 (Eng).

"Le Feu du ciel"

Glauser, *La Poétique de Hugo,* 307–10 (Fr).

Richard B. Grant, "Sequence and Theme in Victor Hugo's 'Les Orientales,'" *PMLA* 94 (October 1979): 896–97, 899 (Eng).

Houston, *Victor Hugo,* 12–13; rev. ed., 24–25 (Eng).

"La Fin de Satan"

Laurence Porter, "Pourquoi 'La Fin de Satan' est-il resté inachevé?" *NCFS* 18 (Spring–Summer 1990): 463–73 (Fr).

"Le Firmament est plein de la vaste clarté"

Frey, *"Les Contemplations,"* 107–9 (Eng).

"Fonction du poète"

Bénichou, *Les Mages romantiques,* 308–10 (Fr).

"Gros temps la nuit"

Glauser, *La Poétique de Hugo,* 319–21 (Fr).

HUGO, VICTOR, "Halte en marchant"

"Halte en marchant"

Houston, *Victor Hugo,* 132–34; rev. ed., 127–29 (Eng).
S. Nash, *"Les Contemplations" of Victor Hugo,* 104–7 (Eng).

"Heureux l'homme, occupé de l'éternel destin"

S. Nash, *"Les Contemplations" of Victor Hugo,* 100–101 (Eng).

"Horror"

Gaudon, *Le Temps de la contemplation,* 209–10, 321 (Fr).

"L'Italie-Ratbert"

Glauser, *La Poétique de Hugo,* 203–4 (Fr).

"Le Jardin des plantes"

Glauser, *La Poétique de Hugo,* 373–76 (Fr).

"Je suis fait d'ombre et de marbre"

Broome and Chesters, *The Appreciation of Modern French Poetry (1850–1950),* 67–70 (Eng).

"Jeune fille, la grâce emplit tes dix-sept ans"

S. Nash, *"Les Contemplations" of Victor Hugo,* 68–71 (Eng).

"La Légende de la nonne"

Houston, *Victor Hugo,* 19–20; rev. ed., 7–9 (Eng).

"Lui"

Marisa Gatti-Taylor, and Steven Taylor, "The God-Man and the Man-God," *NCFS* 18 (Spring–Summer 1990): 456–60 (Eng).

"Les Mages"

Gaillard, *"Les Contemplations": Victor Hugo,* 70–71 (Fr).

Gaudon, *Le Temps de la contemplation,* 263–66, 302–4 (Fr).

Glauser, *La Poétique de Hugo,* 134–36 (Fr).

"Magnitudo parvi"

Frey, *"Les Contemplations,"* 65–66, 100–101 (Eng).

Gaudon, *Le Temps de la contemplation,* 255–58 (Fr).

S. Nash, *"Les Contemplations" of Victor Hugo,* 129–35 (Eng).

"Les Malheureux"

Cogman, *Hugo: Les Contemplations,* 33–34, 39–40 (Eng).

"Mazeppa"

Houston, *Victor Hugo,* 26–27, 30; rev. ed., 15–17 (Eng).

"Mélancholia"

Cogman, *Hugo: Les Contemplations,* 32–33, 37–38 (Eng).

Frey, *"Les Contemplations,"* 26–27, 34, 37, 44, 82–84, 102–3 (Eng).

Gaillard, *"Les Contemplations": Victor Hugo,* 42–44, 61–62 (Fr).

"Le Mendiant"

Cogman, *Hugo: Les Contemplations,* 38–39 (Eng).

"Mes deux filles"

Frey, *"Les Contemplations,"* 64, 91–92 (Eng).

S. Nash, *"Les Contemplations" of Victor Hugo,* 60–63, 85 (Eng).

HUGO, VICTOR, "La Mort du Duc de Berry"

"La Mort du Duc de Berry"

Houston, *Victor Hugo,* rev. ed., 3–4 (Eng).

"Mugitusque boum"

Cogman, *Hugo: Les Contemplations,* 66–67 (Eng).

"Nox"

Gaudon, *Le Temps de la contemplation,* 182–85 (Fr).

"Océan"

Gaudon, *Le Temps de la contemplation,* 205–7, 311 (Fr).
Raitt, *Life and Letters in France,* 66–74 (Eng).

"Les Oiseaux"

S. Nash, *"Les Contemplations" of Victor Hugo,* 94–96 (Eng).

"L'Ombre"

Jean-Bertrand Barrère, "Lecture de 'L'Ombre' *(Les Rayons et les ombres XXXIII),"* *CAIEF* 38 (May 1986): 257–65 (Fr).

"On loge à la nuit"

Wendy Greenberg, "Extended Metaphor in 'On loge à la nuit,' " *RR* 74 (November 1983): 441–54 (Eng).

"O strophe du poète"

Houston, *Victor Hugo,* 136–40; rev. ed., 131–35 (Eng).

S. Nash, *"Les Contemplations" of Victor Hugo,* 74–77 (Eng).

Timothy Raser, "The Fate of Beauty in Romantic Criticism," *NCFS* 14 (Spring–Summer 1986): 255–58 (Eng).

"Paroles sur la dune"

Auffret and Auffret, *Le Commentaire composé,* 91–100 (Fr).

S. Nash, *"Les Contemplations" of Victor Hugo,* 167–69 (Eng).

"Passé"

Py, *Les Mythes grecs,* 152–53 (Fr).

"Pasteurs et troupeaux"

Broome and Chesters, *The Appreciation of Modern French Poetry (1850–1950),* 64–67 (Eng).

Frey, *"Les Contemplations,"* 30, 95–96 (Eng).

Glauser, *La Poétique de Hugo,* 316–18 (Fr).

Houston, *Victor Hugo,* 134–36; rev. ed., 129–31 (Eng).

S. Nash, *"Les Contemplations" of Victor Hugo,* 41–50 (Eng).

"Pensar, dudar"

Edward K. Kaplan, "Victor Hugo and the Poetics of Doubt: The Transition of 1835–1837," *FrF* 6 (May 1981): 150–52 (Eng).

"La Pente de la rêverie"

Victor Brombert, "The Rhetoric of Contemplation: Hugo's 'La Pente de la rêverie,'" in Prendergast, ed., *Nineteenth-Century French Poetry,* 48–61 (Eng).

Gaudon, *Le Temps de la contemplation,* 46–53 (Fr).

Jean Gaudon, "Les Grandes manœuvres de 1829," *CAIEF* 38 (May 1986): 215–27 (Fr).

Glauser, *La Poétique de Hugo,* 54–57 (Fr).

Henri Peyre, *Hugo* (Paris: Presses Universitaires de France, 1972), 25–26 (Fr).

HUGO, VICTOR, "Le Petit Roi de Galice"

"Le Petit Roi de Galice"

Albouy, *La Création mythologique,* 140–41 (Fr).
Glauser, *La Poétique de Hugo,* 209–11, 288–92 (Fr).

"La Pitié suprême"

Glauser, *La Poétique de Hugo,* 158–59, 191–92, 280–83 (Fr).

"Plein ciel"

Glauser, *La Poétique de Hugo,* 483–88 (Fr).

"Pleurs dans la nuit"

Cogman, *Hugo: Les Contemplations,* 72–73, 74–77 (Eng).
Frey, *"Les Contemplations,"* 97, 132–140 (Eng).
Gaudon, *Le Temps de la contemplation,* 226–28 (Fr).
Glauser, *La Poétique de Hugo,* 61–62 (Fr).

"Le Poète bat aux champs"

Py, *Les Mythes grecs,* 94–97 (Fr).

"Le Pont"

S. Nash, *"Les Contemplations" of Victor Hugo,* 77–78, 171–72, 175, 184, 191–92 (Eng).

"La Prière pour tous, VII"

Glauser, *La Poétique de Hugo,* 332–33 (Fr).

"Promenade"

Claude Gély, *Victor Hugo, poète de l'intimité* (Paris: Nizet, 1969), 227–29 (Fr).

HUGO, VICTOR, "Le Sacre de la femme"

"Puits de l'Inde! tombeaux! monuments constellés!"

Glauser, *La Poétique de Hugo,* 327 (Fr).

"Que la musique date du seizième siècle"

Houston, *Victor Hugo,* 79–81, rev. ed., 20–22 (Eng).

"Réponse è un acte d'accusation"

Gaudon, *Le Temps de la contemplation,* 243–44 (Fr).

Glauser, *La Poétique de Hugo,* 338–40 (Fr).

"La République-Constitution"

Nichola Haxell, "Hugo, Gautier, and the Obelisk of Luxor," *NCFS* 18 (Fall–Winter 1989–90): 67–69 (Eng).

"Le Retour de l'empereur"

Gaudon, *Le Temps de la contemplation,* 121–23 (Fr).

"La Rose de l'infante"

Glauser, *La Poétique de Hugo,* 227–39 (Fr).

"Le Rouet d'Omphale"

Cogman, *Hugo: Les Contemplations,* 45–47 (Eng).

S. Nash, *"Les Contemplations" of Victor Hugo,* 63–67, 116–22 (Eng).

"Le Sacre de la femme"

Glauser, *La Poétique de Hugo,* 101–3 (Fr).

HUGO, VICTOR, "Sagesse"

"Sagesse"

Gaudon, *Le Temps de la contemplation,* 114–18 (Fr).

"Saison des semailles"

Patricia A. Ward, "Victor Hugo's Creative Process in 'Saison des semailles,' " *FS* 26 (October 1972): 421–29 (Eng).

Saison des semailles
"Le Soir"

Katz and Hall, *Explicating French Texts,* 46–51 (Fr).

"Sara la baigneuse"

Ross Chambers, "Pour une poétique du vêtement," in Gray, ed., *Poétiques,* 24–29 (Fr).

"Satan dans la nuit"

Albouy, *La Création mythologique,* 279–84 (Fr).

Houston, *Victor Hugo,* 96–98; rev. ed., 68–70 (Eng).

"Le Satyre"

Albouy, *La Création mythologique,* 102, 106, 236–42 (Fr).

Bénichou, *Les Mages romantiques,* 469–74 (Fr).

Paul Comeau, " 'Le Satyre' dans 'La Légende des siècles' de Victor Hugo," *FR* 39 (May 1966): 849–61 (Fr).

Denommé, *Nineteenth-Century French Romantic Poets,* 125–28 (Eng).

Gaudon, *Le Temps de la contemplation,* 375–78 (Fr).

Glauser, *La Poétique de Hugo,* 107–25 (Fr).

Michel Grimaud, "Les Mystères du 'Ptyx': Hypothèses sur la remotivation psychopoétique à partir de Mallarmé et Hugo," in Gray, ed., *Poétiques,* 100–108 (Fr).

Houston, *Victor Hugo,* 120–24; rev. ed., 115–19 (Eng).

Py, *Les Mythes grecs,* 98–103, 161–64, 238–40 (Fr).

Monique Saigal, " 'Le Satyre' de Victor Hugo, poète justicier," *ECr* 16 (Fall 1976): 198–206 (Fr).

"Soleils couchants I"

Glauser, *La Poétique de Hugo,* 303–6 (Fr).

"Sous les arbres"

Frey, *"Les Contemplations,"* 41 (Eng).

"Spes"

Jules Brody, " 'Let There Be Night': Intertextuality in a Poem of Victor Hugo," *RR* 75 (March 1984): 216–29 (Eng).

"La Statue"

Frey, *"Les Contemplations,"* 98–99, 102–3 (Eng).

"Les Statues"

Albouy, *La Création mythologique,* 141–43 (Fr).

"Suite"

Gaudon, *Le Temps de la contemplation,* 246 (Fr).
Glauser, *La Poétique de Hugo,* 179–81 (Fr).

"Ténèbres"

Glauser, *La Poétique de Hugo,* 20–21, 260–61 (Fr).

HUGO, VICTOR, "Les Têtes du sérail"

"Les Têtes du sérail"

Richard B. Grant, "Sequence and Theme in Victor Hugo's 'Les Orientales,'" *PMLA* 94 (October 1979): 897 (Eng).

"Le Titan"

Glauser, *La Poétique de Hugo,* 143–45 (Fr).

Michel Grimaud, "Les Mystères du 'Ptyx': Hypothèses sur la remotivation psychopoétique à partir de Mallarmé et Hugo," in Gray, ed., *Poétiques,* 136–47 (Fr).

Py, *Les Mythes grecs,* 224–25, 228–32 (Fr).

J. Weber, *Genèse de l'œuvre poétique,* 135–38 (Fr).

"Tout le passé et tout l'avenir"

Gaudon, *Le Temps de la contemplation,* 228–30 (Fr).

"Tristesse d'Olympio"

Denommé, *Nineteenth-Century French Romantic Poets,* 96–99 (Eng).

Robert Denommé, "The Palimpsest of the Poet's Remembrance in Hugo's 'Tristesse d'Olympio,'" *KRQ* 29, no. 1 (1982): 15–24 (Eng).

Gaudon, *Le Temps de la contemplation,* 75 (Fr).

Glauser, *La Poétique de Hugo,* 328–31 (Fr).

Patricia A. Ward, " 'Tristesse d'Olympio' and the Romantic Nature Experience," *NCFS* 7 (Fall–Winter 1978–79): 4–6, 11–16 (Eng).

Eléonore M. Zimmermann, "Un Héritage romantique dévoyé: L'Apostrophe dans 'Le Lac,' 'Tristesse d'Olympio,' et 'La Chevelure,'" *FrF* 13 (May 1988): 208–10 (Fr).

"La Trompette du jugement"

Glauser, *La Poétique de Hugo,* 493–96 (Fr).

"Le Vautour"

Albouy, *La Création mythologique,* 111–12, 221–22 (Fr).

Glauser, *La Poétique de Hugo,* 77–78 (Fr).

"La Vie aux champs"

S. Nash, *"Les Contemplations" of Victor Hugo,* 87, 94–96 (Eng).

"La Vision de Dante"

Gaudon, *Le Temps de la contemplation,* 184–89 (Fr).

Glauser, *La Poétique de Hugo,* 59–61 (Fr).

Houston, *Victor Hugo,* rev. ed., 62–64, 91–92 (Eng).

"La Vision d'où est sorti ce livre"

Glauser, *La Poétique de Hugo,* 358–61 (Fr).

Joan Kessler, " 'Cette Babel du monde': Visionary Architecture in the Poetry . . . ," *NCFS* 19 (Spring 1991): 423–25 (Eng).

"Les Voix intérieures"

Denommé, *Nineteenth-Century French Romantic Poets,* 118–19 (Eng).

"Le Voyage"

Claude Gély, *Victor Hugo, poète de l'intimité* (Paris: Nizet, 1969), 230–32 (Fr).

"Zim-Zizimi"

Glauser, *La Poétique de Hugo,* 199–202 (Fr).

JACCOTTET, PHILIPPE

"Airs"

Daniel Delas, "Propositions pour une théorie de la production textuelle et intertextuelle," *RR* 66 (March 1975): 123–39 (Fr).

"A travers un verger"

Richard Stamelman, "The Unseizable Landscape of the Real: The Poetry and Poetics of Philippe Jaccottet," *Studies in Twentieth Century Literature* 13 (Winter 1989): 68–76. Reprinted in Stamelman, ed., *Lost Beyond Telling,* 207–13, 215–18 (Eng).

"La Semaison"

Richard Stamelman, "Landscape and Loss in Yves Bonnefoy and Philippe Jaccottet," *FrF* 5 (January 1980): 43–44 (Eng).

JACOB, MAX

"Avenue du Maine"

Dubosclard and Dubosclard, *Du surréalisme à la Resistance,* 9–15 (Fr).

"Le Christ au cinématographe"

S. I. Lockerbie, "Realism and Fantasy in the Work of Max Jacob," in Beaumont, Cocking, and Cruickshank, eds., *Order and Adventure in Post-Romantic French Poetry,* 157–58 (Eng).

"Honneur de la Sardane et de la Tenora"

S. I. Lockerbie, "Realism and Fantasy in the Work of Max Jacob," in Beaumont, Cocking, and Cruickshank, eds., *Order and Adventure in Post-Romantic French Poetry,* 158–59 (Eng).

JARRY, ALFRED

"Le Sablier"

Groupe Mu, *Rhétorique de la poésie: Lecture linéaire, lecture tabulaire* (Bruxelles: Editions Complexes, 1977): 279–82 (Fr).

JAUFRE RUDEL

"Belhs m'es l'estius"

Topsfield, *Troubadours and Love,* 54–61 (Eng).

"Lanquan li jorn son lonc en mai"

William D. Paden, "Utrum Copularentum of Cors," *ECr* 19 (Winter 1979): 78–79 (Eng).

Topsfield, *Troubadours and Love,* 61–67 (Eng).

"Pro ai del chan essenhadors"

Topsfield, *Troubadours and Love,* 51–54 (Eng).

"Quan lo rius de la fontana"

Topsfield, *Troubadours and Love,* 49–51 (Eng).

"Quan lo rossinhols el folhos"

Topsfield, *Troubadours and Love,* 45–49 (Eng).

JODELLE, ETIENNE

"A Luy mesme"

Gale Crouse, "The Artistic Development of the 'Sonnet rapporté': Jodelle's Unsung Success," *SFr* 29 (January–April 1985): 65 (Eng).

JODELLE, ETIENNE, "Aux communes douleurs"

"Aux communes douleurs qui poindre en ce jour viennent"

Tilde Sankovitch, "Etienne Jodelle and the Mystic-Erotic Experience," *BHR* 40 (May 1978): 250–52 (Eng).

Marcel Tetel, "L'Effacement du 'tu' chez Jodelle," in Kritzman, ed., *Le Signe et le texte,* 70–71 (Fr).

"Chaque temple en ce jour donne argument fort ample"

Tilde Sankovitch, "Etienne Jodelle and the Mystic-Erotic Experience," *BHR* 40 (May 1978): 258–59 (Eng).

"Comme un qui s'est perdu dans la forest profonde"

Bots, *Joachim Du Bellay entre l'histoire littéraire,* 128–35 (Fr).

H. Weber, *La Création poétique au XVIe siècle en France,* 301–2 (Fr).

"De moy-mesme je sui dévotieux, Madame"

Tilde Sankovitch, "Etienne Jodelle and the Mystic-Erotic Experience," *BHR* 40 (May 1978): 252–56 (Eng).

"Des astres, des forests, et d'Acheron l'honneur"

Gale Crouse, "The Artistic Development of the 'Sonnet rapporté': Jodelle's Unsung Success," *SFr* 29 (January–April 1985): 66–67 (Eng).

James Martin, "A Manner of Seeing: Perception in Late Renaissance Poetry," *ECr* 24 (Summer 1984): 77–78 (Eng).

"Des Guerres du Roy Henry Deuxiesme contre l'Empereur
Charles Cinquiesme"

Gale Crouse, "The Artistic Development of the 'Sonnet rapporté': Jodelle's Unsung Success," *SFr* 29 (January–April 1985): 68 (Eng).

JOUVE, PIERRE JEAN, "Hauts-fourneaux"

"L'Epithalame de Madame Marguerite"

Yvonne Bellenger, "Quelques poèmes autobiographiques au XVIe siècle: Fiction et vérité," *SFr* 22 (May–December 1978): 224–25 (Fr).

"Passant dernierement des Alpes au travers"

Marcel Tetel, "L'Effacement du 'tu' chez Jodelle," in Kritzman, ed., *Le Signe et le texte,* 69–70 (Fr).

JOUVE, PIERRE JEAN

"Le 11 novembre 1918, jour de la Victoire"

Callander, *The Poetry of Pierre Jean Jouve,* 61–62 (Eng).

"Les Aéroplanes"

Callander, *The Poetry of Pierre Jean Jouve,* 28–32 (Eng).

"Auguries of Innocence"

Daniel E. Rivas, " 'Noces' et au-delà: Notes sur les morts" (translation of stanza 1 of William Blake's "Auguries of Innocence"), *RLM* 757–61 (1985): 17–19 (Fr).

"La Brouette"

Jean-Michel Solente, "La Poésie de Pierre Jean Jouve: Chant spirituel et champ freudien," *RLM* 757–761 (1985): 41–42 (Fr).

"Coffre de fer"

Stamelman, *Lost Beyond Telling,* 100–101 (Eng).

"Hauts-fourneaux"

Callander, *The Poetry of Pierre Jean Jouve,* 13–14 (Eng).

JOUVE, PIERRE JEAN, "Hélène"

"Hélène"

Martine Broda, *Jouve* (Lausanne: L'Age d'Homme, 1981), 60–73 (Fr).

Stamelman, *Lost Beyond Telling,* 104–6 (Eng).

Jerôme Thélot, "Hélène, Lisbé," *RLM* 757–61 (1985): 83–95 (Fr).

"Hymne à un enfant"

Callander, *The Poetry of Pierre Jean Jouve,* 32–33 (Eng).

Daniel Leuwers, *Jouve avant Jouve; ou, La Naissance d'un poète (1906–1928)* (Paris: Klincksieck, 1984), 71–72 (Fr).

"Mnémosyne"

Daniel E. Rivas, "Jouve's 'Mnémosyne': an Alchemical View," *ECr* 18 (Summer 1978): 53–61 (Eng).

"Nada"

Martine Broda, *Jouve* (Lausanne: L'Age d'Homme, 1981), 50–58 (Fr).

"Noces"

Daniel E. Rivas, " 'Noces' et au-delà: Notes sur les morts," *RLM* 757–61 (1985): 17 (Fr).

"Ode"

Martine Broda, *Jouve* (Lausanne: L'Age d'Homme, 1981), 142–43 (Fr).

"Les Ordres qui changent"

Callander, *The Poetry of Pierre Jean Jouve,* 24–28 (Eng).

JOUVE, PIERRE JEAN, "Le Tableau"

"Le Paradis perdu"

Callander, *The Poetry of Pierre Jean Jouve,* 110–32 (Eng).

Bruno Gelas, "L'Épisode et la scène dans 'Le Paradis perdu,'" *RLM* 757–61 (1985): 25–37 (Fr).

"Pays d'Hélène"

Margaret Callander, "Jouve: 'Pays d'Hélène,' " in Nurse, ed., *The Art of Criticism,* 275–85 (Eng).

"Prière dans la cité d'hiver"

Daniel Leuwers, *Jouve avant Jouve; ou, La Naissance d'un poète (1906–1928)* (Paris: Klincksieck, 1984), 219–21 (Fr).

"La Résurrection des morts"

Mary Anne O'Neil, "Pierre-Jean Jouve's 'La Résurrection des morts': A contemporary devotional sequence," *FrF* 6 (September 1981): 259–72 (Eng).

"Songe"

Daniel E. Rivas, " 'Noces' et au-delà: Notes sur les morts," *RLM* 757–61 (1985): 14–16 (Fr).

"Sueur de sang"

Daniel E. Rivas, "Jouve's 'Suns in the Heart'': Elements for a Poetics," *FrF* 7 (May 1982): 117–31 (Eng).

"Le Tableau"

Stamelman, *Lost Beyond Telling,* 108–10 (Eng).

LABE, LOUISE, "Tempo di Mozart"

"Tempo di Mozart"

Martine Broda, *Jouve* (Lausanne: L'Age d'Homme, 1981), 99–106 (Fr).

"Vie de la tombe d'Hélène"

Stamelman, *Lost Beyond Telling,* 112–14 (Eng).

"La Vierge de Paris"

Daniel E. Rivas, "Jouve's 'Suns in the Heart': Elements for a Poetics," *FrF* 7 (May 1982): 126–29 (Eng).

LABE, LOUISE

"Après qu'un tems la gresle et le tonnere"

Cameron, *Louise Labé,* 77–78 (Eng).

"Au temps qu'Amour, d'hommes et dieus vainquer"

Donaldson-Evans, *Love's Fatal Glance,* 63–65 (Eng).

"Baise m'encor, rebaise moy et baise"

Cameron, *Louise Labé,* 78–80 (Eng).

François Rigolot, "Signature et signification: Les Baisers de Louise Labé," *RR* 75 (January 1984): 16–20 (Fr).

"Car je suis tant navrée en toutes pars"

Cameron, *Louise Labé,* 64–65 (Eng).

"Depuis qu'Amour cruel empoisonna"

Cameron, *Louise Labé,* 65–66 (Eng).

Sandy Petry, "The Character of the Speaker in the Poetry of Louise Labé," *FR* 43 (March 1970): 590–91, 592 (Eng).

LABE, LOUISE, "Lut, compagnon de ma calamité"

"D'un tel vouloir le serf point me désire"

Wilson Baldridge, "Le Langage de la séparation chez Louise Labé," *EL* 20 (Autumn 1987): 70-71 (Fr).

François Rigolot, "Quel genre d'amour pour Louise Labé?" *Poétique* 14 (September 1983): 308–10, 316 (Fr).

"Elégie I"

François Rigolot, "Louise Labé et les 'Dames lionnoises': Les Ambiguïtés de la censure," in Kritzman, ed., *Le Signe et le texte,* 16–17, 20–21 (Fr).

"Elégie III"

François Rigolot, "Louise Labé et les 'Dames lionnoises': Les Ambiguïtés de la censure," in Kritzman, ed., *Le Signe et le texte,* 18–20, 22 (Fr).

"Et quand je suis quasi toute cassée"

Cameron, *Louise Labé,* 66 (Eng).

"Je vis, je meurs, je me brule et noye"

Cameron, *Louise Labé,* 68–69 (Eng).

"Las! que me sert que si parfaitement"

Cameron, *Louise Labé,* 83–84 (Eng).

Donaldson-Evans, *Love's Fatal Glance,* 74–75 (Eng).

"Lut, compagnon de ma calamité"

Paul Audouin, *Maurice Scève, Pernette Du Guillet, Louise Labé: L'Amour à Lyon au temps de la Renaissance* (Paris: Nizet, 1981), 155–56 (Fr).

Donald Stone, "Labé's Sonnet 12: A New Reading," *BHR* 49 (June 1987): 379–82 (Eng).

LABE, LOUISE, "Mais fais Ami, qui ne soit dangereuse"

"Mais fais Ami, qui ne soit dangereuse"

Cameron, *Louise Labé,* 68 (Eng).

"Mais quand je voy si nubileus aprets"

Sharlene Poliner, " 'Signes d'Amants' and the Dispossessed Lover," *BHR* 26 (May 1984): 340–42 (Eng).

"Ne reprenez, Dames, si j'ay aymé"

Cameron, *Louise Labé,* 84–85 (Eng).

"O beaus yeus bruns ô regars destournez"

Wilson Baldridge, "Le Langage de la séparation chez Louise Labé," *ELit* 20 (Autumn 1987): 71–72 (Fr).

Cameron, *Louise Labé,* 62–64 (Eng).

Donaldson-Evans, *Love's Fatal Glance,* 67–68 (Eng).

Nicolas Ruwet, "Analyse structurale d'un poème français: Un Sonnet de Louise Labé," *Linguistics* 3 (1964): 62–83. Reprinted in Nicolas Ruwet, *Musique, langage, poésie* (Paris: Seuil, 1972), 176–99 (Fr).

"O dous regard, o yeus pleins de beauté"

Donaldson-Evans, *Love's Fatal Glance,* 72–73 (Eng).

"Par toy, ami, tant vesqui enflammes"

Cameron, *Louise Labé,* 43–44 (Eng).

"Pour le retour du soleil honorer"

Paul Audouin, *Maurice Scève, Pernette Du Guillet, Louise Labé: L'Amour à Lyon au temps de la Renaissance* (Paris: Nizet, 1981), 156–57 (Fr).

LABE, LOUISE, "Tout aussi to que je commence à prendre"

"Quand j'aperçoy ton blond chef couronné"

Andrea Chan, "The Function of the Beloved in the Poetry of Louise Labé," *AJFS* 17 (January–April 1980): 51–52 (Eng).

"Quand vous lirez, ô Dames Lionnoises"

Cameron, *Louise Labé,* 42–43, 44–45 (Eng).

"Quelle grandeur rend l'homme venerable?"

Cameron, *Louise Labé,* 81–82 (Eng).

Françoise Charpentier, "Les Voix du désir: Le 'Débat de Folie et d'Amour' de Louise Labé" in Kritzman, ed., *Le Signe et le texte,* 28–29 (Fr).

Sandy Petry, "The Character of the Speaker in the Poetry of Louise Labé," *FR* 43 (March 1970): 591–94 (Eng).

"Tant de vertus qui te font estre aymé"

Cameron, *Louise Labé,* 71–72 (Eng).

"Tant que mes yeux pourront larmes espandre"

Cameron, *Louise Labé,* 74–75 (Eng).

Nicolas Ruwet, "L'Analyse structurale de la poésie," *Linguistics* 2 (1963): 38–59. Reprinted in Nicolas Ruwet, *Musique, langage, poésie* (Paris: Seuil, 1972), 160–64, 169–75 (Fr).

"Tel n'ayme point, qu'une Dame aymera"

Cameron, *Louise Labé,* 42, 44–45 (Eng).

"Tout aussi to que je commence à prendre"

Cameron, *Louise Labé,* 69–70 (Eng).

LA CEPPEDE, JEAN DE

Théorèmes, Book 1, Meslanges
"Au Pied de la Croix sanglante"

Cave, *Devotional Poetry,* 181–91 (Eng).

Théorèmes, Book 1, Sonnet 1
"Je chante les amours, les armes, la victoire"

Donaldson-Evans, *Poésie et méditation,* 19–21 (Fr).

Théorèmes, Book 1, Sonnet 8
"Mais qui vous meut, Seigneur, de sortir à cette heure?"

Donaldson-Evans, *Poésie et méditation,* 24–26, 154–55 (Fr).

Théorèmes, Book 1, Sonnet 21
"Quand Rachel s'accoucha (pour son dernier mal-heur)"

Donaldson-Evans, *Poésie et méditation,* 79 (Fr).

Théorèmes, Book 1, Sonnet 38
"S'escartant donc un peu de sa majestueuse"

Donaldson-Evans, *Poésie et méditation,* 168–69 (Fr).

Théorèmes, Book 1, Sonnet 39
"Cette rouge sueur goutte à goutte roulante"

Lance K. Donaldson-Evans, "The Theme of Blood and the Agony of Christ in the Work of French Baroque Poets," *FR* 45 (Special Issue 3) (Fall 1971): 134–35 (Eng).

Gerald Gillespie, "Ceppède's Sonnet ('Cette rouge sueur goutte à goutte roulante')," *Expl* 25 (December 1966): 8–9 (Eng).

Edward Wilson, "Notes on a Sonnet by La Ceppède," *FS* 22 (October 1968): 296–301 (Eng).

Théorèmes, Book 1, Sonnet 41
"Et vous, braves Soldats, de ce Chef tant aimez"

Donaldson-Evans, *Poésie et méditation*, 128–29 (Fr).

Théorèmes, Book 1, Sonnet 49
"Comme il arraisonnoit le traistre Iscarien"

Donaldson-Evans, *Poésie et méditation*, 33–34 (Fr).

Théorèmes, Book 1, Sonnet 77
"Ni des Poles glacez les eternelles nuicts"

Donaldson-Evans, *Poésie et méditation*, 140–41 (Fr).

Théorèmes, Book 1, Sonnet 85
"Et vous sacrez Fleurons que la Bise funeste"

Donaldson-Evans, *Poésie et méditation*, 129–30 (Fr).

Théorèmes, Book 1, Sonnet 86
"Insolente rumeur de la tourbe indiscrète"

Donaldson-Evans, *Poésie et méditation*, 32–33 (Fr).

Théorèmes, Book 1, Sonnet 88
"Maintefois j'ay tenté de vous suivre ô ma vie"

J. D. Lyons, "The Poetic Habit: A Metaphor in La Ceppède and Mallarmé," *FMLS* 11 (July 1975): 227–30, 232–33 (Eng).

Théorèmes, Book 1, Sonnet 91
"Or sus donc serrez fort, liez fort, ô canaille"

Donaldson-Evans, *Poésie et méditation*, 26–28 (Fr).

219

LA CEPPEDE, JEAN DE, *Théorèmes, Book 1, Sonnet 94*

Théorèmes, Book 1, Sonnet 94
"O l'amour de mon âme, ô non pareil Amant"

Paul Chilton, *The Poetry of Jean de La Ceppède: A Study in Text and Context* (Oxford and London: Oxford University Press, 1977), 192–93 (Eng).

Donaldson-Evans, *Poésie et méditation,* 170–71 (Fr).

Théorèmes, Book 2, Sonnet 1
"Erreurs, les horreurs de cette nuict m'esfrayent"

Donaldson-Evans, *Poésie et méditation,* 21–23 (Fr).

Théorèmes, Book 2, Sonnet 31
"L'Apostre n'eut jamais veu l'horreur effroyable"

Donaldson-Evans, *Poésie et méditation,* 171–72 (Fr).

Théorèmes, Book 2, Sonnet 54
"Blanc est le vestement du grand Pere sans âge"

Donaldson-Evans, *Poésie et méditation,* 28–30, 137 (Fr).

Théorèmes, Book 2, Sonnet 63
"Aux Monarques vaincueurs la rouge cotte d'armes"

Calin, *In Defense of French Poetry,* 118–21 (Eng).

Cave, *Devotional Poetry,* 239–42 (Eng).

Donaldson-Evans, *Poésie et méditation,* 30–32, 136–37, 155–56 (Fr).

Théorèmes, Book 2, Sonnet 65
"Nature n'a rien fait qu'on doive mépriser"

Donaldson-Evans, *Poésie et méditation,* 172–73 (Fr).

Théorèmes, Book 2, Sonnet 67
"O Royauté tragique! ô vestement infame!"

Donaldson-Evans, *Poésie et méditation*, 50–53 (Fr).

Théorèmes, Book 2, Sonnet 68
"Mais que dis-je, ô mon Prince, ignorant je diffame"

Donaldson-Evans, *Poésie et méditation*, 50–53 (Fr).

Théorèmes, Book 2, Sonnet 69
"Quand ces prophanes mains du devoir forvoyantes"

Donaldson-Evans, *Poésie et méditation*, 34–35 (Fr).

Théorèmes, Book 2, Sonnet 71
"Jadis ce grand Ouvrier forma ce grand ouvrage"

Donaldson-Evans, *Poésie et méditation*, 80–81 (Fr)

Théorèmes, Book 2, Sonnet 72
"Bon vieillard maudit sa primogeniture"

Donaldson-Evans, *Poésie et méditation*, 81–83 (Fr).

Théorèmes, Book 2, Sonnet 74
"Pilate cuidoit rendre à la pitié playable"

Donaldson-Evans, *Poésie et méditation*, 53–55 (Fr).

Théorèmes, Book 3, Sonnet 1
"Qui m'ouvrira les rangs? Qui me fendra la presse?"

Donaldson-Evans, *Poésie et méditation*, 23–24 (Fr).

Théorèmes, Book 3, Sonnet 23
"L'autel des vieux parfums dans Solyme encensé"

Donaldson-Evans, *Poésie et méditation*, 75–77 (Fr).

LA CEPPEDE, JEAN DE, *Théorèmes, Book 3, Sonnet 24*

Théorèmes, Book 3, Sonnet 24
"Voicy le seur Baston, qui servit de bateau"

Donaldson-Evans, *Poésie et méditation,* 77–79 (Fr).

Théorèmes, Book 3, Sonnet 71
"Si le Père Eternel son cher fils abandonne"

Paul Chilton, *The Poetry of Jean de La Ceppède: A Study in Text and Context* (Oxford and London: Oxford University Press, 1977), 189–90 (Eng).

Théorèmes, Book 3, Sonnet 75
"Amende donc tes mœurs, pauvre Samaritaine"

Donaldson-Evans, *Poésie et méditation,* 73–75 (Fr).

Théorèmes, Book 3, Sonnet 90
"Si la Terre à regret ce Gibet soustenant"

Donaldson-Evans, *Poésie et méditation,* 175–77 (Fr).

LA FONTAINE, JEAN DE

"L'Abbesse"

Lapp, *The Esthetics of Negligence,* 124–26 (Eng).

"Adonis"

Jacqueline Van Baelen, "La Chasse d'Adonis," *ECr* 21 (Winter 1981): 22–27 (Fr).

Emile Bessette, "Présence de Virgile dans l'Adonis' de La Fontaine," *SFr* 12 (May–August 1968): 287–96 (Fr).

William Calin, "Militia and Armor: A Reading of 'Adonis,'" *ECr* 21 (Winter 1981): 28–40 (Eng).

Jean-Pierre Collinet, "La Fontaine et l'Italie," *SFr* 12 (May–August 1968): 119–20 (Fr).

Collinet, *Le Monde littéraire de La Fontaine,* 41–81 (Fr).

Gutwirth, *Un Merveilleux sans éclat,* 43–49 (Fr).

Kohn, *Le Goût de La Fontaine,* 63–64, 95–110 (Fr).

Lapp, *The Brazen Tower,* 65–75, 103–119 (Eng).

John C. Lapp, "Ronsard and La Fontaine: Two Versions of 'Adonis,'" *ECr* 10 (Summer 1970): 132–44 (Eng).

Georges Molinié, "Sur l'Adonis de La Fontaine," *RHL* 75 (September–October 1975): 707–29 (Fr).

Marie-Odile Sweetser, "Adonis, poème d'amour: Conventions et création poétiques," *ECr* 21 (Winter 1981): 41–49 (Fr).

Zobediah Youssef, "Le Temps des amours dans l'onde irréversible: L''Adonis' de La Fontaine," *SFr* 22 (May–December 1978): 241–49 (Fr).

"L'Aigle et la Pie"

Gutwirth, *Un Merveilleux sans éclat,* 103–4 (Fr).

"L'Aigle et le Hibou"

Gutwirth, *Un Merveilleux sans éclat,* 200–202 (Fr).

"L'Aigle et l'Escarbot"

Gutwirth, *Un Merveilleux sans éclat,* 114–16 (Fr).

"L'Aigle, la Laie, et la Chatte"

Guiton, *La Fontaine,* 94–96 (Eng).

"L'Alouette et ses petits avec le Maître d'un champ"

Georges Maurand, "Les 'Enfants' des Fables de La Fontaine: Essai d'analyse actantielle d'un personnage," *LCL* 14 (January 1991): 143–44 (Fr).

A Monsieur de Vendôme
"Prince, qui faites les délices"

Collinet, *Le Monde littéraire de La Fontaine,* 404–5 (Fr).

LA FONTAINE, JEAN DE, *A Monsieur de Vendôme*

A Monsieur de Vendôme
"Quand on croyait la campagne achevée"

Collinet, *Le Monde littéraire de La Fontaine,* 403–4 (Fr).

"L'Amour et la Folie"

Kohn, *Le Goût de La Fontaine,* 246–47 (Fr).

"Les Amours de Psyché et de Cupidon"

Jean Lafond, "La Beauté et la grâce: L'Esthétique 'platonicienne' des 'Amours de Psyché,'" *RHL* 69 (May–August 1969): 475–90 (Fr).

Margaret McGowan, "La Fontaine's Technique of Withdrawal in 'Les Amours de Psyché et de Cupidon,'" *FS* 18 (October 1964): 322–31 (Eng).

Michael Vincent, "Voice and Text: Representations of Reading in La Fontaine's 'Psyché,'" *FR* 57 (December 1983): 179–86 (Eng).

Zobediah Youssef, "Le Thème du miroir dans 'Les Amours de Psyché et de Cupidon,'" *KRQ* 25, no. 3 (1978): 269–81 (Fr).

"Un Animal dans la Lune"

Beverly S. Ridgely, "Astrology and Astronomy in the 'Fables' of La Fontaine," *PMLA* 80 (June 1965): 186–89 (Eng).

Maya Slater, "Butler, La Fontaine, and the Elephant in the Moon," *FSB* 23 (Summer 1987): 5–10 (Eng).

"Les Animaux malades de la peste"

Guiton, *La Fontaine,* 101–4 180–81 (Eng).

J. Moravcevich, "Reason and Rhetoric in the Fables of La Fontaine," *AJFS* 16 (January–April 1979): 357–58 (Eng).

"L'Araignée et l'Hirondelle"

Guiton, *La Fontaine,* 105–6, 182–83 (Eng).

LA FONTAINE, JEAN DE, "Le Berger et le Roi"

"A Son Altesse Monseigneur le Duc de Vendôme"

Collinet, *Le Monde littéraire de La Fontaine,* 399–400 (Fr).

A Son Altesse Sérénissime Monseigneur le Prince de Conti
"Prince vaillant, humain et sage"

Collinet, *Le Monde littéraire de La Fontaine,* 400–403 (Fr).

"L'Astrologue qui se laisse tomber dans un puits"

Beverly S. Ridgely, "Astrology and Astronomy in the 'Fables' of La Fontaine," *PMLA* 80 (June 1965): 181–83 (Eng).

"L'Aveugle et le serpent"

Patrick Dandrey, "Séduction du pouvoir: La Fontaine, le berger, et le roi," *CLDS* 8 (1986): 11–22 (Fr).

"Le Bassa et le Marchand"

Collinet, *Le Monde littéraire de La Fontaine,* 214 (Fr).

"Belphégor"

Kohn, *Le Goût de La Fontaine,* 297–99 (Fr).

"Le Berceau"

Lapp, *The Esthetics of Negligence,* 51–52 (Eng).

"Le Berger et le Roi"

Collinet, *Le Monde littéraire de La Fontaine,* 216–17 (Fr).

Patrick Dandrey, "Séduction du pouvoir" La Fontaine, le berger, et le roi," *CLDS* 8 (1986): 9–32 (Fr).

Gutwirth, *Un Merveilleux sans éclat,* 207–9 (Fr).

LA FONTAINE, JEAN DE, "La Besace"

"La Besace"

Guy Mermier and Yvette Boilly-Widmer Mermier, *Explication de texte, théorie et pratique* (Glenview, Il.: Scott, Foresman, 1972), 72–79 (Fr).

"Le Calendrier des vieillards"

Lapp, *The Esthetics of Negligence,* 71–72, 87 (Eng).

"La Captivité de Saint Malc"

Jean-Dominique Biard, "La Fontaine et Du Bartas," *SFr* 7 (May–August 1963): 279–82 (Fr).

Collinet, *Le Monde littéraire de La Fontaine,* 313–24 (Fr).

Gutwirth, *Un Merveilleux sans éclat,* 49–56 (Fr).

Marcel Gutwirth, "Poésie et sainteté: La Captivité de Saint Malc," *RR* 70 (May 1979): 234–48 (Fr).

Kohn, *Le Goût de La Fontaine,* 254–55 (Fr).

"Cas de conscience"

Catherine Grisé, "La Casuistique dans les 'Contes' de La Fontaine," *SFr* 33 (September–December 1989): 414–15 (Fr).

Gutwirth, *Un Merveilleux sans éclat,* 84–87 (Fr).

Lapp, *The Esthetics of Negligence,* 154–56 (Eng).

"Le Cerf se voyant dans l'eau"

Gutwirth, *Un Merveilleux sans éclat,* 169–71 (Fr).

"Le Chameau et les Bâtons flottants"

Collinet, *Le Monde littéraire de La Fontaine,* 196–98 (Fr).

LA FONTAINE, JEAN DE, "La Chose impossible"

"Le Charlatan"

Gutwirth, *Un Merveilleux sans éclat,* 216–18 (Fr).

René Jasinski, "De quelques contresens sur les 'Fables,'" *Europe* 50 (March 1972): 31–32 (Fr).

"Le Chat et un vieux Rat"

Collinet, *Le Monde littéraire de La Fontaine,* 191–96 (Fr).

"Le Chat, la Belette et le petit Lapin"

Michael Vincent, "Naming names in La Fontaine's 'Le Chat, la Belette et le petit Lapin,'" *RR* 73 (May 1982): 292–301 (Eng).

"La Chatte métamorphosée en Femme"

Danner, *Patterns of Irony,* 139–48 (Eng).

"La Chauve-Souris et les deux Belettes"

René Jasinski, "De quelques contresens sur les 'Fables,'" *Europe* 50 (March 1972): 33–34 (Fr).

"Le Chêne et le Roseau"

Marcel Gutwirth, "'Le Chêne et le Roseau,' ou Les Cheminements de la mimésis," *FR* 48 (March 1975): 695–702 (Fr).

"Le Cheval s'étant voulu venger du Cerf"

Jean-Dominique Biard, "La Fontaine et Du Bartas," *SFr* 7 (May–August 1963): 285–86 (Fr).

"La Chose impossible"

Lapp, *The Esthetics of Negligence,* 144–45 (Eng).

Marc Soriano, "Des contes aux fables," *Europe* 50 (March 1972): 109–10 (Fr).

LA FONTAINE, JEAN DE, "La Cigale et la Fourmi"

"La Cigale et la Fourmi"

Jean-Pierre Collinet, "Une Etude collective de 'La Cigale et la Fourmi,'" *Europe* 50 (March 1972): 142–44 (Fr).

J. H. Fabre, "Une Etude collective de 'La Cigale et la Fourmi,'" *Europe* 50 (March 1972): 134–35 (Fr).

Jean Gartempe, "Une Etude collective de 'La Cigale et la Fourmi,'" *Europe* 50 (March 1972): 144–45 (Fr).

Jacques Gaucheron, "Une Etude collective de 'La Cigale et la Fourmi,'" *Europe* 50 (March 1972): 139–42 (Fr).

Gutwirth, *Un Merveilleux sans éclat,* 160–62 (Fr).

René Jasinski, "Une Etude collective de 'La Cigale et la Fourmi,'" *Europe* 50 (March 1972): 135–39 (Fr).

Jacques-Henri Périvier, "'La Cigale et la Fourmi' comme introduction aux 'Fables,'" *FR* 42 (February 1969): 419–27 (Fr).

J. J. Rousseau, "Avez-vous lu 'La Cigale et la Fourmi'?" *Europe* 50 (March 1972): 132–34 (Fr).

David Lee Rubin, "Four Modes of Double Irony in La Fontaine's 'Fables,'" in Bayley and Coleman, eds., *The Equilibrium of Wit,* 207–8 (Eng).

"Le Cocu battu et content"

Lapp, *The Esthetics of Negligence,* 53–54 (Eng).

"Comment l'esprit vient aux filles"

Gutwirth, *Un Merveilleux sans éclat,* 81–83 (Fr).

"Les Compagnons d'Ulysse"

Pierre Bornecque, "Thèmes et organisation des 'Fables,'" *Europe* 50 (March 1972): 49–50 (Fr).

G. Richard Danner, "La Fontaine's 'Compagnons d'Ulysse': The Merits of Metamorphosis," *FR* 54 (December 1980): 241–47 (Eng).

Danner, *Patterns of Irony,* 116–27 (Eng).

Kohn, *Le Goût de La Fontaine,* 247–48 (Fr).

Jacques-Henri Périvier, "Fondement et mode de l'éthique dans les 'Fables' de La Fontaine," *KRQ* 18, no. 3 (1971): 337–38 (Fr).

David Lee Rubin, "Four Modes of Double Irony in La Fontaine's 'Fables,'" in Bayley and Coleman, eds., *The Equilibrium of Wit,* 208–10 (Eng).

Philip A. Wadsworth, "Le Douzième Livre des 'Fables,' *CAIEF* 26 (May 1974): 108–10 (Fr).

"La Confidente sans le savoir, ou le stratagème"

Lapp, *The Esthetics of Negligence,* 49–50 (Eng).

Merino-Morais, *Différence et répétition,* 54–68 (Fr).

"Conte d'un paysan qui avait offensé son Seigneur"

Gutwirth, *Un Merveilleux sans éclat,* 78–81 (Fr).

"Contre ceux qui ont le goût difficile"

Collinet, *Le Monde littéraire de La Fontaine,* 183–87 (Fr).

Jacques Proust, "Remarques sur la disposition par livres des 'Fables' de La Fontaine," in *De Jean Lemaire de Belges à Jean Giraudoux,* 235–36 (Fr).

David Lee Rubin, "Four Modes of Double Irony in La Fontaine's 'Fables,'" in Bayley and Coleman, eds., *The Equilibrium of Wit,* 202–5 (Eng).

"Le Coq et la Perle"

Collinet, *Le Monde littéraire de La Fontaine,* 181–83 (Fr).

René Jasinski, "De quelques contresens sur les 'Fables,'" *Europe* 50 (March 1972): 30 (Fr).

"Le Coq et le Renard"

Gutwirth, *Un Merveilleux sans éclat,* 142–43 (Fr).

LA FONTAINE, JEAN DE, "Le Corbeau et le Renard"

"Le Corbeau et le Renard"

Xavier Bonnier, "Lecture à clef pour serrure formelle," *Poétique* 20 (November 1989): 460–66, 471–73 (Fr).

Guiton, *La Fontaine,* 2–11 (Eng).

"Le Corbeau, la Gazelle, la Tortue et le Rat"

Gutwirth, *Un Merveilleux sans éclat,* 126–27 (Fr).

"Les Cordeliers de Catalogne"

Lapp, *The Esthetics of Negligence,* 126–27 (Eng).

"La Coupe enchantée"

Kohn, *Le Goût de La Fontaine,* 299–302 (Fr).

Lapp, *The Esthetics of Negligence,* 103–10, 160–63 (Eng).

"La Cour du Lion"

Guiton, *La Fontaine,* 90–91 (Eng).

"La Courtisane amoureuse"

Lapp, *The Esthetics of Negligence,* 151–53 (Eng).

"Le Curé et le Mort"

Collinet, *Le Monde littéraire de La Fontaine,* 212–13 (Fr).

G. Richard Danner, "La Fontaine's Ironic Vision in the 'Fables,'" *FR* 50 (March 1977): 567–68 (Eng).

Danner, *Patterns of Irony,* 53–56 (Eng).

Jacques Proust, "Remarques sur la disposition par livres des 'Fables' de La Fontaine," in *De Jean Lemaire de Belges à Jean Giraudoux,* 240–43 (Fr).

LA FONTAINE, JEAN DE, "Les deux Pigeons"

"Daphné"

Kohn, *Le Goût de La Fontaine,* 335–37 (Fr).

"Daphnis et Alcimadure"

Kohn, *Le Goût de La Fontaine,* 252–53 (Fr).

"Démocrite et les Abdéritains"

Marc Soriano, "Des contes aux fables," *Europe* 50 (March 1972): 123–25, 127 (Fr).

"Le Dépositaire infidèle"

Collinet, *Le Monde littéraire de La Fontaine,* 214–16 (Fr).

"Les deux Amis"

Gutwirth, *Un Merveilleux sans éclat,* 125–26 (Fr).
Merino-Morais, *Différence et répétition,* 36–53 (Fr).

"Les deux Chèvres"

Gutwirth, *Un Merveilleux sans éclat,* 205–7 (Fr).

"Les deux Perroquets, le Roi et son fils"

Gutwirth, *Un Merveilleux sans éclat,* 162–65 (Fr).

"Les deux Pigeons"

Guiton, *La Fontaine,* 155–67 (Eng).
Gutwirth, *Un Merveilleux sans éclat,* 127–30 (Fr).
Kohn, *Le Goût de La Fontaine,* 225–29 (Fr).
Lapp, *The Esthetics of Negligence,* 42–43 (Eng).

LA FONTAINE, JEAN DE, "Le Diable de Papefiguière"

J. Moravcevich, "Reason and Rhetoric in the Fables of La Fontaine," *AJFS* 16 (January–April 1979): 352–53 (Eng).

"Le Diable de Papefiguière"

Lapp, *The Esthetics of Negligence,* 137–39 (Eng).

"Le Diable en Enfer"

Lapp, *The Esthetics of Negligence,* 70–71 (Eng).

"Le Différend de Beaux Yeux, et de Belle Bouche"

Lapp, *The Esthetics of Negligence,* 150–51 (Eng).

Discours à Madame de La Sablière (Premier)
"Iris, je vous louerais"

Guiton, *La Fontaine,* 143–50 (Eng).

Jacques-Henri Périvier, "Fondement et mode de l'éthique dans les 'Fables' de La Fontaine," *KRQ* 18, no. 3 (1971): 336–37 (Fr).

Alain Seznec, "Connaissance philosophique—création poétique: 'Discours à Mme. de La Sablière,' " in Bayley and Coleman, eds., *The Equilibrium of Wit,* 219–30 (Fr).

Discours à Madame de La Sablière, bk. 1 (Second)
"Désormais que ma Muse"

Guiton, *La Fontaine,* 176–78 (Eng).

Lapp, *The Brazen Tower,* 103–14 (Eng).

"Discours à Monsieur le Duc de la Rochefoucauld"

Collinet, *Le Monde littéraire de La Fontaine,* 218–20 (Fr).

"L'Ecolier, le Pédant et le Maître d'un jardin"

Gutwirth, *Un Merveilleux sans éclat,* 99–101 (Fr).

Marie-Odile Sweetser, "Le Jardin: Nature et culture chez La Fontaine," *CAIEF* 34 (May 1982): 67–68 (Fr).

"L'Education"

Georges Maurand, "Les 'Enfants' des Fables de La Fontaine: Essai d'analyse actantielle d'un personnage," *LCL* 14 (January 1991): 148–49 (Fr).

"Elégie 1"

Lapp, *The Brazen Tower,* 114–17 (Eng).

"L'Elégie pour le Malheureux Oronte"

Kohn, *Le Goût de La Fontaine,* 110–14 (Fr),

"Elégies à Clymène"

Marcel Gutwirth, "La Fontaine élégiaque," *FrF* 6 (May 1981): 123–30 (Fr).

Jean Marmier, "La Construction des 'Elégies' de La Fontaine," in Noémi Hepp, Robert Mauzi, and Claude Pichois, eds., *Mélanges de littérature française offerts à M. René Pintard* (Paris: Klincksieck, 1975), 275–82 (Fr).

"L'Epître à M. de Niert"

Kohn, *Le Goût de La Fontaine,* 333–35 (Fr).

"L'Epître dédicatoire au duc de Bourgogne"

Kohn, *Le Goût de La Fontaine,* 240–42 (Fr).

"L'Ermite"

Lapp, *The Esthetics of Negligence,* 127–29 (Eng).

LA FONTAINE, JEAN DE, "Le Faiseur d'oreilles"

"Le Faiseur d'oreilles et le Raccommodeur de moules"

Gutwirth, *Un Merveilleux sans éclat,* 76–78 (Fr).

Lapp, *The Esthetics of Negligence,* 68–70 (Eng).

Merino-Morais, *Différence et répétition,* 69–92 (Fr).

"Le Faucon"

Donna Kuizenga, "La Fontaine's 'Le Faucon': A Lesson of Experience," *FrF* 2, no. 2 (1977): 214–23 (Eng).

Lapp, *The Esthetics of Negligence,* 61–63, 87–88, 166 (Eng).

"La Femme noyée" (conte)

Marc Soriano, "Des contes aux fables," *Europe* 50 (March 1972): 102–9 (Fr).

"La Femme noyée" (fable)

Marc Soriano, "Des contes aux fables," *Europe* 50 (March 1972): 100–109, 114–16 (Fr).

"Le Fermier, le Chien, et le Renard"

A. J. Steele, "La Fontaine: 'Le Fermier, le Chien et le Renard,'" in Nurse, ed., *The Art of Criticism,* 102–12 (Eng).

"Feronde ou le Purgatoire"

Lapp, *The Esthetics of Negligence,* 56–57, 83–84 (Eng).

"La Fiancée du roi de Garbe"

Catherine Grisé, "La Casuistique dans les 'Contes' de La Fontaine," *SFr* 33 (September–December 1989): 415–21 (Fr).

Kohn, *Le Goût de La Fontaine,* 289–93 (Fr).

Lapp, *The Esthetics of Negligence,* 63–68, 156–58, 168–69 (Eng).

Merino-Morais, *Différence et répétition,* 9–35 (Fr).

"Fleuve Scamandre"

Gutwirth, *Un Merveilleux sans éclat,* 87–89 (Fr).

"La Gageure des trois commères"

Lapp, *The Esthetics of Negligence,* 54–56, 86–87 (Eng).

"Le Gascon puni"

Lapp, *The Esthetics of Negligence,* 133–35 (Eng).

"La Génisse, la Chèvre et le Brebis en société"

Alain Seznec, "Connaissance philosophique—création poétique: 'Discours à Mme. de la Sablière,'" in Bayley and Coleman, eds., *The Equilibrium of Wit,* 214 (Fr).

"Le Gland et la Citrouille"

Guiton, *La Fontaine,* 111–12 (Eng).

"La Grenouille et le Rat"

Danner, *Patterns of Irony,* 101–5 (Eng).

Gutwirth, *Un Merveilleux sans éclat,* 150–57 (Fr).

"La Grenouille qui se veut faire aussi grosse que le Boeuf"

David Lee Rubin, "La Fontaine and Phaedrus: A Relation Reargued," in Donald W. Tappan and William A. Mould, eds., *French Studies in Honor of Philip Wadsworth* (Birmingham: Summa, 1985), 21–22 (Eng).

LA FONTAINE, JEAN DE, "Le Héron"

"Le Héron"

Guiton, *La Fontaine,* 25–27 (Eng).

"Le Héron—La Fille"

Collinet, *Le Monde littéraire de La Fontaine,* 205–12 (Fr).

Patrick Dandrey, "L'Emergence du naturel dans les 'Fables' de La Fontaine (à propos du 'Héron et de 'la Fille')," *RHL* 83 (May–June 1983): 371–89 (Fr).

Jacques Proust, "Remarques sur la disposition par livres de 'Fables' de La Fontaine," in *De Jean Lemaire de Belges à Jean Giraudoux,* 236–40 (Fr).

"L'Homme et la Couleuvre"

Pierre Bornecque, "Thémes et organisation des 'Fables,'" *Europe* 50 (March 1972): 47–48 (Fr).

G. Richard Danner, "La Fontaine's 'Fables,' Book X: The Labyrinth Hypothesis," *ECr* 21 (Winter 1981): 93–96 (Eng).

Danner, *Patterns of Irony,* 150–55 (Eng).

Guiton, *La Fontaine,* 119–21 (Eng).

Gutwirth, *Un Merveilleux sans éclat,* 146–50 (Fr).

Alain Seznec, "Connaissance philosophique—création poétique: 'Discours à Mme. de la Sablière,'" in Bayley and Coleman, eds., *The Equilibrium of Wit,* 216–18 (Fr).

"L'Horoscope"

Beverly S. Ridgely, "Astrology and Astronomy in the 'Fables' of La Fontaine," *PMLA* 80 (June 1965): 183–84 (Eng).

"L'Huitre et les Plaideurs"

Gutwirth, *Un Merveilleux sans éclat,* 202–4 (Fr).

Howarth and Walton, *Explications,* 70–79 (Eng).

LA FONTAINE, JEAN DE, "La Laitière et le Pot au Lait"

"Le Jardinier et son Seigneur"

Gutwirth, *Un Merveilleux sans éclat*, 95–97 (Fr).

Marie-Odile Swectser, "Le Jardin: Nature et culture chez La Fontaine," *CAIEF* 34 (May 1982): 69–71 (Fr).

"La Jeune Veuve"

G. Richard Danner, "La Fontaine's Ironic Vision in the 'Fables,'" *FR* 50 (March 1977): 568–70 (Eng).

Danner, *Patterns of Irony*, 56–61 (Eng).

Philippe Jousset, "Jouvence de La Fontaine: Petite physiologie d'un plaisir de lecture," *Poétique* 19 (April 1988): 249–62 (Fr).

"Joconde"

Gutwirth, *Un Merveilleux sans éclat*, 70–75 (Fr).

Lapp, *The Esthetics of Negligence*, 96–102 (Eng).

Merino-Morais, *Différence et répétition*, 93–113 (Fr).

"Le Juge arbitre, l'Hospitalier et le Solitaire"

Gernard Beugnot, "Autour d'un texte: L'Ultime Leçon des 'Fables,'" in Noémi Hepp, Robert Mauzi, and Claude Pichois, eds., *Mélanges de littérature française offerts à M. René Pintard* (Paris: Klincksieck, 1975), 291–301 (Fr).

Gutwirth, *Un Merveilleux sans éclat*, 107–8 (Fr).

Philip A. Wadsworth, "Le Douzième Livre des 'Fables,'" *CAIEF* 26 (May 1974): 111–15 (Fr).

"La Laitière et le Pot au Lait"

Collinet, *Le Monde littéraire de La Fontaine*, 212–13 (Fr).

Jacques Proust, "Remarques sur la disposition par livres des 'Fables' de la Fontaine," in *De Jean Lemaire de Belges à Jean Giraudoux*, 240–43 (Fr).

LA FONTAINE, JEAN DE, "Le Lièvre et la Perdrix"

"Le Lièvre et la Perdrix"

Collinet, *Le Monde littéraire de La Fontaine*, 200–203 (Fr).

"Le Lièvre et la Tortue"

René Jasinski, "De quelques contresens sur les 'Fables,'" *Europe* 50 (March 1972): 37–38 (Fr).

"Le Lièvre et les Grenouilles"

René Jasinski, "De quelques contresens sur les 'Fables,'" *Europe* 50 (March 1972): 29–30 (Fr).

"Le Lion et le Moucheron"

Danner, *Patterns of Irony*, 97–101 (Eng).

Gutwirth, *Un Merveilleux sans éclat*, 162 (Fr).

"Le Lion et le Rat"

Collinet, *Le Monde littéraire de La Fontaine*, 187–91 (Fr).

"Le Lion, Le Loup et le Renard"

Gutwirth, *Un Merveilleux sans éclat*, 141–42 (Fr).

"La Lionne et l'Ourse"

Gutwirth, *Un Merveilleux sans éclat*, 166–67 (Fr).

"Le Loup et l'Agneau"

Guiton, *La Fontaine*, 99–100 (Eng).

Gutwirth, *Un Merveilleux sans éclat*, 133–35 (Fr).

J. Moravcevich, "Reason and Rhetoric in the Fables of La Fontaine," *AJFS* 16 (January–April 1979): 355–56 (Eng).

LA FONTAINE, JEAN DE, "Le Loup, la Chèvre et le Chevreau"

David Lee Rubin, "La Fontaine and Phaedrus: A Relation Reargued," in Donald Tappan and William A. Mould, eds., *French Studies in Honor of Philip Wadsworth* (Birmingham: Summa, 1985), 24–25 (Eng).

"Le Loup et le Chien"

Danner, *Patterns of Irony,* 73–75, 78–84 (Eng).

G. Richard Danner, "Individualism in La Fontaine's 'Le Loup et le Chien,'" *KRQ* 24, no. 2 (1977): 185–90 (Eng).

Gutwirth, *Un Merveilleux sans éclat,* 135–37 (Fr).

Stirling Haig, "La Fontaine's 'Le Loup et le Chien' as a Pedagogical Instrument," *FR* 42 (April 1969): 701–5 (Eng).

David Lee Rubin, "Four Modes of Double Irony in La Fontaine's 'Fables,'" in Bayley and Coleman, eds., *The Equilibrium of Wit,* 205–6 (Eng).

David Lee Rubin, "La Fontaine and Phaedrus: A Relation Reargued," in Donald Tappan and William A. Mould, eds., *French Studies in Honor of Philip Wadsworth* (Birmingham: Summa, 1985), 39–53 (Eng).

"Le Loup et le Renard"

Patrick Dandrey, "Séduction du pouvoir: La Fontaine, le berger, et le roi," *CLDS* 8 (1986): 25–26 (Fr).

Guiton, *La Fontaine,* 97–99 (Eng).

Gutwirth, *Un Merveilleux sans éclat,* 122–24 (Fr).

"Le Loup et les Bergers"

Guiton, *La Fontaine,* 114–15 (Eng).

Gutwirth, *Un Merveilleux sans éclat,* 137–39 (Fr).

"Le Loup, la Chèvre et le Chevreau"

Collinet, *Le Monde littéraire de La Fontaine,* 198–200 (Fr).

LA FONTAINE, JEAN DE, "Les Lunettes"

"Les Lunettes"

Lapp, *The Esthetics of Negligence,* 129–32 (Eng).

"Le Magnifique"

Lapp, *The Esthetics of Negligence,* 48–49, 89–90 (Eng).

"La Mandragore"

Kohn, *Le Goût de La Fontaine,* 293–97 (Fr).

"Le Marchand, le Gentilhomme, le Pâtre et le Fils du Roi"

Marc Soriano, "Des contes aux fables," *Europe* 50 (March 1972): 125–28 (Fr).

"Mazet de Lamporechio"

Lapp, *The Esthetics of Negligence,* 72–73 (Eng).

"Le Milan, le Roi et le Chasseur"

Ross Chambers, "Narrative in Opposition: Reflections on a La Fontaine Fable," *FrF* 8 (September 1983): 216–30 (Eng).

Collinet, *Le Monde littéraire de La Fontaine,* 221–25 (Fr).

Gutwirth, *Un Merveilleux sans éclat,* 209–13 (Fr).

Philip A. Wadsworth, "Le Douzième Livre des 'Fables,'" *CAIEF* 26 (May 1974): 107–8 (Fr).

Philip A. Wadsworth, "Villon's Two Pleas for Absolution," *ECr* 7 (Fall 1967): 189–93 (Eng).

"La Mort et le Bûcheron"

Guiton, *La Fontaine,* 131–33 (Eng).

LA FONTAINE, JEAN DE, "L'Oiseleur, l'Autour, et l'Alouette"

"La Mort et le Malheureux"

Collinet, *Le Monde littéraire de La Fontaine,* 170–76, 178–79 (Fr).

"La Mort et le Mourant"

G. Couton, "Le Livre épicurien des 'Fables': Essai de lecture du livre 8," in Noémi Hepp, Robert Mauzi, and Claude Pichois, eds., *Mélanges de littérature française offerts à M. René Pintard* (Paris: Klincksieck, 1975), 283–84 (Fr).

Guiton, *La.Fontaine,* 173–74 (Eng).

"La Mouche et la Fourmi"

J. Moravcevich, "Reason and Rhetoric in the Fables of La Fontaine," *AJFS* 16 (January–April 1979): 350–51 (Eng).

"Le Muletier"

Lapp, *The Esthetics of Negligence,* 52–53 (Eng).

"Les Obsèques de la Lionne"

Gutwirth, *Un Merveilleux sans éclat,* 167–69 (Fr).

Philip A. Wadsworth, "The Art of Allegory in La Fontaine's Fables," *FR* 45 (May 1972): 1132–35 (Eng).

"Les Oies de Frère Philippe"

Lapp, *The Esthetics of Negligence,* 74–78 (Eng).

"L'Oiseleur, l'Autour, et l'Alouette"

Maurice Delcroix, " 'L'Oiseleur, l'Autour, et l'Alouette': Analyse," *CAIEF* 26 (May 1974): 146–58 (Fr).

LA FONTAINE, JEAN DE, "On ne s'avise jamais de tout"

"On ne s'avise jamais de tout"

Lapp, *The Esthetics of Negligence,* 118 (Eng).

"L'Oraison de Saint Julien"

Kohn, *Le Goût de La Fontaine,* 278–85 (Fr).
Lapp, *The Esthetics of Negligence,* 38, 58–61, 85–86 (Eng).

"Pâté d'anguille"

Lapp, *The Esthetics of Negligence,* 122–24 (Eng).

"Le Pâtre et le Lion"

Collinet, *Le Monde littéraire de La Fontaine,* 203–5 (Fr).

"Le Pâtre et le Lion, le Lion et le Chasseur"

Jacques Proust, "Remarques sur la disposition par livres des 'Fables' de La Fontaine," in *De Jean Lemaire de Belges à Jean Giraudoux,* 232–34 (Fr).

"Le Paysan du Danube"

Gutwirth, *Un Merveilleux sans éclat,* 173–79 (Fr).
Kohn, *Le Goût de La Fontaine,* 211–12 (Fr).

"Le Petit Chien qui secoue de l'argent et des pierreries"

Lapp, *The Esthetics of Negligence,* 110–16 (Eng).

"Philémon et Baucis"

Gutwirth, *Un Merveilleux sans éclat,* 56–58 (Fr).
Kohn, *Le Goût de La Fontaine,* 253–54 (Fr).

"Philomèle et Progné"

Gutwirth, *Un Merveilleux sans éclat,* 171–73 (Fr).

"Le Philosophe scythe"

Gutwirth, *Un Merveilleux sans éclat,* 101–3 (Fr).

"Poème du Quinquina"

Jean-Dominique Biard, "La Fontaine et Du Bartas," *SFr* 7 (May–August 1963): 282–84 (Fr).

Collinet, *Le Monde littéraire de La Fontaine,* 324–32 (Fr).

Gutwirth, *Un Merveilleux sans éclat,* 59–64 (Fr).

Beverly S. Ridgely, "Disciple de Lucrèce une seconde fois: A Study of La Fontaine's 'Poème du Quinquina,' " *ECr* 11 (Summer 1971): 92–122 (Eng).

"Les Poissons et le Cormoran"

Danner, *Patterns of Irony,* 105–12 (Eng).

"Le Pot de terre et le Pot de fer"

Gutwirth, *Un Merveilleux sans éclat,* 116–18 (Fr).

"Le Pouvoir des fables"

Gutwirth, *Un Merveilleux sans éclat,* 223–25 (Fr).

"Les Quiproquo"

Lapp, *The Esthetics of Negligence,* 119–22 (Eng).

"Le Rat et l'Huitre"

Danner, *Patterns of Irony,* 70–72 (Eng).

Guiton, *La Fontaine,* 75–76, 107–8 (Eng).

LA FONTAINE, JEAN DE, "Les Rémois"

"Les Rémois"

Lapp, *The Esthetics of Negligence,* 142–43 (Eng).

"Le Renard et la Cigogne"

David Lee Rubin, "La Fontaine and Phaedrus: A Relation Reargued," in Donald W. Tappan and William A. Mould, eds., *French Studies in Honor of Philip Wadsworth* (Birmingham: Summa, 1985), 20–21 (Eng).

"Le Renard et le Bouc"

Collinet, *Le Monde littéraire de La Fontaine,* 167–69 (Fr).

"Le Renard et l'Ecureuil"

Collinet, *Le Monde littéraire de La Fontaine,* 200–203 (Fr).

"Richard Minutolo"

Lapp, *The Esthetics of Negligence,* 46–48, 51, 85 (Eng).

"Le Satyre et le Passant"

Danner, *Patterns of Irony,* 84–91 (Eng).

"La Servante justifiée"

Lapp, *The Esthetics of Negligence,* 139–40 (Eng).

"Le Singe et le chat"

Katz and Hall, *Explicating French Texts,* 18–23 (Fr).

"Le Singe et le Dauphin"

René Jasinski, "De quelques contresens sur les 'Fables,'" *Europe* 50 (March 1972): 28–29 (Fr).

LA FONTAINE, JEAN DE, "Le Tableau"

"Le Singe et le Léopard"

Anne-Marie Garagnon, "Propos sur une fable de La Fontaine: Le Singe et le Léopard," *CLDS* 6 (1984): 183–90 (Fr).

"Le Songe de Vaux"

Collinet, *Le Monde littéraire de La Fontaine,* 95–106 (Fr).

Guiton, *La Fontaine,* 127–28, 151–52 (Eng).

J. D. Hubert, "La Fontaine et Pellisson ou le mystère des deux acanthes," *RHL* 66 (April–June 1966): 226–30, 232–37 (Fr).

Kohn, *Le Goût de La Fontaine,* 85–92 (Fr).

Robert Nicolich, "The Triumph of Language: The Sister Arts and Creative Activity in La Fontaine's 'Songe de Vaux,' " *ECr* 21 (Winter 1981): 10–21 (Eng).

"Le Songe d'un habitant du Mogol"

Auffret and Auffret, *Le Commentaire composé,* 123–31 (Fr).

Kohn, *Le Goût de La Fontaine,* 231–32 (Fr).

"Les Souhaits"

Gutwirth, *Un Merveilleux sans éclat,* 213–16 (Fr).

"La Souris métamorphosée en fille"

Danner, *Patterns of Irony,* 139–48 (Eng).

"Le Statuaire de la statue de Jupiter"

Gutwirth, *Un Merveilleux sans éclat,* 218–20 (Fr).

Kohn, *Le Goût de La Fontaine,* 199–201 (Fr).

"Le Tableau"

Lapp, *The Esthetics of Negligence,* 36–40 (Eng).

LA FONTAINE, JEAN DE, "Tircis et Amarante"

"Tircis et Amarante"

Jean-Pierre Collinet, "Poésie pastorale et classicisme," *CAIEF* 39 (May 1987): 85–87 (Fr).

"La Tortue et les deux Canards"

Gutwirth, *Un Merveilleux sans éclat,* 104–6 (Fr).

Rubin, *Higher, Hidden Order,* 19–21 (Eng).

"Les Troqueurs"

Lapp, *The Esthetics of Negligence,* 140–42 (Eng).

"Les Vautours et les Pigeons"

Jules Brody, "La Fontaine, 'Les Vautours et les pigeons': An Intertextual Reading," in David Rubin and Mary McKinley, eds., *Convergences: Rhetoric and Poetic in Seventeenth-Century France: Essays for Hugh Davidson* (Colombus: Ohio State University Press, 1989), 143–60 (Eng).

Jules Brody, "Pour une lecture philogogique d'une fable de La Fontaine: 'Les Vautours et les Pigeons,' " *RHL* 89 (March–April 1989): 179–94 (Fr).

"Le Vieillard et l'Ane"

Marc Soriano, "Des contes aux fables," *Europe* 50 (March 1972): 119–23, 127–128 (Fr).

"Le Vieux Chat et la jeune Souris"

Collinet, *Le Monde littéraire de La Fontaine,* 225–26 (Fr).

Gutwirth, *Un Merveilleux sans éclat,* 144–46 (Fr).

LAFORGUE, JULES

"Le Blanc de la complainte"

Jeanne Bem, "Le Blanc de la complainte," *NCFS* 15 (Fall–Winter 1986–87): 119–27 (Eng).

LAFORGUE, JULES, "Complainte du pauvre Chevalier-Errant"

"La Chanson des morts"

Jean-Pierre Bertrand, "Se taire ou se dire: Quelques aspects de l'énonciation dans les premiers poèmes de Jules Laforgue," in Hiddleston, ed., *Laforgue aujourd'hui*, 70–73 (Fr).

"Chanson du petit hypertrophique"

Jean-Pierre Bertrand, "Se taire ou se dire: Quelques aspects de l'énonciation dans les premiers poèmes de Jules Laforgue," in Hiddleston, ed., *Laforgue aujourd'hui*, 80–81 (Fr).

"Complainte de la lune en province"

Broome and Chesters, *The Appreciation of Modern French Poetry (1850–1950)*, 108–11 (Eng).

"La Complainte des blackboulés"

Jeanne Bem, "Le Blackboule," in Hiddleston, ed., *Laforgue aujourd'hui*, 105–16 (Fr).

"Complainte des pianos qu'on entend dans les quartiers aisés"

Collie, *Jules Laforgue*, 40–44 (Eng).

"Complainte du foetus de poète"

Robert L. Mitchell, "Hemorrhoids/Splenectomy/Gestation: Towards Authorial Manipulation, Reader Expectation, and the Perversion of Complicity," *FR* 53 (October 1979): 43–44 (Eng).

"Complainte d'une convalescence en mai"

Collie, *Jules Laforgue*, 49–52 (Eng).

"Complainte du pauvre Chevalier-Errant"

Collie, *Jules Laforgue*, 44–47 (Eng).

LAFORGUE, JULES, "Le Concile féerique"

"Le Concile féerique"

Warren Ramsey, "Phryne, or More Than One Right Word," in Warren Ramsey, ed., *Lules Laforgue: Essays on a Poet's Life and Work* (Carbondale: Southern Illinois University Press, 1969), 152–54 (Eng).

"Désolation"

Jean-Pierre Bertrand, "Se taire ou se dire: Quelques aspects de l'énonciation dans les premiers poèmes de Jules Laforgue," in Hiddleston, ed., *Laforgue aujourd'hui,* 81–82 (Fr).

"Dimanches"

Collie, *Jules Laforgue,* 70–74 (Eng).

Anne Holmes, "Laforgue au travail: Des 'Fleurs' aux 'Derniers Vers,' " in Hiddleston, ed., *Laforgue aujourd'hui,* 128–31 (Fr).

"Dimanches" (from Derniers Vers)

Collie, *Jules Laforgue,* 101–6 (Eng).

"Dimanches" (from Des Fleurs de bonne volonté)

Collie, *Jules Laforgue,* 101–3 (Eng).

"L'Hiver qui vient"

Broome and Chesters, *The Appreciation of Modern French Poetry (1850–1950),* 111–17 (Eng).

Collie, *Jules Laforgue,* 94–101 (Eng).

Peter Collier, "Poetry and Cliché: Laforgue's 'L'Hiver qui vient,' " in Prendergast, ed., *Nineteenth-Century French Poetry,* 199–224 (Eng).

Moreau, *Six Études de métrique,* 40–53 (Fr).

Lawrence Watson, " 'L'Hiver qui vient': Poème-manifeste," in Hiddleston, ed., *Laforgue aujourd'hui,* 135–53 (Fr).

LAFORGUE, JULES, "Sieste éternelle"

"Légende"

Collie, *Jules Laforgue,* 109–11 (Eng).

Warren Ramsey, "Phryne, or More Than One Right Word," in Warren Ramsey, ed., *Lules Laforgue: Essays on a Poet's Life and Work* (Carbondale: Southern Illinois University Press, 1969), 150–52 (Eng).

"Légendes"

Anne Holmes, "Laforgue au travail: Des 'Fleurs' aux 'Derniers Vers,' " in Hiddleston, ed., *Laforgue aujourd'hui,* 128 (Fr).

"Oh! qu'une, d'elle-même, un beau soir"

Warren Ramsey, "Phryne, or More Than One Right Word," in Warren Ramsey, ed., *Lules Laforgue: Essays on a Poet's Life and Work* (Carbondale: Southern Illinois University Press, 1969), 147–49 (Eng).

"Pétition"

Collie, *Jules Laforgue,* 106–7 (Eng).

"Préludes autobiographiques"

Claude Abastado, " 'Préludes autobiographiques' de Jules Laforgue," in *Poésie et société en France au dix-neuvième siècle* (Paris: SEDES [Société d'Edition d'Enseignement Supérieur] CDU, 1983) 143–50 (Fr).

"Salomé"

Michèle Hannoosh, "Laforgue's 'Salomé' and the Poetics of Parody," *RR* 75 (January 1984): 51–69 (Eng).

"Sieste éternelle"

M. Riffaterre, *Semiotics of Poetry,* 145–50 (Eng).

LAFORGUE, JULES, "Solo de Lune"

"Solo de Lune"

Michael Collie, *Jules Laforgue* (London: University of London, Athlone Press, 1977), 66–70 (Eng).

Anne Holmes, "Laforgue au travail: Des 'Fleurs' aux 'Derniers Vers,'" in Hiddleston, ed., *Laforgue aujourd'hui,* 126–27 (Fr).

Warren Ramsey, "Phryne, or More Than One Right Word," in Warren Ramsey, ed., *Jules Laforgue: Essays on a Poet's Life and Work* (Carbondale: Southern Illinois University Press, 1969), 149–50 (Eng).

Clive Scott, *A Question of Syllables: Essays in Nineteenth-Century French Verse* (Cambridge: Cambridge University Press, 1986), 159–88, 194–95 (Eng).

LAMARTINE, ALPHONSE DE

"A Lucy L."

H. Riffaterre, *L'Orphisme dans la poésie,* 172–73 (Fr).

"La Chute d'un ange"

Bénichou, *Les Mages romantiques,* 91–93 (Fr).

Lombard, *Lamartine,* 50–54 (Eng).

"Le Crucifix"

Denommé, *Nineteenth-Century French Romantic Poets,* 52–53 (Eng).

"Le Désert, ou l'Immaterialité de Dieu"

Lombard, *Lamartine,* 91–93 (Eng).

"L'Immortalité"

Simon Jeune, "De Thomas à Lamartine," in *Missions et démarches de la critique: Mélanges offerts au Professeur J. A. Vier* (Paris: Klincksieck, 1973), 377–79 (Fr).

LAMARTINE, ALPHONSE DE, "Le Lac"

"Ischia"

Birkett, *Lamartine and the Poetics of Landscape,* 46–47, 69–70 (Eng).

Mary Ellen Birkett, "Paysage poétique et métaphore musicale chez Lamartine," *FR* 52 (December 1978): 286–93 (Fr).

Mary Ellen Birkett, "Pictura, Poesis and Landscape," *SFR* 2 (Summer 1978): 235–46 (Eng).

"L'Isolement"

Birkett, *Lamartine and the Poetics of Landscape,* 24–26, 37–41, 61–64 (Eng).

Denommé, *Nineteenth-Century French Romantic Poets,* 48–51 (Eng).

Simon Jeune, "De Thomas à Lamartine," in *Missions et démarches de la critique: Mélanges offerts au Prof. J. A. Vier* (Paris: Klincksieck, 1973), 380–81 (Fr).

Katz and Hall, *Explicating French Texts,* 32–39 (Fr).

Erich Köhler, "Alphonse de Lamartine: 'L'Isolement,' " in *Poésie et société en France au dix-neuvième siècle* (Paris: SEDES/CDU, 1983), 97–118 (Fr).

"Le Lac"

Birkett, *Lamartine and the Poetics of Landscape,* 41–43, 64–68 (Eng).

Mary Ellen Birkett, "Paysage poétique et métaphore musicale chez Lamartine," *FR* 52 (December 1978): 289–90 (Fr).

Lloyd Bishop, " 'Le Lac' as Exemplar of the Greater Romantic Lyric," *KRQ* 34, no. 4 (1987): 401–13 (Eng).

Denommé, *Nineteenth-Century French Romantic Poets,* 44–45, 46–48 (Eng).

Eric Gans, "The Poem as Hypothesis of Origin: Lamartine's 'Le Lac,' " in Prendergast, ed., *Nineteenth-Century French Poetry,* 29–47 (Eng).

Simon Jeune, "De Thomas à Lamartine," in *Missions et démarches de la critique: Mélanges offerts au Professeur J. A. Vier* (Paris: Klincksieck, 1973), 374–77 (Fr).

Lombard, *Lamartine,* 24–26 (Eng).

LAMARTINE, ALPHONSE DE, "La Liberté, ou Une Nuit à Rome"

Eléonore M. Zimmerman, "Un Héritage romantique dévoyé: L'Apostrophe dans 'Le Lac,' 'Tristesse d'Olympio,' et 'La Chevelure,' " *FrF* 13 (May 1988): 206–8 (Fr).

"La Liberté, ou Une Nuit à Rome"

Birkett, *Lamartine and the Poetics of Landscape,* 29–31 (Eng).

"Milly ou la terre natale"

Birkett, *Lamartine and the Poetics of Landscape,* 31–34, 47–59 (Eng).

"Novissima verba, ou Mon âme est triste jusqu'à la mort"

Birkett, *Lamartine and the Poetics of Landscape,* 77–85 (Eng).

"L'Occident"

Birkett, *Lamartine and the Poetics of Landscape,* 73–77 (Eng).

"Poésie, ou Paysage dans le Golfe de Gênes"

H. Riffaterre, *L'Orphisme dans la poésie,* 75–77 (Fr).

"Le Premier Regret"

Mary Ellen Birkett, "Lamartine's 'Le Premier Regret': Manuscript, Poem, Commentary," *KRQ* 32, no. 4 (1985): 341–46 (Eng).

"La Prière"

Birkett, *Lamartine and the Poetics of Landscape,* 43–45 (Eng).
Lombard, *Lamartine,* 26–27 (Eng).

"La Vigne et la maison"

Lombard, *Lamartine,* 93–95 (Eng).

LAPOINTE, PAUL-MARIE

"Coup de foudre"

Philippe Haeck, "Naissance de la poésie moderne au Québec," *EF* 9 (May 1973): 110–12 (Fr).

"Le Vierge incendié"

Guy Laflèche, "Ecart, violence et révolte chez Paul-Marie Lapointe," *EF* 6 (November 1970): 395–417 (Fr).

LA ROQUE, SIMEON-GUILLAUME DE

"Psaume 32" (Translation)

Jeannerct, *Poésie et tradition biblique,* 468–69 (Fr).

LA VIGNE, ANDRE DE

"L'Attolitte portus de Gennes"

Brown, *The Shaping of History and Poetry in Late Medieval France,* 43–45, 70 (Eng).

"La Patenostre quis es in celis des Genevois"

Brown, *The Shaping of History and Poetry in Late Medieval France,* 45–47, 70 (Eng).

LECONTE DE LISLE

"L'Albatros"

Denommé, *Leconte de Lisle,* 100–101 (Eng).

LECONTE DE LISLE, "L'anathème"

"L'anathème"

Pich, *Leconte de Lisle,* 195–97 (Fr).

"L'Arc de Civa"

Pich, *Leconte de Lisle,* 229–31 (Fr).

"Les Ascètes"

Pich, *Leconte de Lisle,* 197–201 (Fr).

"Aurore"

Pich, *Leconte de Lisle,* 209–11 (Fr).

"Le Barde de Temrah"

Denommé, *Leconte de Lisle,* 68–70 (Eng).
Pich, *Leconte de Lisle,* 298 (Fr).

"Le Bernica"

Pich, *Leconte de Lisle,* 331–33 (Fr).

"La Bête écarlate"

Denommé, *Leconte de Lisle,* 94–96 (Eng).

"Bhâgavat"

Denommé, *Leconte de Lisle,* 56–58 (Eng).
Pich, *Leconte de Lisle,* 89–93, 167–68 (Fr).

"Les Bucoliastes"

Pich, *Leconte de Lisle,* 370–71 (Fr).

"Chant alterné"

Pich, *Leconte de Lisle,* 126–27 (Fr).

"Christine"

Denommé, *Leconte de Lisle,* 80–81 (Eng).

"La Chute des étoiles"

Pich, *Leconte de Lisle,* 339–40 (Fr).

"Clairs de lune"

Pich, *Leconte de Lisle,* 337–39 (Fr).

"Le Cœur de Hialmar"

Denommé, *The French Parnassian Poets,* 94–96 (Eng).
Denommé, *Leconte de Lisle,* 70–71 (Eng).
Pich, *Leconte de Lisle,* 404–5 (Fr).

"Le Conseil du Fakir"

Pich, *Leconte de Lisle,* 343 (Fr).

"Le Corbeau"

Pich, *Leconte de Lisle,* 313–15 (Fr).

"Un Coucher de soleil"

Pich, *Leconte de Lisle,* 333–35 (Fr).

"Çunacépa"

Pich, *Leconte de Lisle,* 231–35 (Fr).

255

LECONTE DE LISLE, "Dans l'air léger"

"Dans l'air léger"

Denommé, *The French Parnassian Poets*, 109–11 (Eng).

Denommé, *Leconte de Lisle*, 114 (Eng).

"Le Dernier des Maourys"

Christiane Mortelier, "Du 'Vieux Chef' de Thiercelin au 'Dernier des Maourys' de Leconte de Lisle," *RHL:* 90 (March–April 1990): 180–90 (Fr).

"Le Désert"

Pich, *Leconte de Lisle*, 219–21 (Fr).

"Les Deux Glaives"

Pich, *Leconte de Lisle*, 364–66 (Fr).

"Dies irae"

Denommé, *The French Parnassian Poets*, 91–92 (Eng).

Denommé, *Leconte de Lisle*, 62–63 (Eng).

Pich, *Leconte de Lisle*, 140–49, 158–59, 161–63 (Fr).

"Djihan-Arû"

Pich, *Leconte de Lisle*, 345–46 (Fr).

"Effet de lune"

Pich, *Leconte de Lisle*, 335–36 (Fr).

"Eglogue"

Pich, *Leconte de Lisle*, 101–2 (Fr).

LECONTE DE LISLE, "Fultus Hyacintho"

"Fultus Hyacintho"

Pich, *Leconte de Lisle,* 217–19 (Fr).

"La Genèse polynésienne"

Pich, *Leconte de Lisle,* 266 (Fr).

"Glaucé"

Pich, *Leconte de Lisle,* 98–101 (Fr).

"Hélène"

Pich, *Leconte de Lisle,* 65–68, 70–72 (Fr).

"L'Holocauste"

Denommé, *Leconte de Lisle,* 97–98 (Eng).

"Hylas"

Pich, *Leconte de Lisle,* 97–98, 169 (Fr).

"Hypatie"

Pich, *Leconte de Lisle,* 122–26 (Fr).

"Hypatie et Cyrille"

Denommé, *The French Parnassian Poets,* 86–88 (Eng).
Pich, *Leconte de Lisle,* 296–97 (Fr).

"L'Incantation du loup"

Denommé, *Leconte de Lisle,* 101–2 (Eng).

Robert O. Steele, "The Avant-Gardism of Leconte de Lisle," *NCFS* 17 (Spring–Summer 1989): 323–24 (Eng).

LECONTE DE LISLE, "Le Lévier de Magnus"

"Le Jaguar"

Pich, *Leconte de Lisle,* 322–23 (Fr).

"Le Jugement de Komor"

Pich, *Leconte de Lisle,* 343–45 (Fr).

"Les Jungles"

Pich, *Leconte de Lisle,* 236–37 (Fr).

"Khirôn"

Alexandre Embiricos, *Interprétation de Leconte de Lisle* (Paris: Pensée Universelle, 1979), 130–35 (Fr).
Pich, *Leconte de Lisle,* 80–89, 169–72 (Fr).

"Klytie"

Pich, *Leconte de Lisle,* 101 (Fr).

"Les Larmes de l'Ours"

Pich, *Leconte de Lisle,* 456–58 (Fr).

"La Légende des Nornes"

Pich, *Leconte de Lisle,* 311–12 (Fr).

"Lélia dans la solitude"

Irving Putter, "Vers et prose de jeunese de Leconte de Lisle," *SFr* 11 (January–April 1967): 67–74 (Fr).

"Le Lévier de Magnus"

Denommé, *Leconte de Lisle,* 96–97 (Eng).
Pich, *Leconte de Lisle,* 427–29 (Fr).

LECONTE DE LISLE, "Le Manchy"

"Le Manchy"

Denommé, *Leconte de Lisle,* 81–82 (Eng).

"Massacre de Mona"

Pich, *Leconte de Lisle,* 262–66, 281, 298–99 (Fr).

"Midi"

Mary Ann Caws, "Under-Reading at Noon Leconte de Lisle's 'Midi,' " in Prendergast, ed., *Nineteenth-Century French Poetry,* 103–17 (Eng).

Denommé, *The French Parnassian Poets,* 88–91 (Eng).

Denommé, *Leconte de Lisle,* 59–62 (Eng).

"Les Montreurs"

Denommé, *Leconte de Lisle,* 90–91 (Eng).

"La Mort de Valmiki"

Denommé, *Leconte de Lisle,* 56 (Eng).

"La Mort du lion"

Pich, *Leconte de Lisle,* 411–14 (Fr).

Robert O. Steele, "The Avant-Gardism of Leconte de Lisle," *NCFS* 17 (Spring–Summer 1989): 320–21 (Eng).

"Le Nazaréen"

Denommé, *Leconte de Lisle,* 88–89 (Eng).

Pich, *Leconte de Lisle,* 193–95 (Fr).

"Néférou-Ra"

Pich, *Leconte de Lisle,* 349–50 (Fr).

"Niobé"

Alexandre Embiricos, *Interprétation de Leconte de Lisle* (Paris: Pensée Universelle, 1979), 126–30 (Fr).

Pich, *Leconte de Lisle,* 72–79 (Fr).

"Nurmahal"

Pich, *Leconte de Lisle,* 342–43 (Fr).

"L'Oasis"

Pich, *Leconte de Lisle,* 321–22 (Fr).

"Les Oiseaux de proie"

Pich, *Leconte de Lisle,* 405 (Fr).

"La Paix des dieux"

Denommé, *The French Parnassian Poets,* 109, 111–12 (Eng).

Denommé, *Leconte de Lisle,* 111–12 (Eng).

Raitt, *Life and Letters in France,* 101–9 (Eng).

"La Panthère noire"

Pich, *Leconte de Lisle,* 323–24 (Fr).

"Les Paraboles de Dom Guy"

Pich, *Leconte de Lisle,* 306–9 (Fr).

"La Passion"

Pich, *Leconte de Lisle,* 290–95 (Fr).

LECONTE DE LISLE, "Phidylé"

"Phidylé"

Pich, *Leconte de Lisle,* 214–17 (Fr).

"Les Plaintes du Cyclope"

Pich, *Leconte de Lisle,* 368–69 (Fr).

"Qaïn"

Denommé, *The French Parnassian Poets,* 102–7 (Eng).

Denommé, *Leconte de Lisle,* 71–74 (Eng).

Alexandre Embiricos, *Interprétation de Leconte de Lisle* (Paris: Pensée Universelle, 1979), 152–53 (Fr).

Pich, *Leconte de Lisle,* 459–73, 476–86 (Fr).

"Les Raisons du Saint-Père"

Denommé, *Leconte de Lisle,* 110–11 (Eng).

"La Ravine de Saint-Gilles"

Pich, *Leconte de Lisle,* 328–31 (Fr).

"La Recherche de Dieu"

Pich, *Leconte de Lisle,* 150–53 (Fr).

"Requies"

Pich, *Leconte de Lisle,* 222–23 (Fr).

"La Robe du Centaure"

Pich, *Leconte de Lisle,* 124–26 (Fr).

"Le Runoïa"

Denommé, *Leconte de Lisle,* 65–68 (Eng).

Pich, *Leconte de Lisle,* 187–93 (Fr).

"Le Soir d'une bataille"

Pich, *Leconte de Lisle,* 362–64 (Fr).

"Solvet Seclum"

Lewis, *On Reading French Verse,* 4–5 (Eng).

Pich, *Leconte de Lisle,* 315–16 (Fr).

"Le Sommeil du condor"

Denommé, *The French Parnassian Poets,* 99–101 (Eng).

Denommé, *Leconte de Lisle,* 76–78 (Eng).

Pich, *Leconte de Lisle,* 324–28 (Fr).

"La Source"

Pich, *Leconte de Lisle,* 111–13 (Fr).

"Les Spectres"

Peter Hambly, "For an Allegorical reading of Leconte de Lisle's 'Les Spectres,'" *FSB* 18 (Spring 1986): 7–10 (Eng).

Pich, *Leconte de Lisle,* 425–27 (Fr).

"Sûrya"

Denommé, *The French Parnassian Poets,* 84–86 (Eng).

Pich, *Leconte de Lisle,* 116–18 (Fr).

LECONTE DE LISLE, "La Tête de Kenwarc'h"

"La Tête de Kenwarc'h"

Denommé, *Leconte de Lisle,* 98–99 (Eng).

"Thestylis"

Pich, *Leconte de Lisle,* 431–34 (Fr).

"Thyoné"

Pich, *Leconte de Lisle,* 98–101 (Fr).

"La Tristesse du Diable"

Pich, *Leconte de Lisle,* 449–50 (Fr).

"Ultra coelos"

Denommé, *Leconte de Lisle,* 84–85 (Eng).

"Le Vase"

Pich, *Leconte de Lisle,* 226–27 (Fr).

"Le Vent froid de la nuit"

Pich, *Leconte de Lisle,* 211–12 (Fr).

"La Vénus de Milo"

Knight, *Flower Poetics in Nineteenth-Century France,* 164–65 (Eng).

"La Vigne de Naboth"

Pich, *Leconte de Lisle,* 357–60 (Fr).

"La Vipère"

Pich, *Leconte de Lisle,* 103–5 (Fr).

"La Vision de Brahma"

Denommé, *Leconte de Lisle,* 58–59 (Eng).
Pich, *Leconte de Lisle,* 267–70, 279–80 (Fr).

"La Vision de Snorr"

Denommé, *Leconte de Lisle,* 86–87 (Eng).

LEIRIS, MICHEL

"Au vif"

Michael Riffaterre, "Sémantique du poème," *CAIEF* 23 (May 1971): 134–36 (Fr).

Jean-Jacques Thomas, "Michel Leiris, Yvan Goll: 'Touristes nous nous sommes promenés' " *FrF* (May 1978): 215–16 (Fr).

"Ecumes de la Havane"

M. Riffaterre, *Semiotics of Poetry,* 91–93 (Eng).

"La Néréido de la Mer Rouge"

Renée R. Hubert, "l'Image poétique de Michel Leiris," *FrF* 1 (January 1976): 68–78 (Fr).

LEMAIRE DE BELGES, JEAN

"Allégorie contre Jules II"

Jodogne, *Jean Lemaire de Belges,* 392–95 (Fr).

LEMAIRE DE BELGES, JEAN, "Allégorie sur les différends . . ."

"Allégorie sur les différends de la France et de la Papauté"

Brown, *The Shaping of History and Poetry in Late Medieval France,* 99–102, 106–7 (Eng).

"Chansons de Namur"

Jodogne, *Jean Lemaire de Belges,* 299–308 (Fr).

"La Concorde des deux langages"

Frappier, *Du Moyen Age à la Renaissance,* 297–313 (Fr).

Robert Griffin, "Cosmic Metaphor in 'La Concorde des deux langages,'" in Nash, ed., *Pre-Pléiade Poetry,* 15–30 (Eng).

Jodogne, *Jean Lemaire de Belges,* 443–62 (Fr).

Pierre Jodogne, "L'Orientation culturelle de Jean Lemaire de Belges," *CAIEF* 23 (May 1971): 101–3 (Fr).

Michael Randall, "The Flamboyant Design of Jean Lemaire de Belge's 'La Concorde des deux langages,'" *ECr* 28 (Summer 1988): 13–24 (Eng).

Winter, *Visual Variety and Spatial Grandeur,* 63–66 (Eng).

"Temple de Vénus" from "La Concorde des deux langages"

Frappier, *Du Moyen Age à la Renaissance,* 341–45, 350–52 (Fr).

Rigolot, *Poétique et onomastique,* 48–49 (Fr).

"La Concorde du genre humain"

Brown, *The Shaping of History and Poetry in Late Medieval France,* 52–55, 71, 150–51 (Eng).

Jodogne, *Jean Lemaire de Belges,* 312–19 (Fr).

"La Couronne Margaritique"

Frappier, *Du Moyen Age à la Renaissance,* 286–88 (Fr).

Jodogne, *Jean Lemaire de Belges,* 215–54 (Fr).

Rigolot, *Poétique et onomastique,* 33–35 (Fr).

LEMAIRE DE BELGES, JEAN, "Epîtres de l'amant vert, 3"

"Le Dyalogue de Vertu militaire et de Jeunesse françoise"

Jodogne, *Jean Lemaire de Belges,* 387–90 (Fr).

"Epitaphe de Molinet"

Jodogne, *Jean Lemaire de Belges,* 285–89 (Fr).

"Epître du Roy Louis XII à Hector de Troie"

Brown, *The Shaping of History and Poetry in Late Medieval France,* 102–7 (Eng).

Jodogne, *Jean Lemaire de Belges,* 395–403 (Fr).

"Epîtres de l'amant vert"

Jean Frappier, "La Cour de Malines et Jean Lemaire de Belges," *Histoire illustrée des lettres françaises de Belgique* (Bruxelles: La Renaissance du Livre, 1958), 143–50. Reprinted in Frappier, *Du Moyen age à la Renaissance,* 288–92 (Fr).

"Epîtres de l'amant vert, 1"

Frappier, *Du Moyen Age à la Renaissance,* 289–91 (Fr).

Jodogne, *Jean Lemaire de Belges,* 255–60 (Fr).

François Rigolot, "Intentionalité du texte de théorie de la 'persona': Le Cas des 'Epîtres de l'amant vert,'" in Gray, ed., *Poétiques,* 189–206 (Fr).

"Epîtres de l'amant vert, 2"

Jodogne, *Jean Lamaire de Belges,* 260–68 (Fr).

Winter, *Visual Variety and Spatial Grandeur,* 66–69 (Eng).

"Epîtres de l'amant vert, 3"

C. A. Mayer, "'La Tiers epistre de l'amant verd' de Jean Lemaire de Belges," in *De Jean Lemaire de Belges à Jean Giraudoux: Mélanges . . . offerts à Pierre Jourda* (Paris: Nizet, 1970), 27–36 (Fr).

LEMAIRE DE BELGES, JEAN, "Oraison à la Vierge"

"Oraison à la Vierge"

Jodogne, *Jean Lemaire de Belges,* 155–57 (Fr).

"La Plainte du Désiré"

Jodogne, *Jean Lemaire de Belges,* 204–14 (Fr).

John McClelland, "La Poésie à l'époque de l'humanisme: Molinet, Lemaire de Belges et Marot," in *L'Humanisme français au début de la Renaissance* (Paris: Vrin, 1973), 321–23 (Fr).

"Les Regretz de la Dame infortunée"

Jodogne, *Jean Lemaire de Belges,* 269–74 (Fr).

"Le Temple d'Honneur et de Vertus"

Joël Blanchard, *La Pastorale en France aux XIVe et XVe siècles: Recherches sur les structures de l'imaginaire médiévale* (Paris: Champion, 1983), 333–36 (Fr).

Jodogne, *Jean Lemaire de Belges,* 170–203 (Fr).

Pierre Jodogne, "Structure et technique descriptive dans 'le Temple d'honneur et de vertus' de Jean Lemaire de Belges," *SFr* 10 (May–August 1966): 269–78 (Fr).

Winter, *Visual Variety and Spatial Grandeur,* 48–50, 55–62, 64–65 (Eng).

"Les Vingt-quatre Couplets de la Valitude de la Reine"

Jodogne, *Jean Lemaire de Belges,* 392–95 (Fr).

LINGENDES, JEAN DE

"La Chanson à Philis"

Lafay, *La Poésie française du premier XVIIe siècle,* 301–2 (Fr).

LORTIGUE, ANNIBAL DE

"Les Vents qui sont enclos au centre de la terre"

Lafay, *La Poésie française du premier XVIIe siècle,* 203–4 (Fr).

MACHAUT, GUILLAUME DE

"Ami, je t'ay tant amé et cheri"

Johnson, *Poets as Players,* 45–47 (Eng).

"Amours, ma dame et Fortune et mi oueil"

Johnson, *Poets as Players,* 47–50 (Eng).

"De Fortune me doy plaindre et loer"

Johnson, *Poets as Players,* 43–45 (Eng).

"De toutes flours n'avoit et de tous fruis"

Johnson, *Poets as Players,* 51–54 (Eng).

"Dit de la fleur de lis et de la Marguerite"

Calin, *A Poet at the Fountain,* 229–31 (Eng).

"Dit de la Harpe"

Calin, *A Poet at the Fountain,* 227–29 (Eng).

"Dit de l'Alerion"

Kevin Brownlee, "Transformations of the Lyric 'Je': The Example of Guillaume de Machaut," *ECr* 18 (Spring 1978): 9–10 (Eng).

"Dit de la Marguerite"

Calin, *A Poet at the Fountain,* 229–31 (Eng).

"Dit de la Rose"

Calin, *A Poet at the Fountain,* 231–34 (Eng).

MACHAUT, GUILLAUME DE, "Dit du Verger"

"Dit du Verger"

Kevin Brownlee, *Poetic Identity in Guillaume de Machaut* (Madison: University of Wisconsin Press, 1984), 24–37 (Eng).

Calin, *A Poet at the Fountain,* 23–38 (Eng).

"Il m'est avis, qu'il m'est dons de Nature"

Johnson, *Poets as Players,* 42–43 (Eng).

"Je maudi l'eure et le temps et le jour"

Johnson, *Poets as Players,* 50–51 (Eng).

"Ne quier vëoir la biauté d'Absalon"

Friedrich Wolfzettel, "La Poésie lyrique en France comme mode d'appréhension de la réalité," in *Mélanges de langue et le littérature françaises du Moyen Age à la Renaissance, offerts à M. Charles Foulon* vol. 1, 413–14 (Fr).

"Prologue"

Kevin Brownlee, *Poetic Identity in Guillaume de Machaut* (Madison: University of Wisconsin Press, 1984), 16–20 (Eng).

Kevin Brownlee, "Transformations of the Lyric 'Je': The Example of Guillaume de Machaut," *ECr* 18 (Spring 1978): 5–8 (Eng).

Calin, *A Poet at the Fountain,* 234–37 (Eng).

Johnson, *Poets as Players,* 28–34 (Eng).

"Remède de Fortune"

Kelly, *Medieval Imagination,* 100–103 (Eng).

MALHERBE, FRANÇOIS DE, "A Monseigneur le Duc de Bellegarde"

MAETERLINCK, MAURICE

"Les Filles aux yeux bandés"

Eddy Rosseel, "Préliminaires à une lecture des 'Quinze chansons' de Maurice Maeterlinck," *CAIEF* 34 (May 1982): 153–64 (Fr).

MAGNY, OLIVIER DE

Amours de Castianire 10 "Je cherche Paix, et ne trouve que guerre"

Mark Whitney, "Olivier de Magny's 'Amours de Castianire': 'Laura' redux?" *BHR* 45 (May 1983): 261–62 (Eng).

"Les Raiz flambans de vostre oeil foudroyant"

Donaldson-Evans, *Love's Fatal Glance,* 78–79 (Eng).

"Le Sage, doux, chere et divin regard"

Donaldson-Evans, *Love's Fatal Glance,* 85–86 (Eng).

MALHERBE, FRANÇOIS DE

"A la Reine sur sa Bienvenue en France"

Rubin, *Higher, Hidden Order,* 22–36 (Eng).

Rubin, *The Knot of Artifice,* 93–94 (Eng).

Philip A. Wadsworth, "Form and Content in the Odes of Malherbe," *PMLA* 78 (June 1963): 191 (Eng).

"A Monseigneur le Duc de Bellegarde, Grand Escuyer de France"

Rubin, *Higher, Hidden Order,* 68–82 (Eng).

Rubin, *The Knot of Artifice,* 97–98 (Eng).

Philip A. Wadsworth, "Form and Content in the Odes of Malherbe," *PMLA* 78 (June 1963): 192–93 (Eng).

MALHERBE, FRANÇOIS DE, "Au Roy"

"Au Roy"

Nicolas Ruwet, "Malherbe: Hermogène ou Cratyle?" *Poétique* 11 (April 1980): 208–11 (Fr).

"Consolation à M. du Périer, Gentilhomme d'Aix-en-Provence"

Nicolas Ruwet, "Malherbe: Hermogène ou Cratyle?" *Poétique* 11 (April 1980): 201–2 (Fr).

Frank Warnke, "Some Consolations," in Bayley and Coleman, eds., *The Equilibrium of Wit,* 109–11 (Eng).

"Dessein de quitter une dame qui ne le contentait que de promesses"

Lafay, *La Poésie française du premier XVIIe siècle,* 303–8 (Fr).

Nicolas Ruwet, "Malherbe: Hermogène ou Cratyle?" *Poétique* 11 (April 1980): 211–17 (Fr).

"Il n'est rien de si beau comme Caliste est belle"

Henri Fluchère, " 'Beauté, mon beau souci . . . ': Fragment d'un 'Malherbe,' " in Bayley and Coleman, eds., *The Equilibrium of Wit,* 106–8 (Fr).

"Larmes de Saint Pierre"

Cave, *Devotional Poetry,* 253–54 (Eng).

"Larmes du Sieur Malherbe"

Philip A. Wadsworth, "Malherbe's Youthful Elegy," *ECr* 6 (Winter 1966): 264–69 (Eng).

"N'esperons plus, mon âme, aux promesses du monde"

Jeanneret, *Poésie et tradition biblique,* 491, 495–502 (Fr).

MALHERBE, FRANÇOIS DE, "Pour le Roy, allant chastier la rebellion"

"Ode à la Reine sur les heureux succès de sa Régence"

Rubin, *Higher, Hidden Order,* 83–93 (Eng).

Rubin, *The Knot of Artifice,* 98–99 (Eng).

Philip A. Wadsworth, "Form and Content in the Odes of Malherbe," *PMLA* 78 (June 1963): 193 (Eng).

"Ode au feu Roi sur l'heureux succès du voyage de Sedan"

Rubin, *Higher, Hidden Order,* 51–67 (Eng).

Rubin, *The Knot of Artifice,* 96–97 (Eng).

Philip A. Wadsworth, "Form and Content in the Odes of Malherbe," *PMLA* 78 (June 1963): 192 (Eng).

"Ode sur l'Attentat commis en la personne de sa majesté, le 19 de décembre 1605"

Rubin, *Higher, Hidden Order,* 37–50 (Eng).

Rubin, *The Knot of Artifice,* 94–96 (Eng).

Philip A. Wadsworth, "Form and Content in the Odes of Malherbe," *PMLA* 78 (June 1963): 191–92 (Eng).

"Paraphrase sur le Psaume 8"

Jeanneret, *Poésie et tradition biblique,* 491–95 (Fr).

"Pour la Reine mère du Roy pendant sa Régence"

Rubin, *Higher, Hidden Order,* 113–22 (Eng).

Philip A. Wadsworth, "Form and Content in the Odes of Malherbe," *PMLA* 78 (June 1963): 193–94 (Eng).

"Pour le Roy, allant chastier la rebellion des Rochelois, et chasser les Anglois"

Rubin, *Higher, Hidden Order,* 94–107 (Eng).

Rubin, *The Knot of Artifice,* 100–101 (Eng).

Philip A. Wadsworth, "Form and Content in the Odes of Malherbe," *PMLA* 78 (June 1963): 194 (Eng).

MALHERBE, FRANÇOIS DE, "Prière pour le Roy allant en Limousin"

"Prière pour le Roy allant en Limousin"

Rubin, *The Knot of Artifice,* 13–30 (Eng).

David Lee Rubin, "Malherbe and the Poetics of History: A Reading of the 1605 Prayer," *AJFS* 13 (September–December 1976): 244–55 (Eng).

David Lee Rubin, "Unity, Sequence, and the Arts of Compensation: A Perspective on Formal Trends," in *Manifestoes and Movements: French Literature Series,* " vol. 7 (Columbia: University of South Carolina Dept. of Foreign Languages, 1980), 22 (Eng).

Nicolas Ruwet, "Malherbe: Hermogène ou Cratyle?" *Poétique* 11 (April 1980): 202–8 (Fr).

"Psaume 129 (Translation)

Jeanneret, *Poésie et tradition biblique,* 491, 493–99 (Fr).

"Qu'autres que vous soient désirées"

Nicolas Ruwet, "Malherbe: Hermogène ou Cratyle?" *Poétique* 11 (April 1980): 200–201 (Fr).

MALLARME, STEPHANE

"A des heures et sans que tel souffle l'émeuve"

Emilie Noulet, "Remémoration d'amis belges," *AJFS* 1 (January–April 1964): 96–103 (Fr).

"A la nue accablante tu"

Austin, *Poetic Principles and Practice,* 192–200 (Eng).

Lloyd J. Austin, "Meaning in Mallarmé: Remarks on 'A la nue accablante tu,' " *AJFS* 16 (January–April 1979): 217–25. Reprinted in Austin, *Poetic Principles and Practice,* 192–200 (Eng).

Léon Cellier, "Deux notes sur Mallarmé," in Noémi Hepp, Robert Mauzi, and Claude Pichois, eds., *Mélanges de littérature française offerts à M. René Pintard* (Paris: Klincksieck, 1975), 675–78 (Fr).

Chadwick, *Mallarmé,* 132–35 (Fr).

Cohn, *Toward the Poems of Mallarmé,* 229–36 (Eng).

Coleman, *Maurice Scève, Poet of Love,* 3–5, 9–10 (Eng).

Fowlie, *Mallarmé,* 216–18 (Eng).

Houston, *Patterns of Thought,* 124–26 (Eng).

Lloyd, *Mallarmé: Poésies,* 41–43 (Eng).

Robert L. Mitchell, "Poetry of Religion to Religion of Poetry: Hugo, Mallarmé, and the Problematics of Preservation," *FR* 55 (March 1982): 485–87 (Eng).

Gérard Montbertrand, " 'A la nue . . . ,' ou Le Déshabillage d'un poème de Mallarmé," *NCFS* 15 (Spring 1987): 285–301 (Fr).

St. Aubyn, *Stéphane Mallarmé,* 126–27; rev. ed., 113–15 (Eng).

David Scott, "Mallarmé and the Octosyllabic Sonnet," *FS* 31 (April 1977): 158–60 (Eng).

Scott, *Picturialist Poetics,* 113–15 (Eng).

"Angoisse"

Lloyd J. Austin, "Mallarmé disciple de Baudelaire," *RHL* 67 (April–June 1967): 446–47 (Fr).

"Apparition"

Haskell Block, "The Alleged Parallel of Metaphysical and Symbolist Poetry," *CLS* nos. 4, 1–2 (1967): 154–59 (Eng).

Cohn, *Toward the Poems of Mallarmé,* 283–88 (Eng).

Richard, *L'Univers imaginaire de Mallarmé,* 123–24 (Fr).

"L'Après-midi d'un Faune"

Austin, *Poetic Principles and Practice,* 25–26 (Eng).

Jean-Pierre Chausserie-Laprée, "Equilibres mallarméens," *Europe* 54 (April–May 1976): 165–67 (Fr).

Cohn, *Toward the Poems of Mallarmé,* 13–32 (Eng).

MALLARME, STEPHANE, "L'Assaut"

Roseline Crowley, "Toward the Poetics of Juxtapositions: 'L'Après-midi d'un Faune,'" *YFS,* no. 54 (1977): 33–44 (Eng).

Fowlie, *Mallarmé,* 148–67 (Eng).

Hans-Yost Frey, "The Tree of Doubt," *YFS,* no. 54 (1977): 45–54 (Eng).

Richard Goodkin, "Zeno's Paradox: Mallarmé, Valéry, and the Symbolist 'Movement,'" *YFS,* no. 74 (1988): 136–44 (Eng).

Houston, *Patterns of Thought,* 91–93 (Eng).

James Kearns, "A Titian Legacy for Mallarmé's Faun?" *FSB* 31 (Summer 1989): 1–4 (Eng).

Knight, *Flower Poetics in Nineteenth-Century France,* 217–19 (Eng).

Lloyd, *Mallarmé: Poésies,* 57–58, 67–68 (Eng).

S. D. McFarlane, "Pastoral and the Deprived Poet," in Bowie, Fairlie, and Finch, eds., *Baudelaire, Mallarmé, Valéry,* 454–55 (Eng).

Richard, *L'Univers imaginaire de mallarmé,* 117, 295–296 (Fr).

St. Aubyn, *Stéphane Mallarmé,* 74–80; rev. ed., 62–68 (Eng).

Harold Smith, "Mallarmé's Faun: Hero or Anti-Hero?" *RR* 64 (March 1973): 111–24 (Eng).

Albert Sonnenfeld, "Eros and Poetry: Mallarmé's Disappearing Visions," in Beaumont, Cocking, and Cruickshank, eds., *Order and Adventure in Post-Romantic French Poetry,* 89–98 (Eng).

Gretchen Van Slyke, "A la recherche du langage: 'L'Après-midi d'un Faune,'" *NCFS* 12 (Fall–Winter 1983–84): 169–83 (Fr).

Steven Walker, "Mallarmé's Symbolist Eclogue: The 'Faune' as Pastoral," *PMLA* 93 (January 1978): 106–17 (Eng).

J. Weber, *Genèse de l'œuvre poétique,* 264–66 (Fr).

Bernard Weinberg, "Les Limites de l'hermétisme, ou Hermétisme et intelligibilité," *CAIEF* 15 (March 1963): 158–59 (Fr).

"L'Assaut"

Austin Gill, "An Allegory of Love: Mallarmé's 'L'Assaut,'" *AJFS* 6 (May–December 1969): 306–16 (Eng).

"Aumône"

St. Aubyn, *Stéphane Mallarmé,* 45–47; rev. ed., 34–35 (Eng).

Georges Zayed, "Réflexions sur les variantes d'"Aumône' et l'hermétisme mallarméen," *RHL* 72 (January–February 1972): 85–100 (Fr).

"Au seul souci de voyager"

Lloyd J. Austin, "The Mystery of a Name," *ECr* 1 (Fall 1961): 130–38. Reprinted in Austin, ed., *Poetic Principles and Practice,* 73–76 (Eng).

Broome and Chesters, *The Appreciation of Modern French Poetry (1850–1950),* 86–88 (Eng).

Chadwick, *Mallarmé,* 153–55 (Fr).

A. R. Chisholm, "Mallarmé's Vasco Sonnet," *FS* 20 (April 1966): 139–43 (Eng).

Cohn, *Toward the Poems of Mallarmé,* 192–95 (Eng).

Fowlie, *Mallarmé,* 214–15 (Eng).

St. Aubyn, *Stéphane Mallarmé,* 116–17; rev. ed., 104–5 (Eng).

"Autre éventail de mademoiselle Mallarmé"

Broome and Chesters, *The Appreciation of Modern French Poetry (1850–1950),* 83–86 (Eng).

Cohn, *Toward the Poems of Mallarmé,* 113–16 (Eng).

Peter Hambly, "Mallarmé, le crépuscule et les mythes," *AJFS* 22 (September–December 1985): 283–93 (Fr).

Richard, *L'Univers imaginaire de Mallarmé,* 309–13 (Fr).

St. Aubyn, *Stéphane Mallarmé,* 94–95; rev. ed., 82–83 (Eng).

"L'Azur"

Jean-Pierre Chausserie-Laprée, "Equilibres mallarméens," *Europe* 54 (April–May 1976): 161–63 (Fr).

Fowlie, *Mallarmé,* 33–36 (Eng).

MALLARME, STEPHANE, "Billet à Whistler"

Olds, *Desire Seeking Expression,* 58–59 (Eng).

Michael Riffaterre, "Sémantique du poème," *CAIEF* 23 (May 1971): 130–31 (Fr).

Harold Smith, "Dilemma and Dramatic Structure in Mallarmé's Parnasse Poems," *FR* 46 (Special Issue 5) (Spring 1973): 68–69 (Eng).

St. Aubyn, *Stéphane Mallarmé,* 42–44; rev. ed., 31–32 (Eng).

"Billet à Whistler"

A. R. Chisholm, "Two Exegetical Studies (Mallarmé, Rimbaud)," *ECr* 9 (Spring 1969): 28–30 (Eng).

Scott, *Pictorialist Poetics,* 35–36 (Eng).

"Brise marine"

Cohn, *Toward the Poems of Mallarmé,* 288–92 (Eng).

Frank Lestringant, "Rémanence du blanc: À propos d'une réminiscence hugolienne dans l'œuvre de Mallarmé," *RHL* 81 (January–February 1981): 64–72 (Fr).

Lloyd, *Mallarmé: Poésies,* 39–41 (Eng).

Olds, *Desire Seeking Expression,* 59–60 (Eng).

Harold Smith, "Dilemma and Dramatic Structure in Mallarmé's Parnasse Poems," *FR* 46 (Special Issue 5) (Spring 1973): 73–74 (Eng).

St. Aubyn, *Stéphane Mallarmé,* 44–45; rev. ed., 32–34 (Eng).

"Le Château de l'espérance"

Austin Gill, "An Allegory of Love: Mallarmé's L'Assaut, " *AJFS* 6 (May–December 1969): 306–16. Reprinted in Wallace Kirsop, ed., *Studies in Honour of A. R. Chisholm* (Melbourne: Hawthorne Press, 1969), 168–78 (Eng).

"La Chevelure vol d'une flamme"

Edward J. Ahearn, " 'Simplifier avec gloire la femme': Syntax, Synechdoche, Subversion in a Mallarmé Sonnet," *FR* 58 (February 1985): 349–59 (Eng).

Chadwick, *Mallarmé,* 101–4 (Fr).

Cohn, *Toward the Poems of Mallarmé,* 147–52 (Eng).

Fowlie, *Mallarmé,* 39–42 (Eng).

Barbara Johnson, "Poetry and Performative Language," *YFS,* no. 54 (1977): 152–58 (Eng).

Lloyd, *Mallarmé: Poésies,* 63–64 (Eng).

Richard, *L'Univers imaginaire de Mallarmé,* 347–49 (Fr).

St. Aubyn, *Stéphane Mallarmé,* 82–83; rev. ed., 70–71 (Eng).

"Contre un poète parisien"

Austin Gill, "Mallarmé's Use of Christian Imagery for Post-Christian Concepts," in Beaumont, Cocking, and Cruickshank, eds., *Order and Adventure in Post-Romantic French Poetry,* 73–76 (Eng).

"Un Coup de dés"

Richard Anderson, "Hindu Myths in Mallarmé: 'Un coup de dés,'" *CL* 19 (Winter 1967): 28–35 (Eng).

Paul Aron, "Notes sur le 'Coup de dés' de Mallarmé," *SFr* 27 (September–December 1983): 487–92 (Fr).

Austin, ed., "Presence and Poetry of Stéphane Mallarmé" in *Poetic Principles and Practice,* 38–39 (Eng).

Wilson Baldridge, "The Time-Crisis in Mallarmé and Proust," *FR* 59 (March 1986): 564–70 (Eng).

Malcolm Bowie, "The Question of 'Un Coup de dés,'" in Bowie, Fairlie, and Finch, eds., *Baudelaire, Mallarmé, Valéry,* 144–50 (Eng).

Calvin Brown, "De Quincy and the Participles in Mallarmé's 'Coup de dés,'" *CL* 16 (Winter 1964): 65–69 (Eng).

Calvin Brown, "The Musical Analogies in Mallarmé's 'Un Coup de dés'," *CLS* 4 (1967): 67–79 (Eng).

Chadwick, *Mallarmé,* 135–49 (Fr).

Robert G. Cohn, "A Propos du 'Coup de dés,'" *ECr* 1 (Fall 1961): 125–29 (Fr).

MALLARME, STEPHANE, "Un Coup de dés"

Cohn, *Toward the Poems of Mallarmé,* 261–64 (Eng).

Fowlie, *Mallarmé,* 212–13, 218–26 (Eng).

Ursula Franklin, "Segregation and Disintegration of an Image," *NCFS* 12 (Fall–Winter 1983–84): 161–65 (Eng).

Marthe Gonneville, "Poésie et typographie," *EF* 18 (Winter 1983): 21–24 (Fr).

Houston, *Patterns of Thought,* 126–27 (Eng).

Judd Hubert and Renée R. Hubert, "Masson's and Mallarmé's 'Un Coup de dés': An Esthetic Comparison," *NCFS* 18 (Spring–Summer 1990): 508–23 (Eng).

Julia Kristeva, *La Révolution du langage poétique* (Paris: Seuil, 1977): 198–99, 271–314 (Fr).

Julia Kristeva, "Sémianalyse et production de sens: Quelques problèmes de sémiotique," in A. J. Greimas, ed., *Essais de sémiotique poétique* (Paris: Larousse, 1972), 226–34 (Fr).

Longree, *L'Expérience idéo-calligrammatique,* 79–81 (Fr).

Charles Minahen, "Whirling Toward the Void at Dead Center," *RR* 78 (January 1987): 102–13 (Eng).

Emilie Noulet, "Mallarmé and Saint-John Perse," *CAIEF* 27 (May 1975): 314–16 (Fr).

Emilie Noulet, *Suites: Mallarmé, Rimbaud, Valéry* (Paris: Nizet, 1964), 26–30, 68–70 (Fr).

Porter, *The Crisis of French Symbolism,* 72–74 (Eng).

Mitsou Ronat, "Le 'Coup de Dés': Forme fixe?" *CAIEF* 32 (May 1980): 141–47 (Fr).

St. Aubyn, *Stéphane Mallarmé,* 81–82, 144–53; rev. ed., 144–53 (Eng).

Scott, *Pictorialist Poetics,* 138–69 (Eng).

J. Weber, *Genèse de l'œuvre poétique,* 283–90 (Fr).

Bernard Weinberg, "Les Limites de l'hermétisme, ou Hermétisme et intelligibilité," *CAIEF* 15 (March 1963): 159–61 (Fr).

MALLARME, STEPHANE, "Don du poème"

"Dame sans trop d'ardeur à la fois enflammant"

Chadwick, *Mallarmé,* 104–7 (Fr).
Richard, *L'Univers imaginaire de Mallarmé,* 475–76 (Fr).
St. Aubyn, *Stéphane Mallarmé,* rev. ed., 84–85 (Eng).

"La déclaration foraine"

St. Aubyn, *Stéphane Mallarmé,* 136 (Eng).

"De l'orient passé des temps"

Chadwick, *Mallarmé,* 48–50 (Fr).

"Le Démon de l'analogie"

St. Aubyn, *Stéphane Mallarmé,* 132–33 (Eng).
J. Weber, *Genèse de l'œuvre poétique,* 241–46 (Fr).

"Une Dentelle s'abolit"

Chadwick, *Mallarmé,* 44–47 (Fr).
A. R. Chisholm, "Mallarmé and the Act of Creation," *ECr* 1 (Fall 1961): 112–14 (Eng).
Cohn, *Toward the Poems of Mallarmé,* 206–17 (Eng).
Fowlie, *Mallarmé,* 51–54 (Eng).
R. M. Rehder, " 'Une Dentelle s'abolit' de Mallarmé," *NCFS* 1 (May 1973): 162–73 (Eng).
Richard, *L'Univers imaginaire de Mallarmé,* 261–64 (Fr).
St. Aubyn, *Stéphane Mallarmé,* 122–23; rev. ed., 109–10 (Eng).
David Scott, "Mallarmé and the Octosyllabic Sonnet," *FS* 31 (April 1977): 156–57 (Eng).
Eric Wayne, "Mallarmé's Folds: Mallarmé, Boulez, and 'Pli selon pli,' " *NCFS* 9 (Spring–Summer 1981): 227–28 (Eng).

"Don du poème"

Cohn, *Toward the Poems of Mallarmé,* 47–51 (Eng).
Fowlie, *Mallarmé,* 142–44 (Eng).

MALLARME, STEPHANE, "Eventail"

Olds, *Desire Seeking Expression,* 60–61 (Eng).

M. Riffaterre, *Semiotics of Poetry,* 150–63 (Eng).

St. Aubyn, *Stéphane Mallarmé,* 47–48; rev. ed., 35–36 (Eng).

"Eventail"

Sergio Villani, "Mallarmé's Missing Narrative," *ECr* 17 (Fall 1977): 231–32 (Eng).

"Eventail de Madame Mallarmé"

Cohn, *Toward the Poems of Mallarmé,* 111–12 (Eng).

Peter Hambly, "Mallarmé's 'Eventail,' " *FSB* 14 (Spring 1985): 9–12 (Eng).

St. Aubyn, *Stéphane Mallarmé,* 95–97; rev. ed., 83–84 (Eng).

"Les Fenêtres"

Lloyd J. Austin, "Mallarmé disciple de Baudelaire," *RHL* 67 (April–June 1967): 441–42, 447 (Fr).

Robert G. Cohn, " 'Les Fenêtres' de Mallarmé," *CAIEF* 27 (May 1975): 289–98 (Eng).

Robert G. Cohn, "Mallarmé's Windows," *YFS,* no. 54 (1977): 23–31 (Eng).

Fowlie, *Mallarmé,* 31–33, 36 (Eng).

Ursula Franklin, "Segregation and Disintegration of an Image," *NCFS* 12 (Fall–Winter 1983–84): 151–52 (Eng).

Patrick Laude, "Le Poète à sa fenêtre; dualisme et errance métaphysique dans la poésie française du dix-neuvième siècle," *NCFS* 19 (Spring 1991): 361–62 (Fr).

Renée Linkhorn, " 'Les Fenêtres': Propos sur trois poèmes," *FR* 44 (February 1971): 514–16, 517–18 (Fr).

Olds, *Desire Seeking Expression,* 54–58, 61–65 (Eng).

Raitt, *Life and Letters in France,* 135–43 (Eng).

St. Aubyn, *Stéphane Mallarmé,* 37–38; rev. ed., 26–27 (Eng).

Harold Smith, "Dilemma and Dramatic Structure in Mallarmé's Parnasse Poems," *FR* 46 (Special Issue 5) (Spring 1973): 67–68 (Eng).

"Les Fleurs"

Knight, *Flower Poetics in Nineteenth-Century France,* 211–13 (Eng).

"Frisson d'hiver"

Richard, *L'Univers imaginaire de Mallarmé,* 67 (Fr).

St. Aubyn, *Stéphane Mallarmé,* 131–32 (Eng).

"Le Guignon"

Porter, *The Crisis of French Symbolism,* 44–45 (Eng).

St. Aubyn, *Stéphane Mallarmé,* 33–34 (Eng).

J. Weber, *Genèse de l'œuvre poétique,* 256–57 (Fr).

"Hérodiade"

Austin, *Poetic Principles and Practice,* 20, 23–24, 26–28, 30 (Eng).

Georges-Emmanuel Clancier, *La Poésie et ses environs* (Paris: Gallimard, 1973), 115–22 (Fr).

Robert G. Cohn, "New Approaches to 'Hérodiade,'" *RR* 72 (November 1961): 472–81 (Eng).

Cohn, *Toward the Poems of Mallarmé,* 52–90 (Eng).

Gardner Davies, *Mallarmé et le rêve d' 'Hérodiade'* (Paris: Corti, 1978) (Fr).

Gardner Davies, "Paradox and Dénouement in Mallarmé's Poetry," *FS* 17 (October 1963): 352–56 (Eng).

John Erwin, "Claudel and the Lesson of Mallarmé: The Theme of Absence," *ECr* 13 (Spring 1973): 46–47 (Eng).

Fowlie, *Mallarmé,* 125–39 (Eng).

Houston, *Patterns of Thought,* 93–97, 127–28 (Eng).

MALLARME, STEPHANE, *Hérodiade 1* "Ouverture ancienne"

Knight, *Flower Poetics in Nineteenth-Century France,* 213–17 (Eng).

Julia Kristeva, *La Révolution du langage poétique* (Paris: Seuil, 1977), 444–51 (Fr).

Emilie Noulet, "Mallarmé and Saint-John Perse," *CAIEF* 27 (May 1975): 302–3, 313 (Fr).

Porter, *The Crisis of French Symbolism,* 38–39 (Eng).

Ramón Saldívar, "Metaphors of Consciousness in Mallarmé," *CL* 36 (Winter 1984): 61–66 (Eng).

St. Aubyn, *Stéphane Mallarmé,* rev. ed., 38–61 (Eng).

J. Weber, *Genèse de l'œuvre poétique,* 273–78 (Fr).

Hérodiade 1
"Ouverture ancienne"

Jean-Pierre Chausserie-Laprée, "L'Architecture secrète de l'"Ouverture ancienne,'" *Europe* 54 (April–May 1976): 74–103 (Fr).

A. R. Chisholm, "Mallarmé's 'Poétique très nouvelle,'" *AJFS* 6 (May–December 1969): 147–51. Reprinted in Wallace Kirsop, ed., *Studies in Honour of A. R. Chisholm* (Melbourne: Hawthorne Press, 1969), 10–13 (Eng).

Antoine Fongaro, "Hérodiade, le cygne et le poète," *SFr* 23 (January–April 1979): 104–6 (Fr).

Fowlie, *Mallarmé,* 139 (Eng).

Ursula Franklin, "Segregation and Disintegration of an Image," *NCFS* 12 (Fall–Winter 1983–84): 153–55 (Eng).

Rachel Killick, "Mendès, Mallarmé, and 'L'Absente,'" *FSB* 30 (Spring 1989): 1–4 (Eng).

Richard, *L'Univers imaginaire de Mallarmé,* 70–72 (Fr).

St. Aubyn, *Stéphane Mallarmé,* 52–59 (Eng).

Hérodiade 2
"Scène"

Chadwick, *Mallarmé,* 29–32 (Fr).

Fowlie, *Mallarmé,* 139 (Eng).

Lawler, *The Language of French Symbolism,* 15–16 (Eng).

MALLARME, STEPHANE, "Hommage à Richard Wagner"

Richard, *L'Univers imaginaire de Mallarmé*, 173–77 (Fr).

St. Aubyn, *Stéphane Mallarmé*, 59–71 (Eng).

Hérodiade 3
"Cantique de Saint Jean"

Chadwick, *Mallarmé*, 32–34 (Fr).

Wayne Chapman, "Symbolism and its 'Chief' Agent in English: Mallarmé vis à vis Yeats," *KRQ* 37, no. 1 (1990): 24–25 (Eng).

Fowlie, *Mallarmé*, 139–42 (Eng).

J. D. Hubert, "Representations of Decapitation: Mallarmé's 'Hérodiade' and Flaubert's 'Hérodias,'" *FrF* 7 (September 1982): 246–47 (Eng).

Richard, *L'Univers imaginaire de Mallarmé*, 161–64 (Fr).

St. Aubyn, *Stéphane Mallarmé*, 71–73 (Eng).

"Hommage à Puvis de Chavannes"

Cohn, *Toward the Poems of Mallarmé*, 186–88 (Eng).

Richard, *L'Univers imaginaire de Mallarmé*, 268–69 (Fr).

St. Aubyn, *Stéphane Mallarmé*, 115–16; rev. ed., 103–4 (Eng).

"Hommage à Richard Wagner"

Cohn, *Toward the Poems of Mallarmé*, 177–85 (Eng).

Fowlie, *Mallarmé*, 82–85 (Eng).

Peter Hambly, "Deux sonnets de Mallarmé," *AJFS* 25 (January–April 1988): 15–25 (Fr).

James R. Lawler, "Three Sonnets," *YFS*, no. 54 (1977): 91–95 (Eng).

Richard, *L'Univers imaginaire de Mallarmé*, 247–48, 272–73 (Fr).

St. Aubyn, *Stéphane Mallarmé*, 114–15; rev. ed., 101–3 (Eng).

Michael Wroblewski, "Stéphane Mallarmé's 'Hommage à Richard Wagner,'" *KRQ* 27, no. 1 (1980): 97–104 (Eng).

MALLARME, STEPHANE, "Igitur"

"Igitur"

Robert G. Cohn, "Wherefore 'Igitur,' " *RR* 60 (October 1969): 174–77 (Eng).

Nicholas Huckle, "Mallarmé and the Strategy of Transformation in 'Igitur,' " *NCFS* 19 (Winter 1991): 290–303 (Eng).

Lawler, *The Language of French Symbolism,* 12–13 (Eng).

St. Aubyn, *Stéphane Mallarmé,* 139–44; rev. ed., 126–31 (Eng).

J. Weber, *Genèse de l'œuvre poétique,* 278–82 (Fr).

"Las de l'amer repos"

Lloyd J. Austin, "Mallarmé disciple de Baudelaire," *RHL* 67 (April–June 1967): 448–49 (Fr).

Chadwick, *Mallarmé,* 9–19 (Fr).

Wayne Chapman, "Reading the Poem as Sentence and Music: Mallarmé's 'Las de l'amer repos,' " *KRQ* 36, no. 1 (1989): 15–26 (Eng).

Knight, *Flower Poetics in Nineteenth-Century France,* 209–11 (Eng).

Richard, *L'Univers imaginaire de Mallarmé,* 69–70 (Fr).

Harold Smith, "Dilemma and Dramatic Structure in Mallarmé's Parnasse Poems," *FR* 46 (Special Issue 5) (Spring 1973): 74–75 (Eng).

St. Aubyn, *Stéphane Mallarmé,* 39–41; rev. ed., 28–30 (Eng).

"Mes bouquins refermés sur le nom de Paphos"

Wilson Baldridge, "Closing Mallarmé's 'Poésies': A Scève memorial?" *FrF* 15 (May 1990): 195–99 (Eng).

Cohn, *Toward the Poems of Mallarmé,* 237–39 (Eng).

Fowlie, *Mallarmé,* 54–56 (Eng).

Austin Gill, "Mallarmé's Use of Christian Imagery for Post-Christian Concepts," in Beaumont, Cocking, and Cruickshank, eds., *Order and Adventure in Post-Romantic French Poetry,* 78–79 (Eng).

James R. Lawler, "Three Sonnets," *YFS,* no. 54 (1977): 85–88 (Eng).

Lloyd, *Mallarmé: Poésies,* 54–56, 61 (Eng).

St. Aubyn, *Stéphane Mallarmé,* 127–29; rev. ed., 115–16 (Eng).

"M'introduire dans ton histoire"

Anne-Marie Amiot, "La Poétique de l'érotisme mallarméen," *Europe* 564–65 (April–May 1976): 69–73 (Fr).

Chadwick, *Mallarmé,* 96–100 (Fr).

A. R. Chisholm, "Mallarmé: 'M'introduire dans ton histoire,' " *FS* 30 (April 1976): 170–72 (Eng).

Cohn, *Toward the Poems of Mallarmé,* 223–28 (Eng).

Fowlie, *Mallarmé,* 101–4 (Eng).

Lloyd, *Mallarmé: Poésies,* 16–20 (Eng).

St. Aubyn, *Stéphane Mallarmé,* 124–26; rev. ed., 112–13 (Eng).

"Monsieur Mallarmé. Le Pervers"

Ross Chambers, "An Address in the Country: Mallarmé and the Kinds of Literary Context." *FF* 11 (May 1986): 202–15 (Eng).

"Une Négresse"

St. Aubyn, *Stéphane Mallarmé,* 37; rev. ed., 26 (Eng).

"Le Nénuphar blanc"

Richard, *L'Univers imaginaire de Mallarmé,* 99–100 (Fr).

St. Aubyn, *Stéphane Mallarmé,* 136–37 (Eng).

"Les Noces d'Hérodiade"

Gardner Davies, "The 'Scène intermédiaire' in 'Les Noces d'Hérodiade,' " *AJFS* 4 (September–December 1967): 270–86 (Eng).

Gardner Davies, "The Finale of 'Les Noces d'Hérodiade,' " *AJFS* 6 (May–

MALLARME, STEPHANE, "O si chère de loin et proche et blanche"

December 1969): 216–52. Reprinted in Wallace Kirsop, ed., *Studies in Honour of A. R. Chisholm* (Melbourne: Hawthorne Press, 1969): 78–114 (Eng).

Gardner Davies, "The Prelude of 'Les Noces d'Hérodiade,'" *AJFS* 1 (January–April 1964): 71–95 (Eng).

Neal Oxenhandler, "A Hero of Eros: Hysteria and the Question of Closure in Mallarmé's 'Hérodiade,'" *SFR* 9 (Winter 1985): 383–95 (Eng).

Monic Robillard, "De l'œuvre à l'œuvre: 'Les Noces d'Hérodiade,'" *ELit* 22 (Summer 1989): 46–62 (Fr).

Paul Schwartz, "Les Noces d'Hérodiade," *NCFS* 1 (November 1972): 33–42 (Eng).

"O si chère de loin et proche et blanche"

John Erwin, "Méry Laurent and Mallarméan Absence: A New Reading of 'O si chère de loin,'" *FR* 46 (Special Issue 5) (Spring 1973): 87–94 (Eng).

Lloyd, *Mallarmé: Poésies,* 13–14 (Eng).

"Petit air" 1 & 2

St. Aubyn, *Stéphane Mallarmé,* 97–98; rev. ed., 85–86 (Eng).

"Petit air 1"
"Quelconque une Solitude"

Cohn, *Toward the Poems of Mallarmé,* 117–19 (Eng).

Gardner Davies, "Mallarmé's 'Petit air 1,'" in Bowie, Fairlie, and Finch, eds., *Baudelaire, Mallarmé, Valéry,* 158–80 (Eng).

Richard, *L'Univers imaginaire de Mallarmé,* 115–16 (Fr).

Scott, *Pictorialist Poetics,* 111–13 (Eng).

"Petit air 2"
"Indomptablement a dû"

Cohn, *Toward the Poems of Mallarmé,* 292–93 (Eng).

MALLARME, STEPHANE, "Pour un tombeau d'Anatole"

"Petit air (guerrier)"
"Ce me va hormis l'y taire"

Kevin O'Neill, "Mallarmé's 'Petit air (guerrier),' " *SFr* 17 (May–December 1972): 376–79 (Eng).

"Les Phares"

Chadwick, *Mallarmé,* 116–18 (Fr).

"Le Phénomène futur"

Richard, *L'Univers imaginaire de Mallarmé,* 124–25 (Fr).

"Le Pître châtié"

Lloyd J. Austin, "Mallarmé's Reshaping of 'Le Pitre châtié,' " in Beaumont, Cocking, and Cruickshank, eds., *Order and Adventure in Post-Romantic French Poetry* (New York: Harper & Row, 1973), 56–71, Reprinted in Austin, ed., *Poetic Principles and Practice,* 155–69 (Eng).

R. J. Berg, " 'Le Pitre châtié' I et II, ou L'Intertextualité problématique," *NCFS* 15 (Summer 1987): 376–84 (Fr).

Cohn, *Toward the Poems of Mallarmé,* 37–42 (Eng).

Fowlie, *Mallarmé,* 90–96 (Eng).

Ursula Franklin, "Segregation and Disintegration of an Image," *NCFS* 12 (Fall–Winter 1983–84): 157–58 (Eng).

Lloyd, *Mallarmé: Poésies,* 72–75 (Eng).

J. D. Lyons, "The Poetic Habit: A Metaphor in La Ceppède and Mallarmé," *FMLS* 11 (July 1975): 230–33 (Eng).

Joy Newton and Ann Prescott, "Mallarmé's Clown: A Study of 'Le Pitre châtié,' " *KRQ* 30, no. 4 (1983): 435–40 (Eng).

St. Aubyn, *Stéphane Mallarmé,* 35–36; rev. ed., 24–25 (Eng).

"Pour un tombeau d'Anatole"

Porter, *The Crisis of French Symbolism,* 70–72 (Eng).

MALLARME, STEPHANE, "Prose pour des Esseintes"

"Prose pour des Esseintes"

Lloyd Austin, "Mallarmé and the 'Prose pour des Esseintes," *FMLS* 2 (1966), 197–213. (Eng). Reprinted in Austin, *Poetic Principles and Practice,* 77–97 (Eng).

Chadwick, *Mallarmé,* 75–88 (Fr).

Cohn, *Toward the Poems of Mallarmé,* 240–60 (Eng).

Fowlie, *Mallarmé,* 192–209 (Eng).

Austin Gill, "Les Vrais Bosquets de la 'Prose pour Des Esseintes,' " *CAIEF* 15 (March 1963): 87–102 (Fr).

Houston, *Patterns of Thought,* 113–14 (Eng).

Hubert Juin, "Mallarmé et Des Esseintes," *Europe* 54 (April–May 1976): 112–18 (Fr).

Wallace Kirsop, "Brennan as Exegete: Some Documents from the Mallarmé Corpus," *AJFS* 16 (January–April 1979): 235–43 (Eng).

Knight, *Flower Poetics in Nineteenth-Century France,* 232–35 (Eng).

Julia Kristeva, *La Révolution du langage poétique* (Paris: Seuil, 1977), 239–63 (Fr).

D. J. Mossop, "Mallarmé's 'Prose pour Des Esseintes,' " *FS* 18 (April 1964): 123–35 (Eng).

Olds, *Desire Seeking Expression,* 15–48, 74–83 (Eng).

Porter, *The Crisis of French Symbolism,* 66–67 (Eng).

Richard, *L'Univers imaginaire de Mallarmé,* 400–403 (Fr).

St. Aubyn, *Stéphane Mallarmé,* 89–93; rev. ed., 77–81 (Eng).

Karlheinz Stierle, "Position and Negation in Mallarmé's 'Prose pour des Esseintes,' " *YFS,* no. 54 (1977): 96–117 (Eng).

J. P. Verhoeff, "Anciens et modernes devant la 'Prose pour Des Esseintes,' " *RHL* 71 (April 1971): 226–46 (Fr).

"Quand l'ombre menaça de la fatale loi"

Lloyd J. Austin, "The Indubitable Wing," in Cedrick Pickford, ed., *Mélanges de littérature française moderne offerts à Garnet Rees* (Paris: Minard, 1980), 1–14. Reprinted in Austin, ed., *Poetic Principles and Practice,* 201–12 (Eng).

MALLARME, STEPHANE, "Quelle soie aux baumes de temps"

Malcolm Bowie, "Genius at Nightfall: Mallarmé's 'Quand l'ombre menaça de la fatale loi,'" in Prendergast, ed., *Nineteenth-Century French Poetry*, 225–42 (Eng).

Chadwick, *Mallarmé*, 56–60 (Fr).

A. R. Chisholm, "Mallarmé: 'Quand l'ombre menaça . . . ,'" *FS* 15 (April 1961): 146–49 (Eng).

Cohn, *Toward the Poems of Mallarmé*, 120–23 (Eng).

Fowlie, *Mallarmé*, 184–88 (Eng).

Houston, *Patterns of Thought*, 103–4, 122 (Eng).

James R. Lawler, "Three Sonnets," *YFS*, no. 54 (1977): 88–91 (Eng).

Lloyd, *Mallarmé: Poésies*, 44–48 (Eng).

Richard Miller, "Quand l'ombre menaça de la fatale loi," *Expl* 10 (May 1952): 48. Reprinted in Walcutt and Whitesell, eds., *The Explicator Cyclopedia*, vol. 2, 380–81 (Eng).

Richard, *L'Univers imaginaire de Mallarmé*, 180–83 (Fr).

St. Aubyn, *Stéphane Mallarmé*, 99–100; rev. ed., 86–87 (Eng).

"Quelle soie aux baumes de temps"

Lloyd J. Austin, "Les Moyens du mystère chez Mallarmé et chez Valéry," *CAIEF* 15 (March 1963): 104–10 (Fr).

Chadwick, *Mallarmé*, 91–95 (Fr).

A. R. Chisholm, "Mallarmé and the Act of Creation," *ECr* 1 (Fall 1961): 112 (Eng).

Cohn, *Toward the Poems of Mallarmé*, 218–22 (Eng).

Fowlie, *Mallarmé*, 38–39 (Eng).

James R. Lawler, "Expirer comme un diamant . . . Mallarmé and Poetic Language," *FrF* 14 (January 1989): 55–63 (Eng).

Lloyd, *Mallarmé: Poésies*, 70–72 (Eng).

St. Aubyn, *Stéphane Mallarmé*, 123–24; rev. ed., 110–12 (Eng).

Cohn, *Toward the Poems of Mallarmé*, 294–98 (Eng).

MALLARME, STEPHANE, "Réminiscence"

Eric Wayne, "Mallarmé's Folds: Mallarmé, Boulez, and 'Pli selon pli,'"
NCFS 9 (Spring–Summer 1981): 222–27, 229–31 (Eng).

"Réminiscence"

St. Aubyn, *Stéphane Mallarmé,* 135–36 (Eng).

"Sainte"

Jean-Claude Carron, " 'Sainte' de Mallarmé: Poétique et musiques," *KRQ*
26, no. 2 (1979): 133–40 (Fr).

Chadwick, *Mallarmé,* 34–35 (Fr).

Cohn, *Toward the Poems of Mallarmé,* 91–95 (Eng).

Antoine Fongaro, "Pour l'exégèse de 'Sainte,'" *SFr* 10 (September–December 1965): 485–90 (Fr).

Fowlie, *Mallarmé,* 237–38 (Eng).

Austin Gill, "Mallarmé's Use of Christian Imagery for Post-Christian Concepts," in Beaumont, Cocking, and Cruickshank, eds., *Order and Adventure in Post-Romantic French Poetry,* 76–78 (Eng).

Katz and Hall, *Explicating French Texts,* 52–55 (Fr).

Albert Mingelgrun, "Note picturalolinguistique de 'Sainte,'" *Europe* 54
(April–May 1976): 170–73 (Fr).

St. Aubyn, *Stéphane Mallarmé,* 83–85; rev. ed., 71–73 (Eng).

Hans Staub, "Le Mirage interne des mots," *CAIEF* 27 (May 1975): 276–88 (Fr).

"Salut"

Chadwick, *Mallarmé,* 128–32 (Fr).

Cohn, *Toward the Poems of Mallarmé,* 33–36 (Eng).

Robert Giroux and Hélène Dame, "Les Critères de poéticité dans l'histoire
de la poésie québécoise (sémiotique littéraire)," *EL* 14 (April 1981): 134–36
(Fr).

Lloyd, *Mallarmé: Poésies,* 36–39 (Eng).

MALLARME, STEPHANE, "Ses purs ongles très haut dédiant leur onyx"

Robert L. Mitchell, "Poetry of Religion to Religion of Poetry: Hugo, Mallarmé, and the Problematics of 'Preservation,' " *FR* 55 (March 1982): 484–85 (Eng).

François Rastier, "Systématique des isotopies," in A. J. Greimas, ed., *Essais de sémiotique poétique* (Paris: Larousse, 1972), 85–102 (Fr).

St. Aubyn, *Stéphane Mallarmé,* 111–12; rev. ed., 99–100 (Eng).

"Ses purs ongles très haut dédiant leur onyx"

Austin, *Poetic Principles and Practice,* 37–38 (Eng).

Ellen Burt, "Mallarmé's 'Sonnet en yx': The Ambiguities of Speculation," *YFS,* no. 54 (1977): 55–82 (Eng).

Chadwick, *Mallarmé,* 50–54 (Fr).

Charles Chadwick, "Mallarmé le Phénix," *FSB* 25 (Winter 1987–88): 16 (Eng).

A. R. Chisholm, "Mallarmé's Transformation of the Image," in Bowie, Fairlie, and Finch, eds., *Baudelaire, Mallarmé, Valéry,* 154–56 (Eng).

A. R. Chisholm, "The Role of Consciousness in the Poetry of Mallarmé and Valéry," *CLS* 4 (1967): 81–89 (Eng).

Pierre Citron,"Sur le sonnet en -yx de Mallarmé," *RHL* 69 (January–February 1969): 113–16 (Fr).

Cohn, *Toward the Poems of Mallarmé,* 138–46 (Eng).

Fowlie, *Mallarmé,* 77–82 (Eng).

Eric Gans, "La Femme en x: Mallarmé anthropologue," *RR* 72 (May 1981): 285–300 (Eng).

Michel Grimaud, "Les Mystères du 'Ptyx'; Hypothèses sur la remotivation psychopoétique à partir de Mallarmé et Hugo," in Gray, ed., *Poétiques,* 108–23 (Fr).

Houston, *Patterns of Thought,* 100–103 (Eng).

Susan Huston, "The Ideology of Hermeticism: A New Perspective on Mallarmé," *AJFS* 17 (September–December 1980): 268–70 (Eng).

Catherine Lowe, "Le Mirage de ptyx: Implications à la rime," *Poétique* 15 (September 1984): 326–34 (Fr).

Porter, *The Crisis of French Symbolism,* 49–58 (Eng).

MALLARME, STEPHANE, "Le Sonneur"

Laurence Porter, "Erasure of Inspiration in Mallarmé," *RR* 76 (November 1985): 398–404 (Eng).

Deirdre Reynolds, "Illustration, Present or Absent: Reflecting Reflexivity in Mallarmé's 'Sonnet en yx,' " *JES* 19 (December 1989): 311–29 (Eng).

Deirdre Reynolds, "Mallarmé et la transformation esthétique du langage, à l'exemple de 'Ses purs ongles,' " *FrF* 15 (May 1990): 203–20 (Fr).

Richard, *L'Univers imaginaire de Mallarmé*, 167–69, 215–16, 519 (Fr).

M. Riffaterre, *Semiotics of Poetry*, 16–19, 60 (Eng).

Graham Robb, "The Phoenix of Mallarmé's 'Sonnet en -yx,' " *FSB* 24 (Autumn 1987): 13–15 (Eng).

St. Aubyn, *Stéphane Mallarmé*, 103–5; rev. ed., 90–93 (Eng).

Scott, *Pictorialist Poetics*, 83–87 (Eng).

Lawrence Watson, "Some Further Thoughts on Mallarmé's 'Sonnet en -yx,' " *FSB* 27 (Summer 1988): 13–16 (Eng).

J. Weber, *Genèse de l'œuvre poétique*, 270–72 (Fr).

Thomas Williams, "Mallarmé's 'Plusieurs sonnets 4' (Ses purs ongles très haut . . .)," *Expl* 25 (November 1966): 14–16 (Eng).

"Le Sonneur"

Porter, *The Crisis of French Symbolism*, 42–43 (Eng).

"Soupir"

Ramón Saldívar, "Metaphors of Consciousness in Mallarmé," *CL* 36 (Winter 1984): 55–58, 61 (Eng).

"Un Spectacle interrompu"

Maria Assad, "La Production du sens: 'Un Spectacle interrompu,' " *NCFS* 12 (Fall–Winter 1983–84): 186–97 (Fr).

St. Aubyn, *Stéphane Mallarmé*, 134–35 (Eng).

"Surgi de la croupe et du bond"

Lloyd J. Austin, "The Mystery of a Name," *ECr* 1 (Fall 1961): 130–38. Reprinted in Austin, ed., *Poetic Principles and Practice*, 71–73 (Eng).

Chadwick, *Mallarmé*, 41–44 (Fr).

Cohn, *Toward the Poems of Mallarmé*, 201–6 (Eng).

Fowlie, *Mallarmé*, 50–51 (Eng).

Lloyd, *Mallarmé: Poésies*, 50–52 (Eng).

Porter, *The Crisis of French Symbolism*, 67–68 (Eng).

Richard, *L'Univers imaginaire de Mallarmé*, 258–61 (Fr).

David Scott, "Mallarmé and the Octosyllabic Sonnet," *FS* 31 (April 1977): 149–63 (Eng).

St. Aubyn, *Stéphane Mallarmé*, 120–22; rev. ed., 108–9 (Eng).

"Sur les bois oubliés quand passe l'hiver sombre"

Chadwick, *Mallarmé*, 72–74 (Fr).

Ross Chambers, "Parole et poésie: 'Sur les bois oubliés . . . ' de Mallarmé," *Poétique* 10 (February 1979): 56–62 (Fr).

Cohn, *Toward the Poems of Mallarmé*, 43–46 (Eng).

Fowlie, *Mallarmé*, 183–84 (Eng).

Lloyd, *Mallarmé: Poésies*, 14–15 (Eng).

St. Aubyn, *Stéphane Mallarmé*, 106–7; rev. ed., 94–95 (Eng).

Sergio Villani, "Mallarmé's Missing Narrative," *ECr* 17 (Fall 1977): 230–31 (Eng).

"Toast funèbre"

Lloyd J. Austin, "Mallarmé and Gautier: New Light on 'Toast funèbre,' " in Donald G. Charlton, Jean Gaudon, and Anthony Pugh, eds., *Balzac and the Nineteenth Century: Studies in French Literature Presented to Herbert J. Hunt* (Leicester: Leicester University Press, 1972), 335–51. Reprinted in Austin, ed., *Poetic Principles and Practice*, 106–20 (Eng).

Bertocci, *From Symbolism to Baudelaire*, 92–94 (Eng).

MALLARME, STEPHANE, "Le Tombeau de Charles Baudelaire"

Chadwick, *Mallarmé,* 62–69 (Fr).

Jean-Claude Chevalier, "Quelques remarques sur le vocabulaire du 'Toast funèbre' de Stéphane Mallarmé," *CAIEF* 16 (March 1964): 9–19 (Fr).

Cohn, *Toward the Poems of Mallarmé,* 96–110 (Eng).

Fowlie, *Mallarmé,* 171–83 (Eng).

Austin Gill, "Mallarmé's Use of Christian Imagery for Post-Christian Concepts," in Beaumont, Cocking, and Cruickshank, eds., *Order and Adventure in Post-Romantic French Poetry,* 79–81 (Eng).

Lawler, *The Language of French Symbolism,* 4–5, 16–18 (Eng).

Lloyd, *Mallarmé: Poésies,* 27–30, 62–63 (Eng).

Patricia Parker, "Mallarmé's 'Toast funèbre': Some Contexts and a Reading," *RR* 71 (March 1980): 167–82 (Eng).

Richard, *L'Univers imaginaire de Mallarmé,* 246–47, 271–72 (Fr).

St. Aubyn, *Stéphane Mallarmé,* 85–89; rev. ed., 73–77 (Eng).

"Le Tombeau de Charles Baudelaire"

Lloyd J. Austin, " 'Le Tombeau de Charles Baudelaire' by Stéphane Mallarmé: Satire or Homage?" in *Etudes Baudelairiennes: Hommage à W. T. Bandy,* vol. 3 (1973): 185–200. Reprinted in Austin, ed., *Poetic Principles and Practice,* 170–81 (Eng).

Cohn, *Toward the Poems of Mallarmé,* 158–69 (Eng).

Fowlie, *Mallarmé,* 65–68 (Eng).

Austin Gill, "Le Tombeau de Charles Baudelaire," *CLS* 4 (Winter, 1980): 46–65 (Fr).

James R. Lawler, "Mallarmé et le 'poison tutélaire,' " *AJFS* 16 (January–April 1979): 229–32 (Fr).

Lloyd, *Mallarmé: Poésies,* 31–32 (Eng).

D. J. Mossop, "Stéphane Mallarmé: 'Le Tombeau de Charles Baudelaire,' " *FS* 30 (July 1976): 287–300 (Eng).

Jean Pommier, " 'Le Tombeau de Charles Baudelaire' par Stéphane Mallarmé," in *Baudelaire: Actes du Colloque de Nice, 25–27 mai 1967* (Paris: Minard, 1968), 173–82 (Fr).

Richard, *L'Univers imaginaire de Mallarmé*, 248–49 (Fr).

Clive Scott: *A Question of Syllables: Essays in Nineteenth-Century French Verse* (Cambridge: Cambridge University Press, 1986), 141–58 (Eng).

St. Aubyn, *Stéphane Mallarmé*, 109–11; rev. ed., 97–99 (Eng).

"Le Tombeau d'Edgar Poe"

Chadwick, *Mallarmé*, 69–72 (Fr).

Cohn, *Toward the Poems of Mallarmé*, 153–57 (Eng).

Fowlie, *Mallarmé*, 70–74 (Eng).

Ursula Franklin, "Segregation and Disintegration of an Image," *NCFS* 12 (Fall–Winter 1983–84): 158–60 (Eng).

Porter, *The Crisis of French Symbolism*, 47–48 (Eng).

St. Aubyn, *Stéphane Mallarmé*, 107–9; rev. ed., 95–97 (Eng).

Bernard Weinberg, "A Suggested Reading of 'Le Tombeau d'Edgar Poe,'" *ECr* 1 (Fall 1961): 117–24 (Eng).

"Le Tombeau de Verlaine"

Chadwick, *Mallarmé*, 124–27 (Fr).

Cohn, *Toward the Poems of Mallarmé*, 170–76 (Eng).

Fowlie, *Mallarmé*, 75–76 (Eng).

Richard, *L'Univers imaginaire de Mallarmé*, 249–50, 274–75 (Fr).

St. Aubyn, *Stéphane Mallarmé*, 112–13; rev. ed., 100–101 (Eng).

"Toute l'âme résumée"

Ross Chambers, "Le Poète fumeur," *AJFS* 16 (January–April 1979): 146–48 (Fr).

Cohn, *Toward the Poems of Mallarmé*, 189–91 (Eng).

Robert L. Mitchell, "Mint, Thyme, Tobacco: New Possibilities of Affinity in the 'Artes poeticae' of Verlaine and Mallarmé," *FrF* 2 (May 1977): 243–51 (Eng).

MALLARME, STEPHANE, "Tout orgueil fume-t-il du soir"

J. Terrie Quintana, "Mallarmé's 'Toute l'âme résumée,' " *Expl* 35 (Spring 1977): 24–25 (Eng).

Richard, *L'Univers imaginaire de Mallarmé,* 408–9 (Fr).

St. Aubyn, *Stéphane Mallarmé,* 118–19; rev. ed., 105–6 (Eng).

"Tout orgueil fume-t-il du soir"

Chadwick, *Mallarmé,* 36–38 (Fr).

Cohn, *Toward the Poems of Mallarmé,* 197–201 (Eng).

Fowlie, *Mallarmé,* 48–49 (Eng).

Richard, *L'Univers imaginaire de Mallarmé,* 257–58 (Fr).

St. Aubyn, *Stéphane Mallarmé,* 119–20; rev. ed., 107–8 (Eng).

"Tristesse d'été

Fowlie, *Mallarmé,* 37–38 (Eng).

St. Aubyn, *Stéphane Mallarmé,* 41–42 (Eng).

Harold Smith, "Dilemma and Dramatic Structure in Mallarmé's Parnasse Poems," *FR* 46 (Special Issue 5) (Spring 1973): 70–72 (Eng).

J. Weber, *Genèse de l'œuvre poétique,* 260–62 (Fr).

"Victorieusement fui le suicide beau"

Chadwick, *Mallarmé,* 75–88 (Fr).

A. R. Chisholm, "Mallarmé: 'Victorieusement fui le suicide beau,' " *FS* 14 (April 1960): 153–56 (Eng).

Cohn, *Toward the Poems of Mallarmé,* 133–37 (Eng).

Fowlie, *Mallarmé,* 42–48 (Eng).

Peter Hambly, "Mallarmé, le crépuscule et les mythes," *AJFS* 22 (September–December 1985): 272–83 (Fr).

Howarth and Walton, *Explications,* 202–17 (Eng).

Richard, *L'Univers imaginaire de Mallarmé,* 118–19 (Fr).

St. Aubyn, *Stéphane Mallarmé,* 101–3; rev. ed., 88–90 (Eng).

MALLARME, STEPHANE, "Le Vierge, le vivace, et le bel aujourd'hui"

"Le Vierge, le vivace, et le bel aujourd'hui"

Lloyd J. Austin, "How Ambiguous is Mallarmé? Reflections on the Captive Swan," in C. A. Burns, ed., *Literature and Society: Studies in . . . French Literature presented to R. J. North* (Birmingham: Goodman for the University of Birmingham, 1980), 102–14. Reprinted in Austin, ed., *Poetic Principles and Practice,* 213–26 (Eng).

Chadwick, *Mallarmé,* 19–28 (Fr).

Robert Champigny, "The 'Swan' and the Question of Pure Poetry," *ECr* 1 (Fall 1961): 145–55 (Eng).

A. R. Chisholm, "Mallarmé: 'Le Vierge, le vivace et le bel aujourd'hui,' " *FS* 16 (October 1962): 359–63 (Eng).

Cohn, *Toward the Poems of Mallarmé,* 124–32 (Eng).

B. De Cornulier, "Remarques sur le sonnet, 'Le Vierge, le vivace, et le bel aujourd'hui,' " *SF* 22 (January–April1978): 59–75 (Fr).

Philip Cranston, " 'In hoc signo': An Explication of Mallarme's 'Cygne,' " *KRQ* 28, no. 1 (1981): 95–108 (Eng).

Christine Crow, " 'Le Silence au vol de cygne': Baudelaire, Mallarmé, Valéry and the Flight of the Swan," in Bowie, Fairlie, and Finch, eds., *Baudelaire, Mallarmé, Valéry,* 7–12 (Eng).

Fowlie, *Mallarmé,* 96–101 (Eng).

Peter Hambly, "Deux sonnets de Mallarmé," *AJFS* 25 (January–April 1988): 6–14 (Fr).

Timothy Hampton, "Virgil, Baudelaire, and Mallarmé at the Sign of the Swan," *RR* 73 (November 1982): 438, 446–51 (Eng).

Lloyd, *Mallarmé: Poésies,* 75–76 (Eng).

Richard Miller, "Le Vierge, le vivace et le bel aujourd'hui," *Expl* 12 (October 1953): 6. Reprinted in Walcutt and Whitesell, eds., *The Explicator Cyclopedia,* 379–80 (Eng).

Olds, *Desire Seeking Expression,* 66–70 (Eng).

Richard, *L'Univers imaginaire de Mallarmé,* 251–56 (Fr).

St. Aubyn, *Stéphane Mallarmé,* 100–101; rev. ed., 87–88 (Eng).

Harold Smith, "The Bird and the Mirror: A Reading of Mallarmé's 'Le Vierge, le vivace . . . ' " *FR* 63 (October 1989): 57–65 (Eng).

MALLEVILLE, CLAUDE DE, "La Belle matineuse"

Eric Wayne, "Mallarmé's Folds: Mallarmé, Boulez, and 'Pli selon pli,'" *NCFS* 9 (Spring–Summer 1981): 227 (Eng).

R. A. York, "Bonnefoy and Mallarmé: Aspects of Intertextuality," *RR* 71 (May 1980): 309–11 (Eng).

MALLEVILLE, CLAUDE DE

"La Belle matineuse"

Katz and Hall, *Explicating French Texts,* 24–27 (Fr).

MARCABRU

"A la fontana del vergier"

Joël Blanchard, *La Pastorale en France aux XIVe et XVe siècles: Recherches sur les structures de l'imaginaire médiévale* (Paris: Champion, 1983), 63 (Fr).

Frederick Goldin, *Lyrics of the Troubadours and Trouvères: An Anthology and a History* (Garden City, N.Y.: Anchor Books, 1973), 52–53 (Eng).

"Al departir del brau tempier"

Topsfield, *Troubadours and Love,* 75–76 (Eng).

"L'autrier jost'una sebissa"

Topsfield, *Troubadours and Love,* 88–91 (Eng).

"Contra l'ivern"

Topsfield, *Troubadours and Love,* 99–100 (Eng).

"D'aisso laus Dieu"

Topsfield, *Troubadours and Love,* 93–96 (Eng).

MARGUERITE DE NAVARRE, "Las, tant malheureuse je suis"

"Doas cuidas ai compaignier"

Topsfield, *Troubadours and Love,* 96–98 (Eng).

"Pris mos coratges"

Topsfield, *Troubadours and Love,* 84–85 (Eng).

MARGUERITE DE NAVARRE

"L'Art et usage du souverain mirouer du chrestien"

Cottrell, *The Grammar of Silence,* 124–30 (Eng).

"Avès poinct veuz la Peronelle"

Ehsan Ahmed, "Regenerating Feminine Poetic Identity: Marguerite de Navarre's Song of the 'Peronelle,' " *RR* 78 (March 1987): 165–76 (Eng).

"La Coche"

Henri Chamard, *Les Origines de la poésie française de la Renaissance* (Paris: Boccard, 1920; Geneva: Slatkine, 1973), 79–80 (Fr).

Cottrell, *The Grammar of Silence,* 223–41 (Eng).

"Dialogue en forme de vision nocturne"

Cottrell, *The Grammar of Silence,* 35–54 (Eng).

"Las, tant malheureuse je suis"

Ehsan Ahmed, "Marguerite de Navarre's 'Chansons spirituelles,' " *BHR* 52 (March 1990): 41–46 (Eng).

MARGUERITE DE NAVARRE, "Le Miroir de Jhesus Christ crucifié"

"Le Miroir de Jhesus Christ crucifié"

Robert Cottrell, "The Gaze as the Agency of Presence in Marguerite de Navarre's 'Miroir de Jhesus Christ crucifié,'" *FrF* 13 (May 1988): 133–41 (Eng).

"Le Miroir de l'âme pécheresse"

Cottrell, *The Grammar of Silence,* 95–123 (Eng).

"Le Navire"

Cottrell, *The Grammar of Silence,* 203–19 (Eng).

"Oraison à nostre Seigneur Jesus Christ"

Cottrell, *The Grammar of Silence,* 87–91 (Eng).

"Oraison de l'âme fidèle"

Cottrell, *The Grammar of Silence,* 75–87 (Eng).

"Le Petit œuvre dévot et contemplatif"

Cottrell, *The Grammar of Silence,* 57–74 (Eng).

"Pour estre bien vray Chrestien"

Ehsan Ahmed, "Marguerite de Navarre's 'Chansons spirituelles,'" *BHR* 52 (March 1990): 46–48 (Eng).

"Si la douleur de mon esprit"

Ehsan Ahmed, "Marguerite de Navarre's 'Chansons spirituelles,'" *BHR* 52 (March 1990): 37–41 (Eng).

"Le Triomphe de l'Agneau"

Cottrell, *The Grammar of Silence,* 169–92 (Eng).

"Vray Dieu de Ciel, réconfortez mon âme"

Ehsan Ahmed, "Marguerite de Navarre's 'Chansons spirituelles,' " *BHR* 52 (March 1990): 49–50 (Eng).

MARIE DE FRANCE

"Bisclavret"

Clifford, *Marie de France: Lais,* 65–68 (Eng).

Hoepffner, *Les Lais de Marie de France,* 144–50 (Fr).

Pierre Jonin, "Le Roi dans les 'Lais' de Marie de France," in Lacy and Nash, eds., *Essays in Early French Literature Presented to Barbara Craig,* 35–38 (Fr).

Ménard, *Les Lais de Marie de France,* 107–8 (Fr).

Mickel, *Marie de France,* 79–81, 109–10 (Eng).

Rothschild, *Narrative Technique in the Lais,* 92–138 (Eng).

Sienaert, *Les Lais de Marie de France,* 87–96 (Fr).

François Suard, " 'Bisclavret' et les contes du loup-garou: Essai d'interprétation," in *Mélanges de langue et de littérature françaises . . . offerts à M. Charles Foulon,* vol. 2 (Rennes: Institut de Français, 1980), 267–76 (Fr).

"Chaitivel"

Burgess, *The Lais of Marie de France,* 50–64, 143–44 (Eng).

Clifford, *Marie de France: Lais,* 29–35 (Eng).

Hoepffner, *Les Lais de Marie de France,* 159–65 (Fr).

Jean-Charles Huchet, "Nom de femme et écriture féminine au Moyen Age," *Poétique* 48 (November 1981): 428 (Fr).

Mickel, *Marie de France,* 116–17 (Fr).

Sienaert, *Les Lais de Marie de France,* 147–49 (Fr).

"Chèvrefoil"

Burgess, *The Lais of Marie de France,* 65–70 (Eng).

Glyn Burgess, "A Note on Marie de France's 'Chèvrefoil,' " *FSB* 3 (Summer 1982): 1–4 (Eng).

Clifford, *Marie de France: Lais,* 74–77 (Eng).

M. Delbouille, "Chievrefoil," in *Mélanges de langue et de littêrature . . . offerts à Jean Frappier,* vol. 1 (Geneva: Droz, 1970), 207–16 (Fr).

Elizabeth Francis, "A Comment on 'Chevrefoil,' " in F. Whitehead, A. H. Diverres, and F. E. Sutcliffe, eds., *Medieval Miscellany Presented to Eugène Vinaver* (Manchester: Manchester University Press, 1965), 136–45 (Eng).

Jean Frappier, "Contribution au débat sur le Lai du Chèvrefeuille," in *Mélanges de linguistique et de littérature romanes à la mémoire d'Istvan Frank* (Saarlandes:Université des Saarlandes, 1957), 215–24. Reprinted in Frappier, *Du Moyen Age à la Renaissance,* 37–50 (Fr).

Hoepffner, *Les Lais de Marie de France,* 133–38 (Fr).

Jean-Charles Huchet, "Nom de femme et écriture féminine au Moyen Age," *Poétique* 48 (November 1981): 424–26 (Fr).

Guy Mermier, "En relisant le 'Chevrefoil' de Marie de France," *FR* 48 (April 1975): 864–70 (Fr).

Mickel, *Marie de France,* 93–95, 117–18 (Fr).

Sienaert, *Les Lais de Marie de France,* 151–54 (Fr).

Robert Sturges, "Texts and Readers in Marie de France's 'Lais,' " *RR* 71 (May 1980): 249–52 (Eng).

Evelyn B. Vitz, "Orality, Literacy, and the Early Tristan Material," *RR* 78 (May 1987): 307–8 (Eng).

"Les Deus amanz"

Burgess, *The Lais of Marie de France,* 42–49, 106–8 (Eng).

Clifford, *Marie de France: Lais,* 69–71 (Eng).

Hoepffner, *Les Lais de Marie de France,* 125–33 (Fr).

Jean-Charles Huchet, "Nom de femme et écriture féminine au Moyen Age," *Poétique* 48 (November 1981): 420–21 (Fr).

Pierre Jonin, "Le Roi dans les 'Lais' de Marie de France," in Lacy and Nash, eds., *Essays in Early French Literature Presented to Barbara Craig,* 32–34 (Fr).

Mickel, *Marie de France,* 84–86, 110–12 (Fr).

Willem Noomen, "Le Lai des Deus amanz de Marie de France: Contribution pour une description," in *Etudes le langue et de littérature de moyen âge offerts à Félix Lecoy* (Paris: Champion, 1973), 469–81 (Fr).

Rochschild, *Narrative Technique in the Lais,* 139–67 (Eng).

Sienaert, *Les Lais de Marie de France,* 109–19 (Fr).

Jeanne Wathelet-Willem, "Un Lai de Marie de France: 'Les Deux amants,' " in ed., *Mélanges offerts à Rita Lejeune, Professeur à l'Université de Liège,* vol. 2, (Gembloux: Editions Duculot, 1969), 1143–57 (Fr).

"Eliduc"

Leslie Brook, "A Note on the Ending of 'Eliduc,' " *FSB* 32 (Autumn 1989): 14–16 (Eng).

Burgess, *The Lais of Marie de France,* 148–50, 156–57 (Eng).

Clifford, *Marie de France: Lais,* 30–31, 35–43 (Eng).

Donovan, *The Breton Lay,* 32–33 (Eng).

Hoepffner, *Les Lais de Marie de France,* 95–108 (Fr).

Jean-Charles Huchet, "Nom de femme et écriture féminine au Moyen Age," *Poétique* 48 (November 1981): 423–24 (Fr).

Pierre Jonin, "Le Roi dans les 'Lais' de Marie de France," in Lacy and Nash, eds., *Essays in Early French Literature Presented to Barbara Craig,* 26–27 (Fr).

Florence McCulloch, "Length, Recitation, and Meaning of the 'Lais,' " *KRQ* 25, no. 2 (1978): 264–66 (Eng).

Ménard, *Les Lais de Marie de France,* 117–21 (Fr).

Mickel, *Marie de France,* 95–97, 118–20 (Fr).

Deborah Nelson, "Eliduc's Salvation," *FR* 55 (October 1981): 37–42 (Eng).

Jacques Ribard, "Le Lai d''Eliduc': Étude thématique," in *Mélanges de langue et de littérature françaises . . . offerts à M. Charles Foulon* (Rennes: Institut de Français, 1980), vol. 1, 295–99 (Fr).

Howard Robertson, "Love and the Otherworld in Marie de France's 'Eliduc,'" in Cormier and Holmes, eds., *Essays in Honor of Louis Francis Solano,* 167–76 (Eng).

Sienaert, *Les Lais de Marie de France,* 157–73 (Fr).

"Equitan"

Burgess, *The Lais of Marie de France,* 40–42, 102–3, 138–43 (Eng).

Clifford, *Marie de France: Lais,* 44–48 (Eng).

Hoepffner, *Les Lais de Marie de France,* 150–59 (Fr).

Jean-Charles Huchet, "Nom de femme et écriture féminine au Moyen Age," *Poétique* 48 (November 1981): 414–15 (Fr).

Pierre Jonin, "Le Roi dans les 'Lais' de Marie de France," in Lacy and Nash, eds., *Essays in Early French Literature Presented to Barbara Craig,* 30–32 (Fr).

Florence McCulloch, "Length, Recitation, and Meaning of the 'Lais,'" *KRQ* 25, no. 2 (1978): 261–62 (Eng).

Ménard, *Les Lais de Marie de France,* 127–28 (Fr).

Mickel, *Marie de France,* 75–77, 105–7 (Fr).

Rothschild, *Narrative Technique in the Lais,* 21–47 (Eng).

Sienaert, *Les Lais de Marie de France,* 69–76 (Fr).

"Fresne"

Clifford, *Marie de France: Lais,* 49–51 (Eng).

Michelle Freeman, "The Power of Sisterhood: Marie de France's 'Le Fresne,'" *FrF* 12 (January 1987): 5–26 (Eng).

Hoepffner, *Les Lais de Marie de France,* 109–24 (Fr).

Jean-Charles Huchet, "Nom de femme et écriture féminine au Moyen Age," *Poétique* 48 (November 1981): 421–23 (Fr).

Mickel, *Marie de France,* 77–79, 107–9 (Eng).

Rothschild, *Narrative Technique in the Lais,* 48–91 (Eng).

Sienaert, *Les Lais de Marie de France,* 79–85 (Fr).

"Guigemar"

Howard Bloch, "The Lay and the Law: Sexual/Textual Transgression," *SFR* 14 (Spring–Fall 1990): 206–9 (Eng).

Howard Bloch, "The Medieval Text: 'Guigemar' as a Provocation to the Discipline of Medieval Studies," *RR* 79 (January 1988): 63–73 (Eng).

Joan Brumlik, "Thematic Irony in Marie de France's 'Guigemar,' " *FrF* 13 (January 1988): 5–16 (Eng).

Burgess, *The Lais of Marie de France,* 134–38 (Eng).

Clifford, *Marie de France: Lais,* 19–28 (Eng).

Donovan, *The Breton Lay,* 25–26 (Eng).

Hoepffner, *Les Lais de Marie de France,* 82–94 (Fr).

Jean-Charles Huchet, "Nom de femme et écriture féminine au Moyen Age," *Poétique* 48 (November 1981): 418–19 (Fr).

Antoinette Knapton, *Mythe et psychologie chez Marie de France dans "Guigemar"* (Chapel Hill: University of North Carolina Department of Romance Languages, 1975) (Fr).

Florence McCulloch, "Length, Recitation, and Meaning of the 'Lais,' " *KRQ* 25, no. 2 (1978): 261 (Eng).

Charles Mela, "Le Lai de 'Guigemar' selon la lettre et l'écriture," in *Mélanges de langue et de littérature françaises . . . offerts à M. Charles Foulon,* vol. 2 (Rennes: Institut de Français, 1980), 193–202 (Fr).

Mickel, *Marie de France,* 72–75, 103–5 (Fr).

Stephen G. Nichols, "Deflections of the Body in the Old French Lay," *SFR* 14 (Fall 1990): 28–34 (Eng).

Antoinette Saly, "Observations sur le lai de 'Guigemar,' " in *Mélanges de langue et de littérature françaises . . . offerts à M. Charles Foulon,* vol. 1 (Rennes: Institut de Français, 1980), 329–39 (Fr).

Sienaert, *Les Lais de Marie de France,* 51–65 (Fr).

Robert Sturges, "Texts and Readers in Marie de France's 'Lais,' " *RR* 71 (May 1980): 252–56 (Eng).

Evelyn B. Vitz, "The 'Lais' of Marie de France: 'Narrative Grammar' and the Literary Test," *RR* 74 (November 1983): 396–98 (Eng).

"Lanval"

Howard Bloch, "The Lay and the Law: Sexual/Textual Transgression," *SFR* 14 (Spring–Fall 1990): 199–203 (Eng).

Burgess, *The Lais of Marie de France,* 104–6, 122–25 (Eng).

Brigitte Cazelles, "Outrepasser les normes: L'Invention de soi en France médiévale," *SFR* 14 (Spring–Fall 1990): 89–92 (Fr).

Clifford, *Marie de France: Lais,* 55–60 (Eng).

Muriel Davison, "Marie de France's 'Lai de Lanval,' [v.] 31–38," *Expl* 21 (October 1962): 6–7 (Eng).

Hoepffner, *Les Lais de Marie de France,* 56–71 (Fr).

W. T. H. Jackson, "The Arthuricity of Marie de France," *RR* 70 (January 1979): 1–18 (Eng).

Pierre Jonin, "Le Roi dans les 'Lais' de Marie de France," in Lacy and Nash, eds., *Essays in Early French Literature Presented to Barbara Craig,* 28–30 (Fr).

Ménard, *Les Lais de Marie de France,* 106–7, 112, 116 (Fr).

Mickel, *Marie de France,* 81–84 110 (Eng).

Sienaert, *Les Lais de Marie de France,* 99–107 (Fr).

"Laüstic"

Howard Bloch, "The Lay and the Law? Sexual/Textual Transgression," *SFR* 14 (Spring–Fall 1990): 203–6 (Eng).

Kristine Brightenback, "The 'Metamorphosis' and Narrative 'Conjointure' in 'Deus Amanz,' 'Yonec' and 'Le Laüstic,' " *RR* 72 (January 1981): 3–8, 11 (Eng).

Robert Cargo, "Marie de France's 'Le Laüstic' and Ovid's 'Metamorphoses,' " *CL* 18 (Spring 1966): 162–66 (Eng).

Clifford, *Marie de France: Lais,* 71–74 (Eng).

Michelle Freeman, "Marie de France's Poetics of Silence: The Implications for a Feminine 'Translatio,'" *PMLA* 99 (October 1984): 867–71 (Eng).

Hoepffner, *Les Lais de Marie de France,* 138–43 (Fr).

Jean-Charles Huchet, "Nom de femme et écriture féminine au Moyen Age," *Poétique* 48 (November 1981): 417 (Fr).

Florence McCulloch, "Length, Recitation, and Meaning of the 'Lais,'" *KRQ* 25, no. 2 (1978): 263 (Eng).

Mickel, *Marie de France,* 90–91, 113–14 (Eng).

Stephen G. Nichols, "Deflections of the Body in the Old French Lay," *SFR* 14 (Fall 1990): 42–43 (Eng).

Sienaert, *Les Lais de Marie de France,* 131–36 (Fr).

Evelyn B. Vitz, "The 'Lais' of Marie de France: 'Narrative Grammar' and the Literary Test," *RR* 74 (November 1983): 386–89, 399–401 (Eng).

Evelyn B. Vitz, "Orality, Literacy, and the Early Tristan Material," *RR* 78 (May 1987): 306–7 (Eng).

Zumthor, *Essai de poétique médiévale,* 386–90 (Fr).

"Milun"

Burgess, *The Lais of Marie de France,* 79–82, 110–11 (Eng).

Clifford, *Marie de France: Lais,* 51–54 (Eng).

Régine Colliot, "Oiseaux merveilleux dans 'Guillaume d'Angleterre' et les 'Lais' de Marie de France," in *Mélanges de langue et de littérature françaises . . . offerts à M. Charles Foulon,* vol. 1 (Rennes: Institut de Français, 1980), 125–26 (Fr).

Mickel, *Marie de France,* 91–93, 114–16 (Fr).

Rothschild, *Narrative Technique in the Lais,* 211–50 (Eng).

Sienaert, *Les Lais de Marie de France,* 139–44 (Fr).

"Prologue général"

Michelle Freeman, "Marie de France's Poetics of Silence: The Implications for a Feminine 'Translatio,'" *PMLA* 99 (October 1984): 860–64 (Eng).

Sienaert, *Les Lais de Marie de France,* 225–27 (Fr).

MARIE DE FRANCE, "Yonec"

"Yonec"

Kristine Brightenback, "The 'Metamorphosis' and Narrative 'Conjointure' in 'Deus Amanz,' 'Yonec' and 'Le Laüstic,' " *RR* 72 (January 1981): 9–10 (Eng).

Clifford, *Marie de France: Lais,* 60–65 (Eng).

Régine Colliot, "Oiseaux merveilleux dans 'Guillaume d'Angleterre' et les 'Lais' de Marie de France," in *Mélanges de langue et de littérature françaises . . . offerts à M. Charles Foulon,* vol. 1 (Rennes: Institut de Français, 1980), 119–21 (Fr).

Hoepffner, *Les Lais de Marie de France,* 72–81 (Fr).

Jean-Charles Huchet, "Nom de femme et écriture féminine au Moyen Age," *Poétique* 48 (November 1981): 416 (Fr).

Pierre Jonin, "Le Roi dans les 'Lais' de Marie de France," in Lacy and Nash, eds., *Essays in Early French Literature Presented to Barbara Craig,* 34–35 (Fr).

Ménard, *Les Lais de Marie de France,* 138–39 (Fr).

Mickel, *Marie de France,* 86–90, 112–13 (Fr).

Stephen G. Nichols, "Deflections of the Body in the Old French Lay," *SFR* 14 (Fall 1990): 34–39, 45–49 (Eng).

Rothschild, *Narrative Technique in the Lais,* 168–210 (Eng).

Sienaert, *Les Lais de Marie de France,* 121–29 (Fr).

Robert Sturges, "Texts and Readers in Marie de France's 'Lais,' " *RR* 71 (May 1980): 245–47 (Eng).

MAROT, CLEMENT

"Adieu aux dames de la cour"

Vianey, *Les Epîtres de Marot,* 123–24 (Fr).

"A son Amy Lyon"

Jacques Berchtold, "Le Poète-Rat: Villon, Erasme, ou les secrètes alliances de la prison," *BHR* 50 (January 1988): 57–76 (Fr).

Gérard Defaux, "Clément Marot: Une Poétique du silence et le la liberté," in Nash, ed., *Pre-Pléiade Poetry,* 46–49 (Fr).

MAROT, CLEMENT, "Au Roy, pour le deslivrer de prison"

Gérard Defaux, "Rhétorique, silence, et liberté dans l'œuvre de Marot," *BHR* 46 (May 1984): 301–4 (Fr).

Rigolot, *Poétique et onomastique,* 67–68 (Fr).

"Au Conte d'Estampes"

Kenneth Lloyd-Jones, "Une 'supercherie' de Marot," *SFr* 22 (May–December 1978): 369–73 (Fr).

"Au Roy, du temps de son exil à Ferrare"

Griffin, *Clément Marot,* 52–54 (Eng).

Joseph, *Clément Marot,* 131–35 (Eng).

Jourda, *Marot,* 124–26 (Fr).

Richard Katz, "The Lyricism of Clément Marot," *KRQ* 19, supplement no. 1, (1972): 31–33 (Eng).

Plattard, *Marot,* 127–28, 149–50 (Fr).

Vianey, *Les Epîtres de Marot,* 108–13 (Fr).

"Au Roy, pour avoir esté desrobé"

Griffin, *Clément Marot,* 240–43 (Eng).

Joseph, *Clément Marot,* 96–98 (Eng).

Jourda, *Marot,* 119–22 (Fr).

Mayer, *Clément Marot,* 179–86 (Fr).

C. Scollen-Jimack, "Marot and Deschamps: The Rhetoric of Misfortune," *FS* 42 (January 1988): 27–28 (Eng).

Vianey, *Les Epîtres de Marot,* 72–77 (Fr).

"Au Roy, pour le deslivrer de prison"

Joseph, *Clément Marot,* 94–96 (Eng).

Jourda, *Marot,* 118, 120–22 (Fr).

Mayer, *Clément Marot,* 164–66 (Fr).

MAROT, CLEMENT, "Au Roy, pour sa delivrance"

"Au Roy, pour sa delivrance"

Griffin, *Clément Marot,* 252–55 (Eng).

"Au Roy, pour succeder en l'estat de son pere"

Griffin, *Clément Marot,* 78 (Eng).

C. Scollen-Jimack, "Marot and Deschamps: The Rhetoric of Misfortune," *FS* 42 (January 1988): 25–26 (Eng).

"Au tresvertueux prince, Françoys, Daulphin de France"

Vianey, *Les Epîtres de Marot,* 114–16 (Fr).

"Chant d'Amour fugitif" (Second)

Mayer, *Clément Marot,* 188–90 (Fr).

Smith, *Clément Marot, Poet of the French Renaissance,* 207–10 (Eng).

"Chant Nuptial du Mariage de Madame Renée, Fille de France"

Mayer, *Clément Marot,* 196–98 (Fr).

Smith, *Clément Marot, Poet of the French Renaissance,* 175–77 (Eng).

"Complainte de Monsieur de Général Guillaume Preud'homme"

Plattard, *Marot,* 108–12 (Fr).

"Complainte du Baron de Malleville"

Joseph, *Clément Marot,* 48–50 (Eng).

"Complainte d'une Niepce"

Joseph, *Clément Marot,* 50–51 (Eng).

MAROT, CLEMENT, "La Deploration de Florimond Robertet"

"Complainte sur la mort de Anne Lhuilier d'Orléans"

V. Saulnier, *Les Elégies de Clément Marot,* new, expanded edition (Paris: Société d'Enseignement Supérieur, 1968), 23–24 (Fr).

"Coq à l'âne" (Premier)

Plattard, *Marot,* 129–30 (Fr).

"Coq à l'âne" (Seconde)

Griffin, *Clément Marot,* 41–43 (Eng).

Smith, *Clément Marot, Poet of the French Renaissance,* 233–37 (Eng).

Mayer, *Cléément Morot,* 290–300 (Fr).

Plattard, *Marot,* 130–32 (Fr).

"Coq à l'âne" (Troisième)

Plattard, *Marot,* 132–34 (Fr).

"D'Aucunes nonnains"

Tom Conley, "La Poétique dehors: Autour d'un rondeau de Clément Marot," in Gray, ed., *Poétiques,* 53–72 (Fr).

"De celluy qui est demeuré et s'Amye s'en est allée"

Joseph, *Clément Marot,* 61–64 (Eng).

"La Deploration de Florimond Robertet"

Griffin, *Clément Marot,* 129–30 (Eng).

Joseph, *Clément Marot,* 69–76 (Eng).

Jourda, *Marot,* 97–99 (Fr).

MAROT, CLEMENT, "Du baiser de s'Amye"

John McClelland, "La Poésie à l'époque de l'humanisme: Molinet, Lemaire de Belges et Marot," in *L'Humanisme français au début de la Renaissance* (Paris: Vrin, 1973), 323–26 (Fr).

Mayer, *Clément Marot,* 150–63 (Fr).

Plattard, *Marot,* 106–8 (Fr).

Smith, *Clément Marot, Poet of the French Renaissance,* 255–61 (Eng).

"Du baiser de s'Amye"

Smith, *Clément Marot, Poet of the French Renaissance,* 145–47 (Eng).

" Du Coq à l'asne faict à Venise par ledict Marot "

Mayer, *Clément Marot,* 366–69 (Fr).

"Du lieutenant criminel de Paris et de Samblançay"

Rigolot, *Poétique et onomastique,* 68–79 (Fr).

François Rigolot, "Poétique et onomastique: L'Épigramme de Semblançay," *Poétique,* 5 (April 1974): 194–203 (Fr).

"D'ung qu'on appelloit Frère Lubin"

Joseph, *Clément Marot,* 55–56 (Eng).

"Eclogue au Roi soubz les noms de Pan et Robin"

Jourda, *Marot,* 129–30 (Fr).

Annabel Patterson, *Pastoral and Ideology: Virgil to Valéry* (Berkeley and Los Angeles: University of California Press, 1987), 114–16 (Eng).

Smith, *Clément Marot, Poet of the French Renaissance,* 179–82 (Eng).

"Eclogue sur la Naissance du filz de Monseigneur le Daulphin"

Joseph, *Clément Marot,* 80–81 (Eng).

"Eclogue sur le Trespas de ma Dame Loyse de Savoye"

Joseph, *Clément Marot,* 76–80 (Eng).

Jourda, *Marot,* 100–101 (Fr).

Mayer, *Clément Marot,* 198–212 (Fr).

"Elégie pour Louise de Savoie"

Annabel Patterson, *Pastoral and Ideology: Virgil to Valéry* (Berkeley and Los Angeles: University of California Press, 1987), 111–13 (Eng).

"Elégie pour Semblançay"

George Joseph, "Rhetoric, Intertextuality, and Genre in Marot's 'Elégies déploratives,' " *RR* 72 (January 1981): 16–24 (Eng).

V. Saulnier, *Les Elégies de Clément Marot,* new, expanded edition (Paris: Société d'Enseignement Supérieur, 1968), 25–42 (Fr).

"En esperant, espoir me desespere"

T. Conley, "A Last Spending of 'Rhetoricque': Reading Marot's 'Par Contradictions,' " *ECr* 18 (Spring 1978): 82–91 (Eng).

"L'Enfer"

Marcel Françon, " 'L'Enfer' de Clément Marot," *BHR* 29 (January 1967): 157–58 (Fr).

Griffin, *Clément Marot,* 85–88, 232, 234–237 (Eng).

Joseph, *Clément Marot,* 127–31 (Eng).

Jourda, *Marot,* 136–38 (Fr).

Alain Lerond, "Marot et la 'rhétorique': Le Style du début de 'l'Enfer,' "

MAROT, CLEMENT, "Epistre, Au Roy"

in *Mélanges de langue et de littérature . . . offerts à Jean Frappier,* vol. 2 (Geneva: Droz, 1970), 631–44 (Fr).

Mayer, *Clément Marot,* 116–27 (Fr).

Plattard, *Marot,* 122–25 (Fr).

Smith, *Clément Marot, Poet of the French Renaissance,* 197–99, 212–13, 219–31 (Eng).

Vianey, *Les Epîtres de Marot,* 52–54 (Fr).

"Epistre, Au Roy"

Vianey, *Les Epîtres de Marot,* 55–57 (Fr).

"Epistre à la Royne de Navarre"

Vianey, *Les Epîtres de Marot,* 116–17 (Fr).

"Epistre à Lyon Jamet"

Plattard, *Marot,* 148–54 (Fr).

"Epistre à son amy Lyon"

Griffin, *Clément Marot,* 218–20 (Eng).

Joseph, *Clément Marot,* 44–46 (Eng).

Mayer, *Clément Marot,* 112–16 (Fr).

Smith, *Clément Marot, Poet of the French Renaissance,* 95–97, 99–100 (Eng).

Vianey, *Les Epîtres de Marot,* 47–52 (Fr).

"L'Epistre de Frippelippes"

Joseph, *Clément Marot,* 101–3 (Eng).

Jourda, *Marot,* 144–45 (Fr).

Vianey, *Les Epîtres de Marot,* 128–31 (Fr).

MAROT, CLEMENT, "L'Epistre envoyée de Venize"

"L'Epistre de Maguelonne"

Joseph, *Clément Marot,* 34–37 (Eng).

Jourda, *Marot,* 82–84 (Fr).

Mayer, *Clément Marot,* 32–34 (Fr).

Plattard, *Marot,* 98–99 (Fr).

Vianey, *Les Epîtres de Marot,* 34–35 (Fr).

"L'Epistre de Marot à Monsieur Bouchart Docteur en Théologie"

Joseph, *Clément Marot,* 41–44 (Eng).

George Joseph, "Lyric Sequence as a Condition of Meaning: Various Arrangements of Marot's Poems," in Doranne Fenoaltea and David Rubin, eds., *The Ladder of High Designs: Structure and Interpretation of the French Lyric Sequence* (Charlottesville: University of Virginia, 1991), 44–46 (Eng).

Vianey, *Les Epîtres de Marot,* 45–46 (Fr).

"L'Epistre du Camp d'Atigny, à ma dicte Dame d'Alençon"

Joseph, *Clément Marot,* 37–39 (Eng).

Vianey, *Les Epîtres de Marot,* 39–41 (Fr).

"L'Epistre du dépourvu à Mme. la duchesse d'Alençon et de Berry"

Plattard, *Marot,* 141–42 (Fr).

Smith, *Clément Marot, Poet of the French Renaissance,* 68–69, 70–71 (Eng).

Vianey, *Les Epîtres de Marot,* 37–39 (Fr).

"L'Epistre envoyée de Venize à Madame la Duchesse de Ferrare par Clément Marot"

Vianey, *Les Epîtres de Marot,* 105–7 (Fr).

MAROT, CLEMENT, "L'Epistre envoyée par Clément Marot"

"L'Epistre envoyée par Clément Marot, à Monsieur d'Anguyen,
Lieutenant pour le Roy"

George Joseph, "Ronsard's 'Ode' versus Marot's 'Epistle' in Honor of
François de Bourbon, *FR* 54 (May 1981): 789–93 (Eng).

"L'Epistre perdue au jeu contre Madame de Ponts"

Vianey, *Les Epîtres de Marot,* 107–8 (Fr).

"Les Etrennes aux Dames de la Court"

Mayer, *Clément Marot,* 468–71 (Fr).

Smith, *Clément Marot, Poet of the French Renaissance,* 187–91 (Eng).

"Le Jugement de Minos"

Joseph, *Clément Marot,* 29 (Eng).

Jourda, *Marot,* 77–78 (Fr).

"Marot, Prisonnier, escript au Roy pour sa delivrance"

Vianey, *Les Epîtres de Marot,* 57–64 (Fr).

"O notre Dieu et seigneur aimable"

Joseph, *Clément Marot,* 121–26 (Eng).

"O raison contemplative devant le crucifix"

Joseph, *Clément Marot,* 29–30 (Eng).

"Petite Epistre au Roy"

Vianey, *Les Epîtres de Marot,* 36–37 (Fr).

MAROT, CLEMENT, "Psaume 110" (Translation)

"Plaisir n'ai plus, mais vis en déconfort"

Joseph, *Clément Marot,* 65–66 (Eng).

"Pour la petite Princesse de Navarre, à Madame Marguerite"

Smith, *Clément Marot, Poet of the French Renaissance,* 94–95 (Eng).

"Pour une mommerie de deux hermites"

Joseph, *Clément Marot,* 109–11 (Eng).

"Première Eclogue de Virgile" (Translation)

Joseph, *Clément Marot,* 25–26 (Eng).
Jourda, *Marot,* 76–77 (Fr).

"Psaume 4" (Translation)

Jeanneret, *Poésie et tradition biblique,* 54, 69, 82 (Fr).

"Psaume 6" (Translation)

Jeanneret, *Poésie et tradition biblique,* 70–71, 85–86 (Fr).

"Psaume 8" (Translation)

Jeanneret, *Poésie et tradition biblique,* 59, 61, 67, 71, 80 (Fr).

"Psaume 38" (Translation)

Jeanneret, *Poésie et tradition biblique,* 56–57, 67, 69–70, 86 (Fr).

"Psaume 110" (Translation)

Jeanneret, *Poésie et tradition biblique,* 58–59, 63–64, 66–67 (Fr).

MAROT, CLEMENT, "Psaume 118" (Translation)

"Psaume 118" (Translation)

Jeanneret, *Poésie et tradition biblique*, 56, 59–61, 64 (Fr).

"Qu'ay je mesfaict, dictes, ma chere Amye?"

Joseph, *Clément Marot*, 85–89 (Eng).

"Rondeau parfaict à ses amys après sa délivrance"

Gérard Defaux, "Clément Marot: Une Poétique du silence et le la liberté," in Nash, ed., *Pre-Pléiade Poetry*, 49–51 (Fr).

"Sur la traduction des Psaumes de David"

Griffin, *Clément Marot*, 102–4 (Eng).

"Le Temple de Cupido"

Griffin, *Clément Marot*, 221–24 (Eng).

Joseph, *Clément Marot*, 26–29 (Eng).

Jourda, *Marot*, 79–82 (Fr).

Mayer, *Clément Marot*, 29–32 (Fr).

Plattard, *Marot*, 97–98 (Fr).

Smith, *Clément Marot, Poet of the French Renaissance*, 66–68, 70 (Eng).

"Ton gentil cueur si haultement assis"

Griffin, *Clément Marot*, 145–46 (Eng).

"Les Tristes vers de Philippe Béroalde sur le jour du vendredi saint"

Joseph, *Clément Marot*, 29–30 (Eng).

MAYNARD, FRANÇOIS, "Flambeau dont la clarté se résout en fumée"

"Le Valet de Marot contre Sagon"

Mayer, *Clément Marot,* 382–88 (Fr).

MAROT, JEAN

"Epistre d'ung complaignant l'abusif gouvernement du Pape"

Brown, *The Shaping of History and Poetry in Late Medieval France,* 107–11 (Eng).

"Voyage de Gênes"

Brown, *The Shaping of History and Poetry in Late Medieval France,* 47–51, 71, 149 (Eng).

Rigolot, *Poétique et onomastique,* 60–66 (Fr).

MAYNARD, FRANÇOIS

"Alcipe, reviens dans nos Bois"

Rubin, *The Knot of Artifice,* 63–75 (Eng).

"Au cristal de ton front rien ne se parangonne"

Lafay, *La Poésie française du premier XVIIe siècle,* 281–82 (Fr).

"Demeure encore au lit, belle et pompeuse Aurore"

Terence Cave, "Desportes and Maynard: Two Studies in the Poetry of Wit," in Bayley and Coleman, eds., *The Equilibrium of Wit,* 91–93 (Eng).

"Flambeau dont la clarté se résout en fumée"

Lafay, *La Poésie française du premier XVIIe siècle,* 273–75 (Fr).

MAYNARD, FRANÇOIS, "Va-t-en triste soupir vers ma belle Deesse"

"Va-t-en triste soupir vers ma belle Deesse"

Lafay, *La Poésie française du premier XVIIe siècle,* 259–61 (Fr).

MENDES, CATULLE

"L'Absente"

Rachel Killick, "Mendès, Mallarmé, and 'L'Absente,'" *FSB* 30 (Spring 1989): 1–4 (Eng).

MICHAUX, HENRI

"Alphabet"

Peter Broome, "Poetry and Event in the Work of Henri Michaux, 1940–1948," *AJFS* 4 (September–December 1967): 354–55 (Eng).

"Année maudite"

Broome, *Henri Michaux,* 110–11 (Eng).

"Au lit"

Stefano Agosti, "Le Rêve du texte," *Europe* 64 (June–July 1987): 110–16 (Fr).

"Les Centres"

Michel Beaujour, "Michaux et les cygnes," *ECr* 26 (Fall 1986): 97–98 (Fr).

"Le Champ de ma conscience"

Bowie, *Henri Michaux,* 91–96 (Eng).

MICHAUX, HENRI, "L'Espace aux ombres"

"Chant de mort"

Bowie, *Henri Michaux,* 32–33 (Eng).

Lawrence Harvey, "Michaux's 'Chant de mort,'" *Expl* 20 (September 1961): 1–5 (Eng).

"Clown"

Lloyd Bishop, "Michaux's 'Clown,'" *FR* 36 (December 1962): 152–57 (Eng).

Broome, *Henri Michaux,* 122–25 (Eng).

Broome and Chesters, *The Appreciation of Modern French Poetry (1850–1950),* 153–55 (Eng).

Laurie Edson, "Henri Michaux: Between Center and Absence," *FrF* 7 (January 1982): 61–63, 68 (Eng).

"Dans la nuit"

Broome, *Henri Michaux,* 120–21 (Eng).

"La Darelette"

Stefano Agosti, "Le Rêve de texte," *Europe* 64 (June–July 1987): 116–18 (Fr).

"Ecce homo"

Peter Broome, "Poetry and Event in the Work of Henri Michaux, 1940–1948," *AJFS* 4 (September–December 1967): 346, 361 (Eng).

"Emportez-moi"

Broome, *Henri Michaux,* 116–17 (Eng).

"L'Espace aux ombres"

Bowie, *Henri Michaux,* 85–91 (Eng).

MICHAUX, HENRI, "Le Grand combat"

"Le Grand combat"

Bowie, *Henri Michaux,* 158–60 (Eng).

"Icebergs"

Broome and Chesters, *The Appreciation of Modern French Poetry (1850–1950),* 150–52 (Eng).

"Immense voix"

Laurie Edson, "Henri Michaux: Between Center and Absence," *FrF* 7 (January 1982): 65–66 (Eng).

"Injii"

Bowie, *Henri Michaux,* 137–42, 146–50 (Eng).

"Mes propriétés"

Bowie, *Henri Michaux,* 80–84 (Eng).

Broome, *Henri Michaux,* 34–38 (Eng).

"La Mitrailleuse à gifles"

Bowie, *Henri Michaux,* 50–51 (Eng).

"Mon roi"

Bowie, *Henri Michaux,* 28–31 (Eng).

"Nous deux encore"

Peter Broome, "Poetry and Event in the Work of Henri Michaux, 1940–1948," *AJFS* 4 (September–December 1967): 375–78 (Eng).

MICHAUX, HENRI, "Projection"

"Un Oiseau qui traverserait des nuages"

Renée R. Hubert, "Henri Michaux and René Magritte," *SFR* 2 (Spring 1978): 68–69 (Eng).

"Paix dans les brisements"

Bowie, *Henri Michaux,* 126–37, 146–50 (Eng).

Renée R. Hubert, "Paix dans les brisements: Trajectoire verbale et graphique," *ECr* 26 (Fall 1986): 72–86 (Fr).

Reinhard Kuhn, "Prismatic Reflections: Michaux's 'Paix dans les brisements,' " in Caws, ed., *About French Poetry,* 190–202 (Eng).

"Pensées"

Bowie, *Henri Michaux,* 100–101 (Eng).

"Poddema-Ama"

Peter Broome, "Poetry and Event in the Work of Henri Michaux, 1940–1948," *AJFS* 4 (September–December 1967): 363–70 (Eng).

"Poddema-Nara"

Peter Broome, "Poetry and Event in the Work of Henri Michaux, 1940–1948," *AJFS* 4 (September–December 1967): 363, 370–74 (Eng).

"Poésie pour pouvoir"

Bowie, *Henri Michaux,* 114–17 (Eng).

"Portrait des Meidosems"

Bowie, *Henri Michaux,* 73–78 (Eng).

"Projection"

Dubosclard and Dubosclard, *Du surréalisme à la Résistance,* 51–56 (Fr).

MICHAUX, HENRI, "Quelque part, quelqu'un"

"Quelque part, quelqu'un"

Bowie, *Henri Michaux,* 109–12 (Eng).

"Qu'il repose en révolte"

Bowie, *Henri Michaux,* 107–9 (Eng).

"Qui je fus"

Alain Bosquet, *Verbe et vertige: Situations de la poésie* (Paris: Hachette, 1961), 153–54 (Fr).

"Travaux d'Alexandre"

Renée R. Hubert, "Henri Michaux and René Magritte," *SFR* 2 (Spring 1978): 70–71 (Eng).

"Vers la complétude"

Bowie, *Henri Michaux,* 142–60 (Eng).

MILOSZ, OSCAR

"Psaume de l'étoile du matin"

Jean Bellemin-Noël, "Milosz aux limites du poème," *Poétique* 1 (February 1970): 202–23 (Fr).

MOLIERE

"A Monsieur La Mothe le Vayer"

Frank Warnke, "Some Consolations," in Bayley and Coleman, eds., *The Equilibrium of Wit,* 114–16 (Eng).

MOLINET, JEAN

"Complainte pour le trespas de madame Marie de Bourgogne"

Champion, *Histoire poétique du XVe siècle,* vol. 2, 351–53 (Fr).

"Complainte sur la mort de Madame d'Ostrisse"

John McClelland, "La Poésie à l'époque de l'humanisme: Molinet, Lemaire de Belges et Marot," in *L'Humanisme français au début de la Renaissance* (Paris: Vrin, 1973), 319–21 (Fr).

"Dictier sur Tournay"

Rigolot, *Poétique et onomastique,* 44–45 (Fr).

"Le Dit des quatre vins"

Champion, *Histoire poétique du XVe siècle,* vol. 2, 312–16 (Fr).

"Naufrage de la Pucelle"

Champion, *Histoire poétique du XVe siècle,* vol. 2, 349–51 (Fr).

"Oraison sur Maria"

Rigolot, *Poétique et onomastique,* 35–38 (Fr).

"Ressource du petit peuple"

Champion, *Histoire poétique du XVe siècle,* vol. 2, 335–39 (Fr).

"Serventois"

Rigolot, *Poétique et onomastique,* 39–42 (Fr).

MOLINET, JEAN, "Le Temple de Mars"

"Le Temple de Mars"

Champion, *Histoire poétique du XVe siècle,* vol. 2, 339–43 (Fr).

"Throsne d'honneur"

Winter, *Visual Variety and Spatial Grandeur,* 47–48, 54–55 (Eng).

MONTGAILLARD, PIERRE FAUCHERAN

"Desdaigné de mon Prince, et mesprizé de Claire"

Lafay, *La Poésie française du premier XVIIe siècle,* 226–29 (Fr).

"Vieille ha ha vieille hou hou"

Lafay, *La Poésie française du premier XVIIe siècle,* 221–24 (Fr).

MOTIN, PIERRE

"Elégie"

Lafay, *La Poésie française du premier XVIIe siècle,* 284–88 (Fr).

MUSSET, ALFRED DE

"A Julie"

Odoul, *Le Drame intime d'Alfred de Musset,* 80–81 (Fr).

"Après la lecture d'Indiana"

Odoul, *Le Drame intime d'Alfred de Musset,* 51–53 (Fr).

"A quoi rêvent les jeunes filles"

Martine Bercot, "Musset baroque?" *CAIEF* 39 (May 1987): 234–36 (Fr).

L. Bishop, *The Poetry of Alfred de Musset,* 30–32, 114–15 (Eng).

"Chanson de Fortunio"

Uri Eisenzweig, "La Construction de l'objet dans la 'Chanson de Fortunio,'" *Europe* 55 (November–December 1977): 174–91 (Fr).

"La Coupe et les lèvres"

L. Bishop, *The Poetry of Alfred de Musset,* 28–30 (Eng).

Margaret A. Rees, *Alfred de Musset* (New York: Twayne, 1971), 61, 66, 72–73, 76–77, 85 (Eng).

"Don Paez"

Simon Jeune, "Aspects de la narration dans les premières poésies D'Alfred de Musset," *RHL* 76 (March–April 1976): 181–87 (Fr).

Margaret A. Rees, *Alfred de Musset* (New York: Twayne, 1971), 66, 71, 82–85 (Eng).

"L'Espoir en Dieu"

Denommé, *Nineteenth-Century French Romantic Poets,* 147–49 (Eng).

"Impromptu en réponse à cette question: Qu'est-ce que la poésie?"

L. Bishop, *The Poetry of Alfred de Musset,* 63–64 (Eng).

"Lucie"

Odoul, *Le Drame intime d'Alfred de Musset,* 162–67 (Fr).

MUSSET, ALFRED DE, "Mardoche"

"Mardoche"

L. Bishop, *The Poetry of Alfred de Musset,* 6–8 (Eng).

Donald Gamble, "Alfred de Musset et le développement d'une poésie personnelle," *CAIEF* 39 (May 1987): 241–43 (Fr).

Simon Jeune, "Aspects de la narration dans les premières poésies d'Alfred de Musset," *RHL* 76 (March–April 1976): 185–86 (Fr).

"Le Mie Prigioni"

James Hewitt, "Musset apprenti de Byron: Une Nouvelle conception du moi poétique," *RHL* 76 (March–April 1976): 216–18 (Fr).

"Namouna"

Martine Bercot, "Musset baroque?" *CAIEF* 39 (May 1987): 225–26, 233–34 (Fr).

L. Bishop, *The Poetry of Alfred de Musset,* 23, 89–100, 163 (Eng).

Lloyd Bishop, "Romantic Irony in Musset's 'Namouna,'" *NCFS* 7 (Spring–Summer 1979): 182–91 (Eng).

Denommé, *Nineteenth-Century French Romantic Poets,* 136–37 (Eng).

Marc Eigeldinger, "Musset et le mythe de Don Juan," *RHL* 76 (March–April 1976): 219–27 (Fr).

Françoise Han, "Quelques notes sur 'Namouna' et sur la rhétorique," *Europe* 583–84 (November–December 1977): 170–74 (Fr).

James Hewitt, "Musset apprenti de Byron: Une Nouvelle conception du moi poétique," *RHL* 76 (March–April 1976): 213–15 (Fr).

Simon Jeune, "Aspects de la narration dans les premières poésies D'Alfred de Musset," *RHL* 76 (March–April 1976): 185–86 (Fr).

Odoul, *Le Drame intime d'Alfred de Musset,* 57, 89, 91 (Fr).

H. Riffaterre, *L'Orphisme dans la poésie,* 125–26 (Fr).

"La Nuit d'août"

L. Bishop, *The Poetry of Alfred de Musset,* 35–38, 116–117 (Eng).

Bernard Masson, "Relire les 'Nuits': Musset sous la lumière de Jung," *RHL* 76 (March–April 1976): 207–8 (Fr).

MUSSET, ALFRED DE, "Puisque votre moulin tourne"

"La Nuit de décembre"

L. Bishop, *The Poetry of Alfred de Musset,* 34–38 (Eng).

Denommé, *Nineteenth-Century French Romantic Poets,* 144–45 (Eng).

Fournet, *Poètes romantiques,* 88–90 (Fr).

Bernard Masson, "Relire les 'Nuits': Musset sous la lumière de Jung," *RHL* 76 (March–April 1976): 201–7 (Fr).

Odoul, *Le Drame intime d'Alfred de Musset,* 101–2 (Fr).

"La Nuit de mai"

L. Bishop, *The Poetry of Alfred de Musset,* 33–34, 36–38, 58, 115–16 (Eng).

Denommé, *Nineteenth-Century French Romantic Poets,* 141–44 (Eng).

Fournet, *Poètes romantiques,* 87 88 (Fr).

Russell King, "Musset et le dialogue nietochéen d'Apollon et de Dionysos," *Europe* 55 (November–December 1977): 162–69 (Eng).

Bernard Masson, "Relire les 'Nuits': Musset sous la lumière de Jung," *RHL* 76 (March–April 1976): 194–201 (Fr).

Odoul, *Le Drame intime d'Alfred de Musset,* 167–71 (Fr).

"La Nuit d'octobre"

L. Bishop, *The Poetry of Alfred de Musset,* 35–38, 58 (Eng).

Denommé, *Nineteenth-Century French Romantic Poets,* 146–47 (Eng).

Fournet, *Poètes romantiques,* 91–92 (Fr).

Bernard Masson, "Relire les 'Nuits': Musset sous la lumière de Jung," *RHL* 76 (March–April 1976): 209–10 (Fr).

"Puisque votre moulin tourne avec tous les vents"

Graham Falconer, "Notes sur un sonnet d'Alfred de Musset," *RHL* 63 (January–March 1963): 104–8 (Fr).

MUSSET, ALFRED DE, "Que j'aime le premier frisson d'hiver!"

"Que j'aime le premier frisson d'hiver! Le chaume"

Lloyd Bishop, "Musset's First Sonnet: A Semiotic Analysis," *RR* 74 (November 1983): 455–60 (Eng).

L. Bishop, *The Poetry of Alfred de Musset,* 81–88 (Eng).

Phillip Duncan, "Patterns of Stasis and Metamorphosis in Musset's First Sonnet," *NCFS* 16 (Fall–Winter 1987–88): 78–83 (Eng).

"Rolla"

L. Bishop, *The Poetry of Alfred de Musset,* 23–27, 76 (Eng).

Denommé, *Nineteenth-Century French Romantic Poets,* 139–40 (Eng).

Simon Jeune, "Aspects de la narration dans les premières poésies D'Alfred de Musset," *RHL* 76 (March–April 1976): 183–84, 189 (Fr).

Odoul, *Le Drame intime d'Alfred de Musset,* 50–51, 57, 187 (Fr).

"Le Saule"

Simon Jeune, "Aspects de la narration dans les premières poésies d'Alfred de Musset," *RHL* 76 (March–April 1976): 184–89 (Fr).

"Une Soirée perdue"

Denommé, *Nineteenth-Century French Romantic Poets,* 152–54 (Eng).

Monica Nurnberg, "Inspiration and Aspiration: Gautier's 'La Diva' and Musset's 'Une Soirée perdue,'" *AJFS* 15 (September–December 1978): 229–34 (Eng).

"Le Songe du reviewer"

Odoul, *Le Drame intime d'Alfred de Musset,* 85–87 (Fr).

"Souvenir"

Lloyd Bishop, "Musset's 'Souvenir' and the Greater Romantic Lyric," *NCFS* 12–13 (Summer–Fall 1984): 119–30 (Eng).

L. Bishop, *The Poetry of Alfred de Musset,* 101–12 (Eng).

NERVAL, GERARD DE, "A Madame Aguado"

Denommé, *Nineteenth-Century French Romantic Poets,* 149–51 (Eng).

Fournet, *Poètes romantiques,* 94–95 (Fr).

Odoul, *Le Drame intime d'Alfred de Musset,* 300 (Fr).

"Souvenir des alpes"

L. Bishop, *The Poetry of Alfred de Musset,* 169–71 (Eng).

"Stances"

Ladislas Galdi, "Un Aspect peu connu du style poétique de Musset," *CAIEF* 16 (March 1964): 21–30 (Fr).

NELLIGAN, EMILE

"Les Bruns Chêneaux altiers traçaient dans le ciel triste"

Paul Wyczynski, "L'Influence de Verlaine sur Nelligan," *RHL* 69 (September–October 1969): 781–83 (Fr).

"Devant deux portraits de ma mère"

Robert Giroux and Hélène Dame, "Les critères de poéticité dans l'histoire de la poésie québécoise (sémiotique littéraire)," *ELit* 14 (April 1981): 123–62 (Fr).

NERVAL, GERARD DE

"Adieux de Napoléon à la France"

Maurice Blackman, "Byron and the First Poems of Gérard de Nerval," *NCFS* 15 (Fall–Winter 1986–87): 95–99, 103 (Eng).

"A Madame Aguado"

Constans, *Gérard de Nerval devant le destin,* 205–21 (Fr).

NERVAL, GERARD DE, "Antéros"

"Antéros"

Geninasca, *Analyse,* 151–60, 223–36, 269–83 (Fr).

Jasenas, *La Poétique,* 176–85 (Fr).

Knapp, *Gérard de Nerval,* 262–64 (Eng).

Lokke, *Gérard de Nerval,* 112–14 (Eng).

H. Riffaterre, *L'Orphisme dans la poésie,* 101–3 (Fr).

Schärer, *Pour une poétique des "Chimères" de Nerval,* 36–37 (Fr).

Vouga, *Nerval et ses "Chimères,"* 23–40 (Fr).

"Artémis"

Bernadette Caravaggi, "Signification de la polyvalence nervalienne," *SFr* 27 (May–August 1983): 282–86 (Fr).

Constans, *Gérard de Nerval devant le destin,* 11–47, 242–52 (Fr).

Geninasca, *Analyse,* 101–48 (Fr).

Jasenas, *La Poétique,* 196–208 (Fr).

Knapp, *Gérard de Nerval,* 268–72 (Eng).

Knight, *Flower Poetics in Nineteenth-Century France,* 140–41, 147–49 (Eng).

Jean Richer, *Nerval, expérience et création* (Paris: Hachette, 1963), 590–99 (Fr).

Jean Richer, "Notes conjointes sur 'Artémis' de Gérard de Nerval: Sainte napolitaine et sainte de l'abîme," *SFr* 14 (January–April 1970): 96–100 (Fr).

Schärer, *Pour une poétique des "Chimères" de Nerval,* 31–32, 41–42 (Fr).

Vouga, *Nerval et ses "Chimères,"* 117–31 (Fr).

"Avril"

Schärer, *Pour une poétique des "Chimères" de Nerval,* 7–8 (Fr).

"Le Christ aux Oliviers"

Alison Fairlie, "An Approach to Nerval," in L. J. Austin, Garnet Rees, and E. Vinaver, eds., *Studies in Modern French Literature Presented to P. Mansell Jones* (Manchester: Manchester University Press, 1961), 90–91 (Eng).

Geninasca, *Analyse,* 287–346 (Fr).

Jasenas, *La Poétique,* 208–20 (Fr).

Knapp, *Gérard de Nerval,* 272–79 (Eng).

Lokke, *Gérard de Nerval,* 125–27 (Eng).

Schärer, *Pour une poétique des "Chimères" de Nerval,* 29–30, 37–38 (Fr).

"Les Cydalises"

Jean Senelier, "Clartés sur la Cydalise," *SFr* 14 (September–December 1970): 451, 455, 458–60 (Eng).

"Delfica"

Constans, *Gérard de Nerval devant le destin,* 163–81 (Fr).

Geninasca, *Analyse,* 151–68, 191–221 (Fr).

Jasenas, *La Poétique,* 185–96 (Fr).

Knapp, *Gérard de Nerval,* 265–68 (Eng).

Lokke, *Gérard de Nerval,* 131–33 (Eng).

Maurice Piron, "La Composition de 'Delfica,' " *SFr* 6 (January–April 1962): 89–94 (Fr).

Schärer, *Pour une poétique des "Chimères" de Nerval,* 30–32 (Fr).

Vouga, *Nerval et ses "Chimères,"* 41–55 (Fr).

"El Desdichado"

Peter Collier, "Nerval in Apollinaire's 'La Chanson du mal-aimé,' " *FSB* 6 (Spring 1983): 10–13 (Eng).

Constans, *Gérard de Nerval devant le destin,* 252–57 (Fr).

Jacques Dhaenes, "A propos de l'établissement du texte de 'El Desdichado,' " *SFr* 10 (May–August 1966): 286–89 (Fr).

Alison Fairlie, "An Approach to Nerval," in L. J. Austin, Garnet Rees, and E. Vinaver, eds., *Studies in Modern French Literature Presented to P. Mansell Jones* (Manchester: Manchester University Press, 1961), 92–94 (Eng).

Jeanne Genaille, "Sur 'El Desdichado,' " *RHL* 60 (January–March 1960): 1–10 (Fr).

Geninasca, *Analyse,* 49–100, 141–48 (Fr).

Rae Beth Gordon, "The Lyric Persona: Nerval's 'El Desdichado,' " in Prendergast, ed., *Nineteenth-Century French Poetry,* 86–102 (Eng).

Knapp, *Gérard de Nerval,* 246–54 (Eng).

John Kneller, "The Poet and His Moira: 'El Desdichado,' " *PMLA* 75 (September 1960): 402–9 (Eng).

Knight, *Flower Poetics in Nineteenth-Century France,* 149–52 (Eng).

David Martin, "Melancholy of Being, or 'I have sought the "I" of God': Genre, Gender, and Genesis in Nerval's 'El Desdichado,' " *FrF* (January 1990): 25–33 (Eng).

H. Riffaterre, *L'Orphisme dans la poésie,* 100–101 (Fr).

Schärer, *Pour une poétique des "Chimères" de Nerval,* 38–40 (Fr).

Vouga, *Nerval et ses "Chimères,"* 97–115 (Fr).

"Erythréa"

H. Riffaterre, *L'Orphisme dans la poésie,* 111–20 (Fr).

"Horus"

Auffret and Auffret, *Le Commentaire composé,* 132–41 (Fr).

Constans, *Gérard de Nerval devant le destin,* 183–204 (Fr).

Geninasca, *Analyse,* 151–60, 223–36, 237–67 (Fr).

Jasenas, *La Poétique,* 166–76 (Fr).

Knapp, *Gérard de Nerval,* 259–62 (Eng).

Lokke, *Gérard de Nerval,* 114–16 (Eng).

Schärer, *Pour une poétique des "Chimères" de Nerval,* 34–35 (Fr).

"Myrtho"

Broome and Chesters, *The Appreciation of Modern French Poetry (1850–1950)* 71–74 (Eng).

Geninasca, *Analyse,* 151–90 (Fr).

Jasenas, *La Poétique,* 159–66 (Fr).

Knapp, *Gérard de Nerval,* 255–59 (Eng).

Lokke, *Gérard de Nerval,* 130–31 (Eng).

H. Riffaterre, *L'Orphisme dans la poésie,* 255–57 (Fr).

Schärer, *Pour une poétique des "Chimères" de Nerval,* 33–34 (Fr).

Vouga, *Nerval et ses "Chimères,"* 42–55 (Fr).

"Ode à l'étoile de la Légion d'Honneur"

Maurice Blackman, "Byron and the First Poems of Gérard de Nerval," *NCFS* 15 (Fall–Winter 1986–87): 99–103 (Eng).

"Pensée de Byron"

Maurice Blackman, "Byron and the First Poems of Gérard de Nerval," *NCFS* 15 (Fall–Winter 1986–87): 104–6 (Eng).

"Le Relais"

Schärer, *Pour une poétique des "Chimères" de Nerval,* 6–7 (Fr).

"Stances élégiaques"

Maurice Blackman, "Gérard de Nerval et Thomas Moore: Note sur 'Stances élégiaques,'" *RHL* 72 (May–June 1972): 428–31 (Fr).

NERVAL, GERARD DE, "Vers dorés"

"Vers dorés"

Broome and Chesters, *The Appreciation of Modern French Poetry (1850–1950),* 74–76 (Eng).

Geninasca, *Analyse,* 347–55 (Fr).

Jasenas, *La Poétique,* 220–29 (Fr).

Knapp, *Gérard de Nerval,* 279–81 (Eng).

Lokke, *Gérard de Nerval,* 127–30 (Eng).

H. Riffaterre, *L'Orphisme dans la poésie,* 248–50, 254 (Fr).

Schärer, *Pour une poétique des "Chimères" de Nerval,* 43–44 (Fr).

Vouga, *Nerval et ses "Chimères,"* 11–21 (Fr).

NESSON, PIERRE DE

"L'Hommage [L'Oraison] à Notre Dame"

Champion, *Histoire poétique de XVe siècle,* vol. 1, 189–95 (Fr).

"Les Vigiles des morts"

Champion, *Histoire poétique de XVe siècle,* vol. 1, 198–225 (Fr).

Shapley, *Studies in French Poetry,* 1–31 (Eng).

NOEL, BERNARD

"La Chute des temps"

M. Bishop, *The Contemporary Poetry of France,* 114–16 (Eng).

"L'Eté langue morte"

M. Bishop, *The Contemporary Poetry of France,* 111–13 (Eng).

OTON DE GRANDSON

"Complainte de Saint Valentin"

Kelly, *Medieval Imagination,* 179–82 (Eng).

PASQUIER, ETIENNE

"Congratulation au Roy . . . sur l'Edict de Pacification"

Charbonnier, *La Poésie française et les guerres de religion,* 326–30 (Fr).

PEGUY, CHARLES

"La Chanson du Roi Dagobert"

Robert Burac, "La Chanson du Roi Dagobert de Charles Péguy," *AJFS* 22 (September–December 1985): 220–26 (Fr)

Bernard Guyon, *Péguy* (Paris: Hatier, 1973), 116–17, 128–29 (Fr).

F. C. St. Aubyn, *Charles Péguy,* 2d ed. (Boston: Twayne, 1977), 92–93 (Eng).

"Mystère de la Charité de Jeanne d'Arc"

Hume, *Two Against Time,* 152 (Eng).

Nelly Jussem-Wilson, "L'Affaire Jeanne d'Arc et l'affaire Dreyfus: Péguy et 'Notre jeunesse,' " *RHL* 62 (July–September 1962): 400–415 (Fr).

"Le Porche de la deuxième vertu"

Hume, *Two Against Time,* 97–100, 142, 145–46, 162 (Eng).

"Quatrains"

Couffignal, *Zone d'Apollinaire,* 47–52 (Fr).

PEGUY, CHARLES, "La Tapisserie de Notre Dame"

"La Tapisserie de Notre Dame"

Couffignal, *Zone d'Apollinaire,* 52–54 (Fr).

Bernard Guyon, *Péguy,* 2d ed. (Paris: Hatier, 1973), 220–26 (Fr).

F. C. St. Aubyn, *Charles Péguy* (Boston: Twayne, 1977), 104–9 (Eng).

"La Tapisserie de Sainte Geneviève"

Hume, *Two Against Time,* 139–40, 154 (Eng).

"La Tapisserie de Sainte Geneviève et de Jeanne d'Arc"

F. C. St. Aubyn, *Charles Péguy* (Boston: Twayne, 1977), 100–103 (Eng).

PEIRE D'ALVERNHE

"L'airs clars"

Topsfield, *Troubadours and Love,* 171–74 (Eng).

"Al descebrar del païs"

Topsfield, *Troubadours and Love,* 168–69 (Eng).

"Be m'es plazen"

Topsfield, *Troubadours and Love,* 174–78 (Eng).

"Bel m'es quan la roza floris"

Topsfield, *Troubadours and Love,* 178–80 (Eng).

"Cantarai d'aquestz trobadors"

Topsfield, *Troubadours and Love,* 187–89 (Eng).

PELETIER DU MANS, JACQUES, "Louange de la Sciance"

"Deiosta.ls breus iorns e.ls loncs sers"

Topsfield, *Troubadours and Love,* 164–66 (Eng).

"En estiu, qan crida.l iais"

Topsfield, *Troubadours and Love,* 169–71 (Eng).

"Gent es, mentr'om n'a lczer"

Topsfield, *Troubadours and Love,* 180–83 (Eng).

"Sobre.l vieill trobar e.l novel"

Topsfield, *Troubadours and Love,* 183–87 (Eng).

PELETIER DU MANS, JACQUES

"A ceulx qui blament les Mathématiques"

Kathleen M. Hall, "What Did Peletier du Mans Mean By Clarity?" *ECr*
12 (Fall 1972): 211–13 (Eng).

"La Fouche"

H. Weber, *La Création poétique au XVIe siècle en France,* 474–75 (Fr).

"Louange de la Parole"

Chamard, *Histoire de la Pléiade,* vol. 3, 335–36 (Fr).

"Louange de la Sciance"

Chamard, *Histoire de la Pléiade,* vol. 3, 336–40 (Fr).

PELETIER DU MANS, JACQUES, "O ciel puissant!"

"O ciel puissant! o Univers immense!"

Kathleen M. Hall, "What Did Peletier du Mans Mean By Clarity?" *ECr* 12 (Fall 1972): 209–11 (Eng).

"Parnasse"

H. Weber, *La Création poétique au XVIe siècle en France,* 466–69 (Fr).

"Savoye"

Chamard, *Histoire de la Pléiade,* vol. 3, 314–23 (Fr).

"Le Soleïlh"

H. Weber, *La Création poétique au XVIe siècle en France,* 471–72 (Fr).

"Vénus"

H. Weber, *La Création poétique au XVIe siècle en France,* 476–78 (Fr).

PERET, BENJAMIN

"A tout trèfle"

Elizabeth Jackson, " 'Poésie activité de l'esprit': A Study of 'A tout trèfle' by Benjamin Péret," *FR* 44 (May 1971): 1036–47 (Fr).

"Allo"

Caws, *The Inner Theatre,* 85–87 (Eng).

J. H. Mathews, *Benjamin Péret* (Boston: Twayne, 1975), 132–33 (Eng).

"As de pique"

Caws, *The Inner Theatre,* 99–102 (Eng).

PHILIPPE DE VITRY, "Dictz de Franc Gontier"

"Clin d'œil"

Caws, *The Inner Theatre,* 87–90 (Eng).

Mary Ann Caws, "Péret's 'Amour sublime': Just Another 'Amour fou'?" *FR* 40 (November 1966): 210–11 (Eng).

"Des cris étouffés"

Caws, *The Inner Theatre,* 83–85 (Eng).

"Ls Odeurs de l'amour"

Caws, *The Inner Theatre,* 103–5 (Eng).

"Où es-tu"

Caws, *The Inner Theatre,* 90–92 (Eng).

Mary Ann Caws, "Péret's 'Amour sublime': Just Another 'Amour fou'?" *FR* 40 (November 1966): 211–12 (Eng).

"Samson"

Caws, *The Inner Theatre,* 97–99 (Eng).

"Toute une vie"

Caws, *The Inner Theatre,* 80–83 (Eng).

PHILIPPE DE VITRY

"Dictz de Franc Gontier"

Joël Blanchard, *La Pastorale en France aux XIVe et XVe siècles: Recherches sur les structures de l'imaginaire médiévale* (Paris: Champion, 1983), 51–52 (Fr).

PHILIPPE LE BON (BOURGOGNE), "De cueur, de corps . . ."

PHILIPPE LE BON (BOURGOGNE)

"De cueur, de corps et de puissance"

Ann T. Harrison, "Orléans and Burgundy: The literary relationship," *SFR* 4 (Winter 1980): 481–84 (Eng).

"S'il en estoit a mon vouloir"

Ann T. Harrison, "Orléans and Burgundy: The literary relationship," *SFR* 4 (Winter 1980): 479–84 (Eng).

POMPIGNAN, LEFRANC DE

"Ode sur la mort de Jean-Baptiste Rousseau"

Edouard Guitton, "A propos du mythe d'Orphée et de la crise du lyrisme au XVIIIe siècle," in *Approches des lumières: Mélanges offerts à Jean Fabre* (Paris: Klincksieck, 1974), 247–48 (Fr).

PONGE, FRANCIS

"L'Anthracite"

Higgins, *Francis Ponge,* 28–30 (Eng).

"L'Appareil du téléphone"

M. Riffaterre, *Semiotics of Poetry,* 125–38 (Eng).

"L'Araignée"

Rachelle Sherman, "Francis Ponge: Mimesis versus Poiesis," *FR* 52 (October 1978): 64–65 (Eng).

"L'Ardoise"

M. Riffaterre, *Semiotics of Poetry,* 122–24 (Eng).

"Bords de mer"

Ian Higgins, "Francis Ponge," in Cardinal, ed., *Sensibility and Creation,*
198–99 (Eng).

"La Bougie"

Claudine Rousseau, "Francis Ponge et Paul Eluard à la flamme d'une bougie: Lecture à deux voix," *SFr* 25 (September–December 1981): 494–99
(Fr).

"La Cigarette"

Ross Chambers, "Le Poète fumeur," *AJFS* 16 (January–April 1979): 146–
48 (Fr).

"La Crevette"

Nathan Bracher, "Pour ouvrir des abîmes: Les Textes in finis de Fianolo
Ponge," *KRQ* 36 (May 1989): 175–76 (Fr).

"Les Cristaux naturels"

Higgins, *Francis Ponge,* 30–33 (Eng).

M. Riffaterre, *Semiotics of Poetry,* 110–14 (Eng).

"La Danseuse"

Sorrell, *Francis Ponge,* 125–27 (Eng).

"De la nature morte et de Chardin"

Marja Warehime, "Manifestoes and Still Life: Chardin and Ponge," *FrF*
9 (January 1984): 60–67 (Fr).

"Escargots"

Sorrell, *Francis Ponge,* 51–52, 88 (Eng).

PONGE, FRANCIS, "Fable"

"Fable"

Sorrell, *Francis Ponge,* 118–19 (Eng).

"Le Feu"

Higgins, *Francis Ponge,* 56–57 (Eng).

"Flot"

Sorrell, *Francis Ponge,* 117–18 (Eng).

"Le Galet"

Sorrell, *Francis Ponge,* 94 (Eng).

"Le Gui"

Sorrell, *Francis Ponge,* 131–32 (Eng).

"Le Gymnaste"

Sorrell, *Francis Ponge,* 115–17 (Eng).

"Le Mimosa"

Sorrell, *Francis Ponge,* 31–33, 82–83 (Eng).

"Le Ministre"

Sorrell, *Francis Ponge,* 101–2 (Eng).

"La Mousse"

Rachelle Sherman, "Francis Ponge: Mimesis versus Poiesis," *FR* 52 (October 1978): 67–70 (Eng).

"Les Mûres"

Sorrell, *Francis Ponge,* 113–14 (Eng).

"La Nouvelle Araignée"

Sorrell, *Francis Ponge,* 132–40 (Fr).

"Le Nuage"

Sorrell, *Francis Ponge,* 119–20 (Eng).

"Ode inachevée à la boue"

Sorrell, *Francis Ponge,* 89–90 (Eng).

"L'Orange"

Ian Higgins, "Francis Ponge," in Cardinal, ed., *Sensibility and Creation,* 194–97 (Eng).

Cornelia Tenney, "Francis Ponge: La Poétique et l'orange," *SubStance* 1 (Autumn 1971): 11–14 (Fr).

"Le Pain"

Sorrell, *Francis Ponge,* 29–31 (Eng).

"Les Plaisirs de la porte"

Neal Oxenhandler, "Cocteau, Breton, and Ponge: The Situation of the Self," in Caws, ed., *About French Poetry,* 64–5 (Eng).

"Le Platane"

Ian Higgins, "Shrimp, Plane and France: Ponge's Resistance Poetry," *FS* 37 (July 1983): 311–25 (Eng).

PONGE, FRANCIS, "Plat de poissons frits"

"Plat de poissons frits"

Higgins, *Francis Ponge,* 67–93 (Eng).

Jean-Michel Pianca, "Ponge: La Métonymie comme déplacement," *SubStance* 1 (Autumn 1971): 4–10 (Fr).

"Pluie"

Neal Oxenhandler, "Cocteau, Breton, and Ponge: The Situation of the Self," in Caws, ed., *About French Poetry,* 63–4 (Eng).

"Le Pré"

Claudine Giordan, "Ponge et la nomination," *Poétique* 7 (November 1976): 493–59 (Fr).

Higgins, *Francis Ponge,* 58–61 (Eng).

Michel Pierssens, "Sur 'Le Pré,' " *SubStance* 1 (Autumn 1971): 15–19 (Fr).

"Le Savon"

Rachelle Sherman, "Francis Ponge: Mimesis versus Poiesis," *FR* 52 (October 1978): 71–72 (Eng).

"Soir d'août"

Sorrell, *Francis Ponge,* 121–22 (Eng).

"Soleil placé en abîme"

A. Kibedi Varga, "Lire le soleil: Un commentaire de 'Soleil placé en abîme,' " *EF* 17 (April 1981): 112–20 (Fr).

"Sombre période"

Ian Higgins, "Ponge's Resistance Poetry: 'Sombre période,' " *FSB* 8 (Autumn 1983): 7–8 (Eng).

RAIMBAUT D'AURENGA, "Als durs, crus, cozens lauzengiers"

"Trois poésies, 3"

Sorrell, *Francis Ponge,* 110–12 (Eng).

"Le Verre d'eau"

Sorrell, *Francis Ponge,* 65–66, 84–85 (Eng).

PORCHERES, LAUGIER DE

"Sur les yeux de Madame la Marquise de Monceaux"

Lafay, *La Poésie française du premier XVIIe siècle,* 200–202 (Fr).

PREVERT, JACQUES

"Inventaire"

Pierre Weisz, "Langage et imagerie chez Jacques Prévert," *FR* 43 (Special Issue 1) (Winter 1970): 34–35 (Fr).

"Tentative de description d'un dîner de têtes à Paris-France"

Pierre Weisz, "Langage et imagerie chez Jacques Prévert," *FR* 43 (Special Issue 1) (Winter 1970): 36–37 (Fr).

QUENEAU, RAYMOND

"Héraldique"

M. Riffaterre, *Semiotics of Poetry,* 105–9 (Eng).

RAIMBAUT D'AURENGA

"Als durs, crus, cozens lauzengiers"

Topsfield, *Troubadours and Love,* 148–49 (Eng).

RAIMBAUT D'AURENGA, "Ar resplan la flors enversa"

"Ar resplan la flors enversa"

Eliza Miruna Ghil, "Topic and Tropeic: Two Types of Syntagmatic Development in the Old Provençal Canzo," *ECr* 19 (Winter 1979): 63–69 (Eng).

Topsfield, *Troubadours and Love*, 154–58 (Eng).

"Ara.m platz, Giraut de Borneill"

Topsfield, *Troubadours and Love*, 151–52 (Eng).

"Escotatz mas no say que s'es"

Stephen Manning, "Game and Earnest in the Middle English and Provençal Love Lyrics," *CL* 18 (Summer 1966): 234–38 (Eng).

Topsfield, *Troubadours and Love*, 152–54 (Eng).

"Non chant per auzel ni per flor"

Topsfield, *Troubadours and Love*, 149–50 (Eng).

REGNIER, HENRI DE

"Odelette"

Howarth and Walton, *Explications*, 218–26 (Eng).

"Un Petit roseau m'a suffi"

Lewis, *On Reading French Verse*, 2–3, 35–37 (Eng).

REGNIER, MATHURIN

Satire 3
"A Monsieur le Marquis de Coeuvres"

Robert Aulotte, *Mathurin Régnier: "Les Satires"* (Paris: SEDES, 1983), 77–78 (Fr).

Satire 9
"A Monsieur Rapin"

Robert Aulotte, Mathurin Régnier: *"Les Satires"* (Paris: SEDES, 1983), 58–61 (Fr).

Satire 13
"Macette"

Robert Aulotte, *Mathurin Régnier: "Les Satires"* (Paris: SEDES, 1983), 87–101 (Fr).

RENART, JEAN

"Bele Aiglentine"

Zumthor, *Essai de poétique médiévale,* 290–98 (Fr).

"Lai de l'Ombre"

Paula Clifford, *La Chastelaine de Vergi and Jean Renart: "Le Lai de l'ombre"* (London: Grant and Cutler, 1986), 56–88 (Eng).

Donovan, *The Breton Lay,* 89–90 (Eng).

Ménard, *Les Lais de Marie de France,* 74–75 (Fr).

Jean-Charles Payen, "Structure et sens de 'Guillaume de Dole,' " in *Etudes de langue et de littérature du moyen âge offerts à Felix Lecoy* (Paris: Champion, 1973), 496–97 (Fr).

Roger Pensom, "Psychology in the 'Lai de l'ombre,' " *FS* 36 (July 1982): 257–69 (Eng).

RENE D'ANJOU

"Livre du cuer d'amours espris"

Kelly, *Medieval Imagination,* 187–90, 212–18 (Eng).

REVERDY, PIERRE, "Agonie du remords"

REVERDY, PIERRE

"Agonie du remords"

Rothwell, *Textual Spaces,* 163–64 (Eng).

"L'Air de glace"

Caws, *La Main de Pierre Reverdy,* 58–59 (Fr).

"Air"

Rothwell, *Textual Spaces,* 36–44 (Eng).

"L'Ame en péril"

Rothwell, *Textual Spaces,* 170–71 (Eng).

"A travers les signes"

Rothwell, *Textual Spaces,* 244–45 (Eng).

"Au bas-fond"

Rothwell, *Textual Spaces,* 255–56 (Eng).

"Au delà de cette limite"

Rothwell, *Textual Spaces,* 260–61 (Eng).

"Au saut de rêve"

Schroeder, *Pierre Reverdy,* 32–33 (Eng).

"Autres jockeys, alcooliques"

Schroeder, *Pierre Reverdy,* 77–79 (Eng).

REVERDY, PIERRE, "Départ"

"Bande de souvenirs"

Schroeder, *Pierre Reverdy,* 28–30 (Eng).

"Campagne"

Rothwell, *Textual Spaces,* 186–87 (Eng).

"Carrés"

Caws, *La Main de Pierre Reverdy,* 59–61 (Fr).

"Chacun sa part"

Rothwell, *Textual Spaces,* 58–59 (Eng).

"Civil"

Caws, *La Main de Pierre Reverdy,* 44–45, 49–50 (Fr).

"Conscience"

Rothwell, *Textual Spaces,* 214–15 (Eng).

"La Conversion"

Rothwell, *Textual Spaces,* 205–9 (Eng).

"Dehors"

Caws, *La Main de Pierre Reverdy,* 98–100 (Fr).

"Départ"

Robert Greene, "Pierre Reverdy, Poet of Nausea," *PMLA* 85 (January 1970): 48–49 (Eng).

REVERDY, PIERRE, "Dépasse temps"

"Dépasse temps"

Rothwell, *Textual Spaces,* 288–89 (Eng).

"Dernière heure"

Caws, *La Main de Pierre Reverdy,* 37–38 (Fr).

"Détresse du sort"

Caws, *La Main de Pierre Reverdy,* 55–57 (Fr).
Schroeder, *Pierre Reverdy,* 104–5 (Eng).

"Droit vers la mort"

Schroeder, *Pierre Reverdy,* 44–45 (Eng).

"Echo"

Rothwell, *Textual Spaces,* 56–57 (Eng).
Schroeder, *Pierre Reverdy,* 101 (Eng).

"En pente"

Rothwell, *Textual Spaces,* 135–36 (Eng).

"Encore l'amour"

Rothwell, *Textual Spaces,* 277–79 (Eng).

"Espace au fond du couloir"

Caws, *La Main de Pierre Reverdy,* 32–33 (Fr).

"Fausse porte ou portrait"

Caws, *La Main de Pierre Reverdy,* 57–58 (Fr).

REVERDY, PIERRE, "Il devait en effet faire bien froid"

"Fenêtre ou portrait"

Rothwell, *Textual Spaces,* 110–12 (Eng).

"Fétiche"

Robert Greene, "Pierre Reverdy, Poet of Nausea," *PMLA* 85 (January 1970): 49 (Eng).

"Fil d'encre"

Rothwell, *Textual Spaces,* 286–88 (Eng).

"Globe"

Caws, *La Main de Pierre Reverdy,* 80 (Fr).

"La Guitare endormie"

Rothwell, *Textual Spaces,* 155–58 (Eng).

"Un Homme fini"

Caws, *La Main de Pierre Reverdy,* 53–54 (Fr).

"Les Hommes inconnus"

Rothwell, *Textual Spaces,* 101–2 (Eng).

"Il a la tête pleine d'or"

Schroeder, *Pierre Reverdy,* 143–45 (Eng).

"Il devait en effet faire bien froid"

Schroeder, *Pierre Reverdy,* 123–24 (Eng).

REVERDY, PIERRE, "Les Jockeys camouflés"

"Les Jockeys camouflés"

Schroeder, *Pierre Reverdy,* 79–80 (Eng).

"Les Jockeys mécaniques"

Caws, *La Main de Pierre Reverdy,* 25–27 (Fr).
Schroeder, *Pierre Reverdy,* 77 (Eng).

"Joies d'été"

Schroeder, *Pierre Reverdy,* 47–48 (Eng).

"La Langue sèche"

Schroeder, *Pierre Reverdy,* 102–3 (Eng).

"Lendemain de saison"

Caws, *La Main de Pierre Reverdy,* 34–35 (Fr).

"La Ligne des noms et des figures"

Caws, *La Main de Pierre Reverdy,* 36–37 (Fr).

"Lumière dure"

Caws, *La Main de Pierre Reverdy,* 66–67 (Fr).

"Main-morte"

Caws, *La Main de Pierre Reverdy,* 70–71 (Fr).

"Médaille neuve"

Rothwell, *Textual Spaces,* 154–55 (Eng).

REVERDY, PIERRE, "Période hors-texte"

"Moulin à café"

Rothwell, *Textual Spaces,* 133–34 (Eng).

"L'Ombre"

Maryann De Julio, "The Drama of Self in Apollinaire and Reverdy: Play of Light and Shadow," *FrF* 6 (May 1981): 157–59 (Eng).

"L'Ombre du rêve"

Rothwell, *Textual Spaces,* 104 (Eng).

"Outre mesure"

Rothwell, *Textual Spaces,* 263–65 (Eng).

"Papier à musique et chanson"

Rothwell, *Textual Spaces,* 136–38 (Eng).

"La Parole"

Caws, *La Main de Pierre Reverdy,* 105–7 (Fr).

"Le Passant bleu"

Rothwell, *Textual Spaces,* 158–62 (Eng).

"Le Patineur céleste"

Schroeder, *Pierre Reverdy,* 37–38 (Eng).

"Paysage stable"

Caws, *La Main de Pierre Reverdy,* 29–31 (Fr).

"Période hors-texte"

Schroeder, *Pierre Reverdy,* 111–12 (Eng).

REVERDY, PIERRE, "Les Poètes"

"Les Poètes"

Caws, *La Main de Pierre Reverdy,* 79 (Fr).

Schroeder, *Pierre Reverdy,* 34–36 (Eng).

"Pointe"

Anthony Rizzuto, *Style and Theme in Reverdy's "Les Ardoises du toit:* (University: University of Alabama Press, 1971), 155–67 (Eng).

Schroeder, *Pierre Reverdy,* 88–89 (Eng).

"Pour éviter l'écueil qui se tient en arrière"

A. Kibedi Varga, "Syntaxe et rythme chez quelques poètes contemporains," in Monique Parent, ed., *Le Vers français au XXème siècle* (Paris: Klincksieck, 1967), 185–87 (Fr).

"Pour le moment"

Robert Greene, "Pierre Reverdy, Poet of Nausea," *PMLA* 85 (January 1970): 52–53 (Eng).

"Quelque part"

Schroeder, *Pierre Reverdy,* 94–95 (Eng).

"Reflux"

Schroeder, *Pierre Reverdy,* 135–37 (Eng).

"Ronde nocturne"

Dubosclard and Dubosclard, *Du surréalisme à la Résistance,* 22–28 (Fr).

"Ruine achevée"

Robert Greene, "Pierre Reverdy, Poet of Nausea," *PMLA* 85 (January 1970): 51–52 (Eng).

REVERDY, PIERRE, "Temps sec"

"Ruine de la chair"

Eric Sellin, "The Esthetics of Ambiguity: Reverdy's Use of Syntactical Simultaneity," in Caws, ed., *About French Poetry,* 121–24 (Eng).

"Le Sang troublé"

Schroeder, *Pierre Reverdy,* 48–50 (Eng).

"Santé de fer"

Michael Bishop, "Eyes and Seeing in the Poetry of Pierre Reverdy," in Cardinal, ed., *Sensibility and Creation,* 69–70 (Eng).

"Secret"

Roger Cardinal, "Pierre Reverdy and the Reality of Signs," in Beaumont, Cocking, and Cruickshank, eds., *Order and Adventure in Post-Romantic French Poetry,* 207–8 (Eng).

"Le Soir"

Anthony Rizzuto, *Style and Theme in Reverdy's "Les Ardoises du toit"* (University: University of Alabama Press, 1971), 98–100 (Eng).

"Sujets"

Schroeder, *Pierre Reverdy,* 25–28 (Eng).

"Sur le talus"

Anthony Rizzuto, *Style and Theme in Reverdy's "Les Ardoises du toit"* (University: University of Alabama Press, 1971), 100–101 (Eng).

"Temps sec"

Rothwell, *Textual Spaces,* 144–46 (Eng).

REVERDY, PIERRE, "Tentative"

"Tentative"

Schroeder, *Pierre Reverdy,* 23–25 (Eng).

"Tête à tenir"

Rothwell, *Textual Spaces,* 290–92 (Eng).

"La Tête pleine de beauté"

Caws, *La Main de Pierre Reverdy,* 108–9 (Fr).

"Toujours l'amour"

Rothwell, *Textual Spaces,* 279–80 (Eng).

"Les Trois Mousquetaires"

Rothwell, *Textual Spaces,* 162–63 (Eng).

"Les Vides du printemps"

Rothwell, *Textual Spaces,* 81–82 (Eng).
Schroeder, *Pierre Reverdy,* 45–47 (Eng).

"La Voie dans la ville"

Caws, *La Main de Pierre Reverdy,* 20–21, 24–25 (Fr).

"Voix mêlées"

Rothwell, *Textual Spaces,* 48–49 (Eng).

"Voyages trop grands"

Schroeder, *Pierre Reverdy,* 39–40 (Eng).

RIMBAUD, ARTHUR

"Accroupissements"

Edward J. Ahearn, "Rimbaud's 'Images immondes,' " *FR* 40 (February 1967): 505–6 (Eng).

Bays, *The Orphic Vision,* 161–62 (Eng).

Cohn, *The Poetry of Rimbaud,* 96–97 (Eng).

Giusto, *Rimbaud créateur,* 140 (Fr).

Gérald Schaeffer, "Poèmes de la révolte et de la dérision," in Eigeldinger, ed., *Etudes sur les "Poésies" de Rimbaud,* 126–32 (Fr).

"Adieu"

Chadwick, *Rimbaud,* 130–32 (Eng).

Edward K. Kaplan, "The Courage of Baudelaire and Rimbaud: The Anxiety of Faith," *FR* 52 (December 1978): 303–4 (Eng).

"Age d'or"

Bonnefoy, *Rimbaud par lui-même,* 68–71 (Fr).

"Brunel, *Arthur Rimbaud, ou L'Éclatant Désastre,* 119–22 (Fr).

Chadwick, *Rimbaud,* 45–46, 62 (Eng).

Cohn, *The Poetry of Rimbaud,* 204–8 (Eng).

Giusto, *Rimbaud créateur,* 177–80 (Fr).

Hackett, *Rimbaud,* 38–39, 46–47 (Eng).

Kittang, *Discours et jeu,* 122–25 (Fr).

"A la musique"

Cohn, *The Poetry of Rimbaud,* 53–55 (Eng).

Hackett, *Rimbaud,* 7–9 (Eng).

Kittang, *Discours et jeu,* 58–60 (Fr).

Ross, *The Emergence of Social Space,* 77–83 (Eng).

RIMBAUD, ARTHUR, "Alchimie du verbe"

"Alchimie du verbe"

Edward J Ahearn, "Rimbaud's 'Images immondes,'" *FR* 40 (Feb 1967): 511–16 (Eng).

Brunel, *Rimbaud:* Projets et réalisations, 149–72 (Fr).

"Angoisse"

Ahearn, *Rimbaud,* 114, 228–30 (Eng).

Brunel, *Arthur Rimbaud, ou L'Éclatant Désastre,* 209–14 (Fr).

Cohn, *The Poetry of Rimbaud,* 343–46 (Eng).

Giusto, *Rimbaud créateur,* 63, 223–25 (Fr).

Houston, *Patterns of Thought,* 58–59 (Eng).

Keith Macfarlane, "Rimbaud's 'Angoisse,'" *Expl* 34 (January 1976) 11–15 (Eng).

Verstraëte, *La Chasse spirituelle,* 154–61 (Fr).

"Après le déluge"

Ahearn, *Rimbaud,* 15–17, 254–57 (Eng).

Bays, *The Orphic Vision,* 211–12 (Eng).

Gwendolyn Bays, "The Orphic Vision of Nerval, Baudelaire, and Rimbaud," *CLS* 4 (1967): 19–21 (Eng).

Bonnefoy, *Rimbaud par lui-même,* 153–54 (Fr).

Cohn, *The Poetry of Rimbaud,* 246–52 (Eng).

Margaret Davies, "Le Thème de la voyance dans 'Après le déluge,' 'Métropolitain,' et 'Barbare,'" *RLM* 323 (1976): 20–27 (Fr).

Guisto, *Rimbaud créateur,* 213–23 (Fr).

Hackett, *Rimbaud,* 51–55 (Eng).

Houston, *Patterns of Thought,* 74–75 (Eng).

Kittang, *Discours et jeu,* 113–14, 246–47, 315–16 (Fr).

Roger Little, "Rimbaud: Au seuil des 'Illuminations,'" *RLM* 370–73 (1973): 84–85 (Fr).

Porter, *The Crisis of French Symbolism,* 236–37 (Eng).

Marilyn Schuster, "L'Ironie dans les 'Illuminations': Voix empruntées et codes littéraires," *NCFS* 8 (Spring–Summer 1980): 264–66 (Fr).

Verstraëte, *La Chasse spirituelle,* 93–104 (Fr).

"Les Assis"

Marc Ascione and Jean-Pierre Chambon, "Les 'Zolismes' de Rimbaud," *Europe* 51 (May–June 1973): 125–26 (Fr).

Brunel, *Arthur Rimbaud, ou L'Éclatant Désastre,* 51–52 (Fr).

A. R. Chisholm, "Rimbaud's Imagery in 'Les Assis,' " *AJFS* 16 (January–April 1979): 214–16 (Eng).

Cohn, *The Poetry of Rimbaud,* 87–90 (Eng).

Kittang, *Discours et jeu,* 205–11 (Fr).

Robert L. Mitchell, "Hemorrhoids/Splenectomy/Gestation: Towards Authorial Manipulation, Reader Expectation, and the Perversion of Complicity," *FR* 53 (October 1979): 38–41 (Eng).

Noulet, *Le Premier Visage de Rimbaud,* 83–88 (Fr)

Porter, *The Crisis of French Symbolism,* 216–17 (Eng).

"Aube"

Ahearn, *Rimbaud,* 70–73 (Eng).

Bays, *The Orphic Vision,* 214–15 (Eng).

Brunel, *Rimbaud: Projets et réalisations,* 296–304 (Fr).

Cohn, *The Poetry of Rimbaud,* 329–33 (Eng).

Giusto, *Rimbaud créateur,* 101–2, 260–63 (Fr).

Hackett, *Rimbaud,* 68–73 (Eng).

C. A. Hackett, "Rimbaud: 'Illuminations': 'Aube,' " in Nurse, ed., *The Art of Criticism,* 218–24 (Eng).

Houston, *Patterns of Thought,* 72–74 (Eng).

Roger Little, "Aube," *RLM* 370–73 (1973): 83–84 (Fr).

G. M. Macklin, "Rimbaud's 'Trois Contes,' " *FSB* 23 (Summer 1987): 11–12 (Eng).

RIMBAUD, ARTHUR, "Au Cabaret Vert"

Richter, *La Crise du logos,* 51–61 (Fr).

Verstraëte, *La Chasse spirituelle,* 122–26 (Fr).

"Au Cabaret Vert"

Cohn, *The Poetry of Rimbaud,* 76–78 (Eng).

C. A. Hackett, "Verlaine's Influence on Rimbaud," in L. J. Austin, Garnet Rees, and E. Vinaver, eds., *Studies in Modern French Literature Presented to P. Mansell Jones* (Manchester: Manchester University Press, 1961), 167–69 (Eng).

"A une raison"

Brunel, *Rimbaud: Projets et réalisations,* 267–69 (Fr).

Cohn, *The Poetry of Rimbaud,* 287–90 (Eng).

Giusto, *Rimbaud créateur,* 308–10 (Fr).

Houston, *Patterns of Thought,* 59–60 (Eng).

R. Mortier, "La Notion d'harmonie," in Cormier and Holmes, eds., *Essays in Honor of Louis Francis Solano,* 443–44 (Fr).

"Bal des pendus"

Brunel, *Arthur Rimbaud ou l'éclatant désastre,* 48–50 (Fr).

Cohn, *The Poetry of Rimbaud,* 47–49 (Eng).

Porter, *The Crisis of French Symbolism,* 209–10 (Eng).

"Bannières de mai"

Ahearn, *Rimbaud,* 279–82 (Eng).

Brunel, *Arthur Rimbaud, ou L'Éclatant Désastre,* 111–14 (Fr).

Cohn, *The Poetry of Rimbaud,* 194–98 (Eng).

Marc Eigeldinger, *Rimbaud et le mythe solaire* (Neuchâtel: La Baconnière, 1964), 38–41 (Fr).

Giusto, *Rimbaud créateur,* 173–74 (Fr).

Kittang, *Discours et jeu,* 87–88 (Fr).

"Barbare"

Edward J. Ahearn, "Explosions of the Real: Rimbaud's Ecstatic and Political Subversions," *SFR* 9 (Spring 1985): 74–77 (Fr).

Ahearn, *Rimbaud,* 206–12 (Eng).

Bays, *The Orphic Vision,* 236 (Eng).

Chadwick, *Rimbaud,* 92–93, 100, 102–3, 106–7, 109 (Eng).

Cohn, *The Poetry of Rimbaud,* 350–54 (Eng).

Margaret Davies, "Le Thème de la voyance dans 'Après le déluge,' 'Métropolitain' et 'Barbare,' " *RLM* 323 (1972): 34–39 (Fr).

Marc Eigeldinger, "L'Apocalypse dans les 'Illuminations,' " *RHL* 87 (March–April 1987): 189 (Fr).

Giusto, *Rimbaud créateur,* 305–8 (Fr).

Hackett, *Rimbaud,* 74–77 (Eng).

Houston, *Patterns of Thought,* 70–71 (Eng).

Kittang, *Discours et jeu,* 298–304 (Fr).

Porter, *The Crisis of French Symbolism,* 245–49 (Eng).

Verstraëte, *La Chasse spirituelle,* 104–10 (Fr).

Hermann Wetzel, "Un Texte opaque et son interprétation socio-historique: 'Barbare' de Rimbaud," in *Poésie et société en France au dix-neuvième siècle* (Paris: SEDES/CDU, 1983), 127–41 (Fr).

"Le Bateau ivre"

Ahearn, *Rimbaud,* 46–49 (Eng).

Bays, *The Orphic Vision,* 237–41 (Eng).

Bonnefoy, *Rimbaud par lui-même,* 55–57 (Fr).

Brunel, *Rimbaud: Projets et réalisations,* 105–13 (Fr).

Chadwick, *Etudes sur Rimbaud,* 20–26 (Fr).

Chadwick, *Rimbaud,* 18–19, 28 (Eng).

Cohn, *The Poetry of Rimbaud,* 156–72 (Eng).

RIMBAUD, ARTHUR, "Being beauteous"

Marc Eigeldinger, "L'Image crépusculaire dans la poésie de Rimbaud," *RLM* 323 (1972): 11–12, 14 (Fr).

René Etiemble, *Poètes ou faiseurs? Hygiène des lettres,* vol. 4 (Paris: Gallimard, 1966), 23–46 (Fr).

Giusto, *Rimbaud créateur,* 35, 45, 47–50, 65–66, 94–95, 162–69 (Fr).

C. A. Hackett, *Autour de Rimbaud* (Paris: Klincksieck, 1967), 17–28 (Fr).

Hackett, *Rimbaud,* 28–32 (Eng).

Frances Heck, "Rimbaud's 'Le Bateau ivre,' " *Expl* 39 (Summer 1981): 18–20 (Eng).

Houston, *Patterns of Thought,* 17–21 (Eng).

Edward K. Kaplan, "The Courage of Baudelaire and Rimbaud: The Anxiety of Faith," *FR* 52 (December 1978): 299–303, 305–6 (Eng).

Kittang, *Discours et jeu,* 69–72, 84–86, 109–11, 217–18 (Fr).

Knight, *Flower Poetics in Nineteenth-Century France,* 199–201 (Eng).

Noulet, *Le Premier Visage de Rimbaud,* 207–89 (Fr).

Porter, *The Crisis of French Symbolism,* 219–26 (Eng).

Poulet, *Exploding Poetry,* 110–11, 121–22, 124–25 (Eng).

Poulet, *La Poésie éclatée,* 129–30, 141–42, 144–45 (Fr).

Marcel A. Ruff, *Rimbaud* (Paris: Hatier, 1968), 94–100 (Fr).

Bernard Weinberg, "Les Limites de L'hermétisme, ou Hermétisme et intelligibilité," *CAIEF* 15 (March 1963): 156–57 (Fr).

"Being beauteous"

Ahearn, *Rimbaud,* 198–203 (Eng).

Bays, *The Orphic Vision,* 209 (Eng).

Brunel, *Arthur Rimbaud, ou L'Éclatant Désastre,* 182–83 (Fr).

Calin, *In Defense of French Poetry,* 167–73 (Eng).

Cohn, *The Poetry of Rimbaud,* 276–80 (Eng).

Giusto, *Rimbaud créateur,* 292–95 (Fr).

Renée R. Hubert, "The Use of Reversals in Rimbaud's 'Illuminations,' " *ECr* 9 (Spring 1969): 16–18 (Eng).

Kittang, *Discours et jeu,* 277–78, 306–7 (Fr).

James R. Lawler, "The Unity of 'Being Beauteous,'" *FS* 40 (April 1986): 167–73 (Eng).

Whitaker, *La Structure du monde,* 107–10 (Fr).

"Beth-Saïda"

Giusto, *Rimbaud créateur,* 38–39, 101–2 (Fr).

"Bonne pensée du matin"

Ahearn, *Rimbaud,* 344–50 (Eng).

Brunel, *Rimbaud: Projets et réalisations,* 157–59 (Fr).

Chadwick, *Rimbaud,* 46–48, 62 (Eng).

Cohn, *The Poetry of Rimbaud,* 191–94 (Eng).

Margaret Davies, "Rimbaud's 'Bonne pensée du matin,'" *FS* 25 (July 1971): 295–304 (Eng).

Antoine Fongaro, "Obscène Rimbaud," *SFr* 19 (January–April 1975). 94–95 (Fr).

Anne Freadman, "The Tale of the Story-Teller (and the Tale of His Tale): Rimbaud's 'Alchimie du verbe,'" *AJFS* 14 (January–April 1977): 55–57 (Eng).

Giusto, *Rimbaud créateur,* 196–97 (Fr).

J. A. Hiddleston, "Rimbaud's 'Bonne pensée du matin' and the 'Sujets d'un roi de Babylone,'" *SFr* 30 (September–December 1986): 441–44 (Eng).

Houston, *Patterns of Thought,* 29–31 (Eng).

Claude Zilberberg, "Un Essai de lecture de Rimbaud: 'Bonne pensée du matin,'" in A. J. Greimas, ed., *Essais de sémiotique poétique* (Paris: Larousse, 1972), 140–54 (Fr).

"Bottom"

Brunel, *Arthur Rimbaud, ou L'Éclatant Désastre,* 85–91 (Fr).

Chadwick, *Rimbaud,* 88–89 (Eng).

Cohn, *The Poetry of Rimbaud,* 377–80 (Eng).

RIMBAUD, ARTHUR, "La Brise"

Antoine Fongaro, "Obscène Rimbaud 2," *SFr* 24 (September–December 1980: 499–501 (Fr).

Giusto, *Rimbaud créateur,* 27, 245–246 (Fr).

Renée R. Hubert, "The Use of Reversals in Rimbaud's 'Illuminations,' " *ECr* 9 (Spring 1969): 13–14 (Eng).

Kittang, *Discours et jeu,* 262–65 (Fr).

Jean Richer, "Gautier en filigrane dans quelques 'Illuminations,' " *Europe* 51 (May–June 1973): 70–72 (Fr).

M. Riffaterre, *Semiotics of Poetry,* 101–5 (Eng).

Verstraëte, *La Chasse spirituelle,* 84–88 (Fr).

"La Brise"

Marc Ascione and Jean-Pierre Chambon, "Les 'Zolismes' de Rimbaud," *Europe* 51 (May–June 1973): 121–23 (Fr).

"Bruxelles"

Ahearn, *Rimbaud,* 309–10 (Eng).

Brunel, *Arthur Rimbaud, ou L'Éclatant Désastre,* 125–28 (Fr).

Chadwick, *Rimbaud,* 55–56, 63, 64 (Eng).

Jean-Pierre Chambon, "Quelques problèmes de vocabulaire," *RLM* 594–99 (1980): 95–97 (Fr).

Cohn, *The Poetry of Rimbaud,* 212–15 (Eng).

Giusto, *Rimbaud créateur,* 198–202 (Fr).

"Le Buffet"

Cohn, *The Poetry of Rimbaud,* 79–81 (Eng).

"Ce qu'on dit au poète à propos de fleurs"

Ahearn, *Rimbaud,* 249–54 (Eng).

Barrère, *Le Regard d'Orphée,* 143–53 (Fr).

Bonnefoy, *Rimbaud par lui-même,* 54–55 (Fr).

Brunel, *Arthur Rimbaud, ou L'Éclatant Désastre,* 66–68 (Fr).

Chadwick, *Rimbaud,* 32–34 (Eng).

Cohn, *The Poetry of Rimbaud,* 139–46 (Eng).

Giusto, *Rimbaud créateur,* 146–53 (Fr).

Guerdon, *Rimbaud,* 109–27 (Fr).

Hackett, *Rimbaud,* 22–23 (Eng).

Kittang, *Discours et jeu,* 79–80, 83–84, 178–79 (Fr).

Knight, *Flower Poetics in Nineteenth-Century France,* 196–98 (Eng).

Ross, *The Emergence of Social Space,* 42–43, 83–93 (Eng).

"Ce sont des villes"

Renée R. Hubert, "The Use of Reversals in Rimbaud's 'Illuminations,' " *ECr* 9 (Spring 1969): 10–11 (Eng).

"Chanson de la plus haute tour"

Alexandre Amprimoz, "L'Edifice imprimé d'Arthur Rimbaud," *RR* 78 (March 1987): 177–86 (Eng).

Chadwick, *Rimbaud,* 42–44, 62 (Eng).

Cohn, *The Poetry of Rimbaud,* 198–201 (Eng).

Anne Freadman, "The Tale of the Story-Teller (and the Tale of His Tale): Rimbaud's 'Alchimie du verbe,' " *AJFS* 14 (January–April 1977): 57–58 (Eng).

Giusto, *Rimbaud créateur,* 174–75 (Fr).

Kittang, *Discours et jeu,* 125–27 (Fr).

Emilie Noulet, *Suites: Mallarmé, Rimbaud, Valéry* (Paris: Nizet, 1964), 132–46 (Fr).

"Chant de guerre parisien"

Steve Murphy, "Rimbaud's 'Hannetons,' " *FSB* 12 (Autumn 1984): 3–5 (Eng).

Enid Peschel Rhodes, " 'Voici hannetonner leurs tropes': Revolution as a

RIMBAUD, ARTHUR, "Le Châtiment de Tartuffe"

Poetic Adventure in Rimbaud's 'Chant de guerre parisien,' " *SFr* 20 (January–April 1976): 87–88 (Eng).

Gérald Schaeffer, "Poèmes de la révolte et de la dérision," in Eigeldinger, ed., *Etudes sur les "Poésies" de Rimbaud,* 88–100 (Fr).

"Le Châtiment de Tartuffe"

Joseph Bianco, "Rimbaud from Apprentice to Seer," *KRQ* 37, no. 1 (1990): 33–34 (Eng).

Brunel, *Arthur Rimbaud, ou L'Éclatant Désastre,* 55–56 (Fr).

"Les Chercheuses de poux"

Cohn, *The Poetry of Rimbaud,* 153–56 (Eng).

Giusto, *Rimbaud créateur,* 144–45 (Fr).

Ross, *The Emergence of Social Space,* 105–8, 111–12 (Eng).

"Le Cœur du pitre"

Chadwick, *Rimbaud,* 23–24 (Eng).

Giusto, *Rimbaud créateur,* 129–31 (Fr).

Guerdon, *Rimbaud,* 90–95 (Fr).

"Le Cœur supplicié"

Bays, *The Orphic Vision,* 158–61 (Eng).

C. H. L. Bodenham, "Rimbaud's 'Poétique sensationniste' and Some Nineteenth-Century Medical Writing," *FS* 38 (1984): 34–37 (Eng).

Richter, *La Crise du logos,* 37, 44–50 (Fr).

Gérald Schaeffer, "Poèmes de la révolte et de la dérision," in Eigeldinger, ed., *Etudes sur les "Poésies" de Rimbaud,* 100–14 (Fr).

"Le Cœur volé"

Ahearn, *Rimbaud,* 39–41 (Eng).

A. R. Chisholm, "Two Exegetical Studies (Mallarmé, Rimbaud)," *ECr* 9 (Spring 1969): 30–34 (Eng).

Cohn, *The Poetry of Rimbaud,* 109–11 (Eng).

"Comédie de la soif"

Ahearn, *Rimbaud,* 272–77 (Eng).

Bays, *The Orphic Vision,* 227–28 (Eng).

Brunel, *Arthur Rimbaud, ou L'Éclatant Désastre,* 161–63 (Fr).

Chadwick, *Etudes sur Rimbaud,* 68–69 (Fr).

Chadwick, Rimbaud, 41–42, 61 (Eng).

Cohn, *The Poetry of Rimbaud,* 183–91 (Eng).

Giusto, *Rimbaud créateur,* 180–82 (Fr).

"Conte"

Ahearn, *Rimbaud,* 231–33 (Eng).

Bays, *The Orphic Vision,* 207–9 (Eng).

Gwendolyn Bays, "The Orphic Vision of Nerval, Baudelaire, and Rimbaud," *CLS* 4 (1967): 24 (Eng).

Chadwick, *Rimbaud,* 69–71 (Eng).

Cohn, *The Poetry of Rimbaud,* 266–70 (Eng).

Guisto, *Rimbaud créateur,* 326–29 (Fr).

Houston, *Patterns of Thought,* 77–78 (Eng).

Kittang, *Discours et jeu,* 105–6 (Fr).

G. M. Macklin, "Rimbaud's 'Trois Contes,' " *FSB* 23 (Summer 1987): 10–11 (Eng).

R. Mortier, "La Notion d'harmonie," in Cormier and Holmes, eds., *Essays in Honor of Louis Francis Solano,* 445–46 (Fr).

RIMBAUD, ARTHUR, "Les Corbeaux"

Porter, *The Crisis of French Symbolism,* 239–240 (Eng).

Marilyn Schuster, "L'Ironie dans les 'Illuminations': Voix Empruntées et codes littéraires," *NCFS* 8 (Spring–Summer 1980): 267–68 (Fr).

"Les Corbeaux"

Cohn, *The Poetry of Rimbaud,* 84–87 (Eng).

Guerdon, *Rimbaud,* 69–78 (Fr).

Enid Peschel Rhodes, "Rimbaud's 'Les Corbeaux': A Hymn of Hopeless-ness—and of Hope," *FR* 52 (February 1979): 418–22 (Eng).

"Credo in unam"

Brunel, *Arthur Rimbaud, ou L'Éclatant Désastre,* 151–57 (Fr).

Verstraëte, *La Chasse spirituelle,* 19–42 (Fr).

"Délires"

Marie-Joséphine Whitaker, "Les 'Délires' de Rimbaud Un Psychodrame qui s'ignore," *CAIEF* 36 (May 1984): 185–204 (Fr).

"Délires 1, Vierge folle"

Brunel, *Arthur Rimbaud, ou L'Éclatant Désastre,* 77–80 (Fr).

Brunel, *Rimbaud: Projets et réalisations,* 141–47 (Fr).

Chadwick, *Rimbaud,* 115–19 (Eng).

Antoine Fongaro, "Pour Rimbaud," *SFr* 44 (May–August 1971): 228–90 (Fr).

Virginia de La Charité, "Rimbaud and the Johannine Christ: Containment and Liberation," *NCFS* 2 (Fall 1973): 48–51 (Eng).

Porter, *The Crisis of French Symbolism,* 232–33 (Eng).

"Délires 2,
Alchimie du verbe"

Brunel, *Arthur Rimbaud, ou L'Éclatant Désastre,* 130–39 (Fr).

Chadwick, *Rimbaud,* 119–24 (Eng).

Kittang, *Discours et jeu,* 192–96 (Fr).

Virginia de La Charité, "Rimbaud and the Johannine Christ: Containment and Liberation," *NCFS* 2 (Fall 1973): 48–51 (Eng).

Porter, *The Crisis of French Symbolism,* 233–36 (Eng).

"Démocratie"

Ahearn, *Rimbaud,* 337–39 (Eng).

Cohn, *The Poetry of Rimbaud,* 389–90 (Eng).

Enid Peschel Rhodes, "Under the Spell of Africa: Poems and Letters of Arthur Rimbaud Inspired by the Dark Continent," *FR* 44 (Special Issue 2) (Winter 1971): 26 (Eng).

Verstraëte, *La Chasse spirituelle,* 167–69 (Fr).

"Départ"

Brunel, *Arthur Rimbaud, ou L'Éclatant Désastre,* 11–14 (Fr).

Cohn, *The Poetry of Rimbaud,* 285–87 (Eng).

Giusto, *Rimbaud créateur,* 335–37 (Fr).

Hackett, *Rimbaud,* 80–81 (Eng).

"Les Déserts de l'amour"

Bonnefoy, *Rimbaud par lui-même,* 74–78 (Fr).

Brunel, *Arthur Rimbaud, ou L'Éclatant Désastre,* 83–85 (Fr).

(Eng).

André Guyaux, "L'Autre et le rêve," *CAIEF* 36 (May 1984): 229–31 (Fr).

RIMBAUD, ARTHUR, "Dévotion"

"Dévotion"

Ahearn, *Rimbaud,* 203–6 (Eng).

Cohn, *The Poetry of Rimbaud,* 385–89 (Eng).

Margaret Davies, " 'Dévotion' de Rimbaud," *FR* 46 (February 1973): 493–505 (Fr).

Giusto, *Rimbaud créateur,* 329–30 (Fr).

Houston, *Patterns of Thought,* 52–53 (Eng).

Kittang, *Discours et jeu,* 287–97 (Fr).

Roger Little, "Light on Rimbaud's 'Baou' ('Dévotion')," *FSB* 10 (Spring 1984): 3–7 (Eng).

Marilyn Schuster, "L'Ironie dans les 'Illuminations': Voix empruntées et codes littéraires," *NCFS* 8 (Spring–Summer 1980): 262–63 (Fr).

Verstraëte, *La Chasse spirituelle,* 110–16 (Fr).

"Le Dormeur du val"

Suzanne Bernard, "La Palette de Rimbaud," *CAIEF* 12 (May 1960): 107–8 (Fr).

Cohn, *The Poetry of Rimbaud,* 74–76 (Eng).

René-Albert Gutmann, *Introduction a la lecture des poètes français* (Paris: Nizet, 1967), 56–59 (Fr).

Noulet, *Le Premier Visage de Rimbaud,* 69–75 (Fr).

Albert Sonnenfeld, "A Note on 'Le Dormeur du val,' " *FR* 40 (February 1967): 518–21 (Eng).

"L'Éclair"

Chadwick, *Rimbaud,* 129–30 (Eng).

"L'Éclatante Victoire de Sarrebruck"

John P. Houston, "Sexual Allusions and Scholarship: Observations on Rimbaud Studies," *NCFS* 15 (Fall–Winter 1986–1987): 162–72 (Eng).

"Les Effarés"

Broome and Chesters, *The Appreciation of Modern French Poetry* (1850–1950), 101–4 (Eng).

Brunel, *Arthur Rimbaud, ou L'Éclatant Désastre,* 24–26 (Fr).

Cohn, *The Poetry of Rimbaud,* 65–69 (Eng).

Noulet, *Le Premier Visage de Rimbaud,* 55–63 (Fr).

Whitaker, *La Structure du monde,* 34–36 (Fr).

"Enfance"

Bays, *The Orphic Vision,* 213–14 (Eng).

Gwendolyn Bays, "The Orphic Vision of Nerval, Baudelaire, and Rimbaud," *CLS* 4 (1967): 19–21 (Eng).

Cohn, *The Poetry of Rimbaud,* 253–66 (Eng).

Houston, *Patterns of Thought,* 79–80 (Eng).

Roger Little, "Enfance," *RLM* 370–73 (1973): 85–86 (Fr).

Porter, *The Crisis of French Symbolism,* 237–39 (Eng).

Whitaker, *La Structure du monde,* 60–64 (Fr).

"Enfance 1"

Ahearn, *Rimbaud,* 17–19, 74–76 (Eng).

Giusto, *Rimbaud créateur,* 269–71 (Fr).

Kittang, *Discours et jeu,* 228–32 (Fr).

"Enfance 2"

Ahearn, *Rimbaud,* 76–78 (Eng).

Giusto, *Rimbaud créateur,* 271–73 (Fr).

M. Rifaterre, *Semiotics of Poetry,* 120–21 (Eng).

RIMBAUD, ARTHUR, "Enfance 3"

"Enfance 3"

Ahearn, *Rimbaud,* 78–79 (Eng).

Giusto, *Rimbaud* créateur, 273–74 (Fr).

Hackett, *Rimbaud,* 55–59 (Eng).

"Enfance 4"

Ahearn, *Rimbaud,* 79–81 (Eng).

Giusto, *Rimbaud créateur,* 274–76 (Fr).

Kittang, *Discours et jeu,* 261–62 (Fr).

"Enfance 5"

Ahearn, *Rimbaud,* 81–83 (Eng).

Giusto, *Rimbaud créateur,* 84, 276 (Fr).

"Entends comme brame"

Edward J. Ahearn, " 'Entends comme brame' and the Theme of Death in Nature in Rimbaud's Poetry," *FR* 43 (February 1970): 407–17 (Eng).

Chadwick, *Rimbaud,* 57, 63–64 (Eng).

Cohn, *The Poetry of Rimbaud,* 223–25 (Eng).

W. M. Frohock, "Rimbaud's Internal Landscape," in Beaumont, Cocking, and Cruickshank, eds., *Order and Adventure in Post-Romantic French Poetry,* 103–5 (Eng).

Giusto, *Rimbaud créateur,* 205–8 (Fr).

C. A. Hackett, *Autour de Rimbaud* (Paris: Klincksieck, 1967), 39–44 (Fr).

C. A. Hackett, "Verlaine's Influence on Rimbaud," in L. J. Austin, Garnet Rees, and E. Vinaver, eds., *Studies in Modern French Literature Presented to P. Mansell Jones* (Manchester: Manchester University Press, 1961), 172–77 (Eng).

Bernard Meyer, "Une Machine à imaginer: 'Entends comme brame,' " *SFr* 33 (September–December 1989): 423–38 (Fr).

"Est-elle almée?"

Cohn, *The Poetry of Rimbaud,* 215–16 (Eng).

Giusto, *Rimbaud créateur,* 202–3 (Fr).

Kittang, *discours et jeu,* 95–97 (Fr).

"Eternité"

Bays, *The Orphic Vision,* 223–25 (Eng).

Gwendolyn Bays, "The Orphic Vision of Nerval, Baudelaire, and Rimbaud," *CLS* 4 (1967): 25–26 (Eng).

Brunel, *Arthur Rimbaud, ou L'Éclatant Désastre,* 116–18 (Fr).

Brunel, *Rimbaud: Projets et réalisations,* 163–65 (Fr).

Chadwick, *Rimbaud,* 44–45, 62 (Eng).

Cohn, *The Poetry of Rimbaud,* 201 4 (Eng).

René Etiemble, *Rimbaud: Système solaire ou trou noir ?* (Paris: Presses Universitaires de France, 1984), 29, 35–39 (Fr).

Anne Freadman, "The Tale of the Story-Teller (and the Tale of His Tale): Rimbaud's 'Alchimie du verbe,'" *AJFS* 14 (January–April 1977): 57–58 (Eng).

Giusto, *Rimbaud créateur,* 175–77 (Fr).

Hackett, *Rimbaud,* 40–41, 46 (Eng).

J. A. Hiddleston, "The Sea of Brass and the Sun of Righteousness: Two Biblical Illusions in Rimbaud," *FS* 34 (October 1980): 419–20 (Eng).

"L'Etoile a pleuré rose"

Ahearn, *Rimbaud,* 119–22 (Eng).

Cohn, *The Poetry of Rimbaud,* 133–35 (Eng).

Jean-Paul Dumont, " 'Littéralement et dans tous les sens': Essai d'analyse structurale," in A. J. Greimas, ed., *Essais de sémiotique poétique* (Paris: Larousse, 1972), 126–39 (Fr).

René Etiemble, *Le Sonnet des voyelles* (Paris: Gallimard, 1968), 45–49 (Fr).

RIMBAUD, ARTHUR, "Les Etrennes des orphelins"

Giusto, *Rimbaud créateur,* 161–62 (Fr).

Kittang, *Discours et jeu,* 90–91 (Fr).

Noulet, *Le Premier Visage de Rimbaud,* 111–13 (Fr).

"Les Etrennes des orphelins"

Coh, *The Poetry of Rimbaud,* 31–37 (Eng).

André Guyaux, "L'Autre et le rêve," *CAIEF* 36 (May 1984): 223–29 (Fr).

Porter, *The Crisis of French Symbolism,* 201–5 (Eng).

Poulet, *Exploding Poetry,* 76–79 (Eng).

Poulet, *La Poésie éclatée,* 88–92 (Fr).

"Faim"

Anne Freadman, "The Tale of the Story-Teller (and the Tale of His Tale): Rimbaud's 'Alchimie du verbe,' " *AJFS* 14 (January–April 1977): 52–54 (Eng).

"Fairy"

Cohn, *The Poetry of Rimbaud,* 357–60 (Eng).

Margaret Davies, " 'Fairy': Le Rejet du prédécesseur," *CAIEF* 36 (May 1984): 169–84 (Fr).

Giusto, *Rimbaud créateur,* 295–98 (Fr).

Kittang, *Discours et jeu,* 271–77 (Fr).

Verstraëte, *La Chasse spirituelle,* 170–74 (Fr).

"Fête d'hiver"

Cohn, *The Poetry of Rimbaud,* 341–43 (Eng).

David Scott, "Rimbaud and Boucher: 'Fête d'hiver,' " *JES* 9 (September 1979): 185–95 (Eng).

"Fêtes de la faim"

Brunel, *Arthur Rimbaud ou L'Éclatant Désastre,* 116 (Fr).

Cohn, *The Poetry of Rimbaud,* 216–20 (Eng).

Giusto, *Rimbaud créateur,* 182–84 (Fr).

Porter, *The Crisis of French Symbolism,* 229–30 (Eng).

M. Riffaterrre, *Semiotics of Poetry,* 76–80 (Eng).

"Fêtes de la patience"

Cohn, *The Poetry of Rimbaud,* 194–201 (Eng).

"Fleurs"

Edward J. Ahearn, "Explosions of the Real: Rimbaud's Ecstatic and Political Subversions," *SFR* 9 (Spring 1985): 72–74 (Fr).

Ahearn, *Rimbaud,* 245–48 (Eng).

Chadwick, *Rimbaud,* 81–82, 101, 103 (Eng).

Cohn, *The Poetry of Rimbaud,* 333–36 (Eng).

Giusto, *Rimbaud créateur,* 72–73, 263–65 (Fr).

Hackett, *Rimbaud,* 60–62 (Eng).

"Le Forgeron"

Brunel, *Arthur Rimbaud, ou L'Éclatant Désastre,* 56–58 (Fr).

Cohn, *The Poetry of Rimbaud,* 49–53 (Eng).

Kittang, *Discours et jeu,* 74–78 (Fr).

"Génie"

Ahearn, *Rimbaud,* 122, 127–35 (Eng).

Bays, *The Orphic Vision,* 209–11 (Eng).

Bonnefoy, *Rimbaud par lui-même,* 146–52 (Fr).

RIMBAUD, ARTHUR, "Guerre"

Brunel, *Rimbaud: Projets et réalisations,* 264–66 (Fr).

Chadwick, *Rimbaud,* 71–72, 100, 102 (Eng).

Cohn, *The Poetry of Rimbaud,* 390–97 (Eng).

Margaret Davies, "Génie," *RLM* 594–99 (1980): 47–65 (Fr).

René Etiemble, *Rimbaud: Système solaire ou trou noir?* (Paris: Presses Universitaires de France, 1984), 46–74 (Fr).

Giusto, *Rimbaud créateur,* 90, 95–96, 310–15 (Fr).

Hackett, *Rimbaud,* 79–80 (Eng).

Houston, *Patterns of Thought,* 62–65 (Eng).

Kittang, *Discours et jeu,* 220–27 (Fr).

Virginia de La Charité, "Rimbaud and the Johannine Christ: Containment and Liberation," *NCFS* 2 (Fall 1973): 59–60 (Eng).

Lawler, *The Language of French Symbolism,* 76–88, 98–100 (Eng).

Enid Peschel Rhodes, "Ambiguities in Rimbaud's Search for 'Charity,'" *FR* 47 (May 1974): 1090–91, 1093 (Eng).

Marilyn Schuster, "L'Ironie dans les 'Illuminations': Voix empruntées et codes littéraires," *NCFS* 8 (Spring–Summer 1980): 263–67 (Fr).

Verstraëte, *La Chasse spirituelle,* 140–48 (Fr).

"Guerre"

Ahearn, *Rimbaud,* 83–86 (Eng).

Cohn, *The Poetry of Rimbaud,* 360–62 (Eng).

Giusto, *Rimbaud créateur,* 333–35 (Fr).

Marilyn Schuster, "L'Ironie dans les 'Illuminations': Voix empruntées et codes littéraires," *NCFS* 8 (Spring–Summer 1980): 259–62 (Fr).

"H"

Ahearn, *Rimbaud,* 29, 114–16, 136–37 (Eng).

Brunel, *Arthur Rimbaud, ou L'Éclatant Désastre,* 216–17 (Fr).

Cohn, *The Poetry of Rimbaud,* 380–81 (Eng).

Giusto, Rimbaud créateur, 330–32 (Fr).

Guerdon, Rimbaud, 220–24 (Fr).

Charles Stivale, "Corps érotique, corps créateur: 'H' d'Arthur Rimbaud," *SRF* 9 (Spring 1985): 83–90 (Eng).

Verstraëte, La Chasse spirituelle, 116–21 (Fr).

Whitaker, *La Structure du monde,* 144–46 (Fr).

"L'Homme juste"

Brunel, *Arthur Rimbaud, ou L'Éclatant Désastre,* 71–72 (Fr).

Cohn, *The Poetry of Rimbaud,* 135–39 (Eng).

Giusto, *Rimbaud créateur,* 141–43 (Fr).

"Honte"

Brunel, *Arthur Rimbaud, ou L'Éclatant Désastre,* 203–9 (Fr).

Chadwick, *Rimbaud,* 38–39, 59–69 (Eng).

Cohn, *The Poetry of Rimbaud,* 228–29 (Eng).

Giusto, *Rimbaud créateur,* 172 (Fr).

Enid Peschel Rhodes, "Rimbaud's 'Honte' in the Light of his Ambivalence Toward Religion," *SFr* 18 (September–December 1974): 480–84 (Eng).

"Illuminations"

G. M. Macklin, "Perspectives on the Role of Punctuation in Rimbaud's 'Illuminations,' " *JES* 20 (March 1990): 59–72 (Eng).

"L'Impossible"

Bays, *The Orphic Vision,* 243 (Eng).

Chadwick, *Rimbaud,* 128–29 (Eng).

RIMBAUD, ARTHUR, "Jadis, si je me souviens bien"

"Jadis, si je me souviens bien"

Enid Peschel Rhodes, "Ambiguities in Rimbaud's Search for 'Charity,'"
FR 47 (May 1974): 1088–89 (Eng).

"Jeune ménage"

Brunel, *Arthur Rimbaud, ou L'Eclatant Désastre,* 33–35 (Fr).

Chadwick, *Rimbaud,* 53–55, 63 (Eng).

Cohn, *The Poetry of Rimbaud,* 208–11 (Eng).

Giusto, *Rimbaud créateur,* 197–98 (Fr).

Whitaker, *La Structure du monde,* 58–60 (Fr).

"Jeunesse"

Ahearn, *Rimbaud,* 86–96 (Eng).

Cohn, *The Poetry of Rimbaud,* 362–68 (Eng).

Giusto, *Rimbaud créateur,* 337–42 (Fr).

Houston, *Patterns of Thought,* 55–58 (Eng).

James R. Lawler, "The Poet as Self-Critic: Rimbaud's 'Jeunesse,'" *FR* 62
(October 1988): 11–24 (Eng).

Jeunesse I
"Dimanche"

Bays, *The Orphic Vision,* 216–17 (Eng).

Jeunesse II
"Sonnet"

Bays, *The Orphic Vision,* 217–18 (Eng).

Kittang, *Discours et jeu,* 174–77 (Fr).

RIMBAUD, ARTHUR, "Le Loup criait sous les feuilles"

Jeunesse III
"Vingt ans"

Bays, *The Orphic Vision,* 217–18 (Eng).

"Jeunesse IV"

Kittang, Discours et jeu, 186–87 (Fr).

"Larme"

Ahearn, *Rimbaud,* 20–22, 270–71 (Eng).

Brunel, *Rimbaud: Projets et réalisations,* 155–57 (Fr).

Chadwick, *Etudes sur Rimbaud,* 60–64 (Fr).

Chadwick, *Rimbaud,* 48–50, 62, 64 (Eng).

Cohn, *The Poetry of Rimbaud,* 176–80 (Eng).

Anne Freadman, "The Tale of the Story-Teller (and the Tale of His Tale): Rimbaud's 'Alchimie du verbe,' " *AJFS* 14 (January–April 1977): 52–54 (Eng).

W. M. Frohock, "Rimbaud's Internal Landscape," in Beaumont, Cocking, and Cruickshank, eds., *Order and Adventure in Post-Romantic French Poetry,* 102 (Eng).

Guisto, *Rimbaud créateur,* 50–52, 193–94 (Fr).

Kittang, *Discours et jeu,* 131–34 (Fr).

Emilie Noulet, *Suites: Mallarmé, Rimbaud, Valéry* (Paris: Nizet, 1964), 147–59 (Fr).

"Le Loup criait sous les feuilles"

Cohn, *The Poetry of Rimbaud,* 240–42 (Eng).

Anne Freadman, "The Tale of the Story-Teller (and the Tale of His Tale): Rimbaud's 'Alchimie du verbe,' " *AJFS* 14 (January–April 1977): 56–57 (Eng).

J. A. Hiddleston, "Rimbaud," *FS* 35 (October 1981): 510 (Eng).

J. A. Hiddleston, "Rimbaud's Crying Wolf: A Reply," *FS* 35 (July 1981): 296–301 (Eng).

RIMBAUD, ARTHUR, "Ma bohème"

J. A. Hiddleston, "The Sea of Brass and the Sun of Righteousness: Two Biblical Illusions in Rimbaud," *FS* 34 (October 1980): 417–19 (Eng).

Roger Little, "La Mort du Loup?" *FS* 35 (October 1981): 407 (Eng).

Roger Little, "Rimbaud's 'Le Loup criait sous les feuilles': A Further Note," *FS* 35 (April 1981): 148–52 (Eng).

"Ma bohème"

Ahearn, *Rimbaud,* 44–46 (Eng).

Broome and Chesters, *The Appreciation of Modern French Poetry* (1850–1950), 104–7 (Eng).

Cohn, *The Poetry of Rimbaud,* 81–84 (Eng).

Giusto, *Rimbaud créateur,* 33–35, 62 (Fr).

Kittang, *Discours et jeu,* 168–73 (Fr).

Porter, *The Crisis of French Symbolism,* 212–13 (Eng).

Richter, *La Crise du logos,* 27–35 (Fr).

"Les Mains de Jeanne-Marie"

Brunel, *Arthur Rimbaud, ou L'Éclatant Désastre,* 60–61, 64–65 (Fr).

Chadwick, *Rimbaud,* 30–32 (Eng).

Cohn, *The Poetry of Rimbaud,* 114–18 (Eng).

Giusto, *Rimbaud créateur,* 138–39 (Fr).

Kittang, *Discours et jeu,* 211–17 (Fr).

"La Maline"

Brunel, *Arthur Rimbaud, ou L'Éclatant Désastre,* 22–24 (Fr).

"Marine"

Ahearn, *Rimbaud,* 285–89 (Eng).

Brunel, *Rimbaud: Projets et réalisations,* 275–76 (Fr).

Bruno Claisse, "Rimbaud entre Hugo et Michelet," *RHL* 87 (November–December 1987): 1023–32 (Fr).

Cohn, *The Poetry of Rimbaud,* 340–41 (Eng).

Giusto, *Rimbaud créateur,* 228–30 (Fr).

Verstraëte, *La Chasse spirituelle,* 126–29 (Fr).

"Matin"

Chadwick, *Rimbaud,* 130 (Eng).

Virginia de La Charité, "Rimbaud and the Johannine Christ: Containment and Liberation," *NCFS* 2 (Fall 1973): 52–53 (Eng).

"Matinée d'ivresse"

Ahearn, *Rimbaud,* 192–98 (Eng).

Bays, *The Orphic Vision,* 193–97 (Eng).

Bonnefoy, *Rimbaud par lui-même,* 156–60 (Fr).

Brunel, *Rimbaud: Projets et réalisations,* 270–73 (Fr).

Chadwick, *Rimbaud,* 74–76 (Eng)

Cohn, *The Poetry of Rimbaud,* 290–94 (Eng).

Giusto, *Rimbaud créateur,* 288–92 (Fr).

Houston, *Patterns of Thought,* 53–54 (Eng).

Kittang, *Discours et jeu,* 161–168 (Fr).

Virginia de La Charité, "Rimbaud and the Johannine Christ: Containment and Liberation," *NCFS* 2 (Fall 1973): 57–58 (Eng).

R. Mortier, "La Notion d'harmonie," in Cormier and Holmes eds., *Essays in Honor of Louis Francis Solano,* 444–45 (Fr).

Verstraëte, *La Chasse spirituelle,* 56–69 (Fr).

Whitaker, *La Structure du monde,* 132–33 (Fr).

"Mauvais sang"

Barrère, *Le Regard d'Orphée,* 155–85 (Fr).

Brunel, *Rimbaud: Projets et réalisations,* 179–81 (Fr).

Chadwick, *Rimbaud,* 124–27 (Eng).

Virginia de La Charité, "Rimbaud and the Johannine Christ: Containment and Liberation," *NCFS* 2 (Fall 1973): 47–48 (Eng).

Porter, *The Crisis of French Symbolism*, 231–32 (Eng).

Enid Peschel Rhodes, "Under the Spell of Africa: Poems and Letters of Arthur Rimbaud Inspired by the Dark Continent," *FR* 44 (Special Issue 2) (Winter 1971): 22–24 (Eng).

"Mémoire"

Ahearn, *Rimbaud,* 19–20, 268–70 (Eng).

Alexandre Amprimoz, "Mémoire—à quelle boue?" *RLM* 445–49 (1976): 71–80 (Fr).

Bonnefoy, *Rimbaud par lui-même,* 72–74 (Fr).

Brunel, *Arthur Rimbaud, ou L'Éclatant Désastre,* 14–16 (Fr).

Brunel, *Rimbaud: Projets et réalisations,* 166–69 (Fr).

Chadwick, *Rimbaud,* 36–37, 59 (Eng).

Cohn, *The Poetry of Rimbaud,* 230–35 (Eng).

W. M. Frohock, "Rimbaud's Internal Landscape," in Beaumont, Cocking, and Cruickshank, eds., *Order and Adventure in Post-Romantic French Poetry,* 100–01 (Eng).

Guisto, *Rimbaud créateur,* 24–25, 36–38, 65–66, 79–80, 97–99, 187–92 (Fr).

Hackett, *Rimbaud,* 41–45 (Eng).

Houston, *Patterns of Thought,* 23–25 (Eng).

Kittang, *Discours et jeu,* 202–5 (Fr).

John C. Lapp, " 'Mémoire': Art et hallucination chez Rimbaud," *CAIEF* 23 (May 1971): 163–75 (Fr).

Porter, *The Crisis of French Symbolism,* 226–27 (Eng).

Michael Riffaterre, "Sylleptic Symbols Rimbaud's 'Mémoire,' " in Prendergast, ed., *Nineteenth-century French Poetry,* 178–98 (Eng).

Whitaker, *La Structure du monde,* 36–38 (Fr).

Nathaniel Wing, "Metaphor and Ambiguity in Rimbaud's 'Mémoire,' " *RR* 63 (October 1972): 190–210 (Eng).

RIMBAUD, ARTHUR, "Michel et Christine"

"Mes Petites Amoureuses"

Brunel, *Arthur Rimbaud, ou L'Éclatant Désastre,* 52–55 (Fr).

Jean-Pierre Chambon, "Quelques problèmes de vocabulaire," *RLM* 594–99 (1980): 97–8 (Fr).

Cohn, *The Poetry of Rimbaud,* 94–96 (Eng).

Giusto, *Rimbaud créateur,* 131–34 (Fr).

André Guyaux, "Les Niveaux de langue dans la poésie de Rimbaud," *CAIEF* 41 (May 1989): 66–71 (Fr).

Gérald Schaeffer, "Poèmes de la révolte et de la dérision," in Eigeldinger, ed., *Etudes sur les "Poésies" de Rimbaud,* 114–25 (Fr).

"Metropolitain"

Ahearn, *Rimbaud,* 293, 298, 318–21 (Eng).

Cohn, *The Poetry of Rimbaud,* 346–50 (Eng).

Margaret Davies, "Le Thème de la voyance dans 'Après le déluge,' 'Métropolitain' et 'Barbare,'" *RLM* 323 (1972): 27–34 (Fr).

Giusto, *Rimbaud créateur,* 40–42, 283–87 (Fr).

"Michel et Christine"

Brunel, *Arthur Rimbaud, ou L'Éclatant Désastre,* 128–30 (Fr).

Pierre Brunel, "La Fin de L'idylle," *RHL* 87 (March–April 1987): 200–12 (Fr).

Chadwick, *Etudes sur Rimbaud,* 64–68 (Fr).

Chadwick, *Rimbaud,* 39–41, 60–61 (Eng).

Cohn, *The Poetry of Rimbaud,* 225–28 (Eng).

René Etiemble, *Poètes ou faiseurs? Hygiène des lettres,* vol. 4 (Paris: Gallimard, 1966), 47–55 (Fr).

W. M. Frohock, "Rimbaud's Internal Landscape," in Beaumont, Cocking, and Cruickshank, eds., *Order and Adventure in Post-Romantic French Poetry,* 103 (Eng).

RIMBAUD, ARTHUR, "Mouvement"

Guisto, *Rimbaud créateur,* 203–5 (Fr).

Kittang, *Discours et jeu,* 200–202 (Fr).

"Mouvement"

Bays, *The Orphic Vision,* 213 (Eng).

Bonnefoy, *Rimbaud par lui-même,* 161–64 (Fr).

Brunel, *Arthur Rimbaud, ou L'Éclatant Désastre,* 35–36 (Fr).

Michel Charolles, "Le Texte poétique et sa signification," *Europe* 51 (May–June 1973): 97–114 (Fr).

Cohn, *The Poetry of Rimbaud,* 381–85 (Eng).

Giusto, *Rimbaud créateur,* 230–37 (Fr).

Guerdon, *Rimbaud,* 227–29 (Fr).

Kittang, *Discours et jeu,* 93–94, 250–59 (Fr).

Lawler, *The Language of French Symbolism,* 103 (Eng).

Michael Riffaterre, "Sémantique du poème," *CAIEF* 23 (May 1971): 138–39 (Fr).

Verstraëte, *La Chasse spirituelle,* 136–39 (Fr).

Whitaker, *La Structure du monde,* 120–21 (Fr).

"Mystique"

Ahearn, *Rimbaud,* 285–87, 289–91 (Eng).

Bertocci, *From Symbolism to Baudelaire,* 94–96 (Eng).

Cohn, *The Poetry of Rimbaud,* 326–29 (Eng).

Anne Freadman, "To Read Rimbaud, (b) A Reading of 'Mystique,'" *AJFS* 9 (January–April 1974): 65–82 (Eng).

Giusto, *Rimbaud créateur,* 258–60 (Fr).

Renée R. Hubert, "The Use of Reversals in Rimbaud's 'Illuminations'" *ECr* 9 (Spring 1969): 15–16 (Eng).

Roger Little, "Rimbaud's 'Mystique': Some Observations," *FS* 26 (July 1972): 285– 88 (Eng).

"Nocturne vulgaire"

Brunel, *Arthur Rimbaud, ou l'Éclatant Désastre,* 91–94 (Fr).

Chadwick, *Rimbaud,* 79–80 (Eng).

Cohn, *The Poetry of Rimbaud,* 336–40 (Eng).

Giusto, *Rimbaud créateur,* 266–69 (Fr).

Kittang, *Discours et jeu,* 247–50, 307–10 (Fr).

Roger Little, "Nocturne vulgaire," *RLM* 370–73 (1973): 90–91 (Fr).

Verstraëte, *La Chasse spirituelle,* 80–83 (Fr).

"Nuit de l'enfer"

Brunel, *Rimbaud: Projets et réalisations,* 192–96 (Fr).

Chadwick, *Rimbaud,* 127–28 (Eng).

Kittang, *Discours et jeu,* 154–55 (Fr).

Porter, *The Crisis of French Symbolism,* 232 (Eng).

"Ophélie"

Brunel, *Arthur Rimbaud, ou L'Éclatant Désastre,* 103–5 (Fr).

Cohn, *The Poetry of Rimbaud,* 44–47 (Eng).

Knight, *Flower Poetics in Nineteenth-Century France,* 190–92 (Eng).

Valerie Minogue, "Rimbaud's Ophelia," *FS* 43 (October 1989): 423–36 (Eng).

"Ophélie 1"

Kittang, *Discours et jeu,* 114–16 (Fr).

"Ophélie 2"

Kittang, *Discours et jeu,* 120–22 (Fr).

RIMBAUD, ARTHUR, "Oraison du soir"

"Oraison du soir"

Edward J. Ahearn, "Rimbaud's 'Images immondes,'" *FR* 40 (February 1967): 508–10 (Eng).

Cohn, *The Poetry of Rimbaud,* 92–94 (Eng).

"L'Orgie parisienne, ou Paris se repeuple"

Ahearn, *Rimbaud,* 306–7 (Eng).

Cohn, *The Poetry of Rimbaud,* 111–14 (Eng).

Kittang, *Discours et jeu,* 94–95 (Fr).

"Ornières"

Ahearn, *Rimbaud,* 315–18 (Eng).

Cohn, *The Poetry of Rimbaud,* 305–7 (Eng).

Giusto, *Rimbaud créateur,* 256–58 (Fr).

Hackett, *Rimbaud,* 66–68 (Eng).

David Scott, "La Structure spatiale du poème en prose," *Poétique* 15 (September 1984): 306–7 (Fr).

"O Saisons, ô châteaux"

Bays, *The Orphic Vision,* 225–26 (Eng).

Brunel, *Rimbaud: Projets et réalisations,* 169–71 (Fr).

Chadwick, *Rimbaud,* 50–53, 62–63 (Eng).

Cohn, *The Poetry of Rimbaud,* 236–40 (Eng).

Giusto, *Rimbaud créateur,* 185–87 (Fr).

Houston, *Patterns of Thought,* 41–43 (Eng).

"Ouvriers"

Ahearn, *Rimbaud,* 311, 313–14 (Eng).

Brunel, *Arthur Rimbaud, ou L'Éclatant Désastre,* 36–37 (Fr).

Cohn, *The Poetry of Rimbaud,* 299–301 (Eng).

Giusto, *Rimbaud créateur*, 344 (Fr).

Houston, *Patterns of Thought,* 54–55 (Eng).

"Parade"

Ahearn, *Rimbaud,* 157–60 (Eng).

Cohn, *The Poetry of Rimbaud,* 270–75 (Eng).

Giusto, *Rimbaud créateur,* 280–83 (Fr).

Houston, *Patterns of Thought,* 75–76 (Eng).

Kittang, *Discours et jeu,* 311–15 (Fr).

Porter, *The Crisis of French Symbolism,* 240–41 (Eng).

Verstraëte, *La Chasse spirituelle,* 149–54 (Fr).

Whitaker, *La Structure du monde,* 139–42 (Fr).

Nathaniel Wing, "Rimbaud's 'Les Ponts,' 'Parade,' 'Scènes': The Poem as Performance," *FR* 46 (February 1973): 506–21 (Eng).

"Les Pauvres á l'eglise"

Cohn, *The Poetry of Rimbaud,* 106–8 (Eng).

"Phrases"

Chadwick, *Rimbaud,* 78–79, 101 (Eng).

Cohn, *The Poetry of Rimbaud,* 294–98 (Eng).

Giusto, *Rimbaud créateur,* 225–26, 237–38, 243 (Fr).

Daniel Guilbaud, " 'Phrases' de Rimbaud: Essai de lecture," *AJFS* 19 (September–December 1982): 243–65 (Fr).

Porter, *The Crisis of French Symbolism,* 242–44, 250 (Eng).

"Les Poètes de sept ans"

Ahearn, *Rimbaud,* 30–32, 35–37 (Eng).

Yves Bonnefoy, "Madame Rimbaud," in Eigeldinger, ed., *Etudes sur les "Poésies" de Rimbaud,* 9–43 (Fr).

RIMBAUD, ARTHUR, "Les Ponts"

Cohn, *The Poetry of Rimbaud,* 97–106 (Eng).

Guisto, *Rimbaud créateur,* 70–71, 134–35 (Fr).

Hackett, *Rimbaud,* 18–22 (Eng).

Kittang, *Discours et jeu,* 99–100, 116–18, 128–29 (Fr).

Knight, *Flower Poetics in Nineteenth-Century France,* 193–94 (Eng).

Noulet, *Le Premier Visage de Rimbaud,* 95–106 (Fr).

Ross, *The Emergence of Social Space,* 113–19 (Eng).

"Les Ponts"

Ahearn, *Rimbaud,* 321–24 (Eng).

Cohn, *The Poetry of Rimbaud,* 301–3 (Eng).

Guisto, *Rimbaud créateur,* 247–49 (Fr).

Porter, *The Crisis of French Symbolism,* 244–45 (Eng).

Nathaniel Wing, "Rimbaud's 'Les Ponts,' 'Parade,' 'Scènes': The Poem as Performance," *FR* 46 (February 1973): 512–14 (Eng).

"Les Premières Communions"

Cohn, *The Poetry of Rimbaud,* 146–53 (Eng).

Giusto, *Rimbaud créateur,* 143–44 (Fr).

"Première soirée"

Cohn, *The Poetry of Rimbaud,* 57–59 (Eng).

"Promontoire"

Ahearn, *Rimbaud,* 326–28 (Eng).

Brunel, *Rimbaud: Projets et réalisations,* 289–91 (Fr).

Cohn, *The Poetry of Rimbaud,* 368–71 (Eng).

Giusto, *Rimbaud créateur*, 249–51 (Fr).

Renée R. Hubert, "The Use of Reversals in Rimbaud's 'Illuminations,'" *ECr* 9 (Spring 1969): 11–13 (Eng).

Kittang, *Discours et jeu*, 223–38 (Fr).

Michael Riffaterre, "Promontoire," *FR* 55 (April 1982): 625–32 (Fr).

David Scott, "La Structure spatiale du poème en prose," *Poétique* 15 (September 1984): 307 (Fr).

"Qu'est-ce pour nous, mon cœur"

Bonnefoy, *Rimbaud par lui-même*, 91–93 (Fr).

Cohn, *The Poetry of Rimbaud*, 220 (Eng).

"Les Reparties de Nina"

Edward J. Ahearn, "Rimbaud's 'Images immondes,'" *FR* 40 (February 1967): 507–8 (Eng).

Brunel, *Arthur Rimbaud, ou L'Éclatant Désastre*, 20–21 (Fr).

Jean-Pierre Chambon, "Quelques problèmes de vocabulaire," *RLM* 594–99 (1980): 100–101 (Fr).

Cohn, *The Poetry of Rimbaud*, 59–65 (Eng).

Frédérick Eigeldinger, "Futur lyrique et futur épique dans les vers de Rimbaud," in Eigeldinger, ed., *Etudes sur les "Poésies" de Rimbaud*, 69–70 (Fr).

"Rêve"

Hackett, *Rimbaud*, 120–24 (Eng).

Michael Sheringham, "Rimbaud in 1875 and André Breton's 'Forêt noire,'" *FS* 35 (January 1981): 36–40 (Eng).

"Rêvé pour l'hiver"

Cohn, *The Poetry of Rimbaud*, 73–74 (Eng).

Ross, *The Emergence of Social Space*, 33–36 (Eng).

RIMBAUD, ARTHUR, "La Rivière de Cassis"

Kristin Ross, "Rimbaud and the Transformation of Social Space," *YFS*, no. 73 (1987): 107–10 (Eng).

"La Rivière de Cassis"

Brunel, *Arthur Rimbaud, ou L'Éclatant Désastre,* 200–201 (Fr).

Chadwick, *Rimbaud,* 39–60 (Eng).

Jean-Pierre Chambon, "Quelques problèmes de vocabulaire," *RLM* 594–99 (1980): 98–100 (Fr).

Cohn, *The Poetry of Rimbaud,* 180–83 (Eng).

Giusto, *Rimbaud créateur,* 194–96 (Fr).

Guerdon, *Rimbaud,* 54–69 (Fr).

Cohn, *The Poetry of Rimbaud,* 70–73 (Eng).

"Royauté"

Brunel, *Arthur Rimbaud, ou L'Éclatant Désastre,* 37–38 (Fr).

Giusto, *Rimbaud créateur,* 329 (Fr).

Guerdon, *Rimbaud,* 229–32 (Fr).

Houston, *Patterns of Thought,* 71–72 (Eng).

Kittang, *Discours et jeu,* 91–93 (Fr).

G. M. Macklin, "Rimbaud's 'Trois Contes,' " *FSB* 23 (Summer 1987): 11–12 (Eng).

Verstraëte, *La Chasse spirituelle,* 130–36 (Fr).

"Une Saison en enfer"

Ahearn, *Rimbaud,* 26–27, 57–65, 139–50, 177–78, 227–28, 243–44, 307–9, 331, 336 (Eng).

Bonnefoy, *Rimbaud par lui-même,* 107–34 (Fr).

Brunel, *Arthur Rimbaud, ou L'Éclatant Désastre,* 68–83, 94–96 (Fr).

Brunel, *Rimbaud: Projets et réalisations,* 201–21 (Fr).

Chadwick, *Etudes sur Rimbaud,* 145–52 (Fr).

Chadwick, *Rimbaud,* 112–35 (Eng).

Cohn, *The Poetry of Rimbaud,* 401–38 (Eng).

Couffignal, *Zone d'Apollinaire,* 42 (Fr).

Margaret Davis, "Une Saison en enfer," *RLM* 370–73 (1973): 17–40 (Fr).

Margaret Davies, *"Une Saison en enfer"* d'Arthur Rimbaud: Analyse du texte (Paris: Minard, 1975) (Fr).

Laurie Edson, "Rimbaud's 'Une Saison en enfer' and Matisse's 'La Danse,' " *RR* 74 (November 1983): 461–74 (Eng).

Marc Eigeldinger, "L'Image crépusculaire dans la poésie de Rimbaud," *RLM* 323 (1972): 12–14 (Fr).

Mark Eigeldinger, *Rimbaud et le mythe solaire* (Neuchâtel: La Baconnière, 1964), 43–56 (Fr).

Giusto, *Rimbaud créateur,* 84–85, 347–68 (Fr).

Guerdon, *Rimbaud,* 161–217 (Fr).

André Guyaux, "Les Niveaux de langue dans la poésie de Rimbaud," *CAIEF* 41 (May 1989): 75–80 (Fr).

Hackett, *Rimbaud,* 85–119 (Eng).

C. A. Hackett, "Une Saison en enfer: Frénésie et structure," *RLM* 370–73 (1973): 7–15 (Fr).

Houston, *Patterns of Thought,* 46–49 (Eng).

Monique Jutrin, "Parole et silence dans 'Une Saison en enfer': L'Expérience du 'moi' divisé," *RLM* 445–49 (1976): 7–23 (Fr).

Poulet, *Exploding Poetry,* 82–88 (Eng).

Poulet, *La Poésie éclatée,* 96–103 (Fr).

Ross, *The Emergence of Social Space,* 47–71 (Eng).

Kristin Ross, "Rimbaud and the Transformation of Social Space," *YFS* no. 73 (1987): 113–20 (Eng).

Marcel A. Ruff, *Rimbaud* (Paris: Hatier, 1968), 165–89, 206–9 (Fr).

Nathaniel Wing, "The Autobiography of Rhetoric," *FrF* 9 (January 1984): 42–57 (Eng).

RIMBAUD, ARTHUR, "Scénes"

"Scénes"

Cohn, *The Poetry of Rimbaud,* 371–73 (Eng).

Giusto, *Rimbaud créateur,* 251–55 (Fr).

Renée R. Hubert, "The Use of Reversals in Rimbaud's 'Illuminations,' " *ECr* 9 (Spring 1969): 14–15 (Eng).

Kittang, *Discours et jeu,* 266–71 (Fr).

Nathaniel Wing, "Rimbaud's 'Les Ponts,' 'Parade,' 'Scènes': The Poem as Performance," *FR* 46 (February 1973): 518–21 (Eng).

"Sensation"

Brunel, *Arthur Rimbaud, ou L'Éclatant Désastre,* 10–11 (Fr).

Cohn, *The Poetry of Rimbaud,* 37–38 (Eng).

Kittang, *Discours et jeu,* 62–66 (Fr).

Noulet, *Le Premier Visage de Rimbaud,* 45–49 (Fr).

Poulet, *Exploding Poetry,* 88–90 (Eng).

Poulet, *La Poésie éclatée,* 104–6 (Fr).

"Les Sœurs de charité"

Ahearn, *Rimbaud,* 30–32 (Eng).

Cohn, *The Poetry of Rimbaud,* 119–25 (Eng).

Giusto, *Rimbaud créateur,* 23, 64 (Fr).

Enid Peschel Rhodes, "Ambiguities in Rimbaud's Search for 'Charity,' " *FR* 47 (May 1974): 1088, 1090 (Eng).

"Soir historique"

Ahearn, *Rimbaud,* 339–44 (Eng).

Edward J. Ahearn, "Explosions of the Real: Rimbaud's Ecstatic and Political Subversions," *SFR* 9 (Spring 1985): 77–81 (Fr).

Cohn, *The Poetry of Rimbaud,* 374–77 (Eng).

Giusto, *Rimbaud créateur,* 323–26 (Fr).

Houston, *Patterns of Thought,* 60–61 (Eng).

Kittang, *Discours et jeu,* 322–28 (Fr).

Ross, *The Emergence of Social Space,* 95–97 (Eng).

Verstraëte, *La Chasse spirituelle,* 161–66 (Fr).

"Solde"

Ahearn, *Rimbaud,* 122–27, 136–37 (Eng).

Brunel, *Rimbaud: Projets et réalisations,* 291–94 (Fr).

Cohn, *The Poetry of Rimbaud,* 354–57 (Eng).

Giusto, *Rimbaud créateur,* 316–19 (Fr).

Houston, *Patterns of Thought,* 78–79 (Eng).

Verstraëte, *La Chasse spirituelle,* 181–91 (Fr).

"Soleil et chair"

Ahearn, *Rimbaud,* 110–14 (Eng).

Joseph Bianco, "Rimbaud from Apprentice to Seer," *KRQ* 37, no. 1 (1990): 32–33 (Eng).

Cohn, *The Poetry of Rimbaud,* 38–44 (Eng).

Frédérick Eigeldinger, "Futur lyrique et futur épique dans les vers de Rimbaud," in Eigeldinger, ed., *Etudes sur les "Poésies" de Rimbaud,* 67–69 (Fr).

Marc Eigeldinger, *Rimbaud et le mythe solaire* (Neuchâtel: La Baconnière, 1964), 21–27 (Fr).

Giusto, *Rimbaud créateur,* 20–22, 32–33, 43, 55, 69–70, 77 (Fr).

Kittang, *Discours et jeu,* 61–62, 67–69, 73–74, 80–81, 86–87 (Fr).

Porter, *The Crisis of French Symbolism,* 205–8 (Eng).

Poulet, *Exploding Poetry,* 104–6 (Eng).

Poulet, *La Poésie éclatée,* 123–24 (Fr).

RIMBAUD, ARTHUR, "Sonnet"

"Sonnet"

Marcel Schaettel, "Analyse et (re)construction d'un 'Sonnet' de Rimbaud," *RLM* 445–49 (1976): 43–56 (Fr).

"Tête de faune"

Ahearn, *Rimbaud,* 116–19 (Eng).

Cohn, *The Poetry of Rimbaud,* 90–91 (Eng).

Kittang, *Discours et jeu,* 118–20 (Fr).

"Vagabonds"

Brunel, *Arthur Rimbaud, ou L'Éclatant Désastre,* 28–29 (Fr).

Brunel, *Rimbaud: Projets et réalisations,* 141–47 (Fr).

Chadwick, *Rimbaud,* 93–95, 108 (Eng).

Cohn, *The Poetry of Rimbaud,* 314–16 (Eng).

Antoine Fongaro, "Pour Rimbaud," *SFr* 44 (May–August 1971): 285–88 (Fr).

Giusto, *Rimbaud créateur,* 342–44 (Fr).

Guerdon, *Rimbaud,* 224–27 (Fr).

Houston, *Patterns of Thought,* 76–77 (Eng).

Whitaker, *La Structure du monde,* 131–32 (Fr).

"Veillées"

Brunel, *Arthur Rimbaud, ou L'Éclatant Désastre,* 29–33 (Fr).

Cohn, *The Poetry of Rimbaud,* 321–26 (Eng).

Verstraëte, *La Chasse spirituelle,* 72–79 (Fr).

Whitaker, *La Structure du monde,* 130–31 (Fr).

"Veillées 1"

Chadwick, *Rimbaud,* 76–77, 97 (Eng).

Giusto, *Rimbaud créateur,* 226–27 (Fr).

André Guyaux, "Les Trois 'Veillées' de Rimbaud," *SFr* 22 (May–December 1978): 311–16 (Fr).

"Veillées 2"

Giusto, *Rimbaud créateur,* 238–39 (Fr).

André Guyaux, "Les Trois 'Veillées' de Rimbaud," *SFr* 22 (May–December 1978): 311–15, 316–18 (Fr).

"Veillées 3"

Marc Ascione and Jean-Pierre Chambon, "Les 'Zolismes' de Rimbaud," *Europe* 51 (May–June 1973): 127–28 (Fr).

Antoine Fongaro, "La Dernière Phrase," in Cormier and Holmes, eds., *Essays in Honor of Louis Francis Solano,* 451–60 (Fr).

Giusto, *Rimbaud créateur,* 239–43 (Fr).

André Guyaux, "Les Trois 'Veillées' de Rimbaud," *SFr* 22 (May–December 1978): 312–15, 318–21 (Fr).

"Vénus Anadyomène"

Cohn, *The Poetry of Rimbaud,* 56–57 (Eng).

"Vies"

Ahearn, *Rimbaud,* 66–70, 100–102 (Eng).

Chadwick, *Rimbaud,* 95–96 (Eng).

Cohn, *The Poetry of Rimbaud,* 280–85 (Eng).

Giusto, *Rimbaud créateur,* 319–23 (Fr).

RIMBAUD, ARTHUR, "Vies 1"

"Vies 1"

Bays, *The Orphic Vision,* 218–19 (Eng).

"Vies 2"

Bays, *The Orphic Vision,* 219–20 (Eng).

"Vies 3"

Bays, *The Orphic Vision,* 220–21 (Eng).

"Ville"

Ahearn, *Rimbaud,* 311–12, 314–15 (Eng).

Marie-Claire Bancquart, "Une Lecture des 'Ville(s)' d'"Illuminations,'" *RLM* 594–99 (1980): 25–28 (Fr).

Pierre Brunel, "Mythocritique de 'Ville,'" *RLM* 594–99 (1980): 15–23 (Fr).

Cohn, *The Poetry of Rimbaud,* 304–5 (Eng).

Margaret Davies, "Ville," *RLM* 594–99 (1980): 7–14 (Fr).

Giusto, *Rimbaud créateur,* 298–99 (Fr).

C. A. Hackett, "Anglicismes dans les 'Illuminations,'" *RHL* 87 (March–April 1987): 196–97 (Fr).

Hackett, *Rimbaud,* 63–66 (Eng).

Elizabeth Roberts, "Artifice and Ironic Perspective in Rimbaud's 'Ville,'" *AJFS* 24 (January–April 1987): 41–56 (Eng).

Whitaker, *La Structure du monde,* 176–77 (Fr).

"Villes"

Brunel, *Arthur Rimbaud, ou L'Éclatant Désastre,* 158–59 (Fr).

Houston, *Patterns of Thought,* 65–67 (Eng).

RIMBAUD, ARTHUR, "Villes: L'Acropole officiel"

"Villes: Ce sont des villes!"

Ahearn, *Rimbaud,* 212–25, 293–94, 329–30 (Eng).

Marie-Claire Bancquart, 'Une Lecture des 'Ville(s)' d''Illuminations,' " *RLM* 594–99 (1980): 28–30 (Fr).

Chadwick, *Rimbaud,* 84–85, 103 (Eng).

Cohn, *The Poetry of Rimbaud,* 307–14 (Eng).

Giusto, *Rimbaud créateur,* 299–302 (Fr).

Hackctt, *Rimbaud,* 62–63 (Eng).

Kittang, *Discours et jeu,* 239–44 (Fr).

Jean Richer, "Gautier en filigrane dans quelques 'Illuminations,' " *Europe* 51 (May–June 1973): 72–73 (Fr).

Whitaker, *La Structure du monde,* 173–76 (Fr).

"Villes: L'Acropole officiel"

Ahearn, *Rimbaud,* 293–97, 331 (Eng).

Marie-Claire Bancquart, "Une lecture des 'Ville(s)' d''Illuminations,' " *RLM* 594–99 (1980): 31–33 (Fr).

Bays, *The Orphic Vision,* 236–37 (Eng).

Cohn, *The Poetry of Rimbaud,* 316–20 (Eng).

Giusto, *Rimbaud créateur,* 302–5 (Fr).

Hackett, *Rimbaud,* 62–63 (Eng).

Kitang, *Discours et jeu,* 130–31 (Fr).

Jean Richer, "Gautier en filigrane dans quelques 'Illuminations,' " *Europe* 51 (May–June 1973): 73–74 (Fr).

Elizabeth Roberts, "Artifice and Ironic Perspective in Rimbaud's 'Villes 2,' " *AJFS* 24 (May–August 1987): 175–92 (Eng).

L. J. Watson, "Rimbaud's 'Candélabres géants,' " *FSB* 4 (Fall 1982): 6–8 (Eng).

Whitaker, *La Structure du monde,* 170–73 (Fr).

"Voyelles"

Ahearn, *Rimbaud,* 119–22 (Eng).

Barrère, *Le Regard d'Orphée,* 101–27 (Fr).

Jean-Bertrand Barrère, "Les 'Voyelles,' telles quelles?" *RHL* 74 (March–April 1974): 214–22 (Fr).

Bays, *The Orphic Vision,* 231–35 (Eng).

Suzanne Bernard, "La Palette de Rimbaud," *CAIEF* 12 (May 1960): 111–14 (Fr).

C. H. L. Bodenham, "Rimbaud's 'Poetique sensationniste' and Some Nineteenth-Century Medical Writing," *FS* 38 (January 1984): 37–38 (Eng).

Alphonse Bouvet, "Rimbaud, Satan, et 'Voyelles,'" *SFr* 7 (September–December 1963): 499–504 (Fr).

Brunel, *Arthur Rimbaud, ou L'Éclatant Désastre,* 123–25 (Fr).

Chadwick, *Etudes sur Rimbaud,* 27–40 (Fr).

Chadwick, *Rimbaud,* 27, 29, 59 (Eng).

Cohn, *The Poetry of Rimbaud,* 126–33 (Eng).

René Etiemble, *Le Mythe de Rimbaud,* vol. 2 (Paris: Gallimard, 1961), 75–88 (Fr).

René Etiemble, *Le Sonnet des voyelles* (Paris: Gallimard, 1968) (Fr).

Anne-Marie Franc, "Voyelles, un adieu aux vers latins," *Poétique* 15 (1984): 411–22 (Fr).

Jacques Garelli, *La Gravitation poétique* (Paris: Mercure de France, 1966), 201–10 (Fr).

Giusto, *Rimbaud créateur,* 153–60 (Fr).

Victor Graham, "Rimbaud's 'Voyelles,'" *KRQ* 11, no. 4 (1964): 192–99 (Eng).

Guerdon, *Rimbaud,* 129–54 (Fr).

Hackett, *Rimbaud,* 23–27 (Eng).

Claudine Hunting, "La Voix de Rimbaud: Nouveau point de vue sur les 'naissances latentes' des 'Voyelles,'" *PMLA* 88 (May 1973): 472–83 (Fr).

Kittang, *Discours et jeu,* 279–86 (Fr).

RONSARD, PIERRE DE, "A Antoine de Chasteigner"

Knight, *Flower Poetics in Nineteenth-Century France,* 198–99 (Eng).

Lawler, *The Language of French Symbolism,* 105–10 (Eng).

Henry Lubienski-Bodenham, "Theology and Medicine in Rimbaud's Sonnet 'Voyelles,'" *CLS* 13 (December 1976): 359–71 (Eng).

Stamos Metzidakis, "Did Rimbaud Really Know His Alphabet?" *NCFS* 14 (Spring–Summer 1986): 278–83 (Eng).

Noulet, *Le Premier Visage de Rimbaud,* 119–97 (Fr).

Marcel A. Ruff, *Rimbaud* (Paris: Hatier, 1968), 91–94 (Fr).

ROCHE, DENIS

"Le Mécrit, texte 2"

Sarah Lawall, "Yves Bonnefoy and Denis Roche: Art and the Art of Poetry," in Caws, ed., *About French Poetry,* 87–90 (Eng).

"Le Mécrit, texte 3"

M. Bishop, *The Contemporary Poetry of France,* 74–77 (Eng).

RODENBACH, GEORGES

"Les Malades aux fenêtres"

Patrick Laude, "Le Poète à sa fenêtre . . . ," *NCFS* 19 (Spring 1991): 365 (Fr).

RONSARD, PIERRE DE

"A Antoine de Chasteigner, de la Roche de Posé"

Quainton, *Ronsard's Ordered Chaos,* 39–40 (Eng).

RONSARD, PIERRE DE, "L'Absence, ny l'oubly, ny la course du jour"

"L'Absence, ny l'oubly, ny la course du jour"

Desonay, *Ronsard, poète de l'amour,* vol. 1, 221–23 (Fr).

Stone, *Ronsard's Sonnet Cycles,* 135–39 (Eng).

"Adonis"

Lapp, *The Brazen Tower,* 58–65 (Eng).

John C. Lapp, "Ronsard and La Fontaine: Two Versions of 'Adonis,'" *ECr* 10 (Summer 1970): 126–32, 141–44 (Eng).

"A Joachim Du Bellay: Dedans ce grand monde"

Quainton, *Ronsard's Ordered Chaos,* 199–201 (Eng).

"A la Fontaine Bellerie"

Desonay, *Ronsard, poète de l'amour,* vol. 1, 183–84 (Fr).

"Amour, qui as ton regne en ce monde si ample"

H. Weber, *La Création poétique au XVIe siècle en France,* 279–81 (Fr).

"Les Amours d'Eurymedon et de Callirée"

Marcel Raymond, "Sur 'Les Amours d'Eurymedon et de Callirée,'" in *De Jean Lemaire de Belges à Jean Giraudoux: Mélanges . . . offerts à Pierre Jourda* (Paris: Nizet, 1970), 59–74 (Fr).

Amours de Cassandre (Preface)
"Voeu"

Terence Cave, "Ronsard as Apollo: Myth, Poetry and Experience in a Renaissance Sonnet Cycle," *YFS,* no. 47 (1972): 76–78 (Eng).

Amours de Cassandre 1
"Qui voudra voir comme Amour me surmonte"

Brian Mallett, "Some Uses of 'Sententiae' in Ronsard's Love Sonnets," *FS* 27 (April 1973): 135–37 (Eng).

Stone, *Ronsard's Sonnet Cycles,* 35–36 (Eng).

Amours de Cassandre 2
"Nature ornant Cassandre qui devoit"

John McClelland, "Setting the Sonnet to Music," *AJFS* 21 (September–December 1984): 230–38 (Eng).

Amours de Cassandre 3
"Entre les rais de sa jumelle flame"

Grahame Castor, "Petrarchism and the Quest for Beauty," in Cave, ed., *Ronsard the Poet,* 88–90 (Eng).

Dassonville, *Ronsard,* vol. 3, 63–64 (Fr).

Amours de Cassandre 4
"Je ne suis point, ma guerrière Cassandre"

Alphonse Bouvet, "Fantaisies humanistes: Ronsard, Amours de Cassandre I, 4," *AJFS* 2 (January–April 1965): 39–44 (Fr).

Amours de Cassandre 13
"Pour aller trop tes beaux soleils aimant"

Dassonville, *Ronsard,* vol. 3, 57–59 (Fr).

Amours de Cassandre 19
"Avant le temps tes temples fleuriront"

Jerome Schwartz, "The Ambitious Augury in Ronsard's Sonnet 'Avant le temps,'" *ECr* 10 (Summer 1970): 145–49 (Eng).

Stone, *Ronsard's Sonnet Cycles,* 47–48 (Eng).

Amours de Cassandre 20
"Je vouldroy bien richement jaunissant"

Baker, *Narcissus and the Lover,* 127–28 (Eng).

Calin, *In Defense of French Poetry,* 37–39 (Eng).

Grahame Castor, "Petrarchism and the Quest for Beauty," in Cave, ed., *Ronsard the Poet,* 90–91 (Eng).

Mary Cisar, "From Reality to Dream: Ronsard's 'Je voudroy bien richement jaunissant' and the Tradition of the Medieval 'Alba,' " *FR* 55 (December 1981): 181–87 (Eng).

Gendre, *Ronsard, poète de la conquête amoureuse,* 470–72 (Fr).

Lapp, *The Brazen Tower,* 43–55 (Eng).

John McClelland, "Lieu commun et poésie de la Renaissance," *EF* 16 (1980): 66–69 (Fr).

Stone, *Ronsard's Sonnet Cycles,* 36–38 (Eng).

Sara Sturm-Maddox, "Ronsard's Metamorphoses: Petrarchan Play in the Amours of 1552," *CLS* 23 (Summer 1986): 110–15 (Eng).

Amours de Cassandre 23
"Ce beau coral, ce marbre qui souspire"

Desonay, *Ronsard, poète de l'amour,* vol. 1, 82–85 (Fr).

Amours de Cassandre 29
"Si mille oeilletz, si mille liz j'embrasse"

H. Weber, *La Création poétique au XVIe siècle en France,* 361–62 (Fr).

Amours de Cassandre 32
"Quand en naissant la Dame que j'adore"

Stone, *Ronsard's Sonnet Cycles,* 27–32 (Eng).

Amours de Cassandre 36
"Pour la douleur, qu'amour veult que je sente"

H. Weber, *La Création poétique au XVIe siècle en France,* 316–17 (Fr).

Amours de Cassandre 38
"Doulx fut le traict, qu'Amour hors de sa trousse"

Gendre, *Ronsard, poète de la conquête amoureuse,* 331–32 (Fr).

Amours de Cassandre 40
"Que de Beautez, que de Graces écloses"

Stone, *Ronsard's Sonnet Cycles,* 39–40 (Eng).

Amours de Cassandre 41
"Quand au matin ma Deesse s'habille"

Gendre, *Ronsard, poète de la conquête amoureuse,* 324–26 (Fr).

Amours de Cassandre 42
"Avant qu'Amour du Chaos ocieux"

Isidore Silver, "Ronsard's Reflections on Cosmogony and Nature," *PMLA* 79 (June 1964): 223 (Eng).

Amours de Cassandre 46
"Je veus mourir pour tes beautés, Maistresse"

Gendre, *Ronsard, poète de la conquête amoureuse,* 462–63 (Fr).

Brian Mallett, "Some Notes on the 'Sensuality' of Ronsard's 'Amours de Cassandre,' " *KRQ* 19, no. 4 (1972): 437–38 (Eng).

Amours de Cassandre 59
"Comme un chevreuil quand le printemps destruit"

Dassonville, *Ronsard,* vol. 3, 35–37 (Fr).

H. Weber, *La Création poétique au XVIe siècle en France,* 239–41 (Fr).

François Rigolot, "Rhétorique de la métamorphose chez Ronsard," in Floyd Gray and Marcel Tetel, eds., *Textes et intertextes: Etudes sur le XVIe siècle pour Alfred Glauser* (Paris: Nizet, 1979), 148–52 (Fr).

RONSARD, PIERRE DE, *Amours de Cassandre 64*

Amours de Cassandre 64
"Tant de couleurs le grand arc ne varie"

André Gendre, "Fixité et mobilité du sonnet: L'Expérience de Ronsard," *CAIEF* 32 (May 1980): 111–21 (Fr).

Amours de Cassandre 66
"Ciel, air, et vents, plains et montz descouvers"

H. Weber, *La Création poétique au XVIe siècle en France,* 320–21 (Fr).

Stone, *Ronsard's Sonnet Cycles,* 32–34 (Eng).

Winter, *Visual Variety and Spatial Grandeur,* 108–9 (Eng).

Amours de Cassandre 79
"Si je trépasse entre tes bras, Madame"

Brian Mallett, "Some Notes on the 'Sensuality' of Ronsard's 'Amours de Cassandre,' " *KRQ* 19, no. 4 (1972): 438–39 (Eng).

Amours de Cassandre 82
"Je meurs, Paschal, quand je la voy si belle"

Desonay, *Ronsard, poète de l'amour,* vol. 2, 223–24 (Fr).

Amours de Cassandre 92
"Soubz le cristal d'une argenteuse rive"

H. Weber, *La Création poétique au XVIe siècle en France,* 245–46 (Fr).

Amours de Cassandre 94
"Soit que son or se crespe lentement"

Tom Conley, "Ronsard, le sonnet et la lettre: Amorces de 'Soit que son or se crespe lentement,' " in Kritzman, ed., *Le Signe et le texte,* 117–26 (Fr).

I. D. McFarlane, "Aspects of Ronsard's Poetic Vision," in Cave, ed., *Ronsard the Poet,* 31–32 (Eng).

Amours de Cassandre 106
"Je suis larron pour vous aymer Madame"

Stone, *Ronsard's Sonnet Cycles,* 150–53 (Eng).

Amours de Cassandre 120
"Franc de raison, esclave de fureur"

Grahame Castor, "Petrarchism and the Quest for Beauty in the 'Amours' of Cassandre and the 'Sonets pour Hélène,'" in Cave, ed., *Ronsard the Poet,* 82–84 (Eng).

Amours de Cassandre 127
"Non la chaleur de la terre, qui fume"

Gendre, *Ronsard, poète de la conquête amoureuse,* 204–5 (Fr).

Amours de Cassandre 143
"Ce ris plus doulx que l'oeuvre d'une abeille"

H. Weber, *La Création poétique au XVIe siècle en France,* 269–70 (Fr).

Amours de Cassandre 144
"J'iray tousjours et resoant et songeant"

H. Weber, *La Création poétique au XVIe siècle en France,* 277–78 (Fr).

Amours de Cassandre 160
"Or que Jupin espoint de sa semence"

Desonay, *Ronsard,* poète de l'amour, vol. 1, 85–87 (Fr).

RONSARD, PIERRE DE, *Amours de Cassandre 163*

Amours de Cassandre 163
"Voicy le bois que ma sainte Angelette"

Desonay, *Ronsard, poète de l'amour,* vol. 1, 101–2 (Fr).

Amours de Cassandre 175
"Je ne suis point, Muses, accoustumé"

William Kennedy, "Ronsard's Petrarchan Textuality," *RR* 77 (March 1986): 88–91 (Eng).

Lapp, *The Brazen Tower,* 42–43 (Eng).

Amours de Cassandre 181
"Jamais au cuoeur ne sera que je n'aye"

Brian Mallett, "Some Notes on the 'Sensuality' of Ronsard's 'Amours de Cassandre,'" *KRQ* 19, no. 4 (1972): 441–42 (Eng).

Amours de Cassandre 193
"Ces flotz jumeaulx de laict bien espoissi"

H. Weber, *La Création poétique au XVIe siècle en France,* 286–87 (Fr).

Amours de Cassandre 213
"Je suis, je suis plus aise que les Dieus"
Variant: "Je suis aise en mon coeur que les Dieux"

Brian Mallett, "Some Notes on the 'Sensuality' of Ronsard's 'Amours de Cassandre,'" *KRQ* 19, no. 4 (1972): 439–40 (Eng).

Amours de Cassandre
"Elégie à Janet peintre du Roi"

Desonay, *Ronsard,* poète de l'amour, vol. 1, 191–92 (Fr).

RONSARD, PIERRE DE, *Amours de Marie, Chanson*

Amours de Marie 1
"Tyard, chacun disoit à mon commencement"
Variant: "Tyard, on me blasmoit, à mon commencement"

Richard Griffiths, "Humor and Complicity in Ronsard's 'Continuation des Amours,'" in Bayley and Coleman, eds., *The Equilibrium of Wit,* 47–49 (Eng).

Amours de Marie 19
"Marie, levez-vous, ma jeune paresseuse"

Stone, *Ronsard's Sonnet Cycles,* 64–67 (Eng).

Amours de Marie 42
"Si j'estois Jupiter, Marie, vous seriez"

Desonay, *Ronsard,* poète de l'amour, vol. 2, 151–52, 156–57 (Fr).

R. A. Sayce, "Epilogue: A Sonnet by Ronsard," in Cave, eds., *Ronsard the Poet,* 319–31 (Eng).

Amours de Marie 44
"Marie, baisez-moy; non, ne me baisez pas"

Desonay, *Ronsard, poète de l'amour,* vol. 2, 153–54 (Fr).

Amours de Marie 61
"J'ay l'ame pour un lict de regrets si touchée"

Stone, *Ronsard's Sonnet Cycles,* 55–56 (Eng).

Amours de Marie, Chanson
"Douce Maistresse, touche"

Desonay, *Ronsard, poète de l'amour,* vol. 2, 203–4 (Fr).

411

RONSARD, PIERRE DE, *Amours de Marie, Chanson*

Amours de Marie, Chanson
"Je suis un demidieu quand assis vis à vis"

H. Weber, *La Création poétique au XVIe siècle en France*, 256–58 (Fr).

Amours de Marie, Chanson
"Quand ce beau Printemps je vay"

Desonay, *Ronsard, poète de l'amour*, vol. 2, 204–5 (Fr).

Amours de Marie, Chanson
"Quand je te veux raconter mes douleurs"

H. Weber, *La Création poétique au XVIe siècle en France*, 255–56 (Fr).

Amours de Marie
"Elégie à Marie"

Desonay, *Ronsard, poète de l'amour*, vol. 2, 171–75 (Fr).

Amours de Marie
"Elégie à son lìvre"

Desonay, *Ronsard, poète de l'amour*, vol. 2, 24–26, 103 (Fr).
Stone, *Ronsard's Sonnet Cycles*, 67–74 (Eng).

Amours de Marie
"Quenoille"

Desonay, *Ronsard, poète de l'amour*, vol. 2, 163–64 (Fr).

Amours diverses 12
"Petit nombril, que mon penser adore"

Brian Mallett, "Some Notes on the 'Sensuality' of Ronsard's 'Amours de Cassandre,'" *KRQ* 19, no. 4 (1972): 434–36 (Eng).

RONSARD, PIERRE DE, "Au Seigneur de Carnavalet"

Amours diverses, Elégie 2
"Cherche, Maistresse, un poète nouveau"

Desonay, *Ronsard, poète de l'amour,* vol. 1, 219–21 (Fr).

"Ange divin, qui mes playes embasme"

H. Weber, *La Création poétique au XVIe siècle en France,* 360–61 (Fr).

"L'An se rajeunissoit en sa verde jouvence"

Stone, *Ronsard's Sonnet Cycles,* 80–81 (Eng).

"A Pierre de Paschal"

Yvonne Bellenger, "Quelques poèmes autobiographiques au XVIe siècle: Fiction et vérité," *SFr* 22 (May–December 1978): 225–29 (Fr).

Les Armes
"À Jean Brinon"

Elizabeth Armstrong, *Ronsard and the Age of Gold* (Cambridge: Cambridge University Press, 1968), 19–21 (Eng).

"A son âme"

Silver, *Ronsard and the Hellenic Renaissance in France,* vol. 2, *Ronsard and the Grecian Lyre,* pt. 1, 418–20 (Eng).

"A son retour de Gascongne voiant de loin Paris"

Py, *Imitation et Renaissance dans la poésie de Ronsard,* 47–48 (Fr).

"Au Seigneur de Carnavalet"

Jones, *Pierre de Ronsard,* 29–31 (Eng).

RONSARD, PIERRE DE, "Au Tresorier de l'Espargne"

"Au Tresorier de l'Espargne"

Ménager, *Ronsard,* 102–4 (Fr).

Silver, *The Intellectual Evolution of Ronsard,* vol. 1, 280–81 (Eng).

Silver, *Ronsard and the Hellenic Renaissance in France,* vol. 2, pt. 1, 380–82 (Eng).

"Avantentrée du Rois treschrestien à Paris"

H. Weber, *La Création poétique au XVIe siècle en France,* 478–81 (Fr).

"L'Avant-Venu du Printemps"

Jones, *Pierre de Ronsard,* 33–36 (Eng).

"Bacchanales"

Terence, Cave, "Ronsard's Bacchic Poetry from the Bacchanales to the 'Hymme de l'autonne,'" *ECr* 10 (Summer 1970): 104–6 (Eng).

"Les Bacchanales ou le folastrissime voyage d'Hercueil près Paris"

Isidore Silver, "Ronsard's Ethical Thought," *BHR* 24 (January 1962): 108–9 (Fr).

"Baïf, il semble à voir tes rimes langoureuses"

Richard Griffiths, "Humor and Complicity in Ronsard's 'Continuation des Amours,'" in Bayley and Coleman, eds., *The Equilibrium of Wit,* 49–51 (Eng).

"Bel aubepin verdissant"

Stone, *Ronsard's Sonnet Cycles,* 86–90 (Eng).

RONSARD, PIERRE DE, "Complainte contre Fortune"

"Chant pastoral sur les nopces de Monseigneur Charles,
Duc de Lorraine"

Terence Cave, "Ronsard's Mythological Universe," in Cave, ed., *Ronsard the Poet,* 176–77 (Eng).

Dassonville, *Ronsard,* vol. 4, 48–49 (Fr).

Moss, *Poetry and Fable,* 122–24 (Eng).

"Un Chaste feu qui les cuoeurs illumine"

H. Weber, *La Création poétique au XVIe siècle en France,* 270–72 (Fr).

"Le Chat"

Silver, *Three Ronsard Studies,* 65–67 (Eng).

H. Weber, *A travers le seizième siècle,* 131–32 (Fr).

"Chef, escole des arts, le sejour de science"

Isidore Silver, "Ronsard's Reflections on the Heavens and Time," *PMLA* 80 (September 1965): 357–58 (Eng).

"Complainte à la Royne mere du Roy"

Silver, *The Intellectual Evolution of Ronsard,* vol. 1, 290–92 (Eng).

Silver, *Ronsard and the Hellenic Renaissance in France,* vol. 2, pt. 1, 376–78 (Eng).

"Complainte contre Fortune"

Philip Ford, "Ronsard and the Theme of Inspiration," in Bayley and Coleman, eds., *The Equilibrium of Wit,* 67–68 (Eng).

Py, *Imitation et Renaissance dans la poésie de Ronsard,* 57–60 (Fr).

RONSARD, PIERRE DE, "Continuation du Discours des Misères"

Silver, *The Intellectual Evolution of Ronsard,* vol. 1, 284–86 (Eng).

Silver, *Ronsard and the Hellenic Renaissance in France,* vol. 2, pt. 1, 372–74; vol. 2, pt. 2, 368–69 (Eng).

"Continuation du Discours des Misères de ce temps"

Jones, *Pierre de Ronsard,* 105–8 (Eng).

Ménager, *Ronsard,* 202–15, 231–34 (Fr).

John Nothnagle, "The Drama of 'Les Discours' of Ronsard," *ECr* 10 (Summer 1970): 120–21 (Eng).

Marguerite Soulié, "Ronsard et la Bible," *Europe* 691–92 (November–December 1986): 75–78 (Fr).

H. Weber, *La Création poétique au XVIe siècle en France,* 569–70, 575–78 (Fr).

"Contre les bucherons de la forêt de Gastins"

Henri Chamard, *Histoire de la Pléiade,* vol. 3, 393–96 (Fr).

Wilson, *Ronsard, Poet of Nature,* 56–58 (Eng).

"Le Cyclope amoureux"

Dassonville, *Ronsard,* vol. 4, 100–102, 107–8 (Fr).

H. Weber, *La Création poétique au XVIe siècle en France,* 282–83 (Fr).

"Dans le serain de sa jumelle flamme"

Michel Dassonville, "Réflexions sur le pétrarquisme," in *Missions et démarches de la critique: Mélanges offerts au Prof. J. A. Vier* (Paris: Klincksieck, 1973), 590 (Fr).

"Dedans des Prez je vis une Dryade"

H. Weber, *La Création poétique au XVIe siècle en France,* 247–49 (Fr).

RONSARD, PIERRE DE, "Discours à la Reine"

"De l'election de son sepulchre"

H. Weber, *A travers le seizième siècle,* 98–103 (Fr).

Henri Weber, "Structure des odes chez Ronsard," *CAIEF* 22 (May 1970): 112–17 (Fr).

"De moy seul ennemy, voire traistre je suis"

Desonay, *Ronsard, poète de l'amour,* vol. 2, 210–12 (Fr).

"De Posidippe sur l'image du tems"

Malcolm Quainton, "Ronsard's Philosophical and Cosmological Conceptions of Time," *FS* 23 (January 1969): 14–16 (Eng).

"Des Peintures contenues dedans un tableau"

Philip Ford, "Ronsard the Painter: A Reading of 'Des Peintures contenues dedans un tableau,' " *FS* 40 (January 1986): 32–44 (Eng).

"Discours 1 en forme d'élégie"

Desonay, *Ronsard, poète de l'amour,* vol. 2, 216–19 (Fr).

"Discours à Guillaume des Autels"

John Nothnagle, "The Drama of 'Les Discours' of Ronsard," *ECr* 10 (Summer 1970): 117–18 (Eng).

"Discours à Jean Morel, Ambrunois"

Desonay, *Ronsard, poète de l'amour,* vol. 2, 101–2 (Fr).

"Discours à la Reine"

Yvonne Bellenger, "L'Allégorie dans les poèmes de style élevé de Ronsard," *CAIEF* 28 (May 1976): 73–76 (Fr).

H. Weber, *La Création poétique au XVIe siècle en France,* 567–69 (Fr).

RONSARD, PIERRE DE, "Discours à Louis des Masures"

"Discours à Louis des Masures"

John Nothnagle, "The Drama of 'Les Discours' of Ronsard," *ECr* 10 (Summer 1970): 117–18 (Eng).

"Discours à Odet de Colligny, Cardinal de Chastillon"

Dassonville, *Ronsard,* vol. 4, 36–37 (Fr).

"Discours à très illustre et vertueux Prince, Philibert, Duc de Savoye et de Piedmont"

Quainton, *Ronsard's Ordered Chaos,* 65–67 (Eng).

"Discours au duc de Savoie"

Francis Higman, "Ronsard's Political and Polemical Poetry," in Cave, ed., *Ronsard the Poet,* 253–54 (Eng).

Quainton, *Ronsard's Ordered Chaos,* 65–67 (Eng).

"Discours au Roy, après son retour de Pologne"

Chamard, *Histoire de la Pléiade,* vol. 3, 373–75 (Fr).

Silver, *Ronsard and the Hellenic Renaissance in France,* vol. 2, pt. 1, 397–402 (Eng).

"Discours contre Fortune"

Quainton, *Ronsard's Ordered Chaos,* 78–82 (Eng).

"Discours de l'alteration et change des choses humaines"

Quainton, *Ronsard's Ordered Chaos,* 31–37 (Eng).

"Discours de l'équité des vieux Gaulois"

Chamard, *Histoire de la Pléiade,* vol. 3, 389–92 (Fr).

RONSARD, PIERRE DE, "Douce, belle, amoureuse"

"Discours des Misères de ce Temps"

Edwin Duval, "The Place of the Present: Ronsard, Aubigné, and the 'Misères de ce temps,' " *YFS,* no. 80 (1991): 14–18, 29 (Eng).

Jones, *Pierre de Ronsard,* 105 (Eng).

Ménager, *Ronsard,* 197–202, 226–31 (Fr).

John Nothnagle, "The Drama of 'Les Discours' of Ronsard," *ECr* 10 (Summer 1970): 119–20 (Eng).

"Discours d'un amoureux desesperé"

Silver, *The Intellectual Evolution of Ronsard,* vol. 1, 192–94 (Eng).

"Discours ou Dialogue entre les Muses deslogées et Ronsard"

Silver, *The Intellectual Evolution of Ronsard,* vol. 1, 320–23 (Eng).

Silver, *Ronsard and the Hellenic Renaissance in France,* vol. 2, pt. 1, 416–17; vol. 2, pt. 2, 397–98 (Eng).

"Dithyrambes"

Terence Cave, "Ronsard's Bacchic Poetry . . .," *ECr* 10 (Summer 1970): 106–10 (Eng).

"Dois-je voler emplumé d'esperance"

Marc Eigeldinger, "Le Mythe d'Icare dans la poésie française du XVIe siècle," *CAIEF* 25 (May 1973): 271–73 (Fr).

"Douce, belle, amoureuse et bien-fleurante Rose"

Jones, *Pierre de Ronsard,* 59–61 (Eng).

H. Weber, *La Création poétique au XVIe siècle en France,* 334–36 (Fr).

RONSARD, PIERRE DE, "Du malheur de recevoir"

"Du malheur de recevoir"

Chamard, *Histoire de la Pléiade,* vol. 2, 59–62 (Fr).

"D'un foyble vol, je vole après l'espoyr"

Desonay, *Ronsard, poéte de l'amour,* vol. 1, 87–88 (Fr).

Elégie 5
"Madame, oyez le mal que je reçoy"

Desonay, *Ronsard, poète de l'amour,* vol. 2, 208–10 (Fr).

"Elegie à Chretophle de Choiseul, abbé de Mureaux"

Desonay, *Ronsard, poète de l'amour,* vol. 2, 103–4 (Fr).

"Elégie à Des Autels"

Ménager, *Ronsard,* 187–93 (Fr).

"Elégie à Janet, peintre du Roi"

Roberto Campo, "A Poem to a Painter: The 'Elegie à Janet' and Ronsard's Dilemma of Ambivalence," *FrF* 12 (September 1987): 273–87 (Eng).

R. A. Sayce, "Ronsard and Mannerism: The 'Elégie à Janet,'" *ECr* 6 (Winter 1966): 234–47 (Eng).

"Elégie à Lois des Masures"

Jones, *Pierre de Ronsard,* 102–4 (Eng).

"Elégie à Marie"

Stone, *Ronsard's Sonnet Cycles,* 99–101 (Eng).

RONSARD, PIERRE DE, "Elégie pour Genèvre 1"

"Elégie à Nicolas de Nicolay"

Ménager, *Ronsard,* 93–95 (Fr).

"Elégie à Philippes des Portes, Chartrain"

Quainton, *Ronsard's Ordered Chaos,* 141–43 (Eng).

"Elégie à Pierre L'Escot"

Philip Ford, "Ronsard and the Theme of Inspiration," in Bayley and Coleman, ed., *The Equilibrium of Wit,* 65–67 (Eng).

Danielle Trudeau, "Ronsard côté cour et côté jardin," *Poétique* 20 (November 1989): 446–48 (Fr).

"Elégie à Robert de la Haye"

Elizabeth Armstrong, *Ronsard and the Age of Gold* (Cambridge: Cambridge University Press, 1968), 28–31 (Eng).

Dassonville, *Ronsard,* vol. 4, 63–66 (Fr).

"Elégie au Roy"

Silver, *Ronsard and the Hellenic Renaissance in France,* vol. 2, pt. 1, 386–87, 410–11 (Eng).

"Elégie du Verre"

Ullrich Langer, "La Poudre à canon et la transgression poétique: 'L'Elégie du verre' de Ronsard," *RR* 73 (March 1982): 190–94 (Fr).

"Elégie pour Genèvre 1"

Berry, *Ronsard,* 175–77 (Fr).

RONSARD, PIERRE DE, "Elégie pour Genèvre 3"

"Elégie pour Genèvre 3"

Desonay, *Ronsard, poète de l'amour,* vol. 2, 220–22 (Fr).

Stone, *Ronsard's Sonnet Cycles,* 128–32 (Eng).

Elégie
"Pour vous monstrer que j'ay parfaité envie"

Desonay, *Ronsard, poète de l'amour,* vol. 3, 50–52 (Fr).

"Elégies, mascarades et bergeries"

M. C. Smith, "Ronsard and Queen Elizabeth I," *BHR* 29 (May 1967): 93–100 (Fr).

"En choisissant l'esprit vous estes mal-apprise"

Desonay, *Ronsard, poète de l'amour,* vol. 3, 301–2 (Fr).

"Epistre au Cardinal de Lorraine"

Silver, *Ronsard and the Hellenic Renaissance in France,* vol. 2, pt. 1, 357–60 (Eng).

"Epitaphe d'André Blondet"

Silver, *Ronsard and the Hellenic Renaissance in France,* vol. 2, pt. 2, 377–88 (Eng).

"Epitaphe de feu Monseigneur D'Annebault"

Quainton, *Ronsard's Ordered Chaos,* 167–68 (Eng).

"Epitaphe de François Rabelais"

Chamard, *Histoire de la Pléiade,* vol. 2, 78–80 (Fr).

RONSARD, PIERRE DE, "Le Folastrissime voyage d'Hercueil"

"Epître à Charles de Lorraine"

Py, *Imitation et Renaissance dans la poésie de Ronsard,* 52–54 (Fr).

Quainton, *Ronsard's Ordered Chaos,* 103–4 (Eng).

Malcolm Quainton, "Ronsard's Philosophical and Cosmological Conceptions of Time," *FS* 23 (January 1969): 6–7 (Eng).

"Epître à Charles de Pisseleu"

Malcolm Quainton, "Ronsard's Philosophical and Cosmological Conceptions of Time," *FS* 23 (January 1969): 7–9 (Eng).

"Estreines au Roy Henry III, Envoyées à Sa Majesté
au mois de decembre"

Silver, *The Intellectual Evolution of Ronsard,* vol. 1, 317–19 (Eng).

Silver, *Ronsard and the Hellenic Renaissance in France,* vol. 2, pt. 1, 403–6 (Eng).

"Exhortation au camp du roy pour bien combattre le jour de la bataille"

Dassonville, *Ronsard,* vol. 4, 30–32 (Fr).

"Exhortation pour la paix"

Dassonville, *Ronsard,* vol. 4, 32–35 (Fr).

"Fantaisie à sa dame"

Sara Sturm-Maddox, "Ronsard's Metamorphoses: Petrarchan Play in the Amours of 1552," *CLS* 23 (Summer 1986): 104–5, 115 (Eng).

"Le Folastrissime voyage d'Hercueil"

Dassonville, *Ronsard,* vol. 2, 133–37 (Fr).

RONSARD, PIERRE DE, "Le Fourmy, à Remy Belleau"

"Le Fourmy, à Remy Belleau"

Chamard, *Histoire de la Pléiade,* vol. 2, 82–87 (Fr).

"Franc de raison, esclave de fureur"

Sara Sturm-Maddox, "Ronsard's Metamorphoses: Petrarchan Play in the Amours of 1552," *CLS* 23 (Summer 1986): 105–6 (Eng).

"Hé! que me sert, Pasquier, ceste belle verdure"

Stone, *Ronsard's Sonnet Cycles,* 48–49, 53–55 (Eng).

"Hercule chrestien"

Jean Céard, "Dieu, les hommes, et le poète; Structure, sens et fonction des mythes dans les 'Hymnes' de Ronsard," in Lazard, ed., *Autour des "Hymnes" de Ronsard,* 100 (Fr).

Claude Faisant, "Le Sens religieux de 'L'Hercule chrestien,'" in Lazard, ed., *Autour des "Hymnes" de Ronsard,* 243–57 (Fr).

Silver, *The Intellectual Evolution of Ronsard,* vol. 2, 398–401 (Eng).

Isidore Silver, "Ronsard's Ethical Thought," *BHR* 24 (May 1962): 346–48 (Eng).

R. Trousson, "Ronsard et la légende d'Hercule." *BHR* 24 (January 1962): 86–87 (Fr).

"Le Houx"

Quainton, *Ronsard's Ordered Chaos,* 46–47 (Eng).

"L'Huillier, si nous perdons ceste belle princesse"

Desonay, *Ronsard, poète de l'amour,* vol. 2, 206–8 (Fr).

RONSARD, PIERRE DE, "Hymne de la Mort"

"Hymne de Bacchus"

Terence Cave, "Ronsard's Bacchic Poetry . . .," *ECr* 10 (Summer 1970): 110–11 (Eng).

"Hymne de Bacus"

Dassonville, *Ronsard,* vol. 3, 128–29 (Fr).

"Hymne de Charles, Cardinal de Lorraine"

Dassonville, *Ronsard,* vol. 4, 42–47 (Fr).

"Hymne de France"

Silver, *The Intellectual Evolution of Ronsard,* vol. 2, 19–23 (Eng).

"Hymne de la Justice"

Calin, *In Defense of French Poetry,* 78–80 (Eng).

Jean Céard, "Dieu, les hommes, et le poète: Structure, sens et fonction des mythes dans les 'Hymnes' de Ronsard," in Lazard, ed., *Autour des "Hymnes" de Ronsard,* 90–91, 96–100 (Fr).

Chamard, *Histoire de la Pléiade,* vol. 2, 194–97 (Fr).

Françoise Joukovsky, "Temps et éternité dans les 'Hymnes,' " in Lazard, ed., *Autour des "Hymnes" de Ronsard,* 63–65, 68, 78–80 (Fr).

Lafeuille, *Cinq hymnes de Ronsard,* 83–126 (Fr).

Ménager, *Ronsard,* 72–81, 139–42 (Fr).

Marguerite Soulié, "Ronsard et la Bible," *Europe* 64 (November–December 1986): 70–75 (Fr).

"Hymne de la Mort"

Jean Céard, "Dieu, les hommes, et le poète; Structure, sens et fonction des mythes dans les 'Hymnes' de Ronsard," in Lazard, ed., *Autour des "Hymnes" de Ronsard,* 88–89, 92–94, 97–98 (Fr).

RONSARD, PIERRE DE, "Hymne de la Philosophie"

Chamard, *Histoire de la Pléiade,* vol. 2, 201–5 (Fr).

Joyce Hanks, "Ronsard's Debt to Marot in 'L'Hymne de la mort,' " *ECr* 12 (Fall 1972): 189–92 (Eng).

Françoise Joukovsky, "Temps et éternité dans les 'Hymnes,' " in Lazard, ed., *Autour des "Hymnes" de Ronsard,* 55, 71–72, 81–82 (Fr).

Lapp, *The Brazen Tower,* 51–53 (Eng).

Ménager, *Ronsard,* 85–91, (Fr).

Quainton, *Ronsard's Ordered Chaos,* 132–33, 135–36, 144–46 (Eng).

H. Weber, *La Création poétique au XVIe siècle en France,* 508–14 (Fr).

Wilson, *Ronsard, Poet of Nature,* 64–68 (Eng).

"Hymne de la Philosophie"

Jean Céard, "Dieu, les hommes, et le poète; Structure, sens et fonction des mythes dans les 'Hymnes' de Ronsard," in Lazard, ed., *Autour des "Hymnes" de Ronsard,* 86–87 (Fr).

Chamard, *Histoire de la Pléiade,* vol. 2, 186–87 (Fr).

Dassonville, *Ronsard,* vol. 3, 133–38 (Fr).

Lafeuille, *Cinq hymnes de Ronsard,* 61–82 (Fr).

Silver, *Ronsard and the Hellenic Renaissance in France,* vol. 2, pt. 2, 382–85 (Eng).

Isidore Silver, "Ronsard's Reflections on Cosmogony and Nature," *PMLA* 79 (June 1964): 219–21 (Eng).

Silver, *Three Ronsard Studies,* 13–15, 84, 92–93 (Eng).

Mark Whitney, *Critical Reactions and the Christian Element in the Poetry of Pierre de Ronsard* (Chapel Hill: University of North Carolina Press, 1971), 36–42 (Eng).

"Hymne de l'Automne"

Terence Cave, "Ronsard's Bacchic Poetry . . .," *ECr* 10 (Summer 1970): 111–16 (Eng).

Chamard, *Histoire de la Pléiade,* vol. 3, 22–23 (Fr).

RONSARD, PIERRE DE, "Hymne de L'Eternité"

Philip Ford, "Ronsard and the Theme of Inspiration," in Bayley and Coleman, eds., *The Equilibrium of Wit,* 57–58, 62–65 (Eng).

Elliott Forsyth, "Le Concept de l'inspiration poétique chez Ronsard," *RHL* 75 (July–August 1975): 525, 528–29 (Fr).

Moss, *Poetry and Fable,* 137–39 (Eng).

Py, *Imitation et Renaissance dans la poésie de Ronsard,* 43–45, 49–51 (Fr).

Quainton, *Ronsard's Ordered Chaos,* 96–99 (Eng).

Stone, *Ronsard's Sonnet Cycles,* 109–13 (Eng).

Danielle Trudeau, "Ronsard côté cour et côté jardin," *Poétique* 20 (November 1989): 445–51, 453–85 (Fr).

Wilson, *Ronsard, Poet of Nature,* 102–5 (Eng).

"Hymne de l'Eté"

Quainton, *Ronsard's Ordered Chaos,* 96–99 (Eng).

Stone, *Ronsard's Sonnet Cycles,* 113–15 (Eng).

H. Weber, *La Création poétique au XVIe siècle en France,* 500–503 (Fr).

"Hymne de L'Eternité"

Chamard, *Histoire de la Pléiade,* vol. 2, 199–201 (Eng).

Françoise Joukovsky, "Temps et éternité dans les 'Hymnes,'" in Lazard, ed., *Autour des "Hymnes" de Ronsard,* 53–55, 57–59, 66, 74, 79 (Fr).

Lafeuille, *Cinq hymnes de Ronsard,* 41–60 (Fr).

Quainton, *Ronsard's Ordered Chaos,* 101–3, 169–71 (Eng).

Silver, *Three Ronsard Studies,* 103–7 (Eng).

Isidore Silver, "Ronsard's Reflections on the Heavens and Time," *PMLA* 80 (September 1965): 346, 354, 363–64 (Eng).

Wilson, *Ronsard, Poet of Nature,* 71–73 (Eng).

RONSARD, PIERRE DE, "Hymne de l'Hyver"

"Hymne de l'Hyver"

Moss, *Poetry and Fable,* 140 (Eng).

Quainton, *Ronsard's Ordered Chaos,* 96–99 (Eng).

H. Weber, *La Création poétique au XVIe siècle en France,* 503–7 (Fr).

"Hymne de l'or"

Chamard, *Histoire de la Pléiade,* vol. 2, 191–94 (Fr).

Jean-Claude Margolin, " 'L'Hymne de l'Or' et son ambiguité," *BHR* 28 (May 1966): 271–93 (Fr).

Ménager, *Ronsard,* 97–103, 106–15 (Fr).

Silver, *Ronsard and the Hellenic Renaissance in France,* vol. 2, pt. 1, 340–43 (Eng).

Maurice Verdier, "A propos d'une controverse sur 'L'Hymne de l'Or' de Pierre de Ronsard," *BHR* 35 (January 1973): 7–18 (Fr).

H. Weber, *A travers le seizième siècle,* 145–47 (Fr).

Henri Weber, "La Philosophie de Ronsard dans 'Les Hymnes,' " in Lazard, ed., *Autour des "Hymnes" de Ronsard,* 47–51 (Fr).

"Hymne de Mercure"

Ménager, *Ronsard,* 116–28 (Fr).

"Hymne des Astres"

Jean Céard, "Dieu, les hommes, et le poète; Structure, sens et fonction des mythes dans les 'Hymnes' de Ronsard," in Lazard, ed., *Autour des "Hymnes" de Ronsard,* 92–94 (Fr).

Isidore Silver, "Ronsard's Reflections on the Heavens and Time," *PMLA* 80 (September 1965): 350–54 (Eng).

Silver, *Three Ronsard Studies,* 70–72, 76 (Eng).

H. Weber, *La Création poétique au XVIe siècle en France,* 497–99 (Fr).

"Hymne des Daimons"

Berry, *Ronsard,* 131–34 (Fr).

Jean Céard, "Dieu, les hommes, et le poète; Structure, sens et fonction des mythes dans les 'Hymnes,' de Ronsard," in Lazard, ed., *Autour des "Hymnes" de Ronsard,* 90–92 (Fr).

Françoise Joukovsky, "Temps et éternité dans les 'Hymnes,' " in Lazard, ed., *Autour des "Hymnes" de Ronsard,* 73–75 (Fr).

Hélène Moreau, "Les 'Daimons,' ou De la fantaisie," in Lazard, ed., *Autour des "Hymnes" de Ronsard,* 215–42 (Fr).

Michel Simonin, "Sur le personnel du premier livre des 'Hymnes': A l'ombre de Dieu," in Lazard, ed., *Autour des "Hymnes" de Ronsard,* 156–59 (Fr).

H. Weber, *A travers le seizième siècle,* 137–39 (Fr).

H. Weber, *La Création poétique au XVIe siècle en France,* 515–21 (Fr).

Henri Weber, "La Philosophie de Ronsard dans 'Les Hymnes,' " in Lazard, ed., *Autour des "Hymnes" de Ronsard,* 44–47 (Fr).

Mark Whitney, *Critical Reactions and the Christian Element in the Poetry of Pierre de Ronsard* (Chapel Hill: University of North Carolina Press, 1971), 42–47 (Eng).

Wilson, *Ronsard, Poet of Nature,* 68–71 (Eng).

"Hymne des Estoiles"

Odette de Mourgues, "Ronsard's Later Poetry," in Cave, ed., *Ronsard the Poet,* 295–300 (Eng).

Quainton, *Ronsard's Ordered Chaos,* 75–76 (Eng).

H. Weber, *La Création poétique au XVIe siècle en France,* 488–93 (Fr).

Wilson, *Ronsard, Poet of Nature,* 84–86 (Eng).

"Hymne du Ciel"

Françoise Joukovsky, "Temps et éternité dans les 'Hymnes,' " in Lazard, ed., *Autour des "Hymnes" de Ronsard,* 57–61, 80–81 (Fr).

Lafeuille, *Cinq hymnes de Ronsard,* 19–39 (Fr).

RONSARD, PIERRE DE, "Hymne du Printemps"

Isabelle Pantin, "L'Hymne du Ciel," in Lazard, ed., *Autour des "Hymnes" de Ronsard,* 187–214 (Fr).

Quainton, *Ronsard's Ordered Chaos,* 8–9, 99–101 (Eng).

Isidore Silver, " Ronsard's Reflections on Cosmogony and Nature," *PMLA* 79 (June 1964): 221, 225–26 (Eng).

Silver, *Three Ronsard Studies,* 28–31, 55–56, 59–60, 67–70, 72–76, 81–82, 93–94, 99–100 (Eng).

H. Weber, *La Création poétique au XVIe siècle en France,* 485–87, 493–96 (Fr).

"Hymne du Printemps"

Quainton, *Ronsard's Ordered Chaos,* 96–99 (Eng).

"Hymne du tres-chrestien Roy de France Henri II de ce nom"

Chamard, *Histoire de la Pléiade,* vol. 2, 179–80 (Fr).

Dassonville, *Ronsard,* vol. 3, 213–14 (Fr).

Françoise Joukovsky, "Temps et éternité dans les 'Hymnes,' " in Lazard, ed., *Autour des "Hymnes" de Ronsard,* 67–69, 77–79 (Fr).

Francis Higman, "Ronsard's Political and Polemical Poetry," in Cave, ed., *Ronsard the Poet,* 243–44 (Eng).

Daniel Ménager, "L'Hymne du Treschrestien Roy de France Henri II de ce nom," in Lazard, ed., *Autour des "Hymnes" de Ronsard,* 161–85 (Fr).

"Hymne Triomphal de Marguerite de Valois, royne de Navarre"

Dassonville, *Ronsard; étude historique,* vol. 3, 127–28 (Fr).

"Hymne . . . du trèsillustre prince Charles, Cardinal de Lorraine"

Silver, *Ronsard and the Hellenic Renaissance in France,* vol. 2, pt. 1, 361–65; vol. 2, pt. 2, 70–71, 92–94 (Eng).

RONSARD, PIERRE DE, "Je vous envoye un bouquet de ma main"

"Il faut laisser maison et vergers et jardins"

Odette de Mourgues, "Ronsard's Later Poetry," in Cave, ed., *Ronsard the Poet*, 317–18 (Eng).

H. Weber, *A travers le seizième siècle*, 153–60 (Fr).

"L'Institution pour l'adolescence du roy Charles IX"

Chamard, *Histoire de la Pléiade*, vol. 2, 360–66 (Fr).

Dassonville, *Ronsard*, vol. 4, 116–19 (Fr).

John Nothnagle, "The Drama of 'Les Discours' of Ronsard," *ECr* 10 (Summer 1970: 118–19 (Eng).

"Les Isles Fortunées: A Marc Antoine de Muret"

Elizabeth Armstrong, *Ronsard and the Age of Gold* (Cambridge: Cambridge University Press, 1968), 14–17 (Eng).

Terence Cave, "Ronsard as Apollo: Myth, Poetry and Experience in a Renaissance Sonnet Cycle," *YFS* no. 47 (1972): 80 (Eng).

Dassonville, *Ronsard*, vol. 4, 68–70 (Fr).

Silver, *Ronsard and the Hellenic Renaissance in France*, vol. 2, pt. 2, 248–49 (Eng).

"Je vous donne des œufs. L'œuf en sa forme ronde"

Silver, *Three Ronsard Studies*, 57–59 (Eng).

"Je vous envoye un bouquet de ma main"

Auffret and Affret, *Le Commentaire composé*, 59–69 (Fr).

Mary Crumpacker, " 'Quand vous serez bien vieille': The Development of a Lyric Form," *BHR* 41 (May 1979): 305–12 (Eng).

Dassonville, *Ronsard*, vol. 3, 184–85 (Fr).

Quainton, *Ronsard's Ordered Chaos*, 121–22 (Eng).

H. Weber, *La Création poétique au XVIe siècle en France*, 348–49 (Fr).

RONSARD, PIERRE DE, "La Lyre"

"La Lyre"

Terence Cave, "Mythes de l'abondance et de la privation chez Ronsard," *CAIEF* 25 (May 1973): 247–50 (Fr).

Terence Cave, "Ronsard as Apollo: Myth, Poetry and Experience in a Renaissance Sonnet Cycle," *YFS*, no. 47 (1972): 86–88 (Eng).

Terence Cave, "Ronsard's Mythological Universe," in Cave, ed., *Ronsard the Poet,* 190–92 (Eng).

"La Mort de Narcisse, en forme d'élégie"

Ullrich Langer, "Ronsard's 'La mort de Narcisse': Imitation and the Melancholy Subject," *FrF* 9 (January 1984): 7–16 (Eng).

"Le Narssis"

Quainton, *Ronsard's Ordered Chaos,* 45–46 (Eng).

"Le Nuage, ou L'Yorogne"

Desonay, *Ronsard, poète de l'amour,* vol. 1, 53–54 (Fr).

"Nues, ou Nouvelles"

Ménager, *Ronsard,* 268–77, 323–25 (Fr).

Ode 13, Book 3, "A sa maistresse"
"Jeune beauté, mais trop outrecuidée"

Dassonville, *Ronsard,* vol. 4, 177–83 (Fr).

Ode 16, Book 2, "A sa maistresse"
"Ma petite columbelle"

François Rigolot, "Rhétorique de la métamorphose chez Ronsard," in Floyd Gray and Marcel Tetel, eds., *Textes et intertextes: Etudes sur le XVIe siècle pour Alfred Glauser* (Paris: Nizet, 1979), 152–53 (Fr).

H. Weber, *La Création poétique au XVIe siècle en France,* 370–72 (Fr).

RONSARD, PIERRE DE, "Ode à Joachim Du Bellay"

Ode 25, Book 2
"O pucelle plus tendre"

H. Weber, *La Création poétique au XVIe siècle en France,* 381–84 (Fr).

"Ode à Anthoine Chasteigner"

Malcolm Quainton, "Ronsard's Philosophical and Cosmological Conceptions of Time," *FS* 23 (January 1969): 4–6 (Eng).

"Ode à Cassandre"
"Mignonne, allon voir si la rose"

Calin, *In Defense of French Poetry,* 33–36 (Eng).

Dassonville, *Ronsard,* vol. 3, 106–9 (Fr).

Desonay, *Ronsard, poète de l'amour,* vol. 1, 168–71 (Fr).

Howarth and Walton, *Explications,* 13–24 (Eng).

Stone, *Ronsard's Sonnet Cycles,* 4–12 (Eng).

H. Weber, *La Création poétique au XVIe siècle en France,* 345–48 (Fr).

"Ode à Charles Cardinal de Lorraine"

Silver, *Ronsard and the Hellenic Renaissance in France,* vol. 2, pt. 2, 91–92 (Eng).

"Ode à Guy Pacate"

Quainton, *Ronsard's Ordered Chaos,* 147–49 (Eng).

"Ode à Joachim Du Bellay"

H. Weber, A travers le seizième siècle, 91–98 (Fr).

Henri Weber, "Structure des odes chez Ronsard," *CAIEF* 22 (May 1970): 104–12 (Fr).

RONSARD, PIERRE DE, "Ode à la Forêt de Gastine"

"Ode à la Forêt de Gastine"

Chamard, *Histoire de la Pléiade,* vol. 1, 333–35 (Fr).

H. M. Richmond, "Rural Lyricism: A Renaissance Mutation of the Pastoral," *CL* 16 (Summer 1964): 197–99 (Eng).

"Ode à Michel de l'Hospital"

Terence Cave, "Ronsard as Apollo: Myth, Poetry and Experience in a Renaissance Sonnet Cycle," *YFS,* no. 47 (1972): 77, 87 (Eng).

Terence Cave, "Ronsard's Mythological Universe," in Cave, ed., *Ronsard the Poet,* 187–90 (Eng).

Dassonville, *Ronsard,* vol. 3, 15–16 (Fr).

Jones, *Pierre de Ronsard,* 37–40 (Eng).

Françoise Joukovsky-Micha, "La Guerre des dieux et des géants chez les poètes français du seizième siècle (1500–1585)," *BHR* 29 (January 1967): 74–84 (Fr).

Lapp, *The Brazen Tower,* 34, 44–48 (Eng).

Silver, *The Intellectual Evolution of Ronsard,* vol. 1, 302–7; vol. 2, 43–44, 165–66, 394 (Eng).

Silver, *Ronsard and the Hellenic Renaissance in France,* vol. 2, pt. 2, 245–46 (Eng).

Isidore Silver, "Ronsard débutant et la 'Théogonie d'Hésiode,'" *RHL* 60 (April–June 1960): 153–64 (Fr).

Wilson, *Ronsard, Poet of Nature,* 30–32 (Eng).

Winter, *Visual Variety and Spatial Grandeur,* 110–16 (Eng).

"Ode à Monsieur de Verdun"

Quainton, *Ronsard's Ordered Chaos,* 122–24 (Eng).

"Ode à Nicolas Denisot"

Isidore Silver, "Ronsard's Reflections on Cosmogony and Nature," *PMLA* 79 (June 1964): 224–25 (Eng).

RONSARD, PIERRE DE, "La Paix, au roi Henry II"

"Ode à sa maistresse"
"Quand au temple nous serons"

Dassonville, *Ronsard,* vol. 4, 184–85 (Fr).

"Ode a un rossignol"

Dassonville, *Ronsard,* vol. 4, 183–84 (Fr).

"Ode au roi"

H. Weber, *La Création poétique au XVIe siècle en France,* 481–83 (Fr).

"Ode au Roy Henri II"

Silver, *Ronsard and the Hellenic Renaissance in France,* vol. 2, pt. 1, 301–3 (Eng).

"Ode de la Paix"

Chamard, *Histoire de la Pléiade,* vol. 1, 344–46, 349–50 (Fr).
Quainton, *Ronsard's Ordered Chaos,* 55–59 (Eng).
Silver, *Ronsard and the Hellenic Renaissance in France,* vol. 2, pt. 1, 299–301, 348–49; vol. 2, pt. 2, 31–32, 96–101, 165–66, 239–42 (Eng).

"Ode"
"Celuy qui est mort aujourd' huy"

Quainton, *Ronsard's Ordered Chaos,* 136–40 (Eng).

"L'Ombre du cheval"

Isidore Silver, *Ronsard and the Hellenic Renaissance in France,* vol. 1, 156–58 (Eng).

"Or que Jupin espoint de sa semence"

Jones, *Pierre de Ronsard,* 48–51 (Eng).

"La Paix, au roi Henry II"

Dassonville, *Ronsard,* vol. 4, 51–53(Fr).

RONSARD, PIERRE DE, "Panegyrique de la Renommée"

"Panegyrique de la Renommée"

Silver, *Ronsard and the Hellenic Renaissance in France,* vol. 2, pt. 1, 206–7, 406–10 (Eng).

"Par un destin dedans mon cuoeur demeure"

Moss, *Poetry and Fable,* 132–33 (Eng).

"Le Pensement, qui me fait devenir"

Gendre, *Ronsard, poète de la conquête amoureuse,* 326–27 (Fr).

"Le Petit enfant Amour"

Chamard, *Histoire de la Pléiade,* vol. 2, 62–64 (Fr).

"Le Pin"

Terence Cave, "Mythes de l'abondance et de la privation chez Ronsard," *CAIEF* 25 (May 1973): 251–54 (Fr).

Quainton, *Ronsard's Ordered Chaos,* 48–49 (Eng).

"Plus estroit que la vigne à l'ormeau se marie"

Desonay, *Ronsard, poète de l'amour,* vol. 3, 332–35 (Fr).

Gendre, *Ronsard, poète de la conquête amoureuse,* 464–66 (Fr).

H. Weber, *La Création poétique au XVIe siècle en France,* 382–85 (Fr).

"Plus que mes yeux j'aime tes beaux cheveux"

Brian Mallett, "Some Uses of 'Sententiae' in Ronsard's Love Sonnets," *FS* 27 (April 1973): 134–50 (Eng).

"Pour boire dessus l'herbe tendre"

Jones, *Pierre de Ronsard,* 67–69 (Eng).

RONSARD, PIERRE DE, "Quand je suis vingt ou trente mois"

"Pour estre an vain tes beaulz soleilz aymant"

H. Weber, *A travers le seizième siècle,* 79–80 (Fr).

"Pour son tombeau"

Silver, *Ronsard and the Hellenic Renaissance in France,* vol. 2: *Ronsard and the Grecian Lyre,* pt. 1, 418–20 (Eng).

"Prière à la Fortune"

Malcolm Quainton, "Some Classical References, Sources, and Identities in Ronsard's 'Prière a la Fortune,'" *FS* 21 (October 1967): 293–301 (Eng).

Silver, *Ronsard and the Hellenic Renaissance in France,* vol. 2: *Ronsard and the Grecian Lyre,* pt. 2, 366–68 (Eng).

"Le Procès, à trèsillustre prince Charles, Cardinal de Lorraine"

Silver, *Ronsard and the Hellenic Renaissance in France,* vol. 2: *Ronsard and the Grecian Lyre,* pt. 1, 368–69 (Eng).

"La Promesse: A la Royne"

Silver, *Ronsard and the Hellenic Renaissance in France,* vol. 2: *Ronsard and the Grecian Lyre,* pt. 1, 378–80 (Eng).

"Quand en songeant ma follastre j'accolle"

Grahame Castor, "Petrarchism and the Quest for Beauty," in Terrence Cave, ed., *Ronsard the Poet,* 92–95 (Eng).

Grahame Castor, "Ronsard: 'Les Amours,' 'Quand en songeant ma follastre j'acolle,'" in Nurse, ed., *The Art of Criticism,* 19–26 (Eng).

"Quand je suis vingt ou trente mois"

Desonay, *Ronsard, poète de l'amour,* vol. 1, 198–202 (Fr).

RONSARD, PIERRE DE, "Quand je vous voy, ma gentille maistresse"

"Quand je vous voy, ma gentille maistresse"

H. Weber, *La Création poétique au XVIe siècle en France,* 254–55 (Fr).

"Que laschement vous me trompez, mes yeulz"

Ullrich Langer, "Ronsard's 'La Mort de Narcisse': Imitation and the Melancholy Subject," *FrF* 9 (January 1984): 6–7 (Eng).

"Quinconque aura premier la main embesognée"

Hélène Fredrickson, "L'Orphelin de la forêt: L'Elégie 24 de Ronsard," *SFR* 4 (Winter 1980): 435–51 (Fr).

"Le Ravissement de Cephale"

Moss, *Poetry and Fable,* 125–32 (Eng).

"Remonstrance au peuple de France"

Yvonne Bellenger, "L'Allégorie dans les poèmes de style élevé de Ronsard," *CAIEF* 28 (May 1976): 76–77 (Fr).

Chamard, *Histoire de la Pléiade,* vol. 2, 382–84 (Fr).

Charbonnier, *La Poésie francaise et les guerres de religion,* 50–56 (Fr).

Ménager, *Ronsard,* 234–39 (Fr).

John Nothnagle, "The Drama of 'Les Discours' of Ronsard," *ECr* 10 (Summer 1970): 121–22 (Eng).

Quainton, *Ronsard's Ordered Chaos,* 158–59 (Eng).

H. Weber, *La Création poétique au XVIe siècle en France,* 571, 573–74, 580–82, 586–87, 591–95 (Fr).

Wilson, *Ronsard, Poet of Nature,* 108–10 (Eng).

"Réponse de Pierre de Ronsard aux injures et calomnies de je
ne sçay quels predicontereaux et ministreaux de Génève"

Chamard, *Histoire de la Pléiade,* vol. 2, 387–90 (Fr).

Charbonnier, *La Poésie française et les guerres de religion,* 77–91 (Fr).

Jones, *Pierre de Ronsard,* 110–12, 269–73 (Eng).

Ménager, *Ronsard,* 170–71, 253–70 (Fr).

Py, *Imitation et Renaissance dans la poésie de Ronsard,* 36–41 (Fr).

"Response de Pierre de Ronsard aux injures et calomnies . . . "

Berry, *Ronsard,* 171–73 (Fr).

John Nothnagle, "The Drama of 'Les Discours' of Ronsard," *ECr* 10 (Summer 1970): 122–24 (Fr).

"Le Rossignol"

Desonay, *Ronsard, poète de l'amour,* vol. 2, 224–25 (Fr).

Quainton, *Ronsard's Ordered Chaos,* 47–48 (Eng).

"La Salade"

Wilson, *Ronsard, Poet of Nature,* 109–11 (Eng).

"Le Satyre"

Moss, *Poetry and Fable,* 142–48 (Eng).

"Le Seul penser, qui me fait devenir"

Grahame Castor, "Petrarchism and the Quest for Beauty," in Cave, ed., *Ronsard the Poet,* 95–96 (Eng).

"Si la foy des amans que l'Amour favorise"

Desonay, *Ronsard, poète de l'amour,* vol. 2, 206–8 (Fr).

H. Weber, *La Création poétique au XVIe siècle en France,* 314–15 (Fr).

Sonnets pur Hélène, Book 1, 1
"Le premier jour de may, Hélène, je vous jure"

Grahame Castor, "Petrarchism and the Quest for Beauty," in Cave, ed., *Ronsard the Poet,* 100–101 (Eng).

Desonay, *Ronsard, poète de l'amour,* vol. 3, 324–25 (Fr).

RONSARD, PIERRE DE, *Sonnets pour Hélène, Book 1, 3*

Alan Nagel, "Literary and Historical Context in Ronsard's 'Sonnets pour Hélène,'" *PMLA* 94 (May 1979): 410–11, 414–15 (Eng).

Sonnets pour Hélène, Book 1, 3
"Ma douce Hélène, non, mais bien ma douce haleine"

Stone, *Ronsard's Sonnet Cycles,* 166–67, 171 (Eng).

Sonnets pour Hélène, Book 1, 24
"Je liay d'un filet de soye cramoisie"

Desonay, *Ronsard, poète de l'amour,* vol. 3, 300 (Fr).

Sonnets pour Hélène, Book 1, 27
"Chef, escole des arts, le sejour de science"

Silver, *Ronsard and the Hellenic Renaissance in France,* vol. 2, pt. 1, 235–36 (Eng).

Silver, *Three Ronsard Studies,* 89–90 (Eng).

Sonnets pour Hélène, Book 1, 29
"De voz yeux, le mirouer du ciel et de nature"

André Gendre, "Fixité et mobilité du sonnet: L'Expérience de Ronsard," *CAIEF* 32 (May 1980): 111–21 (Fr).

Sonnets pour Hélène, Book 1, 49
"D'un solitaire pas je ne marche en nul lieu"

Stone, *Ronsard's Sonnet Cycles,* 199–202 (Eng).

Sonnets pour Hélène, Book 1, 52
"Dessus l'autel d'Amour planté sur vostre table"

Stone, *Ronsard's Sonnet Cycles,* 212–14 (Eng).

RONSARD, PIERRE DE, *Sonnets pour Hélène, Book 2, 42*

Sonnets pour Hélène, Book 1, 61
"Madame se levoit un beau matin d'Esté"

Lapp, *The Brazen Tower*, 56–57 (Eng).

Sonnets pour Hélène, Book 1, 63
"Je faisois ces sonnets en l'antre Pieride"

Alan Nagel, "Literary and Historial Context in Ronsard's 'Sonnets pour Hélène,'" *PMLA* 94 (May 1979): 414 (Eng).

Sonnets pour Hélène, Book 1, Madrigal
"Si c'est aimer, Madame et de jour et de nuict"

Gendre, *Ronsard, poète de la conquête amoureuse,* 182–83 (Fr).

Sonnets pour Hélène, Book 2, 2
"Afin qu'à tout jamais de siècle en siècle vive"

Odette de Mourgues, "Ronsard's Later Poetry," in Cave, ed., *Ronsard the Poet,* 300–302 (Eng).

Sonnets pour Hélène, Book 2, 3
"Amour, qui as ton regne en ce monde si ample"

Stone, *Ronsard's Sonnet Cycles,* 206–11 (Eng).

Sonnets pour Hélène, Book 2, 29
"Vous triomphez de moy, et pource je vous donne"

Desonay, *Ronsard, poète de l'amour,* vol. 3, 335–37 (Fr).

Sonnets pour Hélène, Book 2, 42
"Ces longues nuicts d'Hyver, où la Lune ocieuse"

Grahame Castor, "Petrarchism and the Quest for Beauty," in Cave, ed., *Ronsard the Poet,* 116–18 (Eng).

Grahame Castor, "The Theme of Illusion in Ronsard's 'Sonnets pour Hélène' and the Variants of the 1552 'Amours,' " *FMLS* 7 (October 1971): 364–65 (Eng).

Sonnets pour Hélène, Book 2, 43
"Quand vous serez bien vieille"

Elizabeth Armstrong, "Une vieille accroupie," *FSB* 27 (Summer 1988): 12–13 (Eng).

Tom Conley, "Ronsard, le sonnet et la lettre: Amorces de 'Soit que son or se crespe lentement,' " in Kritzman, ed., *Le Signe et le texte,* 126–30 (Fr).

Mary Crumpacker, " 'Quand vous serez bien vieille': The Development of a Lyric Form," *BHR* 41 (May 1979): 312–16 (Eng).

Dassonville, *Ronsard,* vol. 4, 185–86 (Fr).

Desonay, *Ronsard, poète de l'amour,* vol. 3, 337–38 (Fr).

Gendre, *Ronsard, poète de la conquête amoureuse,* 294–96 (Fr).

Ruth Murphy, " 'Devidant et filant': A New Reading of Ronsard's 'Quand vous serez bien vieille,' " *FSB* 25 (Winter 1987–88): 5–7 (Eng).

Stone, *Ronsard's Sonnet Cycles,* 4–12 (Eng).

Sonnets pour Hélène, Book 2, 44
"Genévres herissez, et vous Houx espineux"

Stone, *Ronsard's Sonnet Cycles,* 203–6 (Eng).

Sonnets pour Hélène, Book 2, 49
"Le Soir qu'Amour vous fist en la salle descendre"

Grahame Castor, "Petrarchism and the Quest for Beauty," in Cave, ed., *Ronsard the Poet,* 113–15 (Eng).

Sonnets pour Hélène, Book 2, 56
"J'errois en mon jardin, quand au bout d'une allée"

Stone, *Ronsard Sonnet Cycles,* 195–99 (Eng).

RONSARD, PIERRE DE, "Suyte de l'Hymne de tres illustre"

Sonnets pour Hélène, Book 2, 60
"Passant dessus la tombe où Lucrèce repose"

Desonay, *Ronsard, poète de l'amour,* vol. 3, 306–7 (Fr).

Sonnets pour Hélène, Book 2, 66
"Mon ame mille fois m'a predit mon dommage"

Brian Mallett, "Some Uses of 'Sententiae' in Ronsard's Love Sonnets," *FS* 27 (1973): 145–48 (Eng).

Sonnets pour Hélène, Book 2, 77
"Je chantois ces sonnets amoureux d'une Hélène"

Alan Nagel, "Literary and Historical Context in Ronsard's 'Sonnets pour Hélène,' " *PMLA* 94 (May 1979): 406–19 (Eng).

"Stances de la fontaine d'Hélène"

Stone, *Ronsard Sonnet Cycles,* 177–78, 182–83 (Eng).

Sur la Mort de Marie 4
"Comme on voit sur la branche au mois de mai la rose"

Calin, *In Defense of French Poetry,* 36–37 (Eng).

Lewis, *On Reading French Verse,* 193–209 (Eng).

Leo Spitzer, "Sur la morte de Marie," *Expl* 2 (October 1951): 1. Reprinted in Walcutt and Whitesell, eds., *The Explicator Cyclopedia,* 384–86 (Eng).

Stone, *Ronsard Sonnet Cycles,* 139–40 (Eng).

H. Weber, *La Création poétique au XVIe siècle en France,* 350–53 (Fr).

"Suyte de l'Hymne de tres illustre Prince Charles,
Cardinal de Lorraine"

Silver, *Ronsard and the Hellenic Renaissance in France,* vol. 2, pt. 1, 365–68 (Eng).

RONSARD, PIERRE DE, "Tombeau de Très Illustre"

"Tombeau de Très Illustre Princesse
Marguerite de France"

Chamard, *Histoire de la Pléiade,* vol. 3, 371–73 (Fr).

Jones, *Pierre de Ronsard,* 126–27 (Eng).

"Trois temps, Seigneurs, icy bas ont naissance"

Quainton, *Ronsard's Ordered Chaos,* 119–20 (Eng).

Malcolm Quainton, "Ronsard's Philosophical and Cosmological Conceptions of Time," *FS* 23 (January 1969): 9–11 (Eng).

"Verson ces roses pres ce vin"

Wilson, *Ronsard, Poet of Nature,* 67–70 (Eng).

"La Vertu amoureuse à tresillustre Prelat
Hieronyme de la Rovère"

Silver, *Ronsard and the Hellenic Renaissance in France,* vol. 2, pt. 2, 385–87 (Eng).

"La Victoire de François de Bourbon,
Comte d'Anguien à Cerisoles"

Dassonville, *Ronsard,* vol. 2, 17–19 (Fr).

George Joseph, "Ronsard's 'Ode' Versus Marot's 'Epistle' in Honor of François de Bourbon," *FR* 54 (May 1981): 788–89, 793–96 (Eng).

"La Victoire de Gui de Chabot, seigneur de Jarnac"

Silver, *Ronsard and the Hellenic Renaissance in France,* vol. 2, pt. 2, 267–68 (Eng).

"Vous ne le voulez pas? et bien, j'en suis contant"

Desonay, *Ronsard, poète de l'amour,* vol. 2, 125–27 (Fr).

RUTEBEUF, "Complainte du roi de Navarre"

"Le Voyage de Tours"

Elizabeth Armstrong, *Ronsard and the Age of Gold* (Cambridge: Cambridge University Press, 1968), 166–68 (Eng).

Berry, *Ronsard,* 152–55 (Fr).

Terence Cave, "Ronsard's Mythological Universe," in Cave, ed., *Ronsard the Poet,* 179–80 (Eng).

Chamard, *Histoire de la Pléiade,* vol. 2, 169–70 (Fr).

Dassonville, *Ronsard,* vol. 4, 99–100 (Fr).

Desonay, *Ronsard, poète de l'amour,* vol. 2, 169–71 (Fr).

Jones, *Pierre de Ronsard,* 61–63 (Eng).

Hélène Moreau, "Variations sur la métamorphose: Ronsard, 'Le Voyage de Tours,'" in Guy Demerson, ed., *Poétiques de la métamorphose* (N.p.: Publications de l'Université de Saint-Etienne, 1981), 108–23 (Fr).

Stone, *Ronsard's Sonnet Cycles,* 95–99 (Eng).

"Le Voyage d'Herceuil"

Berry, *Ronsard,* 62–66 (Fr).

Wilson, *Ronsard, Poet of Nature,* 33–37 (Eng).

RUTEBEUF

"La Bataille des vices contre les vertus"

Regalado, *Poetic Patterns in Rutebeuf,* 152–54 (Eng).

Serper, *Rutebeuf, poète satirique,* 139–45 (Fr).

"Complainte du comte de Poitiers"

Regalado, *Poetic Patterns in Rutebeuf,* 58–61 (Eng).

"Complainte du roi de Navarre"

Regalado, *Poetic Patterns in Rutebeuf,* 57–58 (Eng).

RUTEBEUF, "Complainte Maître Guillaume de Saint-Amour"

"Complainte Maître Guillaume de Saint-Amour"

Regalado, *Poetic Patterns in Rutebeuf,* 163–67 (Eng).

"La Complainte Rutebeuf"

Jean Frappier, "Rutebeuf, poète du jeu, du guignon et de la misère" dans *Les Pharaons* (*La Voix des poètes,* no. 39), no. 4, 1970, pp. 47–57. Reprinted in Frappier, *Du Moyen Age à la Renaissance,* 129–30 (Fr).

Regalado, *Poetic Patterns in Rutebeuf,* 300–303 (Eng).

"De Frère Denise"

Regalado, *Poetic Patterns in Rutebeuf,* 180–82 (Eng).

"Dit d'Hypocrisie"

Regalado, *Poetic Patterns in Rutebeuf,* 146–51 (Eng).

Serper, *Rutebeuf, poète satirique,* 126–32 (Fr).

"Dit de Guillaume de Saint-Amour"

Brian Levy, "Rutebeuf's Change of Address," *FSB* 11 (Summer 1984): 1–3 (Eng).

Regalado, *Poetic Patterns in Rutebeuf,* 160–63 (Eng).

"Dit des Cordeliers"

Regalado, *Poetic Patterns in Rutebeuf,* 73–78 (Eng).

"Du Pharisien"

Regalado, *Poetic Patterns in Rutebeuf,* 201–4 (Eng).

Serper, *Rutebeuf, poète satirique,* 132–39 (Fr).

RUTEBEUF, "Nouvelle complainte d'outremer"

"Du Secrestain et de la femme au chevalier"

Regalado, *Poetic Patterns in Rutebeuf,* 241–46 (Eng).

"Griesche d'Este"

Regalado, *Poetic Patterns in Rutebeuf,* 309–11 (Eng).

"Griesche d'Hiver"

Jean Frappier, "Rutebeuf, poèts du jeu, du guignon et de la misère" dans *Les Pharaons (La Voix des poètes,* no. 39), no. 4, 1970, pp. 47–57. Reprinted in Frappier, *Du Moyen Age à la Renaissance,* 126–27 (Fr).

Regalado, *Poetic Patterns in Rutebeuf,* 304–9 (Eng).

Serper, *Rutebeuf, poète satirique,* 55–56 (Fr).

Michel Zink, "Bonheurs de l'inconséquence dans le texte de Rutebeuf," *ECr* 27 (Spring 1987): 86–88 (Fr).

"Le Mariage Rutebeuf"

Jean Frappier, "Rutebeuf, poète du jeu, du guignon et de la misère," dans *Les Pharaons (La Voix des poètes,* no. 39), no. 4, 1970, pp. 47–57. Reprinted in Frappier, *Du Moyen Age à la Renaissance,* 128–29 (Fr).

"La Mort Rutebeuf"

Jean Frappier, "Rutebeuf, poète du jeu, du guignon et de la misère," dans *Les Pharaons (La Voix des poètes,* no. 39), no. 4, 1970, pp. 47–57. Reprinted in Frappier, *Du Moyen Age à la Renaissance,* 131–32 (Fr).

Regalado, *Poetic Patterns in Rutebeuf,* 271–82 (Eng).

Michel Zink, "Bonheurs de l'inconséquence dans le texte de Rutebeuf," *ECr* 27 (Spring 1987):79–82 (Fr).

"Nouvelle complainte d'outremer"

Regalado, *Poetic Patterns in Rutebeuf,* 48–54 (Eng).

RUTEBEUF, "Renart le Bestourné"

"Renart le Bestourné"

Serper, *Rutebeuf, poète satirique,* 106–26 (Fr).

"La Vie de Sainte Marie l'Egyptienne"

Suzanne Nash, "Rutebeuf's Contribution to the Saint Mary the Egyptian Legend," *FR* 44 (March 1971): 695–705 (Eng).

Elizabeth Wilson, "Name Games in Rutebeuf and Villon," *ECr* 18 (Spring 1978): 48–51 (Eng).

"Voie de Paradis"

Regalado, *Poetic Patterns in Rutebeuf,* 29–39(Eng).

Serper, *Rutebeuf, poète satirique,* 145–53 (Fr).

Michel Zink, "Bonheurs de l'inconséquence dans le texte de Rutebeuf," *ECr* 27 (Spring 1987): 83–86 (Fr).

SAGON, FRANCOIS

"Elegie par F. S. se complaignant à luy mesmes d'aucuns qui ne prennent bien l'intention de son Coup d'Essay, dont il frappa Marot"

Christine M. Scollen, *The Birth of the Elegy in France* (Geneva: Droz, 1967), 71–76 (Eng).

SAINT-AMANT, GIRARD DE

"L'Albion"

Gourier, Etude des *œuvres* poétiques de Saint-Amant, 104–5, 109–11, 124 (Fr).

Lagny, *Le Poète Saint-Amant,* 273–76, 279–85 (Fr).

"L'Amarante"

Lagny, *Le Poète Saint-Amant,* 222–26 (Fr).

"L'Andromède"

Gourier, *Etude des œuvres poétiques de Saint-Amant,* 161–64 (Fr).

Richard Mazzara, "Saint-Amant's 'L'Andromède' and Lope de Vega's 'La Andromeda,' " *KRQ* 8, no. 1 (1961): 7–14 (Eng).

"L'Arion"

Jean-Pierre Chauveau, "La Voix des poètes," *LCL* 12 (1990): 200–202 (Fr).

Edwin Duval, *Poesis and Poetic Tradition in the Early Works of Saint-Amant: Four Essays in Contextual Reading* (York, S.C.: French Literature Publications, 1981), 93–135 (Eng).

William Roberts, "Classical Sources of Saint-Amant's 'L'Arion,' " *FS* 17 (October 1963): 341–50 (Eng).

"L'Automne des Canaries"

Corum, *Other Worlds and Other Seas,* 137–42 (Eng).

Gourier, *Etude des œuvres poétiques de Saint-Amant,* 174–75 (Fr).

Donna Kuizenga, "Saint-Amant's Seasonal Cycle: "A Baroque Myth," *FR* 56 (February 1983): 387–91 (Eng).

Francis Lawrence, "A Post-Structuralist Critique of Saint-Amant's Four Season Sonnets," *ECr* 20 (Winter 1980): 26–28 (Eng).

"L'Avant-Satire"

Lagny, *Le Poète Saint-Amant,* 248–49 (Fr).

"Le Barberot"

Lagny, *Le Poète Saint-Amant,* 276–78 (Fr).

"Le Cantal"

Elizabeth Davis, "Originality and Imitation in Four Poems by Saint-Amant," *JES* 10 (March 1980): 4–5 (Eng).

Lagny, *Le Poète Saint-Amant,* 221–22 (Fr).

SAINT-AMANT, GIRARD DE, "Caprice"

"Caprice"

Lagny, *Le Poète Saint-Amant,* 164–65 (Fr).

"La Chambre du débauché"

Gourier, *Etude des œuvres poétiques de Saint-Amant,* 147–49 (Fr).

Richard Mazzara, "The 'Anti-Hero' in Saint-Amant," *KRQ* 9, no. 3 (1962): 123–29 (Eng).

William Roberts, "Berni's 'Malo Alloggio' motif in Saint-Amant," *SFr* 10 (September–December 1965): 466–71 (Eng).

"Les Committimus"

Lagny, *Le Poète Saint-Amant,* 215–17 (Fr).

"Le Comtemplateur"

D. Dale Casper, "Saint-Amant: Pictorialism and the Devotional Style," *SFr* 22 (May–December 1978): 390–91 (Eng).

Corum, *Other Worlds and Other Seas,* 32–68 (Eng).

Gourier, *Etude des œuvres poétiques de Saint-Amant,* 185–90 (Fr).

Lagny, *Le Poète Saint-Amant,* 131–33, 184 (Fr).

Francis Lawrence, "Time and the Individual Consciousness in Saint-Amant's 'La Solitude' and 'Le Contemplateur,'" *FR* 46 (Special Issue 5) (Spring 1973): 36–39 (Eng).

Richard Mazzara, "Théophile de Viau, Saint-Amant, and the Spanish Soledad," *KRQ* 14, no. 4 (1967): 401–2 (Eng).

"Epître à l'Abbé de Villeloin"

Gourier, *Etude des œuvres poétiques de Saint-Amant,* 63–66 (Fr).

"Epître à l'Hyver, sur le voyage de Sa Serenissime Majesté en Pologne"

Lagny, *Le Poète Saint-Amant,* 301–2 (Fr).

SAINT-AMANT, GIRARD DE, "Fragment d'une Meditation"

"Epître à M. le baron de Melay"

Elizabeth Davies, "Originality and Imitation in Four Poems by Saint-Amant," *JES* 10 (March 1980): 9–11 (Eng).

Lagny, *Le Poète Saint-Amant,* 260–66 (Fr).

"Epître à M. le baron de Villarnoul"

Lagny, *Le Poète Saint-Amant,* 304–8 (Fr).

"Epître diversifiée à M. Des Noyens"

Lagny, *Le Poète Saint-Amant,* 310–16 (Fr).

"Epître héroï-comique à Mgr. le duc d'Orléans"

Lagny, *Le Poète Saint-Amant,* 290–96 (Fr).

"L'Este de Rome"

Corum, *Other Worlds and Other Seas,* 130–36 (Fr).

Donna Kuizenga, "Saint-Amant's Seasonal Cycle: A Baroque Myth," *FR* 56 (February 1983): 386–91 (Eng).

Lagny, *Le Poète Saint-Amant,* 202–3 (Fr).

Francis Lawrence, "A Post-Structuralist Critique of Saint-Amant's Four Season Sonnets," *ECr* (Winter 1980): 22–25 (Eng).

"Fragment d'une Meditation sur le Crucifix"

D. Dale Casper, "Saint-Amant: Pictorialism and the Devotional Style," *SFr* 22 (May–December 1978): 388–90 (Eng).

Gourier, *Etude des œuvres poétiques de Saint-Amant,* 196–98 (Fr).

SAINT-AMANT, GIRARD DE, "Le Fromage"

"Le Fromage"

Elizabeth Davies, "Originality and Imitation in Four Poems by Saint-Amant," *JES* 10 (March 1980): 4–6, 8 (Eng).

Edwin Duval, *Poesis and Poetic Tradition in the Early Works of Saint-Amant: Four Essays in Contextual Reading* (York, S.C.: French Literature Publications, 1981), 69–92 (Eng).

"Le Fumeur"

Gourier, *Etude des œuvres poétiques de Saint-Amant,* 153–55 (Fr).

"Galanterie champestre"

Lagny, *Le Poète Saint-Amant,* 350–51 (Fr).

"La Généreuse"

Lagny, *Le Poète Saint-Amant,* 385–94 (Fr).

"L'Hyver des Alpes"

Corum, *Other Worlds and Other Seas,* 122–29 (Eng).

Gourier, *Etude des œuvres poétiques de Saint-Amant,* 175–76 (Fr).

Donna Kuizenga, "Saint-Amant's Seasonal Cycle: A Baroque Myth," *FR* 56 (February 1983): 388–92 (Eng).

Francis Lawrence, "A Post-Structuralist Critique of Saint-Amant's Four Season Sonnets," *ECr* 20 (Winter 1980): 19–25, 28 (Eng).

Francis Lawrence, "Saint-Amant's 'L'Hyver des Alpes': A Structural Analysis," *RR* 68 (November 1977): 247–53 (Eng).

William Roberts, "Sources and Style of Saint-Amant's 'L'Hyver des Alpes,'" *ECr* 20 (Winter 1980): 85–95 (Eng).

"La Lune parlante"

Lagny, *Le Poète Saint-Amant,* 403–9 (Fr).

SAINT-AMANT, GIRARD DE, "Les Nobles Triolets"

"Le Mauvais logement"

Rubin, *The Knot of Artifice,* 31–46 (Eng).

"Le Melon"

D. Dale Casper, "Saint-Amant: Pictorialism and the Devotional Style," *SFr* 22 (May–December 1978): 391–92 (Eng).

Elizabeth Davies, "Originality and Imitation in Four Poems by Saint-Amant," *JES* 10 (March 1980): 6, 9–10 (Eng).

Edwin Duval, *Poesis and Poetic Tradition in the Early Works of Saint-Amant: Four Essays in Contextual Reading* (York, S.C.: French Literature Publications, 1981), 137–68 (Eng).

Gourier, *Etude des œuvres poétiques de Saint-Amant,* 88–90, 133–35 (Fr).

"La Métamorphose de Lyrian et de Sylvie"

Gourier, *Etude des œuvres poétiques de Saint-Amant,* 165–68 (Fr).

"Moyse sauvé"

Jacques Bailbé, "Les Paysages chez Saint-Amant," *CAIEF* 29 (May 1977): 33–35, 38–42 (Fr).

Gérard Genette, *Figures,* 3 vols. (Paris: Seuil, 1966–1972). Vol. 1, 13–16; vol. 2, 195–222 (Fr).

Gourier, *Etude des œuvres poétiques de Saint-Amant,* 193–96, 199–225 (Fr).

Fernand Hallyn, "Saint-Amant et les discours sur la peinture," *ECr* 20 (Winter 1980): 46–47, 49–51 (Eng).

"Moyse sauvé, seconde partie"

Lagny, *Le Poète Saint-Amant,* 308–9 (Fr).

"Les Nobles Triolets"

Lagny, *Le Poète Saint-Amant,* 320–28 (Fr).

SAINT-AMANT, GIRARD DE, "La Nuict"

"La Nuict"

Corum, *Other Worlds and Other Seas,* 102–14 (Eng).

"Ode héroï-comique pour Monseigneur le Prince
lors Duc d'Anguien"

Gourier, *Etude des œuvres poétiques de Saint-Amant,* 46, 48–49 (Fr).

Lagny, *Le Poète Saint-Amant,* 297–99 (Fr).

"Le Passage de Gibraltar"

Gourier, *Etude des œuvres poétiques de Saint-Amant,* 47–49, 122–24 (Fr).

"La Petarde aux Rondeaux"

Lagny, *Le Poète Saint-Amant,* 249–50 (Fr).

"La Pluye"

Corum, *Other Worlds and Other Seas,* 69–83 (Eng).

"Poème sur la Suspension d'armes"

Lagny, *Le Poète Saint-Amant,* 400–402 (Fr).

"Le Poète crotté"

Gourier, *Etude des œuvres poétiques de Saint-Amant,* 111–13 (Fr).

Lagny, *Le Poète Saint-Amant,* 152–58 (Fr).

"La Polonaise"

Gourier, *Etude des œuvres poétiques de Saint-Amant,* 61–62 (Fr).

Lagny, *Le Poète Saint-Amant,* 334–39 (Fr).

SAINT-AMANT, GIRARD DE, "La Solitude"

"Les Pourveus bachiques"

Lagny, *Le Poète Saint-Amant,* 258–60 (Fr).

"Le Printemps des environs de Paris"

Corum, *Other Worlds and Other Seas,* 115–21 (Eng).

Gourier, *Etude des œuvres poétiques de Saint-Amant,* 173–74 (Fr).

Donna Kuizenga, "Saint-Amant's Seasonal Cycle: A Baroque Myth," *FR* 56 (February 1983): 385–88 (Eng).

Francis Lawrence, "A Poet-Structuralist Critique of Saint-Amant's Four Season Sonnets," *ECr* 20 (Winter 1980): 25–26 (Eng).

"La Rome ridicule"

Gourier, *Etude des œuvres poétiques de Saint-Amant,* 105–7, 125–30 (Fr).

Lagny, *Le Poète Saint-Amant,* 182–83, 189–209 (Fr).

"La Rude"

Christopher Rolfe, "The Flemish Connection: Saint-Amant and the Genre-Painters," *SFr* 17 (September–December 1973): 477–78 (Eng).

"La Seine extravagante"

Lagny, *Le Poète Saint-Amant,* 395–97 (Fr).

"Le Soleil levant"

Corum, *Other Worlds and Other Seas,* 84–101 (Eng).

"La Solitude"

Jacques Bailbé, "Les Payages chez Saint-Amant," *CAIEF* 29 (May 1977): 30–31 (Fr).

Corum, *Other Worlds and Other Seas,* 11–31 (Eng).

SAINT-AMANT, GIRARD DE, "Sonnet à feu Monsieur des Yvetaux"

Edwin Duval, *Poesis and Poetic Tradition in the Early Works of Saint-Amant: Four Essays in Contextual Reading* (York, S.C.: French Literature Publications, 1981), 17–68 (Eng).

Gourier, *Etude des œuvres poétiques de Saint-Amant,* 176–83 (Fr).

Catherine Ingold and Robert Corum Ingold, "Perceptions sur 'La Solitude' " *O&C* 5 (Autumn 1980): 41–49 (Fr).

Lagny, *Le Poète Saint-Amant,* 53–56, 63–65, 92–94 (Fr).

Francis Lawrence, "Time and the Individual Consciousness in Saint-Amant's 'La Solitude' and 'Le Contemplateur,' " *FR* 46 (Special Issue 5) (Spring 1973): 34–36 (Eng).

Richard Mazzara, "Théophile de Viau, Saint-Amant, and the Spanish Soledad," *KRQ* 14, no. 4 (1967): 393–400 (Eng).

Tamara Root, " 'La Solitude': Saint-Amant's Expression of Unrest," *FR* 50 (October 1976): 12–20 (Eng).

"Sonnet à feu Monsieur des Yvetaux"

Corum, *Other Worlds and Other Seas,* 143–49 (Eng).

"Sonnet sur la moisson d'un lieu proche de Paris"

Corum, *Other Worlds and Other Seas,* 150–55 (Eng).

"Stances à Monsieur Corneille sur son Imitation de Jésus-Christ"

Lagny, *Le Poète Saint-Amant,* 372–78 (Fr).

"La Vigne"

Lagny, *Le Poète Saint-Amant,* 115–19, 128–29 (Fr).

"Les Visions"

Gourier, *Etude des œuvres poétiques de Saint-Amant,* 145–47, 149–51 (Fr).

SAINT-GELAIS, OCTAVIEN DE, "Tous nobles cueurs"

"La Vistule sollicitée"

Lagny, *Le Poète Saint-Amant,* 29–30, 340–41 (Fr).

SAINTE-BEUVE, CHARLES

"Les Rayons jaunes"

Patrick Laude, "Le Poète à sa fenêtre; dualisme et errance métaphysique dans la poésie française du dix-neuvième siècle," *NCFS* 19 (Spring 1991): 355–59 (Fr).

SAINT-GELAIS, MELLIN DE

"Déploration de Vénus sur la mort du bel Adonis"

V. L. Saulnier, "Mellin de Saint-Gelais, Pernette Du Guillet et l'air 'Conde Claros,' " *BHR* 32 (September 1970): 525–28, 531–32 (Fr).

"Laissez la verde couleur"

Donald Stone, "Saint-Gelais and the Epigrammatic Mode," in Nash, ed., *Pre-Pléiade Poetry,* 37–38 (Eng).

"Ne craignez point, plume bien fortunée"

Marc Eigeldinger, "Le Mythe d'Icare dans la poésie française du XVIe siècle," *CAIEF* 25 (May 1973): 263–64 (Fr).

SAINT-GELAIS, OCTAVIEN DE

"Tous nobles cueurs"

Mary Beth Marvin, "Complainte sur la mort d'une passeroute appellée Marguerite," *BHR* 39 (January 1977): 26–32 (Fr).

SAINT-JOHN PERSE

"Amers"

Alain Bosquet, *Verbe et vertige: Situations de la poésie* (Paris: Hachette, 1961), 145–48 (Fr).

Francis Carmody, "Saint-John Perse and Several Oriental Sources," *CLS* 2 (1965): 143–46 (Eng).

Mechthild Cranston, " 'L'Activité du songe' in the Poetry of Saint-John Perse," *FMLS* 2 (October 1966): 365–67 (Eng).

Curnier, *Pages commentées d'auteurs contemporains,* vol. 1, 211–22 (Fr).

Little, *Saint-John Perse,* 40–53 (Eng).

Roger Little, "The World and the Word in the Work of Saint-John Perse," in Cardinal, ed., *Sensibility and Creation,* 131–32 (Eng).

Emilie Noulet, "Mallarmé and Saint-John Perse," *CAIEF* 27 (May 1975): 315–19 (Fr).

"Amitié du Prince"

Little, *Saint-John Perse,* 15–16 (Eng).

Robichez, *Sur Saint-John Perse,* 129–40 (Fr).

"Anabase"

Peter Baker, "The Sexuation of Poetic Language in Saint-John Perse's 'Anabase,' " *FrF* 12 (January 1987): 109–18 (Eng).

Alain Bosquet, *Verbe et vertige: Situations de la poésie* (Paris: Hachette, 1979), 140–42 (Fr).

Nathan Bracher, "En quête radicale de Saint-John Perse: Simplicité, duplicité, ou complicité de l'etymologie?" *FR* 61 (December 1987): 188 (Fr).

Calin, *In Defense of French Poetry,* 329–43 (Eng).

Francis Carmody, "Saint-John Perse and Several Oriental Sources," *CLS* 2 (1965): 125–28, 133–39 (Eng).

Mechthild Cranston, " 'L'Activité du songe' in the Poetry of Saint-John Perse," *FMLS* 2 (October 1966): 361–62 (Eng).

Arthur Knodel, "Towards an Understanding of 'Anabase,'" *PMLA* 79 (June 1964): 329–43 (Eng).

Little, *Saint-John Perse,* 17–21 (Eng).

Robichez, *Sur Saint-John Perse,* 147–211 (Fr).

Jacques Robichez, "A propos d'"Anabase': Trois Approches du texte," *RHL* 78 (May–June 1978): 428–34 (Fr).

Maurice Tournier, 'Mots mémoriels: L'"Anabase' de Saint-John Perse et le mythe de Babel," *RHL* 78 (May–June 1978): 379–403 (Fr).

"Berceuse"

Robichez, *Sur Saint-John Perse,* 112–13, 117–19, 142–43 (Fr).

"Chant pour un équinoxe"

Walter Strauss, "Exile to Equinox," *SRF* 11 (Summer 1987): 235–36 (Eng).

"Chronique"

Michel Benamou, " 'Chronique' de Saint-John Perse," *FR* 34 (April 1961): 480–82 (Fr).

Francis Carmody, "Saint-John Perse and Several Oriental Sources," *CLS* 2 (1965): 146–48 (Eng).

Little, *Saint-John Perse,* 53–54 (Eng).

"Les Cloches"

Robichez, *Sur Saint-John Perse,* 43–44 (Fr).

"Cohorte"

Little, *Saint-John Perse,* 71–73 (Eng).

SAINT-JOHN PERSE, "Des Villes sur trois modes"

"Des Villes sur trois modes"

René Galand, "En Marge d' 'Eloges,' " *FR* 46 (Special Issue 5) (Spring 1973): 112–19 (Fr).

"Ecrit sur la porte"

Elizabeth Jackson, " 'Eloges': Cadre et récit," *FrF* 6 (September 1981): 254 (Fr).

Little, *Saint-John Perse,* 8–9 (Eng).

Robichez, *Sur Saint-John Perse,* 33–39 (Fr).

"Eloges"

Mechthild Cranston, " 'L'Activité du songe' in the Poetry of Saint-John Perse," *FMLS* 2 (October 1966): 357–60 (Eng).

Elizabeth Jackson, " 'Eloges': Cadre et récit," *FrF* 6 (September 1981): 254–57 (Fr).

Little, *Saint-John Perse,* 11–12 (Eng).

Robert Mauzi, "Composition et signification d'"Eloges,' " *RHL* 78 (May–June 1978): 404–13 (Fr).

Robichez, *Sur Saint-John Perse,* 67–107 (Fr).

"Eloges III: Les Rythmes de l'orgueil descendent les mornes rouges"

Robichez, *Sur Saint-John Perse,* 77–79 (Fr).

"Eloges IV: Azur! nos bêtes sont bondées d'un cri!"

Robichez, *Sur Saint-John Perse,* 76–77, 127–28 (Fr).

"Eloges V: Et d'autres montent, à leur tour, sur le pont"

Marie-Laure Ryan, "L'Instant de la bascule: sur un poème d' 'Eloges' de Saint-John Perse," *KRQ* 25, no. 2 (1978): 185–94 (Fr).

"Eloges VIII: Au négociant le porche sur la mer,
et le toit au Faiseur d'almanachs!"

Robichez, *Sur Saint-John Perse*, 89–91 (Fr).

"Eloges XII: Nous avous un clergé, de la chaux"

Robichez, *Sur Saint-John Perse*, 97–98 (Fr).

"Eloges XIII: La Tête de poisson ricane"

Robichez, *Sur Saint-John Perse*, 98–100 (Fr).

"Exil"

Francis Carmody, "Saint-John Perse and Several Oriental Sources," *CLS* 2 (1965): 139–43 (Eng).

Little, *Saint-John Perse*, 21–24 (Eng).

"Exil I, II, III: I. Portes ouvertes sur les sables; II. A nulles rives dédiée, a nulle pages confiée; III. . . . . Toujours il y eut cette clameur"

Nathan Bracher, "En quête radicale de Saint-John Perse: Simplicité, duplicité, ou complicité de l'etymologie?" *FR* 61 (December 1987): 188–92 (Fr).

"Exil VI. . . . Celui qui erre, à la mi-nuit, sur les galeries de pierre"

Nathan Bracher, "Rigeur et ouverture chez Saint-John Perse: Exil VI," *FrF* 14 (May 1989): 187–97 (Fr).

"La Gloire des Rois"

Robichez, *Sur Saint-John Perse*, 111–43 (Fr).

SAINT-JOHN PERSE, "Images à Crusoé"

"Images à Crusoé"

Mechthild Cranston, " 'L'Activité du songe' in the Poetry of Saint-John Perse," *FMLS* 2 (October 1966): 356–57 (Eng).

Philippe Jaccottet, *L'Entretien des Muses* (Paris: Gallimard, 1968), 38–39 (Fr).

Elizabeth Jackson, " 'Eloges': Cadre et récit," *FrF* 6 (September 1981): 250–52 (Fr).

Little, *Saint-John Perse,* 12–14 (Eng).

Robichez, *Sur Saint-John Perse,* 40–47 (Fr).

"Jadis Londres"

Little, *Saint-John Perse,* 73 (Eng).

"Le Livre"

Robichez, *Sur Saint-John Perse,* 42, 44 (Fr).

"Neiges"

Cécile Koerber, "Saint-John Perse: 'Neiges,' " *FR* 37 (October 1963): 22–30 (Fr).

Little, *Saint-John Perse,* 25–26 (Eng).

Marie-Laure Ryan, "Genèse du discours et discours de la genèse: 'Pluies' et 'Neiges,' " *SRF* 5 (Winter 1981): 345–52 (Fr).

"Oiseaux"

Little, *Saint-John Perse,* 54–55 (Eng).

Stephen Winspur, "Saint-John Perse's 'Oiseaux': The Poem, the Painting, and Beyond," *ECr* 22 (Winter 1982): 47–55 (Eng).

SAINT-JOHN PERSE, "Pour fêter une enfance IV"

"Pluies"

Mechthild Cranston, " 'L'Activité du songe' in the Poetry of Saint-John Perse," *FMLS* 2 (October 1966): 363 (Eng).

Charles Dolamore, "The Love and Aggression of Saint-John Perse's 'Pluies,' " *FMLS* 7 (July 1971): 211–20 (Eng).

Little, *Saint-John Perse,* 24–25 (Eng).

Roger Little, "The World and the Word in the Work of Saint-John Perse," in Cardinal, ed., *Sensibility and Creation,* 124–25 (Eng).

Marie-Laure Ryan, "Genèse du discours et discours de la genèse: 'Pluies' et 'Neiges,' " *SRF* 5 (Winter 1981): 342–45, 348–52 (Fr).

"Poème à l'étrangère"

Little, *Saint-John Perse,* 26–27 (Eng).

"Pour fêter une enfance"

Elizabeth Jackson, " 'Eloges': Cadre et récit," *FrF* 6 (September 1981): 252–54 (Fr).

Little, *Saint-John Perse,* 9–11 (Eng).

"Pour fêter une enfance I: Palmes . . . ! Alors ou te baignait daus l'eau-de-feuilles-vertes"

Robichez, *Sur Saint-John Perse,* 48, 50, 53 (Fr).

"Pour fêter une enfance II: Et les servantes de ma mère, grandes filles luisantes . . ."

Dubosclard and Dubosclard, *Du surréalisme à la Resistance,* 44–50 (Fr).

"Pour fêter une enfance IV: Et tout m'était que règne, et confins de lueurs"

Robichez, *Sur Saint-John Perse,* 50–52, 54–55 (Fr).

SAINT-JOHN PERSE, "Pour fêter une enfance V"

"Pour fêter une enfance V: . . . O! j'ai lieu de louer!"

Robichez, *Sur Saint-John Perse,* 61–64 (Fr).

"Pour fêter une enfance VI: Palmes! et sur la craquante demeure
tant de lances de flamme!"

Robichez, *Sur Saint-John Perse,* 52–53, 60–61, 64–66 (Fr).

"Récitation à l'éloge d'une reine"

Little, *Saint-John Perse,* 14–15 (Eng).

Robichez, *Sur Saint-John Perse,* 111–12, 120–23 (Fr).

"Sécheresse"

Walter Strauss, "Exil to Equinox," *SFR* 11 (Summer 1987): 233–35 (Eng).

"Vendredi"

Robichez, *Sur Saint-John Perse,* 43–44 (Fr).

"Vents"

Nathan Bracher, "En quête radicale de Saint-John Perse: Simplicité, duplicité, ou complicité de l'etymologie?" *FR* 61 (December 1987): 188 (Fr).

Nathan Bracher, "Là où se trame 'l'histoire à vif et convulsive': Les réseaux
dans 'Vents,'" *KRQ* 35, no. 2 (1988): 151–59 (Fr).

Francis Carmody, "Saint-John Perse and Several Oriental Sources," *CLS*
2 (1965): 130–33 (Eng).

Mechthild Cranston, " 'L'Activité du songe' in the Poetry of Saint-John
Perse," *FMLS* 2 (October 1966): 364–65 (Eng).

Little, *Saint-John Perse,* 27–40 (Eng).

SAVOIE, LOUISE DE, "Ce n'est qu'ung cueur, ung vouloir, ung penser"

"Vents I, 4: Tout à reprendre. Tout à redire.
Et la faux du regard sur tout l'avoir menée!"

Moreau, *Six Études de métrique,* 68–79 (Fr).

"Vents III, 4: Mais c'est de l'homme qu'il s'agit!"

Ann Churchman, "L'Enumération chez Saint-John Perse: A propos d'une page de 'Vents,'" in *Studies in Modern French Literature Presented to P. Mansell Jones* (Manchester: Manchester University Press, 1961), 62–70 (Fr).

SAINT-POL-ROUX

"Seul et la flamme"

Anne-Marie Amiot, "Les Fondements mystiques de la poétique de Saint-Pol-Roux," in *Approches: Essais sur la poésie moderne de langue française* (Paris: Les Belles Lettres, 1971), 90–97 (Fr).

SARASIN, JEAN-FRANÇOIS

"Myrtil ou le Nautonier"

Janis Pallister, "Jean-François Sarasin: Lyric Poet," *ECr* 20 (Winter 1980): 58–59 (Eng).

"Orphée"

Janis Pallister, "Jean-François Sarasin: Lyric Poet," *ECr* 20 (Winter 1980): 59–61 (Eng).

SAVOIE, LOUISE DE

"Ce n'est qu'ung cueur, ung vouloir, ung penser"

June Kane, "Louise de Savoie, Poetess," *SFr* 22 (May–December 1978): 352–53 (Eng).

SAVOIE, LOUISE DE, "De desirer et de regrect avoir"

"De desirer et de regrect avoir"

June Kane, "Louise de Savoie, Poetess," *SFr* 22 (May–December 1978): 353–55 (Eng).

"Pensant passer passaige si piteux"

June Kane, "Louise de Savoie, Poetess," *SFr* 22 (May–December 1978): 355–56 (Eng).

"Reveoir meslé d'amertume et douleur"

June Kane, "Louise de Savoie, Poetess," *SFr* 22 (May–December 1978): 356–57 (Eng).

SCEVE, MAURICE

A Sa Délie
"Non de Venus les ardentz estincelles"

Coleman, *Maurice Scève, Poet of Love,* 44–45 (Eng).

Joseph Pivato, "Maurice Scève's 'Délie," Unpetrarchan and Hermetic," *SFr* 27 (January–April 1983): 16–17 (Eng).

"Blason du soupir"

Quignard, *La Parole de Délie,* 75–76 (Fr).

"Délie"

Gregory de Rocher, "The Curing Text: Maurice Scève's Délie as the 'Délie,'" *RR* 78 (January 1987): 10–24 (Eng).

"Délie" (Emblems)

Randolph Runyon, "'Continuelz discors': The Silent Discourse of Délie's Emblems," *ECr* 28 (Summer 1988): 58–67 (Eng).

Délie 1
"L'Oeil trop ardent en mes jeunes erreurs"

Baker, *Narcissus and the Lover,* 32–34 (Eng).

Terence Cave, "Scéve's 'Délie': Correcting Petrarch's Errors," in Nash, ed., *Pre-Pléiade Poetry,* 112–13 (Eng).

Coleman, *Maurice Scève, Poet of Love,* 24–26 (Eng).

Della Neva, *Song and Counter-Song,* 93–96, 98 (Eng).

Lance K. Donaldson-Evans, "Love Divine, All Loves Excelling," *FrF* 14 (January 1989): 6–7 (Eng).

Donaldson-Evans, *Love's Fatal Glance,* 100–102 (Eng).

Doranne Fenoaltea, "Three Animal Images in the 'Délie': New Perspectives," *BHR* 34 (September 1972): 418–22, 425–26 (Eng).

Joseph Pivato, "Maurice Scève's 'Délie,' Unpetrarchan and Hermetic," *SFr* 27 (January–April 1983): 17–18 (Eng).

H. Weber, *La Création poétique au XVIe siècle en France,* 179–80 (Fr).

Délie 2
"Le Naturant par ses haultes Idées"

Coleman, *Maurice Scève, Poet of Love,* 134–36 (Eng).

Dorothy G. Coleman, "Scève's Choice of the Name 'Délie,' " *FS* 18 (January 1964): 7–8 (Eng).

Délie 3
"Ton doulx venin, grace tienne, me fit"

Donaldson-Evans, *Love's Fatal Glance,* 121–23 (Eng).

Délie 5
"Ma Dame ayant l'arc d'Amour en son poing"

Donaldson-Evans, *Love's Fatal Glance,* 102–4 (Eng).

Délie 6
"Libre vivois en l'avril de mon âge"

Baker, *Narcissus and the Lover,* 38–39, 42 (Eng).

Daniel Bergez, "Sur un poème de Maurice Scève," *RHL* 88 (July–August 1988): 635–49 (Fr).

Dorothy G. Coleman, "Les Emblesmes dans la 'Délie' de Maurice Scève," *SFr* 8 (January–April 1964): 11–12 (Fr).

Lance K. Donaldson-Evans, "Love Divine, All Loves Excelling," *FrF* 14 (January 1989): 7–8 (Eng).

Donaldson-Evans, *Love's Fatal Glance,* 104–5 (Eng).

Délie 7
"Celle beaulté, qui embellit le monde"

Coleman, *Maurice Scève, Poet of Love,* 127–29 (Eng).

Dorothy G. Coleman, "Scève's Choice of the Name 'Délie,' " *FS* 18 (January 1964): 12–13 (Eng).

Dorothy G. Coleman, "Sound-Play and Verbal Delight in Scève's 'Délie,' " *FS* 30 (July 1976): 261–63 (Eng).

H. Weber, *La Création poétique au XVIe siècle en France,* 181–83 (Fr).

Délie 9
"Non de Paphos, délices de Cypris"

Wilson Baldridge, "Closing Mallarmé's 'Poésies': A Scève memorial?" *FrF* 15 (May 1990): 189–95 (Eng).

Coleman, *Maurice Scève, Poet of Love,* 118–20, 124 (Eng).

Dorothy G. Coleman, "Scève's Choice of the Name 'Délie,' " *FS* 18 (January 1964): 2–3 (Eng).

Doranne Fenoaltea, "Establishing Contrasts: An Aspect of Scève's Use of Petrarch's Poetry in the 'Délie,' " *SFr* 19 (January–April 1975): 31–33 (Eng).

Délie 10
"Suave odeur: mais le goust trop amer"

Doranne Fenoaltea, "Establishing Contrasts: An Aspect of Scève's Use of Petrarch's Poetry in the 'Délie,'" *SFr* 19 (January–April 1975): 32–33 (Eng).

Délie 11
"De l'océan, l'adultère obstiné"

Paul Audouin, *Maurice Scève, Pernette Du Guillet, Louise Labé: L'Amour à Lyon au temps de la Renaissance* (Paris: Nizet, 1981), 231–32 (Fr).

Délie 12
"Ce lyen d'or, raiz de toy mon Soleil"

Donalson-Evans, *Love's Fatal Glance,* 135–36 (Eng).

Délie 14
"Elle me tient par ces cheveulx lyé"

Coleman, *Maurice Scève, Poet of Love,* 130–31 (Eng).

Délie 16
"Je preteroys a tous Dieux ma Maistresse"

Donaldson-Evans, *Love's Fatal Glance,* 105–6 (Eng).

Délie 17
"Plus tost seront Rhosne, et Saone desjoinctz"

Alfred Glauser, " 'Souffrir non souffrir': Formule de l'écriture scévienne," in Kirtzman, ed., *Le Signe et le texte,* 44–48 (Fr).

Délie 22
"Comme Hecaté tu me feras errer"

Baker, *Narcissus and the Lover,* 28–29 (Eng).

Coleman, *Maurice Scève, Poet of Love,* 138–40 (Eng).

Dorothy G. Colemand, "Scève's Choice of the Name 'Délie,'" *FS* 18 (January 1964): 10–11 (Eng).

Lance K. Donaldson-Evans, "Love Divine, All Loves Excelling," *FrF* 14 (January 1989): 8–9 (Eng).

Edwin Duval, " 'Comme Hecaté': Mythography and the Macrocoasm in an Epigramme by Maurice Scéve," *BHR* 41 (January 1979): 7–22 (Eng).

Guy Mermier and Yvette Boilly-Widmer, *Explication de texte, théorie et pratique* (Glenview, Ill.: Scott, Foresman, 1972), 68–72 (Fr).

Rigolot, *Poétique et onomastique,* 112–14 (Fr).

H. Weber, *La Création poétique au XVIe siècle en France,* 210–11 (Fr).

Délie 24
"Quand l'oeil aux champs est d'esclairs esblouy"

Donaldson-Evans, *Love's Fatal Glance,* 130–32 (Eng).

Délie 26
"Je voy en moy estre ce Mont Forvière"

Lance K. Donaldson-Evans, "Love Divine, All Loves Excelling," *FrF* 14 (January 1989): 9–10 (Eng).

Délie 27
"Voyant soubdain rougir la blanche neige"

Baker, *Narcissus and the Lover,* 85–86 (Eng).

Délie 30
"Des yeulx, ausquelz s'enniche le Soleil"

Donald-Evans, *Love's Fatal Glance,* 106–7 (Eng).

Jane Drake-Brockman, "Scève, the Snake and the Herb," *FS* 33 (April 1979): 129–36 (Eng).

Peter Sharrat, "Scève, the Snake and the Herb Again," *FS* 35 (July 1981): 257–60 (Eng).

Délie 31
"Les Tristes Sœurs plaingnoient l'antique offense"

Thomas Greene, "Styles of Experience in Scève's 'Délie,'" *YFS*, no. 47 (1972): 61–62 (Eng).

Délie 33
"Tant est Nature en volenté puissante"

Baker, *Narcissus and the Lover,* 84–85 (Eng).

François Lecercle, "Du Phénix au pot au feu: Les Emblèmes de 'Délie,'" *Europe* 64 (November–December 1986): 98–100 (Fr).

Délie 42
"Si doulcement le venin de tes yeulx"

Donaldson-Evans, *Love's Fatal Glance,* 123–24 (Eng).

Délie 46
"Si le desir, image de la chose"

Coleman, *Maurice Scève, Poet of Love,* 172–73 (Eng).

Doranne Fenoaltea, "Three Animal Images in the 'Délie': New Perspectives," *BHR* 34 (September 1972): 415–16, 425 (Eng).

Délie 48
"Si onc la Mort fut tresdoulcement chere"

Dorothy Coleman, "Scève: A Virile Intellect Aereated by Sensibility," in Bayley and Coleman, eds., *The Equilibrium of Wit,* 25–26 (Eng).

Délie 50
"Perseverant en l'obstination"

Beverley Ormerod, "Scève's 'Délie' and the Mythographers' Diana," *SFr* 23 (January–April 1979): 86–87 (Eng).

Délie 57
"Comme celuy, qui jouant à la Mousche"

Baker, *Narcissus and the Lover,* 101–3 (Eng).

Délie 58
"Quand j'apperceu au serain de ses yeulx"

Coleman, *Maurice Scève, Poet of Love,* 163–67 (Eng).

Délie 59
"Taire, ou parler soit permis a chascun"

Dorothy G. Coleman, "Scève's Choice of the Name 'Délie,' " *FS* 18 (January 1964: 11–12 (Eng).

Délie 60
"Si c'est Amour, pourquoy m'occit-il doncques"

Baker, *Narcissus and the Lover,* 2–5 (Eng).

Colemane, *Maurice Scève, Poet of Love,* 77–79 (Eng).

Dorothy G. Coleman, "Les emblesmes dans la 'Délie' de Maurice Scève," *SFr* 8 (January–April 1964): 13–14 (Fr).

Jo Ann Della Neva, "Scattered Rhymes: Petrarchan Fragments in Scève's 'Délie 60,' " *FS* 41 (April 1987): 129–40 (Eng).

Gisèle Mathieu-Castellani, "Emblèmes de la mort," *Europe* 64 (November–December 1986): 128–31 (Fr).

Délie 64
"Des Montz hautains descendent les ruisseaulx"

Dorothy G. Coleman, "Sound-Play and Verbal Delight in Scève's 'Délie,' " *FS* 30 (July 1976): 260–61 (Eng).

Délie 70
"Decrepité en vieilles esperances"

Beverley Ormerod, "Scève's 'Délie' and the Mythographers' Diana," *SFr* 23 (January–April 1979): 86–87 (Eng).

Délie 75
"Pour me despendre en si heureux service"

Dorothy Coleman, "Scève: A Virile Intellect Aereated by Sensibility," Bayley and Coleman, eds., *The Equilibrium of Wit,* 18–20 (Eng).

Délie 77
"Au Caucasus de mon souffrir lyé"

Coleman, *Maurice Scève, Poet of Love,* 151–53 (Eng).

Alfred Glauser, " 'Souffrir non souffrir': Formule de l'écriture scévienne," in Kritzman, ed., *Le Signe et le texte,* 43–44 (Fr).

Lori Walters, "Un Mythe fondamental de la 'Délie'—Maurice Scève—La Prométhée," *RR* 80 (March 1989): 172–74 (Fr).

H. Weber, *A travers le seizième siècle,* 74–75 (Fr).

Délie 79
"L'Aulbe estaingnoit Estoilles a foison"

Coleman, *Maurice Scève, Poet of Love,* 158–60 (Eng).

Thomas Greene, "Styles of Experience in Scève's 'Délie,' " *YFS,* no. 47 (1972): 72–74 (Eng).

Hans Staub, "Le Thème de la lumière chez Maurice Scève," *CAIEF* 20 (May 1968): 126–27 (Fr).

Délie 80
"Au recevoir l'aigu de tes esclairs"

Donaldson-Evans, *Love's Fatal Glance,* 132–34 (Eng).

Délie 84
"Ou le contraire est certes vérité"

Baker, *Narcissus and the Lover,* 87–88 (Eng).

SCEVE, MAURICE, *Délie 92* "Sur nostre chef gettant Phebus ses rayz"

Délie 92
"Sur nostre chef gettant Phebus ses rayz"

Donaldson-Evans, *Love's Fatal Glance,* 136–37 (Eng).

Dorrane Fenoaltea, "Establishing Contrasts: An Aspect of Scève's Use of Petrarch's Poetry in the 'Délie,'" *SFr* 19 (January–April 1975): 26–27 (Eng).

Délie 95
"Ton hault sommet, ô Mont a Venus saincte"

Quignard, *La Parole de Délie,* 73–74 (Fr).

Délie 96
"Te voyant rire avecques si grand' grace"

Baker, *Narcissus and the Lover,* 88–89 (Eng).

Délie 98
"Le Dieu Imberbe au giron de Thetys"

Thomas Greene, "Styles of Experience in Scève's 'Délie'" *YFS,* no. 47 (1972): 59–61 (Eng).

Délie 99
"Fusse le moins de ma calamité"

Baker, *Narcissus and the Lover,* 89–90 (Eng).

Délie 100
"L'Oysiveté des delicates plumes"

Coleman, *Maurice Scève, Poet of Love,* 167–69 (Eng).

Délie 106
"J'attens ma paix du repos de la nuict"

Dorothy G. Coleman, "Scève's Choice of the Name 'Délie,'" *FS* 18 (January 1964): 14 (Eng).

Della Neva, *Song and Counter-Song,* 53–59 (Eng).

Donaldson-Evans, *Love's Fatal Glance,* 141–42 (Eng).

SCEVE, MAURICE, *Délie 126* "A l'embrunir des heures tenebreuses"

Délie 112
"Longue silence, ou je m'avainissoys"

Fenoaltea, *"Si haulte architecture,"* 71–72, 74 (Eng).

Quignard, *La Parole de Délie,* 70–71 (Fr).

Donald Stone, "Scève's Emblems," *RR* 60 (April 1969): 100–101 (Eng).

Délie 114
"O ans, ô moys, sepmaines, jours, et heures"

Coleman, *Maurice Scève, Poet of Love,* 106–8 (Eng).

Délie 115
"Par ton regard severement piteux"

Donaldson-Evans, *Love's Fatal Glance,* 127–28 (Eng).

Délie 118
"Le Hault penser de mes frailes desirs"

Baker, *Narcissus and the Lover,* 96–97, 123–24 (Eng).

Coleman, *Maurice Scève, Poet of Love,* 153–55 (Eng).

Délie 120
"L'Aigle des Cieux pour proye descendit"

Baker, *Narcissus and the Lover,* 99–100 (Eng).

Délie 124
"Si Apollo restrainct ses raiz dorez"

Della Neva, *Song and Counter-Song,* 45–50 (Eng).

Délie 126
"A l'embrunir des heures tenebreuses"

Coleman, *Maurice Scève, Poet of Love,* 125–27 (Eng).

Dorothy G. Coleman, "Scève's Choice of the Name 'Délie' " *FS* 18 (January 1964): 3–4 (Eng).

SCEVE, MAURICE, *Délie 129* "Le jour passé de ta doulce presence"

Dorothy G. Coleman, "Some Notes on Scève and Petrarch," *FS* 14 (October 1960): 297–99 (Eng).

Délie 129
"Le jour passé de ta doulce presence"

Coleman, *Maurice Scève, Poet of Love,* 169–71 (Eng).

Lance K. Donaldson-Evans, "Love Divine, All Loves Excelling," *FrF* 14 (January 1989): 10–11 (Eng).

Beverley Ormerod, "Délie and the Hare," *FS* 30 (October 1976): 385–92 (Eng).

Joseph Pivato, "Maurice Scève's 'Délie,' Unpetrarchan and Hermetic," *SFr* 27 (January–April 1983): 20–21 (Eng).

Quignard, *La Parole de Délie,* 77–80 (Fr).

Délie 131
"Delia ceincte, hault sa cotte attournée"

Donaldson-Evans, *Love's Fatal Glance,* 109–11 (Eng).

Délie 140
"A Cupido je fes maintz traictz briser"

Donaldson-Evans, *Love's Fatal Glance,* 111–12 (Eng).

Délie 141
"Comme des raiz du Soleil gracieux"

Baker, *Narcissus and the Lover,* 67–68 (Eng).

Délie 143
"Le Souvenir, ame de ma pensée"

Coleman, *Maurice Scève, Poet of Love,* 146–48 (Eng).

Délie 144
"En toy je vis, ou que tu sois absente"

Nancy Frelick, "Absence in Presence, Death in Life: A Study of the Poetics of Desire in Scève's 'Délie' " *RR* 80 (May 1989): 350–62 (Eng).

H. Weber, *La Création poétique au XVIe siècle en France*, 195–96 (Fr).

Délie 148
"Voy que l'Hyver tremblant en son sejour"

Coleman, *Maurice Scève, Poet of Love*, 181–82 (Eng).

Délie 149
"Et Helicon, ensemble et Parnasus"

Doranne Fenoaltea, "Establishing Contrasts: An Aspect of Scève's Use of Petrarch's Poetry in the 'Délie' " *SFr* 19 (January–April 1975): 23–24 (Eng).

Délie 150
"Ou sa bonté par vertu attractive"

Coleman, *Maurice Scève, Poet of Love*, 111–12 (Eng).

Beverley Ormerod, "The Ivy Emblem in Scève's Dizain 150," *AJFS* 17 (January–April 1980): 58–64 (Eng).

Délie 156
"Estre ne peult le bien de mon malheur"

Dorothy Coleman, "The Poetic Sensibility of Scève," in Nash, ed., *Pre-Pléiade Poetry*, 131–32 (Eng).

Délie 158
"L'air tout esmeu de la tant longue peine"

Dorothy G. Coleman, "Some Notes on Scève and Petrarch," *FS* 14 (October 1960): 293–94 (Eng).

SCEVE, MAURICE, *Délie 159* "Si de sa main ma fatale ennemye"

Délie 159
"Si de sa main ma fatale ennemye"

Donald Stone, "Scève's Emblems," *RR* 60 (April 1969): 98–99 (Eng).

Délie 161
"Seul avec moy, elle avec sa partie"

Baker, *Narcissus and the Lover,* 78–81 (Eng).

Coleman, *Maurice Scève, Poet of Love,* 145–46 (Eng).

Joseph Pivato, "Maurice Scève's 'Délie,' Unpetrarchan and Hermetic," *SFr* 27 (January–April 1983): 19–20 (Eng).

Délie 164
"Comme corps mort vagant en haulte Mer"

Baker, *Narcissus and the Lover,* 125–27 (Eng).

Coleman, *Maurice Scève, Poet of Love,* 175–76 (Eng).

Délie 165
"Mes pleurs clouantz au front ses tristes yeulx"

Dorothy Coleman, "The Poetic Sensibility of Scève," in Nash, ed., *Pre-Pléiade Poetry,* 134 (Eng).

Délie 168
"Toutes les fois qu'en mon entendement"

Coleman, *Maurice Scève, Poet of Love,* 99–103 (Eng).

Doranne, Fenoaltea, "Three Animal Images in the 'Délie': New Perspectives," *BHR* 34 (September 1972): 422–26 (Eng).

Délie 174
"Encores vit ce peu de l'esperance"

Coleman, *Maurice Scève, Poet of Love,* 173–74 (Eng).

SCEVE, MAURICE, *Délie 199* "Sans lesion le Serpent Royal vit"

Délie 175
"Voy le jour cler ruyner en tenebres"

Coleman, *Maurice Scève, Poet of Love,* 185–86 (Eng).

H. Weber, *La Création poétique au XVIe siècle en France,* 198–99 (Fr).

Délie 176
"Diane on voit ses deux cornes jecter"

Donaldson-Evans, *Love's Fatal Glance,* 142–44 (Eng).

Délie 179
"Amour me presse, et me force de suyvre"

Jerry C. Nash, "Logic and Lyric: Poetic Closure in Scève's 'Délie' " *FS* 38 (October 1984): 386–88 (Eng).

Délie 186
"Je m'esjouys quand votre face se monstre"

Donaldson-Evans, *Love's Fatal Glance,* 112–13 (Eng).

Délie 195
"Desir, souhait, esperance, et plaisir"

Joseph Pivato, "Maurice Scève's 'Délie,' Unpetrarchan and Hermetic," *SFr* 27 (January–April 1983): 24–27 (Eng).

Délie 197
"Doulce ennemye, en qui ma dolente ame"

Donaldson-Evans, *Love's Fatal Glance,* 113–15 (Eng).

Délie 199
"Sans lesion le Serpent Royal vit"

H. Weber, *La Création poétique au XVIe siècle en France,* 177–78 (Fr).

SCEVE, MAURICE, *Délie 200* "Phebé luysant par ce Globe terrestre"

Délie 200
"Phebé luysant par ce Globe terrestre"

Coleman, *Maurice Scève, Poet of Love,* 174–75 (Eng).

Doranne Fenoaltea, "Establishing Contrasts: An Aspect of Scève's Use of Petrarch's Poetry in the 'Délie'" *SFr* 19 (January–April 1975): 20–22 (Eng).

Délie 201
"Soubz doulx penser ie me voy congeler"

Doranne Fenoaltea, "Establishing Contrasts: An Aspect of Scève's Use of Petrarch's Poetry in the 'Délie'" *SFr* 19 (January–April 1975): 22–23 (Eng).

Délie 204
"Ce hault desir de doulce pipperie"

Coleman, *Maurice Scève, Poet of Love,* 84 –86 (Eng).

Délie 207
"Je m'asseurois, non tant de liberté"

Donaldson-Evans, *Love's Fatal Glance,* 128–29 (Eng).

Délie 212
"Tes beaulx yeulx clers fouldroyamment luisantz

Baker, *Narcissus and the Lover,* 42–42 (Eng).

Dorothy G. Coleman, "Sound-Play and Verbal Delight in Scève's 'Délie'" *FS* 30 (July 1976): 259–60 (Eng).

Donaldson-Evans, *Love's Fatal Glance,* 134–35 (Eng).

Délie 213
"Si droit n'estoit, qu'il ne fust scrupuleux"

Baker, *Narcissus and the Lover,* 100–101 (Eng).

Délie 224
"Nouvelle amour, nouvelle affection"

Fenoaltea, *"Si haulte architecture,"* 71–72 (Eng).

Doranne Fenoaltea, "Establishing Contrasts: An Aspect of Scève's Use of Petrarch's Poetry in the 'Délie'" *SFr* 19 (January–April 1975): 27–28 (Eng).

François Rigolot, "Prosodie et sémantique: Une Hypothèse sur le sens des quatrains atypiques dans la 'Délie' de Maurice Scève," in Bayley and Coleman, eds., *The Equilibrium of Wit,* 31–34 (Fr).

Délie 227
"Pour m'efforcer a degluer les yeulx"

Doranne Fenoaltea, "Establishing Contrasts: An Aspect of Scève's Use of Petrarch's Poetry in the 'Délie'" *SFr* 19 (January–April 1975): 25–26 (Eng).

Délie 229
"Dens son poly ce tien Criotal opaque"

Baker, *Narcissus and the Lover,* 69–71 (Eng).

Délie 230
"Quand ie te vy orner ton chef doré"

Baker, *Narcissus and the Lover,* 54–56 (Eng).

Délie 231
"Incessament mon grief martyre tire"

Coleman, *Maurice Scève, Poet of Love,* 103–6 (Eng).

Délie 235
"Au moins toy, clere et heureuse fontaine"

Baker, *Narcissus and the Lover,* 47–49 (Eng).

Dorothy G. Coleman, "Some Notes on Scève and Petrarch," *FS* 14 (October 1960): 302 (Eng).

Délie 236
"Bienheureux champs et unbrageux costaulx"

Dorothy G. Coleman, "Some Notes on Scève and Petrarch," *FS* 14 (October 1960): 302–3 (Eng).

Délie 243
"Ces tiens, non yeulx, mais estoilles celestes"

Doranne Fenoaltea, "Establishing Contrasts: An Aspect of Scève's Use of Petrarch's Poetry in the 'Délie'" *SFr* 19 (January–April 1975): 28–29 (Eng).

Délie 253
"Par tes vertuz excellentement rares"

Cynthia Skenazi, "La mise en jeu politique dans la 'Délie'" *BHR* 52 (June 1990): 303–4 (Fr).

Délie 254
"Si le blanc pur est Foy immaculée"

Cynthia Skenazi, "La Mise en jeu politique dans la 'Délie'" *BHR* 52 (June 1990): 293–307 (Fr).

Délie 255
"De la clere unde yssant hors Cytharée"

Diane Cook, "The Political Dizains of the 'Délie'" *BHR* 29 (May 1967): 348–49 (Eng).

Délie 259
"De toute mer tout long, et large espace"

Coleman, *Maurice Scève, Poet of Love,* 184–85 (Eng).

Délie 262
"Je vois cherchant les lieux plus solitaires"

Doranne Fenoaltea, "The Poet in Nature: Sources of Scève's 'Délie' in Petrarch's 'Rime'" *FS* 27 (July 1973): 265–69 (Eng).

Délie 267
"Au doulx record de son nom je me sens"

Coleman, *Maurice Scève, Poet of Love,* 108–9 (Eng).

Jerry C. Nash, "Logic and Lyric: Poetic Closure in Scève's 'Délie' " *FS* 38 (October 1984): 388–89 (Eng).

Délie 269
"Ces deux Soleilz nuisamment penetrantz"

Donaldson-Evans, *Love's Fatal Glance,* 137–39 (Eng).

Délie 270
"Amour lustrant tes sourcilz Hebenins"

Donaldson-Evans, *Love's Fatal Glance,* 115–16 (Eng).

Délie 271
"J'espere, et crains, que l'esperance excede"

Baker, *Narcissus and the Lover,* 103–5 (Eng).

Délie 278
"Qui veult scavoir par commune evidence"

Della Neva, *Song and Counter-Song,* 41–45 (Eng).

Michael Giordana, "Scève's Dizain 278: Advertisement as Retraction," *KRQ* 27, no. 2 (1980): 151–61 (Eng).

Délie 288
"Plus ie poursuis par le discours des yeulx"

Baker, *Narcissus and the Lover,* 58–59 (Eng).

Délie 290
"Comme gelée au monter du Soleil"

Coleman, *Maurice Scève, Poet of Love,* 155–56 (Eng).
Donaldson-Evans, *Love's Fatal Glance,* 116–18 (Eng).

Délie 306
"Ta beaulté fut premier, et doulx Tyrant"

Diane Cook, "The Political 'Dizains' of the 'Délie' " *BHR* 29 (May 1967): 340–41 (Eng).

Délie 307
"Plus ie la voy, plus i'adore sa face"

Baker, *Narcissus and the Lover,* 51–53 (Eng).

Délie 310
"Tu te verras ton yvoire cresper"

Della Neva, *Song and Counter-Song,* 77–84 (Eng).

Jo Anne Della Neva, "Poetry, Metamorphosis, and the Laurel: Ovid, Petrarch, and Scève," *FrF* 7 (September 1982): 203–8 (Eng).

Délie 330
"Au centre heureux, au coeur impenetrable"

Donald Stone, "Scève's Emblems," *RR* 60 (April 1969): 99–100, 102 (Eng).

Délie 335
"Pour la fraischeur, Delie se dormoit"

Baker, *Narcissus and the Lover,* 49–51 (Eng).

Délie 336
"Ne cuydez point entre vous, qui suyvistes"

Fenoaltea, "*Si haulte architecture,*" 164–65 (Eng).

Délie 341
"Quasi moins vraye alors ie l'apperçoy"

Baker, *Narcissus and the Lover,* 108–10 (Eng).

Délie 344
"Leuth resonnant, et le doulx son des cordes"

Quignard, *La Parole de Délie,* 65–68 (Eng).

Délie 346
"A si hault bien de tant saincte amytié"

Coleman, *Maurice Scève, Poet of Love,* 6–7, 10–12 (Eng).

Délie 348
"Par ce penser tempestant ma pensée"

Diane Cook, "The Political Dizains of the 'Délie,' " *BHR* 29 (May 1967): 353–54 (Eng).

Délie 352
"Non moins ardoir je me sens en l'absence"

Doranne Fenoaltea, "Three Animal Images in the 'Délie': New Perspectives," *BHR* 34 (September 1972): 416–18, 425 (Eng).

Délie 353
"Sa vertu veult estre aymée et servie"

Coleman, *Maurice Scève, Poet of Love,* 132–34 (Eng).
Dorothy G. Coleman, "Scève's Choice of the Name 'Délie' " *FS* 18 (January 1964): 5–7 (Eng).

Délie 355
"L'Aulbe venant pour nous rendre apparent"

Fenoaltea, *"Si haulte architecture,"* 48–49, 51 (Eng).

Délie 356
"Quand Titan a sué le long du jour"

Della Neva, *Song and Counter-Song,* 59–68 (Eng).
Fenoaltea, *"Si haulte architecture,"* 48–49, 51 (Eng).

SCEVE, MAURICE, *Délie 362* "Ne du passé la recente memoyre"

Délie 362
"Ne du passé la recente memoyre"

Jerry C. Nash, "Logic and Lyric: Poetic Closure in Scève's 'Délie' " *FS* 38 (October 1984): 392–95 (Eng).

Délie 365
"La Lune au plein par sa clarté puissante"

Hans Staub, "Le Thème de la lumière chez Maurice Scève," *CAIEF* 20 (May 1968): 127–28 (Fr).

Délie 367
"Assez plus long, qu'un siècle platonique"

Coleman, *Maurice Scève, Poet of Love,* 112–14, 176–77 (Eng).

Ida Fasel, "Scève's 'Délie' 367, 7–10," *Expl* 23 (March 1965): 8–9 (Eng).

Joseph Pivato, "Maurice Scève's 'Délie,' Unpetrarchan and Hermetic," *SFr* 27 (January–April 1983): 22–23 (Eng).

Délie 372
"Tu m'es le Cedre encontre le venin"

Coleman, *Maurice Scève, Poet of Love,* 149–51 (Eng).

Donaldson-Evans, *Love's Fatal Glance,* 124–26 (Eng).

Délie 373
"A son aspect mon oeil reveremment"

Coleman, *Maurice Scève, Poet of Love,* 91–92 (Eng).

Délie 376
"Tu es le Corps, *Dame, et je suis ton umbre*"

Coleman, *Maurice Scève, Poet of Love,* 137–38 (Eng).

Dorothy G. Coleman, "Scève's Choice of the Name 'Délie' " *FS* 18 (January 1964): 5–7 (Eng).

Délie 378
"La Blanche Aurore à peine finyssoit"

Baker, *Narcissus and the Lover,* 132–34 (Eng).

Coleman, *Maurice Scève, Poet of Love,* 157–60 (Eng).

Doranne Fenoaltea, "Establishing Contrasts: An Aspect of Scève's Use of Petrarch's Poetry in the 'Délie' " *SFr* 19 (January–April 1975): 30–31 (Eng).

Fenoaltea, *"Si haulte architecture,"* 174–75 (Eng).

Délie 385
"Dessus ce Mont, qui la Gaule descouvre"

Doranne Fenoaltea, "The Poet in Nature: Sources of Scève's 'Délie' in Petrarch's 'Rime' " *FS* (July 1973): 258–60 (Eng).

Fenoaltea, *"Si haulte architecture,* 49–51 (Eng).

Délie 386
"Quand Apollo après l'Aulbe vermeille"

Donaldson-Evans, *Love's Fatal Glance,* 139–40 (Eng).

Fenoaltea, *"Si haulte architecture,"* 49–51 (Eng).

Délie 388
"Ce doulx venin, qui de tes yeulx distille"

Baker, *Narcissus and the Lover,* 42–44 (Eng).

Coleman, *Maurice Scève, Poet of Love,* 123–24 (Eng).

Della Neva, *Song and Counter-Song,* 25–32 (Eng).

Doranne Fenoaltea, "Establishing Contrasts: An Aspect of Scève's Use of Petrarch's Poetry in the 'Délie' " *SFr* 19 (January–April 1975): 18–19 (Eng).

Délie 389
"Elle a le coeur en si hault lieu assis"

Diane Cook, "The Political Dizains of the 'Délie' " *BHR* 29 (May 1967): 351–52 (Eng).

SCEVE, MAURICE, *Délie 390* "Toutes les fois que je voy eslever"

Délie 390
"Toutes les fois que je voy eslever"

Donaldson-Evans, *Love's Fatal Glance*, 118–19 (Eng).

Délie 408
"Quand Mort aura, après long endurer"

Coleman, *Maurice Scève, Poet of Love*, 188–90 (Eng).

Alfred Glauser, " 'Souffrir non souffrir': Formule de l'écriture scévienne," in Kritzman, ed., *Le Signe et le texte*, 42–43 (Fr).

Délie 409
"Apperceuant cest Ange en forme humaine"

Baker, *Narcissus and the Lover*, 97–98 (Eng).

Délie 412
"Mont costoyant le fleuve et la cité"

Doranne Fenoaltea, "The Poet in Nature: Sources of Scève's 'Délie' in Petrarch's 'Rime' " *FS* 27 (July 1973): 260–62 (Eng).

Délie 414
"Plaisant repos du sejour solitaire"

Doranne Fenoaltea, "The Poet in Nature: Sources of Scève's 'Délie' in Petrarch's 'Rime' " *FS* 27 (July 1973): 260–62 (Eng).

Délie 415
"Quant je te vy, miroir de ma pensée"

W. Blandford Kay, "Scève's 'Délie 415' " *Expl* 23 (May 1965): 6–7 (Eng).

Marie-Claire Wrage, "Scève's 'Délie 415' " *Expl* 25 (September 1966): 14–15 (Eng).

Délie 417
"Fleuve rongeant pour t'attiltrer le nom"

Coleman, *Maurice Scève, Poet of Love,* 121–23 (Eng).

Della Neva, *Song and Counter-Song,* 32–38 (Eng).

Doranne Fenoaltea, "Establishing Contrasts: An Aspect of Scève's Use of Petrarch's Poetry in the 'Délie'" *SFr* 19 (January–April 1975): 19–20 (Eng).

Délie 422
"Touché au vif et de ma conscience"

Beverley Ormerod, "Scève's 'Délie' and the Mythographers' Diana," *SFr* 23 (January–April 1979): 87–88 (Eng).

Délie 423
"Respect du lieu, soulacieux esbat"

Coleman, *Maurice Scève, Poet of Love,* 179 (Eng).

Dorothy G. Coleman, "Some Notes on Scève and Petrarch," *FS* 14 (October 1960): 299–301 (Eng).

Doranne Fenoaltea, "The Poet in Nature: Sources of Scève's 'Délie' in Petrarch's 'Rime'" *FS* 27 (July 1973): 262–65 (Eng).

Délie 424
"De corps tresbelle et d'ame bellissime"

Donaldson-Evans, *Love's Fatal Glance,* 119–21 (Eng).

Doranne Fenoaltea, "The Final Dizains of Scève's 'Délie' and the 'Dialogo d'Amore' of Sperone Speroni," *SFr* 20 (May–August 1976): 204–5 (Eng).

Délie 425
"Bien que ie sache amour, et ialousie"

Doranne Fenoaltea, "The Final Dizains of Scève's 'Délie' and the 'Dialogo d'Amore' of Sperone Speroni," *SFr* 20 (May–August 1976): 205–6 (Eng).

Délie 426
"Finablement prodigue d'esperance"

Doranne Fenoaltea, "The Final Dizains of Scève's 'Délie' and the 'Dialogo d'Amore' of Sperone Speroni," *SFr* 20 (May–August 1976): 206–7 (Eng).

Délie 428
"Quoy que ce soit, amour, ou ialousie"

Doranne Fenoaltea, "The Final Dizains of Scève's 'Délie' and the 'Dialogo d'Amore' of Sperone Speroni," *SFr* 20 (May–August 1976): 207–8 (Eng).

Délie 430
"Quoy q'a malheur ie vueille attribuer"

Doranne Fenoaltea, "The Final Dizains of Scève's 'Délie' and the 'Dialogo d'Amore' of Sperone Speroni," *SFr* 20 (May–August 1976): 208–9 (Eng).

Délie 431
"Respect de toy me rendant tout indigne"

Doranne Fenoaltea, "The Final Dizains of Scève's 'Délie' and the 'Dialogo d'Amore' of Sperone Speroni," *SFr* 20 (May–August 1976): 209 (Eng).

Délie 433
"Je m'en esloigne, et souvent m'en absente"

Doranne Fenoaltea, "The Final Dizains of Scève's 'Délie' and the 'Dialogo d'Amore' of Sperone Speroni," *SFr* 20 (May–August 1976): 210–12 (Eng).

Délie 434
"Ainsi absent la memoyre posée"

Doranne Fenoaltea, "The Final Dizains of Scève's 'Délie' and the 'Dialogo d'Amore' of Sperone Speroni," *SFr* 20 (May–August 1976): 210–12 (Eng).

Délie 436
"Incessament travaillant en moy celle"

Diane Cook, "The Political 'Dizains' of the 'Délie' " *BHR* 29 (May 1967): 340–41 (Eng).

Doranne Fenoaltea, "The Final Dizains of Scève's 'Délie' and the 'Dialogo d'Amore' of Sperone Speroni," *SFr* 20 (May–August 1976): 213–15 (Eng).

SCEVE, MAURICE, *Délie 444* "Nature au Ciel, mon Peripatetique"

Délie 439
"Bien que raison soit nourrice de l'ame"

Doranne Fenoaltea, "The Final Dizains of Scève's 'Délie' and the 'Dialogo d'Amore' of Speronc Speroni," *SFr* 20 (May–August 1976): 215–16 (Eng).

Délie 440
"Resplendissantz les doulx rayz de ta grace"

Doranne Fenoaltea, "The Final Dizains of Scève's 'Délie' and the 'Dialogo d'Amore' of Spcrone Speroni," *SFr* 20 (May–August 1976): 216–17 (Eng).

Délie 441
"Donques apres mille trauaulx et mille"

Doranne Fenoaltea, "The Final Dizains of Scève's 'Délie' and the 'Dialogo d'Amore' of Sperone Speroni," *SFr* 20 (May–August 1976): 217–18 (Eng).

Délie 442
"Pourroit donc bien (non que ie le demande)"

Doranne Fenoaltea, "The Final Dizains of Scève's 'Délie' and the 'Dialogo d'Amore' of Sperone Speroni," *SFr* 20 (May–August 1976): 219–20 (Eng).

Délie 443
"Combien qu'a nous soit cause le Soleil"

Coleman, *Maurice Scève, Poet of Love,* 156–57 (Eng).

Donaldson-Evans, *Love's Fatal Glance,* 140–41 (Eng).

Doranne Fenoaltea, "The Final Dizains of Scève's 'Délie' and the 'Dialogo d'Amore' of Sperone Speroni," *SFr* 20 (May–August 1976): 220–21 (Eng).

Délie 444
"Nature au Ciel, mon Peripatetique"

Doranne Fenoaltea, "The Final Dizains of Scève's 'Délie' and the 'Dialogo d'Amore' of Sperone Speroni," *SFr* 20 (May–August 1976): 221–22 (Eng).

SCEVE, MAURICE, *Délie 445* "Ainsi qu'Amour en la face au plus beau"

Délie 445
"Ainsi qu'Amour en la face au plus beau"

Terence Cave, "Scève's 'Délie': Correcting Petrarch's Errors," in Nash, ed., *Pre-Pléiade Poetry,* 120–21 (Eng).

Doranne Fenoaltea, "The Final Dizains of Scève's 'Délie' and the 'Dialogo d'Amore' of Sperone Speroni," *SFr* 20 (May–August 1976): 222–23 (Eng).

Délie 446
"Rien, ou bien peu, faudroit pour me dissoudre"

Doranne Fenoaltea, "The Final Dizains of Scève's 'Délie' and the 'Dialogo d'Amore' of Sperone Speroni," *SFr* 20 (May–August 1976): 223–24 (Eng).

Jerry C. Nash, "Logic and Lyric: Poetic Closure in Scève's 'Délie' " *FS* 38 (October 1984): 389–90 (Eng).

Délie 447
"Si tu t'enquiers pourquoy sur mon tombeau"

Baker, *Narcissus and the Lover,* 135–37 (Eng).

François Cornilliat, "Le Discours et les signes: Lecture du dizain 447 de 'Delie' " *Europe* 64 (November–December 1986): 116–24 (Fr).

Gisèle Mathieu-Castellani, "Emblèmes de la mort," *Europe* 64 (November–December 1986): 130–34 (Fr).

Délie 449
"Flamme si saincte en son cler durera"

Baker, *Narcissus and the Lover,* 135–39 (Eng).

Della Neva, *Song and Counter-Song,* 96–98 (Eng).

Lance K. Donaldson-Evans, "Love Divine, All Loves Excelling," *FrF* 14 (Jan 1989): 13–14 (Eng).

"Le Front"

Robert D. Cottrell, "Scève's 'Blasons' and the Logic of the Gaze," *ECr* 28 (Summer 1988): 69–70 (Eng).

SCEVE, MAURICE, "Le Sourcil"

"La Gorge"

Robert D. Cottrell, "Scève's 'Blasons' and the Logic of the Gaze," *ECr* 28 (Summer 1988): 74–76 (Eng).

"La Larme"

Robert D. Cottrell, "Scève's 'Blasons' and the Logic of the Gaze," *ECr* 28 (Summer 1988): 72–73 (Eng).

"Le Microcosme"

Françoise Rigolot, "Le Figuier et le coudrier: Allégorie et reflexivité dans le 'Microcosme' " *BHR* 49 (January 1987): 7–25 (Fr).

"Microcosme," Book I

Baker, *Narcissus and the Lover,* 62–66 (Eng).

"Non de Venus les ardentz estincelles"

Coleman, *Maurice Scève, Poet of Love,* 44–45 (Eng).

"La Saulsaye"

Ruth Mulhauser, *Maurice Scève* (Boston: Twayne, 1977), 101–3 (Eng).

"Le Soupir"

Robert D. Cottrell, "Scève's 'Blasons' and the Logic of the Gaze," *ECr* 28 (Summer 1988): 73–74 (Eng).

"Le Sourcil"

Robert D. Cottrell, "Scève's 'Blasons' and the Logic of the Gaze," *ECr* 28 (Summer 1988): 70–72 (Eng).

Donaldson-Evans, *Love's Fatal Glance,* 95–99 (Eng).

SCEVE, MAURICE, "Le Souvenir, ame de ma pensée"

"Le Souvenir, ame de ma pensée"

Coleman, *Maurice Scève, Poet of Love,* 146–48 (Eng).

SEGALEN, VICTOR

"Trahison fidèle"

Michel Deguy, "Constèlation," *Europe* 64 (April 1987): 73–74 (Fr).

SEGHERS, PIERRE

"Dans la nuit"

Ian Higgins, "Tradition and Myth in French Resistance Poetry: Reaction or Subversion?" *FMLS* 21 (January 1985): 55–56 (Eng).

SENGHOR, LEOPOLD SEDAR

"L'Absente"

Guibert, *Léopold Sédar Senghor,* 68–71 (Fr).

Lebaud, *Lépold Sédar Senghor,* 47–48 (Fr).

Jean-Luc Steinmetz, "A la rencontre de la reine de Saba," in Leuwers, ed., *Léopold Sédar Senghor,* 218–22 (Fr).

"A l'appel de la race de Saba"

Guibert, *L'éopold Sédar Senghor,* 56–58 (Fr).

Spleth, *Léopold Sédar Senghor,* 76–77 (Eng).

Jean-Luc Steinmetz, "A la rencontre de la reine de Saba," in Leuwers, ed., *Léopold Sédar Senghor,* 212–18 (Eng).

"A New York"

Alain Baudot, "Ré-écouter 'A New York' de Senghor," *ELit* 7 (December 1974): 369–79 (Fr).

Jacqueline Leiner, "Etude comparative des structures de l'imaginaire d'Aimé Césaire et de Léopold Sédar Senghor," *CAIEF* 30 (May 1978): 209–24 (Fr).

Mezu, *The Poetry of L. S. Senghor,* 59–65 (Eng).

Spleth, *Lépold Sédar Senghor,* 121–22 (Eng).

"Aux soldats Négro-Américains"

Mezu, *The Poetry of L. S. Senghor,* 41–42 (Eng).

"Aux tirailleurs sénégalais morts pour la France"

Lebaud, *Léopold Sédar Senghor,* 15–16 (Fr).

Mezu, *The Poetry of L. S. Senghor,* 33–34 (Eng).

"Chaka"

Jean-Louis Joubert, "Sur le 'Chaka' de Léopold Sédar Senghor," *RHL* 88 (March–April 1988): 215–24 (Fr).

Mezu, *The Poetry of L. S. Senghor,* 65–67 (Eng).

"Chant de l'initié"

Martha Climo, "L. S. Senghor's Imagery: An Expression of His Negritude," in *Hommage à Léopold Sédar Senghor, homme de culture* (Paris: Présence Africaine, 1976), 271–72 (Eng).

Lebaud, *Léopold Sédar Senghor,* 51–53 (Fr).

Serge Meitinger, "Les Dimensions de temps et de monde dans le 'Chant de l'initié' " in Leuwers, ed., *Léopold Sédar Senghor,* 121–41 (Fr).

SENGHOR, LEOPOLD SEDAR, "Chant de printemps"

"Chant de printemps"

Spleth, *Léopold Sédar Senghor,* 85–86 (Eng).

"Chants pour Signare"

Elisabeth Cardonne-Arlyck, "Effets de noms," in Leuwers, ed., *Léopold Sédar Senghor,* 36–40 (Fr).

"Congo"

Martha Climo, "L. S. Senghor's Imagery: An Expression of His Negritude," in *Hommage à Léopold Sédar Senghor, homme de culture* (Paris: Présence Africaine, 1976), 272–74 (Eng).

"Désespoir d'un volontaire libre"

Lebaud, *Léopold Sédar Senghor,* 17–20 (Fr).

Spleth, *Léopold Sédar Senghor,* 79–80 (Eng).

"Elégie de minuit"

Guibert, *Léopold Sédar Senghor,* 91–93 (Fr).

Mezu, *The Poetry of L. S. Senghor,* 71–78 (Eng).

Spleth, *Léopold Sédar Senghor,* 126–28 (Eng).

"Elégie des Aligés"

Spleth, *Léopold Sédar Senghor,* 135–38 (Eng).

"Elégie des circoncis"

Guibert, *Léopold Sédar Senghor,* 98–101 (Fr).

Spleth, *Léopold Sédar Senghor,* 128–29 (Eng).

SENGHOR, LEOPOLD SEDAR, "Etait-ce une nuit maghrebine?"

"Elégie des eaux"

Spleth, *Léopold Sédar Senghor,* 129–30 (Eng).

"Elégie des saudades"

Spleth, *Léopold Sédar Senghor,* 132–33 (Eng).

"Elégie pour Aynina Fall"

Spleth, *Léopold Sédar Senghor,* 130–32 (Eng).

"Elégie pour Georges Pompidou"

Spleth, *Léopold Sédar Senghor,* 153–55 (Eng).

"Elégie pour Jean-Marie"

Spleth, *Léopold Sédar Senghor,* 151–52 (Eng).

"Elégie pour la reine de Saba"

Spleth, *Léopold Sédar Senghor,* 155–57 (Eng).

Jean-Luc Seinmetz, "A la rencontre de la reine de Saba,"in Leuwers, ed., *Léopold Sédar Senghor,* 225–37 (Fr).

"Elégie pour Martin Luther King"

Spleth, *Léopold Sédar Senghor,* 152–53 (Eng).

"Epîtres à la Princesse"

Jean-Luc Steinmetz, "A la rencontre de la reine de Saba," in Leuwers, ed., *Léopold Sédar Senghor,* 222–25 (Fr).

"Etait-ce une nuit maghrebine?"

Guibert, *Léopold Sédar Senghor,* 85–86 (Fr).

SENGHOR, LEOPOLD SEDAR, "Femme noire"

"Femme noire"

Sylvia Washington Ba, *The Concept of Negritude in the Poetry of Léopold Sédar Senghor* (Princeton: Princeton University Press, 1973), 132–35 (Eng).

Martha Climo, "L. S. Senghor's Imagery: An Expression of His Negritude," in *Hommage à Léopold Sédar Senghor, homme de culture* (Paris: Présence Africaine, 1976), 256–58 (Eng).

Mezu, *The Poetry of L. S. Senghor,* 20–25 (Eng).

Spleth, *Léopold Sédar Senghor,* 56–57 (Eng).

"L'Homme et la bête"

Sylvia Washington Ba, *The Concept of Negritude in the Poetry of Léopold Sédar Senghor* (Princeton: Princeton University Press, 1973), 135–40 (Eng).

Lebaud, *Léopold Sédar Senghor,* 60 (Fr).

Mezu, *The Poetry of L. S. Senghor,* 55–57 (Eng).

Spleth, *Léopold Sédar Senghor,* 111–12 (Eng).

"In memoriam"

Martha Climo, "L. S. Senghor's Imagery: An Expression of His Negritude," in *Hommage à Léopold Sédar Senghor, homme de culture* Paris: Présence Africaine, 1976), 251–53, 267–68 (Eng).

Daniel Leuwers, "Léopold Sédar Senghor, ou La Naissance au poème," in Leuwers, ed., *Léopold Sédar Senghor,* 22–25 (Fr).

Spleth, *Léopold Sédar Senghor,* 50–52 (Eng).

"Joal"

Martha Climo, 'L. S. Senghor's Imagery: An Expression of His Negritude," in *Hommage à Léopold Sédar Senghor, homme de culture,* (Paris: Présence Africaine, 1976), 259–62 (Eng).

Mezu, *The Poetry of L. S. Senghor,* 18–20 (Eng).

Charles O'Keefe, "Recall in Lépold Sédar Senghor's 'Joal' " *FR* 57 (April 1984): 625–33 (Eng).

SENGHOR, LEOPOLD SEDAR, "Neige sur Paris"

"Le Kaya-Magan"

Mezu, *The Poetry of L. S. Senghor,* 53–55 (Eng).

"Libération"

Spleth, *Léopold Sédar Senghor,* 63–64 (Eng).

"Luxembourg 1939"

Mezu, *The Poetry of L. S. Senghor,* 34–35 (Eng).

"Mais ces routes de l'insomnie"

Guibert, *Léopold Sédar Senghor,* 74–76 (Fr).

"Masque nègre"

Guibert, *Léopold Sédar Senghor,* 36–37 (Fr).

"Le Message"

Spleth, *Léopold Sédar Senghor,* 58–59 (Eng).

"Messages"

Mezu, *The Poetry of L. S. Senghor,* 58–59 (Eng).

"Ndessé"

Martha Climo, "L. S. Senghor's Imagery: An Expression of his Negritude," in *Hommage à Léopold Sédar Senghor, homme de culture* (Paris: Présence Africaine, 1976), 254–56 (Eng).

Lebaud, *Léopold Sédar Senghor,* 14–15 (Fr).

"Neige sur Paris"

Guibert, *Léopold Sédar Senghor,* 44–45 (Fr).

SENGHOR, LEOPOLD SEDAR, "Nuit de Sine"

"Nuit de Sine"

Mezu, *The Poetry of L. S. Senghor,* 16–18 (Eng).

Spleth, *Léopold Sédar Senghor,* 54–55 (Eng).

"Or ce matin"

Elisabeth Cardonne-Arlyck, "Effets de noms," in Leuwers, ed., *Léopold Sédar Senghor,* 33–5 (Fr).

"Par-delà Erôs"

Spleth, *Léopold Sédar Senghor,* 67–68 (Eng).

Poème liminaire
"Hosties noires"

Mezu, *The Poetry of L. S. Senghor,* 29–31 (Eng).

Spleth, *Léopold Sédar Senghor,* 74–75 (Eng).

"Prière aux masques"

Guibert, *Léopold Sédar Senghor,* 40–41 (Fr).

"Prière de paix"

Mezu, *The Poetry of L. S. Senghor,* 43–45 (Eng).

Spleth, *Léopold Sédar Senghor,* 87–88 (Eng).

"Prière des tirailleurs senégalais"

Spleth, *Léopold Sédar Senghor,* 80–81 (Eng).

Mezu, *The Poetry of L. S. Senghor,* 36–38 (Eng).

"Que m'accompagnent kôraset et balafong"

Spleth, *Léopold Sédar Senghor,* 64–67 (Eng).

"Le Retour de l'enfant prodigue"

Martha Climo, "L. S. Senghor's Imagery: An Expression of His Negritude," in *Hommage à Léopold Sédar Senghor, homme de culture* (Paris: Présence Africaine, 1976), 263–65 (Eng).

Spleth, *Léopold Sédar Senghor,* 68–70 (Eng).

"Taga de Mbaye Dijôb"

Mezu, *The Poetry of L. S. Senghor,* 40–41 (Eng).

"Ton visage beauté des temps anciens"

Guibert, *Léopold Sédar Senghor,* 79–81 (Fr).

SPONDE, JEAN DE

Sonnets d'Amour 5
"Je meurs, et les soucis qui sortent du martyre"

Terence Cave, "The Love-Sonnets of Jean de Sponde: A Reconsideration," *FMLS* 3 (January 1967): 53–54 (Eng).

Sonnets d'Amour 7
"Si j'avois comme vous, mignardes colombelles"

Lafay, *La Poésie française du premier XVIIe siècle,* 198–99 (Fr).

Sonnets d'Amour 18
"Ne vous estonnez point si mon esprit, qui passe"

Terence Cave, "The Love-Sonnets of Jean de Sponde: A Reconsideration," *FMLS* 3 (January 1967): 57–58 (Eng).

Sonnets d'Amour 26
"Les Vents grondaient en l'air, les plus sombres nuages"

Gisèle Mathieu-Castellani, "The Poetics of Place: The Space of the Emblem by Sponde," *YFS,* no. 80 (1991): 34–40 (Eng).

"Sonnets de la Mort"

Jean-Claude Carron, "Jean de Sponde: 'Et quel bien de la mort?' ", *FS* 31 (April 1977): 129–38 (Fr).

Sonnets de la Mort 1
"Mortels, qui des mortels avez pris vostre vie"

Edelgard Dubruck, *The Theme of Death in French Poetry of the Middle Ages and the Renaissance* (The Hague: Mouton, 1964), 126–28 (Eng).

Susan Hills, " 'Stances le la mort' and 'Autres sonnets sur le mesme sujet': Losing to the Angel," *FrF* 4 (January 1979): 76 (Eng).

Winn, *Jean de Sponde,* 66–69 (Fr).

Sonnets de la Mort 2
"Mais si faut-il mourir, et la vie orgueilleuse"

Susan Hills, " 'Stances de la mort' and 'Autres sonnets sur le mesme sujet': Losing to the Angel," *FrF* 4 (January 1979): 77–78 (Eng).

Winn, *Jean de Sponde,* 50–64 (Fr).

Sonnets de la Mort 3
"Ha! que j'en voy bien peu songer à ceste mort"

Edelgard Dubruck, *The Theme of Death in French Poetry of the Middle Ages and the Renaissance* (The Hague: Mouton, 1964), 128–29 (Eng).

Susan Hills, " 'Stances de la mort' and 'Autres sonnets sur le mesme sujet': Losing to the Angel," *FrF* 4 (January 1979): 78 (Eng).

Sonnets de la Mort 4
"Pour qui tant de travaux? Pour vous? de qui l'haleine"

Susan Hills, " 'Stances de la mort' and 'Autres sonnets sur le mesme sujet':
Losing to the Angel," *FrF* 4 (January 1979): 78–79 (Eng).

Sonnets de la Mort 5
"Hélas! contez vos jours: les jours qui sont passez"

Susan Hills, " 'Stances de la mort' and 'Autres sonnets sur le mesme sujet':
Losing to the Angel," *FrF* 4 (January 1979): 79 (Eng).

Winn, *Jean de Sponde,* 25–37 (Fr).

Sonnets de la Mort 6
"Tout le monde se plaint de la cruelle envie"

Susan Hills, " 'Stances de la mort' and 'Autres sonnets sur le mesme sujet':
Losing to the Angel," *FrF* 4 (January 1979): 79–80 (Eng).

Sonnets de la Mort 7
"Tandis que dedans l'air un autre air je respire"

Susan Hills, " 'Stances de la mort' and 'Autres sonnets sur le mesme sujet':
Losing to the Angel," *FrF* 4 (January 1979): 80–81 (Eng).

Sonnets de la Mort 8
"Voulez-vous voir ce traict qui si roide s'eslance"

Susan Hills, " 'Stances de la mort' and 'Autres sonnets sur le mesme sujet':
Losing to the Angel," *FrF* 4 (January 1979): 81–82 (Eng).

Kurt Weinberg, "Verbal Labyrinths in Sponde's 'Stances et sonnets de la
mort,' " *ECr* 16 (Winter 1976): 138–45 (Eng).

SPONDE, JEAN DE, Sonnets de la Mort 9

Sonnets de la Mort 9
"Qui sont, qui sont ceux-là, dont le coeur idolatre"

Calin, *In Defense of French Poetry,* 115–18 (Eng).

Susan Hills, " 'Stances de la mort' and 'Autres sonnets sur le mesme sujet': Losing to the Angel," *FrF* 4 (January 1979): 82–83 (Eng).

Winn, *Jean de Sponde,* 15–16 (Fr).

Sonnets de la Mort 10
"Mais si mon foible corps, qui comme l'eau s'escoule"

Susan Hills, " 'Stances de la mort' and 'Autres sonnets sur le mesme sujet': Losing to the Angel," *FrF* 4 (January 1979): 83–84 (Eng).

Mario Richter, "Sponde: 'Sonnets de la mort' 10," *BHR* 38 (January 1976): 73–76 (Fr).

Sonnets de la Mort 11
"Et quel bien de la Mort? où la vermine ronge"

Laura Durand, "Sponde and Donne: Lens and Prism," *CL* 21 (Fall 1969): 319–36 (Eng).

Sonnets de la Mort 12
"Tout s'enfle contre moy, tout m'assaut, tout me tente"

Edelgard Dubruck, *The Theme of Death in French Poetry of the Middle Ages and the Renaissance* (The Hague: Mouton, 1964), 129–31 (Eng).

Lafay, *La Poésie française du premier XVIIe siècle,* 202–3 (Fr).

"Stances de la Mort"

Susan Hills, " 'Stances de la mort' and 'Autres sonnets sur le mesme sujet': Losing to the Angel," *FrF* 4 (January 1979): 69–75 (Eng).

Stances de la Mort 1
"Mes yeux ne lancez plus vostre point esblouye"

Cave, *Devotional Poetry,* 171–75 (Eng).

Kurt Weinberg, "Verbal Labyrinths in Sponde's 'Stances et sonnets de la mort,' " *ECr* 16 (Winter 1976): 137–41 (Eng).

Stances de la Mort 8
"Et puis c'est ta main qui façonna le monde"

Kurt Weinberg, "Verbal Labyrinths in Sponde's 'Stances et sonnets de la mort,' " *ECr* 16 (Winter 1976): 138–45 (Eng).

Stances de la Mort 16
"Quelle plaine en l'Enfer de ces pointus encombres?"

Kurt Weinberg, "Verbal Labyrinths in Sponde's 'Stances et sonnets de la mort,' " *ECr* 16 (Winter 1976): 146–47 (Eng).

Stances de la Mort 18
"Ton mal, c'est ta prison, et ta prison encore"

Kurt Weinberg, "Verbal Labyrinths in Sponde's 'Stances et sonnets de la mort,' " *ECr* 16 (Winter 1976): 147–48 (Eng).

Stances de la Mort 19
"O la plaisante mort qui nous pousse à la vie"

Kurt Weinberg, "Verbal Labyrinths in Sponde's 'Stances et sonnets de la mort,' " *ECr* 16 (Winter 1976): 148–49 (Eng).

Stances de la Mort 22
"Invisibles beautez, délices invisibles!"

Kurt Weinberg, "Verbal Labyrinths in Sponde's 'Stances et sonnets de la mort,' " *ECr* 16 (Winter 1976): 149–51 (Eng).

SPONDE, JEAN DE, "Stances du sacré banquet"

"Stances du sacré banquet et convive de Jésus-Christ"

Cave, *Devotional Poetry*, 208–11 (Eng).

"Tandis que dedans l'air un autre air je respire"

Winn, *Jean de Sponde*, 39–49 (Fr).

SULLY-PRUDHOMME, ARMAND

"Le Vase brisé"

Howarth and Walton, *Explications*, 175–82 (Eng).

SUPERVIELLE, JULES

"Docilité"

Dubosclard and Dubosclard, *Du surréalisme à la Resistance*, 37–43 (Fr).

"Haute mer"

Broome and Chesters, *The Appreciation of Modern French Poetry (1850–1950)*, 140–42 (Eng).

"Montévidéo"

Broome and Chesters, *The Appreciation of Modern French Poetry (1850–1950)*, 138–40 (Eng).

TAHUREAU, JACQUES

"Si en un lieu solitaire"

H. Weber, *La Création poétique au XVIe siècle en France*, 317–18 (Fr).

TORTEL, JEAN

"Après les saisons de pluies"

Bernard Vargaftig, "Les Vers sont en travail," *Europe* 68 (January–February 1990): 182–83 (Fr).

TOULET, PAUL-JEAN

"Etranger, je sens bon. Cucille-moi sans remords"

Groupe Mu, *Rhétorique de la poésie: Lecture linéaire, lecture tabulaire* (Bruxelles: Editions Complexe, 1977), 230–46 (Fr).

TRELLON, G. DE

"Voicy la belle main et pasle et potelée"

Lafay, *La Poésie française du premier XVIIe siècle,* 219–21 (Fr).

TRISTAN L'HERMITE

"Les Forges D'Antoigné"

Robert T. Corum, "Perceptions of the External World in Tristan L'Hermite," *ECr* 20 (Winter 1980): 78–81 (Eng).

"La Gouvernante importune"

Francis Lawrence, "Tristan L'Hermite's 'La Gouvernante importune': The Structure of a Pastoral Satire," *FrF* 4 (July 1979): 239–48 (Eng).

"La Mer"

Claude Abraham, *Tristan L'Hermite* (Boston: Twayne, 1980), 50–51, 56–57, 58–59 (Eng).

Robert T. Corum, "Perceptions of the External World in Tristan L'Hermite," *ECr* 20 (Winter 1980), 76–78 (Eng).

TRISTAN L'HERMITE, "Miserere"

Doris Guillumette, *La Libre Pensée dans l'œvre de Tristan L'Hermite* (Paris: Nizet, 1972), 157–59 (Fr).

"Miserere"

Claude Abraham, *Tristan L'Hermite* (Boston: Twayne, 1980), 76–77 (Eng).

"Orphée

Jean-Pierre Chauveau, "La Voix des poètes," *LCL* 12 (1990); 202–4 (Fr).

Catherine Grisé, "Italian Sources of Tristan L'Hermite's Poetry," *SFr* 14 (May–August 1970): 289–90 (Eng).

Doris Guillumette, *La Libre Pensée dans l'œuvre de Tristan L'Hermite* (Paris: Nizet, 1972), 161–64 (Fr).

Lapp, *The Brazen Tower,* 99–103 (Eng).

"Les Plaintes d'Acante"

Doris Guillumette, *La Libre Pensée dans l'œuvre de Tristan L'Hermite* (Paris: Nizet, 1972), 148–52 (Fr).

"Pour une excellente beauté qui se mirait"

Lapp, *The Brazen Tower,* 93–95 (Eng).

"Le Promenoir des deux amants"

Claude Abraham, *Tristan L'Hermite* (Boston: Twayne, 1980), 59–61 (Eng).

Doris Guillumette, *La Libre Pensée dans l'œuvre de Tristan L'Hermite* (Paris: Nizet, 1972), 165 (Fr).

Lapp, *The Brazen Tower,* 98–99 (Eng).

"Les Terreurs nocturnes"

Robert T. Corum, "Perceptions of the External World in Tristan L'Hermite," *ECr* 20 (1980): 81–84 (Eng).

TYARD, PONTUS DE

"Au plus haut de l'humain chef"

Eva Kushner, "The Role of Platonic Symbols in the Poetry of Pontus de Tyard," *YFS*, no. 47 (1972): 138–39 (Eng).

"Blond cheveu d'or plus fin et délié"

H. Weber *A travers le seizième siècle,* 75–76 (Fr).

"Caverneuse montagne"

Carron, *Discours de l'errance amoureuse,* 84–86 (Fr).

"Cest or filé, ce marbre, cest yvoire"

Carron, *Discours de l'errance amoureuse,* 117–19 (Fr).

"Chant a son Leut"

Donaldson-Evans, *Love's Fatal Glance,* 86–88 (Eng).

"Chant de chaste amour"

Carron, *Discours de l'errance amoureuse,* 35–36, 114–16 (Fr).

"Dequoy me sert, quand la douleur me presse"

Eva Kushner, "The Role of Platonic Symbols in the Poetry of Pontus de Tyard," *YFS*, no. 47 (1972): 136–37 (Eng).

"Disgrace"

Carron, *Discours de l'errance amoureuse,* 65–67 (Fr).

Kathleen M. Hall, "Pontus de Tyard and his 'Disgrace,'" *ECr* 5 (Summer 1965): 102–9 (Eng).

TYARD, PONTUS DE, "Du Riche oiseau de Junon les cent yeux"

Eva Kushner, "The Role of Platonic Symbols in the Poetry of Pontus de Tyard," *YFS*, no. 47 (1972): 142–44 (Eng).

H. Weber, *A travers le siezième siècle,* 10–12 (Fr).

Henri Weber, "Y a-t-il une poésie hermétique au XVe siècle en France?" *CAIEF* 15 (March 1963): 45–47 (Fr).

"Du Riche oiseau de Junon les cent yeux"

Lapp, *The Brazen Tower,* 19–20 (Eng).

"Elégie à Pierre de Ronsard"

Robert Griffin, "Pontus de Tyard's 'Le Curieux' and the Forbidden Fruit," *ECr* 12 (Fall 1972): 224–25 (Eng).

Lapp, *The Brazen Tower,* 22–23 (Eng).

Errances amoureuses, Book 1, 30
"Doulx de ces yeux le traict qui me foudroye"

André Gendre, "Enfance du sonnet français: Les Premières 'Erreurs amoureuses' de Pontus de Tyard," in Bellenger, ed., *Le Sonnet à la Renaissance,* 51–52 (Fr).

Errances amoureuses, Book 1, 38
"Au temps premier qu'Amour se vint loger"

André Gendre, "Enfance du sonnet français: Les Premières 'Erreurs amoureuses' de Pontus de Tyard," in Bellenger, ed., *Le Sonnet à la Renaissance,* 47–48 (Fr).

Errances amoureuses, Book 1, 55
"J'ay haultement esté recompensé"

André Gendre, "Enfance du sonnet français: Les Premières 'Erreurs amoureuses' de Pontus de Tyard," in Bellenger, ed., *Le Sonnet à la Renaissance,* 45–46 (Fr).

"Favorite"

Carron, *Discours de l'errance amoureuse,* 62–63 (Fr).

TYARD, PONTUS DE, "Un Jour Amour voltigeoit dens tes yeux"

"Le Ferme dueil prenant en mon cœur vie"

Carron, *Discours de l'errance amoureuse,* 57–58 (Fr).

"Les Grenouilles"

Lapp, *The Brazen Tower,* 17–18 (Eng).

"Ha bien permis ma Dame (helas) trop dure"

Carron, *Discours de l'errance amoureuse,* 97–98 (Fr).

"Heureux le mois, heureuse la journée"

Eva Kushner, "The Role of Platonic Symbols in the Poetry of Pontus de Tyard," *YFS,* no. 47 (1972): 134–36 (Eng).

"Idyll of the Roses"

Lapp, *The Brazen Tower,* 16 (Eng).

"Je mesurois pas à pas et la plaine"

Carron, *Discours de l'errance amoureuse,* 83–84 (Fr).

"Je n'ay encor de la sainte eau sceu boire"

Carron, *Discours de l'errance amoureuse,* 25–26 (Fr).

"Je veis rougir son blanc poly ivoire"

Eva Kushner, "The Role of Platonic Symbols in the Poetry of Pontus de Tyard," *YFS,* no. 47 (1972): 133 (Eng).

"Un Jour Amour voltigeoit dens tes yeux"

Donaldson-Evans, *Love's Fatal Glance,* 88–89 (Eng).

511

TYARD, PONTUS DE, "Le Long souffrir de mes morts languissantes"

"Le Long souffrir de mes morts languissantes"

Carron, *Discours de l'errance amoureuse,* 107–8, 117 (Fr).

"Lors que je veis ces cheveux d'or dorer"

Eva Kushner, "The Role of Platonic Symbols in the Poetry of Pontus de Tyard," *YFS,* no. 47 (1972): 128–30 (Eng).

"Mal de guida, las, la sage Déesse"

H. Weber, *A travers le seizième siècle,* 8–10, 76–77 (Fr).

"Mon cueur suyvant la cause de ma peine"

Carron, *Discours de l'errance amoureuse,* 74–76 (Fr).

"Mon oeil aux traits de ta beauté"

Carron, *Discours de l'errance amoureuse,* 43–46 (Fr).

"Mon oeil peu caut buvant alterement"

Carron, *Discours de l'errance amoureuse,* 124–25 (Fr).

"Pere divin, sapience eternelle"

Carron, *Discours de l'errance amoureuse,* 125–26 (Fr).

"Pere du doux repos, Sommeil pere du songe"

H. Weber, *La Création poétique au XVIe siècle en France,* 366–68 (Fr).

"Le Plus ardant de tous les elemens"

Eva Kushner, "The Role of Platonic Symbols in the Poetry of Pontus de Tyard," *YFS,* no. 47 (1972): 131–32 (Eng).

TZARA, TRISTAN, "Circuit total par la lune et par la couleur"

"Le Premier curieux"

Robert Griffin, "Pontus de Tyard's 'Le Curieux' and the Forbidden Fruit," *ECr* 12 (Fall 1972): 214–16, 220–21 (Eng).

"Le Second curieux"

Robert Griffin, "Pontus de Tyard's 'Le Curieux' and the Forbidden Fruit," *ECr* 12 (Fall 1972): 216–17 (Eng).

"Quand le desir de ma haulte pensée"

Carron, *Discours de l'errance amoureuse,* 61–62 (Fr).

"Quand le doux fruit, sur ma foy s'assure"

Carron, *Discours de l'errance amoureuse,* 91–93 (Fr).

"Si follement je me le persuade"

Carron, *Discours de l'errance amoureuse,* 122–24 (Fr).

"Le Solitaire premier"

Robert Griffin, "Pontus de Tyard's 'Le Curieux' and the Forbidden Fruit," *ECr* 12 (Fall 1972): 218–19 (Eng).

"Sur la mort de la petite chienne de Jane, nommée Flore"

Lapp, *The Brazen Tower,* 14–15 (Eng).

TZARA, TRISTAN

"Circuit total par la lune et par la couleur"

Caws, *The Inner Theatre,* 62–64 (Eng).

TZARA, TRISTAN, "Gare"

"Gare"

Caws, *The Inner Theatre,* 58–62 (Eng).

Mary Ann Caws, "Motion, Vision, and Coherence in the Dada Poetry of Tristan Tzara," *FR* 43 (Special Issue 1) (Winter 1970): 3–4 (Eng).

VALERY, PAUL

"L'Abeille"

Jon Beeker, "Symbolism of Ternary Structures in Paul Valéry's 'Charmes,'" *KRQ* 24, no. 4 (1977): 443 (Eng).

Crow, *Paul Valéry,* 110–15 (Eng).

Lawler, *The Language of French Symbolism,* 140–44 (Eng).

Charles G. Whiting, "Préciosité in 'La Jeune Parque' and 'Charmes,'" *YFS,* no. 44 (1970): 123–25 (Eng).

"Air de Sémiramis"

Franklin, *The Broken Angel,* 80–81 (Eng).

James R. Lawler, "Existe! . . . Sois enfin toi-même . . . ," *AJFS* 8 (May–August 1971): 146–74 (Eng).

S. Nash, *Paul Valéry's "Album,"* 254–64 (Eng).

Nicole Schön-Pietri, "Paul Valéry et le réveil," *EFr* 6 (November 1970): 436–37 (Fr).

Charles Whiting, *Paul Valéry* (London: Athlone Press, 1978), 20–21 (Eng).

"A l'aurore"

James R. Lawler, "Light in Valéry," *AJFS* 6 (May–December 1969): 355–60 (Eng).

Lawler, *The Poet as Analyst,* 175–81 (Eng).

VALERY, PAUL, "Au platane"

"L'Amateur de poèmes"

S. Nash, *Paul Valéry's "Album,"* 264–67 (Eng).

"L'Ame et la danse"

Michel Mansuy, "Valéry, l'objet et l'imagination," *SFR* 2 (Spring 1978): 35–38 (Fr).

"L'Ange"

Franklin, *The Broken Angel,* 102–21 (Eng).

"Anne"

Lawler, *The Poet as Analyst,* 155–57 (Eng).
S. Nash, *Paul Valéry's "Album,"* 240–54 (Eng).
Whiting, *Valéry jeune poète,* 131–37 (Fr).

"Apparition"

Mossop, *Pure Poetry,* 114–15 (Eng).

"Au bois dormant"

S. Nash, *Paul Valéry's "Album,"* 163–69 (Eng).

"Au platane"

Lloyd J. Austin, "The Negative Plane Tree," *ECr* 4 (Spring 1964): 3–10. Reprinted in Austin, ed., *Poetic Principles and Practice,* 246–53 (Eng).

Crow, *Paul Valéry,* 131–37 (Eng).

Pierre Laurette, *Le Thème de l'arbre chez P. Valéry* (Paris: Klincksieck, 1967), 30–42 (Fr).

James R. Lawler, "An Ironic Elegy: Valéry's 'Au Platane,' " *FR* 36 (February 1963): 339–51 (Eng).

VALERY, PAUL, "Aurore"

Pierre Parent and Monique Parent, "Réflexions sur la valeur des motifs de l'eau et du vent dans 'La Jeune Parque' et dans 'Charmes,'" *RLM* 413–18 (1974): 82–84 (Fr).

J. Weber, *Genèse de l'œuvre poétique,* 420–22 (Fr).

"Aurore"

Jon Beeker, "Symbolism of Ternary Structures in Paul Valéry's 'Charmes,'" *KRQ* 24, no. 4 (1977): 444–45 (Eng).

Crow, *Paul Valéry,* 116–30 (Eng).

Franklin, *The Broken Angel,* 58–60 (Eng).

Emilie Noulet, " 'Aurore': Essai d'exégèse," *RLM* 413–18 (1974): 103–19 (Fr).

Pierre Parent and Monique Parent, "Réflexions sur la valeur des motifs de l'eau et du vent dans 'La Jeune Parque' et dans 'Charmes,'" *RLM* 413–18 (1974): 81–82 (Fr).

J. Weber, *Genèse de l'œuvre poétique,* 418–20 (Fr).

Charles G. Whiting, "Préciosité in 'La Jeune Parque and 'Charmes,'" *YFS,* no. 44 (1970): 125–26 (Eng).

"Baignée"

S. Nash, *Paul Valéry's "Album,"* 169–75 (Eng).

Whiting, *Valéry jeune poète,* 75–80 (Fr).

"Ballet"

Lawler, *The Poet as Analyst,* 154–55 (Eng).

"La Belle au bois dormant"

Lawler, *The Poet as Analyst,* 152–54 (Eng).

S. Nash, *Paul Valéry's "Album,"* 163–69 (Eng).

Whiting, *Valéry jeune poète,* 10–16 (Fr).

VALERY, PAUL, "Celle qui sort de l'onde"

"Blanc"

Whiting, *Valéry jeune poète,* 5–9 (Fr).

"Le Bois amical"

Whiting, *Valéry jeune poète,* 87–94 (Fr).

"Cantabile"

Céline Sabbagh, "Le 'Corps de l'eau,' " *RLM* 938–45 (1989): 68–71 (Fr).

"Cantiques des colonnes"

Crow, *Paul Valéry,* 137–43 (Eng).

Pierre Parent and Monique Parent, "Réflexions sur la valeur des motifs de l'eau et du vent dans 'La Jeune Parque' et dans 'Charmes,' " *RLM* 413–18 (1974): 84–85 (Fr).

"Les Cantiques des colonnes" (Stanzas 2, 9–11)

Daniel Kaylor, "Valéry's 'Les Cantiques des colonnes" Stanzas 2, 9–11, *Expl* 24 (September 1965): 6–7 (Eng).

"La Ceinture"

Lloyd J. Austin, "Modulation and Movement in Valéry's Verse," *YFS,* no. 44 (1970): 29–30. Reprinted in Austin, ed., *Poetic Principles and Practice,* 262–63 (Eng).

Serge Bourjea, "L'Ombre-majuscule: Une Exégèse de 'La Ceinture,' " *RLM* 413–18 (1974): 121–45 (Fr).

Broome and Chesters, *The Appreciation of Modern French Poetry (1850–1950),* 118–20 (Eng).

Crow, *Paul Valéry,* 150–53 (Eng).

"Celle qui sort de l'onde"

Whiting, *Valéry jeune poète,* 69–73 (Fr).

VALERY, PAUL, "César"

"César"

Whiting, *Valéry jeune poète,* 113–18 (Fr).

"Chanson à part"

Lawler, *The Poet as Analyst,* 209–17 (Eng).

James R. Lawler, "Valéry's Later Poetry," *AJFS* 4 (September–December 1967): 307–13 (Eng).

"Le Cimetière marin"

Lloyd J. Austin, "Modulation and Movement in Valéry's Verse," *YFS,* no. 44 (1970): 25–29, 31–32. Reprinted in Austin, ed., *Poetic Principles and Practice,* 257–61, 263–69 (Eng).

Jon Beeker, "Symbolism of Ternary Structures in Paul Valéry's 'Charmes,'" *KRQ* 24, no. 4, (1977): 442–45 (Eng).

Broome and Chesters, *The Appreciation of Modern French Poetry (1850–1950),* 124–31 (Eng).

Donald Bruce, "Marooned in a Cemetery: Paul Valéry and Dylan Thomas," *JES* 18 (March 1988): 1–4 (Eng).

Nicole Celeyrette-Pietri, "La Psychanalyse et le cas Valéry," *O&C* 9, no. 1 (1984): 117–20 (Fr).

A. R. Chisholm, "Moods of the Intellect in 'Le Cimetière marin,'" *YFS,* no. 44 (1970): 72–86 (Eng).

Crow, *Paul Valéry,* 21–22, 63–64, 201–15 (Eng).

Franklin, *The Broken Angel,* 61–65 (Eng).

Elizabeth de Gelsey, "L'Architecture du 'Cimetière marin,'" *RHL* 63 (July–September 1963): 458–64 (Fr).

Richard Goodkin, "Zeno's Paradox: Mallarmé, Valéry, and the Symbolist 'Movement,'" *YFS,* no. 74 (1988): 144–56 (Eng).

Jean Hytier, *La Poétique de Valéry* (Paris: Armand Colin, 1970), 185–86, 188, 227 (Fr).

Huguette Laurenti, "Musique et monologue: Notes pour une approche valéryenne du poème," *RLM* 413–18 (1974): 61–63 (Fr).

James Lawler, *Form and Meaning in Valéry's 'Le Cimetière marin'* (London: Cambridge University Press, 1960) (Eng).

Garrett McCutchan, "Sun, Consciousness, Sound, and Identity in 'Le Cimetière marin,'" *KRQ* 25 no. 2 (1978): 195–204 (Fr).

Mossop, *Pure Poetry,* 225–48 (Eng).

S. Nash, *Paul Valéry's "Album,"* 104–7 (Eng).

Emilie Noulet, "Tone in the Poems of Paul Valéry," *YFS,* no. 44 (1970): 47–49 (Eng).

Pierre Parent and Monique Parent, "Réflexions sur la valeur des motifs de l'eau et du vent dans 'La Jeune Parque' et dans 'Charmes,'" *RLM* 413–18 (1974): 92–95 (Fr).

Keith Sinclair, "Valéry, Villon, and the 'Ubi sunt?' Theme," *SFr* 15 (September–December 1971): 495–501 (Eng).

Léon Tauman, *Paul Valéry, ou Le Mal de l'art* (Paris: Nizet, 1969), 85–116 (Fr).

J. Weber, *Genèse de l'œuvre poétique,* 438–46 (Fr).

Charles G. Whiting, "'Profusion du soir' and Le Cimetière marin,'" *PMLA* 77 (March 1962): 134–39 (Eng).

Le Cimetière marin
"Zénon! Cruel Zénon! Zénon d'Elée!"

Robert Champigny, "The Zeno Stanza," *ECr* 4 (Spring 1964): 11–18 (Eng).

"Dialogue de l'arbre"

Pierre Laurette, *Le thème de l'arbre chez P. Valéry* (Paris: Klincksieck, 1967), 55–66 (Fr).

Michel Mansuy, "Valéry, l'objet et l'imagination," *SFR* 2 (Spring 1978): 30–32 (Fr).

"La Dormeuse"

Crow, *Paul Valéry,* 153–55 (Eng).

Brian Stimpson, *Paul Valéry and Music: A Study of the Techniques of Composition in Valéry's Poetry* (Cambridge: Cambridge University Press, 1984), 237–58 (Eng).

VALERY, PAUL, "Ebauche d'un serpent"

Charles G. Whiting, "Préciosité in 'La Jeune Parque and 'Charmes,'"
YFS, no. 44 (1970): 122–23 (Eng).

Charles G. Whiting, "Sexual Imagery in La Jeune Parque' and
'Charmes,'" *PMLA* 86 (October 1971): 942–44 (Eng).

"Ebauche d'un serpent"

A. R.Chisholm, "Victorous Eve (Ebauche d'un serpent)," *AJFS* 8 (May–
August 1971): 139–45 (Eng).

Crow, *Paul Valéry,* 180–87 (Eng).

Curnier, *Pages commentées d'auteurs contemporains,* vol. 1, 15–30 (Fr).

Franklin, *The Broken Angel,* 65–68 (Eng).

R. Fromilhague, "Sur la poésie pure de paul Valéry," *RHL* 76 (May–June
1976): 407–9 (Fr).

Paul Gifford, "Dimension humoristique de Paul Valéry," *RHL* 75 (July–
August 1975): 597–607 (Fr).

Pierre Laurette, *Le Thème de l'arbre chez P. Valéry* (Paris: Klincksieck,
1967), 43–49 (Fr).

Marcel Muller, "Satan contre Dieu, ou Paul Valéry face à Victor Hugo:
Pour une lecture allégorique de 'Ebauche d'un serpent,'" *SFR* 12 (1988):
328–44 (Fr).

Emilie Noulet, "Tone in the Poems of Paul Valéry," *YFS,* no. 44 (1970):
39–40 (Eng).

J. Weber, *Genèse de l'œuvre poétique,* 433–36 (Fr).

Charles Whiting, *Paul Valéry* (London: Athlone Press, 1978), 40–41 (Eng).

"Episode"

S. Nash, *Paul Valéry's "Album,"* 197–205 (Eng).

"Equinoxe"

Lawler, *The Language of French Symbolism,* 197–217 (Eng).

"Eté"

S. Nash, *Paul Valéry's "Album,"* 217–28 (Eng).

Whiting, *Valéry jeune poète,* 105–12 (Fr).

"La Fausse Morte"

Crow, *Paul Valéry,* 188–89 (Eng).

Jacques Thomas, "Source de 'La Fausse Morte' de Paul Valéry," *RHL* 61 (April–June 1961): 238–42 (Fr).

Charles G. Whiting, "Sexual Imagery in 'La Jeune Parque' and 'Charmes,'" *PMLA* 86 (October 1971): 942–43 (Eng).

"Féerie"

Henry A. Grubbs, *Paul Valéry* (New York: Twayne, 1968), 49–52 (Eng).

S. Nash, *Paul Valéry's "Album,"* 157–60 (Eng).

J. Weber, *Genèse de l'œuvre poétique,* 400–401 (Fr).

"Un Feu distinct"

James R. Lawler, "Valéry's 'Un feu distinct . . . ,'" *FS* 28 (April 1974): 169–76 (Eng).

S. Nash, *Paul Valéry's "Album,"* 175–80 (Eng).

Nicole Schön-Pietri, "Note sur 'Un Feu distinct' de Paul Valéry," *FS* 26 (October 1972): 434–38 (Fr).

Whiting, *Valéry jeune poète,* 139–42 (Fr).

"La Fileuse"

Jean Dubu, "Valéry et Courbet, origine de 'La Fileuse,'" *RHL* 65 (April–June 1965): 239–43 (Eng).

Lawler, *The Poet as Analyst,* 151–52 (Eng).

S. Nash, *Paul Valéry's "Album,"* 115–41 (Eng).

VALERY, PAUL, "Fragments du Narcisse"

J. Weber, *Genèse de l'œuvre poétique,* 396–98 (Fr).

Whiting, *Valéry jeune poète,* 17–33 (Fr).

"Fragments du Narcisse"

Anne Boyman, *Lecture du Narcisse: Sémiotique du texte de Valéry* (Québec: Didier, 1982) (Fr).

Nicole Celeyrette-Pietri, "Métamorphoses de Narcisse," *RLM* 413–18 (1974): 9–28 (Fr).

Crow, *Paul Valéry,* 157–66 (Eng).

Franklin, *The Broken Angel,* 79–80 (Eng).

Michel Gauthier, " 'Gammes' et 'transactions' dans les 'Fragments du Narcisse,' " *RLM* 791–96 (1987): 135–67 (Fr).

Mossop, *Pure Poetry,* 217–23 (Eng).

Jean Onimus, "Lectures du 'Rameur,' " *RLM* 413–18 (1974): 147–60 (Fr).

Pierre Parent and Monique Parent, "Réflexions sur la valeur des motifs de l'eau et du vent dans 'La Jeune Parque' et dans 'Charmes,' " *RLM* 413–18 (1974): 86–89 (Fr).

Whiting, *Valéry jeune poète,* 81–85 (Fr).

Charles G. Whiting, "Sexual Imagery in 'La Jeune Parque' and 'Charmes,' " *PMLA* 86 (October 1971): 941–43 (Eng).

"Les Grenades"

Crow, *Paul Valéry,* 189–93 (Eng).

René Etiemble, *Poètes ou faiseurs? Hygiène des lettres,* vol. 4 (Paris: Gallimard, 1966), 232–50 (Fr).

W. N. Ince, "An Exercise in Artistry: Valéry's 'Les Grenades,' " *RR* 55 (October 1964): 190–202 (Eng).

Katz and Hall, *Explicating French Texts,* 64–67 (Fr).

David Scott, "Valéry and the Sonnet: A Critical Re-examination of his Theory and Practice," *AJFS* 14 (September–December 1977): 271–74 (Eng).

VALERY, PAUL, "La Jeune Parque"

"Hélène, la reine triste"

S. Nash, *Paul Valéry's "Album,"* 141–49 (Eng).

Whiting, *Valéry jeune poète,* 35–41 (Fr).

"Heure"

James R. Lawler, "Light in Valéry," *AJFS* 6 (May–December 1969): 360–74 (Eng).

Lawler, *The Poet as Analyst,* 182–84, 193–200 (Eng).

"L'Insinuant"

Crow, *Paul Valéry,* 187–88 (Eng).

Emilie Noulet, "Tone in the Poems of Paul Valéry," *YFS,* no. 44 (1970): 43–45 (Eng).

"Intérieur"

Crow, *Paul Valéry,* 199–200 (Eng).

James R. Lawler, "Light in Valéry," *AJFS* 6 (May–December 1969): 362–64, 366–70 (Eng).

Lawler, *The Poet as Analyst,* 184–87 (Eng).

"La Jeune Parque"

Lloyd J. Austin, "Modulation and Movement in Valéry's Verse," *YFS,* no. 44 (1970): 22–25, 32–35. Reprinted in Austin, ed., *Poetic Principles and Practice,* 235–37, 256–58, 263, 265–67 (Eng).

Serge Bourjea, "Sang et soleil de la Parque: 'La Jeune Parque' et l'éternel retour," *RLM* 498–503 (1985): 123–46 (Fr).

Louise Cazeault, "Le Symbole du serpent: Étude des cahiers de 1910 à 1913," *RLM* 498–503 (1985): 77–87 (Fr).

Nicole Celeyrette-Pietri, "La Parque et la mort," *RLM* 498–503 (1985): 7–32 (Fr).

Jean-Pierre Chausserie-Laprée, "Constructions valéryennes: Un Motif dominant du fragment 15 de 'La Jeune Parque,' " *RLM* 791–96 (1987): 115–34 (Fr).

Crow, *Paul Valéry,* 66–102 (Eng).

Jacques Duchesne-Guillemin, "Introduction to 'La Jeune Parque,' " *YFS,* no. 44 (1970): 87–105 (Eng).

K. R. Dutton, "Valéry's 'La Jeune Parque': Towards a Critical Close Reading," *AJFS* 11 (January–April 1974): 83–108 (Eng).

Franklin, *The Broken Angel,* 56–58 (Eng).

R. Fromilhague, "Sur la poésie pure de Paul Valéry," *RHL* 76 (May–June 1976): 393–94, 398–406 (Fr).

Henry A. Grubbs, *Paul Valéry* (New York: Twayne, 1968), 52–60 (Eng).

Werner Hamacher, "History, Theory: Some Remarks on 'La Jeune Parque,' " *YFS,* no. 74 (1988): 67–94 (Eng).

Jean Hytier, *La Poétique de Valéry* (Paris: Armand Colin, 1970), 31–33, 173–74, 183–85, 188, 297 (Fr).

Jean Hytier, *Questions de littérature: Études valéryennes et autres* (New York: Columbia University Press, 1967), 3–39 (Fr).

Helmut Kohler, "Rencontres: 'La Jeune Parque' aux miroirs: Essai de traduction comparée," *O&C* 2 (Winter 1977–1978): 125–34 (Fr).

Huguette Laurenti, "Le Contexte de 'La Jeune Parque,' " *RLM* 498–503 (1985): 89–106 (Fr).

Huguette Laurenti, "Musique et monologue: Notes pour une approche valéryenne du poème," *RLM* 413–18 (1974): 53–59 (Fr).

Lawler, *The Poet as Analyst,* 139–47, 150–51, 263–65 (Eng).

Florence De Lussy, "Les Astres et la mer dans 'La Jeune Parque,' " *RLM* 498–503 (1985): 107–22 (Fr).

Florence De Lussy, *La Genèse de "La Jeune Parque" de Paul Valéry: Essai de chronologie* (Paris: Lettres Modernes, 1975) (Fr).

Daniel Moutote, "L'Egotisme poétique de Valéry dans 'Charmes,' " *RLM* 413–18 (1974): 39–40 (Fr).

Daniel Moutote, "Le Fonctionnement du langage poétique dans 'La Jeune Parque,' " *RLM* 498–503 (1985): 57–75 (Fr).

Emilie Noulet, "Tone in the Poems of Paul Valéry," *YFS,* no. 44 (1970): 45–47 (Eng).

Pierre Parent and Monique Parent, "Réflexions sur la valeur des motifs de l'eau et du vent dans 'La Jeune Parque' et dans 'Charmes,'" *RLM* 413–18 (1974): 78–80 (Fr).

Judith Robinson, "'La Jeune Parque': Poème de l'adolescence," *RLM* 498–503 (1985): 33–55 (Fr).

Judith Robinson, "L'Architecture ouverte de 'La Jeune Parque,'" *Poétique* 10 (February 1979): 63–82 (Fr).

Brian Stimpson, *Paul Valéry and Music: A Study of the Techniques of Composition in Valéry's Poetry* (Cambridge: Cambridge University Press, 1984), 211–12, 214–16, 228–33 (Eng).

J. Weber, *Genèse de l'œuvre poétique,* 411–18 (Fr).

Charles Whiting, *Paul Valéry* (London: Athlone Press, 1978), 21–35 (Eng).

Charles G. Whiting, "Préciosité in 'La Jeune Parque' and 'Charmes,'" *YFS,* no. 44 (1970): 119–20, 124–27 (Eng).

Charles G. Whiting, "Sexual Imagery in 'La Jeune Parque' and 'Charmes,'" *PMLA* 86 (October 1971): 940–42, 944 (Eng).

Robert Wilbur, "Valéry's 'La Jeune Parque' (Lines 495–512)," *Expl* 20 (May 1962): 8–9 (Eng).

"Ma Nuit"

Lawler, *The Poet as Analyst,* 157–60 (Eng).

"Même féerie"

S. Nash, *Paul Valéry's "Album,"* 160–63 (Eng).

"Naissance de Vénus"

S. Nash, *Paul Valéry's "Album,"* 149–57 (Eng).

VALERY, PAUL, "Narcisse parle"

"Narcisse parle"

S. Nash, *Paul Valéry's "Album,"* 180–97 (Eng).

J. Weber, *Genèse de l'œuvre poétique,* 406–8 (Fr).

Whiting, *Valéry jeune poète,* 59–68 (Fr).

"Neige"

James R. Lawler, "Light in Valéry," *AJFS* 6 (May–December 1969): 348–55 (Eng).

Lawler, *The Poet as Analyst,* 166–75 (Eng).

"Ode secrète"

Lloyd J. Austin, " Les Moyens du mystère chez Mallarmé et chez Valéry," *CAIEF* 15 (March 1963): 110–17 (Fr).

Crow, *Paul Valéry,* 215–26 (Eng).

Graham Martin, "Valéry's 'Ode secrète': The Enigma Solved?" *FS* 31 (October 1977): 425–36 (Eng).

"L'Oiseau cruel"

Lawler, *The Poet as Analyst,* 206–9 (Eng).

James R. Lawler, "Valéry's Later Poetry," *AJFS* 4 (September–December 1967): 295–301 (Eng).

"Orphée"

Whiting, *Valéry jeune poète,* 43–51 (Fr).

"Palme"

Crow, *Paul Valéry,* 236–44 (Fr).

Franklin, *The Broken Angel,* 58–61 (Eng).

Tatiana Greene, " 'Palme' de Paul Valéry et le cantique de Racine 'Sur les vaines occupations des gens du siècle,' " *KRQ* 19, no. 1 (1972): 83–97 (Fr).

Pierre Laurette, *Le Thème de l'arbre chez P. Valéry* (Paris: Klincksieck, 1967), 50–54 (Fr).

Daniel Moutote, "L'Égotisme poétique de Valéry dans 'Charmes,' " *RLM* 413–18 (1974): 43–44, 46–47 (Fr).

Pauline Roth-Mascagni, *Petite prose pour "Palme," à partir du texte et des brouillons inédits de Valéry* (Paris: Lettres Modernes, 1977): (Fr).

Charles Whiting, *Paul Valéry* (London: Athlone Press, 1978), 37 (Eng).

"Les Pas"

Lloyd J. Austin, "Modulation and Movement in Valéry's Verse," *YFS*, no. 44 (1970): 35–37. Reprinted in Austin, ed., *Poetic Principles and Practice,* 267–68 (Eng).

Crow, *Paul Valéry,* 147–50 (Eng).

Elizabeth Jackson, "Sense and Sensitivity in Valéry's Poetry: A Study of 'Les Pas,' " *FR* 50 (October 1976): 46–53 (Eng).

Lawler, *The Poet as Analyst,* 264–66 (Eng).

Yannick Viers, "Le 'Faire' valéryen: Désir et subversion de l'égo scriptor," *FrF* 12 (January 1987): 68–71 (Fr).

Charles G. Whiting, "Sexual Imagery in 'la Jeune Parque' and 'Charmes,' " *PMLA* 86 (October 1971): 942–43 (Eng).

"Le Philosophe et la Jeune Parque"

James R. Lawler, "Valéry's Later Poetry," *AJFS* 4 (September–December 1967): 313–22 (Eng).

"Poésie"

Crow, *Paul Valéry,* 143–46 (Eng).

Pierre Parent and Monique Parent, "Réflexions sur la valeur des motifs de l'eau et du vent dans 'La Jeune Parque' et dans 'Charmes,' " *RLM* 413–18 (1974): 85 (Fr).

J. Weber, *Genèse de l'œuvre poétique,* 430–31 (Fr).

VALERY, PAUL, "Profusion du soir"

"Profusion du soir"

Franklin, *The Broken Angel,* 54–56 (Eng).

Lawler, *The Poet as Analyst,* 74–116 (Eng).

S. Nash, *Paul Valéry's "Album,"* 228–39 (Eng).

Céline Sabbagh, "Le 'Corps de l'eau,'" *RLM* 938–45 (1989): 84–86 (Fr).

Whiting, *Valéry jeune poète,* 119–29 (Fr).

Charles G. Whiting, "'Profusion du soir' and 'Le Cimetière marin,'" *PMLA* 77 (March 1962): 134–39 (Eng).

"Psaume sur une voix"

Lawler, *The Poet as Analyst,* 127–30 (Eng).

"La Pythie"

Crow, *Paul Valéry,* 166–79 (Eng).

Lawler, *The Poet as Analyst,* 147–48 (Eng).

Pierre Parent and Monique Parent, "Réflexions sur la valeur des motifs de l'eau et du vent dans 'La Jeune Parque' et dans 'Charmes,'" *RLM* 413–18 (1974): 89–90 (Fr).

"Le Rameur"

Crow, *Paul Valéry,* 226–36 (Eng).

"Sémiramis"

Lawler, *The Poet as Analyst,* 36–73 (Eng).

Emilie Noulet, *Suites: Mallarmé, Rimbaud, Valéry* (Paris: Nizet, 1964) 202–4 (Fr).

Whiting, *Valéry jeune poète,* 143–52 (Fr).

"Sinistre"

Lawler, *The Poet as Analyst,* 1–35 (Eng).

VALERY, PAUL, "Le Vin perdu"

"Sonnet d'Irène"

James R. Lawler, "Paul Valéry et Saint Ambroise," *CAIEF* 17 (March 1965): 233–34, 240–42 (Fr).

Lawler, *The Poet as Analyst,* 238–43 (Eng).

James R. Lawler, "Valéry's Later Poetry," *AJFS* 4 (September–December 1967): 301–7 (Eng).

"Soupir"

Mossop, *Pure Poetry,* 115–16 (Eng).

"Le Sylphe"

Emilie Noulet, "Tone in the Poems of Paul Valéry," *YFS,* no. 44 (1970): 42–43 (Eng).

"Les Vaines danseuses"

J. Weber, *Genèse de l'œuvre poétique,* 404–5 (Fr).

Whiting, *Valéry jeune poète,* 53–57 (Fr).

"Valvins"

Lawler, *The Poet as Analyst,* 120–26 (Eng).

S. Nash, *Paul Valéry's "Album,"* 210–17 (Eng).

Whiting, *Valéry jeune poète,* 99–103 (Fr).

"Le Vin perdu"

Crow, *Paul Valéry,* 194–99 (Eng).

James R. Lawler, "The Meaning of Valéry's 'Le Vin perdu,'" *FS* 14 (October 1960): 340–51 (Eng).

VALERY, PAUL, "Vue"

"Vue"

S. Nash, *Paul Valéry's "Album,"* 205–10 (Eng).

Whiting, *Valéry jeune poète,* 95–98 (Fr).

VAUQUELIN DE LA FRESNAYE, JEAN

"Pour la Monarchie de ce Royaume contre la Division"

Charbonnier, *Le Poésie française et les guerres de religion,* 247–50 (Fr).

VERGIER, JACQUES

"La Culotte"

Jacques Lemaire, "Un Emule 'libertin' de La Fontaine: Jacques Vergier," *SFr* 23 (May–August 1979): 271–85 (Fr).

VERLAINE, PAUL

"A Clymène"

Bornecque, *Etudes verlainiennes,* 168–70 (Fr).

Alphonse Bouvet, "Verlaine et la poésie des 'Fêtes galantes': Ambiguïté et mal du siècle," *AJFS* 4 (September–December 1967): 267–68 (Fr).

Howarth and Walton, *Explications,* 183–90 (Eng).

Taylor-Horrex, *Verlaine,* 38–40, 65, 74 (Eng).

"Ah! l'inspiration superbe et souveraine"

Claude Abraham, "Verlaine: Étude d'une évolution poétique," *KRQ* 10, no. 1, (1963): 1–2 (Fr).

"A la promenade"

Bornecque, *Etudes verlainiennes,* 154–56 (Fr).

VERLAINE, PAUL, "Ariettes oubliées"

"L'Allée"

Bornecque, *Etudes verlainiennes,* 154 (Fr).

Claude Cuénot, "Technique et esthétique du sonnet chez Paul Verlaine," *SFr* 4 (September–December 1960): 469–70 (Fr).

Taylor-Horrex, *Verlaine,* 31–32, 41–42 (Eng).

"Allégorie"

Lawler, *The Language of French Symbolism,* 65–66 (Eng).

"L'Angélus du matin"

Diana Festa-McCormick, "Y a-t-il un impressionisme littéraire? Le cas Verlaine," *NCFS* 2 (Spring–Summer 1974): 147–50 (Fr).

"L'Angoisse"

Bornecque, *Les Poèmes saturniens de Paul Verlaine,* 210–12 (Fr).

Claude Cuénot, "Technique et esthétique du sonnet chez Paul Verlaine," *SFr* 4 (September–December 1960): 461–62 (Fr).

Porter, *The Crisis of French Symbolism,* 85–87 (Eng).

"Après trois ans"

Bornecque, *Les Poèmes saturniens de Paul Verlaine,* 203–5 (Fr).

Nadal, *Paul Verlaine,* 27–28 (Fr).

J. Weber, *Genèse de l'œuvre poétique,* 311–13 (Fr).

"Ariettes oubliées"

Daniel Bergez, "Incertitude et vacuité du moi dans les 'Ariettes oubliées' de Verlaine," *RHL* 82 (May–June 1982): 412–23 (Fr).

Nadal, *Paul Verlaine,* 51–54, 128–29 (Fr).

VERLAINE, PAUL, "Ariettes oubliées III"

Robichez, *Verlaine entre Rimbaud et Dieu*, 58–69 (Fr).

Taylor-Horrex, *Verlaine*, 50–54, 59–61, 67–70, 72–74 (Eng).

"Ariettes oubliées III"

Chadwick, *Verlaine*, 36–37, 49 (Eng).

Paul Delbouille, *Poésie et sonorités: Les Nouvelles Recherches*, vol. 2 (Paris: Les Belles Lettres, 1984), 214–22 (Fr).

"Art poétique"

Chadwick, *Verlaine*, 80–82 (Eng).

Michel Deguy, *Choses de la poésie et affaire culturelle* (Paris: Hachette, 1986), 42–46 (Fr).

Michel Grimaud, "Questions de méthode: Verlaine et la critique structuraliste," *O&C* 9, no. 2 (1984): 125–26 (Fr).

Robert L. Mitchell, "Mint, Thyme, Tobacco: New Possibilities of Affinity in the 'Artes poeticae' of Verlaine and Mallarmé," *FrF* 2 (May 1977): 238–43, 248–51 (Eng).

Porter, *The Crisis of French Symbolism*, 109–11 (Eng).

Raitt, *Life and Letters in France*, 153–61 (Eng).

Carol de Dobay Rifelj, "Familiar and Unfamiliar: Verlaine's Poetic Diction," *KRQ* 29, no. 4 (1982): 373–74 (Eng).

Taylor-Horrex, *Verlaine*, 64–65, 70 (Eng).

"L'Auberge"

Carol de Dobay Rifelj, "Familiar and Unfamiliar: Verlaine's Poetic Diction," *KRQ* 29, no. 4 (1982): 368–69 (Eng).

"A une femme"

Bornecque, *Les Poèmes saturniens de Paul Verlaine*, 209–10 (Fr).

Claude Cuénot, "Technique et esthétique du sonnet chez Paul Verlaine," *SFr* 4 (September–December 1960): 463–64 (Fr).

VERLAINE, PAUL, "César Borgia"

"Avant que tu ne t'en ailles"

Chadwick, *Verlaine,* 32–34 (Eng).

"Beams"

D. D. R. Owen, "Beams," *FS* 25 (April 1971): 156–61 (Eng).
Robichez, *Verlaine entre Rimbaud et Dieu,* 76–77 (Fr).

"Birds in the night"

Robichez, *Verlaine entre Rimbaud et Dieu,* 72, 74–75 (Fr).
Taylor-Horrex, *Verlaine,* 56, 61–62 (Eng).

Bruxelles "Simples fresques"

Taylor-Horrex, *Verlaine,* 55 (Eng).

"Cauchemar"

Bornecque, *Les Poèmes saturniens de Paul Verlaine,* 216–17 (Fr).

"Çavitri"

Bornecque, *Les Poèmes saturniens de Paul Verlaine,* 231 (Fr).

"Certes, si tu le veux mériter, mon fils, oui"

Claude Cuénot, "Technique et esthétique du sonnet chez Paul Verlaine,"
SFr 4 (September–December 1960): 467 (Fr).

"César Borgia"

Bornecque, *Les Poèmes saturniens de Paul Verlaine,* 239–40 (Fr).

VERLAINE, PAUL, "C'est l'extase langoureuse"

"C'est l'extase langoureuse"

Antoine Adam, *Verlaine,* new edition (Paris: Hatier, 1965), 110–11 (Fr).

"Chanson d'automne"

Bornecque, *Les Poèmes saturniens de Paul Verlaine,* 119–20, 226–27 (Fr).

Broome and Chesters, *The Appreciation of Modern French Poetry (1850–1950),* 96–98 (Eng).

Mourot, *Verlaine,* 119–29 (Fr).

"La Chanson des ingénues"

Porter, *The Crisis of French Symbolism,* 90 (Eng).

"Charleroi"

Russell King, "Le Paysage verbal verlainien," *Europe* 52 (September–October 1974): 97–107 (Fr).

"Chevaux de bois"

Bernhard Frank, "Verlaine's 'Wooden Steeds,'" *Expl* 46 (Winter 1988): 29–31 (Eng).

"Child Wife"

Taylor-Horrex, *Verlaine,* 58–59, 62 (Eng).

"Le Ciel est par-dessus le toit"

Nadal, *Paul Verlaine,* 67–68 (Fr).

"Clair de lune"

Auffret and Auffret, *Le Commentaire composé,* 153–57 (Fr).

Bornecque, *Etudes verlainiennes,* 70–73, 75–78, 147–52 (Fr).

Alphonse Bouvet, "Verlaine et la poésie des 'Fêtes galantes': Ambiguïté et mal du siècle," *AJFS* 4 (September–December 1967): 264–65 (Fr).

Mourot, *Verlaine,* 105, 109–10 (Fr).

Taylor-Horrex, *Verlaine,* 29–30, 68–69 (Eng).

Hallam Walker, "Visual and Spatial Imagery in Verlaine's 'Fêtes galantes," *PMLA* 87 (October 1972): 1007, 1009–10 (Eng).

"Colloque sentimental"

Bornecque, *Etudes verlainiennes,* 100–101, 177–81 (Fr).

Alphonse Bouvet, "Verlaine et la poésie des 'Fêtes galantes': Ambiguïté et mal du siècle," *AJFS* 4 (September–December 1967): 265–66 (Fr).

Broome and Chesters, *The Appreciation of Modern French Poetry (1850–1950),* 98–100 (Eng).

Jean Dubu, "Du 'Banc de pierre' de Gautier au 'Colloque sentimental' de Verlaine," *SFr* 11 (September–December 1967): 486–87 (Fr).

Mourot, *Verlaine,* 114, 129–38 (Fr).

Taylor-Horrex, *Verlaine,* 30–31, 36 (Eng).

Hallam Walker, "Visual and Spatial Imagery in Verlaine's 'Fêtes galantes,'" *PMLA* 87 (October 1972): 1014–15 (Eng).

Susan Youens, "To Tell a Tale: Symbolist Narrative in Debussy's 'Fêtes galantes II,'" *NCFS* 6 (Fall–Winter 1987–88): 185–88, 191 (Eng).

"Colombine"

Bornecque, *Etudes verlainiennes,* 173–75 (Fr).

"Crépuscule du soir mystique"

Bornecque, *Les Poèmes saturniens de Paul Verlaine,* 221–23 (Fr).

Nadal, *Paul Verlaine,* 125–27 (Fr).

"Crimen amoris"

Antoine Adam, *Verlaine,* new edition (Paris: Hatier, 1965), 123–25 (Fr).

Chadwick, *Verlaine,* 73–77 (Eng).

Houston, *Patterns of Thought,* 45–46 (Eng).

Nadal, *Paul Verlaine,* 72–75, 156–58 (Fr).

VERLAINE, PAUL, "Croquis parisien"

"Croquis parisien"

Bornecque, *Les Poèmes saturniens de Paul Verlaine,* 213–16 (Fr).

Carol de Dobay Rifelj, "Familiar and Unfamiliar: Verlaine's Poetic Diction," *KRQ* 29, no. 4 (1982): 370–72 (Eng).

"Cythère"

Taylor-Horrex, *Verlaine,* 34, 42, 65–66 (Eng).

"Dans la grotte"

Bornecque, *Etudes verlainiennes,* 156–58 (Fr).

"Du Fond du grabat"

John P. Houston, "Rimbaud, Mysticism, and Verlaine's Poetry of 1873–74," *ECr* 9 (Spring 1969): 24–27 (Eng).

"L'Echelonnement des haies"

Pierre Creignou, "Variations du paysage chez Verlaine," *Europe* 52 (September–October 1974): 94–95 (Fr).

Nadal, *Paul Verlaine,* 113–18 (Fr).

Maurice Regard, "La Critique des createurs," *EF* 1 (October 1965): 72–73 (Fr).

Scott, *Pictorialist Poetics,* 107–8 (Eng).

"Effet de nuit"

Bornecque, *Les Poèmes saturniens de Paul Verlaine,* 217–18 (Fr).

"En bateau"

Bornecque, *Etudes verlainiennes,* 165–66 (Fr).

"En patinant"

Bornecque, *Etudes verlainiennes*, 160–63 (Fr).

Hallam Walker, "Visual and Spatial Imagery in Verlaine's 'Fêtes galantes,'" *PMLA* 87 (October 1972): 1011–12 (Eng).

"En sourdine"

Bornecque, *Etudes verlainiennes*, 176–77 (Fr).

Alphonse Bouvet, "Verlaine et la poésie des 'Fêtes galanges': Ambiguîté et mal du siècle," *AJFS* 4 (September–December 1967): 262–64 (Fr).

Mourot, *Verlaine*, 113–14 (Fr).

Taylor-Horrex, *Verlaine*, 42–44, 66 (Eng).

"Epilogue"

Bornecque, *Les Poèmes saturniens de Paul Verlaine*, 241–48 (Fr).

Mourot, *Verlaine*, 62–64, 82–84 (Fr).

"L'Espoir luit comme un brin de paille dans l'étable"

Lawler, *The Language of French Symbolism*, 36–40, 55–63 (Eng).

Eléonore M. Zimmermann, "Verlaine: 'Vieux et nouveaux coppées: Une Analyse de 'L'Espoir luit . . . ,'" *SFr* 8 (September–December 1964): 482–88 (Fr).

"Fantoches"

Bornecque, *Etudes verlainiennes*, 163–64 (Fr).

"Le Faune"

Bornecque, *Etudes verlainiennes*, 166–67 (Fr).

Susan Youens, "To Tell a Tale: Symbolist Narrative in Debussy's 'Fêtes galantes II,'" *NCFS* 16 (Fall–Winter 1987–88): 184–85 (Eng).

VERLAINE, PAUL, "Final"

"Final"

Robichez, *Verlaine entre Rimbaud et Dieu*, 126–28 (Fr).

"Green"

Robichez, *Verlaine entre Rimbaud et Dieu*, 75–77 (Fr).

Taylor-Horrex, *Verlaine*, 57 (Eng).

"Grotesques"

Bornecque, *Les Poèmes saturniens de Paul Verlaine*, 218–20 (Fr).

"L'Heure du berger"

Jeanne Bem, "Verlaine, poète lunaire: Mythe et langage poétique," *SFR* 4 (Winter 1980): 384–86 (Fr).

"Il faut m'aimer . . ."

Claude Cuénot, "Technique et esthétique du sonnet chez Paul Verlaine," *SFr* 4 (September–December 1960): 465 (Fr).

"Il pleure dans mon cœur"

Marie-Georgette Steisel, "Verlaine's 'Il pleure dans mon cœur,'" *Expl* 32 (January 1974): 4–5 (Eng).

"Images d'un sou"

Nadal, *Paul Verlaine*, 55–56 (Fr).

"Les Indolents"

Bornecque, *Etudes verlainiennes*, 172–73 (Fr).

"Les Ingénus"

Susan Youens, "To Tell a Tale: Symbolist Narrative in Debussy's 'Fêtes galantes II,'" *NCFS* 16 (Fall–Winter 1987–88): 182–84 (Eng).

"Je ne sais pourquoi"

Pierre Creignou, "Variations du paysage chez Verlaine," *Europe* 52 (September–October 1974): 91–92 (Fr).

"Kaléidoscope"

Diana Festa-McCormick, "Y a-t-il un impressionisme littéraire? Le cas Verlaine," *NCFS* 2 (Spring–Summer 1974): 150–52 (Fr).

Nadal, *Paul Verlaine,* 57–59 (Fr).

"Lassitude"

Bornecque, *Les Poèmes saturniens de Paul Verlaine,* 206 (Fr).

"Lettre"

Bornecque, *Etudes verlainiennes,* 170–72 (Fr).

Porter, *The Crisis of French Symbolism,* 99–101 (Eng).

"La Lune blanche"

Chadwick, *Verlaine,* 31–32 (Eng).

C. A. Hackett, *Autour de Rimbaud* (Paris: Klincksieck, 1967), 39–44 (Fr).

"Mandoline"

Bornecque, *Etudes verlainiennes,* 167–78 (Fr).

Laurence M. Porter, "Text Versus Music in the French Art Song: Debussy, Fauré, and Verlaine's 'Mandoline,'" *FS* 12 (Fall–Winter 1983–84): 139–43 (Eng).

Taylor-Horrex, *Verlaine,* 33–36, 42, 66, 68–69 (Eng).

VERLAINE, PAUL, "Marco"

"Marco"

Bornecque, *Les Poèmes saturniens de Paul Verlaine*, 238–39 (Fr).

"Mon rêve familier"

Bornecque, *Les Poèmes saturniens de Paul Verlaine*, 207–9 (Fr).

"Monsieur Prudhomme"

Carol de Dobay Rifelj, "Familiar and Unfamiliar: Verlaine's Poetic Diction," *KRQ* 29, no. 4 (1982): 367–68 (Eng).

"Mort!"

Nadal, *Paul Verlaine*, 76–77, 79–82 (Fr).

"Nevermore"

Bornecque, *Les Poèmes saturniens de Paul Verlaine*, 201–3 (Fr).

Porter, *The Crisis of French Symbolism*, 91–92 (Eng).

"Nocturne parisien"

Bornecque, *Les Poèmes saturniens de Paul Verlaine*, 235–38 (Fr).

"Nouvelles variations sur le point du jour"

Carol de Dobay Rifelj, "Familiar and Unfamiliar: Verlaine's Poetic Diction," *KRQ* 29, no. 4 (1982): 375–77 (Eng).

"Nuit du Walpurgis classique"

Bornecque, *Les Poèmes saturniens de Paul Verlaine*, 223–26 (Fr).

Porter, *The Crisis of French Symbolism*, 88–90 (Eng).

VERLAINE, PAUL, "Soleils couchants"

"Pantomime"

Porter, *The Crisis of French Symbolism,* 95–96 (Eng).

Taylor-Horrex, *Verlaine,* 31, 34–35, 37, 41, 65–66 (Eng).

Richard Whitmore, "Verlaine's 'Pantomime,' " *Expl* 34 (May 1976): 15–18 (Eng).

"Prologue"

Bornecque, *Les Poèmes saturniens de Paul Verlaine,* 193–99 (Fr).

Mourot, *Verlaine,* 60–62, 82–83 (Fr).

"Résignation"

Bornecque, *Les Poèmes saturniens de Paul Verlaine,* 200–201 (Fr).

Claude Cuénot: "Technque et esthétique du sonnet chez Paul Verlaine," *SFr* 4 (September–December 1960): 470 (Fr).

"Le Rossignol"

Nadal, *Paul Verlaine,* 127–29 (Fr).

M. Riffaterre, *Semiotics of Poetry,* 37–39 (Eng).

"Les Sages d'autrefois"

Bornecque, *Les Poèmes saturniens de Paul Verlaine,* 192–93 (Fr).

"Un Soir d'octobre"

J. Weber, *Genèse de l'œuvre poétique,* 298–99 (Fr).

"Soleils couchants"

George Combet, "Un Poème de l'attente frustrée: 'Soleils couchants' de Paul Verlaine," *Poétique* 11 (April 1980): 225–33 (Fr).

Michel Grimaud, "Questions de méthode: Verlaine et la critique structuraliste," *O&C* 9, no. 2 (1984): 120–24 (Fr).

VERLAINE, PAUL, "Le Son du cor s'afflige vers les bois"

Mourot, *Verlaine*, 143–45 (Fr).

Porter, *The Crisis of French Symbolism*, 88 (Eng).

"Le Son du cor s'afflige vers les bois"

Claude Cuénot: "Technque et esthétique du sonnet chez Paul Verlaine," *SFr* 4 (September–December 1960): 462–63 (Fr).

Moreau, *Six Études de métrique*, 26–37 (Fr).

"Spleen"

Taylor-Horrex, *Verlaine*, 57–58 (Eng).

"Sub urbe"

Bornecque, *Les Poèmes saturniens de Paul Verlaine*, 232–33 (Fr).

"Sur l'herbe"

Bornecque, *Etudes verlainiennes*, 152–54 (Fr).

"Les Vaincus"

Nadal, *Paul Verlaine*, 79–82 (Fr).

"Via dolorosa"

Robichez, *Verlaine entre Rimbaud et Dieu*, 125–28 (Fr).

"Vœu"

Bornecque, *Les Poèmes saturniens de Paul Verlaine*, 205–6 (Fr).

"Walcourt"

Robichez, *Verlaine entre Rimbaud et Dieu*, 69–70 (Fr).

VERMEIL, ABRAHAM DE

"Belle, je sers vos yeux et vos cheveux dorez"

Lafay, *La Poésie française du premier XVIIe siècle,* 204–5 (Fr).

"Heureux celui qui d'un brave courage"

David Lee Rubin, "Mannerism and Love," *ECr* 6 (Winter 1966): 258–60 (Eng).

"Je chante et pleure, et veux faire et defaire"

Lafay, *La Poésie française du premier XVIIe siècle,* 224–26 (Fr).

"Je couve dans mon sein un océan de pleurs"

Lafay, *La Poésie française du premier XVIIe siècle,* 271–73 (Fr).

"Je ne suis plus un homme, ou bien si je le suis"

David Lee Rubin, "Mannerism and Love," *ECr* 6 (Winter 1966): 260–62 (Eng).

"Un Jour mon beau soleil miroit sa tresse blonde"

Lafay, *La Poésie française du premier XVIIe siècle,* 251–53 (Fr).

"Mon cœur hautain médisait de l'Amour"

David Lee Rubin, "Mannerism and Love," *ECr* 6 (Winter 1966): 257–58 (Eng).

"Puissant sorcier d'Amour transformé en abeille"

Lafay, *La Poésie française du premier XVIIe siècle,* 283–84 (Fr).

VIAN, BORIS

"Le Déserteur"

Charlotte Gerrard, "Anti-militarism in Vian's Minor Texts," *FR* 45 (May 1972): 1117–20 (Eng).

THÉOPHILE DE VIAU

"Cloris lorsque je songe en te voyant si belle"

John Lyons, "Temporality in the Lyrics of Théophile de Viau," *AJFS* 16 (May–August 1979): 372–74 (Eng).

"Un Corbeau devant moy croasse"

Alvin Eustis, "A Deciphering of Théophile's 'Un Corbeau devant moy croasse,' " *ECr* 20 (Winter 1980): 107–19 (Eng).

Rubin, *The Knot of Artifice,* 84–87 (Eng).

"Courtisans qui passez vos jours dans les delices"

John Lyons, "Temporality in the Lyrics of Théophile de Viau," *AJFS* 16 (May–August 1979): 374–75 (Eng).

"Lettre à son frère"

John Lyons, "Temporality in the Lyrics of Théophile de Viau," *AJFS* 16 (May–August 1979): 363–71 (Eng).

"La Maison de Sylvie"

Jean-Pierre Chauveau, "La Voix des poètes," *LCL* 12 (1990): 209–12 (Fr).

Richard Mazzara, "The Philosophical-Religious Evolution of Théophile du Viau," *FR* 14 (April 1968): 622–23 (Eng).

VIGNY, ALFRED DE, "Les Amants de Montmorency"

"La Maison de Sylvie 2"

Beverley Ormerod, "Nature as a Source of Imagery in the Work of Théophile de Viau," *FMLS* 6 (July 1970): 305–7 (Eng).

"Le Matin"

Rubin, *The Knot of Artifice,* 47–59 (Eng).

"La Solitude"

Robert Hill, "In Context: Théophile de Viau's 'La Solitude,'" *BHR* 30, no. 3 (1968): 499–536 (Eng).

Richard Mazzara, "Théophile du Viau, Saint-Amant, and the Spanish Soledad," *KRQ* 14 no. 4 (1967): 394–98, 403 (Eng).

Anthony Pugh, "The Unity of Théophile's 'La Solitude,' '': *FR* 45 (Special Issue 3) (Fall 1971): 117–26 (Eng).

Donald Stone, "Théophile's 'La Solitude': An Appraisal of Poem and Poet," *FR* 40 (December 1966): 321–28 (Eng).

"Traicté de l'immortalité de l'âme"

Richard Mazzara, "The *Phaedo* and Théophile de Viau's 'Traicté de l'immortalité de l'âme,' '' *FR* 40 (December 1966): 329–40 (Eng).

VIELE-GRIFFIN, FRANCIS

"La Partenza"

J. M. Aguirre, "Francis Vielé-Griffin, 'La Partenza': A Symbolist Poem," *SFr* 24 (January–April 1980): 102–13 (Fr).

VIGNY, ALFRED DE

"Les Amants de Montmorency"

Doolittle, *Alfred de Vigny,* 81–82 (Eng).

VIGNY, ALFRED DE, "Le Bal"

"Le Bal"

J. Weber, *Genèse de l'œuvre poétique,* 78–81 (Fr).

"La Bouteille à la mer"

Bénichou, *Les Mages romantiques,* 235–37 (Fr).

Castex, *"Les Destinées,"* 211–40 (Fr).

Denommé, *Nineteenth-Century French Romantic Poets,* 81–82 (Eng).

Doolittle, *Alfred de Vigny,* 111 (Eng).

Fournet, *Poètes romantiques,* 116–17 (Fr).

La Salle, *Alfred de Vigny,* 234–37 (Fr).

Wren, *Vigny: "Les Destinées,"* 62–71 (Eng).

"La Colère de Samson"

Bénichou, *Les Mages romantiques,* 249–53 (Fr).

Doolittle, *Alfred de Vigny,* 96–98 (Eng).

La Salle, *Alfred de Vigny,* 184–87 (Fr).

Wren, *Vigny: "Les Destinées,"* 29–31 (Eng).

"Le Déluge"

Denommé, *Nineteenth-Century French Romantic Poets,* 68–69 (Eng).

J. Weber, *Genèse de l'œuvre poétique,* 74–75 (Fr).

"Les Destinées"

Bénichou, *Les Mages romantiques,* 253–63 (Fr).

Castex, *"Les Destinées,"* 245–55, 294–96 (Fr).

Stirling Haig, "The Double Register of Les Destinées,' " *SFr* 22 (January–April 1978): 104–6 (Eng).

Wren, *Vigny: "Les Destinées,"* 21–24, 26–28 (Eng).

VIGNY, ALFRED DE, "La Maison du berger"

"Eloa, ou La Sœur des anges"

Doolittle, *Alfred de Vigny,* 65–72 (Eng).

La Salle, *Alfred de Vigny,* 64–66 (Fr).

J. Weber, *Genèse de l'œuvre poétique,* 72–73 (Fr).

"L'Esprit pur"

Bénichou, *Les Mages romantiques,* 263–68 (Fr).

Castex, *"Les Destinées,"* 271–90 (Fr).

Denommé, *Nineteenth-Century French Romantic Poets,* 82–84 (Eng).

Doolittle, *Alfred de Vigny,* 112–13 (Eng).

La Salle, *Alfred de Vigny,* 270–76 (Fr).

Wren, *Vigny: "Les Destinées,"* 71–74 (Eng).

"La Femme adultère"

Doolittle, *Alfred de Vigny,* 58–61 (Eng).

"La Fille de Jephté"

Doolittle, *Alfred de Vigny,* 58, 60–61 (Eng).

"La Flûte"

Bénichou, *Les Mages romantiques,* 233–35 (Fr).

Castex, *"Les Destinées,"* 139–43 (Fr).

Doolittle, *Alfred de Vigny,* 110–11 (Eng).

Wren, *Vigny: "Les Destinées,"* 60–61 (Eng).

"La Maison du berger"

Bénichou, *Les Mages romantiques,* 237–49 (Fr).

Castex, *"Les Destinées,"* 145–210, 292–94 (Fr).

Denommé, *Nineteenth-Century French Romantic Poets,* 74–77 (Eng).

VIGNY, ALFRED DE, "Moïse"

Doolittle, *Alfred de Vigny,* 101–9 (Eng).

Martha Evans, "Mirror Images in 'La Maison du berger,' " *FR* 56 (February 1983): 393–99 (Eng).

François Germain, "Saveur de la gravité," *RHL* 64 (April–June 1964): 190–92 (Fr).

René-Albert Gutmann, *Introduction à la lecture des poètes français* (Paris: Nizet, 1967), 76–82 (Fr).

La Salle, *Alfred de Vigny,* 207–23 (Fr).

Henry Majewski, "Alfred de Vigny and the Poetic Experience," *RR* 67 (November 1976): 268–89 (Eng).

Jean-Pierre Richard, *Etudes sur le romantisme* (Paris: Seuil, 1970), 171–75 (Fr).

Wren, *Vigny: "Les Destinées,"* 42–56 (Eng).

"Moïse"

Fernande Bartfield, *Vigny et la figure de Moïse* (Paris: Minard, 1968) (Fr).

Denommé, *Nineteenth-Century French Romantic Poets,* 66–68 (Eng).

Doolittle, *Alfred de Vigny,* 78–81 (Eng).

J. Weber, *Genèse de l'œuvre poétique,* 71–72 (Fr).

"Le Mont des Oliviers"

Bénichou, *Les Mages romantiques,* 223–29 (Fr).

Lloyd Bishop, "Jesus as Romantic Hero: 'Le Mont des Oliviers,' " *FR* 46 (Special issue 5) (Spring 1973): 41–48 (Eng).

Castex, *"Les Destinées,"* 107–32 (Fr).

Denommé, *Nineteenth-Century French Romantic Poets,* 70–74 (Eng).

Doolittle, *Alfred de Vigny,* 98–101 (Eng).

Fournet, *Poètes romantiques,* 107–9 (Fr).

Malcolm McGoldrick, "Vigny's 'Le Mont des Oliviers' and Amos," *FSB* 32 (Autumn 1989): 5–8 (Eng).

Wren, *Vigny: "Les Destinées,"* 20–21, 24–26 (Eng).

"La Mort du loup"

Bénichou, *Les Mages romantiques,* 229–31 (Fr).

Castex, *"Les Destinés,"* 75–83 (Fr).

Denommé, *Nineteenth-Century French Romantic Poets,* 77–79 (Eng).

Fournet, *Poètes romantiques,* 109–10, 113–15 (Fr).

Robert O. Steele, "The Avant-Gardism of Leconte de Lisle," *NCFS* 17 (Spring–Summer 1989): 318–19 (Eng).

Wren, *Vigny: "Les Destinées,"* 31–34 (Eng).

"Les Oracles"

Castex, *"Les Destinées,"* 257–69 (Fr).

Wren, *Vigny: "Les Destinées,"* 39–42, 50 (Eng).

"Paris"

Pierre Citron, *La Poésie de Paris lans la littérature française de Rousseau à Baudelaire* (Paris: Editions de Minuit, 1961), vol. 1, 264–78 (Fr).

Doolittle, *Alfred de Vigny,* 82–83 (Eng).

"La Prison"

Doolittle, *Alfred de Vigny,* 61–65 (Eng).

"La Sauvage"

Bénichou, *Les Mages romantiques,* 231–33 (Fr).

Castex, *"Les Destinées,"* 133–38 (Fr).

Wren, *Vigny: "Les Destinées,"* 57–60 (Eng).

"Wanda"

V. B. and A. D. Nikolski Bikoulitch, "Une Correspondance avec la comtesse Kossakovskaia," *Europe* 56 (May 1978): 24–28 (Fr).

Castex, *"Les Destinées,"* 241–44 (Fr).

Wren, *Vigny: "Les Destinées,"* 35–39 (Eng).

VILLON, FRANÇOIS

Ballade des menus propos
"Je congnois bien mouches en let"

Emilie Kostoroski, "Two Ballads of Villon Reconsidered," *FR* 46 (Special Issue 5) (Spring 1973): 24–27 (Eng).

Ballade des pendus
"Frères humains qui aprè nous vivez"

Fox, *Villon: Poems,* 96–98 (Eng).

Le Gentil, *Villon,* 73–74, 108–110, 134–37 (Fr).

Ballade des proverbes
"Tant grate chievre que mau gist"

Emilie Kostoroski, "Two Ballads of Villon Reconsidered," *FR* 46 (Special Issue 5) (Spring 1973): 22–24 (Eng).

Ballade du concours de Blois
"Je meurs de soif auprès de la fontaine"

Fox, *The Poetry of Villon,* 115–16 (Eng).

Emilie Kostoroski, "Two Ballads of Villon Reconsidered," *FR* 46 (Special Issue 5) (Spring 1973): 27–31 (Eng).

"Le Débat de Villon et de son cœur"

Fox, *The Poetry of Villon,* 22–23, 28–32 (Eng).

Fox, *Villon: Poems,* 93–96 (Eng).

Le Gentil, *Villon,* 119–22 (Fr).

"Epitaphe Villon"

Fox, *The Poetry of Villon,* 32, 56 (Eng).

VILLON, FRANÇOIS, *Lais* "Item, au Chevalier du guet" (v. 145–52)

Epître à ses amis
"Aiez pitié, aiez pitié de moy"

Anacker, *François Villon,* 89–91 (Eng).

Jean Frappier, "Contribution au commentaire de Villon," in *Studi in onore di Italo Siciliano,* vol. 1 (Florence: L. S. Olschki, 1966), 437–56. Reprinted in Frappier, *Du Moyen Age à la Renaissance,* 173–78 (Fr).

"Je suis Françoys dont ce me poise"

Dufournet, *Nouvelles recherches sur Villon,* 239–46 (Fr).

Kuhn, *La Poétique de François Villon,* 13–21 (Fr).

"Lais"

Anacker, *François Villon,* 37–42 (Eng).

William Calin, "Observations on Point of View and the Poet's Voice in Villon," *ECr* 7 (Fall 1967): 184–85 (Eng).

Pierre Demarolle, *Villon: un testament ambigu* (Paris: Larousse, 1973), 19–22 (Fr).

Jean Dufournet, *Recherches sur le "Testament" de Villon,* 2nd ed., vol. 1 (Paris: SEDES, 1971–73), 66–67, 93–98, 262–263 (Fr).

Kuhn, *La Poétique de François Villon,* 99–130, 401–431 (Fr).

Le Gentil, *Villon,* 31–49 (Fr).

Henri Peyre, *The Crossroads of Intentions: A Study of Symbolic Expression in the Poetry of François Villon* (The Hague and Paris: Mouton, 1974), 49–50, 71–72, 116–118 (Eng).

Lais
"An quatre cens cinquante six" (v. 1–8)

Fox, *The Poetry of Villon,* 84–85 (Eng).

Lais
"Item, au Chevalier du guet" (v. 145–52)

Dufournet, *Nouvelles recherches sur Villon,* 89–93 (Fr).

551

VILLON, FRANÇOIS, *Lais* "Item, au seigneur de Grigny" (v. 137–44)

Lais
"Item, au seigneur de Grigny" (v. 137–44)

Dufournet, *Nouvelles recherches sur Villon,* 173–78, 184–86 (Fr).

Lais
"Item, laisse et donne en pur don" (v. 121–28)

Dufournet, *Nouvelles recherches sur Villon,* 149–50, 153–54 (Fr).

"Prière"

Elizabeth Wilson, "Name Games in Rutebeuf and Villon," *ECr* 18 (Spring 1978): 54–56 (Eng).

"Testament"

Champion, *Histoire poétique du XVe siècle,* vol. 2, 107–20, 125–31 (Fr).

Pierre Demarolle, *Villon: Un Testament ambigu* (Paris: Larousse, 1973), 22–34, 96–196 (Fr).

Jean Dufournet, *Recherches sur le "Testament" de Villon,* 2nd ed., vol. 1 (Paris: SEDES, 1971–73), 37–93, 98–307 (Fr).

Fox, *Villon: Poems,* 11 (Eng).

Grace Frank, "Villon's Poetry and the Biographical Approach," *ECr* 7 (Fall 1967): 164–68 (Eng).

Reginald Hyatte, "Villon's 'Testament,' " *Expl* 43 (Fall 1984): 9–11 (Eng).

Le Gentil, *Villon,* 50–70 (Fr).

Daniel Poirion, "Opposition et composition dans le 'Testament' de Villon," *ECr* 7 (Fall 1967): 170–79 (Fr).

Nancy F. Regalado, "Testament: La Fonction poétique des noms propres dans le 'Testament'' de François Villon," *CAIEF* 32 (May 1980): 51–68 (Fr).

Barbara Sargent, "On Certain Lines of Villon's 'Testament,' " *ECr* 7 (Fall 1967): 197–204 (Eng).

Richard Terdiman, "The Structure of Villon's 'Testament,' " *PMLA* 82 (December 1967): 622–33 (Eng).

VILLON, FRANÇOIS, *Testament* "Ballade de conclusion"

Heinz Weinmann, "L'Economie du 'Testament' de François Villon," *EF* 16 (April 1980): 35–62 (Fr).

Testament
"A chartreux et a celestins" (v. 1968–1995)

Kuhn, *La Poétique de François Villon*, 313–15 (Fr).

Testament
"Au cappitaine Jehan Riou" (v. 1126–1141)

Dufournet, *Nouvelles recherches sur Villon*, 113–24 (Fr).

Testament
"Ballade à s'amye" (v. 942–969)

Dufournet, *Nouvelles recherches sur Villon*, 265–69 (Fr).

Jean Dufournet, *Recherches sur le "Testament" de Villon*, 2nd ed., vol. 1 (Paris: SEDES, 1971–73), 71–80, 98–109 (Fr).

Fox, *Villon: Poems*, 83–84 (Eng).

Testament
"Ballade de bonne doctrine" (v. 1692–1719)

Kuhn, *La Poétique de François Villon*, 450–52 (Fr).

Jean-Charles Payen, "Le Coup de l'étrier: Villon martyr et Goliard ou comment se faire oublier quand on est immortel?," *EF* 16 (April 1980): 21–34 (Fr).

Testament
"Ballade de conclusion" (v. 1996–2023)

Fein, *A Reading of Villon's "Testament,"* 75–80 (Eng).

Kuhn, *La Poétique de François Villon*, 325–34, 455–57 (Fr).

VILLON, FRANÇOIS, *Testament* "Ballade de Jehan Cotart"

Testament
"Ballade de Jehan Cotart" (v. 1238–1265)

Kuhn, *La Poétique de François Villon,* 378–83 (Fr).

Testament
"Ballade de la Belle Heaulmière" (v. 533–560)

William Calin, "Observations on Point of View and the Poet's Voice in Villon," *ECr* 7 (Fall 1967): 181–82 (Eng).

Testament
"Ballade de la Grosse Margot" (v. 1591–1627)

Calin, *In Defense of French Poetry,* 66–69 (Eng).

William Calin, "Observations on Point of View and the Poet's Voice in Villon," *ECr* 7 (Fall 1967): 186 (Eng).

Fein, *A Reading of Villon's "Testament,"* 64–67 (Eng).

Kuhn, *La Poétique de François Villon,* 25–38 (Fr).

Elizabeth Wilson, "Name Games in Rutebeuf and Villon," *ECr* 18 (Spring 1978): 55–56 (Eng).

Testament
"Ballade des Dames du temps jadis" (v. 329–356)

Anacker, *François Villon,* 49–53 (Eng).

Fein, *A Reading of Villon's "Testament,"* 14–17 (Eng).

Fox, *The Poetry of Villon,* 69–70, 113, 118–19, 148–51 (Eng).

Fox, *Villon: Poems,* 47–52 (Eng).

Jean Frappier, "Les Trois Ballades du temps jadis," *BCLSMP* (Academie Royale de Belgique, *Bulletin de la Classe des Lettres et des Sciences Morales et Politiques*) 5th ser., 57 (1971): 316–41. Reprinted in Frappier, *Du Moyen Age à la Renaissance,* 197–214 (Fr).

Emilie Kostoroski, "Two Ballads of Villon Reconsidered," *FR* 46 (Special Issue 5) (Spring 1973): 20–22 (Eng).

Kuhn, *La Poétique de François Villon,* 77–92 (Fr).

VILLON, FRANÇOIS, *Testament* "Ballade pour prier Nostre Dame"

Le Gentil, *Villon,* 103–4, 133–34 (Fr).

Jean-Marcel Paquette, "Temps, écriture et change: Pour une sémiosis du 'Testament' de Villon," *EF* 16 (April 1980): 11–12 (Fr). ¹

Testament
"Ballade des langues ennuyeuses" (v. 1440–1456)

Jean Frappier, "Contribution au commentaire de Villon," in *Studi in onore di Italo Siciliano,* vol. 1 (Florence: L. S. Olschki, 1966), 437–56. Reprinted in Frappier, *Du Moyen Age à la Renaissance,* 168–70 (Fr).

Testament
"Ballade des Seigneurs du temps jadis" (v. 357–384)

Dufournet, *Nouvelles recherches sur Villon,* 29–43 (Fr).

Fox, *Villon: Poems,* 52–54 (Eng).

Jean Frappier, "Les Trois Ballades du temps jadis," *BCLSMP* 5th ser., 57 (1971): 316–41. Reprinted in Frappier, *Du Moyen Age à la Renaissance,* 214–19 (Fr).

Jean-Marcel Paquette, "Temps, écriture et change: Pour une sémiosis du 'Testament' de Villon," *EF* 16 (April 1980): 12–14 (Fr).

Testament
"Ballade en vieil langage françoys" (v. 385–412)

Fox, *Villon: Poems,* 54–57 (Eng).

Jean Frappier, "Les Trois Ballades du temps jadis," *BCLSMP* 5th ser., 57 (1971): 316–41. Reprinted in Frappier, *Du Moyen Age à la Renaissance,* 219–22 (Fr).

Testament
"Ballade pour prier Nostre Dame" (v. 873–909)

William Calin, "Observations on Point of View and the Poet's Voice in Villon," *ECr* 7 (Fall 1967): 180–81 (Eng).

Edelgard Dubruck, "Villon's Two Pleas for Absolution," *ECr* 7 (Fall 1967): 189–93 (Eng).

VILLON, FRANÇOIS, *Testament* "Ballade pour Robert d'Estouteville"

Fein, *A Reading of Villon's "Testament,"* 35–39 (Eng).

Kuhn, *La Poétique de François Villon,* 43 (Fr).

Testament
"Ballade pour Robert d'Estouteville" (v. 1378–1405)

Dufournet, *Nouvelles recherches sur Villon,* 191–212 (Fr).

Fein, *A Reading of Villon's "Testament,"* 59–61 (Eng).

Fox, *Villon: Poems,* 87–88 (Eng).

Jean Frappier, "Contribution au commentaire de Villon," in *Studi in onore di Italo Siciliano,* vol. 1 (Florence: L. S. Olschki, 1966), 437–56. Reprinted in Frappier, *Du Moyen Age à la Renaissance,* 162–68 (Fr).

La Testament
"Belle Heaulmière" (v. 533–560)

Anacker, *François Villon,* 56–59 (Eng).

Fein, *A Reading of Villon's "Testament,"* 19–21 (Eng).

Fox, *Villon: Poems,* 59–64 (Eng).

Testament
"Ce monde n'est perpetuel" (v. 421–428)

Zumthor, *Essai de poétique médiévale,* 421–28 (Fr).

Testament
"Combien, au plus fort de mes maulx" (v. 97–104)

Kuhn, *La Poétique de François Villon,* 139–76, 196–201 (Fr).

Testament
"Contreditz de Franc Gontier" (v. 1473–1506)

Fein, *A Reading of Villon's "Testament,"* 62–64 (Eng).

VILLON, FRANÇOIS, *Testament* "Item, a maistre Andry Courault"

Testament
"Cy gist et dort en ce sollier" (v. 1884–1891)

Kuhn, *La Poétique de François Villon,* 441–43 (Fr).

Testament
"Dieu mercy . . . et Taque Thibault" (v. 737–752)

Kuhn, *La Poétique de François Villon,* 297–312 (Fr).

Testament
"Double ballade" (v. 625–672)

Anacker, *François Villon,* 60–62 (Eng).

Fein, *A Reading of Villon's "Testament,"* 29–33 (Eng).

Fox, *Villon: Poems,* 67–69 (Eng).

Testament
"Ecrit l'ail'an soixante et un" (v. 81–88)

Jean-Marcel Paquette, "Temps, écriture et change: Pour une sémiosis du 'Testament' de Villon," *EF* 16 (April 1980): 9–11 (Fr).

Testament
"En l'an trentieme de mon âge" (v. 1–16)

Fox, *The Poetry of Villon,* 78–82 (Eng).

Jean-Marcel Paquette, "Temps, écriture et change: Pour une sémiosis du 'Testament' de Villon," *EF* 16 (April 1980): 7–9 (Fr).

Nancy F. Regalado, "Effet de réel, effet du réel: Representation and Reference in Villon's 'Testament,' " *YFS,* no. 70 (1987): 66–68 (Eng).

Testament
"Item, a maistre Andry Courault" (v. 1457–1463)

Dufournet, *Nouvelles recherches sur Villon,* 217–22 (Fr).

VILLON, FRANÇOIS, *Testament* "Item, a maistre Jacques James"

Testament
"Item, a maistre Jacques James" (v. 1812–1819)

Nancy F. Regalado, "Effet de réel, effet du réel: Representation and Reference in Villon's 'Testament,'" *YFS,* no. 70 (1987): 71–72 (Eng).

Testament
"Item, a maistre Jehan Cornu" (v. 990–997)

Dufournet, *Nouvelles recherches sur Villon,* 51–61 (Fr).

Testament
"Item, a mes povres clergons" (v. 1306–1337)

Dufournet, *Nouvelles recherches sur Villon,* 158–61 (Fr).

Testament
"Item, au seigneur de Grigny" (v. 1346–1353)

Dufournet, *Nouvelles recherches sur Villon,* 180–83 (Fr).

Testament
"Item, aux Unze Vings sergens" (v. 1086–1093)

Dufournet, *Nouvelles recherches sur Villon,* 138–42 (Fr).

Testament
"Item, et parce que la femme" (v. 1006–1013)

Dufournet, *Nouvelles recherches sur Villon,* 76–86 (Fr).

Testament
"Item, je donne a maistre Jacques" (v. 1038–1044)

Dufournet, *Nouvelles recherches sur Villon,* 93–98 (Fr).

VILLON, FRANÇOIS, *Testament* "Mon seigneur n'est ne mon evesque"

Testament
"Item, ne sçay qu'a l'Ostel Dieu" (v. 1644–1651)

Dufournet, *Nouvelles recherches sur Villon,* 225–36 (Fr).

Testament
"Item, quant est de Merebuef" (v. 1046–1053)

Dufournet, *Nouvelles recherches sur Villon,* 103–9 (Fr).

Testament
"Item, riens a Jacquet Cardon" (v. 1776–1783)

Dufournet, *Nouvelles recherches sur Villon,* 151–53, 154–58, 162–64 (Fr).

Testament
"Item, vueil que le jeune Marle" (v. 1266–1273)

Dufournet, *Nouvelles recherches sur Villon,* 144–46 (Fr).

Testament
"Je congnois que povres et riches" (v. 305–328)

Jean Frappier, "Essai d'analyse stylistique," in *Etudes de langue et de littérature du Moyen Age offerts à Felix Lecoy* (Paris: Champion, 1973), 125–38. Reprinted in Frappier, *Du Moyen Age à la Renaissance,* 231–39 (Fr).

Testament
"L'Epitaphe Villon" (v. 1996–2023)

William Calin, "Observations on Point of View and the Poet's Voice in Villon," *ECr* 7 (Fall 1967): 183–84 (Eng).

Edelgard Dubruck, "Villon's Two Pleas for Absolution," *ECr* 7 (Fall 1967): 193–96 (Eng).

Testament
"Mon seigneur n'est ne mon evesque" (v. 9–16)

Kuhn, *La Poétique de François Villon,* 220–53 (Fr).

VILLON, FRANÇOIS, *Testament* "Or est vray qu'après plains et pleurs"

Testament
"Or est vray qu'après plains et pleurs" (v. 89–96)

Kuhn, *La Poétique de François Villon,* 185–96, 201–214 (Fr).

Testament
"Par faulte d'un huys q'y perdiz" (v. 998–1005)

Dufournet, *Nouvelles recherches sur Villon,* 52–61 (Fr).

Testament
"Puisque pappes, roys, filz de roys" (v. 413–420)

Jean Frappier, "Les Trois Ballades du temps jadis," *BCLSMP* 5th ser., 57 (1971): 316–41. Reprinted in Frappier, *Du Moyen Age à la Renaissance,* 222–24 (Fr).

Testament
"Quant des auditeurs messeigneurs" (v. 1206–1213)

Dufournet, *Nouvelles recherches sur Villon,* 127–33 (Fr).

Testament
"Regrets de la Belle Heaulmière" (v. 533–560)

Fox, *The Poetry of Villon,* 69, 112, 114–15, 133–37 (Eng).

Testament
"Si aperçois le grand danger" (v. 569–720)

Jean-Marcel Paquette, "Temps, écriture et change: Pour une sémiosis du 'Testament' de Villon," *EF* 16 (April 1980): 5–19 (Fr).

Testament
"Si prieray pour luy de bon cueur" (v. 33–48)

Jean Frappier, "Contribution au commentaire de Villon," in *Studi in onore di Italo Siciliano,* vol. 1 (Florence: L. S. Olschki, 1966), 437–56. Reprinted in Frappier, *Du Moyen Age à la Renaissance,* 151–62 (Fr).

VOLTAIRE, "Connue sous le nom des *vous* et des *tu*"

VITRY, PHILIPPE DE

"Dictz de Franc Gontier"

Winter, *Visual Variety and Spatial Grandeur,* 41–42 (Eng).

VOITURE, VINCENT

"Pour vous servir j'ay pû me desgager"

Odette de Mourgues, "Voiture and the Question of Wit," *ECr* 20 (Winter 1980): 11–12 (Eng).

"Le Soleil ne voit icy bas"

Odette de Mourgues, "Voiture and the Question of Wit," *ECr* 20 (Winter 1980): 7–18 (Eng).

"La Terre brillante de fleurs"

Odette de Mourgues, "Voiture and the Question of Wit," *ECr* 20 (Winter 1980): 9–11 (Eng).

VOLTAIRE

"A Monsieur de la Noue, auteru de Mahomet II, tragédie, en lui envoyant celle de Mahomet le prophète"

Calin, *In Defense of French Poetry,* 74–76 (Eng).

"Connue sous le nom des *vous* et des *tu*"

Calin, *In Defense of French Poetry,* 76–77 (Eng).

Main Sources Consulted

Books listed as Main Sources contain five or more explications. Books with fewer explications appear with full publication information in the Checklist itself. Periodicals listed here publish French poetry explications frequently. The list of periodical abbreviations on pages xiii–xv identifies all periodicals cited.

AGUETTANT, LOUIS. *Baudelaire.* Paris: Editions du Cerf, 1978.

AHEARN, EDWARD J. *Rimbaud: Visions and Habitations.* Berkeley: University of California Press, 1983.

ALBOUY, PIERRE. *La Création mythologique chez Victor Hugo.* Paris: José Corti, 1968.

ANACKER, ROBERT H. *François Villon.* New York: Twayne, 1968.

ANGELET, CHRISTIAN. *La Poétique de Tristan Corbière.* Brussels: Palais des Académies, 1961.

ARNOLD, A. JAMES. *Modernism and Negritude: The Poetry and Poetics of Aimé Césaire.* Cambridge, Mass.: Harvard University Press, 1981.

AUDOIN, PHILIPPE. *Breton.* Paris: Gallimard, 1970.

AUFFRET, SERGE, and **HELENE AUFFRET.** *Le Commentaire composé.* Paris: Hachette, 1968.

AUSTIN, LLOYD. *Poetic Principles and Practice: Occasional Papers on Baudelaire, Mallarmé and Valéry.* Cambridge: Cambridge University Press, 1987.

Australian Journal of French Studies 1 (1963)–25 (1988).

BAKER, DEBORAH L. *Narcissus and the Lover: Mythic Recovery and Reinvention in Scève's "Délie."* Saratoga, Calif.: Anma Libri, 1986.

BALAKIAN, ANNA. *André Breton: Magus of Surrealism.* New York: Oxford University Press, 1971.

BARRERE, JEAN-BERTRAND. *Claudel: Le Destin et l'œuvre.* Paris: Société d'Edition d'Enseignement Supérieure, 1979.

———. *Le Regard d'Orphée, ou L'Échange poétique: Hugo—Baudelaire—Rimbaud—Apollinaire.* Paris: Société d'Edition d'Enseignement Supérieur (SEDES), 1977.

BATES, SCOTT. *Guillaume Apollinaire.* New York: Twayne, 1967. Rev. ed. Boston: Twayne, 1989.

BAYLEY, PETER, and **DOROTHY COLEMAN,** eds. *The Equilibrium of Wit: Essays for Odette de Mourgues.* Lexington, Ky.: French Forum, 1982.

BAYS, GWENDOLYN. *The Orphic Vision: Seer Poets from Novalis to Rimbaud.* Lincoln: University of Nebraska Press, 1964.

BEAUMONT, E.M., J. M. COCKING, and **J. CRUICKSHANK,** eds. *Order and Adventure in Post-Romantic French Poetry.* New York: Harper and Row, 1973.

BELLENGER, YVONNE, ed. *Le Sonnet à la Renaissance, des origines au XVIIe siècle.* Paris: Aux Amateurs de Livres, 1988.

BENICHOU, PAUL. *Les Mages romantiques.* Paris: Gallimard, 1988.

BERRY, ANDRE. *Ronsard.* Paris: Flammarion, 1961.

BERTOCCI, ANGELO P. *From Symbolism to Baudelaire.* Carbondale: Southern Illinois University Press, 1964.

Bibliothèque d'Humanisme et Renaissance 22 (1960)–51 (1989).

BIRKETT, MARY ELLEN. *Lamartine and the Poetics of Landscape.* Lexington, Ky.: French Forum, 1982.

BISHOP, LLOYD. *The Poetry of Alfred de Musset: Styles and Genres.* New York: Peter Lang, 1987.

BISHOP, MICHAEL. *The Contemporary Poetry of France: Eight Studies.* Amsterdam: Rodopi, 1985.

BLOOM, HAROLD, ed. *Charles Baudelaire.* New York: Chelsea House, 1987.

BONNEFOY, YVES. *Rimbaud par lui-même.* Paris: Editions du Seuil, 1964.

BORNECQUE, JACQUES-HENRY. *Etudes verlainiennes: Lumières sur les "Fêtes galantes" de Paul Verlaine.* Paris: Nizet, 1969.

————, ed. *Les Poèmes saturniens de Paul Verlaine.* Enlarged edition. Paris: Nizet, 1967.

BOTS, WILHELMUS JOSEPHUS ALOYSIUS. *Joachim Du Bellay entre l'histoire littéraire et la stylistique: Essai de synthèse.* Groningen: Drukkerij van Denderen, 1970.

BOWIE, MALCOLM. *Henri Michaux: A Study of His Literary Works.* Oxford: Clarendon Press, 1973.

BOWIE, MALCOLM, ALISON FAIRLIE, and ALISON FINCH, eds. *Baudelaire, Mallarmé, Valéry: New Essays in Honour of Lloyd Austin.* Cambridge: Cambridge University Press, 1982.

BRAY, RENE. *Boileau:L'Homme et l'œuvre.* Paris: Nizet, 1962.

BROOME, PETER. *Henri Michaux.* London: Athlone Press, 1977.

BROOME, PETER, and GRAHAM CHESTERS. *The Appreciation of Modern French Poetry (1850–1950)*. Cambridge: Cambridge University Press, 1976.

BROWN, CYNTHIA J. *The Shaping of History and Poetry in Late Medieval France: Propaganda and Artistic Expression in the Works of the Rhétoriqueurs*. Birmingham, Ala.: Summa, 1985.

BRUNEL, PIERRE. *Arthur Rimbaud, ou L'Eclatant Désastre*. Paris: Champ Vallon, 1983.

——. *Rimbaud: Projets et réalisations*. Geneva: Slatkine, 1983.

BURGESS, GLYNN S. *The Lais of Marie de France: Text and Context*. Athens: University of Georgia Press, 1987.

CAILLER, BERNADETTE. *Proposition poétique: Une Lecture de l'œuvre d'Aimé Césaire*. Sherbrooke, Québec: Editions Naaman, 1976.

CALIN, WILLIAM. *In Defense of French Poetry: An Essay in Revaluation*. University Park: Pennsylvania State University Press, 1987.

——. *A Poet at the Fountain: Essays on the Narrative Verse of Guillaume de Machaut*. Lexington: University Press of Kentucky, 1974.

CALLANDER, MARGARET. *The Poetry of Pierre Jean Jouve*. Manchester: The University Press, 1965.

CAMERON, KEITH. *Agrippa d'Aubigné*. Boston: Twayne, 1977.

——. *Louise Labé, Renaissance Poet and Feminist*. New York: Berg, 1990.

CARDINAL, ROGER, ed. *Sensibility and Creation: Studies in Twentieth-Century French Poetry*. London: Croom Helm; New York: Barnes and Noble, 1977.

CARRON, JEAN-CLAUDE. *Discours de l'errance amoureuse: Une lecture du canzoniere de Pontus de Tyard*. Paris: Vrin, 1986.

CARTER, ALFRED EDWARD. *Charles Baudelaire*. Boston: Twayne, 1977.

CASSOU-YAGER, HELENE. *La Polyvalence du thème de la mort dans "Les Fleurs du Mal" de Baudelaire.* Paris: Nizet, 1979.

CASTEX, PIERRE-GEORGES. *"Les Destinées" d'Alfred de Vigny.* Paris: Société d'Edition d'Enseignement Supérieur (SEDES), 1964.

CAVE, TERENCE C. *Devotional Poetry in France, c. 1570–1613.* Cambridge: Cambridge University Press, 1969.

——, ed. *Ronsard the Poet.* London: Methuen, 1973.

CAWS, MARY ANN. *The Inner Theatre of Recent French Poetry: Cendrars, Tzara, Péret, Artaud, Bonnefoy.* Princeton: Princeton University Press, 1972.

——. *La Main de Pierre Reverdy.* Geneva: Droz, 1979.

——. *The Presence of René Char.* Princeton: Princeton University Press, 1976.

——. *René Char.* Boston: Twayne, 1977.

——. *Yves Bonnefoy.* Boston: Twayne, 1984.

——, ed. *About French Poetry from Dada to "Tel Quel": Text and Theory.* Detroit: Wayne State University Press, 1974.

CHADWICK, CHARLES. *Etudes sur Rimbaud.* Paris: Nizet, 1960.

——. *Mallarmé: Sa Pensée dans sa poésie.* Paris: Corti, 1962.

——. *Rimbaud.* London: Athlone Press, 1979.

——. *Verlaine.* London: Athlone Press, 1973.

CHAMARD, HENRI. *Histoire de la Pléiade.* 4 vols. Paris: Didier, 1939. Reprint. Paris: Didier, 1961–63.

CHAMPION, PIERRE. *Histoire poétique du XVe siècle.* 2 vols. Paris: Champion, 1923. Reprint. Paris: Champion, 1966.

CHARBONNIER, F. *La Poésie française et les guerres de religion (1560–*

1574): Etude historique et littéraire sur la poésie militante depuis la conjuration d'Amboise jusqu'à la mort de Charles IX. Paris: Bureau de la Revue des Œuvres Nouvelles, 1919. Reprint. Geneva: Slatkine Reprints, 1970.

CHESTERS, GRAHAM. *Baudelaire and the Poetics of Craft.* Cambridge: Cambridge University Press, 1988.

CHOLAKIAN, ROUBEN C. *Deflection/Reflection in the Lyric Poetry of Charles d'Orléans.* Potomac, Md.: Scripta Humanistica, 1984.

CLANCIER, G. E. *André Frénaud.* Paris: Seghers, 1963.

CLIFFORD, PAULA. *Marie de France: Lais.* London: Grant and Cutler, 1982.

CLIMO, MARTHA. *Hommage à Léopold Sédar Senghor, homme de culture.* Paris: Présence Africaine, 1976.

COGMAN, PETER. *Hugo: Les Contemplations.* London: Grant and Cutler, 1984.

COHN, ROBERT G. *The Poetry of Rimbaud.* Princeton: Princeton University Press, 1973.

———. *Toward the Poems of Mallarmé.* Expanded ed. Berkeley and Los Angeles: Univesity of California Press, 1980.

COLEMAN, DOROTHY G. *The Chaste Muse: A Study of Joachim Du Bellay's Poetry.* Leyden: Brill, 1980.

———. *Maurice Scève, Poet of Love: Tradition and Originality.* Cambridge: Cambridge University Press, 1975.

COLLIE, MICHAEL. *Jules Laforgue.* London: Athlone Press, 1977.

COLLINET, JEAN-PIERRE. *Le Monde littéraire de La Fontaine.* Paris: Presses Universitaires de France, 1970.

CONSTANS, FRANÇOIS. *Gérard de Nerval devant le destin.* Paris: Nizet, 1979.

CORMIER, RAYMOND and **URBAN HOLMES,** eds. *Essays in Honor* *of Louis Francis Solano.* Chapel Hill: University of North Carolina Press, 1970.

CORUM, ROBERT T. *Other Worlds and Other Seas: Art and Vision in Saint-Amant's Nature Poetry.* Lexington, Ky.: French Forum, 1979.

COTTRELL, ROBERT D. *The Grammar of Silence: A Reading of Marguerite de Navarre's Poetry.* Washington, D.C.: Catholic University of America Press, 1986.

COUFFIGNAL, ROBERT. *Apollinaire.* Paris: Desclée de Brouwer, 1966.

——. *Apollinaire.* Trans. Eda Levitine. University, Ala.: University of Alabama Press, 1975.

——. *L'Inspiration biblique dans l'œuvre de Guillaume Apollinaire.* Paris: Minard, 1966.

——. *Zone d'Apollinaire: Structure et confrontations.* Paris: Minard, 1970.

CROW, CHRISTINE M. *Paul Valéry and the Poetry of Voice.* Cambridge: Cambridge University Press, 1982.

CURNIER, PIERRE. *Pages commentées d'auteurs contemporains.* 2 vols. Paris: Larouse, 1962–65.

DANNER, RICHARD. *Patterns of Irony in the "Fables" of La Fontaine.* Athens: Ohio University Press, 1985.

DASSONVILLE, MICHEL. *Ronsard: Etude historique et littéraire.* 4 vols. Geneva: Droz, 1968–85.

DAVIS, GREGSON, ed. and trans. *Non-Vicious Circle: Twenty Poems of Aimé Césaire, Translated with an Introduction and Commentary.* Stanford: Stanford University Press, 1984.

DECAUDIN, MICHEL, ed. *Apollinaire et la musique: Actes du Colloque, Stavelot, 27–29 août 1965.* Stvelot: Editions des Amis de G. Apollinaire, 1967.

DE FABRY, ANNE, and **MARIE-FRANCE HILGAR,** eds. *Etudes autour d'"Alcools."* Birmingham, Ala.: Summa, 1985.

DEGUY, MICHEL. *Tombeau de Du Bellay.* Paris: Gallimard, 1973.

De Jean Lemaire de Belges à Jean Giraudoux. Mélanges d'histoire et de critique littéraire offerts à Pierre Jourda par ses collègues, ses élèves et ses amis. Paris: Nizet, 1970.

DELCROIX, MAURICE, and **WALTER GEERTS,** eds. *"Les Chats" de Baudelaire: Une Confrontation de méthodes.* Namur: Presse Universitaire de Namur, 1980.

DELLA NEVA, JO ANN. *Song and Counter-Song: Scève's "Délie" and Petrarch's "Rime."* Lexington, Ky.: French Forum, 1983.

DENOMME, ROBERT. *The French Parnassian Poets.* Carbondale: Southern Illinois University Press; London: Feffer and Simons, 1972.

———. *Leconte de Lisle.* New York: Twayne, 1973.

———. *Nineteenth-Century French Romantic Poets.* Carbondale: Southern Illinois University Press; London: Feffer and Simons, 1969.

DESONAY, FERNAND. *Ronsard, poète de l'amour.* 3 vols. Brussels: Palais des Académies, 1952–1959. Reprint. 1965.

DONALDSON-EVANS, LANCE K. *Love's Fatal Glance: A Study of Eye Imagery in the Poets of the "Ecole lyonnaise."* University, Mich.: Romance Monographs, 1980.

———. *Poésie et méditation chez Jean de La Ceppède.* Geneva: Droz, 1969.

DONOVAN, MORTIMER J. *The Breton Lay: A Guide to Varieties.* Notre Dame, Ind.: University of Notre Dame Press, 1969.

DOOLITTLE, JAMES. *Alfred de Vigny.* New York: Twayne, 1967.

DUBOSCLARD, ANNE-YVONNE, and **JOEL DUBOSCLARD.** *Du surréalisme à la Résistance: Dix poèmes expliqués.* Paris: Hatier, 1984.

DUFOURNET, JEAN. *Nouvelles recherches sur Villon.* Paris: Champion, 1980.

DUMAS, MARIE-CLAIRE, ed. *Moi qui suis Robert Desnos.* Paris: José Corti, 1987.

DURRY, MARIE-JEANNE. *Guillaume Apollinaire: Alcools.* 3 vols. Paris: SEDES, 1964. 3d ed., 1979.

ECKHARDT, ALEXANDRE. *Rémy Belleau, sa vie, sa Bergerie: Etude historique et critique.* Budapest: Joseph Nemeth, 1917. Reprint. Geneva: Slatkine, 1969.

EIGELDINGER, MARC, ed. *Etudes sur les "Poésies" de Rimbaud.* Neuchâtel: La Baconnière, 1979.

EMERY, LEON. *Trois poètes cosmiques.* Lyon: Les Cahiers Libres, 1964.

Esprit créateur 1 (1961)–30 (1990).

Etudes litteraires 1 (1968)–22 (1990).

FAIRLIE, ALISON. *Baudelaire: "Les Fleurs du mal."* Great Neck, N.Y.: Barron's 1960.

FEIN, DAVID A. *Charles d'Orléans.* Boston: Twayne, 1983.

————. *A Reading of Villon's "Testament."* Birmingham, Ala.: Summa, 1984.

FENOALTEA, DORANNE. *"Si haulte architecture": The Design of Scève's "Délie."* Lexington, Ky.: French Forum, 1982.

FOURNET, CHARLES. *Poètes romantiques: Etudes littéraires.* Geneva: Georg, 1962.

FOWLIE, WALLACE. *Mallarmé.* Chicago: University of Chicago Press, 1962.

FOX, JOHN. *The Poetry of Villon.* London: Thomas Nelson and Sons, 1962.

————. *Villon: Poems.* London: Grant and Cutler, 1984.

FRANKLIN, URSULA. *The Broken Angel: Myth and Method in Valéry.* Chapel Hill: University of North Carolina Department of Romance Languages, 1984.

FRAPPIER, JEAN. *Du Moyen Age à la Renaissance: Etudes d'histoire et de critique littéraire.* Paris: Champion, 1976.

French Review 33 (1959–60)–63 (1989–90).

French Studies 14 (1960)–43 (1989).

FREY, JOHN A. *"Les Contemplations" of Victor Hugo: The Ash Wednesday Liturgy.* Charlottesville: University Press of Virginia, 1988.

GAILLARD, POL. *"Les Contemplations": Victor Hugo.* Paris: Hatier, 1981.

GALAND, RENE. *Baudelaire: Poétiques et poésie.* Paris: Nizet, 1969.

GAUDON, JEAN. *Le Temps de la contemplation: L'Œuvre poétique de Victor Hugo des "Misères" au "Seuil du gouffre" (1845–1856).* Paris: Flammarion, 1969.

GENDRE, ANDRE. *Ronsard, poète de la conquête amoureuse.* Neuchâtel: La Baconnière, 1970.

GENINASCA, JACQUES. *Analyse structurale des "Chimères" de Nerval.* Neuchâtel: La Baconnière, 1971.

GIUSTO, JEAN-PIERRE. *Rimbaud créateur.* Paris: Presses Universitaires de France, 1980.

GLAUSER, ALFRED. *La Poétique de Hugo.* Paris: Nizet, 1978.

GOODRICH, NORMA L. *Charles of Orléans: A Study of Themes in His French and in His English Poetry.* Geneva: Droz, 1967.

GOURIER, FRANÇOISE. *Etude des œuvres poétiques de Saint-Amant.* Geneva: Droz, 1961.

GRANT, RICHARD B. *Théophile Gautier.* Boston: Twayne, 1975.

GRAY, FLOYD. *La Poétique de Du Bellay.* Paris: Nizet, 1978.

————, ed. *Poétiques: Théorie et critique littéraires.* Ann Arbor: Department of Foreign Languages, University of Michigan, 1980.

GRIFFIN, ROBERT. *Clément Marot and the Inflections of Poetic Voice.* Berkeley: University of California Press, 1974.

GUERDON, DAVID. *Rimbaud: La Clef alchimique.* Paris: Robert Laffont, 1980.

GUIBERT, ARMAND. *Léopold Sédar Senghor: L'Homme et l'œuvre.* Paris: Présence Africaine, 1962.

GUITON, MARGARET. *La Fontaine: Poet and Counterpoet.* New Brunswick, N.J.: Rutgers University Press, 1961.

GUTWIRTH, MARCEL. *Un Merveilleux sans éclat: La Fontaine, ou La Poésie exilée.* Geneva: Droz, 1987.

HACKETT, C. A. *Rimbaud: A Critical Introduction.* Cambridge: Cambridge University Press, 1981.

HALL, KATHLEEN M., and MARGARET B. WELLS. *Du Bellay: Poems.* London: Grant and Cutler, 1985.

HARMS, ALVIN. *Théodore de Banville.* Boston: Twayne, 1983.

HARRISON, ANN TUKEY. *Charles d'Orléans and the Allegorical Mode.* Chapel Hill: University of North Carolina Department of Romance Languages, 1975.

HIDDLESTON, JAMES, ed. *Laforgue aujourd'hui.* Paris: Corti, 1988.

HIGGINS, IAN. *Francis Ponge.* London: Athlone Press, 1979.

HOEPFFNER, ERNEST. *Les Lais de Marie de France.* Paris: Nizet, 1966.

HOUSTON, JOHN PORTER. *Patterns of Thought in Rimbaud and Mallarmé.* Lexington, Ky.: French Forum, 1986.

————. *Victor Hugo.* Boston: Twayne, 1974. Rev. ed. 1988.

573

HOWARTH, W. D., and **C. L. WALTON.** *Explications: The Technique of French Literary Appreciation.* London: Oxford University Press, 1971.

HUME, JOY N. *Two Against Time: A Study of the Very Present Worlds of Paul Claudel and Charles Péguy.* Chapel Hill: University of North Carolina Department of Romance Languages, 1978.

JASENAS, ELIANE. *La Poétique: Desbordes-Valmore et Nerval.* Paris: Jean-Pierre Delarge, 1975.

JEANNERET, MICHEL. *Poésie et tradition biblique au XVIe siècle: Recherches stylistiques sur les paraphrases des psaumes de Marot à Malherbe.* Paris: Corti, 1969.

JODOGNE, PIERRE. *Jean Lemaire de Belges: Ecrivain franco-bourguignon.* Brussels: Académie Royale de de Belgique, 1972.

JOHNSON, LEONARD. *Poets as Players: Theme and Variation in Late Medieval French Poetry.* Stanford: Stanford University Press, 1990.

JONES, K. R. W. *Pierre de Ronsard.* New York: Twayne, 1970.

JOSEPH, GEORGE. *Clément Marot.* Boston: Twayne, 1985.

JOURDA, PIERRE. *Marot.* New ed. Paris: Hatier, 1967.

KATZ, EVE, and **DONALD R. HALL.** *Explicating French Texts: Poetry, Prose, Drama.* New York: Harper and Row, 1970.

KEATING, L. CLARK. *Joachim Du Bellay.* New York: Twayne, 1971.

KELLY, DOUGLAS. *Medieval Imagination: Rhetoric and the Poetry of Courtly Love.* Madison: University of Wisconsin Press, 1978.

KITTANG, ATLE. *Discours et jeu: Essai d'analyse des textes d'Arthur Rimbaud.* Bergen: Universitetsforlaget; Grenoble: Presses Universitaires de Grenoble, 1975.

KNAPP, BETTINA L. *Gérard de Nerval: The Mystic's Dilemma.* University: University of Alabama Press, 1980.

KNIGHT, PHILIP. *Flower Poetics in Nineteenth-Century France.* Oxford: Clarendon Press, 1986.

KOHN, RENEE. *Le Goût de La Fontaine.* Paris: Presses Universitaires de France, 1962.

KRITZMAN, LAWRENCE, ed. *Le Signe et le texte: Etudes sur l'écriture au XVIe siècle en France.* Lexington, Ky.: French Forum, 1990.

KUHN, DAVID. *La Poétique de François Villon.* Paris: Armand Colin, 1967.

LA CHARITE, VIRGINIA DE. *The Poetry and the Poetics of René Char.* Chapel Hill: University of North Carolina Press, 1968.

LACY, NORRIS, and **JERRY NASH,** eds., *Essays in Early French Literature Presented to Barbara Craig.* York, S.C.: French Literature, 1982.

LAFAY, HENRI. *La Poésie française du premier XVIIe siècle (1598–1630): Esquisse pour un tableau.* Paris: Nizet, 1975.

LAFEUILLE, GERMAINE. *Cinq hymnes de Ronsard.* Geneva: Droz, 1973.

LAGNY, JEAN. *Le Poète Saint-Amant (1594–1661): Essai sur sa vie et ses œuvres.* Paris: Nizet, 1964.

LAPP, JOHN C. *The Brazen Tower.* Saratoga, Calif.: Anma Libri, 1977.

———. *The Esthetics of Negligence: La Fontaine's "Contes."* Cambridge: Cambridge University Press, 1971.

LA SALLE, BERTRAND DE. *Alfred de Vigny.* Paris: Fayard, 1963.

LAWLER, JAMES R. *The Language of French Symbolism.* Princeton: Princeton University Press, 1969.

———. *The Poet as Analyst: Essays on Paul Valéry.* Berkeley: University of California Press, 1974.

———. *René Char: The Myth and the Poem.* Princeton: Princeton University Press, 1978.

MAIN SOURCES CONSULTED

LAZARD, MADELEINE, ed. *Autour des "Hymnes" de Ronsard.* Paris: Champion, 1984.

——. *Studies in Modern French Literature Presented to P. Mansell Jones.* Manchester: Manchester University Press, 1961.

LEAKEY, F. W. *Baudelaire: Collected Essays 1953–88 of F. W. Leakey.* Ed. Eva Jacobs. Cambridge: Cambridge University Press, 1990.

LEBAUD, GENEVIEVE. *Léopold Sédar Senghor, ou La Poésie du royaume d'enfance.* Dakar: Nouvelles Editions Africaines, 1976.

LE GENTIL, PIERRE. *Villon.* Paris: Hatier, 1967.

LESTRINGANT, FRANK. *Agrippa d'Aubigné: Les Tragiques.* Paris: Presses Universitaires de France, 1986.

LEUWERS, DANIEL, ed. *Léopold Sédar Senghor: Colloque de Cerisy-la-Salle, 14 au 21 août 1986.* N.p.: Sud, 1987.

LEWIS, ROY. *On Reading French Verse: A Study of the Poetic Form.* Oxford: Clarendon Press, 1982.

LITTLE, ROGER. *Saint-John Perse.* London: Athlone Press; New York: Humanities Press, 1973.

LLOYD, ROSEMARY. *Mallarmé: Poésies.* London: Grant and Cutler, 1984.

LOKKE, KARI. *Gérard de Nerval: The Poet as Social Visionary.* Lexington, Ky.: French Forum, 1987.

LOMBARD, CHARLES M. *Lamartine.* New York: Twayne, 1973.

LONGREE, GEORGES H. F. *L'Expérience idéo-calligrammatique d'Apollinaire.* Liège: Noël, 1984.

McLEOD, ENID. *The Order of the Rose: The Life and Ideas of Christine de Pisan.* London: Chatto and Windus, 1976.

MAYER, C. A. *Clément Marot.* Paris: Nizet, 1972.

Mélanges de langue et de littérature du Moyen Age et de la Renaissance offerts à Jean Frappier, Professeur à la Sorbonne, par ses collègues, ses élèves et ses amis. Geneva: Droz, 1970.

Mélanges de langue et de littérature française du Moyen âge et de la Renaissance, offerts à M. Charles Foulon. Rennes: Institut de Français, 1980.

MENAGER, DANIEL. *Ronsard, le roi, le poète et les hommes.* Geneva: Droz, 1979.

MENARD, PHILIPPE. *Les Lais de Marie de France: Contes d'amour et d'aventure du Moyen Age.* Paris: Presses Universitaires de France, 1979.

MERINO-MORAIS, JANE. *Différence et répétition dans les "Contes" de La Fontaine.* Gainesville: University Presses of Florida, 1981.

MEZU, S. OKECHUKWU. *The Poetry of L. S. Senghor.* London: Heinemann, 1973; New York: Twayne, 1974.

MICKEL, EMANUEL. *Marie de France.* Paris: Klincksieck, 1973; New York: Twayne, 1974.

MITCHELL, ROBERT L. *The Poetic Voice of Charles Cros: A Centennial Study of His Songs.* University, Miss.: Romance Monographs, 1976.

———. *Tristan Corbière.* Boston: Twayne, 1979.

MOREAU, FRANÇOIS. *Six Etudes de métrique, de l'alexandrin romantique au verset contemporain, avec un choix de textes et de questions.* Paris: Société d'Edition d'Enseignement Supérieur (SEDES), 1987.

MORHANGE-BEGUE, CLAUDE, and **PIERRE LARTIGUE.** *Alcools Apollinaire: Analyse critique.* Paris: Cambridge University Press, 1984.

MOSS, ANN. *Poetry and Fable: Studies in Mythological Narrative in Sixteenth-Century France.* Cambridge: Cambridge University Press, 1984.

MOSSOP, D. J. *Pure Poetry: Studies in French Poetic Theory and Practice, 1746 to 1945.* Oxford: Clarendon Press, 1971.

MOUROT, JEAN. *Verlaine.* Nancy: Presses Universitaires de Nancy, 1988.

NADAL, OCTAVE. *Paul Verlaine.* Paris: Mercure de France, 1961.

NASH, J. C., ed. *Pre-Pléiade Poetry.* Lexington, Ky.: French Forum, 1985.

NASH, SUZANNE. *"Les Contemplations" of Victor Hugo: An Allegory of the Creative Process.* Princeton: Princeton University Press, 1976.

————. *Paul Valéry's "Album de vers anciens": A Past Transfigured.* Princeton: Princeton University Press, 1983.

Nineteenth-Century French Studies 1 (1973)–18 (1990).

NOULET, EMILIE. *Le Premier Visage de Rimbaud: Huit poèmes de jeunesse, choix et commentaire.* 2d ed. Brussels: Palais des Académies, 1973.

NUGENT, ROBERT. *Paul Eluard.* New York: Twayne, 1974.

NURSE, PETER, ed. *The Art of Criticism: Essays in French Literary Analysis.* Edinburgh: Edinburgh University Press, 1969.

ODOUL, PIERRE. *Le Drame intime d'Alfred de Musset.* Paris: Pensée Universelle, 1974.

OLDS, MARSHALL C. *Desire Seeking Expression: Mallarmé's "Prose pour des Esseintes."* Lexington, Ky.: French Forum, 1983.

Papers on French Seventeenth Century Literature 1 (1973)–34 (1991).

PERCHE, LOUIS. *Paul Eluard.* Paris: Editions Universitaires, 1963.

PICH, EDGARD. *Leconte de Lisle et sa création poétique: "Poèmes antiques" et "Poèmes barbares," 1852–1874.* Lyon: Imprimerie Chirat, 1975.

PLANCHE, ALICE. *Charles d'Orléans, ou La Recherche d'un langage.* Paris: Champion, 1975.

PLATTARD, JEAN. *Marot: Sa carrière poétique, son œuvre.* Paris: 1938. Reprint. Geneva: Slatkine Reprints, 1972.

POCOCK, GORDON. *Boileau and the Nature of Neo-Classicism.* Cambridge: Cambridge University Press, 1980.

PORTER, LAURENCE. *The Crisis of French Symbolism.* Ithaca: Cornell University Press, 1990.

POULET, GEORGES. *Exploding Poetry.* Translated by Françoise Meltzer. Chicago: University of Chicago Press, 1984.

———. *La Poésie éclatée: Baudelaire/Rimbaud.* Paris: Presses Universitaires de France, 1980.

PRENDERGAST, CHRISTOPHER, ed. *Nineteenth-Century French Poetry: Introductions to Close Reading.* Cambridge: Cambridge University Press, 1990.

PREVOST, JEAN. *Baudelaire: Essai sur l'inspiration poétique.* 1953. Reprint. Paris: Mercure de France, 1964.

PY, ALBERT. *Imitation et Renaissance dans la poésie de Ronsard.* Geneva: Droz, 1984.

———. *Les Mythes grecs dans la poésie de Victor Hugo.* Geneva: Droz, 1963.

QUAINTON, MALCOLM. *Ronsard's Ordered Chaos: Visions of Flux and Stability in the Poetry of Pierre de Ronsard.* Manchester: Manchester University Press, 1980.

QUESNEL, MICHEL. *Baudelaire solaire et clandestin: Les Données singulières de la sensibilité et de l'imaginaire dans les "Fleurs du mal."* Paris: Presses Universitaires de France, 1987.

QUIGNARD, PASCAL. *La Parole de Délie.* Paris: Mercure de France, 1974.

RAITT, A. W., *Life and Letters in France: The Nineteenth Century.* New York: Charles Scribner's Sons, 1965.

REGALADO, NANCY F. *Poetic Patterns in Rutebeuf.* New Haven: Yale University Press, 1970.

REGOSIN, RICHARD L. *The Poetry of Inspiration: Agrippa d'Aubigné's "Les Tragiques."* Chapel Hill: University of North Carolina Press, 1970.

RENAUD, PHILIPPE. *Lecture d'Apollinaire.* Lausanne: Editions L'Age d'Homme, 1969.

Revue d'Histoire Littéraire de la France 60 (1960)–90 (1990).

RICHARD, JEAN-PIERRE. *L'Univers imaginaire de Mallarmé.* Paris: Seuil, 1961.

RICHTER, MARIO. *La Crise du logos et la quête du mythe: Baudelaire, Rimbaud, Cendrars, Apollinaire.* Neuchâtel: La Baconnière, 1976.

RIFFATERRE, HERMINE B. *L'Orphisme dans la poésie: Thèmes et style surnaturalistes.* Paris: Nizet, 1970.

RIFFATERRE, MICHAEL. *Semiotics of Poetry.* Bloomington: Indiana University Press, 1978.

RIGOLOT, FRANÇOIS. *Poétique et onomastique: L'Exemple de la Renaissance.* Geneva: Droz, 1977.

ROBICHEZ, JACQUES. *Sur Saint-John Perse: "Eloges," "La Gloire des rois," "Anabase."* 2d ed. Paris: SEDES, 1982.

———. *Verlaine entre Rimbaud et Dieu des "Romances sans paroles" à "Sagesse."* Paris: SEDES/CDU, 1982.

Romance Quarterly 7 (1960)–37 (1990).

ROSS, KRISTIN. *The Emergence of Social Space: Rimbaud and the Paris Commune.* Minneapolis: University of Minnesota Press, 1988.

ROTHSCHILD, JUDITH R. *Narrative Technique in the Lais of Marie de France: Themes and Variations,* Vol. 1. *North Carolina Studies in the Romance Languages and Literatures,* no. 39. Chapel Hill: University of North Carolina Department of Romance Languages, 1974.

ROTHWELL, ANDREW. *Textual Spaces: The Poetry of Pierre Reverdy.* Amsterdan: Rodopi, 1989.

RUBIN, DAVID L. *Higher, Hidden Order: Design and Meaning in the Odes of Malherbe. North Carolina Studies in the Romance Languages and Literatures,* no. 117. Chapel Hill: University of North Carolina Press, 1972.

——. *The Knot of Artifice: A Poetic of the French Lyric in the Early Seventeenth Century.* Columbus: Ohio State University Press, 1981.

ST. AUBYN, F. C. *Stéphane Mallarmé.* Boston: Twayne, 1969. rev. ed. 1989.

SCHÄRER, KURT. *Pour une poétique des "Chimères" de Nerval.* Paris: Lettres Modernes, 1981.

SCHARFMAN, R. *"Engagement" and the Language of the Subject in the Poetry of Aimé Césaire.* Gainesville: University of Florida Press, 1987.

SCHROEDER, JEAN. *Pierre de Reverdy.* Boston: Twayne, 1981.

SCOTT, DAVID. *Pictorialist Poetics: Poetry and the Visual Arts in Nineteenth-Century France.* Cambridge: Cambridge University Press, 1988.

SERPER, ARIE. *Rutebeuf, poète satirique.* Paris: Klincksieck, 1969.

SHAPLEY, C. S., ed. *Studies in French Poetry of the Fifteenth Century.* The Hague: Martinus Nijhoff, 1970.

SIENAERT, EDGARD. *Les Lais de Marie de France: Du conte merveilleux à la nouvelle psychologique.* Paris: Champion, 1984.

SILVER, ISIDORE. *The Intellectual Evolution of Ronsard.* 2 vols. St. Louis: Washington University, 1969.

——. *Ronsard and the Hellenic Renaissance in France.* Vol. 1: *Ronsard and the Greek Epic.* St. Louis: Washington University, 1961.

——. *Ronsard and the Hellenic Renaissance in France.* Vol. 2: *Ronsard and the Grecian Lyre.* Geneva: Droz, 1981–85.

——. *Three Ronsard Studies.* Geneva: Droz, 1978.

SMERNOFF, RICHARD A. *André Chénier.* Boston: Twayne, 1977.

SMITH, PAULINE M. *Clément Marot, Poet of the French Renaissance.* London: Athlone Press, 1970.

SORRELL, MARTIN. *Francis Ponge.* Boston: Twayne, 1981.

MAIN SOURCES CONSULTED

SPLETH, JANICE. *Leopold Sédar Senghor.* Boston: Twayne, 1985.

STAMELMAN, RICHARD. *The Drama of Self in Guillaume Apollinaire's "Alcools."* Chapel Hill: University of North Caroline Department of Romance Languages, 1976.

———. *Lost Beyond Telling: Representations of Death and Absence in Modern French Poetry.* Ithaca: Cornell University Press, 1990.

Stanford French Review 1 (1977)–14 (1991).

STONE, DONALD. *Ronsard's Sonnet Cycles: A Study in Tone and Vision.* New Haven: Yale University Press, 1966.

TAYLOR-HORREX, SUSAN. *Verlaine: "Fêtes galantes" and "Romances sans paroles."* London: Grant and Cutler, 1988.

TOPSFIELD, L. T. *Troubadours and Love.* Cambridge: Cambridge University Press, 1975.

TURNELL, MARTIN. *Baudelaire: A Study of His Poetry.* New York: New Directions, 1972.

VERSTRAETE, DANIEL. *La Chasse spirituelle d'Arthur Rimbaud: Les "Illuminations."* Paris: Cerf, 1980.

VIANEY, JOSEPH. *Les Epîtres de Marot.* Paris: Nizet, 1962.

VOUGA, DANIEL. *Nerval et ses "Chimères."* Paris: Corti, 1981.

WALCUTT, CHARLES CHILD, and **J. EDWIN WHITESELL,** eds. *The Explicator Cyclopedia.* Vol. 2, *Traditional Poetry: Medieval to Late Victorian.* Chicago: Quadrangle Books, 1986.

WEBER, HENRI. *A travers le seizième siècle.* Paris: Nizet, 1985.

———. *La Création poétique au XVIe siècle en France de Maurice Scève à Agrippa d'Aubigné.* 1955. Reprint. Paris: Nizet, 1969.

WEBER, JEAN-PAUL. *Genèse de l'œuvre poétique.* Paris: Gallimard, 1960.

WHITAKER, MARIE-JOSEPHINE. *La Structure du monde imaginaire de Rimbaud.* Paris: Nizet, 1972.

WHITE, JULIAN E. *Nicolas Boileau.* New York: Twayne, 1969.

WHITING, CHARLES G. *Valéry jeune poète.* New Haven: Yale University Press; Paris: Presses Universitaires de France, 1960.

WILLARD, CHARITY. *Christine de Pisan: Her Life and Works.* New York: Persea Books, 1984.

WILSON, D. B. *Ronsard, Poet of Nature.* Manchester: Manchester University Press, 1961.

WINN, COLETTE H. *Jean de Sponde: Les "Sonnets de la Mort," ou La Poétique de l'accoutumance.* Potomac, Md.: Scripta Humanistica, 1984.

WINTER, JOHN F. *Visual Variety and Spatial Grandeur: A Study of the Transition from the Sixteenth to the Seventeenth Century in France.* Chapel Hill: University of North Carolina Department of Romance Languages, 1974.

WREN, KEITH. *Vigny: "Les Destinées."* London: Grant and Cutler, 1985.

ZILBERBERG, CLAUDE. *Une Lecture des "Fleurs du Mal."* Paris: Mame, 1972.

ZUMTHOR, PAUL. *Essai de poétique médiévale.* Paris: Seuil, 1972.

Index of Critics

585

Index of Critics

Index of Critics

Index of Critics

Index of Critics

Potts, D. C., 11
Pouilliart, Raymond, 20
Poulet, Georges, 46, 78, 366, 378, 395, 396, 397
Poupon, Marc, 10, 14, 15, 17, 20, 24
Prendergast, Christopher, 182
Prescott, Ann, 289
Price, John, 90, 91
Price, L. Brian, 44
Prothin, Annie, 89, 91
Proust, Jacques, 229, 230, 236, 237, 242
Prévost, Jean, 41, 42, 44, 45, 46, 47, 48, 49, 52,
    53, 54, 55, 56, 57, 59, 60, 62, 63, 64, 65,
    66, 67, 68, 69, 70, 71, 72, 73, 74, 75, 76, 77,
    78
Pugh, Anthony, 545
Putter, Irving, 259
Py, Albert, 189, 194, 201, 202, 205, 206, 414,
    415, 423, 427

Quainton, Malcolm, 31, 35, 37, 403, 404, 422,
    423, 424, 426, 427, 428, 429, 430, 431, 432,
    433, 434, 435, 436, 437, 438, 439, 444
Quesnel, Michel, 41, 42, 44, 45, 46, 49, 51, 53,
    55, 56, 57, 58, 59, 60, 61, 62, 63, 65, 66,
    67, 68, 70, 71, 72, 73, 74, 75, 76, 78
Quignard, Pascal, 466, 474, 475, 476, 485
Quilligan, Maureen, 134
Quintana, J. Terrie, 298

Raillard, Georges, 170, 171
Raitt, A. W., 53, 200, 261, 282, 532
Ramsey, Warren, 248, 249, 250
Randall, Michael, 266
Ranwez, Alain, 49
Raser, Timothy, 43, 46, 73, 200
Rastier, François, 293
Raymond, Marcel, 404
Read, Peter, 27
Reed, Arden, 69
Reed, J., 2
Rees, Margaret A., 329
Regalado, Nancy F., 445, 446, 447, 448, 552,
    557, 558
Regard, Maurice, 536
Regosin, Richard L., 32, 33, 34, 35
Rehder, R. M., 281
Renaud, Philippe, 6, 7, 8, 9, 10, 11, 12, 13, 14,
    15, 16, 17, 18, 19, 20, 21, 22, 23, 24, 25, 26
Reynolds, Deirdre, 294
Rhodes, Enid Peschel, 152, 369, 373, 380, 382,
    386, 396
Ribard, Jacques, 139, 306
Richard, Jean-Pierre, 44, 275, 276, 277, 279,
    281, 283, 284, 285, 286, 287, 288, 289, 290,
    291, 294, 295, 296, 297, 298, 299, 548
Richer, Jean, 8, 9, 13, 15, 16, 334, 368, 401
Richmond, H. M., 433
Richter, Mario, 7, 20, 25, 41, 100, 363, 370, 504
Ridgely, Beverly S., 224, 225, 236, 243
Ries, Garnet, 27
Rifelj, Carol de Dobay, 532, 536, 540
Riffaterre, H., 37, 38, 40, 181, 182, 183, 250,
    252, 330, 334, 336, 337, 338
Riffaterre, Michael, 36, 46, 51, 74, 75, 94, 96,
    97, 98, 138, 167, 175, 182, 249, 265, 278,
    282, 294, 344, 345, 349, 368, 379, 386, 388,
    393, 541
Rigolot, François, 35, 153, 159, 160, 214, 215,
    266, 267, 311, 314, 321, 327, 408, 413, 470,
    481, 493
Rinsler, Norma, 28
Rivas, Daniel, E., 172, 211, 212, 213, 214
Rizzuto, Anthony, 358, 359

Robb, Graham, 51, 294
Roberts, Elizabeth, 400, 401
Roberts, William, 449, 450, 452
Robertson, Howard, 306
Robichez, Jacques, 458, 459, 460, 461, 462, 463,
    464, 532, 533, 538, 542
Robillard, Monic, 288
Robinson, Judith, 525
Rodriguez, Antonio, 93
Rolfe, Christopher, 455
Ronat, Mitsou, 280
Root, Tamara, 456
Rosenthal, Alan, 57
Ross, Kristin, 369, 370, 392, 393, 394, 395, 397
Rosseel, Eddy, 271
Roth-Mascagni, Pauline, 527
Rothschild, Judith R., 303, 305, 306, 307, 309,
    310
Rothwell, Andrew, 352, 353, 354, 355, 356, 357,
    359, 360
Rousseau, Claudine, 177, 345
Rousseau, J. J., 228
Rousselot, Jean, 31
Rowland, Michael, 15
Rubin, David Lee, 228, 229, 235, 239, 244, 246,
    271, 273, 274, 321, 453, 543, 544, 545
Ruff, Marcel A., 366, 395, 403
Runyon, Randolph, 466
Russell, Daniel, 154, 155
Russo, Adelaide, 150, 151
Ruwet, Nicolas, 59, 64, 216, 217, 272, 274
Ryan, Marie-Laure, 460, 462, 463
Ryding, Erik S., 29

Sabbagh, Céline, 517, 528
Saigal, Monique, 205
Saldívar, Ramón, 284, 294
Saly, Antoinette, 307
Samaras, Zoé, 184, 185
Sankovitch, Tilde, 210
Sargent, Barbara, 552
Sasaki, Shigemi, 126
Saulnier, V. L., 168, 313, 315, 457
Sayce, R. A., 411, 420
Scarfe, Francis, 132
Schaeffer, Gérald, 97, 361, 370, 387
Sckhaettel, Marcel, 398
Scharfman, Ronnie, 102, 103, 104, 105, 107
Schoenfeld, Jean, 93, 96
Schroeder, Jean, 352, 353, 354, 355, 356, 357,
    358, 359, 360
Schuster, Marilyn, 362, 372, 374, 380
Schwartz, Jerome, 405
Schwartz, Paul, 288
Schärer, Kurt, 334, 335, 336, 337, 338
Schön-Pietri, Nicole, 514, 521
Scollen, Christine M., 169, 448
Scollen-Jimack, C., 311, 312
Scott, Clive, 46, 47, 188, 250, 275, 278, 280, 288,
    294, 297, 536
Scott, David, 275, 281, 295, 378, 390, 393, 522
Sellin, Eric, 186, 359
Senelier, Jean, 335
Serper, Arie, 445, 446, 447, 448
Seznec, Alain, 232, 235, 236
Shapley, C. S., 127, 128, 129, 338
Sharrat, Peter, 470
Shaw, D. J., 160
Sheringham, Michael, 93, 94, 95, 96, 98, 393
Sherman, Rachelle, 344, 346, 348
Sieburth, Richard, 47
Sienaert, Edgard, 303, 304, 305, 306, 307, 308,
    309, 310